# NEW WORKS IN ACCOUNTING HISTORY

Richard P. Brief, *Series Editor*

*Leonard N. Stern School of Business*
*New York University*

A Garland Series

# RECURRING ISSUES IN AUDITING

*Professional Debate 1875–1900*

---

*Edited by*
**Roy A. Chandler and
John Richard Edwards**

---

WITHDRAWN

Garland Publishing, Inc.
New York and London 1994

Introduction copyright © 1994 by Roy A. Chandler and
John Richard Edwards

**Library of Congress Cataloging-in-Publication Data**

Recurring issues in auditing: professional debate 1875–1900 / edited by Roy A.
Chandler and John Richard Edwards.
   p. cm.—(New works in accounting history)
 Includes bibliographical references and index.
 ISBN 0-8153-1719-0
1. Auditing—Great Britain—History—19th century. 2. Auditing—Great Britain—
History—19th century—Sources. I. Chandler, Roy. II. Edwards, J.R. III. Series.
HF5667.R39    1994    93–29294
657'.45'0941034—dc20       CIP

*All volumes printed on acid-free, 250-year-life paper.*
*Manufactured in the United States of America.*

Design by Marisel Tavarez

# CONTENTS

# INTRODUCTION

The period 1875–1900 has been chosen because its start is close to the first publication in 1874, of the weekly journal *The Accountant,* from which the articles and items in this book have been taken. *The Accountant* represented the forum for debate among practitioners of the issues which were of greatest importance at the time.

The period is also noteworthy since it covers the granting of the Royal Charter to the Institute of Chartered Accountants in England and Wales (ICAEW) in 1880. Though not the first accounting body in the United Kingdom to be granted such a charter, the ICAEW quickly became influential in the development of the accountancy profession.

The year 1900 has been chosen to end the period under review since it saw the introduction of a major piece of company legislation, the Companies Act 1900, which contained important new audit requirements. This marked the beginning of a new era in company auditing.

By the end of the nineteenth century, the limits of auditors' legal liabilities were becoming much more closely defined. It was during the 1890s that the land-mark cases of re Kingston Cotton Mills and re London and General Bank took place and provided the basis for further developments in the concept of auditors' liabilities (for reports on these and other contemporary cases see the companion text, *British Audit Practice 1884–1900: A Case Law Perspective*).

## THE SELECTION AND ORGANIZATION OF THE MATERIAL

As with all similar anthologies of historical material the selection of items to be included is a very subjective process. The compiler is always open to criticism for including certain items while omitting others. Our intention is not to produce a book of readings which could compete with a comprehensive history of the auditing profession. Rather it is our aim to give a flavor of the issues that concerned auditing practitioners more than one hundred years ago and which appear to retain a certain relevance to us today.

We were faced at an early stage with having to make a decision as to whether to organize the items into "themes" or simply present them in chronological order. The thematic approach has an obvious appeal in that material on a single subject such as fraud detection or audit reporting is brought together in a way that allows easy comparison of different views. However, the subject of auditing is much more difficult to organize in such a manner than, say, accounting issues because of the inter-relationship of the issues involved. For example, the views on the fraud detection role of auditing naturally involve some consideration of the practical limitations on the scope of audit work, not least the adequacy of the fee which the client was willing to pay. This illustrates the difficulty of finding items which touch only on one issue. The work of categorization of material into neat self-contained compartments therefore became impossible.

We have opted instead for the approach of presenting the items in chronological order, which has the advantages of emphasizing the interconnections between the issues and, we believe, conveying the overall depth and flavor of the debate. (There are some minor exceptions involving a continuing debate or related correspondence concerning a single issue which we felt were better located together, even if this slightly disrupts the strict chronological sequence.)

## THE ISSUES

It is interesting for us now to review the issues which exercised the minds of professional accountants a century ago. One aspect which will strike the modern reader immediately is the apparent timelessness of the issues raised more than one hundred years ago. Today many of these issues remain unresolved, indicating either the failure of the profession to deal with crucial matters or the permanent insolubility of vital auditing questions.

### *Independence*

The need for the auditor to be independent of his client and its management was appreciated at an early stage. An editorial commented:

> The idea of the importance of the post of auditor must be thoroughly grasped; and the necessity of his utter independence of any influences which may color his conclusions, must be insisted upon.

> (Item 4, *The Accountant,* May 8, 1875, p. 3)

Such independence extends to freedom from management's influence on the scope of audit work and this too was realized: "the audit should be unlimited as to its scope, and . . . the auditors should not be tied down to prescribed times for their work" (*Item 11, The Accountant,* March 15, 1879, p. 4).

That the full importance of independence was understood at least by some is evidenced in a letter to *Vanity Fair* (reproduced in Item 21, *The Accountant,* November 3, 1883, p. 12): "An auditor, to be of the slightest value, must be independent and free. If he is not, his certificate is not worth the paper it is written on. To ensure independence is the problem to be solved". The passage of another 110 years has not diminished the relevance of this observation.

The current concern that auditors are only nominally appointed by shareholders but actually appointed by directors may be found in Item 87, p. 615. *The Accountant* documents particular cases illustrating how disagreements between auditors and directors (for example, Items 91 and 101) could lead to a change of auditor. The tone of the editorials is clearly in support of auditors seeking to take an independent stand in making their report, if necessary even against the wishes of directors. The lack of security of auditors' tenure is seen as a threat to independence (see Item 68). The suggestion that accountants should stand together and refuse to act for directors who have dismissed predecessor auditors has been heard many times during the intervening years.

## Audit Fees

A recurring theme throughout the period under review is the level of fees which clients were prepared to pay for the audit service. One explanation for the poor quality of audit work was often the lack of adequate fees to enable the auditor to perform a competent audit. An editorial in *The Accountant* complained that it was common "to find that [a] small fee paid is accepted on the footing that services of corresponding value are expected" (Item 5, *The Accountant,* June 12, 1875, p. 3). This was one of the issues put by D. Chadwick to an audience who resolved that "It is the duty of an Auditor to fully perform his work, whatever the amount of the fee he receives" (Item 14, *The Accountant,* November 3, 1883, p. 18).

However, many took the more commercial view that "you get what you pay for." A cheap audit could not possibly be expected to do the same job as a more expensive engagement. The existence of the 'amateur auditor' hindered attempts to ensure that undercutting of fees did not result in substandard work since if the fees of a professional auditor appeared too high, the amateur could always be hired at a lower cost (see for example Item 17, *The Accountant,* October 20, 1883, p. 12). But competitive pressures between professional auditors also played a part; it is interesting to see that the phenomenon now known as "lowballing" is not new (see Item 26).

## Auditors' Responsibilities

There were calls for the development of a clear definition of the duties of auditors (see Item 8, *The Accountant,* May 13, 1876, the article 'Auditing' contributed by Z). The extent of the auditor's responsibility for detecting and preventing fraud received as much attention in the 1890s as it has done in the 1990s. There was much discussion in those formative days as to whether the primary objective of the audit was fraud detection or the verification of financial statements, (see Item 45).

## The Impact of Case Law

Prior to the 1880s there had been few cases involving the work of auditors or accountants. However, as time went on and more cases came before the courts it is not surprising to find members of the profession devoting more consideration to their legal responsibilities. F. Whinney's contribution to the ICAEW Autumnal meeting in 1888 (Item 29) provides an early example of the concern with legal aspects. A little later W.H. Nairne (Item 81) provides a detailed analysis of the legal position of auditors following the two landmark cases of the mid-1890s, re Kingston Cotton Mills and re London and General Bank.

## Extent of Audit Work

As the auditing profession developed, debate continued on the manner in which the audit should be conducted, the methods to be used and the extent of the auditor's examination of the company's books and records.

At one extreme there were those who apparently thought that the auditor was required merely to check the agreement of the balance sheet with the balances in the books:

> Many consider an audit has nothing more in it than certifying the agreement of the balances in a balance sheet with those in the ledgers from which they were taken.
>
> (Item 2, *The Accountant,* February 6, 1875, p. 6)

At the other extreme, others expected a much more thorough job even to the extent of checking every entry in the books with supporting documentation. One editorial suggested that a 'rudimentary' audit would insist on vouchers being produced to support every payment as well as checking the correspondence of the balance sheet with the books. The editorial went on to illustrate an even more sophisticated feature of the audit:

> At the other end of the scale is the audit which whilst relying on the certificates of skilled officials for the quantity and value of stocks and plant, exercises a certain supervision even over matters such as these, and includes a thorough analysis of all ledger accounts. (Item 5, *The Accountant,* June 12, 1875, p. 2)

In the first of a series of articles on auditing penned anonymously, "X" indicated a move away from the rudimentary type of auditing:

> To look over, in a hurried and cursory manner, the accounts rendered for inspection, was at one period frequently the mode of conducting an audit, but this fashion of auditing has proved to be entirely insufficient.
>
> (Item 1, *The Accountant,* January 9, 1875, p. 7)

It is to give a flavor of the nature of audits as then conducted that we have included articles giving details of audit procedures actually followed (for example, Items 13, 14, 24, 30, 42). One aspect of auditing which is worthy of separate mention is reliance on the adequacy of control systems to reduce the extent of tests of the detail of transactions and balances, which we now refer to as "substantive tests" (see for example, Item 8, *The Accountant,* May 13, 1876, the article "Auditing," contributed by "Z," pp. 3 and 4, Item 14 by D. Chadwick, p. 8).

There are indications that other aspects of modern auditing, such as *directional testing* and notions of varying quality of audit evidence, were also appreciated: "In his examination of the cash book the income side must be checked from the most independent source the auditor can find available" (Item 13, F.W. Pixley, *The Accountant,* May 26 1883, p. 8). C.R. Trevor (Item 33) recommended the circularization of debtors as a source of independent confirmation.

Extracts (Item 103) from a series of articles published in 1900 illustrate the degree of sophistication attained by the views on audit procedures in contrast to those expressed a quarter of a century before.

## Manner of Audit Reporting

The way in which audit findings were to be reported was a further topic of much discussion among leading practitioners. On the one hand there were those who considered that the simple signature of a reputable accountant was sufficient to attest to the reliability of the accounts. The short phrase "audited and found correct" at the foot of the balance sheet was a frequent method of audit reporting.

Others favored strict adherence to the form of words contained in a company's articles of association, while some preferred even longer, more detailed reports covering not only a description of the audit work carried out but also specific comments on individual aspects of the company's performance and position, (see Item 38).

## Code of Audit

The differences in approaches to the audit, the varying quality of its performance and different reporting styles led some even in those early days to call for the codification of the duties of the auditor and the manner in which those duties could be sufficiently discharged. In the early part of the period there was relatively little literature to guide auditors in practice. It was not until 1881 that F. W. Pixley produced the first textbook on auditing. The need for guidance felt by practitioners can be seen from a letter which bemoaned the lack of literature, pleaded for the series of articles by "X" to be continued and suggested:

> The public as well as the profession . . . would be gainers by the duties of an auditor being properly understood, defined, and performed as a bona fide service, instead of, as it appears to be a mere sham, and as fees paid and various forms of certifying prove it to be at present.

> (Item 2, *The Accountant,* February 6, 1875, p. 6)

The topic was picked up in the second article by "X":

> A code embracing the most important points relative to the duties of auditors, drawn up and adopted by the various London and Provincial Societies, would without doubt, give universal satisfaction. This would demonstrate to the public the amount of security afforded by the employment as auditors of Accountants actuated by a full appreciation of their obligations and duties.

> (Item 3, *The Accountant,* February 13, 1875, p. 4)

Arguments for a "Manual on Auditing" are persuasively put forward by Milburne in Item 12 *(The Accountant,* 1881, pp. 11–13). In 1883 *The Accountant* asked readers for their suggestions for a uniform audit certificate (Item 15, October 13, 1883, p. 7).

In 1888 (Item 28) it appears that *The Accountant is* less enthusiastic about the Institute codifying audit practice and audit reporting. However, Pixley is reported (by Carter, Item 45, p. 15) as supporting the call for the Institute to settle "what would constitute a thorough audit". J.G. Barry, in 1894, repeated this call in respect of audit reports (see Item 53).

The Council of the ICAEW was not disposed to provide detailed guidance although in 1893 a statement was issued to the press setting out the general nature of an audit (see Item 66, p. 958). This reluctance to provide guidance to members went against advice from no less a source than Mr. Justice Vaughan Williams (see Item 89, p. 775).

The only significant step taken by the ICAEW in providing detailed guidance during the period 1875–1900 was in obtaining and publishing Counsels' opinion on the form of audit report following the Companies Act 1900 (Item 104). This, it will be seen, interpreted the auditor's reporting obligation in terms of the minimum needed to satisfy the strict legal requirement (in the case of the unqualified auditor's report). This approach found favor with the accounting bodies which continued until very recently to produce reporting guidance of a minimalist nature.

## Criticism of Auditing

Throughout the period under review the accounting profession had to deal with a level of public concern about the value of audits that seems very familiar to us today. The language used by parties to the debate was provocative: on the one hand, critics referred to the audit certificate "a delusion and a snare" (Item 21, p. 10), "a simple farce" (Item 50) and called the audit "valueless as a means of detecting fraud" (Item 57); and on the other hand *The Accountant* accused the critics of "desiring to throw mud at an honorable profession" (Item 48, p. 214). Then, as now, the criticism was provoked by the financial failure of well-known companies which had previously been held in high regard. Articles containing attacks on accountants and auditors frequently appeared in contemporary journals such as *Vanity Fair, The Economist, Money, The Bullionist,* in specialist journals such as *The Building Societies Gazette, The Warehouseman, The Journal of Gas Lighting,* and in the wider press including, *The Financial Times, The Pall Mall Gazette, The Daily Chronicle, The Westminster Gazette, The Scotsman,* and *The Western Press.* The profession was anxious to respond to criticism and to defend its position. *The Accountant* assisted by reproducing the critical articles, by producing replies in the form of editorials and by generating debate within the profession.

The self-regulatory role of the professional bodies was also called into question at an early stage (see Item 19, October 27, 1883, p. 11), a criticism which was to be repeated many times. *The Accountant* was keen to defend the profession, citing the fact that the ICAEW's disciplinary powers had been "frequently exercised" (Item 95, p. 742).

## *Government Auditors*

It is difficult now to judge the effectiveness of such criticism in terms of motivating the profession to improve its performance. However, there must have been some concern in professional circles that, at an extreme, the criticism might stimulate the government to intervene in the regulation and operation of the auditing industry. A letter from a Mr. John Lowe to an unnamed contemporary of *The Accountant* (reproduced in *The Accountant)* complaining of the quality of auditing provides an early example of the call for greater government supervision:

> If a body of independent auditors were attached to the Board of Trade, to whom all new schemes [of company formation] would be referred for approval or otherwise, and, if sanctioned, were periodically audited by this body, a powerful check would, in my opinion, be put upon the issuing of many delusive schemes which now cause incalculable ruin.
> (Item 7, *The Accountant,* November 20, 1875, p. 13)

For an example of the same call in relation to the auditing of banks, see Item 9, *The Accountant,* 1879, p. 8. *The Accountant* considered the proposition sufficiently controversial to deem it worthy of consideration (see Item 46). Of course in a period in which the laissez-faire attitude towards business activity was at its height, the threat of government intervention may not have been taken very seriously, a fact admitted even by the profession's critics (see Item 95, p. 761).

## CONCLUSION

The aim of presenting the following extracts from nineteenth-century auditing literature is to give an idea of the historical roots from which today's highly sophisticated and highly lucrative auditing profession is descended. The events and discussions of one century ago may seem remote indeed, yet in reading the material, the immediate impression is the familiarity of the issues under discussion.

## AUDITORS.

### No. 1.—AUDITING.

One of the most important requirements in an Accountant is the capability of fulfilling faithfully and with satisfaction to his clients and himself, the manifold duties which he undertakes in accepting a position of the above nature. To look over, in a hurried and cursory manner, the accounts rendered for inspection, was at one period frequently the mode of conducting an audit, but this fashion of auditing has proved to be entirely insufficient. Errors and discrepancies, unavoidably passed unnoticed, in the course of a short and superficial investigation, were subsequently exposed in the settlement of business transactions; consequently professional men have found it absolutely necessary to alter in its entirety the system of auditing, and to adopt a more perfect method of determining the accuracy of the various accounts placed in their hands for verification. It would be out of place, in these columns, to refer particularly to the enormous frauds that have remained for great lengths of time undiscovered, owing rather to the laxity or ineffacacy of the system of Audit, than to the want of efficiency or fidelity in the Auditors; but that many such malpractices have been unwittingly favoured by the former cause cannot be disputed. For many years a fraud may have been creeping gradually along in the security afforded by the want of thorough examination; when the stringent exercise of their duty by those employed to detect irregularities and discrepancies, would have checked it in its infancy. There are many systems now in use, one, the most general, being to follow and check the various items, which culminate in the details forming the Balance Sheet, or whatever Statement requires authentication; another and more laborious mode is to analyze the whole of the transactions in abstracts specially prepared for the purpose, something in the manner adopted in compiling a statistical return. Some Auditors however, are satisfied with simply checking the totals here and there of the Cash and other books, ascertaining that the statement rendered, agrees with the Ledgers, and that the result tallies with precedents. There exist many more ways of auditing, some more or less complicated, but the three quoted will serve to illustrate the work of an Auditor, who, notwithstanding the smallness of his fee, is expected to verify accounts which, perhaps on a thorough investigation would be found teeming with errors and inaccuracies. In a subsequent article I propose to refer in detail to the duties of auditors, and in a third 'contribution to their responsibilities.

X.

## AUDITORS AND AUDITING.

A correspondent writes to us as follows:—"I am glad to observe that this subject has been taken up by a writer in the ACCOUNTANT, who promises two more articles thereon. I am sure it is one which demands attention, with the view to defining what the duties of an auditor really are, and the value of the service, when properly rendered. It would be well for Accountants' Societies generally to move in this matter, as also in that of accountants' charges, which like the duties of an auditor, require to be defined with the object of securing uniformity. I believe no dozen men would have the same view as to the said duties; nor do directors, or the public, appreciate as they ought, the immense value of them, if honestly performed. Many consider an audit has nothing more in it than certifying to the agreement of balances in a balance-sheet with those in the ledgers from which they are taken; and that cash at the bankers is stated conformably with the pass book, (cash in hand being in some cases absolutely ignored). An auditors' duties are much more important, and should embrace his right to have the accounts kept on such a system that he can *really* get at the essence of affairs; and that his supervision should extend *throughout* a year, and not merely at the end of it. His signature to a balance-sheet then would mean something, and responsibility in the shape of a guarantee, would rest upon him towards the shareholders, for which fees should be paid equivalent. See the various forms of certifying accounts, daily appearing on balance-sheets, and you at once detect how very vague are the views of the different parties signing the accounts on the subject. At any rate, whether I take a wrong view of the matter or not, it is certainly one which must sooner or later be discussed. The public as well as the profession (which would gain also in status very considerably), would be gainers by the duties of an auditor being properly understood, defined, and performed as a *bona fide* service, instead of, as it appears to be a mere sham, and as fees paid and various forms of certifying prove it to be at present."

Our correspondent adds :—" I am glad also to notice an article in the ACCOUNTANT of 2nd inst., on those who style themselves accountants, professing at the same time to be Jacks-of-all-trades, and touters accordingly. What we want is a feeling of *esprit de corps*, in the profession, and a determination on the part of its respectable members to set their faces against anything of the sort. Touting should be denounced, and those descending to it should be shown up. I am in hopes that the profession of a P. A., may some day be looked upon as the most honorable of honorable callings.

## AUDITORS.
### No. 2.—(THEIR DUTIES.)

In continuation of the article on the above subject, we now proceed to deal with the duties and obligations of professional auditors. For the purpose of avoiding complication, it must be borne in mind that there are two distinct classes of general audits, which, for the sake of convenience, may be briefly characterized, one as of a *restricted*, and the other of an *unrestricted*, nature. Regarding the former, it may be taken for granted that a definition of the duties is at the outset arranged with the client; and the extent and period of the investigation determined; and it follows that any subsequent dissatisfaction and personal responsibility become disposed of so long as the mechanical work undertaken is performed as agreed. Such audits, however, being mere affairs of routine and of but little practical value, need not be further discussed, it being obvious that unless an investigation can be carried on in an *unrestricted* and independent manner its utility is insignificant. One of the most essential qualities in an auditor should be a stern determination to fulfil his obligations in a free and unfettered manner. In far too many cases personal feelings tend to bias the professional man in the performance of that which should be divested of the minutest taint of partiality. Again, he may find himself obliged to co-operate with unprofessional men, who, however praiseworthy their intentions may be, are unfortunately so carried away by the fact of holding an appointment, or are so flustered and timid in consequence of their inexperience in matters of business, that it verges almost on the impossible to maintain a systematic regularity in examining accounts under such circumstances. Hence arises the imperative duty of ascertaining beforehand the qualities of the colleagues with whom it may become necessary to act. In public companies the inconveniences of such associations is more particularly manifested, and the Accountant-auditor should use every endeavour to clear himself from the opinionated impedimenta known as co-auditors. To those who are young and growing up in the profession, it cannot be too strongly pointed out that officials and others having some latent purpose to serve, will, by a plausible argument, or an off-hand representation, seek to hide the importance of an auxiliary book or document, thereby successfully concealing transactions which, if brought to light, might possibly lead to an awkward exposure of carelessness, neglect, or fraud. Consequently, the principle of self-reliance is by no means the smallest of the qualifications for the post of Auditor. Referring more particularly to the auditing of companies' accounts, it must be remembered that a large portion of the public will as a rule rely more implicitly on the Report of the auditor than on any other statement submitted to them, so that the authentication of this class of accounts should not be undertaken without the strictest scrutiny. Many whose tendencies lead them to a connection with concerns either for the purposes of investment or speculation, place the utmost faith in the auditor's certificate, and rather than permit the publication of half-audited accounts, his testimony of their correctness should decidedly be withheld. To detail the duties of those who make this their special business would be impossible in these columns; but among the general matters requiring careful scrutiny may be mentioned the vouchers, and cash securities. A code embracing the most important points relative to the duties of auditors, drawn up and adopted by the various London and Provincial Societies, would without doubt, give universal satisfaction. This would demonstrate to the public the amount of security afforded by the employment as auditors of Accountants actuated by a full appreciation of their obligations and duties.  X.

# The Accountant.

## MAY 8, 1875.

The meeting of the Manchester Society of Accountants has been followed by the meeting of the Institute of Accountants; and the reports which we gave of the proceedings on both occasions cannot fail to prove highly gratifying to all who are interested in the well-being of the profession. There was the same strongly marked feeling that the time had come for the decided recognition of accountants as a body, and the same marked determination to uphold their position and their privileges. These meetings, and the publicity given to them, do much towards the great step of thorough union and consolidation. The remarks of the Chairman at the Institute gathering were especially valuable, as directing attention to one very important branch of an accountant's duties, that of auditing. The cry against accountants is, that they are in reality a body of men who have sprung into existence since the Bankruptcy and Companies' Acts, and flourish simply on the ruins of once prosperous undertakings, and the wrecks of private fortunes. This cry is echoed, not only in the columns of mere professional organs, which may naturally be expected to utter shrieks of indignation at any thing which may threaten their interests, but obtains a wider publicity by letters to the daily press. It is true, of course, that the accountant is the man to whom is entrusted the task of saving as much as possible out of the fire ; but there is another aspect of his duties to which we have frequently directed attention, and on which Mr. Kemp dwelt at some length, —that of protection of shareholders and creditors by means of fearless and rigorous auditing. Here is a ground on which no professional jealousy can give rise to any hostility, and on which the public can yield to the profession a sincere and hearty support. It is not too much to say, that but few of the terrible financial scandals which have sprung into such disgraceful notoriety could have taken place, if a thorough and independent system of auditing had been in force. Let the Institute follow up the principles enunciated by Mr. Kemp. Let them hold the professional honour of an accountant to be so high, that it forces him to decline to certify to the correctness of any accounts where he has not been allowed the fullest means of investigation. Let them stand by the man whose fearless discharge of his duty has brought about his dismissal, and let them insist upon his reinstatement. In this course they will carry with them the warm sympathy of the public ; and they will find that those whom it is most necessary to hold in check, will soon cease to contend against them. The fact of an auditor of any company having been dismissed, and all men of eminence and standing in their profession refusing, with the support of the general body, to succeed to his post, will be proof positive to the world that the affairs of the company in question are not able to bear the light of publicity, and the necessary inferences will be readily drawn. Moreover, shareholders and investors will scrutinise carefully the audited account, and see the first threatenings of an impending danger which they may avert or escape from in time. A sound and solvent company need not fear the closest scrutiny into its affairs ; and in answer to any alarming or disquieting rumours as to its stability, may point calmly to the signed approval of the auditors. A shaky concern will dread submitting its accounts to the keen eyes of a trained investigator, for fear of having its instability exposed to the world ; and the dread of independent examination will tell its own tale. If the Institute of Accountants will persist in directing attention to these points, they will have done a very great service to the world, and laid the foundations of a really sound commercial prosperity. But they must attempt to educate the mind of the public. The idea of the importance of the post of auditor must be thoroughly grasped ; and the necessity of his utter independence of any influences which may colour his conclusions, must be insisted upon. Where the auditor or examiner is a mere official of the company, his results cannot invariably be implicitly relied on.

It is to be hoped, also, for the honour and dignity of the profession, that the Council of the Institute will receive that support which they have a right to expect. The name of accountant is often used as a term of reproach, and he is wilfully and maliciously confounded with the outsiders of every calling who do the dirty work, if any. But to be a member of a large and influential body, trained for his work by a well-directed course of study, subject to the keen checks of professional restraint,—to feel that his fiat is looked upon as the test of the stability of many a seemingly prosperous undertaking, and that to his honour, integrity and skill numbers look for the safety of their fortune,—is a position, beyond all dispute, as high as can well be attained. The movement has now fairly begun ; the progress towards the realisation of the wishes of the chief and best members of the profession is rapid ; and we shall soon see, we trust, all working towards the same end, to place the profession of an accountant on the same level as those older professions which may be at present more dignified, but in no degree call forth greater skill or deeper responsibility.

# The Accountant.

JUNE 12, 1875.

In speaking of an audit, it is of the first importance to distinguish whether or not a thorough and efficient one is meant, and also to consider how far the matters to be audited admit of exhaustive treatment, without such heavy expense as would be considered intolerable by any body of shareholders. Many accountants appear to consider that in demonstrating that they really understand book-keeping by double entry, and that they can, if left to follow their own course and take their own time, fully explore all the intricacies of a business concern,—they have shown their fitness for the highest tasks. And many shareholders, on the other hand, practically adopt the idea that they have secured all the advantages of a true audit when they have voted a sum for that purpose, which so far from sufficiently remunerating a careful and plodding inquirer, would hardly pay a man of genius for accountancy for the trouble of superficially glancing at their accounts.

There is a rudimentary kind of audit, which consists in ascertaining that some sort of voucher can be produced for every payment, and that the printed balance-sheet corresponds with balances which can be found in the ledger. Such an audit is supposed to be completed by checking the additions of the cash-book and balance-sheet, and glancing at the banker's pass-book. It was in the days when such audits were common, and were frequently performed (as well they might be) by unprofessional men, that the custom of voting a trifling pittance of ten or twenty guineas to the auditor originated. At the other end of the scale is the audit which, whilst relying on the certificates of skilled officials for the quantity and value of stocks and plant, exercises a certain supervision even over matters such as these, and includes a thorough analysis of all ledger accounts, particularly the impersonal ones. An auditor who does his work well, endeavours to watch every thing with the eye of a prudent and careful master, not flattering himself with the existence of profit until every unfavourable possibility has been gauged. We have known cases where the ill-judged parsimony of shareholders has failed to hinder an effectual audit, because the directors chose to regard the *honorarium* voted to the auditors as a mere fee due in respect of the responsibility assumed by them, and the personal supervision they bestowed ; paying them in addition a much larger sum for the time and travelling expenses of their clerks. But the directors, we believe, would have done no such thing, had not their sense of responsibility been quickened by the fact that they themselves held enormous stakes in the concern. It is more common by far to find that the small fee paid is accepted on the footing that services of corresponding value are expected, and that any investigation of accounts, however desirable in itself, which would render the auditorship a losing affair, is to be left undone. No doubt, the most cursory examination of a balance-sheet by a trained accountant must tend to prevent gross mistakes; but the professional man little considers what is due to himself, who accepts a task (on whatever terms) without a fixed determination, cost what it may, to perform that task effectually. A resolute adherence to this principle would soon lead to important results; for auditors of any eminence would either free themselves from the most anxious and responsible of their professional duties, or they would enforce the payment of an adequate fee.

Some of the artifices against which an auditor has to be on his guard, are very difficult of detection. He has to rely on human testimony after all, and cannot hope to do more than excite a salutary terror in the breasts of evil-doers. There was once a case, for instance, of a railway company, whose officers presented a schedule showing the tonnage of unused rails in stock. The piles were some of them minutely described, the number and lengths of the rails being given. Other piles were briefly stated to consist of so many tons. The auditor's suspicions were excited; he demanded to see the man who had made out the inventory, and at length elicited that some of the piles were purely imaginary. Renewals or other expensive outlays had taken place in the past half-year which some official thought it expedient to place to a certain extent against the revenue of the next half-year; hence the creation of this imaginary asset, which it was meant should be written off before the next audit. Small blame would have attached to the auditor, in the minds of reasonable men, had he been taken in by such a contrivance as this: for the possibilities of deceit are infinite, whilst the vigilance of any man must necessarily be finite.

In the case of banks an enormous mass of details must be taken for granted, unless the expense of the audit is to be very much augmented. The auditor can, and does, compare as many pass-books as he can obtain with the balances in the ledgers, and he examines the securities, and the profit and loss account: but any one who knows what it is to count bonds and other securities by thousands, must be aware that errors are possible—at the least, coupons may be missing; and

the accounts of individual depositors may be manipulated by clerks, who will know how to secrete, temporarily, the pass-books of such depositors. Worst of all, the counting of coin, and of securities takes place at a date which is foreknown by all concerned; and there is nothing to prevent a deficiency being momentarily covered by a short loan of cash, to be re-taken out of the bank till, soon after the auditor's scrutiny is over.

We need not comment on the fact that the amounts due to banks and other institutions on current bills and loans (or overdrawn balances, so common in the North) may or may not be recoverable. An auditor can never know who is insolvent or embarrassed, except by mere chance, until some visible sign of difficulty appears on the face of the accounts. The chance of detecting any rottenness in the assets is much diminished when the debtors reside in distant cities; and, again, when a Company may have entered into contracts of the most hazardous nature, in respect of which no entry can be made in a balance-sheet.

Experienced auditors have always endeavoured to limit their responsibility by using guarded language in their certificates. Let shareholders look to such language closely; and if they see fit, let them call for explanations from the auditors at their meetings. The result will generally be most wholesome.

## AUDITING.

The following letter recently appeared in a daily contemporary. We give insertion to Mr. Lowe's communication, although his conclusions apply to honorary and ornamental auditing, rather than to the work of a paid accountant :—

"Arthur-street, Rochdale, Oct. 31.

"Sir,—It must have been a matter of painful surprise and astonishment to the outside public that so many great frauds on the public elude detection. Day after day we are accustomed to find in our morning paper the account of some serious defalcation on the part of some officer of trust who has been successfully deluding his employers for a number of years, and whose discovery is generally mainly attributable to the chapter of accidents. It is not only in the affairs of private firms that these practices obtain success, but equally in the accounts of public bodies, corporate or otherwise, who employ disinterested persons periodically to audit and certify the same to be found correct. An effort to supply some remedy that would prevent this anomaly, and nip in the bud these gigantic frauds which so frequently startle us, is a simple duty.

"It must be admitted that there must be a serious defect in the system of auditing as at present generally exercised, else it were a total impossibility that these evils should obtain. I am inclined to think, indeed I know, that the majority of gentlemen who discharge the duties of auditor content themselves with the examination of the balance-sheet as prepared by the secretary or book-keeper who submits it for their perusal. This examination consists—firstly, of a simple comparing of the balances shown in the balance-sheet with the balances as they appear in the ledgers; secondly, the comparing of the vouchers with the payments as entered in the cash-book; and lastly, a general checking of the various additions in the different books. This completed, the auditor signs his name to the balance-sheet, and his work is ended. No means are adopted by him to ascertain if every thing is in the books that ought to be there; that point he considers to be out of his province.

"I would ask, then, if this set form of procedure is all the public or the auditor's employers have a right to expect? Take, for instance, the affairs of a private firm who employ an auditor. The books are put through the process as described above, but there are probably some hundred or two of accounts represented as debtors to the firm, but which are never applied to by the auditor to ascertain if their debit balances as shown by the ledger are correct or not. If any of these have paid money which has not been passed to their credit, but which has been appropriated by the dishonest servant, no means are adopted whereby this wide door to fraud can be early and promptly closed. Again, take an instance of a Corporation, where a rate of so much in the pound is laid upon a certain assessed value. The balances as shown to be owing by the books are invariably assumed to be correct without any further inquiry, and so fraud may go on from year to year, duly audited and found correct. In the latter case, it may be argued that it is an impossibility to frame a check, as the number of debtors are so numerous. I am not of that opinion. The amount of the rate to be realised is known. The amount actually paid is easily traceable. The difference between the

two should be represented by the balances owing. Now, I would suggest that in the case of a private firm, all the debtors should be furnished with a statement of their indebtedness as shown by the books, and requested to verify or otherwise the same; and in the case where collectors are employed, as in corporate or public bodies, inspectors should at certain periods either acccompany them or go independently and check off what amounts are unaccounted for. These reports being submitted to an auditor, would render him wholly independent of the fair copied books, and I believe effectually remedy this great evil.

"It is time that audits ceased to be matters of routine, and that they became what the outside world understand them to be—thorough investigations. Honest men will not shrink at any thing that proves them to be worthy of trust.

"I hope, Sir, you will excuse my addressing you, but the interest I have long taken in this subject must be my apology.

"Your obedient servant,

"JOHN LOWE."

## AUDITING.

The following additional communication on the subject of auditing is extracted from a contemporary :—

" Arthur-street, Rochdale, Nov. 5.

" Sir,—In my letter which appeared in your columns of the 2nd inst. I called attention to the loose system of auditing as at present exercised, and ventured to point out some means whereby it might be improved. Your remarks of yesterday are exceedingly pertinent to the question, and your suggestion of the formation of a wholly independent body of professional auditors is one that would dissipate many of the existing evils.

" Your correspondent 'Auditor' remarks 'that audits are too often regarded as tedious formalities, to be disposed of at the least possible amount of expense ; and the fee allowed is frequently such as to make it well understood that merely a superficial discharge of the duties is required.' If any thing were required to confirm the justice of my remarks it is to be found in this sentence, where we are gravely told by a professional gentleman that we are to judge of the worth of the audit by the amount of fee paid for its performance. Such is not my opinion of the duty. Either a gentleman should refuse to audit where the fee is insufficient, or the public should be informed of its relative value. An auditor's certificate should be based upon totally disinterested grounds, the result of careful and honest investigation.

" If you will allow me, Sir, to make another remark on this subject, I would like to suggest that, when such a body as you refer to has been formed, every proposed new company should submit its plans to the Board of Trade, and receive its sanction before the public are invited by specious prospectuses to invest their capital. This would have, palpably, a very beneficial effect in keeping out fraud. The promoters of any new company that was honest would not complain of such a step as this on the ground of unwarrantable interference, as the public have a perfect right to a proper guarantee against the designs of schemers and those who make their fortunes by plausible representations and by cleverly working the share markets. If a body of independent auditors were attached to the Board of Trade, to whom all new schemes would be referred for approval or otherwise, and, if sanctioned, were periodically audited by this body, a powerful check would, in my opinion, be put upon the issuing of many delusive schemes which now cause incalculable ruin.

" Permit me also to hope that measures will be taken to amend the clause in the Municipal Act which has been recently defined as confining the duties of an auditor to the examination of the books and vouchers in a borough treasurer's department only, and which, through being so interpreted by the legal adviser of a corporation, has materially helped to prevent an earlier discovery of the defalcations lately reported in a neighbouring borough.

" Allow me to thank you for your assistance, and I hope it will promote an improvement in our commercial system of auditing.

" Your obedient servant,
" JOHN LOWE."

## Communicated Articles.

### AUDITING.

What is an audit? in what does the duty of auditing consist? If it were a duty about the performance of which no doubt, or any difference of opinion existed, the simple attestation "Audited" at the foot of a balance sheet, followed by the auditor's signature, would and should be sufficient; but the fact of there being so many forms of attestation in use, none of which can be said to carry a specific meaning, is a proof that this very important subject has not had that attention given to it which it deserves, and that the shadow and not the substance, as in other formal matters, is what is deemed sufficient.

The time, I think, has now arrived for a clear definition of the duties of an auditor being decided and acted upon, so that the farce of auditing as hitherto sanctioned may end, and the real value of the service, when properly rendered, be explained and demanded, as well as adequately paid for. The following are my ideas on the subject:—

1. An auditor, like a barrister or medical man, should be *unable to depute a subordinate to do his work;* individual character being the first qualification for the duties, otherwise confidence is misplaced, &c.

2. The auditor's signature should imply that *he himself* had checked the figures and vouchers in the balance-sheet put before him.

3. The fees payable should be for the *individual* service rendered, and they should be such that men of experience and honour would feel it worth their while to accept, and not such as are about equivalent to a principal's charge for a poorly paid clerk, who can have no feeling of responsibility in the performance of what he can but consider ordinary *clerical* duties.

4. The balance sheet being made out and submitted to the auditor, there remains no *clerical* work to be done; what is required is, that Mr. A., the duly appointed auditor, "do now proceed personally to verify the figures thereon stated," his signature is then of value to those who have reposed their confidence in him; but how can it be of value otherwise? and yet, as a rule nine audits out of ten are those of clerks: the auditor himself takes his clerk's figures for granted, and by so doing admits his position to be of little or no actual value—in fact, lowers the status of his profession in this branch of it. As regards going concerns, clerks are employed to the most advantage by those whose business needs their services; but it seems absurd to employ accountants' clerks in solvent businesses, where to devise a clear system of account and the supervision thereof is the duty of the accountant himself.

5. This view being admitted, what are the auditor's duties? I think they ought to begin by the system on which the accounts are to be kept being submitted to and

approved of by him before opening the books, and if he be not satisfied that the system is one which will enable him to ascertain clearly the result of transactions at the end of a period, he should, in the event of opposition to his views for that purpose, at once resign.

6. No account of a "leakage" character should be opened without his sanction, such as for "extension of business," "special extra services," &c., and if sanctioned he should have the right to approve of the extent to which such payment should be made, after consultation with the directors. It is no use his objecting to such account when the money has already been spent.

7. According to the magnitude of the business, the auditor should determine whether it be necessary for him to attend, say monthly throughout the year, so that he may see that the various accounts which merge in profit and loss at balancing time are properly treated.

8. The auditor should see that all expenditure accounts are properly analysed, and that the various totals of items agree with the total debits of the respective accounts in ledger; the general and petty cash being audited (if monthly visits are decided upon) and the balances in hand verified each visit.

9. Personal accounts would only be referred to at the time of balancing, and then the age of the various balances should be looked into, also the nature of the accounts, so that the auditor himself can thus form his own opinion of their *bonâ fides* and value; and this being understood by those who conduct the business, care would be taken that due provision is periodically made for bad or doubtful assets in the shape of book debts, or the risk would be run of the auditor declining to sign the balance sheet.

10. All securities (other than stock), including bills receivable, and cash, should be carefully checked; the bills being examined as to their *bonâ fides;* stock, as to the value of which an auditor can have no personal knowledge beyond an asked for assurance that it is taken at *cost* price, should be vouched for by a certificate from a responsible party to that effect, and that due allowance has been made for any depreciation.

11. The balance sheet should be accompanied by a clearly stated profit and loss account (for without this I do not see much value to shareholders of the balance sheet only), and also an equally clear statement of expenses account, showing all the headings of the various items, so that no large item of "sundries" appears; this, however, need not be printed, but it should be open to any shareholder to inspect at the office.

12. If cheques are all crossed and made payable to order by the printing, and they are each numbered, the number being entered with the entry in cash book, and are attached in order to the counterparts on their return paid by the bank, it does not seem necessary that any other receipts should be produced to the auditor; the petty cash being the only channel for robbery, and this is checked by the analysis of expenses I suggest, the various headings denoting to the auditor whether payments are apparently excessive or not.

13. An audit conducted in this way, whereby the auditor himself knows the whole working of the accounts (they of course being kept on a proper and clear system), I consider to be of every use and of immense value, the mere looking at receipts and checking postings being superlative labour; and if it were understood that the auditor (subject only to the value of stock, which every two years might be independently valued by a competent person to be appointed by the auditor, or better still by the shareholders) not only vouches for the agreement of the balances as shown in the balance sheet with those in the ledger, but that he has superintended the accountancy throughout, has sanctioned any expenditure standing at debit of an account to be reduced in the course of years, has himself personally looked at all the book debts, and is satisfied, as far as it is possible, that they are *bonâ fide*, and not old ones of years' standing, has been assured by certificate from the responsible party that all invoices for goods bought to date of balance sheet are credited the personal accounts to debit of the respective impersonal ones, that other assets have been looked to by him, &c., &c., then if this is what an audit is understood to be, the word

" AUDITED "

should be quite sufficient, and the auditor bears a responsibility for which his reputation stands guarantee; and the remuneration should be adequate. I am fully aware that others take quite a different view of the subject, the discussion of which, however, at the present time, I cannot but think desirable for the benefit of all concerned.

Z.

*14th April*, 1876.

## AUDIT OF BANKING ACCOUNTS.

The publication of the following reports and extracts relating to the establishment of a more efficient system of auditing bank accounts has been delayed by reason of pressure on our space during the last two or three weeks :

At a meeting of the National Association for the Promotion of Social Science, held at Adam-street, Adelphi, Professor Bonamy Price in the chair, a paper was read by Mr. Harold Brown, entitled " Defects of Joint-Stock Banks, and Suggestions for their Remedy." In the course of his paper Mr. Brown discussed the the four defects which, in his view, vitiated the whole system of joint-stock banks—namely, the publicity necessarily given to their transactions as embodied in their periodical balance-sheets and accounts; the evils incidental to their management; the want of an efficient audit ; and, lastly, the principle of unlimited liability. The publicity which was inseparable from the system almost compelled the directors to show on their balance-sheets a profit, whether earned or not. Private traders, who were not forced to publish their returns year by year, could write off their losses in a bad year ; but joint-stock banks could not do so without a serious diminution of their credit. The management of such banks was inherently faulty, both as regards the divided responsibility of the directors and the want of any definite code to regulate their duties or disabilities as to their dealings with the banks with which they were themselves connected. As for the auditors, the average shareholder believed, and was even intended to believe, that the audit meant something more than the mere checking of the arithmetical calculations appearing in the books and summarized in the annual balance-sheet; but, as a matter of fact, audits seldom had any deeper significance, as the independent valuation of the assets represented in the balance-sheet could only be made by the managers and directors themselves. Finally, unlimited liability rendered investments in bank shares undesirable, save for a comparatively small class of persons. The faults to which he alluded were, Mr. Brown contended, all susceptible of remedy. In particular, as it was not likely that the great banks would, by any concerted action, invite simultaneous inspection, a compulsory Government audit was necessary ; and to meet the other most prominent evil he suggested the abolition of unlimited liability. Limited liability, pure and simple, he did not advocate ; but he desired that the liability should be small enough to be comprehended and clearly taken into account by the average investor, and yet large enough to give the confidence essential to a healthy trading credit. The exact limit he could not pretend to assign, but he believed that any statesman who dealt judiciously with the subject would deserve well of his country. The chairman said that they were not discussing good or bad banking, but only the specific evils attendant on one kind of banks. The question was whether those evils called for legislative interference, and upon what principle could the Legislature be invoked. For his own part, he considered legislative interference justified in matters of trade wherever a large body of the community could not, from the nature of the case, protect itself. The catastrophe of the City of Glasgow Bank proved the necessity of adopting some safeguards by which, without undue publication of a bank's affairs, a true and faithful account of the debts and assets might be given. Sir R. Torrens expressed his opinion that the reader of the paper had depicted an abnormal and exceptional state of things, and that the evils he had mentioned were by no means widespread. Mr. Chadwick, M.P., believed that publicity, so far from being a defect, was one of the very great advantages of the joint-stock system. He agreed, however, with Mr. Brown that audits might be made more efficient, and that an increased liability should attach to the auditor. After a few words from Sir J. M'Kenna, M.P., Mr. F. Hill said that the burden of proof lay with those who desired the interference of the Legislature. There was no reason for departing from the principle of commercial non-interference ; and, instead of a compulsory Government audit, an investigation made on the application of a moderate number of shareholders, as under the provisions of the Friendly Societies Act, would be equally efficacious. Mr. J. Brown, Q.C., remarked that it was too late to discuss the question whether the Legislature ought or ought not to interfere, considering that joint-stock banks were already the creations of Parliament and were regulated by the Companies Acts of 1862 and 1867. It was only doubtful how far Parliament should go. In his opinion, a compulsory audit was necessary, the present system being little better than a farce, as the auditor was practically, though not nominally, chosen by the directors. It would, of course, be borne in mind that a compulsory audit would cast no undeserved slur on the credit of any one bank.

The discussion was continued at an adjourned meeting, at which Mr. Chadwick, M.P., presided. Mr. C. Walford, who resumed the debate, having briefly stated the history of joint-stock banking, expressed his opinion that one of the most important remedies that could be adopted would be to prevent a bank, under any circumstances, purchasing or making advances upon its own shares. With regard to the publication of proceedings connected with banking he held that a reasonable amount of publicity, coupled with audit made by public accountants of acknowledged status, would tend to the advantage, not only of the shareholders, but of the banks themselves. In proof of this the speaker pointed out that, as far as he knew, no bank had been known to fail the accounts of which were audited by public accountants. In concluding, Mr. Walford contended that the most important step to be taken for the remedy of existing evils connected with banking was to put an end to banking with unlimited liability. Mr. Haughton, who followed, maintained that a Government audit would be advantageous, not only to the shareholders but to the banks themselves, if they were strong, and their business was conducted on sound principles. Mr. Finch held that the main reason for the failure of joint-stock banks in late years had been the habit of investing their money in uncertain and dead securities, which put it beyond the power of the directors to realize the money of the bank at short notice, when occasion required. With regard to the accounts of banks he held

that real publicity was of vital importance, and that the audit ought to be placed in the hands of a public body, which should arrange for the frequent publication of accounts, as was the case with the Bank of England. Mr. Tait called attention to the anomalous state of the law in Scotland in regard to trustees, and maintained that there the three principal remedies to be adopted for the existing state of things would be the prevention of banks speculating in their own shares, the establishment of a Government audit, and the establishment of a universal system of limited liability in banking business. Mr. Addison strongly opposed the suggestion of a Government audit, mainly on the ground that the business transacted by banks was so various that no single auditor could possibly cope with all its details. In his point of view, the most effectual step to be taken would be to subdivide the form of accounts to a greater extent than at present, and to insure the fullest possible publicity for them. Mr. M'Ewen, speaking as a bank manager, complained that the account which had been given by the author of the paper of the mode in which joint-stock banks were conducted was a most grotesque production, and conveyed an unjust view of the manner in which the business was carried on. With regard to the question of audit, he felt sure that no Government, however adventurous, would ever be found to endorse the accounts of any joint-stock bank. Mr. Welton thought that, as regarded a good alteration of the power of directors, it would be very hard to draw up a plan. Mr. Denny Wilson, with reference to the question of audit, thought it a matter of grave doubt whether the Government would ever undertake the audit of the balance-sheets of banks. He recommended an independent audit by respectable auditors. The Chairman expressed the opinion that there ought to be a limitation of deposits bearing proportion to the paid-up capital of the bank, and proposed a vote of thanks to Mr. Harold Brown for his paper, and it was adopted by acclamation, after which Mr. Harold Brown proceeded to say that what was wanted was true publicity. With reference to the auditor he should be a person above the board, and should be able to speak with authority. The amount of deposits was sufficient to show the public interest involved. He thought there were many grounds for justifying judicious parliamentary legislation.

Mr. Thomson Hankey writes as follows in *The Times.*—" I venture to express a very decided opinion that an attempt to carry out a systematic audit in any of the various modes proposed would be both futile and mischievous—futile because no professional auditor can really ascertain whether the assets of a bank have been properly valued, and mischievous because, if attempted, it would tend to relieve the directors of a responsibility which they are bound to undertake, and which duty if they are incapable of performing they are unfit to continue to be directors. I believe that in 99 out of every 100 cases of failure of a bank it can be shown to have arisen from one of three causes :—(1) Ignorance of bookkeeping ; (2) investments in other than banking securities ; (3) ignoring the difference between a bill of exchange and a mortgage. I will endeavour to explain my meaning respecting these three points. 1. As to bookkeeping. I consider it an axiom in all good bookkeeping that no profits can be considered as earned until it has been clearly shown that the capital account is perfectly intact. In many trading concerns it may be difficult to effect this perfectly at an annual balance of accounts, because goods or other property may have been sent to various parts of the world ; and as long as these have not been realized, it may be impossible to estimate their actual value at any one moment. Not so, however, with the accounts of a bank. If the assets of a bank are invested in proper securities, these securities are always capable of being valued within such limits as cannot materially affect the accuracy of the accounts. 2. What are proper securities for a bank in which to employ money deposited and liable to be recalled at the will of the depositor ? First of all, it is absolutely necessary to have a certain amount kept in ready money. I do not consider that money lent to a bill broker or discount house (however safe for certain purposes) should ever be considered as ready money, which is cash or Bank of England notes. What is the normal amount or proportion of deposits so to be retained must depend on the nature of the business carried on by the bank. One-fifth or one-sixth may in some banks be as little as should be so kept; others, perhaps, may consider that one-tenth may be sufficient; but some regular proportion is absolutely necessary. After this provision has been made the most undoubted security for investment is in good bills of exchange—that is, in engagements by persons whose financial position is considered above suspicion to pay their engagements at maturity. A term of three months is long enough for such banking securities; but if ever longer, it should be only under exceptional circumstances; and above all it is indispensable for a good banking security that the acceptor intends to pay his acceptance at the date of maturity and not to contemplate a renewal of the bill. It is also essential that the engagement to pay should be perfectly independent of any external circumstances, such as the realization of goods, &c. There are various other kinds of good banking securities, but one feature must necessarily pervade them all—viz., that they must be of a marketable nature, so that the banker may safely depend, under all ordinary circumstances, on being able to realize them within a very short time. 3. To understand the difference between a bill of exchange and a mortgage. I have already said that a bill of exchange must be a document which the acceptor intends to discharge at maturity, and cannot be made to depend on any external circumstances, such as the sale of goods or a counter-engagement of any other person. This I hold to be the main difference between a bill of exchange and a mortgage. A bill of exchange may be the form in which a person may give a security to a banker for a loan, and he may intend to pay it if he is able to sell a ship or a house or a landed estate; but it does not come under the proper character of a bill of exchange if dependent on any such external contingency; and it is the refusal to recognize this difference which, I venture to assert, is generally the first cause of a bank becoming involved in difficulties and locking up the money of depositors in investments which cannot be realized when the depositor requires to withdraw his money. Before any public bank declares a dividend the balance-sheet ought to be most carefully examined by a committee of four or five of the oldest and most experienced directors, who should sign a declaration (to be read before every meeting of shareholders for dividends), stating that they had gone over every item of the securities held by the bank, and, according to the best opinion they could form, each separate item was properly stated in the money column according to its marketable value. If these rules were followed, no further audit would be necessary; and if shareholders would take care to elect as directors only gentlemen of acknowledged character and position, I do not believe that we should often hear of any public banking establishment getting into difficulties.

---

THE *Times* City Editor writes as follows in commenting upon the form of certificate adopted by the auditors of the Alliance Bank :—A considerable change has been made in the auditors' certificate appended to the report, and it is worth quoting entire as a fair sample of what an auditor could reasonably be called upon to certify about a bank. The common objection to audit is that " it would be impossible for any auditor to assess the value of securities which may be good in themselves." No reasonable person expects that an auditor should certify to values. He can, however, certify to the correctness of the books, and whether a bank really has securities against its loans, and such a certification the following covers :—" We have examined the foregoing accounts in detail, with the books and vouchers of the bank, and find them to be correct. Further, we have ascertained by actual enumeration the correctness of the items of cash and bills of exchange in hand, and have inspected the securities representing the bank's own investments in Government stocks, &c., and also those held on account of advances and loans, as well as those belonging to customers, and we find them to be in due accordance with the books and accounts of the bank,

" WILLIAM QUILTER (Quilter, Ball & Co.) }
" JOHN YOUNG (Turquand, Youngs & Co.) } Auditors."

With a more complete balance-sheet, such as all banks must in time be induced to give, this formula would be also nearly complete.

### EFFICIENT AUDITING.

It is a relief to turn from a contemplation of the varied piece of legal patchwork known as bankruptcy legislation to a subject which is at least of equal importance, viz. the necessity of a compulsory audit for banking and other concerns of a joint-stock nature.

As things at present exist, it is too much the rule to call in the aid of an accountant only when the commercial patient is in a moribund or defunct condition, and hence arises no small part of the odium which, in the popular mind, attaches to the accountants' profession, because, forsooth, the expert is unable to bring about a resurrection, or cure the hopelessly diseased. Evidences, however, are not wanting that business men are beginning to see the expediency of a somewhat more rational process. Great banking failures, and the consequent collapse of parasitical mercantile houses, have led men to feel that every possible precaution of a preventive nature must be taken—and it is now becoming a generally accepted conclusion that a more thorough and efficient system of auditing is not amongst the least of such safeguards. Independent examinations, and searching investigations from without of the modes of doing business, are indeed essential, whether it be fraud or incapacity which it is advisable to guard against. It is only a truism of the stalest character to say that it is for the general weal that rotten trading and fraudulent transactions should be nipped in the bud, before they culminate in the ruin of innocent shareholders; and it is to accountants that the public look for the performance of the duties thus indicated. As the *Times* put it in an article a few days ago on the subject of amendments in the Banking Laws, "our main trust would be in a greatly increased rigour in the audit of accounts." Of course no one regards compulsory audit as a panacea for commercial ailments. Isolated cases are sure to occur, in which misdirected abilities will set at defiance all audits, and particularly such as are of a restricted character; but, as our contemporary says, "an honest system of auditing" would at least serve in most instances "to arrest folly or fraud at the outset." Such a system would indeed make it impossible "for the experts of other banks not to perceive that a business which owed ten millions in November was not in a position to pay a twelve per cent. dividend in July."

As the tide of public opinion thus appears to be setting in a direction which will undoubtedly serve to raise the tone and enhance the value of the services rendered to commerce by the profession, it is, we think, important that accountants should express their opinions in some decided and authoritative form, with the view, not only to clearing away some of the misconceptions which exist on the subject, but also to defining the requirements and extent of an efficient audit. There is,

unfortunately, a considerable amount of selfish reticence amongst accountants: they have been, up to the present, too much disposed to stand quietly by, without making any vigorous protest or suggestion, whilst others frame laws which accountants have to carry out, with the inevitable consequence of also bearing the blame of inherent defects. This subject of audit, for instance, is one vitally affecting accountants, and on which an authoritative statement of a practical character would receive the consideration due to the judgment of an expert, and would probably serve to affect the result beneficially, not only for accountants themselves, but for the public. There are many fallacies and stumbling-blocks in the way of an efficient audit, which some official statement as to the broad principles that ought to govern such a survey would tend to clear away. We may simply instance two conditions, without which we think it will be generally agreed that no audit can lay claim to be considered really *efficient*—i.e. serving the purpose of its creation, which we take to be, broadly speaking, the supplying an assurance that the statements put forth by the management as to earnings and general position are accurate and trustworthy, having regard specially to the fact that this assurance is intended mainly for the benefit of such persons interested in joint-stock concerns as are unable from various causes to obtain it for themselves. And these conditions are, that the audit should be unlimited as to its scope, and that the auditors should not be tied down to prescribed times for their work; or, since the two are necessarily blended—that the auditing should be *unrestricted* in the full sense of the word. The value of the auditor's labours is insignificant when his inspection is limited beforehand to certain books, in respect of which he is simply required to give a certificate that certain totals and balances agree, and that certain numerical conclusions are logically correct, provided always that the premises are also unassailable—which latter fact he is not allowed to ascertain for himself. The intrinsic value of such work is in fact proportionate to the fee paid for it. What is wanted is that the discretion to limit the inquiry of an auditor in this way should be entirely taken away from directors and managers. Then as to the periods prescribed for the audit, nothing can be more subversive of the desired end than to fix the dates of such examinations long beforehand. It is thus always possible to clear the decks and make everything as trim as possible for the occasion. Books can be put out of the way, and reasons concocted for non-production, and deficiencies covered by temporary loans; and he would be a very smart auditor who did not occasionally fail to discover some concealed rottenness when every preparation had been made for his arrival. Failures do not necessarily begin either in frauds or gross blunders, but originate often enough in the desire on the part of the management to make things a little *couleur de rose* for the shareholders. And it is precisely such insidious deviations from the path of commercial rectitude which could frequently be easiest concealed from an auditor, who is in many cases (to use a Yankeeism) " put through " his official visit. There must indeed be an element of *continuity* in the inspection of an auditor: he should have full liberty to look into the affairs of the concern at his own promptings and at his own seasons. And there need be no fear that such a privilege would be abused by any respectable auditor; although the profession is yet a young one, we need not hesitate to assert that there are plenty of men in it who have as high a sense of their duty, and may be trusted to act up to it as implicitly, as the family lawyer and the family doctor. And as to the check which a *régime* of this kind would give to shady practices on the part of directors and managers—it is surely not necessary to commend an advantage which is so apparent. Another subject on which it is desirable that there should be some expressed agreement amongst auditors as a body is as to the extent, and the form of the certificate given as the result of their audit. It is unquestionably the duty of an auditor to make the shareholder fully cognisant of the extent of his examination, and with that view the employment of any general phrase should be repudiated; and on this point we may draw attention to the certificate of the auditors of the Alliance Bank, which we reprinted in our issue of the 1st inst. Some avowed understanding amongst leading accountants on this head is, it appears to us, very desirable. It would strengthen the hands of auditors against any attempted pressure on the part of directors, and it would serve to show shareholders that accountants are cognisant of the reliance placed on their work by the public, and anxious to carry out their trust in the most effectual manner.

## "THE NECESSITY OF A MANUAL ON AUDITING."*

The proceedings of the Co-operative Congress at Leeds would not have been entirely barren if they had resulted

* The title of a paper which is printed on another page of this issue.—ED.

in nothing more important than a discussion upon the above subject. We shall be glad to find that a well-considered series of resolutions are arrived at by the Committee to whom the matter has been referred, indicating what work ought in the opinion of practical men to be performed by the auditor.

Mr. Milburne himself possesses a grasp of the subject which sufficiently evidences a practical acquaintance with its difficulties. But perhaps his paper is not free from the failings which are incidental to a hasty treatment of a matter the intricacy of which demands the calmest consideration and the most deliberate judgment.

We take the liberty at the outset to differ with Mr. Milburne as to the main purpose of an audit. It is not the chief duty of an auditor to ascertain as to the integrity or otherwise of the officials of a Company. His primary work is to ascertain the state of the Company's affairs at a certain time, and the results of its transactions within a given period; not to verify every particular transaction and to follow every item of value. Incidentally, he must test both the honesty, the intelligence, and the fairness of the officials, as well as their capacity to do the work entrusted to them. And Mr. Milburne is perfectly correct in attaching importance to this portion of their labours.

The nature of the business of a Co-operative Store is such, that a thorough test by the auditor of all transactions would be too laborious and too costly a process. It is often thought impracticable to carry out efficiently a system of accounting for stock. It has happened sometimes that through want of efficient control, through diversity of duties and consequent interruptions in the work, or from the occurrence of frequent changes in the staff, a stock account, when attempted, has been incompletely worked out, and has therefore been unserviceable though costly. The nomenclature of articles may sometimes become a source of difficulty, the same thing being called by several names, or points of distinction being recorded at one time and not at another. Junior clerks are apt enough, when puzzled, to omit to write up their work, and to fail in applying to their chiefs for guidance. However that may be, the keeping of a stock account is part of the work of the staff, if it is to be done at all, and the auditor should see that very good reasons exist for the absence of such a record, if none is placed before him.

Mr. Milburne's general remarks are very true. He sees that the most honest officer may commit errors of judgment, and that such a man, more than any one, will seek the support only to be given him by an efficient and searching audit. But when he goes on to say that a diligent auditor without a certain mental grasp may fail to detect fraud, and may even pass over mistakes and errors of judgment without noting them, we can only infer that he is thinking of the inherent difficulties of the subject, and inferentially asserting that they can all be overcome, when practically such is not the case.

Now, as to the belief Mr. Milburne seems to entertain, that whilst many audits where due diligence has been shown " in tracing that all cash shown to be received has passed into the hands of the bankers, fail in proving that the amount as shown to be the cash received is correct," something better may be attained by the help of this "mental grasp"—we fail to follow his idea. What more can be done than to trace the receipts from the counter to the till and thence to the bank? If the staff be inadequate, some one may cheat, and remain undetected, through want of supervision; if there be dishonesty all through, anything nearly is possible in the way of fraud without a trace. How does the auditor combat this kind of thing? We think he has little chance of doing more than to arrive at a fair estimate of what the gross profit should be on the business done, having regard to the cost of given articles, their retail price, and the extent of the turnover. He may want *data* for such an estimate, if no complete account of stock received and issued is kept, or if such account is rendered unreliable by fraud.

Whilst then we would guard against fallacious hopes, pointing to absolute certainty as the result of an efficient audit, we would endorse what Mr. Milburne says, as to the possibility of a great deal of good and careful work being done to little purpose, if the field is not properly covered. A fraudulent man will soon see what details there are which escape the auditor's eye and what opportunities for fraud are thus presented. He has all the year to devise his plans : the auditor but a few hurried days in which to unearth the subterranean plots which may exist.

As to a Society being on the high road to ruin if, out of £30,000 receipts, a portion such as £500 has been embezzled, we would only say that the balance-sheet is sure to show its position in its worst aspect, if well arranged and vouched, and supposing the office is so far free from fraud that the accounts current can be relied upon. Cash sales suppressed would operate exactly as low prices would do in decreasing receipts ; but receipts from customers embezzled and not credited in their accounts would not have such an effect ; and the only consolation is that such errors are bound to be discovered if the books are kept written up to date, if the work of keeping accounts current in ledgers and writing up customers' pass-books is frequently transferred from one member of the staff to another, and if any one of the ledger keepers is honest.

W. A. T.

*(To be continued.)*

### CO-OPERATIVE CONGRESS: MANUAL OF AUDITING.

At the thirteenth annual Co-operative Congress, held at Leeds last week, a paper was read by Mr. R. J. Milburne on "The Necessity of a Manual on Auditing." The following is a copy of the paper, to which reference is made elsewhere by W. A. T. :—

The first element necessary to the success of a co-operative store, or any financial institution, may be fairly considered to be public confidence in its stability and the integrity of its working.

If this be true with regard to a store and its members, it is quite as true in the relations which exist between the board of management and the employés. Confidence—thorough, hearty and intelligent confidence—must be felt by the board of management in both the financial ability and the integrity of the secretary, treasurer, and other officials of the store. This confidence must be based upon a thorough and efficient system of check, and also upon reliance on the integrity of all who have to do with the manipulation of accounts, the receiving and paying of cash or dealing with securities. This intelligent confidence can only be established and maintained either upon the part of themselves in the store, or upon the part of the board of management in the officials of the store, by more than a simple reliance upon the personal honesty of the individuals upon whom special responsibility rests. Errors of judgment lead, if not detected and corrected in time, to serious evils, and these errors are committed by persons of the most unimpeachable characters ; but further experience teaches us that it is not wise to allow any man to have charge of, and deal with, the funds of others without the safeguard of efficient check and supervision. So true is this, that no sensible man would undertake any position of trust in which his actions would be free from the safeguard of supervision, because, however honestly he might fulfil his duties, he would know that he had no means of establishing his integrity by external testimony. The true end of any system of audit is an external check-supervision and testimony of the honesty and integrity of the officials and the soundness of the society. Auditors must have a mental grasp of the aim of the accounts to be examined, and when this is obtained a vast amount of detail may be dispensed with. Place an engine into the hands of a practical engineer, and he will direct his attention to the special parts of its mechanism upon which its right action depends, and in which any defect will have serious consequences, without wasting his time over a minute examination of every rod, shaft, bolt, nut, and washer, simply because he knows the character and object of every part of the complex machine. He does not need to scrutinise each part, as a man knowing nothing of its structure might do, in order to ascertain that it is in proper working order. Without this mental grasp the auditors' most diligent labours may utterly fail to attain the object for which they were appointed, and they may find, after spending hour upon hour in comparing entries, adding up cash column after cash column, multiplying, dividing and subtracting, that all their labours have ended in the entire concealment of mistakes and frauds which it was their duty to find out and expose ; and also, instead of affording satisfactory evidence of security, they have, through ignorance and mis-direction, proved to be nothing better than "a mockery, a delusion and a snare,"—that is, they have either established a false confidence, aided systematic fraud, or perhaps extinguished the sparks of what may have been a just suspicion, and, further, have neglected to find out errors of judgment. Many audits—very complete in checking cash trans-actions and comparing postings from cash books to ledger, and also in tracing that all cash shown to be received has passed into the hands of the bankers, and, also, further seeing that each amount has been expended or paid away for legitimate purposes, and ascertaining that for every payment there is a voucher—fail in proving that the amount as shown to be the cash received is correct. It is quite possible, after all the above examination and checking has been done, for an official to have actually received £30,000 in the course of a year, but by fraud it is quite possible that only £29,500 may appear upon the received side of the cash book, and *that sum* may be duly accounted for and properly dis-bursed, and every voucher for the same presented with care, in proper order, and yet, if their researches stop there, the society may be on the high road to ruin. As to the mode of appointing auditors, the Industrial and Provident Societies Act of 1876 (39 and 40 Vict., chap. 45) prescribes that the accounts of all societies registered under this Act shall be duly audited, but it does not lay down any rule as to how they shall be appointed beyond stating that they shall be appointed as the rules of each society provide. The Treasury may from time to time appoint public auditors, but it is optional with the societies whether they employ any of these public auditors or choose others to fill the appointments.

(Extract)—"Every society shall once at least in every year submit its accounts for audit either to one of the public auditors appointed as herein mentioned, or to two or more persons appointed as the rules of the society provide, who shall have access to all the books and accounts of the society, and shall examine the general statements of the receipts and expenditure, funds and effects of the society, and verify the same with the accounts and vouchers relating thereto, and should either sign the same as found by them to be correct, duly vouched, and in accordance with law, or specially report to the society in what respects they find them incorrect or not in accordance with law. Once in every year, before the first day of June, send to the registrar a general statement (to be called the Annual Return) of the receipts and expenditure, funds and effects of the society as audited." It is evident that the duties of an auditor are not only onerous and responsible, but frequently intricate, and at times even disagreeable. It may happen that he differs with the board of management as to the manner in which the accounts should be stated, or as to other matters connected with his office. As the representative of the members his principal obligation is, of course, to have regard to their interests, and, though he may be accused by the board of interfering with what they may con-sider their own particular duties, he should not allow these arguments to influence him when he is persuaded that his suggested alterations would be to the advantage of the members. In prosperous times an auditor's duties, in connection with the secretary and the board of management, are pleasant, and usually very little trouble is experienced in arranging for a proper allowance for depreciation of stock-in-trade, fixtures, land and buildings, &c., to be charged against revenue account ; but when a depression in trade arises there is frequently great difficulty in pursuading the board to continue this wholesome practice ; a variety of excuses are made, and if a point-blank refusal is given it is not always easy to resolve what course to pursue. It may be argued that each member is a partner in the society, and ought to know that the dividend is not calculated upon the strict basis as hitherto, but, on the other hand, this information may be made use of by a single member to depreciate the position of the society, or even totally destroy the future of the store. It may be as well here to see how far the auditors are the agents of the members. H. B. Buckley, in his work upon the Companies Acts, says :—" The auditors are agents of the shareholders so far as relates to the audit of the accounts, and for the purpose of the audit they will bind the shareholders. But they are not the agents of the shareholders so as to conclude the shareholders by any knowledge which, in the course of the audit, they may have acquired of any unauthorised acts on the part of the directors. It is no part of their office to inquire into the validity of any transactions appearing in the accounts of the company."—(*Spackman* v. *Evans*, L.R., 3 H.L., 171, 196, 236). " It was said by Lord Justice Turner, in *Nichol's* case (3 D.G. and I. 387, 441) with respect to fraudulent misrepresentation made by the directors as to the position of the company, that ' there were auditors of the company appointed by the shareholders. These auditors were, within the scope of their duty, at least as much the agents of the shareholders as the directors were, and the false and fraudulent representations were discoverable by them,' but Lord Chelmsford expressed himself as unable to agree with the Lord Justice in treating the auditors as agents of the share-holders for that purpose." An auditor should be able, not only to check and verify accounts placed before him, but also if he find the books are kept in a careless manner or on a bad system, be able to suggest a better method, the adoption of which might not only save expense, but also ensure greater accuracy in recording the transactions of the society. After he has ascer-tained that there are neither errors of omission or commission he should see that there are no errors of principle, and this last point is the one upon which many audits fail, because no system is laid down to work upon nor manual to refer to. After investi-gating the accounts it is the duty of the auditor to inspect the securities representing the assets, and ascertain that they are in the possession of the society, free and unencumbered with mort-gages or charges, unless the fact of their being so charged is clearly stated in the accounts. This is another point frequently omitted by auditors for want of a guide to their duties. No form of certificate is fixed by either the Industrial and Provident or Friendly Societies Acts ; it is therefore left to the auditor to convey his opinion of the accounts. It would be an advantage if a form of certificate were drawn up for general use, stating that the auditors had performed certain duties, and so dispense with that phrase " Examined and found correct, Brown and Robinson, auditors," which may only refer to the additions of the balance-sheet. I extract the following remarks from one issue of the *News*, which gives a tabulated statement of the balance-sheets of twenty-five societies, scattered over all parts of the kingdom, and the comments upon twelve of them clearly show that there is a necessity for a manual upon auditing to instruct and guide the auditors who have audited the accounts and allowed them to be published :—1. " Non-members' dividend paid should not be included among general expenses in cash account." 2. " The depreciation of fixed stock should be shown in the assets." 3. " But why cannot interest due on shares and loans be entered next their principals and added thereto, so that the claims and total loans would each appear as one item ? " 4. " Is it not misleading to include balance disposable as part of the reserve fund ? " 5. " There is no expenses account." 6. " The several trade accounts show a profit which is neither gross nor net." 7. " Why is interest on members' claims included as part of balance disposable ? " 8. " In consequence of the absence of trade and expenses account the members' claims are not entered correctly." 9. " There are departmental accounts, the profit of which are not shown to agree with the other accounts." 10. " There is no expenses account ; one portion of expenses is charged to trade account and the other to profit and loss account. The consequence is that the profit shown in trade account is neither gross nor net." 11. " The profit shown in trade account is neither net nor gross." 12. " The net profit from trade does not appear in the capital account." The further necessity for a Manual upon Auditing is proved by the fact that there is no one system adopted by co-operative auditors. It may fairly be said that they have followed every one his own way, and many of them have gone astray. They have done the things that they ought not to have done, and left undone the things which they ought to have done. For instance, in my experience, I have known cases where the auditors have not checked the members' pass books or compared them with the societies' books ; others where they have examined and checked the additions and calculated out the stock books and the balance sheets, but have never seen any other books of the society ; others, again, where the shopmen's pass books with the treasurer are never seen by the auditors ; and again, in others the deeds and securities are never asked for, and the treasurer's balance at the end of the quarter never proved ; in some the stock books have never been signed or stocks vouched for by any one. Indeed many audits are conducted upon the orange woman's principle, who bought ninety-six oranges at two for a penny and ninety-six oranges at three for a penny, and sold them at five for twopence, and audited the transaction thus :—" I bought two oranges for one penny and three oranges for the other penny, therefore I cannot lose anything by selling them at five for twopence," and was prepared to give a certificate, " audited and certified," omitting to carry out the totals, which would have shown her that, while they cost her 80d., she would get only 76½d. by selling them. Having shown the necessity for a Manual of Auditing, I would suggest that it be prepared in a similar form to Beeton's Handbooks on Insurance, Agency, &c., with an index, and that its contents should be as follows :—1. What auditing is. 2. The qualifications and duties of an auditor. 3. An effective audit. 4. Errors to be avoided in auditing. 5. Appendix, containing copy of the annual return, and other legal forms, tables, &c. In conclusion, a Manual of Auditing would be a fit and proper addition to the Manual of Bookkeeping, and, as we are already reaping such a great benefit from the latter in the improved style in which the books of many societies are kept and their balance sheets are now issued, so may we expect that if a guide was published for auditors many defalcations and errors of judgment would be nipped in the bud. The cost of the Manual would be repaid, as it is a well-known fact that the most prosperous commercial firms are they who have their books best kept and audited ; indeed, I have no hesitation in saying that the soundest and most prosperous co-operative societies (and there are many both prosperous and sound) are those whose books are most carefully kept and audited ; and that amongst the commercial firms and societies who get into bankruptcy or liquidation, it is the exception to find that their accounts have been duly audited and their books well kept.

As a result of the reading of the above paper, Mr. B. Jones moved that Mr. R. Bailey, Mr. Wood, and Mr. Milburne be appointed a committee to make a draft of a Manual of Auditing, and submit it to the sections and the united board for their revision and approval. Mr. Foster seconded the motion. The motion was carried by a large majority.

## "THE NECESSITY OF A MANUAL ON AUDITING."° (II.)

In our last issue we referred to the fact that if only the account-books of a Society with its customers and suppliers are correctly kept, the balance-sheet must display the effects of any errors of judgment and even of any frauds which may have occurred, so far as they affect " profit and loss " account immediately. But we do not of course ignore the fact that much may be done by means of a deceptive stock account to conceal such consequences as must otherwise be apparent.

One form of fraud, which in the absence of a stock account may easily occur, is the double charging of a payment for goods. Now and then double receipts are inadvertently furnished. The orders for supplies may consist to a great extent of " repeats." The man who keeps the cash book can then draw a second cheque, to match the second receipt, and pocket the proceeds. The vouchers will be right, and the auditor effectually deceived ; but it depends npon the system adopted, how far it would be possible to obtain a second cheque, without for instance the co-operation of the store-keeper, who should verify the receipt of goods.

We do not entertain the view that an auditor's opinion " as to how the accounts should be stated " ought to prevail. But questions of depreciation of assets are distinctly within his province, and should he detect any deviation from a course admitted to be correct, his duty is plain, viz. to call attention to the facts in his certificate. It is not a matter for him to consider, whether a single member may be enabled to depreciate the position of the Society. He should do nothing willingly which could be turned to accoun by such a person, but without regard to consequences, his duty, when it lies quite distinctly before him, *must* be done.

The practical point for the Committee, who have Mr. Milburne's paper before them to consider, is, how much work they want done by the auditor, thus :—

Must he compare every current balance with the pass-books in the hands of members, or post a notification to members which would have the effect of disclosing any discrepancy ?

Must he insist upon a stock account being kept, and verify that all articles paid for have been entered at debit of such account?

Must he trace the receipt of cash from the shopmen's pass-books upwards until they reach the bank?

Must he exercise any supervision over the prices attached to the stocks of various articles at the stocktaking ? And is it incumbent on him to require an independent stock-taking, or will that of the officers of the association be sufficient ?

Must he require a fixed principle to be laid down and adhered to with reference to depreciations ?

Questions such as these are much more important than those raised upon twelve balance-sheets as shown by Mr. Milburne ; and the internal evidence rather makes us think that he who wrote the twelve comments quoted was a far less able man than Mr. Milburne himself. For example :—" 2. The depreciation of fixed stock should be shown in the assets " reads to us rather like nonsense. " The amount deducted in respect of depreciation of fixed stock should be shown on the asset side " is probably what is meant. No. 4 is to us almost unintelligible in the

° (*Vide* No. 341, p. 4.—ED.)

absence of the balance-sheet on which it is a comment. But it leads up to a remark concerning reserve funds which it may be well to make, viz. that the form in which a reserve is held may be, in some cases, that of permanent investments in Consols and other convertible securities ; in other cases it may be merged in the assets of the business; and it depends entirely on the nature of the business carried on, whether the one mode of treatment or the other is wisest.    In the case of a co-operative concern, a reserve may be created to provide for replacement of fixed plant, or it may be intended to equalise dividends, or possibly it may be destined to guard against fluctuations of prices. In the first case it may be necessary to have an invested reserve ; in the second it is convenient to have so much invested or in cash as might probably be wanted at one time ; in the third it is enough if the reserve exists without any special investment.    We regard it as a pure craze when shareholders, as a matter of principle, demand that reserves should *always* exist in an invested form.

Subject to the above remarks, we see no objection to the five headings under which Mr. Milburne would arrange the desired Manual ; assuming that the third head would include a full description of the work to be done.

W. A. T.

## CHARTERED ACCOUNTANTS' STUDENTS' SOCIETY OF LONDON.

### AUDITING.

At the Second Meeting of the above Society, held on the 8th inst., Mr. F. W. Pixley, F.C.A., read the following paper on "Auditing":—

In every profession varied duties are undertaken by its members, but on examination it will be found they all are offshoots of one which forms the mainstay of the professional work.

The members of the profession among whom you aspire to enroll your names, are called upon to undertake positions of great public responsibility and trust, and the reason why we are selected for these offices is because of our knowledge of Auditing, or that particular branch of our professional work upon which I have the honour of addressing you this evening. In addition to our acting as the auditors of the accounts of private individuals, of firms, and of public companies, we are now naturally selected for the offices of arbitrators, receivers, and official liquidators in the Chancery Division of the High Courts of Justice, and receivers and trustees in the Court of Bankruptcy; and the only reason there can be for selecting us for these responsible positions is, that our experience as auditors renders us familiar with the intricacies of accounts which those who hold the above offices are in nearly every instance called upon to deal with. Until within the last few years the only qualification for an auditor of the accounts of a joint stock company was the holding of shares in the undertaking, and he was usually a friend of one of the directors, who recommended him as being willing to subscribe for one or more shares on condition of his receiving the appointment. Having been chosen by the board, the auditor was almost certain to retain his appointment, as the shareholders seldom took the trouble to question his fitness for the office, his duties being looked upon as merely nominal. A rude awakening, however, came upon both directors and shareholders. Companies whose financial position was looked upon as beyond the slightest suspicion, fell with a crash which startled both the commercial and the social world, and on examination it was found that the revenue accounts which had been periodically presented, authorising large dividends, and balance-sheets showing ample assets to meet the liabilities, together with reserve funds, rested on no proper foundation, and were merely prepared to look well before the shareholders and the public. It is true these accounts had been audited, but who could blame an auditor who never pretended to have any special qualifications for the duties entrusted to him beyond what were supposed to be possessed by every other shareholder, many of whom would have been willing to have accepted his appointment should a vacancy have occurred. The Companies Act of 1862, under which by far the greater number of companies are registered, does not require the accounts of companies to be audited unless they are registered without articles of association, when certain clauses in the first schedule, usually known as Table A, which provide that the accounts should be audited, come into effect. This seems a curious omission, as it was passed seventeen years after the Companies Clauses Act, 1845, which governs all companies incorporated by special Act of Parliament. This Act contains many clauses relating to the appointment of auditors and the audit of accounts, but the great blot as regards the subject on which I am now treating is that it compels the shareholders to select the auditor from among their own body. There are many objections to this. First, unless a professional accountant either happens to be a member, or is willing to qualify himself by taking at least one share, the shareholders may be compelled to appoint a thoroughly incompetent person; and in the second place, I think you will all agree with me that no person who has any interest whatever in the company should be appointed to a position which demands the strictest impartiality. Where an auditor is interested in a company as a shareholder it may often be to his personal disadvantage to act in accordance with what he knows is his duty as the representative of his brother members. If he considers the accounts are too favourably presented, and he has a large holding, he knows that in the event of his objecting to the accounts and having them altered to suit his own views, his own property may be seriously depreciated. On the other hand, he may be tempted to recommend a too favourable revenue account and balance-sheet, in order that his property may be materially increased in value. No man ought to be placed in such a position, and it is to be hoped that in any future Act that may be passed relating to companies of every description, a clause may be inserted that no person who is a shareholder shall be eligible for the appointment of auditor. It is, of course, proper that the directors should hold shares, as the larger their holding the more interested they will be in looking after their own interests which are identical with those of the shareholders by careful attention to the management.

I will not deal with the training of an auditor, as the Institute of Chartered Accountants has prescribed the nature of the examinations which you will have to pass before obtaining your certificates; but of the many subjects you have to study the theory and practice of, bookkeeping is above all others the most important, which you should thoroughly comprehend and master in every detail. A knowledge, however, of bookkeeping is not the only qualification an auditor should possess. It is merely the foundation on which his training is based, as it does not by any means follow that a most accomplished bookkeeper, and one able to keep the accounts of a large banking and mercantile firm, is capable of effectually auditing the books of a small retail business. The duties of a bookkeeper are confined to recording the financial transactions, and his skill can go no higher than performing these operations in a manner which combines the greatest accuracy with the simplest method, the least possible labour, and the least possible consumption of time. An auditor, on the other hand, is a critic of the bookkeeper's work, and in some cases also a check upon his employers, for it is not only the auditor's duty to check the accounts of the bookkeeper, but also to see that he has received full and proper information of the transactions of the business, and that they are all duly entered in the books.

Previous to commencing an audit, the auditor should thoroughly comprehend the nature of his responsibilities with regard to that particular audit. Where he is acting for one or a few persons who tell him to take certain things for granted, and merely make a partial investigation, such as putting into proper shape the accounts presented to him, or seeing that the statements as prepared by the accountant or bookkeeper are correct, his responsibilities are very light as compared with those he is under when he is called upon to audit accounts on behalf of a number of persons who do not give him any particular instructions, but leave the matter entirely in his hands as to what may be necessary he should inquire into on their behalf. Audits of the accounts of private individuals or firms come principally under the first class of audits; and those of the accounts of public companies, where the auditor acts for the general body of shareholders, who leave themselves entirely in his hands, and also where he is investigating accounts on behalf of executors or trustees, come under the latter.

In the case of firms the auditor usually receives his instructions at an interview with one or more of the partners.

In the case of companies his appointment rests in the first place with the directors, but subsequently with the shareholders, who elect him at their annual general meetings. When a new company is formed it is now the practice for the directors to insert the names of auditors in the prospectus, and their appointment is usually confirmed by the shareholders; but no matter from whom the auditor receives his appointment, he must always remember that he is acting on behalf of the general body of shareholders, who are, therefore, his clients. An auditor by allowing his name to be placed upon the prospectus of a new company does not, of course, render himself liable for any statement there may be in the prospectus, unless such refer to him personally. The promoters, the directors, and the solicitors are, of course, responsible for the statements, but the auditor's name on the prospectus merely notifies the fact that he is the person selected by the directors to audit the accounts when they are placed before him for that purpose.

As to whether an auditor should allow his name to be placed on the prospectus of a company where he has reason to believe it is not promoted with *bonâ fide* intentions is a matter fairly open to discussion. By some it will undoubtedly be argued that no accountant ought to allow his name to be connected with any company until he is perfectly satisfied that everybody connected with it is thoroughly respectable, and that the expectations of those who invest their money have at least a fair chance of being realised, as his name may induce clients and others who have confidence in him to invest in the company's shares. Others may contend that as auditors by allowing their names to be placed on the prospectus do not in any way make themselves responsible for anything beyond the fact that they intend to investigate the accounts when called upon to do so, it is their duty to allow their names to be placed indiscriminately on any prospectus that may be placed before them, so that should there be anything wrong in the accounts as submitted to the members they may be able to expose the fraud; but I fancy that the most respectable accountants would prefer not to have their names associated at all with unsound schemes, and this is the view that I should recommend you in your future careers to strictly follow.

In Table A, or the first schedule of the Companies Act of 1862, and in the articles of association of many companies there is inserted a clause that the accounts of a company shall be examined by one or more auditor or auditors; and the question was raised some time ago as to whether the appointment of a firm of accountants by name was in legal compliance with the Act or the articles of association; and a case was submitted to counsel by the Institute of Chartered Accountants, which was fully reported in *The Accountant*, No. 390, p. 5.

Before commencing the actual examination of the accounts, the auditor should make himself familiar with the arrangements by which his clients are jointly interested in the business which he is to investigate. In the case of a private partnership they are usually contained in the articles of partnership. In investigating the accounts of executors or trustees, he will be guided by the will, together with any codicils attached thereto, while in the case of a public company, the public Acts of Parliament relating to companies, taken in conjunction with either the private Acts of Parliament of the company or in the case of a limited company the Memorandum or Articles of Association, or the first schedule of the Companies Act, 1862, already referred to as Table A.

Chartered Accountants are, of course, supposed to be intimately acquainted with the public Acts of Parliament bearing upon any of their professional duties, and those acts specially referring to the subject of accounts and auditing are the following:—Apportionment Act, 1870; Companies Act, 1862; Companies Act, 1879; Companies Act, 1880; Companies Clauses Consolidation Act, 1845; Companies Clauses Act, 1863; Railway Companies Securities Act, 1866; Railway Companies Act, 1867; Regulation of Railways Act, 1868; Gas Works Clauses Act, 1847; Do. 1871; Waterworks Clauses Act, 1847; Metropolis Water Act, 1852; Do. 1871; Life Assurance Companies Act, 1870; Friendly Societies Act, 1875; Friendly Societies Amendment Act, 1876; Industrial and Provident Societies Act, 1876; the Falsification of Accounts Act, 1875. Some of the above are of course special Acts, containing regulations relating to the accounts of companies referred to in their titles, but professional auditors should be familiar with the above Acts, especially with the clauses relating to the books of accounts and the duties of auditors. An auditor, therefore, before commencing his duties, should also peruse the articles of partnership, the will, the private Acts of Parliament, or the articles of association of the company, as the case may be, and he should take notes of any clauses affecting the preparation of the accounts, the manner in which they should be presented, and his own duties. Where he finds anything unusual, he should take a careful note. And here it will not be out of place to strongly impress upon you the desirability of making careful notes of anything that may come under your observation during an audit which is not perfectly clear or satisfactory. Notes taken during an audit should be recorded systematically, and in such a manner that both the queries raised and the answers given can be referred to at any time, in case any explanation be required as to any matter relating to the audit. The entries in every paper referring to the audit should be in ink, and each document should be endorsed and put away amongst the papers, as it is extremely important that nothing should be destroyed, so that a record can always be found of the queries raised and the manner in which they were answered.

It is impossible to prescribe any fixed rules as to the manner in which an audit should be proceeded with, because in nearly every case they vary according to circumstances. Demands made by an auditor which to one of his clients would be particularly pleasing, might in another instance be looked upon as an unwarrantable assumption of authority and a useless interference. The general principle of an audit when conducted on behalf of private individuals or partners, is that the auditor investigates accounts on behalf of the proprietor or proprietors of the business who have neither the time, the inclination, nor the ability to do so for themselves; but he should understand his instructions clearly, and should also let his client know what would be the result of their being carried out. If, in the auditor's opinion, they are not sufficient, he should make that clear to his client, and point out what risks he may be under through not having the work done more completely. It is desirable in both interests that this should be clearly understood at the commencement of the audit, so that there may be afterwards no ground for complaint by the client that a sufficiently searching investigation has not been made, or on the other hand that more has been done than the client intended, and consequently a heavier expense incurred than he is willing to pay.

Where an auditor is acting on behalf of partners who, on appointing him, do not give him any instructions—such as, for example, in the case of the appointment of the auditor of a public company, or also in the case of executors or trustees—then his responsibilities are very great, as he is, of course, relied upon for the accuracy of the accounts in every particular, his clients looking to him to protect their interests in every possible way. An auditor of a company, however, although entrusted with the fullest powers, must always remember that he is in no sense responsible for the acts of the directors, managers, or employés of the company. The directors of a company are solely answerable to the shareholders for the management, and it is the duty of the auditor merely to see that the results of the transactions as carried on under the superintendence of the directors are properly placed before the shareholders in the accounts submitted to them. It is, however, quite within his province if, in his opinion, a certain class of transactions are not likely to conduce to the prosperity of the company, to point this out to the directors, and also to call their attention to any faulty system in the bookkeeping, and to suggest improvements. The auditor thus has it very often in his power to prove of great assistance to the directors, by bringing to their notice matters of this sort which might otherwise escape their attention; and in this way he also benefits his clients. He must, however, remember that he has no power to enforce his views on the directors, nor interfere in any way with the management except by making these suggestions in a friendly spirit.

Having perused the private Acts of Parliament, the articles of association, the articles of partnership, or the testator's will, as the case may be, the auditor should then make himself familiar with the method on which the general principles of bookkeeping are adapted to recording the transactions of the particular business he is investigating, and he then proceeds with the practical part of his duties. As most of you are aware, the details of an audit are in the offices of Chartered Accountants performed by clerks under superintendence, the principals devoting themselves more particularly to seeing that the statements which result from the bookkeeping are properly drawn, and represent all that they profess to do. It need scarcely be said that the greatest attention must be paid to performing every detail of an audit, and the most mechanical operation, namely, the checking, which is usually performed by one clerk calling over to another, requires the greatest care, as the slightest inaccuracy may often make it necessary for the whole of the checking to be done over again. One of the most common sources of error in this respect is when an entry, which ought to be posted to the debit, has been posted to the credit, or *vice versa*. A clerk who is only paying attention to the figures, and is not careful to see that every item called out to him is posted to the right side of the account, frequently passes a mistake of this nature, and ticks it as correct. Every item thus passed creates an error of double the amount. Where the audit fee is fixed it makes it far less profitable if the calling over has to be done twice, or possibly more times, and where the work is paid for by time it unduly swells the bill, and is unsatisfactory to the client as it is to the auditor. In his examination of the cash book the income side must be checked from the most independent source the auditor can find available—for example, the counterfoils of receipt books, the customer's pass books of a bank, although of course in this instance he can only attempt a few test cases, or a rough cash book, but the items on the credit or payment side should be checked with the vouchers, and although this is a mere mechanical process still it ought to be performed very carefully. The auditor has, of course, the right to demand that the vouchers should be handed to him in a proper manner, either in a guard-book or filed in some way, so that they may come to his hand in the order in which they are entered in the cash-book. They should consist of actual receipts, and, with the exception of those made by bills payable, the payments to merchants or tradesmen should be vouched by proper receipted accounts. In some cases the endorsements on cheques may be accepted, especially where crossed "not negotiable," as then there can be no doubt that they have been paid to the persons represented on the face of the cheques. The balance as it appears in the cash-book should be reconciled with the balance as shown in the banker's pass-book. It is seldom they are identical, as cheques drawn by the company on or before the day on which the books are closed may not have been presented for payment, neither will the bankers, unless a special arrangement has been made with them, have given credit for country cheques not cleared on that day. A reconciliation statement should, therefore, be prepared, and either entered in the cash-book or given to the auditor in a proper form to place amongst his own papers. An auditor must use his own discretion, guided by his experience, as to how far it may be necessary to check the details found in the subsidiary books. He should, however, make as much use as possible of documents obtained from independent sources, to guard against omissions. The checking being completed, and the cash payments vouched, the balances are then taken out from the ledger into what is technically called the trial balance, from which the revenue account and balance-sheet are prepared. At this point the duties of auditors vary. In some cases the trial balance is given them, also the revenue account and balance-sheet. In other cases they have to take out the trial balance themselves, and prepare the statements either for the shareholders, the executors, or the partners, as the case may be. It is far preferable for the auditor to prepare his own statements if his clients are willing he should do so, as he can then draft them in any form he pleases, whereas where the accounts are submitted to him already prepared he may have to certify them, when perhaps he may not approve of the form, but cannot object as there may be nothing actually wrong in them.

In the case of a firm, he usually prepares, in addition to a revenue account and balance-sheet, capital accounts of each of the partners, while in the preparation or audit of executorship accounts, he usually prepares a statement showing the position of the testator on the day of his death, and statements showing the position of the separate trusts created by the will. Occasionally the revenue account and balance-sheet of a company are accompanied by a cash account, while sometimes the cash account is substituted for the revenue account. When a cash account alone accompanies a balance-sheet, shareholders are very apt to suppose it is a revenue account, and the auditor should be very careful to prevent their falling into such a mistake. The difference between a revenue and a cash account is, that the former shows the results of the transactions for the period, and beyond making due provision for bad and doubtful debts, does not take into consideration whether contracts have been settled or not; while on the other hand the cash account is merely an abstract of the cash book, and it is, therefore, very easy for an account of this nature to be made as favourable as possible by not paying accounts due by the company until after the close of the period under audit, and on the other hand by collecting as much money as possible, and for this purpose even allowing illegitimate discounts before the date on which the books are closed. An auditor should of course be careful not to sanction the payment of a dividend declared on the strength of a mere cash account, but should in all cases require the revenue account to be prepared before the declaration of the dividend, although the statement may not be issued to the shareholders.

In the case of a trading company, the best form of revenue account is one divided into three parts,—the first showing the gross profit on the difference between buying and selling, the second part showing how this gross profit after charging it with the profit and loss items has resulted in a net profit or a net loss, while in the third part should be put the balance brought from the previous revenue account, the balance of the second part of the statement and the dividend or bonus declared, if any, while the balance of this third part will then be carried into the balance-sheet.

In the case of a non-trading company the first and second part of the revenue account will be included in one. By means of a revenue account prepared in the above manner shareholders are enabled to see in what the trading of the period has actually resulted and whether in the event of a dividend being declared it has been earned out of the profits of the period, or taken partly or wholly out of the balance of the undivided profit brought forward from the previous accounts. In examining the revenue account, the auditor should see that it is properly charged with all the expenses incidental to carrying on the business. When either the firm or company have not been successful during the period embraced by the audit, the revenue account is often prepared on too favourable a basis, and items which ought to be properly included therein are frequently carried to a suspense account, and thus included amongst the assets in the balance-sheet.

In the case of a firm the auditor should draw the attention of the partners to any items which he thinks ought to be charged against revenue, and suggest their being thus treated. If this proposal be not carried out, he should protect himself in his report on the accounts, and clearly point out that the partners have not sufficiently charged the revenue account, and that it would be unwise for them to divide as profits the amount assumed to be such in the statements so prepared.

In the case of a company, the auditor should be firm, as, of course, the amount to be written off for depreciation is most certainly a question affecting him and his duty, and is not solely one of management, and he can very justly be blamed by the shareholders if he passes accounts without comment where the revenue is not properly charged with all the outgoings incidental to the period embraced by the audit. For example, the auditor should see that a proper provision is made for bad and doubtful debts; and for this purpose, should go through the schedule of the debtors, and where any of them are beyond a certain age he should inquire the reason they have not been paid. If the answer be not satisfactory, he should include such items in an amount to be raised for bad and doubtful debts, and charge it against the revenue account. Unless due provision be made periodically for bad and doubtful debts, there will appear among the assets in successive balance-sheets an increasing amount due from debtors to the company, which will ultimately attract the attention of the shareholders; and on inquiry being made, and the true value of this outstanding amount ascertained, it will be found by writing this asset down to its value that the difference absorbs part or whole of the net profits taken credit for in the period under audit, and that consequently a dividend cannot be declared.

The auditor should also see that a proper amount is written off any leases the company may hold, and charged against the revenue account, so that the balance standing in the books as the value of the leases may represent their proper value at that date. This remark applies whether the business is carried on in the leasehold premises or whether they are held as an investment. In the latter case the rents received should be included amongst the income in the revenue account after the deduction of the incidental expenses connected therewith. When the leasehold premises are in the possession of the company for its own business, the proportion written off is equivalent, of course, to a rent paid, and should be treated accordingly. All amounts expended for renewals and repairs should be charged against the revenue account. There are, however, two ways at least of treating items of this sort. In some cases all amounts expended on plant, premises, &c., are added to the plant account, and a certain percentage is periodically written off the balance. In other cases no addition is made to the plant account except for actual purchases, and the whole expenditure incurred in keeping it in a state of efficiency is charged against the revenue account, and this plan is in my opinion preferable to the other.

In all trading companies the value of the stock-in-hand at the commencement and end of the periods is brought into the trading or revenue account. The auditor is not, of course, responsible for the accuracy of this item, but should inquire into the method on which the stock has been taken, and require a certificate of its accuracy from some responsible official. It should be stated in the accounts on what basis the value is arrived at, whether at cost price or at an increased or less value. It is, of course, impossible in a lecture of this nature to discuss in detail the various items of receipt and expenditure which can be brought under the notice of auditors in their investigations of revenue accounts. I merely now repeat what I have already remarked—that this statement should show the actual profit or loss of the period, and that it will not do so unless every item of expenditure be properly charged against the revenue.

The balance-sheet or statement of assets and liabilities contains, in the case of a company, amongst its liabilities its shareholders' capital, and in the case of a firm the capital of the partners; and there is no doubt the most correct form of preparing this statement would be to divide it into two parts, the first part showing the assets and the amounts due to creditors of every description, while the balance, showing what is the value of the assets after providing for these outstanding liabilities, should be brought into the second part. The second part will then consist solely of the shareholders' or partners' capital on the liabilities side, with the balance of the assets after paying the outstanding liabilities on the other side; and the shareholders or partners would then distinctly see whether they were solvent or otherwise, and in the latter case how much in the £ they were worth. This method of preparing a balance-sheet is, however, contrary to the usual practice, where the capital is placed first, and is, in fact, merely given as my own idea as to the best form, and you, of course, understand that any particular form for a revenue account or balance-sheet can only be *suggested* by an auditor, and that he has no power to require the accounts to be presented as he may wish unless his forms are prescribed by Act of Parliament.

In the case of railway, gas, water, and life assurance companies the forms of accounts are prescribed, as are also those for societies registered under the Friendly Societies Act, 1875; but in the majority of companies, viz. those registered under the Companies Act, 1862, the directors are allowed to present accounts in any form they may please, except in the case of companies to which Table A applies, where the form of balance-sheet is given. The only special point calling for notice in this account is that any debt due from the directors or other officials of the company is to be separately stated amongst the assets. With the exception of the companies just referred to, the auditor is obliged to accept the accounts in any form the directors may think proper to place before him; but on the other hand any suggestions he may make are likely to receive attention, for the directors are aware that although the auditor has no authority to prescribe the form of accounts except as already stated, still he has a power which can keep in check a board of directors, however unwilling they may be to fall in with his views, for they know that he has the power of making a special report to the shareholders. In strict accordance with the Act, and with the clauses usually contained in the articles of association, directors are required to furnish the auditor with the balance-sheets and accounts as they propose to present them to the shareholders, and he can return them with a certificate thereon refusing to vouch their correctness, and make any remarks he may think proper, and the directors will be bound to place the accounts before the shareholders with this certificate. Such a course, however, would be most unusual; and, in fact, I have never yet heard of the letter of the Act being so strictly adhered to. It is the recognised practice amongst Chartered Accountants that where an auditor disapproves of the accounts submitted to him, he either sees the chairman or manager, or addresses a letter to them on the subject of the accounts suggesting alterations which he thinks it advisable to make, and these suggestions are usually carefully considered, and if not at once acquiesced in, are discussed in a businesslike manner with the auditor. If the directors absolutely refuse to agree with the auditor's request, the latter is very often in a position of great difficulty, for the shareholders are his clients, and anything that may damage the reputation of the company must necessarily be injurious to their interests. It is impossible, however, to lay down rules as to what course should be taken in the event of a disagreement between an auditor and the board. It is only experience that can teach this, but the auditor should remember he has a twofold duty, that towards the shareholders, and that towards himself. He must protect the shareholders as much as possible, and at the same time, he must have regard to his own character and reputation.

Should a company whose shares are not fully paid-up hold any shares as an investment, it should be clearly shown in the balance-sheet, as otherwise the shareholders would not be fully aware of the extent of their liability in the event of the company going into liquidation, for should this happen, the shareholders would be liable in proportion to their holdings to pay the amount which would otherwise be raised by the payments on these shares were they in the hands of private owners, in addition to having to meet the calls on their own shares.

Occasionally an auditor may not be satisfied with reconciling the balance as shown in the cash book with that of the banker's pass book. In order, therefore, to guard against any fraud, he may call on the bankers of the company informing them of his position, and request them to show him in confidence their ledger account with the company, as instances have been known of a cashier having kept duplicate pass books, and this, of course, can only be found out by application to the bankers.

In the balance-sheets of all companies are to be found included amongst the assets amounts representing expenditure, which cannot be said to be represented by realisable assets, such as, for example, the amounts paid for the good-will of a business, preliminary expenses, establishment of agencies, &c. In the event of the company going into liquidation it is evident that these items in the balance-sheet would not turn out to be realisable assets, and it is therefore desirable that a reserve fund should be raised to meet contingencies. In the case of preliminary expenses a certain amount should be charged against the revenue account, say for the first five or ten years at the most, until this fictitious asset disappears. Where plant, machinery, or property of any description is purchased under a hiring agreement, that is, an agreement in which it is provided that after the lessee has paid a rent for the use of the

article for a certain number of years, it shall become his absolute property on payment of a nominal sum at the expiration of the period, the company is entitled to take credit amongst its assets for a proportionate part, after charging the revenue account with a fair and reasonable amount for wear and tear during the period under audit. Having finally settled the form of balance-sheet, the securities should be inspected by the auditor, previous to which he should be supplied with a proper schedule dividing them into their various classes. When freehold or leasehold property forms part of the assets, the deeds should be produced, and also receipts for the last premiums on policies of insurance of perishable property. Where a company holds stock, shares, or debentures, they should be counted; and in the case of bonds to bearer, the auditor should see that the coupons next due, and those up to the date of repayment of the bond are attached.

The investments should stand in the names of the trustees of the company, where there are properly appointed trustees. Should there be none, then in the names of two or more of the directors, but investments should not stand in the names of the manager or secretary alone.

Should the securities be in the custody of the company's bankers, and it is not stated in the accounts that they are held as security for a loan, the auditor should be careful to ascertain that this is the fact.

Where the company has branches it is impossible, of course, for the auditor to make such a thorough investigation as where all the records of the business are kept in one office. The returns must be examined, and the auditor must ascertain that they are properly amalgamated with the books kept at the head office; and in giving his certificate he should be careful to certify the correctness of the accounts, subject to the returns from the branches representing accurately the transactions of their particular business.

Having completed his investigation, the auditor then appends his certificate to the accounts. If he makes a report to the directors on any matter on which he considers the shareholders should be informed, he should be careful to intimate in his certificate that such report exists, so that the shareholders may ask for it at the meeting, or he may, of course, require an undertaking from the directors that they read his report to the meeting.

I have endeavoured in the foregoing remarks to give an outline of the general principles of an audit and the duties of an auditor without going into those details which can only be acquired by experience, but I trust I have made it evident that auditing is accompanied with many responsibilities, and that before any one undertakes the appointment of auditor he should be carefully trained.

The Chartered Accountants' Students' Society of London has been formed for the express purpose of assisting those who are desirous of acquiring amongst other technical accomplishments a knowledge of these duties; and, in conclusion, I hope that the few words I have addressed to you this evening may contribute in a small way towards the furtherance of the Society's aim.

The meeting terminated with a vote of thanks to the lecturer.

## CHARTERED ACCOUNTANTS' STUDENTS' SOCIETY OF LONDON.

#### AUDITORS.

At a Meeting of the above Society, held on the 25th inst., Mr. David Chadwick, F.C.A. read the following paper on the Duties of a Professional Auditor :—

No subject falling within the range of duties of a public, or Chartered Accountant, can be considered of more importance than the proper audit of public and private accounts. The subject must, therefore, be of great interest to the Students and Associates of the Institute of Chartered Accountants.

The business or profession of an accountant is of comparatively modern origin, and like that of the business of an engineer, has grown in importance with the extension of trades, manufactures, and commerce.

I presume that I am addressing intelligent students, who have acquired a knowledge of the various books and forms used in bookkeeping by double entry.

The transactions of every private firm, joint stock company, or incorporation of any kind, and all trustees' and executors' accounts should be kept by *double entry*.

In other words, the receipts and expenditure, and the credits and debits, should, in addition to personal accounts, be shown under general and convenient heads known as "Nominal Accounts."

The number and division of these heads or nominal accounts is a matter of judgment and discretion.

The main object of an audit is to detect errors, and to secure corrections in accounts.

The occurrence of frauds like those recently exposed in the cases of the City of Glasgow Bank, and the Army and Navy Stores, and numerous other cases, should be rendered impossible by the services of experienced professional auditors.

We have, therefore, now to answer the inquiry : what are the duties of a professional auditor ?

They should include generally a careful examination and comparison with the vouchers of every item of receipt and payment in the cash book, and of the correctness of the balances : of the entries generally in the day books and journals, the classification of the nominal accounts, and the postings to the personal and nominal accounts in the ledger.

The trial balances and the closing entries should be verified.

The profit and loss account and the balance-sheet should be carefully examined.

The mode of taking and valuing outstanding debts owing by and to the concern, and of taking and valuing stocks on hand, requires careful attention.

The statutory system of auditing the accounts of railways, poor law boards, and other public bodies, has proved of great value : and when the employment of Chartered Accountants as auditors by all public bodies is made compulsory, the public will feel still greater confidence and satisfaction.

Being a member of parliament when the Joint Stock Companies' Amendment Act of 1880 was introduced, authorising existing joint stock banks to adopt the principle of limited liability, I had the opportunity of conferring with the Government, as the only professional accountant in the House : I placed amendments on the paper with a statutory form of balance-sheet, and a form of auditor's certificate ; but I only succeeded, with the support of Sir Richard Cross, the Home Secretary, and himself a banker, in carrying clause 8, requiring every bank balance-sheet to be signed by three directors as well as the auditors and secretary or manager.

The power to deduct depreciation on machinery is by a recent Act rendered legal, and is acknowledged by the Income Tax Commissioners ; there is, therefore, no longer any reason for not clearly showing on the face of a balance-sheet the amount of deduction for depreciation.

Having described generally the importance of the business of auditing, I will now refer in some detail to the nature of the duties of clerks and principals engaged in this important duty.

The following instructions to auditors were prepared by me many years ago, and have as far as practicable been carried out by my firm and their clerks in a large and varied business.

The particular duties of an auditor may be stated as follows :—

1. In commencing a new audit you should obtain a list of all the books kept, and of all persons authorised to receive or pay money and order goods.

2. In the case of a joint stock company, examine the articles and board minutes respecting the receipt and payment of money, and the drawing of cheques, acceptances, &c.

3. Ascertain and take note of the general system upon which the books are constructed, and the plan of checking the correctness of the accounts paid, and whether exclusively or generally by cheques.

4. Report if the accounts and vouchers are submitted to the board of directors by an account committee or otherwise, and whether they are systematically checked and certified ; and note any discrepancies.

5. Examine all the items in the cash-book with the bank pass books and vouchers, and put your usual audit initials in the pass-book and to every item in the cash-book. Ascertain if the bankers' pass-book is frequently entered up and examined.

6. Note any unusual or extraordinary payments or receipts.

7. In regard to the payments for wages and petty cash, note any unusual items and see that vouchers for all payments are kept and produced.

8. Report whether a rough cash book is kept, and whether the fair cash book is regularly and punctually posted and balanced, and if the balance is checked.

9. Report also if the entries in the fair cash book are in arrear,

on account of the current year; and if so, to what extent? and why?

10. In all cases where branch establishments are included in one business, you will be careful to examine into the mode of bringing the returns of work, accounts, and expenses to the head office.

11. Examine all the day books, and see that the proper returns of purchases and sales are made by each department, and that the bought and sold books are properly entered up: that the invoices are properly checked as to quantities and prices; obtain a declaration, or otherwise satisfy yourself, that every liability of the year is brought into account.

12. The postings in the personal ledgers must be checked from the bought and sold day books and the cash book, and also from the bill books and journal.

13. The postings in the nominal or impersonal ledgers must be checked from the journalising of the bought and sold day books, the bill books, the invoice books, and the cash books, and the mode and correctness of the journalising must be carefully proved.

14. Examine the bills receivable and bills payable books, and note any item of past due, renewed or dishonoured bills, and make list of same and of the securities, if any.

15. Examine the entries and transfers passed through the journal, and check the postings; and although you are not held responsible for the details of classification, it is desirable you should make any suggestions required, and note any discrepancies, especially in relation to the division of expenditure, on account of capital and profit and loss accounts respectively.

16. Examine the share register, and see that the amounts received for calls agree with the entries in the bank pass books, and that they are correctly posted to the credit of the respective shareholders in the share ledger; that all transfers from the transfer deeds are duly stamped and entered in the register of transfers; and also that the amount of the subscibed and paid-up capital and arrears corresponds with the balance-sheet.

17. Examine the register of all mortgages on the company's property, and all debenture bonds issued, and note and check the amount of capital paid in advance of calls and of the receipts and payments in respect thereof with the bank pass book.

18. In the accounts of stock-taking see that all stock sheets and returns are duly signed by the heads of departments, and that the same are correctly carried forward to the general stock account; and ascertain and note whether goods finished or in progress are taken at cost price or otherwise; also report whether in large concerns an independent check clerk or valuer has verified the stock returns in regard to prices and quantities.

19. In checking the profit and loss account note whether the usual and proper deductions are made for wear and tear and depreciation, and for recouping of capital on works or premises held on short leases.

20. Take care that in the balance-sheet no additions are made to expenditure on capital account except such as are duly authorised by the board of directors, and note the distinction between new works and mere replacements.

21. Ascertain whether the conveyance deeds and other securities specified in the agreement of purchase and articles of association have been duly executed, and the sums paid by the company on account of purchase have been duly endorsed thereon or otherwise acknowledged to the satisfaction of the solicitors or board of directors; also that the existence and safe custody of these documents has been duly certified; ascertain by application to the bankers the correctness of any balances, bills or securities lodged with them.

22. Ascertain the correctness of the cash balances, bills and other securities in hand, and take note of every exceptional transaction.

Having referred generally to the importance of auditing as part of the business of an accountant, I may refer briefly to the mode in which the accounts of large concerns are usually kept and stated.

In my experience as a professional auditor during a period of 40 years, including the audit of some of the very largest trading, banking, and manufacturing businesses, I have not attempted to mould all of them to any one system of journalising and classification for the nominal accounts; but I have accepted different forms of profit and loss statements and balance-sheets, if they have been clearly and correctly stated.

In balance-sheets, I have adopted generally the usual form of placing on the left side, and debiting the firm or company with the capital and liabilities, and crediting them on the right side with the property and assets; but in special cases, by charter, special Act, or old custom, the reverse mode has been continued without any material inconvenience.

Whilst I recommend statutory uniformity, I do not think the "form" in such cases is of such consequence as the "substance," by which I mean the intelligent and correct classification under proper heads of all items of receipt and expenditure, and of assets and liabilities.

The importance and necessity of a professional audit of the accounts of all public trusts, and Government departments, and of all railway, insurance, banking, and joint stock companies, is now generally acknowledged; and the compulsory forms of account in regard to railways, insurance and friendly societies, will, I believe, soon be extended.

I think it is a matter of regret that the balance-sheet in table "A" of the Companies Act, 1862, was not made compulsory on all joint stock companies.

The certificate which an auditor should give, should be made compulsory.

The book on "Auditors: their Duties and Responsibilities," by Mr. Pixley, gives copies of the audit clauses in various Acts, and the statutory forms of balance-sheets, and much useful and valuable information.

As the object of this address is to create an intelligent interest in the duties and responsibilities of auditors, it should always be remembered that the main necessity of auditing is to secure absolute honesty in the case of all persons who touch or have control over other people's money or goods.

It may well be asked whether the great losses or frauds could have occurred in the case of the City of Glasgow Bank, if the accounts had been audited by professional accountants, and the auditors had done their duty? A similar inquiry might be made in regard to the great losses in connection with other well-known and similarly disastrous concerns.

It would be an interesting investigation to estimate the advantages of the official system of auditing now adopted in some of the great departments of Government; and whether a system of auditing by Chartered Accountants could not be extended to every department of the public service.

The following are samples of difficult cases in which auditors are called upon to exercise their judgment and firmness:—

1. In the balance-sheet of a manufacturing concern the directors and managers on one occasion estimated the value of stocks on hand without taking any inventories, and the auditors referred to the fact in their report, and were consequently not reappointed by the shareholders.

In this case the auditors suffered for doing their duty honestly.

2. In the balance-sheet of a large concern the managers included as a good debt an overdue acceptance held without security, to which the auditors objected, and which turned out bad. To what extent and in what way should an auditor, in a serious case within his knowledge, insist upon communicating his opinions to the shareholders?

3. The chairman of a large concern refused to allow an auditor's junior partner and managing clerk to check the details, but insisted on the auditor himself being present during the whole time occupied in the examination. The auditor resigned. Should he have reported the facts to the shareholders?

4. In the balance-sheet of a colliery the managing owners, a few years ago, largely increased the value of the property, as the profits were then exceedingly large, and each partner's capital on the books was increased by a corresponding amount. Since that time the property has decreased in value, and the profits are now very moderate; but the proprietors retain the excessive value in their books, and no reserve fund exists.

Some of the owners have never fully understood the case. In the case of the death of a proprietor, great difficulty would arise. What course should the auditor take in this case?

5. In the balance-sheet of a large concern, where a great number of wagons are used, they stand now, after yearly depreciation, at an average value of £50 each, having cost £70 each, but they are now only worth on an average £30 each, as new wagons can be bought at £45. For every thousand wagons there is therefore in the balance-sheet an over value of £20,000. With a full knowledge of these facts, is the auditor justified in certifying the balance-sheet without calling special attention thereto?

6. Numerous cases have occurred where the annual depreciation for short leases is not adequately provided for in the annual balance-sheets.

Is it the auditor's duty to call the attention of shareholders thereto? or can he properly sign the balance-sheet as "correct according to the books?"

7. Many cases have occurred where proprietors and companies have fixed the audit fees at so low an amount as to render it impossible without a positive loss for the requisite time and work to be devoted to the audit.

In such cases, is the auditor justified, when requested by the proprietors, in omitting such an examination of the accounts in detail as he would consider necessary if the audit fee were a fair and reasonable amount? And if not justified, has he any other remedy than either resigning the audit, or suffering the loss?

I cannot conclude without a word of congratulation on the passing of the excellent new Bankruptcy Act of 1883; and expressing my entire approval of the provisions contained therein for closing old accounts, and for auditing the accounts of trustees under the Act.

It is one of the main objects of the Institute of Chartered Accountants to improve the status of its members, and to render their services of increasing value to the public; this can only be done effectually by supporting their independent actions against ignorance, prejudice, apathy, and self-interest.

Another great object of the Institute is to limit the entrance into the profession to those only who by education, ability, and aptitude have proved themselves qualified to perform the important duties of Chartered Accountants.

The success of the Institute has been undoubted, and no better proof of that success could be given than the fact that it has attracted to the profession so intelligent a body of students as the members of the Chartered Accountants' Students' Society of London.

## CHARTERED ACCOUNTANTS' STUDENTS' SOCIETY OF LONDON.

### AUDITORS: THEIR DUTIES AND RESPONSIBILITIES.

At a meeting of the above Society, held at St. Michael's Hall, George Yard, Lombard Street, on the 9th ult., Mr. T. A. Welton, F.C.A., in the chair, a discussion took place on the paper read at the previous meeting by Mr. David Chadwick, F.C.A. The following were the points under discussion, together with the resolutions that were passed :—

1. In the balance-sheet of a manufacturing concern the Directors and Managers on one occasion estimated the value of stocks on hand without taking any inventories, and the Auditors referred to the fact in their report; and were consequently not re-appointed by the Shareholders.

   In this case the Auditors suffered for doing their duty honestly.

   *Resolution.*—That the Auditors acted quite right in drawing the attention of the Shareholders to the fact that no inventory had been taken of the stocks, and it was to the detriment of the profession that another member should accept that auditorship.

2. In the balance-sheet of a large concern the Managers included as a good debt, an overdue acceptance held without security, to which the Auditors objected, and which turned out bad. To what extent and in what way should an Auditor, in a serious case within his knowledge, insist upon communicating his opinions to the Shareholders?

   *Resolution.*—When an Auditor is well warranted in the belief that insufficient provision had been made for probable loss by a bad debt, he should mention the fact in his certificate.

3. The Chairman of a large concern refused to allow an Auditor's junior partner and managing clerk to check the details, but insisted on the Auditor himself being present during the whole time occupied in the examination. The Auditor resigned. Should he have reported the facts to the Shareholders?

   *Resolution.*—That it be part of an Auditor's duty not to resign his position after having been elected by the Shareholders without stating his reason for so doing.

4. In the balance-sheet of a colliery the Managing Owners, a few years ago, largely increased the value of the property, as the profits were then exceedingly large, and each partner's capital on the books was increased by a corresponding amount. Since that time the property has decreased in value, and the profits are now very moderate; but the proprietors retain the excessive value in their books, and no reserve fund exists.

   Some of the owners have never fully understood the case. In the case of the death of a proprietor great difficulty would arise. What course should the Auditor take in this case?

   *Resolution.*—The Auditors should suggest a fresh valuation, or

introduce a marginal note intimating the decrease in value of the property.

5. In the balance-sheet of a large concern, where a great number of waggons are used, they stand now, after yearly depreciation, at an average value of £50 each, having cost £70 each, but they are now only worth on an average £30 each, as new waggons can be bought at £45. For every thousand waggons there is therefore in the balance-sheet an over value of £20,000. With a full knowledge of these facts, is the Auditor justified in certifying the balance-sheet, without calling special attention thereto?

   *Resolution.*—That the capital and revenue accounts being distinct, the Auditor is fully justified in certifying the balance-sheet without calling special attention thereto.

6. Numerous cases have occurred where the annual depreciation for short leases is not adequately provided for in the annual balance-sheets.

   Is it the Auditor's duty to call the attention of Shareholders thereto? or can he properly sign the balance-sheet as "*correct according to the books?*"

   *Resolution.*—It is the Auditor's duty to call the attention of the Shareholders to the absence of adequate depreciation in the case of short leases.

7. Many cases have occurred where proprietors and companies have fixed the Audit fees at so low an amount as to render it impossible without a positive loss for the requisite time and work to be devoted to the Audit.

   In such cases is the Auditor justified when requested by the proprietors in omitting such an examination of the accounts in detail as he would consider necessary if the Audit fee were a fair and reasonable amount? And if not justified, has he any other remedy than either resigning the Audit or suffering the loss?

   *Resolution.*—It is the duty of an Auditor to fully perform his work, whatever the amount of the fee he receives.

## AUDITORS' CERTIFICATES TO BALANCE-SHEETS.

The following important article on the question of auditors' certificates appeared in *Vanity Fair* of the 6th inst. As the matter is of the utmost importance to the profession, we shall be glad to receive the suggestions of our readers as to a uniform certificate :—

In our issue of July 14th last we devoted some attention to the affairs of the Trading Steamship Company, Limited. In the course of our remarks upon the manner in which the accounts of this undertaking were drawn up, we made reference to the certificate to the balance-sheet, to which the auditor of the company, a Chartered Accountant of the name of W. L. Hamilton, had put his signature. We then said, concerning this certificate, that it amounted to a mere mechanical auditing, which had in itself no practical value. In the following week this remark drew a reply, amongst others, from Messrs. Harrison and Bond, the managers of the Trading Steamship Company, to the effect that our criticism of Mr. Hamilton's certificate was beyond fair journalistic comment. Nothing was further from our thoughts than to attack the reputation of a single individual accountant, who for all we know is as straight and painstaking an auditor as any one in the profession. What we condemned was the system of auditing as at present carried on; and we assert that by far the greater number of the certificates which professional auditors attach to the foot of a balance-sheet are in no degree a proof of the stability of the financial position of the companies to which they apply. Neither do these certificates in themselves, as a general rule, pledge the reputation or word of the gentlemen who give them, that the companies are solvent and that their capital is intact. Like the misty utterances of the Delphian oracles, these certificates can generally be read in two ways. The share-holder—for whose benefit they are intended—pays his money and takes his choice. It is confidently believed by many credulous persons that the very fact of a firm of accountants running over the totals of the balances of a bank, or a trading concern, or a shipping company, once a half-year or once a year, and then signifying in the various devious terms which it delights these exponents of arithmetical science to adopt in giving their certificate, proves these totals of necessity to be correct, and that the magic wand of the accountant having been waved, all is serene, and no fraud can be perpetrated. This is quite a fallacy. Accountants for years past have been employed in auditing the affairs of Joint Stock Companies. We do not remember one single instance amongst the hundreds of frauds and misrepresentations which have taken place since the establishment of the Act of 1862 which has been detected or laid bare by the hands of the professional auditor. But, on the other hand, it has been painfully apparent that in companies whose accounts have been supposed to have been strictly audited large defalcations have taken place. We purposely abstain from quoting the names of the companies to which we refer. It would be unfair to specifically mark the fallacy of one or two auditors' certificates when, as we contend, it is the system, and not the auditor, who is at fault. Neither do we remember any striking example of the power that an auditor can exert for saving a company from that bourne to which the generality of them wander—the mazes of the Court of Chancery. This is not the auditors' fault under the present system. Accordingly they do all they can to make their duties as light as possible.

When the end of the half-year or year arrives, and the books of a company have been made up, and the directors and managers are satisfied that this delicate culinary operation has been conducted with a due amount of solemnity, the appointed auditor is sent for. As a rule, this responsible office is the creation of the board, and not of the shareholders. If the auditor be, in professional parlance, a small man, he attends himself, and is as keen in his examination of the accounts as he possibly can be. He probably carps at a few insignificant items, but mostly passes lightly over generalities involving the fate of thousands. Vouchers are examined—what they represent he is not supposed to inquire into. If there is any cash in the till he counts it. Securities are looked to; whether they really represent the full value at which they stand in the balance-sheet is not always ascertained. The time of day is passed between himself and the manager, and after a quiet chop and a glass or two of dry sherry, the balance-sheet is passed, and the certificate signed.

When it is borne in mind what an immense amount of work and dealing with detail is necessary to properly keep the books of a bank or a company which is doing any business at all, it is obvious that the little time which accountants generally devote to an audit is not sufficient to convince them of its true financial position. The fault does not lie with the accountants. They do as much as they can for the money they receive for their work, and we honestly believe that if a company pay ten guineas for an audit, they get the equivalent out of the firm of accountants they employ. But at the finish what does an audit amount to? Frauds go on unchecked, directors and managers advance on rotten paper, or produce just the same, and shareholders lose their money, all the while imagining that the accountant is a check upon irregularity and insolvency.

For many years professional auditing was only applied to joint-stock trading companies. Shareholders in banks were formerly contented with the dual auditorial certificate of the manager and a director. The unpleasant circumstances surrounding the suspension of the City of Glasgow Bank changed all that, and now banking accounts are vouched for by professional men. That this circumstance in any way diminishes the risk which shareholders in these concerns run of being deceived by the directors or being robbed by their managers we fail to perceive, for auditing as at present carried on is mechanical, and, as a rule, the addendum of an accountant's certificate to a balance-sheet is of no practical value.

We will take as an example the certificate which Messrs. Turquand, Youngs and Co., accountants, who are not obscure in their profession, appended to the balance-sheet and accounts of the Indo-China Steam Navigation Company, Limited. The following is a copy:—

"We have examined the above balance-sheet and revenue account with the books and vouchers kept by the company in London, and with the statements received from the General Managers in China, and find them in accordance therewith; and we are of opinion that the balance-sheet is a full and fair balance-sheet, properly drawn up so as to exhibit a true and correct view of the state of the company's affairs.—TURQUAND, YOUNGS & CO."

"London, June 9th, 1883."

Our readers will recollect that in our review of the accounts of the company, which appeared in *Vanity Fair* on the 8th and 15th ult., we showed that the depreciation account of this company had been under-estimated about 1½ per cent., and that the directors, whilst accounting for the results of only eleven months' working, had drawn twelve months' salary. Neither one of these two important inaccuracies appears to have struck the auditors. But, as their certificate shows, they saw that the items in the balance-sheet tallied with the totals in the books; and we suppose their duties carried them no farther.

We will next proceed to quote the certificate given by Messrs. Howard Smith and Slocombe, the auditors of the Union Bank of Birmingham, which was attached to the balance-sheet presented to the proprietors of this bank at the annual meeting held on the 25th of July last:—

"We have examined the books and accounts of the company, tested by actual enumeration the assets and securities in their possession, and certify that the balance-sheet is in accordance therewith, and that in our opinion it truly sets forth the position of the company on the 30th day of June last.

"July 11th, 1883. "HOWARD SMITH AND SLOCOMBE, Auditors."

Now as auditors' certificates go, this one is comprehensive and good. It sets forth that in their opinion the balance-sheet clearly shows the true position of the bank, and we should have gathered from this that the auditors had satisfied themselves as to the nature and value of all the assets of the bank. At the same time we contend that in signing such a certificate Messrs. Howard Smith and Slocombe accepted a very serious responsibility.

For what do we find? Scarcely is the ink of the accountants' signature dry when we read that the manager of the Union Bank of Birmingham has absconded, leaving defalcations to the extent of £20,000, which must have extended over a long period of time; and that the bank has to be merged with another local affair in order to escape the clutch of the official liquidator. A Birmingham contemporary, in reporting some details of this case, said naively, "The means by which the transaction was carried out was simple enough. The books of the bank were properly kept, but the manager presented to the directors false returns as to his operations in bills, and also as to his own account with the bank." Whether the accountants, who were responsible for the above certificate, were not supposed to be more astute than the directors we know not. It is evident that they were not ; and this being the case, i auditors are unable to detect frauds of this nature, their confirmation of the correctness of the accounts degenerates into a farce, and they receive pay for duties which are of no earthly benefit to shareholders.

Such a fraud as the above having occurred in an apparently flourishing bank only a few days ago, it may be worth while to examine the true worth in plain language of the auditorial certificates which accompany the balance-sheets of a few of the leading London joint-stock banks. We have picked them out haphazard from the last half-yearly reports. One or two will be sufficient for our purpose.

For example, let us take the certificate which the auditors of the Imperial Bank affixed to the last half-yearly report of that establishment. Here it is :—

"We have compared the balances as set forth in this balance-sheet with the *books*, and find the same *correct*.

" FREDERICK FEARON, GEORGE BROOM, Auditors."

Now, in the name of common sense, what does this declaration amount to? This certificate, we take it, put into plain English, reads thus :—"We have visited the Imperial Bank ; " we have seen the insides of the books of that institution, " and certify that the balances as brought down therein on the " 30th June last are the same as those printed in the balance- " sheet." It must be perfectly apparent to the most obtuse that in the remote possibility of any irregularity occurring in the books, or of the assets of the bank proving hopelessly bad, Messrs. Fearon and Broom did not attempt to investigate the matter. At any rate, these gentlemen appear to think that their duties began and ended with the performance of that task which they have recorded as above.

We next come to the certificate furnished by the auditors of the Alliance Bank, which is annexed : —

" *We have examined the foregoing accounts in detail, with the books and vouchers of the Bank, and find them to be correct.* Further, we have ascertained by actual enumeration the correctness of the items of cash and bills of exchange in hand, and have inspected the securities representing the bank's own investments in Government stocks, &c., and also those held on account of advances and loans as well as those belonging to customers, and we find them to be in due accordance with the books and accounts of the bank.

" WILLIAM QUILTER (Quilter, Ball, and Co.) } Auditors."
" JOHN YOUNG (Turquand, Youngs and Co.) }

This it must be admitted is a very rambling specimen. We find that the auditors admit having examined the accounts *with the books*, and having satisfied themselves that they are correct. They have also examined certain securities representing the investments of the bank. They further proceed to say that they have examined securities held by the bank on account of advances and loans, and they add they found them *in due accordance with the books and accounts of the bank.* In the first statement the word "correct" we take it means "agree therewith." This practically amounts to the farce of comparing items in the books with the published details of the balance-sheet. With regard to the securities held against advances, we can scarcely think the shareholders should rest entirely satisfied. There is no pledge here from the auditors that the securities in hand equal or exceed the amount of advances which borrowers have obtained upon them. Yet this is one of the most vital questions affecting the stability of a bank. It is an indisputable fact that banks have suffered most of their heaviest losses from the circumstance that the securities on which customers have obtained loans proved totally inadequate to realise the amount advanced.

We will next take the certificate which the auditors of the London and South-Western Bank have thought fit to attach to the balance-sheet of that institution, which reads as follows :—

" We have compared the above statements with the books and vouchers at the head office, and with the certified returns from the several branches, and certify that we found the cash in hand, and at Bank of England, bills discounted, loans, and other items, as stated in the balance-sheet to be duly in accordance therewith. We have likewise examined the securities for cash at call and short notice, as also the investments of the bank, standing in the balance-sheet at £733,603 17s. 6d. and £95,235 7s. 2d., and found the same correct.

"(Signed) JAMES EDMESTON,
     "JAMES WORLEY, Chartered Accountant, } Auditors.
" Dated this 11th day of July, 1883."

This we take to be a rare specimen of auditorial casuistry. In fact, its proper position should be amongst the "hard cases" of which it is the pleasure of many readers of this paper to give a solution. We have read it in the English style, in the Hebraic style, and in the Chinese. We do not suppose that Mr. Edmeston and Mr. Worley intended to concoct a puzzle ; but if they did, they have been singularly successful.

At the first glance it looks as if the auditors had done what auditors should—counted the cash, verified the balance at the Bank of England, and inspected the bill-case. But if we understand the meaning of the English language, the certificate reads thus :—"We have compared the above balance-sheet with the books and vouchers at the head office of the bank and with the certified returns from the several branches, and we find it to be duly in accordance therewith." In other words, we have been careful to see that in making a fair copy of the balance-sheet from the books of the company no clerical errors have occurred. The last part of this certificate is somewhat clearer than the foregoing, in this respect. The auditors specifically state that they have examined the securities for cash at call and short notice, and also the investments of the bank, standing in the balance-sheet at £733,000 and £95,000 respectively. "*Standing in the balance-sheet at.*" This is a phrase indefinite in the extreme, and may cover a multitude of sins. What does it really mean? An old lady we know holds Honduras Bonds "*standing at*"—in her mind—eighty, the price she paid for them. All her friends, practically social auditors, tell her that these securities should be valued at what they will fetch—the market price. But if the old lady made up her own balance-sheet, we feel sure that she would insist on having her stock as an asset *standing at* eighty. The securities for the London and South-Western are doubtless fully worth what they stand at in the balance-sheet. But the auditors' certificate is no assurance to this effect.

The last auditors' certificate which we shall give at present is that attached to the balance-sheet of one of the best banks in the world, the London Joint Stock Bank, which reads as follows :—

" We have audited the above statement of liabilities and assets, and we report that in our opinion it is a full and fair balance-sheet, properly drawn up so as to exhibit a true and correct view of the state of the bank's affairs, *as shown in the books of the bank.*

" WILLIAM CROSBIE (Quilter, Ball & Co.)
" JOHN G. GRIFFITHS (Deloitte, Dever, Griffiths & Co.)
             Auditors."

In this case the auditors state that they have audited the statement of the liabilities and assets of the bank, and they report that in their opinion the balance-sheet is full and fair, and properly drawn up so as to exhibit a full and correct view of the state of the bank's affairs. But there is a rift in the lute. The whole of these pleasant assertions hinge on the important qualification that they are shown by the books of the bank. The last few words, in our opinion, bring the certificate into the same category as the preceding documents to which we have referred.

Without citing any further cases, of which there are plenty, we think we have sufficiently proved our assertion that auditing, as carried on under the present system, is of no practical value as evidence of the true financial position of a company. The general expression of auditors' certificates all tends in the same direction, and, although the terms may vary in minor details, they all agree in the essential point that they merely certify that the balance-sheet is correctly copied from the books, sometimes with the addition that the auditors have counted the cash and inspected the bill-case and the security-box.  Audits under such conditions are a delusion and a snare.  In this we are quite sure that the general body of accountants will agree with us.

The fault does not lie with the profession, the members of which are capable—if their duties were properly defined and understood by the shareholding community—of exercising great good, and of being the means of saving to the public millions per annum.  But as long as the accounts are left out of consideration until the time of audit arrives at the end of the year or half-year, as is now the case, the value of the supposed check that auditors can exert is simply infinitesimal.  And such a condition of affairs will always prevail until responsibility is imposed upon the givers of these certificates, and until they are paid in a degree proportionate to the importance of the duties they execute.

It is time that audits should cease to be a mere matter of routine and custom, and become what in the true sense of the word they should be—thorough investigations.

[It is a pity the editor of *Vanity Fair* does not keep himself better posted up in regard to current matters, as he would then not have fallen foul of the actual facts in regard to the audit of the Union Bank, Birmingham, the defalcations on which were acknowledged by one of the directors, in the report which appeared in the *Times* of the 10th inst., to be the discovery of Mr. Joseph Slocombe, one of the auditors.  The editor of *Vanity Fair* has either a bad memory, or, as indicated above, he suffers from a dearth of knowledge when he says that he does not "remember one single instance" of fraud "being laid bare by the hands of the professional auditor"—the latest notorious instance in which the auditors were instrumental in discovering fraud being the River Plate Bank.  However, the subject is much too important to be dismissed in a single paragraph, and we shall devote a leading article to the matter in our next issue.—ED. *The Accountant.*]

##### AUDITORS' CERTIFICATES TO BALANCESHEETS.

In these days of almost boundless commercial enterprise the question of Auditors' Certificates to Balancesheets is of the utmost importance, not only to the profession which we represent, but also to the investing public.  It is, therefore, with great satisfaction that we find the matter has been opened in the columns of *Vanity Fair*, and with a view to thoroughly ventilating the question, we reproduced the first article from our contemporary in our last issue, while this issue contains further editorial comments and correspondence from the same paper.

In replying to the editor of *Vanity Fair* we forwarded him a copy of No. 896 of *The Accountant*, which contains a letter pointing out that the defects in the laws relating to auditing are the real cause of the present unsatisfactory position of an auditor.  We do not entirely endorse the views expressed by "Anti-Twaddle" in our present issue, as we regard the subject in a much more important light than that of twaddle, and there is, unfortunately, a deal of truth in the comments of the editor of *Vanity Fair*, but we admit that our correspondent has put his finger on some of the reasons why an auditor is, in company work, unable to exercise the same efficient control as he is able to exercise in examining the accounts of a private undertaking.

We are agreed with our contemporary that, although excellent in some respects, Mr. Welton's letter does not touch the real question under discussion, which is as to the form of auditorial certificate : and we must admit that Mr. Welton's assertion that banks, with independent professional men as auditors *do not fail*, is not borne out by facts.  We imagine that what Mr. Welton wished to convey was that where professional men are allowed to exercise that independence and authority which is conferred upon them by private clients, failure does not ensue. If that is Mr. Welton's meaning we agree with him, as we could quote many instances where clients, by acting upon the advice given by their auditors, have been saved from embarking in serious risks; deterred from taking too sanguine views of their position; and, consequently, have attained a prosperity beyond their anticipation.

The letter of "H., F.C.A.," is much more to the point, for he calls attention to the difficulty an auditor has to contend with where a board persists in adopting views which he cannot honestly endorse.

*Vanity Fair*, however, clearly misunderstands the powers of an auditor. As things exist at present, the balance-sheet does not emanate from him, but from the directors, whose statement it is. In substance, every Act relating to accounts contains clauses to the following effect:—"Once at least in every year the directors shall lay before the company in general meeting a statement of the income and expenditure for the past year made up to a date not more than three months before such meeting, and every auditor shall be supplied with a copy of the balance-sheet, and it shall be his duty to examine the same with the accounts and vouchers relating thereto," &c.

It is doubtless desirable as suggested by "Anti-Twaddle" that the balance-sheet should emanate from the auditors and not from the directors, but this could only be done by special legislation.

Some of the real difficulties an auditor has to encounter in connection with joint stock auditing are— (1) that in most instances he is not allowed to audit, say from month to month, but only once a year, when the balance-sheet is ready; (2) that too little time is allowed for the auditor to make an exhaustive report, as the documents are required for the printer, consequently a short certificate becomes a necessity; (3) that, as a rule, shareholders, in spite of the assertion of *Vanity Fair* to the contrary, are generally impatient to get through the business; (4) that the fee, as instanced by "H," is usually out of all proportion to the work required to be done; (5) that in nearly every instance the voting power is in the absolute control of the Board.

Notwithstanding what has been said by our contemporary to the contrary, the present practice of giving certificates in lieu of special reports has been found to work well in most instances, inasmuch as every auditor who values his reputation always falls back upon the latter when he feels that he cannot conscientiously endorse the statements put forward by the directors.

In every case where the auditor is a man of honour and ability, the very absence of a special report is in itself evidence that he is satisfied with the *bonà fides* of the directors' accounts.

Since writing the above we have received a communication on this subject from an F.C.A., in which he censures us for calling the Editor of *Vanity Fair* to account for not having read a report on the Union Bank, which appeared subsequent to his article. We had overlooked this fact when writing last week, but at the same time it was very well known about a month ago that it was entirely owing to the auditors that the fraud was discovered, and the Editor of *Vanity Fair* should have made himself acquainted with the absolute facts. We must defer further comment until our next issue.

———

##### Auditors' Certificates to Balance Sheets.

*To the Editor of The Accountant.*

Sir,—I shall look forward with considerable interest, as doubtless will most other readers of your journal, to your promised article upon the above subject. But pending its appearance I would just suggest that we must be just whilst we are critical, and that we shall do well to consider whether the Editor of *Vanity Fair* has not done or commenced to do a good service to auditors in the article in his paper to which you are about to reply. And in passing allow me to suggest that you are a little hard in reproaching him for not having read a report which appeared in the *Times* of the 10th inst. before writing his of the 6th.

The Editor of *Vanity Fair* is evidently labouring under some strange delusion as to the meaning of the words quoted from the several certificates, which certify that certain figures in the respective balance-sheets are correct in accordance with the companies' books ; and you, or those gentlemen whom he has criticised, will soon put him right upon that point.

With regard, however, to one of the broader questions raised, as to the use or uselessness of independent audits, I venture to suggest that the Editor of *Vanity Fair* will have rendered a real service to the profession, if only his letter is the means of ventilating this important subject— if, in fact, the outside public are informed as to what an audit can effect and what it cannot. And whilst upon this subject I am tempted to refer to a remark made by Mr. Chadwick in his address to the students of the London Institute of Accountants on the 25th September last.

That gentleman is reported in your journal of the 29th of September to have said that "the occurrence of frauds like those recently exposed in the cases of the Glasgow Bank and the Army and Navy Stores should have been rendered impossible by experienced auditors." Now an efficient audit should detect fraud certainly, but is it not too much to say that it is bound to prevent it?

With regard to bank auditing and the certificates that should be given, I shall be glad if your invitation for an exchange of views through the medium of your journal is responded to by some gentlemen more experienced in this particular than myself. Meanwhile I take the fact to be that the several auditors mentioned by the Editor of *Vanity Fair* have intended nothing more than to certify as to the figures in the respective balance-sheets-being supported by the existence of securities, and that they in no way hold themselves responsible for the accuracy of the revenue account, or indeed the accuracy of the figures in the balance-sheet; and if the words referring to the bank books, to which that gentleman takes exception, have led the shareholders to any other conclusion, the sooner they are undeceived the better.

The Editor suggests that banking accounts should be thoroughly investigated. Has he taken the trouble to ascertain the probable cost of such an operation, and the delay that would take place in publishing the returns?

Again, he suggests that what is now done is but a delusion and a snare. This is only partly true. It is certainly no delusion to the shareholders to be informed that their property as stated by the directors is intact, and their position sound, at the end of a given year; but whether the appearance of the auditors' signatures at the foot of the balance-sheet ensnares them into the belief that all is bound to remain intact until the appearance of the next annual report is another matter: and here I think the question arises whether it should not be made a practice for banks to draw monthly statements of their affairs (not for publication), that the auditors might check the securities twelve times in lieu of once in each year.

Since writing the above, I observe that Mr. Deloitte was asked on Tuesday last, when he appeared as a witness in the case of the River Plate Bank, whether there was any particular reason why an examination of securities should not take place monthly; and I was somewhat surprised at his reply. He is reported to have said, "Not if the directors wanted it." I have yet to learn that the directors have anything to do with the matter. Is it not rather a question for the auditors to decide or to recommend to the shareholders?

In conclusion, I would suggest that there is a large amount of truth in the article in *Vanity Fair* of the 6th inst.; and notwithstanding that the tenor of it must necessarily be very unpalatable to the profession at large, there is upon the whole a spirit of fairness evinced towards auditors, and inasmuch as it must be tolerably clear to all that public accountants and auditors are just now on their trial before the bar of public opinion, it behoves us to be careful how we meet this attack.

Yours, &c.

AUDITOR, F.C.A.

17th October, 1883.

For the benefit of our readers we give the evidence of Mr. Deloitte referred to by our correspondent:—

Mr. William Welch Deloitte, examined by Mr. Poland— I am a member of the firm of Deloitte, Dever, Griffiths, and Co., chartered accountants, 4 Lothbury, and am one of the auditors to the River Plate Bank. The other auditor is Mr. John Banner, who is not a member of our firm. I have been in the habit from time to time of auditing the accounts of the bank, and it has been my practice to see the securities on which the bank has made advances. I was at the bank on Monday, the 1st October, to audit the accounts. I had previously received the following letter from Mr. Warden:— "September 20.—Dear Sir,—I beg to remind you that we shall as usual require the attendance of yourself and Mr. Banner on Monday, the 1st of October, for the purpose of verifying the bills and securities on the close of the financial year. I have not arranged with Mr. Banner, but leave you to arrange with him. The 1st being Monday, say 12 o'clock.—I am yours obediently, Geo. Warden."—I and Mr. Banner met at the bank at the appointed time. Mr. Warden was there. We proceeded to examine the securities in the secretary and manager's room. To facilitate the audit a list of the securities was handed to us. The list produced, which is in the writing of Mr. Warden, is a list of the securities up to Sept. 30 on which the bank had made advances. It was part of my duty to see that these securities were there. Amongst others in the list there is "Commercial Bank, Alexandria (Limited) against loan of £25,000, £30,000 Egyptian Preference Stock." Were these securities produced to you?—They were. By whom?—By Mr. Warden. And I see the item is ticked as being correct?—It is. The tick is mine. Mr. Banner and myself examined them together. What time of day was that?—It was after the bills were produced. These were then handed in. I can't say the time exactly, but it was between 12 and 2. The figures £3000 in red ink have been added since. How many following lots of securities mentioned in that list were handed to you?—Nine. They were produced to you by whom?—Mr. Warden. And all found to be correct?—They were examined by Mr. Banner and myself and ticked by me. Then there follow other four lots. When you had ticked the last of the nine lots did Mr. Warden say anything to you?—He said he would go into the treasury and fetch the remainder of the securities. The Alderman— What did he mean by the "treasury"?—That is the expression he made use of. Mr. Poland—I believe the strong-room is called the treasury at the bank. (To witness) What time was it when he said that?—It was about half-past one. He went out of the room, apparently for the purpose which he mentioned, and he did not return. You waited some time and he did not return?—Yes. Did you communicate with the director on duty?—No, I communicated with Mr. Langton one of the staff—the chief bookkeeper. I waited some time and Mr. Warden never returned. You never saw him again until he was in custody?—No. [A list of the securities was then handed to the Alderman.] Mr. Poland: Were the bonds you found correct produced from time to time?—They were produced one after another, as called for, and examined. Of course you do not have to examine the securities left for safe custody?— Certainly not. The previous time we had examined the securities was, I believe, on the 2nd of October last year. I do not think that before this time the securities were personally produced by Mr. Warden. They have always up to this year been found correct. The Alderman: A half-yearly audit has been spoken of—did you take any part in that?—Witness: That was intermediate. The accounts were made up to date merely. Then in point of fact the whole of the securities were not checked half-yearly?—Certainly not; only once a year. Is it usual for the audit of a bank only to take place once a year?—It all depends upon how the accounts are made up. Here there was an interim dividend unaccompanied by a statement of accounts. It was the duty of the auditors to submit the accounts only at the end of the financial year. Is there any particular reason why an examination of securities should not take place monthly?—Not if the directors wanted it. Mr. Poland: I suppose that after the securities were examined and the list ticked they were handed back to Mr. Warden. Witness: Yes, they were laid on the table for us to check. We counted every one individually.

### To the Editor of The Accountant.

SIR,—Doubtless in common with many of your readers, I have read with considerable amusement the article republished in your last issue from the columns of *Vanity Fair*.

I had thought that critics were supposed to know *something* about what they undertook to write upon, but it is evident that, like the hobbledehoy who eschewed the delights of Punch and Judy in favour of the nauseating effects of colouring his first meerschaum, the editor of *Vanity Fair* is "much above that sort of thing."

Would the said editor be surprised to hear :—

1. That an auditor has no power to go beyond the figures contained in the books unless it be to protest in a special report against any manifest inaccuracy, such as carrying forward at 20s. in the pound bills which have been dishonoured.

2. That an auditor has no power to value book debts to test their accuracy by communicating with such debtors, or by the doubtful information derivable from trade protection inquiry offices.

3. That the balance-sheet, for which the directors are responsible, is generally submitted to the auditor but a very short time before the day fixed for issuing it, and that it is then not infrequently imperfect.

4. That the auditorial fee is generally out of all proportion to what would be fair remuneration for an efficient audit.

5. That the auditor's responsibility is limited to the verification of the figures submitted to him as being the outcome of the contents of the books.

6. That in every certificate he has quoted there is an evident desire to show to what extent the respective auditors take the responsibility of the figures certified to.

7. That the power of electing auditors is almost invariably in the absolute control of the directors, and that any difference of opinion is almost certain to result in the supersession of the cavilling auditor.

8. That shareholders (like other people) sometimes have a strong objection to knowing the truth, and

9. That directors, however honest, do not like to look at the worst side of affairs, but rather tend to admire the rosy side?

The editor of *Vanity Fair*, far from recognising the above facts, and especially the evident desire of the respective auditors to do justice to the interests they were appointed to protect, contents himself, like the average critic, with pulling others' work to pieces without suggesting any form of certificate which would suit his fastidious taste. So far as I can gather from his remarks a special pamphlet (which nobody would read) *might* content him provided every *i* was dotted and every *t* crossed.

That the responsibility of an auditor *should* be great no accountant will deny, but for an auditor to be responsible for the full contents of the accounts it is evident that very material alterations must first take place in the existing laws on the subject—in fact, a special law on auditorial duties would have to be passed.

Even in an ordinary undertaking the amount of knowledge requisite would be practically outside the control of the auditor without assistance from others. An admirable Crichton would break down in acquiring the knowledge necessary to control even twenty fairly important audits, for it would involve the obligation of knowing the position of every debtor, the intricate customs and future of each trade, the future of each investment, the "life" of the machinery, plant, utensils, &c., of each undertaking, &c., so that the calling in of others would become an absolute necessity.

Under present circumstances, therefore, common sense (scarce commodity, alas!) should have taught the critic in question that the responsibility of the accounts must rest with the board, and that of the verification thereof *as contained in the company's books* with the auditor.

If the said critic wishes to distinguish himself and make an auditor fully responsible, let him obtain the passing of a law containing *inter alia* the following provisions :—

1. That no director shall vote on the election of auditor.

2. That no proxies shall be issued for that purpose or be given to any director or official of the company.

3. That the books shall be audited at least once a month, *and not as at present too often happens once a year against time.*

4. That every debt not duly met at maturity shall be treated as bad, and the proceeds thereof be credited to profit and loss when received.

5. That the auditor shall, if he thinks fit, have power at the expense of the company to employ suitable persons to value book debts and other assets, or portions thereof.

6. That the balance-sheet and accounts shall be prepared by the auditor, and not by the board or its officers, but that they shall render any requisite information and assistance in connection therewith.

7. That due provision shall be made for the remuneration of the auditor and others engaged upon the accounts.

When such a law is passed, it will be reasonable to hold auditors responsible, but not till then.

When the editor of *Vanity Fair* has ["done this great thing," his opinion on auditorial duties and responsibilities will be of value ; and I do not doubt that every auditor will consult him on the exact words to put in his certificate.

I would add that I am not interested in his attempted "slaughter of the innocents."

Yours, &c.

ANTI-TWADDLE.

15th October, 1883.

## AUDITORS' CERTIFICATES TO BALANCE-SHEETS.

The following article and correspondence on this matter appeared in *Vanity Fair* of the 13th inst. :—

The remarks on this subject which appeared in our last issue have evidently been taken to heart by auditors and accountants.

We have received a great many letters from various members of the profession in reference to the above question. Not one of them gives anything like a specific denial to our assertions that auditors' certificates to balance-sheets as a rule mean nothing further than that balance-sheets so audited simply agree with the books, and contain no assurance that the assets of a company are intact and that the profits have been properly realised. The letters of most of our correspondents are much like some auditorial certificates—difficult to understand. But the following seem entitled to insertion :—

"*To the Editor of 'Vanity Fair.'*

"SIR,—Your article to-day will be of much service if it induces shareholders and the public to closely scan the certificates appended to accounts in which they are interested.

"It is not my purpose to answer your remarks, but merely to point out some facts which do not perhaps lie on the surface, and to which you do not appear to refer.

"1. A great feature in most concerns, particularly banks, is the amount due from sundry debtors. Country bankers allow overdrafts, the same accommodation being given in London by way of loans ; either way, hundreds and thousands of debtor balances are called into being.

"Now, no person, even the bank manager, can be *certain* of these balances ; all must accept the testimony of the books. But in the facts (*a*) that the accounts are open to the whole body of clerks ; (*b*) that they are frequently balanced, and the result compared with a summary book kept by the chief manager ; and (*c*) that if an error exists, the public (*i.e.*, the customer who is interested) will bring it sooner or later to light, lies *almost* perfect security. The auditor cannot do more than the manager in this case. The above remark applies to creditor balances.

"2. The idea that a large defalcation *must* be the result of operations extending 'over a long period of time' is incorrect. A manager might do much between audit and audit, and so long as he puts everything straight at the date of the audit, no impropriety would appear. It is when he makes a heavy loss or determines upon flight that he can in a very short time abstract large sums, and then not so that the clerks will perceive it ; but the auditors' examination of securities, including, it may be, bonds to bearer for many thousands, will at once disclose the fraud.

"3. That the auditor should say ' the securities in hand equal or exceed the amount of advances made upon' them involves two suppositions—(*a*) That every advance is made upon security of at least equal value, and (*b*) that the auditor is a judge of values, so as to take the responsibility of what is in effect a valuation of very varied matters and things. Neither of these is absolutely true. The risk where a banker advances without security is often much less serious than when he makes an advance *solely* on the strength of a security which may fall in value Accordingly such advances, when they occur, are not treated as wrong in themselves, but simply as matters requiring grave attention. The auditor cannot tell what value to attach to ships, factories, and many other subjects held as security. All he can do is to use ordinary common sense, and call attention privately to any case in which he thinks better security ought to be obtained. Also, he can form an opinion as to the reserve against doubtful debts, and ensure a prudent policy being adopted in the way of raising this reserve as high as may be expedient.

"4. You will no doubt concur with me in thinking that an auditor, who cannot express *all* he has done within the four corners of a short certificate, ought to err on the side of reticence, understating rather than overstating the checks he has employed. One of the securities which the public are entitled to presume when a competent auditor is employed is this, that he will be so unwilling that his name should ever be associated with failure that he will ally himself with all that is conservative in the management and prevent the distribution of a penny in dividend that is really wanted for safety. He is interested in keeping down appearances, and never suffers a flourishing aspect to be put on by a concern which has need of all its resources. Now the mere presence of an independent auditor stops many things. Bear in mind that as respects the dealings of a bank with its ordinary customers, who may owe various sums up to a thousand or two, no real risk worth mentioning is ever incurred ; such small accounts are like the grass, nutritious beyond anything, but, taken separately, of no consequence at all. It is when a bank has a customer of importance, like Booker in the case of the West of England Bank, that real benefit results from auditorial care. That bank had no auditor ; it had perhaps a hundred large and unsafe accounts. No rational man, acting as auditor, would have allowed the distribution of large dividends until a good private reserve had been accumulated to counterbalance the risk. If an auditor did no more than look with the proverbial 'master's eye' into the largest accounts, he would earn his fee many times over.

"5. In conclusion, I will simply observe that, according to my experience, banks with independent professional men as auditors *do not fail.*—Your obedient servant,   THOS. A. WELTON.

"Quilter, Ball, and Co.,

"5 Moorgate Street, London, E.C.

"6th October, 1883."

It will be noticed that our correspondent states that it is not his purpose to answer our remarks. This we regret, as we should have been glad to have received a definite opinion on this important subject from so trustworthy a source. Mr. Welton has, however, been so good as to inform us of some facts which he states do not lie on the surface.

These facts appear from his letter to amount to this—that auditors do a great deal more than one would imagine from their certificates. He also proceeds to explain various details into which we need not enter, inasmuch as it is not our purpose to enter into a discussion of the technicalities of auditing.

We fully accept the statements of Mr. Welton. He says that auditors do a great deal more than is implied in their certificates ; but all we can say is—and we feel sure that it will be re-echoed by our readers—that if, after all this labour has been expended, the result to which we have drawn attention is to be the only result, a great deal of labour is apparently thrown away, and much ado made about nothing. But as will be seen from Mr. Welton's remarks, he tacitly admits the justice of our criticisms. It is only due to ourselves, however, to remark that he diverts attention from the main issue raised by us. We never questioned the ability of accountants to do anything that lies in human power ; but giving them credit for this, and also for that desirable possession of a "master's eye," we reiterate our original assertions—that their certificates are commonly of no practical value. In paragraph 2 of his letter Mr. Welton—unintentionally no doubt —misrepresents our statement. We had no idea that a large defalcation must be the result of irregularities extending over a long period of time. What we said was that the fact of the large defalcations of the manager of the Union Bank of Birmingham being discovered so soon after the publication of the balance-sheet was evidence that, in this case, the irregularities had extended over a long period of time. This statement is up to the present uncontradicted, so we are entitled to assume that it is correct. A passage in paragraph 3 strikes us as unsound. What does Mr. Welton mean when he tells us that an auditor should call attention *privately* to the case when the manager of a bank in taking undue risks? This might suggest the idea of collusion between the manager and the auditor, which is certainly not the purpose of the institution of the latter office.

In paragraph 4 Mr. Welton says an "auditor cannot express all he has done within the four corners of a short certificate, and that he ought to err rather on the side of reticence." But why should the certificate be so very short? Why should it be reduced to the few unmeaning sentences which it generally amounts to? Our experience leads us to believe that the more they are told about the true position of their property the more shareholders are pleased. We are certainly unaware of the existence of any Act of Parliament which forbids the rendering of a complete and exhaustive certificate, showing actually where the audit has been of value. Mr. Welton says that the "mere presence of an auditor stops many things." What are we to learn from this? We can but suppose that our correspondent has accidentally omitted what would have been the most interesting part of his communication—viz., what it really is that the presence of an auditor does put a stop to.

We disagree entirely with the statement that the mere fact of a competent auditor being employed should be considered as a security by the public that an artificially flourishing aspect is never put on the affairs of a company. The many failures of banks and of myriads of public companies where auditors have been employed are in direct contradiction to this.

Mr. Welton's description of the value of small accounts is noteworthy. He says they are "like the grass, nutritious beyond anything, but taken separately of no consequence at all." The simile can scarcely be called a happy one, for grass is supposed to symbolise that which perishes in a day. It is only natural that Mr. Welton should magnify his office; but when we come to the remark that an auditor looks into accounts with the proverbial "master's eye," we must confess that we can scarcely accept it as final. Who is to determine that every auditor possesses this superlative attribute? Can the Institute of Chartered Accountants or its learned Council impart the gift?

The sting of Mr. Welton's letter however lies, like the scorpion's, in the tail. Mr. Welton says that, "according to his experience, banks with independent auditors do not fail." We, on the contrary, assert that many banks, not to speak of companies, have either reduced their capital, wound up, or failed, notwithstanding the fact that they were audited by independent or professional auditors. We will name a few—The Bank of Hindustan, China, and Japan; the New Zealand Banking Corporation, Limited; the London, Bombay, and Mediterranean Bank; the Metropolitan Bank, Limited; and the Standard Bank of London, Limited. These we remember failing within our recollection. Whether the gentlemen who audited these accounts possessed the mystic qualification of a "master's eye" we know not. Either therefore Mr. Welton's memory is deficient, or his experience is limited. Until we receive more convincing proof than Mr. Welton's letter affords us, of the fallacy of our contention, we must unhesitatingly reiterate our belief that, for all the general good that the exercise of the "master's eye" by auditors may do, auditing, as at present carried on, is commonly a delusion and a snare.

*"To the Editor of 'Vanity Fair.'*

"SIR,—I read with great interest your powerful article on "Auditors' Certificates to Balance Sheets." As a chartered accountant, and with many years' experience, I feel delighted at the singularly correct insight of the writer into the matter. I can fully confirm your opinion that in too many instances the certificates of professional auditors are a delusion and a snare. Permit me to illustrate, by one case in my own experience, the difficulties against which professional auditors have to contend. I was appointed by the directors of a manufacturing company newly formed to take over a large and profitable business. In the first year's audit, to satisfy myself that the balance-sheet

was not only in accordance with the books, but also with the true value of their assets and the full extent of their liabilities, and further to satisfy myself that the manufactured results of the revenue and expenditure had all been faithfully recorded in the books of the company, and also to satisfy myself on other important points, I endeavoured to establish a sound and satisfactory audit. What were the results? Considerable alterations in the balance-sheet, the ill-will of the managing director, and an altercation with the chairman at the company's office. At the general meeting a bank clerk in the town was put forward by the directors to take my place on these grounds:—They fully recognised the ability of the auditor, but 'the business could not bear the expense.' The fee I asked was £80 for twelve months' audit, including two balance-sheets. The bank clerk put forward was willing to check the books and sign the balance-sheets for £20 per annum. In this case the shareholders at the general meeting would not consent to the proposal of the board, and I was re-elected, provided I consented to a future fee of £30 per annum. Well, Sir, I have this audit still, and it occupies over six weeks yearly 'of my clerk's' and two weeks of my own time, besides involving travelling and hotel expenses. If it were not that many thousands of pounds of my friends' money were placed on my recommendation in the company, how could I afford sufficient time to this audit to enable me to give a satisfactory certificate to two half-yearly balance-sheets for £30 per annum? It is very essential that skilled and experienced accountants should be employed to audit the balance-sheets of public companies; but as the wording of the Companies Acts is vague as to the full scope of the duties, the responsibility of the audit rests in a great measure with the shareholders themselves. If the shareholders require a satisfactory certificate they must pay a fair price for it—according to fee so must necessarily be the value of the certificate. As a professional accountant I thank you for your very fair and just article.—Your obedient servant,                                    "H., F.C.A."

# The Accountant.

## OCTOBER 27, 1883.

### AUDITORS' CERTIFICATES TO BALANCE-SHEETS.

While we willingly recognise the fact that *Vanity Fair* has opened a discussion which ought to lead to an improvement in the status and power of auditors, we feel bound to assert that that paper is not acting with that spirit of fairness which should be the guiding power of everybody who assumes to act as a censor of public morality.

We have called the attention of *Vanity Fair* to an

article which appeared long ago in our columns, complaining of the manner in which auditors found themselves stultified in their duties, and to our knowledge similar communications have been made to that paper, but unless they can be distorted to support the views of the writer of the articles, they are quietly ignored, or at best twisted to suit the present purposes of that paper.

It must be evident to every reasoning mind that an auditor's first wish must be that he should be independent of influence or control, and that not only for the sake of those who were perhaps induced by his name to embark capital in a company, but also for his own sake his great desire must be to hold the power necessary to be able to exercise that decision and vigilance which he so successfully exercises on behalf of private clients.

Far be it from us to complain of the object which *Vanity Fair* has in view. On the contrary, we thoroughly appreciate it, as we feel convinced that the more the powers of auditors are strengthened the better it will be both for the public and themselves. All we complain of is, that in seeking to attain a laudable object, our contemporary, following the jesuitical proverb, acts as if "the end justified the means."

Surely all auditors are not imbecile. The various forms of certificate published by *Vanity Fair* show that the respective auditors have striven to convey to the shareholders a fair idea of the extent to which they are, or are not, responsible for the figures certified to.

The most unscrupulous—and we use the word advisedly—attack is that upon Mr. Deloitte, under the heading of "Auditing in Excelsis." We *had* thought that while matters remained *sub judice* journalistic and legal etiquette required that comments should be withheld. *Vanity Fair* is, however, evidently superior to anything which does not accord with its views. We shall, however, not fall into the trap laid or abandon the line of decency so generally recognised, and we doubt not that Mr. Deloitte will in the ordinary course of evidence furnish an explanation as to his position and powers in the matter.

While writing thus strongly on the undoubted bad taste of our contemporary, we wish it to be distinctly understood that we approve of the motive of that paper.

The powers of an auditor ought to be such as are daily exercised by accountants in relation to private clients. We are frequently receiving communications from members of the profession, all tending to show that if the auditor were invested with proper powers and made independent of the directors, the former would for the sake of his reputation insist upon his own balance-sheet being substituted for that of the directors. Instance after instance is furnished in the audit of private firms showing that even where the accountant has thought it right and proper to adopt a view different from that held by his client, the client has finished by thanking him for his discreet and advantageous intervention.

The editor of *Vanity Fair* acknowledges that one of his correspondents states that further legislation is required. This further legislation he asserts is unnecessary, while he recognises the fact that the remuneration of auditors is by no means commensurate with the duties which he alleges ought to be required of them. Yet in the face of this negation of the necessity of further legislation, he apparently endorses the views of his correspondent, Mr. Fraser, F.C.A., that no remedy can be found until the proxy system is done away with, and the power of an auditor is made such as to render him not only independent of the directors, but entitled to substitute his figures for those which they submit for his verification.

In auditing the affairs of a private concern the auditor does not, as a rule, wait until the end of the financial year or half-year, but attends weekly or monthly. As a consequence he can frequently detect errors of judgment, nip fraud in the bud, and generally prevent disaster.

The material point is, however, that which *Vanity Fair* carefully avoids, viz. the form of certificate which under existing laws would satisfy his fastidious fancy.

## AUDITORS' CERTIFICATES TO BALANCE-SHEETS.

### To the Editor of The Accountant.

SIR,—In these days of vast commercial enterprise, carried on in a great measure by joint stock companies, the question of auditing accounts, and the certificates to be given by auditors, is a matter far too important to the profession, as well as to the investing public, to be passed over lightly. The Editor of *Vanity Fair* in his article—although he has not dealt as fairly with the matter as he might have—has done a certain amount of service, by calling public attention to the form and significance of these certificates. I must ask your pardon if I appear to take up too much of the space which might be better allotted to an abler pen, but the subject being one which has occupied my attention for some years must be my only excuse.

In the first place it must be understood that the position of auditor, whether to a private partnership or a public company, is a singularly onerous and responsible one, representing as the auditor does, in the case of a joint stock company, the whole body of shareholders, who, relying upon his integrity and ability, are content with his scrutiny of the accounts of the undertaking in which they are concerned. Now in order that an auditor should be properly able to carry out his duties, he must be an experienced accountant, and one whose study and training have been properly directed to this particular class of work ; but it appears to be a practice amongst shareholders to appoint some one to fill this position without any regard to qualifications for carrying out the duties of the appointment ; such a matter, indeed, seldom entering their minds when filling the post : and oftentimes the only qualification which a candidate may possess is the fact that he is a shareholder in the concern. I cannot now spare time to argue the question as to whether or not it is desirable for an auditor to hold shares in the company to which he is appointed ; suffice it to say here, that the bare fact of his being a shareholder does not give him the qualifications necessary to carry out his duties effectually. It is positively ridiculous the way some accounts are left which have been presumably audited by some of these shareholders. I have on several occasions had accounts placed in my hands for investigation which bear the certificate of the former auditors, and upon examination have found that the books of the concern have not been balanced for years, and that the accounts were absurdly incorrect and misleading.

Now it is a matter much to be regretted, looking at it from a broad commercial point of view, that the appointment of an auditor to every public company, or associations of every kind registered under any Act of Parliament, has not been rendered compulsory. The extent, moreover, of the power frequently vested in directors and managers of companies, places the auditor in a very peculiar and unpleasant position. The mode of appointment too is such, that if he offend the directors or officers in carrying into effect such corrections, or alterations, which to him appear absolutely essential, he is frequently looked upon as assuming a position, and usurping a power, to which he has no right ; and so long as the power of voting by proxy is permitted to apply to these appointments, and until companies are compelled to have their accounts audited by professional accountants, the dangers to which too-confiding shareholders and the commercial public are exposed cannot be in any degree lessened. It is to be hoped that in the passing of all future Acts in any way dealing with these matters, that due provision will be made for such appointments being filled by competent persons.

Now as to the responsibility of auditors. An auditor's certificate should be positive and complete, and not admit of any qualification. Accounts are either correct or they are incorrect. If correct, the auditor need have no hesitation in saying so ; if incorrect, he should not sign them at all. The greatest difficulty with which an auditor has to deal—being held responsible for the correctness of the account he certifies—is the value of the assets as represented by the several securities. This is perhaps more the case in audits of the accounts of banks, and concerns of a kindred nature, where amounts are advanced upon all kinds of securities ; and in such cases, if the auditor is not satisfied as to the actual value of any such security, he should be empowered to have the opinion of an expert produced, in order to protect himself from the possibility of a charge being brought against him of issuing a false account with his certificate attached. Of course, in the case of concerns where money is laid out in the construction of works, plant, &c., the actual expenditure can be set forth, and depreciation provided for and written off against the profits of the concern. In every case there is a possibility of an auditor satisfying himself as to the value of a security held, or as to a fair amount of depreciation chargeable against any period of trading ; and although it would be perfectly impossible in an article like the present to set forth all descriptions of trades and enterprises carried on by joint stock companies, &c., I contend that an auditor should not attach his signature to any accounts for the accuracy of which, in every shape and form, against fraudulent representations, he is not prepared to be responsible. An auditor cannot, of course, be held responsible for the defalcations of clerks and managers. An efficient audit should detect and expose such ; but no auditor nor system of accounts in existence can prevent such taking place, although the auditor can, by getting a carefully and well devised system of accounts adopted, lessen the opportunities for such occurrences. The end of every system of accounts and audit should be — in addition to mere mechanical account keeping—to make it difficult to defraud and do wrong. I cannot leave this part of my subject without first expressing the astonishment with which I read in the letter of " Auditor, F.C.A.," in your last issue, the following remarks :— " Meanwhile I take the fact to be that the several auditors mentioned by the Editor of *Vanity Fair* have intended nothing more than to certify as to the figures in the respective balance-sheets being supported by the existence of securities, and that they in no way hold themselves responsible for the accuracy of the revenue account, or indeed the accuracy of the figures in the balance-sheet." If this is the principle upon which accounts have been hitherto audited, the whole system has been a sham and a delusion. An auditor must be responsible, or his certificate is not of the value of the paper upon which it is written.

As to the remuneration of professional accountants as auditors ; there are so many persons now-a-days styling themselves accountants, who scarcely understand the significance of the terms ' debit ' and ' credit,' much less the principles of bookkeeping ; and who are so hungry after fees, putting their signatures to accounts, without any examination of the items comprised therein, for a few guineas, that there is no difficulty in procuring an auditor's certificate to the most rotten and false statement, and rendering it extremely difficult for experienced professional men to obtain anything like a fair remuneration for their responsible services.

If, however, any professional accountant accepts the position of auditor to a company at a nominal remuneration, he is bound in duty to his profession and his own reputation, to act as carefully, cautiously, and discreetly as if he were paid upon the highest scale of charges for his services ; so that the fact—rather urged by the editor of *Vanity Fair* as an excuse for the neglect of their duties—that auditors are often so poorly remunerated for their services, should have no weight in deciding upon this question.

I will refrain from entering upon the question as to whether audits should be continuous, and not periodical, in order to be most effectual, as I have ready occupied so much of your valuable space.

Yours, &c.

ARTHUR H. ROBERTS,

Cardiff, 23rd October, 1883.     Chartered Accountant.

## AUDITORS' CERTIFICATES TO BALANCE-SHEETS.

The following further article and correspondence appeared in the issue of *Vanity Fair* for October 20th :—

We have received an interesting communication on this question from a Chartered Accountant highly esteemed in his profession. We regret that we are unable to publish the same, owing to the express interdiction of the writer. But having regard to the importance of the subject, we feel constrained to refer to two passages in this letter worthy of notice. In the first place, our correspondent thoroughly agrees with us in the general view we have taken of this question, and adds that " auditors' certificates might be longer and at the same time better." But to accomplish this he thinks " legislation is needed." We are not in accord with this latter view. In a simple matter such as an auditor's certificate we fail to see why any legal interference is called for. What the public and shareholders want is a readable assurance from the accountants, stating in plain English what they really have done. Such certificates as these are seldom given. Speaking of the expense which would be entailed by a thorough and comprehensive audit, our correspondent says that it would be a serious drawback to the success of any public company " which has to face continually increasing competition, cutting down profits, and making it almost fatal to be even so slightly handicapped." We are quite aware that a thorough audit would entail a far greater outlay than is generally applied to this most important part of the administration of a public company. But an addition to the auditors' remuneration, in order to get the work done thoroughly, would not be money thrown away ; and if the companies could not bear the expense, the services of a director might, we think, usually be more easily spared than those of a competent auditor.

We have not as yet, amongst the numerous letters we have received on this subject, been favoured with a contradiction to our original assertion that auditors' certificates in their present shape are misleading and of no practical value whatever.

In support of this assertion it may be useful to quote the certificates which are attached to the reports and balance-sheets of two great banks which have been published within the last few days. The first in chronological order is that affixed to the balance-sheet of the Oriental Bank Corporation (Limited), which is as follows :—

" Examined and found correct.

" J. R. ROBERTSON, }
" S. RAWSON,     } Auditors."

The gentlemen who have given this certificate are not, so far as we are aware, professional accountants ; but that circumstance has nothing to do with the main issue, which is, what they mean by " examined and found correct." In our opinion this certificate either means a great deal or it means nothing. We incline to the latter opinion, because, in a glance, we find in the balance-sheet an item, " Debts *secured* by landed or other property, £281,422." It is manifestly impossible for an auditor on this side of the world to give an opinion as to whether this property does truly and actually represent the value advanced upon it ; so one must suppose that Messrs. Robertson and Rawson have simply accepted the statement of the bank officials. There is no check in such a proceeding as this, and the duties of an auditor under these circumstances, for all the benefit they are to the shareholders, might just as well be carried out by the bank porters. The question of auditing might be profitably drawn attention to by some of the shareholders of the Oriental Bank at the Special General Meeting called for the 25th inst.

We next come to the auditors' certificate attached to the report and balance-sheet of the Chartered Mercantile Bank of India, London, and China, adopted at the half-yearly meeting of the shareholders held on Tuesday last. It reads thus :—

" London, 3rd October, 1883.—We have examined the *returns* of Bills of Exchange, Local Bills discounted, and other Securities held by the Bank, and its several agencies, as transmitted from the several managers, and are satisfied that such Bills and Securities are available. We consider that sufficient provision has been ma le for bad and doubtful debts.

"Geo. Christian, } Auditors."
"F. Tendron,     }

It will be remembered that in the letter of Mr. Welton addressed to us last week he stated that he considered our remarks on auditors' certificates would do great good even if they did no more than induce shareholders to more closely scan the wording of these documents. We are afraid that our remarks have been thrown on barren ground. At any rate, the shareholders of the above Bank could scarcely have glanced at this last certificate, or they would surely not have let it pass unquestioned, as they did. They apparently read the magic word "auditors," and did not trouble to attempt to analyse the exact meaning of the words immediately preceding. We assert that this certificate is actually no certificate at all, and that, for all the evidence it affords that the assets of the Bank are good and the capital intact, it is not worth the trouble of printing. Messrs Christian and Tendron apparently have not even gone through the farce of examining the balances shown in the balance sheet, together with the books. They are content with the *returns* of bills of exchange, local bills discounted, and other securities held by the Bank and its agencies. We are aware that as regards what the Bank holds abroad the returns must be taken for granted. But as regards securities, &c., held by the Bank in London, the auditors do not, from this certificate, appear to have taken the trouble to ascertain whether they exist or not. This so-called certificate is one of the worst we have yet called attention to.

We publish the following, as being the most practical of the letters we have this week received on this subject:—

### To the Editor of "Vanity Fair."

Sir,—I have read with satisfaction the remarks contained in your issue of the 6th inst, on this important subject, which has interested me for many years; and I trust that the criticism and discussion which it has excited in various quarters will not cease until some improvement in the present system of auditing has been effected. Most people will admit the general principle you enunciate of the audits of accounts of Public Companies, as usually conducted, being mere shams and delusions, and therefore practically worthless. This arises principally from evasions of wise legislative enactments and the abuse of the powers with which directors are invested under ordinary circumstances. The audit of Public Companies' accounts was designed to control and check the action of directors in their administration of the affairs of Public Companies; and yet, as a rule, the auditors who are chosen for this purpose owe their employment to the very directors whom they are presumed so to control and check in the interests of the shareholders. This is one of the evils arising out of the proxy system, which I trust we may some day see abolished, as being utterly pernicious and vicious in root and branch. It should be laid down as an invariable rule that directors, trustees, or other persons in fiduciary positions should never be allowed the direct or indirect use of proxies in voting, or in fact to vote personally, on any subject affecting the performance of the duties imposed upon them by the trusts under which they act, or on the passing of the accounts as presented by them to their proprietary or *cestui que* trust. Parliament intended that shareholders should elect their own auditors, and, in order to their protection it was designed that the auditors to be so chosen should be clothed with ample powers; for, by section 94 of "Table A," which is appended to the Companies Act, 1862, passed for the regulation and management of Limited Companies, it is provided that "the auditors shall make a report to the members "upon the balance-sheet and amounts, and in every such "report they shall state whether, in their opinion, the balance-"sheet is a full and fair balance-sheet, properly drawn up so "as to exhibit a true and correct view of the state of the "Company's affairs; and in case they have called for explana-"tions or information from the directors, whether such

"explanations or information have been given by the directors, "and whether they have been satisfactory; and such report "shall be read, together with the report of the directors, at "the ordinary meeting."

The schedule to the same Act moreover, in making provision for the specification of the Company's assets in the balance-sheets of the company, oddly enough stipulates for detailing separately, under the heading "*Debts considered doubtful and* "*bad*, any debt due from a director or other officer of the "Company;" so that the position of directors and officers of the Company was intended to be strictly and specially scrutinised by the auditors and made clear by them to the members.

Auditors, however, notwithstanding these provisions, are at times induced by directors to *make things look pleasant*, and deem it prudent to append bald, ambiguous, and evasive certificates to the accounts submitted for their approval. The fees allowed are moreover, as a rule, wholly inadequate to insure a thorough and conscientious audit and investigation being undertaken, and you very properly make this apparent, and condemn the *system* and not the auditors engaged.

The valuation of property, stock-in-trade, and plant of Public Companies is an element of the utmost importance, but it is to a great extent disregarded. The Companies Act requires provision to be made by a charge to profit and loss for deterioration in value or maintenance; and there cannot be a doubt that periodical valuations of this class of assets should be made by independent and competent valuers unconnected with the Company, and that their certificates should be added to the Company's published accounts.

The value of all other assets of the Company which are capable and admit of valuation should in like manner be ascertained and duly certified; and every item of the assets should be open to the inspection of, and if possible be examined by, the auditors. Experience proves that, unless some such precautions as I have referred to are rigidly enforced, no reliance can safely be placed on the balance-sheets of Public Companies as accurately indicating the true position of affairs, although they may be audited by accountants of the highest standing.— I am, Sir, your obedient servant,      John Fraser, F.I.C.A.

Billiter House, London, 18th October, 1883.

Commenting on the prospectus of The Southend Hotel Company, Limited, which has been formed for the purchase of the Royal Hotel, Southend, the Editor of *Vanity Fair* gives us a still further contribution on the subject of auditors' certificates, and says:—

"The next temptation which the directors offer is the following wonderful certificate concerning the present working of the business, which has been compiled by Messrs. Good, Daniels, and Co., of 7 Poultry, E.C. Here it is:—

"New Poultry Chambers, 7 Poultry, London, E.C.,
"25th September, 1883.

"*To the Directors of* The Hotels and City Properties Share "Trust, Limited, 20 Bucklersbury, E.C.
"The Royal Hotel and Stores, Southend-on-Sea.

"Dear Sirs,—We have examined the books of the above for the four months from 12th May to 12th September, 1883, inclusive, and find that the net profit for that period amounts to £1,277 17s. 9d.—We remain, dear sirs, yours faithfully,
"(Signed) Good, Daniels, and Co., Chartered Accountants."

Now we have devoted some little attention to auditors' certificates lately, and must confess that, as these documents go, there is nothing to find fault with such a one as the above.

Messrs. Good, Daniels, and Co. were, we suppose, asked to give a certificate of the result of four months' working of the Royal Hotel, and they have done so. But the directors stand in a very different position. These gentlemen are responsible for the following daring statement. Speaking in reference to the above certificate, they say:—

"These figures, which are for *four* months, show a very satisfactory result of the present working of the business, and if it is calculated that the profits will only be doubled for the *whole year*, the result will be a net return of upwards of 14 per cent. upon the present issue of the capital."

We must confess we are struck with the calm assurance of this assumption built on an "if." The directors are but three, and perhaps we are not far wrong in assuming that Mr. B. P. Daniels, chartered accountant, of 7 Poultry, E.C., and partner in the firm whose signature is attached to the above certificate, is the man of business on the board. We will therefore ask Mr. B. P. Daniels whether in his professional capacity as chartered accountant it is consistent with his position as a director of the Southend Hotel Company to allow such an extraordinary estimate of profits to be framed on so flimsy a foundation. Mr. Daniels has furnished the public with the result of working the Royal during the best four months of the year. But are we to understand that he pledges his professional reputation that *any* appreciable profit can be made during the remaining eight months, when Southend is little better than a howling wilderness, and when a stray Londoner at the Royal is looked upon with as much curiosity as if he were a friendly Zulu? During those dark and dreary months is there not an entire absence of excursionists, and as a rule are not the only occupants and best customers of that spacious bar which the prospectus says is a great source of profit, the neglected piermaster and the boatman?

We would further ask Mr. Daniels whether it is not customary for accountants, when estimating the value of a business, whether it be an hotel or a street-crossing, to take as a basis for their calculation, not the result of the *best* four months' working, but an average derived from *three* whole years' trading previous and up to the date of the proposed transfer. The necessity of such a method may not strike the massive brain of the ordinary director. He is very often content with having his directorial qualification found for him, and taking for granted all that the promoters may put in the prospectus. But Mr. Daniels is not an ordinary director. He is, as we have said, a chartered accountant, and knows, or should know, that such a course as that to which we have alluded is the only trustworthy one to pursue. In either case we are of opinion that, were Mr. Daniels about to purchase the Royal Hotel with his own instead of with other people's money, he would not be content to base his calculations solely on the figures which he and his co-directors have given to the public. It is to be regretted that at the present time, when so much attention is being directed to the doings of accountants, it is not in the power of the Council of the Institute of Chartered Accountants to put some check upon one of their profession following the mistaken course which it appears to us has been adopted by Mr. Daniels.

The prospectus contains no information of terms or details of the purchase of the hotel, but states ;—

"The following contracts have been entered into : – Contract dated the 22nd day of March, 1883, and made between William Reeves Fuller of the one part, and the Hotels and City Properties Share Trust, Limited, of the other part. Supplemental Contract dated the 11th day of May, 1883, made between the same parties, and a Contract dated the 25th day of September, 1883, made between the Hotels and City Properties Share Trust, Limited, of the one part, and the Southend Hotel Company, Limited, of the other part."

It would be interesting to know who it is that constitutes the Hotels and City Properties Share Trust Company, Limited, and also whether there is any, and if so what, difference in price between the contract dated the 22nd March, 1883, and that dated 25th September, 1883.

### AUDITING IN EXCELSIS.

The evidence in the case of the robbery of securities from the London and River Plate Bank shows that on the very day of the audit Warden abstracted stock to the value of £25,000, which a few minutes before had been checked and passed by Mr. Deloitte, and that with the proceeds he proceeded to obtain other securities to be "checked" by the auditor. But for the mere accident of a stockbroker refusing to take Warden's confederate's cheque for the necessary amount, this brief formality would have been complied with. Warden would then have obtained the loan of the securities for the five minutes required to flash them before the "master-eye" of the auditor, and all would have been well. Such is auditing.— *Vanity Fair.*

AUDITORS' CERTIFICATES TO BALANCE-SHEETS.

In acknowledging our contributions on the above subject, the editor of *Vanity Fair* has somewhat distorted our statements ; but perhaps we ought not to take it much to heart, since it has given him an opportunity of displaying his talent as a doggrel rhymester, and what is doubtless more important, his poetical effusion and comicalities have probably had the effect of inducing his readers to wade through a technical subject that, but for his facile pen and the glamour he has thrown on the subject, would have been the reverse of fascinating.

Though startled at an attack from such a quarter, we recognise the good service of *Vanity Fair* in bringing forward a topic which was discussed in our columns long ago ; but *Vanity Fair's* manner of treating such a subject is not certainly such as to evoke a blessing, while to curse is alien to our principles. The complaint we make against our contemporary is that of treating the subject from a too narrow-minded point of view. We allege that the defects in connection with Joint Stock Auditing are mainly attributable to the existing laws in relation thereto. *Vanity Fair*, on the other hand, confines itself to cavilling at the form of certificate, and instead of making a practical suggestion upon a serious subject takes refuge in comicalities. We think that ample reasons have been shown for the necessity of further legislature ; while *Vanity Fair* denies that necessity, and avoids the main point.

The editor of *Vanity Fair* has misunderstood the scope of the article which appeared in *The Accountant* of the 20th ult. ; but if he will take the trouble to refer again he will find that our object was not to give an exhaustive leader on the duties of an auditor, but simply to enumerate "some of the real difficulties an auditor has to encounter in connection with Joint Stock Auditing."

If shareholders are satisfied with the responsibility that attaches to the certificates that are continually being quoted by *Vanity Fair*, they have their money's worth ; if not, and our contemporary does not concede the fact of fresh legislation being necessary, it is for the shareholders to cure the evil by giving the auditor the powers necessary to justify him in increasing his responsibility. Audits will continue to be unsatisfactory as long as the conditions exist whereby directors control the balance-sheet and accounts and auditors are prevented from exercising that vigilance which they exercise on behalf of private clients ; while the voting power is left practically in the control of the board ; and while, moreover, audits are not continuous. Has it struck our contemporary that there is a certain stigma attaching to auditors who are not re-elected ? and has he ever inquired how many auditors have been superseded for their *bona fide* endeavour to protect shareholders ? or what are the fees usually attaching to the post of auditor ? There is a fair field for discussion   An evil exists the removal of which would be welcomed by all auditors. We seek to deal with the subject as a whole ; *Vanity Fair* prefers to discuss a side issue, cavilling at facts and refusing to recognise the necessity for a remedy.

We are not going to defend our correspondent " Anti-Twaddle," but we have generally found that when arguments are unassailable attempts are made to pick holes in one another's grammar.

<hr>

### Auditors' Certificates to Balance-Sheets.

*To the Editor of The Accountant.*

Sir,—In your issue of the 13th ult. you ask for suggestions to be sent in for a uniform Certificate to be used by all accountants in connection with the balance-sheets they sign, and as I understand the correspondence which has taken place on this subject, that the said Certificate should clearly define the auditor's responsibilities in the matter.

Now I fail to see how under the existing state of things this end is to be arrived at, as a uniform certificate would attach the same amount of responsibility whether the audit had only been a partial one and the auditor's fee a small one, as if the audit had been a complete one and the remuneration proportionate. What I would suggest is, that every accountant on contracting for an audit should clearly state in writing the actual work he engages to do for a certain sum, that is, that he should give a complete list of the books, &c. that he checked, and the nature of the checking.

The shareholders should be at liberty to receive a copy of this list for a nominal fee ; and thus every shareholder who took sufficient interest in his investments, would know the exact amount of checking done by the auditor, and if the said shareholder did not think everything was checked that ought to be he could at the Annual General Meeting make known his grievance.

This would, I think, meet all requirements, as the auditor would define his responsibility in the list of work that he did. Of course, those companies who considered the checking of the vouchers and securities sufficient, and only cared to pay a small sum for the audit, could do so, and the auditor would then be responsible only for what he checked.

If thought desirable, the books, documents, &c. submitted to the auditor could be endorsed on the balance-sheet, along with the nature of the checking done thereto.

This is just a rough sketch of a system which I think might be adopted with advantage.

Apologising for taking up so much of your valuable space,

Yours, &c.

CHAS. LITCHFIELD, A.C.A.

Manchester, October 26th, 1883.

---

*To the Editor of The Accountant.*

Sir,—Will you allow me to state, by way of reply to a portion of Mr. Roberts's letter in your issue of the 27th ult., that I did [not attempt to express an opinion as to what a bank audit should consist in. Upon this point I am anxious to be informed ; and believing as I do that it would be practically impossible for any firm of public accountants to effect a complete audit of the affairs of a large bank at the end of any given year, I am willing to sit at the feet and learn from any competent authority upon the subject who is prepared to prove otherwise.

What I intended was, to suggest that if asked the plain question, the gentlemen to whom I was alluding would one and all admit that they had not *audited* the accounts, but merely *checked the securities* as against the totals which appeared in the several companies' books, and which totals were faithfully repeated in the respective balance-sheets ; and I must confess I am at a loss to conceive how it would be possible to do more in the time usually occupied at so-called bank audits.

Mr. Roberts's opinion as to the desirability of an unqualified certificate being given in all cases is good in theory, but in practice there must ever be many exceptions to such a rule, and I question whether the certificates to bankers' balance-sheets will not always form one of those exceptions.

This is a large question, and it seems to me matter for regret that it has not been taken up through your journal by one or more of those gentlemen whose names have been so freely used by the editor of *Vanity Fair*. If bank auditors *do* audit the books, let them state so, and give the unqualified certificates which Mr. Roberts asks for. If they do not, then let the frank avowal be made, that all that is attempted is a verification of the securities; and do not let this business, important and beneficial as it is to the shareholders, be dignified with a title which it does not deserve.

Yours, &c.

AUDITOR, F.C.A.

29th October, 1883.

---

### To the Editor of The Accountant.

SIR,—Whether intentionally or not, the Editor of *Vanity Fair* has paid me a great compliment. Either from ignorance of the meaning of words or from some other cause he has confused " Anti " with " Aunty." I accept the cognomen he has conferred upon me. My aunties have been to me protectresses, guiding my steps in childhood, and helping me with their fostering care in times of sickness and distress. The examples set by my aunties are symbolical of the care which should be given by auditors to those placed under their care, and those examples I have endeavoured to follow. In some instances success has rewarded my efforts; in other instances my desire to justify the confidence reposed in me has led to some more convenient person being put in my place.

For your guidance, but not as an advertisement, I hand you a list of audits which I lost because I could not conscientiously certify to the figures submitted. Among this list you will observe two insurance, a co-operative, and three mining companies, where I was not re-elected because I insisted upon stating the reasons for my objections. In other instances I withdrew my name because I declined to be associated with persons after I had reason to doubt their good faith.

In several of these instances I was elected by the shareholders, but when the differences of opinion arose the directors had it their own way.

I assert that in many cases shareholders will not look at anything but results. So long as dividends are forthcoming they are satisfied, and do not seek to learn how such dividends are created.

To the credit of my profession I can say, that in one instance only did a professed accountant accept the position from which I had been ejected.

Another instance I can cite where, having warned the board by letter that I should be compelled to report my refusal to pass certain entries, I was not allowed to audit, though nominated and appointed in public meeting, another person of more facile disposition was called in, and in spite of a formal report as auditor and a protest as a shareholder, the accounts were accepted in general meeting, the result being that the company not very long afterwards had to go into liquidation, and heavy calls had to be made to cover the mischief created by the very person I had warned the board against.

*Vanity Fair* calls me rude, illogical, and ungrammatical.

To the first I reply, *Tu quoque;* to the second, I say that I am content to leave your readers to say which of us two is wanting in logic ; and to the third, I retort that in the House of Commons (admittedly the most critical of audiences) common sense and fair reasoning are held to be superior to mere grammatical precision.

*Vanity Fair* may or may not be witty, but I assert that it is not honest—while abusing a system which all admit to be faulty—to persistently decline to recognise the need for a remedy, and at the same time to attack those who in order to protect reputations which are not made in a day, seek to show upon the face of their certificates to what extent they are responsible for the figures submitted to them for *more* or *less* verification. In conclusion, I would add that if my former communication was rude, it was because I endeavoured to bring myself down to the level of *Vanity Fair*. I have not apparently succeeded in this attempt.

Yours, &c.

AUNTY.

---

## AUDITORS' CERTIFICATES TO BALANCE-SHEETS.

We extract the following from the issue of *Vanity Fair* of the 27th ult.

A series of articles and letters has appeared in the *Accountant* with regard to our treatment of this matter. The Editor of that journal and his correspondents bless us and curse us in the same breath. On the one hand, they are fain to admit that we have done well what we have done in calling attention to the matter; on the other hand they hold that we have left undone ill what we have not done.

The *Accountant* says that we clearly misunderstand the powers of an auditor, and then proceeds to give what we should call a very incomplete account of his duties and his difficulties. As to the latter, it assures us that he is not allowed to audit often enough, that when he does audit he is not allowed sufficient time, that his fees are inadequate, and that he is under the control of the Board.

All this does not in the least touch our original assertion.

What we asserted and made good on the 6th of October was that by far the greater number of the certificates which professional auditors attach to the foot of a balance-sheet are in no degree a proof of the stability of the financial position of the Company to which they apply. Neither do these certificates in themselves, as a general rule, pledge the reputation or word of the gentlemen who give them that the Companies are solvent, and that their capital is intact. Nobody has hitherto ventured to dispute these propositions. The *Accountant*, indeed, so far from denying that they are true, gives reasons to explain *why* they are true, every one of the reasons having already been given by ourselves in the original article. We don't attach much importance to the reasons—no more importance, in fact, than Richelieu attached to the reasons alleged by the thief who was brought before him and who urged his necessities. What we look to are the facts, and the facts are strengthened by the reasons for them. We would suggest that in future auditors' certificates should, in accordance with the defence now made for them, run thus:—We having been allowed to audit not from month to month, but only once a year; having had too little time to make an exhaustive report, because the documents are required for the printer; knowing that shareholders are generally impatient to get through the business; being paid a fee out of all proportion to the work required to be done; and being aware that the voting power is in the absolute control of the Board—certify that, so far as we, under these disabilities, can ascertain and dare disclose the facts, it is all right. This would at any rate let shareholders know from the certificate, as we know from the general chorus of certifiers, what the true meaning and value of the certificate really amount to. Our complaint was and is that at present they do not know this, but that they are led and are meant to imagine that bladders are lanterns and auditors' certificates proofs of all excellences and complete solvency and security. It is now quite clear that they are nothing of the kind, for one accountant after another tells us *why* they cannot be so.

We are not to be drawn off the scent by any invitation to discuss the powers of auditors or the technicalities of auditing. That is not the question. The question is—What is the worth, and what, therefore, the use of an auditorial certificate in its various forms as it is now commonly given? We say it is worth next to nothing. Our critics say, not that it is worth much, but that it is very hard to make it worth anything. Very well. Then we and our critics are agreed. The certificate *is* worth next to nothing; and this being so, it is a delusion and a snare.

There is however one correspondent of the *Accountant* who signs himself "Anti-Twaddle," and who deserves special remark. He is very rude, but not more rude than illogical and ungrammatical. He too sets forth the difficulties of the poor auditor, and so feelingly that he has evidently suffered from them. The auditor gets no power, no time, and no money to talk of; he is not responsible except for the verification of figures put before him; he is the slave of the directors, who do not like to look at the worst side of affairs, and he has to satisfy also the shareholders, who sometimes have a strong objection to knowing the truth. But, dear ingenuous Aunty Twaddle, that is exactly what we complain of—except indeed as to the shareholders, for we believe that if they have sometimes a strong objection to knowing the truth, they have at least as often as strong an objection to having lies told to them. And it is quite clear that, if this venerable Aunty were herself set to audit accounts and to frame thereon an auditorial certificate, she would unhesitatingly avoid any difference of opinion with directors, would carefully abstain from looking at the worst side of affairs, would very generously indulge the shareholders' strong objection to knowing the truth, and would, in spite of the insufficient time, power, and money, frame and publish a certificate that would make everything pleasant for everybody, and above all for Aunty. This is exactly what we complain of.

And yet, in spite of this injurious disclosure of the way in which certificates are moulded from the dirty mud of facts by the Sculptor-Director, and invested with artistic merit by the Ghost-Auditor, Aunty wants to have herself fastened on all concerns by an Act of Parliament which shall supersede directors and everybody else, and make Aunty a first charge on the concern, just as though she were an official liquidator or trustee. And she proposes that *we* should get her Act passed for her! No; we cannot do this. On the contrary, we say—Amend your Certificates and not your Statutes; tell the truth if you know it, and shame the Director. If you don't know and can't find it out—why say that; but in any case, cease making those merely damnable faces which are now called Auditors' Certificates.

The *Accountant* also contained a letter from a correspondent signing himself "Auditor, F.C.A." This contains no points worthy of notice, other than the statement that we are evidently under some strange delusion as to the meaning of the words we have quoted from the various certificates, and expressing surprise that the gentlemen whose certificates we have criticised have not set us right. As a matter of fact, amongst the many letters, which we have received on this question, letters of contradiction or explanation from those gentlemen to whose certificates we have drawn attention have been singularly absent. Silence in this case may be fairly taken as assent, for it is certain that if any explanation could have been furnished it would have been forthcoming long ago. Take, for instance, our analysis of the accounts of the Indo-China Steam Navigation Company. Messrs. Turquand, Youngs, and Co., tacitly admit that they passed some errors which should be apparent to a schoolboy. It is evident therefore, as we have already stated, that not only our critics and ourselves are agreed, but also that those whose certificates we have criticised concur in the justice of our remarks.

With regard to the statement that we clearly misunderstand the powers of an auditor, that is an assertion which raises the point whether the gentlemen who sign these certificates are clear in their own minds on this subject. It will be remembered that in our last issue we published a letter from Mr. John Fraser, F.C.A., which contained a suggestion appended to the Companies Act, 1862, for the guidance of auditors in giving their certificates. This suggestion if acted upon would no doubt be of service, but the fact is that auditors' duties are generally defined by the Articles of Association of every limited company at its formation. Whether auditors fully take advantage of their powers under these Articles is very open to question.

We will take as an example the clause of the Articles of Association which relates to the auditing of the accounts of a bank, the auditors' certificate to which we first mentioned—

THE IMPERIAL BANK, LIMITED.

The clause runs as follows:—

The account and balance-sheet shall be received from the Board and be examined by the auditor, who, within fourteen days after the receipt thereof, either shall approve thereof and report *generally* thereon, or shall report *specially* thereon, and shall deliver the account and balance-sheet with his report thereon to the Board, in order that the same may be presented and read with the Directors' report on the state of the Bank to the ordinary meeting.

We have quoted this clause merely as a sample of what we may fairly presume are the powers given to auditors under the generality of Articles of Association. Our contemporary, the *Accountant*, urges as an excuse for short certificates that too little time is allowed for the auditor to make an exhaustive report, as the documents are required for the *printer*, consequently a short certificate becomes a necessity. But in the case of the Imperial Bank we cannot accept this excuse for the certificate attached to the balance-sheet by the auditors. We reproduce it for the benefit of the *Accountant* :—

We have compared the balances as set forth in the balance-sheet with the *Books*, and find the same correct.

> FREDERICK FEARON, } Auditors.
> GEORGE BROOME, }

We leave it to our readers to decide whether in this certificate the auditors have properly performed their duties, as defined by the powers conferred upon them. The high social standing of most of the directors of this Bank renders it surprising that they in justice to themselves should allow such a certificate as this to be appended to their report.

At the time of writing, the yearly report and balance-sheet of the Commercial Bank of Alexandria, Limited, has just appeared. In the balance-sheet appear the following items:—

Advances against security    ...    ...    £220,790
Current and other accounts ...    ...    170,163
Cash in London and Alexandria    ...    216,029

Here is the certificate of the auditors :—

18th October, 1883.—Examined with the *books* and *vouchers* in *London*, and found correct.

W. W. DELOITTE, } Auditors.
JOHN ELIN,

It will be observed that Messrs. Deloitte and Elin carefully abstain from committing themselves to any statement regarding the existence or the value of the above assets. The shareholders of the Commercial Bank of Alexandria would seem therefore to be spending money in the maintenance of an office which is of no service to them whatever.

---

We have received the following letter from an influential source. The writer has had much experience in Indian banking business. As both of the half-yearly meetings of the two banks mentioned are now over, it is too late for the shareholders to insist upon the reforms suggested by our correspondent. But it would be well to bear them in mind, and endeavour to carry them out on a future occasion :—

*To the Editor of " Vanity Fair."*

SIR,—Having for a long period taken considerable trouble in pointing out to my fellow-shareholders in Indian banks the manner in which their auditors are appointed, what their qualifications are and ought to be, I shall be much obliged if you will permit me to repeat my views for the benefit of a wider circle through the medium of your columns, and to refer to the certificates attached to the balance-sheets of the Oriental and Chartered Mercantile Banks quoted by you. I have been interested in both banks, and am one of the largest shareholders in the latter.

As regards the Oriental, neither Mr. Robertson nor Mr. Rawson is a professional accountant, and their certificate affords no guarantee to the shareholders that the position of the bank is as stated in the balance-sheet. Managers abroad report to managers at home ; the latter report to directors, and occasionally to auditors. Matters are made pleasant all round, until one day the shareholders are startled by the loss of the reserved fund, then by diminishing dividends, then by none at all. Had the auditors been capable men they could not have prevented the losses, but they could and should have refused to allow them to be bottled up until the bottle burst. We are promised some interesting explanations at the meeting of the Oriental Band on 25th inst., especially as regards the value of estates in Mauritius and Ceylon, upon which enormous advances have been made and cannot be realised. I wonder if any shareholder can ascertain who paid and employed the valuators, for a servant is sometimes apt to serve his master, and what was the average price per acre on coffee properties in Ceylon ?

As to the Chartered Mercantile Bank, Mr. Tendron is a professional accountant, but neither he nor Mr. Christian knows anything of Indian banking. They may go over certain securities, but are totally incompetent to certify that the balance-sheet represents all things as they are. For years they passed the value of moneys lodged in India, but payable in London, at 1s. 9d. per rupee, and it was left, not to the directors, but to shareholders, to point out a mistake of over £100,000 which has since been rectified. Even, however, in the last balance-sheet they pass the item, Capital £750,000, fixed abroad at par =750,000, whereas it is not fixed abroad at par at all—par means parity of exchange, i.e., interchangeable values. The

value of this capital at par is therefore—taking the rupee at 1s. 7⅗d.—not £750,000, but rather less than £620,000, only a difference of £130,000. If the bank cannot afford to estimate their capital at its current value, surely they might say it was fixed abroad at the equivalent of 2s. per rupee. I mean of course, in their balance-sheets.

Nearly the whole evil is caused by the auditors being practically appointed by the directors, the very last persons who ought to have the remotest influence on their election, for auditors are the servants of either directors or shareholders. They are appointed by the former, paid by the former, and come in contact with the former, so they naturally make things pleasant. Banks have failed before now—was it ever found that auditors had done their duty ?

Speaking on Indian banks, one auditor should be a professional accountant, another a gentleman thoroughly conversant with the minutest details of Indian banking, and neither should be eligible for a seat at the board. Apologising for the length of this letter, I am, Sir, your obedient servant,

AN INDIAN BANK SHAREHOLDER.

London, October 20th, 1883.

---

We have also received, among others, the following letters, which are well worth attention :—

*To the Editor of " Vanity Fair."*

SIR,—Auditors of Public Companies and the investing public ought to feel greatly indebted to you for the interest your incisive remarks have excited on a subject of very great importance to them. Your original assertion that auditors' certificates in their present shape are misleading, and of no practical value whatever, is a sweeping statement which it is difficult to refute. The Act 42 and 43 Vict. c. 76, provides that auditors should state in a report—

That, in his or their opinion, the balance-sheet referred to in the report is a full and fair balance-sheet, properly drawn up, so as to exhibit a true and correct view of the state of the Company's affairs as shown by the books of the Company.

The purpose of the audit of Public Companies is to satisfy the shareholders that the balance-sheet is a correct and faithful account of the assets and liabilities of the business, and that their property is intact, as shown in the balance-sheet.

The certificate expresses, or should express, the auditor's *opinion.* The auditor's *opinion* is expressed more or less positively, just in proportion to the care and attention he has bestowed in forming it, and that depends upon his fee, and the amount of the fee depends upon the shareholders. The amount of remuneration voted represents the exact importance the shareholders attach to the value of an audit. Therefore this is a matter which rests in the hands of the shareholders. Let them bargain for the form and strength of certificate they require to be embodied in the auditor's report, and pay for it accordingly. If they insure their property according to the amount of premium, so is the sum insured, and, indeed, the auditor's fee is a premium of insurance—insurance against fraud and deception.

The auditor should be required to state in his certificate that he has called at the offices, without previous notice, from time to time, and examined the books and checked the securities. If you engage a detective to watch a suspect, and give the latter due notice of when and how he is to be watched, the detective must not be blamed if the suspect checkmates him. The shareholders should also require in their contract with the auditor that the securities or other property entrusted to the care of their manager be also duly registered and checked, no matter whether the Company is legally or morally or expediently responsible for the safety of such property. The auditors should represent the shareholders in the very important matter of auditing, and the directors (as such) should have no voice in the matter.

As to the importance of a proper auditorial certificate, practically valuable, surely by this time, and after your invaluable remarks, shareholders will see that it is as important to have it clear and precise as it is to have a policy of insurance legally drawn, and should be paid for in proportion to the peace of mind they wish to have.—Yours, &c.,

CHARLES HIGHT, F.C.A.

3, Copthall Buildings, E.C., October 24, 1883.

*To the Editor of " Vanity Fair."*

SIR,—You are quite right. Auditing as at present carried on is commonly a delusion and a snare.

One very important reason is that in very many Companies the auditor is appointed by the promoters for services rendered in the promotion of the Company, and very frequently he is an actual promoter directly interested in that mysterious promotion money which in the majority of prospectuses has not been, neither will be paid.

It is a very difficult subject to deal with, and the profession is in my opinion indebted to you for starting the discussion.

An auditor, to be of the slightest value, must be independent and fr e. If he is not, his certificate is not worth the paper it is written on. To ensure independence is the problem to be solved.—Yours obediently,                    C.A.
23rd October, 1883.

## THE AUDITOR AUDITED.

Quod facit per alium facit per se
Is the rule of an Auditor—*as to the fee ;*
But, when the accounts are not up to the mark,
Then it was not the Auditor—*only his clerk.*

The following report has reference to the above subject :—

## THE CHARTERED MERCANTILE BANK OF INDIA, LONDON, AND CHINA.

A correspondent writes to us to the effect that we are in error in stating that the auditors' certificate to the balance-sheet of this Bank passed unquestioned at the meeting held on the 16th inst. He says that the Chairman, Mr. J. N. Bullen, referred to the subject. We will repeat what we wrote on this matter :—The shareholders of this Bank could scarcely have glanced at this certificate, or they would surely not have let it pass unquestioned as they did. They apparently read the magic word auditors, and did not trouble to attempt to analyse the exact meaning of the words immediately preceding. Mr. J. N. Bullen, it is true, did refer to the certificate. This is what he said, according to the report which appeared in the *Times* on the day following :—All their securities were in the joint custody of the manager and chief accountant, and a written certificate was sent in by the auditors that the whole of them had been examined and found correct. As to the securities held by the Bank belonging to customers, they did not hold much. They had just been examined and found all in order.

The shareholders said nothing.

But we maintain that the certificate affixed by the auditors did not state, what Mr. Bullen affirms as a fact, that the auditors had furnished a written certificate that the *whole of the securities* belonging to the Bank had been examined and found correct. Here is the certificate :—

London, 3rd October, 1883.—We have examined the *returns* of Bills of Exchange, Local Bills discounted, and other Securities held by the Bank, and its several Agencies, as transmitted from the several Managers, and are satisfied that such Bills and Securities are available. We consider that sufficient provision has been made for bad and doubtful debts.

GEO. CHRISTIAN, } Auditors.
F. TENDRON,

From the above evidence it will be admitted that Mr. J. N. Bullen, unintentionally no doubt, fell into the error of making statements which were not borne out by actual facts—or at any rate by the certificate which is supposed to state and verify the facts.

## AUDITORS' CERTIFICATES TO BALANCE SHEETS.

*Vanity Fair,* as will be seen from the article we reprint elsewhere, again finds fault with auditors' certificates to balance sheets, and asserts that in the cases it quotes they are not in accordance with the Act of Parliament. If the writer merely means that in many cases they do not comply with the exact phraseology laid down in the act, we admit that it is so, but, looking at it from a more liberal point of view, we assert, that these certificates not only cover all the requirements of the act, but, in most cases, give more information than they are required to afford.

The writer also, by quoting section 6 of the act, gives unconsciously the answer to all his objections ; that section reduced to every-day phrases, and with all superfluous verbiage eliminated may be taken to read as follows : "The auditors are to state whether the balance sheet submitted to them exhibits a correct view of the company's affairs as shown by the books."

Anyone understanding book-keeping will know that a balance sheet properly drawn up and agreeing with the books must show the correct state of the company's affairs as shown by the books, the books and the balance sheet being so closely connected, and the former so necessary to the latter, that any discrepancy must become at once apparent on intelligent audit.

Taking the balance sheets quoted by *Vanity Fair* seriatim we come to—

(1).—The old balance sheet of the Imperial Bank which has the following certificate : " We have compared the balances as set forth in the balance sheet with the books and find the same correct.

(2).—The balance sheet of the same bank presented and passed January 15th, which bears the same certificate with the addition of the following words interpolated, " and examined the securities representing the investments of the Bank." *Vanity Fair* considers that the alteration in No. 2 has been brought about through its criticisms, but still is not happy ; now, we contend that the first certificate contains all the information required by the act, and the second states that the auditors have, in addition, done what they were not required to do, viz., examined the securities. Now, in the first certificate the auditors practically state that the balance sheet and balances in the books agree, and this must show the correct position of the bank *as shown by the books*, all that is required by the act.

*Vanity Fair* notes particularly the absence of any assurance that the auditors consider that the balance sheet exhibits a true state of the bank's affairs, or that the profits to be divided have been properly earned.  As we state above, if the book balances and balance sheet agree, the latter *must* show the true state of affairs, as far as an auditor's duties go as at present defined by the act, although, we think, they might easily be extended and made more comprehensive, a matter we propose to deal with next week, and on which in our previous articles we contended fresh legislation is required; and the objection about the profits is a matter for the directors and manager, the auditor *qua* auditor, having nothing to do with the question.

(3).—The Alliance Bank.

The writer finds fault with the general vagueness of this certificate, but we fail to see the vagueness ; the auditors have examined the foregoing accounts (including the balance sheet) in detail with the books and vouchers of the bank, and find them to be correct.  This fulfils all that is required of the auditors, but they have gone further, and thoroughly investigated the correctness of the amount of cash in hand, checked all the bills of exchange, inspected the securities representing the bank investments, those held against advances and loans, and those belonging to customers.  This is a most thorough and searching investigation, and instead of the vagueness of which the writer complains, we think, it is most precise, and gives details unexpected because unlooked for.

(4)—The London and South Western Bank.

The auditors here appear to have been as searching as in the previous case, with the exception that they have not checked the securities held against advances and loans, or those belonging to customers. The objection that they do not state whether the balance sheet is properly drawn up or not is absurd ; if it agrees with the books it must be properly drawn up ; the further objection that they have not checked the books shows an equal ignorance of book-keeping, if they were required to check the books it would take the two auditors months to accomplish their task, or require a number of auditors in the proportion of one to ten of the number of clerks employed ; and the final one that they have been content to accept the directors own estimate as to the value of investments is beside the question, the directors and manager being responsible for those figures, and all the auditor has to do is to see that they appear in the books, and also in the balance sheet.

(5).—The Central Bank of London.

" Audited and approved."

The writer is not happy even in his little pleasantry, he states this certificate is like a maiden's kiss—short and sweet—exactly so, but ask any young man, and how long will it take him to tell you all the joys, bliss and sensations contained in that short act of osculation ; in the same way what is not comprehended in those three words ?  "Audited and approved"—written and signed by men thoroughly understanding their duties, they comprise everything that is required of an auditor ; and although, perhaps, it would be well in these days of carping criticism to comply exactly with the wording of the act, we consider this form of certificate, signed by conscientious men thoroughly acquainted with their duties, the most complete, because the most simple ever devised.  Can the writer recall his schooldays, and Cœsar's famous despatch, *Veni, Vidi, Vici,*—what can be shorter and yet more comprehensive than this.

(6).—The City Bank.

The writer finds fault with the auditors for stating that the balance sheet shows a correct view of affairs as shown by the books, whereas that is exactly what they are required to do by the Act, and not check cash, securities, &c.

(7).—The Consolidated Bank.

The flippant remark that the certificate appears to mean, " We have signed what the directors put before us, and we hope that everything is going on as it should," would be in bad taste in any serious discussion like the present, but is simply absurd when you look at the names, attached to the certificate.

(8).—The London Joint Stock Bank.

This certificate, the same as all enumerated above, fulfils in our opinion all the requirements of the Act, and notwithstanding the uncalled-for sneer with regard to one of the auditors we consider they have done their duty.

(9).—London and Westminster Bank.

(10).—Union Bank of London.

The writer comments on the glaring incompleteness of the certificates of the above banks, whereas they comply word for word with the act, and in addition give further information with regard to the securities, &c.

*Vanity Fair's* idea that the Council of the Institute of Chartered Accountants should impress on auditors the necessity of giving more complete certificates, is good in itself; but we all know the value the world puts on unasked-for advice, and the Council very properly ignore such suggestions, and will do so until asked by the responsible authorities, when no doubt they will give their valuable assistance in defining—

(1)—What the duties of an auditor should be.

(2)—To what extent he should be expected to check securities, value the same, and estimate and value book debts, &c.

(3)—What remuneration he should receive.

We have shown that all these certificates comply with the requirements of the act, and even go beyond them; the question formerly propounded by us, and carefully avoided by *Vanity Fair* still remains, " Is fresh legislation required ? "

AUDITORS' CERTIFICATES TO BALANCE-SHEETS.

Our Contemporary *Vanity Fair*, has again taken up this subject in their issue of the 9th inst., as per the following article :—

There is nothing like pegging away at an abuse until it is remedied.  So we make no excuse for recurring to this subject.  We may be pardoned when we confess that when we started this question of the value of auditorial certificates to balance-sheets as then rendered, we were unaware that special enactments of Parliament had been passed to guide and control auditors in this respect.

The Act was entitled " An Act to amend the laws with respect to the liability of members of banking and other joint stock Companies, and for other purposes."  It was dated August 15th, 1879.

Here are the sections relating to the special subject of auditing under this Act :—

" (5.) Every auditor shall have a list delivered to him of all books kept by the Company, and shall at all reasonable times have access to the books and accounts of the Company ; and any auditor may, in relation to such books and accounts, examine the directors or any other officer of the Company : Provided that if a Banking Company has branch banks beyond the limits of Europe, it shall be sufficient if the auditor is allowed access to such copies of and extracts from the books and accounts of any such branch as may have been transmitted to the head office of the Banking Company in the United Kingdom.

" (6.) The auditor or auditors shall make a *report to the members on the accounts examined by him or them, and on every balance-sheet laid before the Company in general meeting* during his or their tenure of office ; *and in every such report shall state whether, in his or their opinion, the balance-sheet referred to in the report is a full and fair balance-sheet properly drawn up, so as to exhibit a true and correct view of the state of the Company's affairs*, as shown by the books of the Company ; and such report shall, be read before the Company in general meeting."

The leading London joint-stock banks having now concluded their half-yearly meetings and passed their reports, it will not be out of place to ascertain how far, from external evidence, the auditors whose names appear on the various balance-sheets have acted in compliance with the specifications of the above Act, and also how far they have amended their ways since the discussion raised by us.

The first certificate which we will reproduce is that which was appended to the balance-sheet of the IMPERIAL BANK, and to which we directed some attention in the article on this subject which appeared in *Vanity Fair* of October 6th. This certificate read thus:—

" We have compared the balances as set forth in the balance-sheet with the books, and find the same correct.

" FREDERICK FEARON, ⎫ *Auditors.*"
" GEORGE BROOM, ⎭

The following is the certificate which appeared affixed to the balance-sheet presented and passed at the meeting of this Bank which was held January 15th, and for which the auditors received the usual vote of thanks from confiding shareholders, and—the usual fees.

" We have *compared* the balances as set forth in this balance-sheet with the *books* and examined the securities representing the investments of the Bank, and find the same correct.

" FREDERICK FEARON, ⎫ *Auditors.*"
" GEORGE BROOM, ⎭

The criticisms of *Vanity Fair* have no doubt brought about this slight change ; but this change, like the character of the famous hotel chambermaid, is nothing to boast about. It certainly does contain the small consolation which the shareholders of the Imperial Bank did not get before—that their investments have been counted and checked by independent persons at least once during the last six months.

Otherwise we do not see of what use this certificate is, because if we are to take as gospel that which Messrs. Fearon and Broom convey by it, it might just as well have never been given. We note particularly the absence of any assurance that the auditors consider that the balance-sheet exhibits a true state of the Bank's affairs, or that the profits to be divided have been properly earned. Let our reader first peruse the Act and then this, which it is a disgrace to the English language to call a certificate. Then let them decide between the directors and auditors of the Imperial Bank and ourselves as to whether such a production is not a violation of the Companies' Act.

We next come to the certificate to the balance-sheet and accounts of the ALLIANCE BANK. It is the same as that which we criticised in our issue of October 6th, and is as follows :—

" We have examined the foregoing accounts in detail with the books and vouchers of the Bank, and find them to be correct. Further, we have ascertained by actual enumeration the correctness of the items of cash and Bills of Exchange in hand, and have inspected the securities representing the Bank's own investments in Government Stocks, &c., and also those held on account of advances and loans as well as those belonging to customers, and we find them to be in due accordance with the books and accounts of the Bank.

" WILLIAM QUILTER (*Quilter, Ball, & Co.*), ⎫ *Auditors.*"
" JOHN YOUNG (*Turquand, Youngs, & Co.*), ⎭

There is no occasion to repeat our adverse criticisms which appeared in this paper on this special certificate in October last, the truth of which criticisms its concoctors admitted by allowing them to pass unquestioned and uncontradicted. We will merely state that, in addition to general vagueness, this certificate egregiously fails under the terms of the Act, in the important respect that the shareholders in the Alliance Bank have not received the assurance from their auditors that the balance-sheet and accounts which they have passed are " properly drawn up so as to exhibit a true and correct view of the Company's affairs." What a chance for a cantankerous shareholder ! In the strict letter of the law this balance-sheet is incomplete, and therefore irregular.

We next come to the certificate attached to the balance sheet of the LONDON AND SOUTH-WESTERN BANK. In October last we called it a Chinese puzzle ; we call it so still, and reproduce it for the edification of Bank shareholders.

" We have compared the above statements with the Books and Vouchers at the Head Office, and with the Certified Returns from the several Branches, and certify that we found the Cash in hand, and at Bank of England, Bills discounted, Loans, and other items, as stated in the Balance-sheet, to be duly in accordance therewith. We have likewise examined the Securities for Cash at Call and Short Notice, as also the Investments of the Bank, standing in the Balance-sheet at £718,694 5s. 0d. and £107,547 17s. 2d., and found the same correct.

" (Signed)  JAMES EDMESTON, ⎫ *Auditors.*
" JAMES WORLEY ⎭
(Chartered Accountants.)

" *Dated this 10th day of January*, 1884."

This is certainly one of the greatest delusions in the shape of a certificate which we have yet criticised. The one which is attached to the Imperial Bank is bad, but this is delusion. In the first place, the auditors do not state whether the balance-sheet is properly drawn up or no. They have not checked the books—they have only compared balances. Moreover they have not, in the face of the express stipulation of the Act, audited the books of the branch offices. They have been content with " *the certified returns therefrom.*" Finally, they have been content to accept the directors' own estimate of the investments, without any inquiry as to whether these investments are really worth what they are valued at.

The certificate of the balance-sheet of the CENTRAL BANK OF LONDON reads thus :—

" Audited and Approved.

" JOHN YOUNG
" (*Turquand, Youngs, and Co.*), ⎫
" H. L. HAMMACK, ⎬ *Auditors.*
" E. H. BYAS, ⎭

" *9th January*, 1884."

This certificate is like a maiden's kiss—short and sweet. But what are we to understand by these three words, " Audited and Approved ?"

This is what we should feel inclined to call a good specimen of an after-lunch certificate. The chop has been discussed, the last glass of dry sherry been drained, digestion is going on well, and the auditors are in that happy frame of mind when they will approve of anything. The smiling manager or secretary accordingly brings in a statement which they accept, approve of and sign, apparently on superficial evidence. The fee is taken, and the auditors waltz away till next half-year. This is all very pleasant, but is it auditing, and have these three gentlemen complied with the Act of 1879?

The auditors of the CITY BANK say :—

" We beg to report that, in our opinion, the foregoing is a full and fair balance-sheet, properly drawn up, and that it exhibits a true and correct view of the Company's affairs, *as shown by the books of the Company.*

" JOHN CURRY, ⎫ *Auditors*
" WILLIAM E. EAST, ⎭

Now this certificate entirely excludes any reference that the assets of this Bank, such as cash, bills, and securities, really exist. The auditors say " as shown by the books." Books can be kept in such a way as to show anything, and although we do not believe that the City Bank directors would be capable of deceiving their auditors or their customers, they might have their bill-case full of gingerbread-nuts, or they might—as did the directors of the City of Glasgow Bank—say they held so many hundred of thousands of Consols, when really they did not hold sixpennyworth. Essential inquiries such as these Messrs. Curry and East have apparently not troubled themselves to make.

The certificate of the auditors of the CONSOLIDATED BANK reads as follows ;—

" We have to report that we have examined the Accounts and Balance-sheet of the Bank for the half-year ending 31st December 1883, and have signed the same as exhibiting a true and correct view of the Company's affairs, in conformity with the Deed of Settlement.

> " ARTHUR COOPER (*Cooper Brothers & Co*,) } *Auditors.*
> " EDWIN COLLIER,
> " *10th January, 1884.*"

This is not a whit better than the preceding one which we have quoted. It appears to us to mean, " We have signed what the directors put before us, and we hope that everything is going on as it should."

The following is the certificate attached to the balance-sheet of the LONDON JOINT-STOCK BANK :—

> " We have audited the above Statement of Liabilities and Assets, and we report that in our opinion it is a full and fair Balance-sheet, properly drawn up so as to exhibit a true and correct view of the state of the Bank's affairs, as *shown in the Books of the Bank.*
> " WILLIAM CROSBIE (*Quilter, Ball, & Co.*),
> " JOHN G. GRIFFITHS                                      } *Auditors.*"
> (*Deloitte, Dever, Griffiths & Co.*)

We must confess we are much disappointed with this certificate. Considering the special and unpleasant experience which one of these gentlemen has had through the recent disclosures concerning the efficacy of his partner's auditing at the London and River Plate Bank, we expected something better. As is apparent, the shareholders of the London Joint-Stock Bank have no assurance from their auditors that the existence of certain securities has been verified.

We will conclude our review of these certificates by giving the copies of the auditors' certificates to the two largest London banks. The first is that attached to the balance-sheet of the LONDON AND WESTMINSTER BANK ; the second that of the UNION BANK OF LONDON :—

> "· We have satisfied ourselves of the correctness of the Cash Balances, and have examined the Securities held against the Money at Call and Short Notice and representing the Investments of the Bank, and in accordance with the provisions of the Companies' Act, we have examined the foregoing Balance-sheet and Profit and Loss Account with the *Books of the Company*, and beg to report, that in our opinion such Accounts are properly drawn up, so as to exhibit a true and correct view of the state of the Company's affairs as shown by the *Books of the Company.*
> " WILLIAM TURQUAND, } *Auditors.*"
> " EDWIN WATERHOUSE,

" We certify that we have verified the correctness of the cash Balances, of the Investments held by the Bank, of the Securities held against Monies at Call and Short Notice, and of the Bills discounted : and having examined the foregoing Balance-sheet and Profit and Loss Account with the books of the Company, we beg to report in accordance with the provisions of the Companies' Act, 1879, that in our opinion such Balance-sheet and Account are properly drawn up so as to exhibit a true and correct view of the state of the Company's affairs as shown by the books of the Company.

> " R. P. HARDING, } *Audttors.*"
> " R. MACKAY,

Our readers will admit that if anything were needed to prove the glaring incompleteness of the preceding certificates, as compared with those designed by the Act of 1879, these last two would be sufficient. The question arises, if it is possible for one set of auditors to give a certificate which appears to endeavour to fulfil the requirements of the Act, why should they not all? From the certificates to the Union, and London and Westminster Banks we gather that the auditors who gave them have actually read the Act of 1879, and have endeavoured to frame their reports accordingly. We suppose that their *confrères* have not. But we should have been more pleased with these two reports if they had expressed themselves distinctly as to whether the audit extended only to the head offices of these banks, and whether they had taken for granted the correctness of returns received from branches. As they now stand, this last fact is left to the imagination.

From seven out of the nine certificates which we have quoted, it appears that auditors themselves have a very incomplete notion of their duty towards the shareholder. And the question naturally arises, who is to teach them their duty? *Vanity Fair* does not aspire to the proud distinction. We can only fix this responsibility upon that select few of the accountants' profession who have banded themselves together, obtained a charter, formed an " Institute," and dubbed themselves members of the Council of the Institute of Chartered Accountants. It is for the " Council " to effect this much-needed reform, and by virtue of their office they are the right people to impress upon the profession the advisability of its followers giving intelligible certificates, in accordance with the Act which the Legislature has framed to meet its requirements. Occurrences in bank history during the past six months have shown that frauds go on unchecked despite the presence of the " master's eye " of the auditor, who nevertheless takes his fee, while all the world wonders. And that robbers are undismayed by the twinkle of his magisterial optic is further shown by the disclosures of the Blakeway fraud. In this case we are brought face to face with the fact, that owing to the blind belief which the Directors had in an old name, the London Chartered Bank of Australia have been plundered to the tune of £120,000, and the Colonial Bank to that of £40,000. In addition to these two banks, there are rumours of others which have also been hit to a considerable extent. In every instance these banks have auditors, and have published within a month or so half-yearly accounts, which their auditors have certified as being correct, notwithstanding the fact that, as events have proved, certain securities supposed to have been held against advances had no material existence. The means adopted by Blakeway to rob the banks was by obtaining loans on what is known as a " bank transfer " of certain registered stock of which he was supposed to be the owner, but which stock he either never possessed, or he had previously pledged to some other lender. The directors of these banks were only too glad to lend their spare cash on the bare signature of a firm which boasted of an existence of a century, and, we must suppose, did not take the trouble to ascertain whether it really held security or not. Had the auditors of these banks properly fulfilled their duties, in seeing to their own satisfaction that proper and actual security was held against loans, we imagine that these frauds could not have been perpetrated. We shudder to think how many such exposures of this nature would have to be faced if auditors properly fulfilled their duties towards the shareholders. For the latter class the experience would at first perhaps be painful. But the end would be that business would be placed on a sound footing.

Thursday, Feb. 7, 1884.

## CHARTERED ACCOUNTANTS' STUDENTS' SOCIETY OF LONDON.

### THE PREPARATION AND AUDIT OF INCOME AND EXPENDITURE ACCOUNTS.

#### By Mr. G. Van de Linde, F.C.A., F.S.S.

At a meeting of this Society, Mr. G. Van de Linde, read the following paper on the above subject:—

The lecturer said:—Doubtless you are all, in a measure, familiar with the accounts that form the subject of the present lecture, they being those that generally first come before you in the discharge of your duties. What I have more particularly before me at the present time are those relating to Charities, Clubs, Institutes, Corporations, and other organizations of a kindred nature, where the bulk, if not the whole, of the year's operations are focussed in an Annual Statement of Income and Expenditure. Such accounts have, until recent years, been to a great extent audited by non-professional gentlemen with, in many cases, no fixed principles to guide them, nor technical knowledge or experience, the result often proving to be of no practical use as regards the object intended to be attained. The conviction as to the existence of such a state of things has for the last few years been steadily gaining ground, and the incorporation of our Institute, some five years ago, offered a practical solution to the vague doubts and misgivings that were occupying and perplexing many thoughtful minds. It is a satisfaction to be able to state that the outcome of all this has been, that professional Audits are daily becoming more general, and it can safely be asserted that they will soon be the rule instead of, as formerly, only the exception.

Bear in mind, however, that with such an altered state of things, the audit that once passed muster would not do so now. The public are quite alive to this fact, and to what they have a right to, and do expect, from professional Auditors. It is our policy, as well as our duty, therefore, to be in every way qualified to respond effectively to the functions we are thus called upon to discharge, and which necessarily bring with them certain responsibilities, if our audit is to be of practical use and inspire confidence.

What is worth doing at all is worth doing thoroughly, and, as the President of our Institute mentioned the other day, when referring to the Bankruptcy Act, 1883, although we have no vested rights in such matters, we should have no difficulty, by our special training, experience, and knowledge, in satisfying all that we can do our work better than those gentlemen who have had neither training, experience, nor knowledge herein.

There are two classes of Accounts that come under the heading of Income and Expenditure.

    A. Cash Receipts and Payments, *or* Receipts and Disbursements.

    B. Income and Expenditure.

A is simply an abstract of the Cash Book, commencing with the Cash Balance, being the amount in hand or at the bankers at the beginning of the financial year, and ending with the Cash Balance at its close, and it is frequently the only record of the year's transactions; neither outstanding assets nor outstanding liabilities being taken into account, there is consequently no Balance Sheet.

B on the other hand, is an account of all Income and Expenditure appertaining to the period involved, and by means of the Assets and Capital and Liabilities, comprised in the Balance Sheet, includes every item both of Income and Expenditure, whether received or paid in cash or still due.

B form, therefore, commends itself in every way, except in such simple cases where all items can be brought into the Cash Book in the year to which they refer, and thus for the time being absorb every transaction, both of Income and Expenditure. For present purposes, therefore, while advocating B form whenever possible, I must not pass over and ignore A form.

Accountants are not unfrequently called in to prepare such Annual Statements from the *quasi* cash book, or other memoranda that have hitherto been kept, and for that purpose they have to abstract and summarize the various items on both sides, in order to bring them under their respective heads, and evolve order out of chaos.

Although there certainly is a short method of arriving at the result required, its adoption in such cases cannot be recommended. It is preferable that the opportunity should be availed of, with the materials and data at hand, to at once recommend and obtain permission to start books on a proper and permanent basis.

If A form is to be adopted, a Cash Book, Petty Cash Book and Ledger are all that, for the moment, will be needed, but with B form a Journal will also be required. Of course, there will be other books of a subsidiary character, which will require to be kept according to the nature of the respective accounts, which will naturally suggest themselves in due course.

Let us for the present confine ourselves to A form, "Receipts and Payments:" and of which the Cash Book is the principal factor. But before commencing to write it up, we have first to consider what Ledger accounts are necessary. These require care as to their classification: it is convenient that they should be opened in the same order in which they will be shown in the final Annual Statement, receipts, under their various heads and sub-heads, having the respective openings first ; next payments must be dealt with in a similar manner ; and lastly, there will require to be opened a Ledger Account, entitled " Receipts and Payments," to which the totals of all the Ledger Accounts are transferred at the end of the year ; and these, with the Cash Balances, will give the information for the annual statement.

Sufficient Ledger Accounts need to be opened to meet every requirement, being in fact self-explanatory, and when once opened, there must be uniformity in their adoption in subsequent years, having recourse to further openings only if new classes of receipts and payments arise. This is important for purposes of comparison, and drawing up statistical and tabular forms relating to the accounts.

As regards the Petty Cash Book, this, besides one total column, should be ruled with such columns as may be required for the respective heads of payments that will be made through the petty cash ; there might be also one additional column to be used for " Sundries," each item of which would have to be passed out separately. By the adoption of the Imprest System referred to in the next paragraph, the whole of the payments by petty cash can be passed, systematically and regularly, to their respective Ledger Accounts without difficulty or confusion.

To give effect to the Imprest System, a round sum, say £15 or £20, should in the first instance be drawn for the petty cashier, which sum, at the commencement and end of the financial year, is always intact. At regular periodical intervals the cast of the Petty Cash Book is taken, and a cheque drawn for the exact amount disbursed : this is passed out through the general Cash Book to the debit of the various Ledger Accounts, as per the respective heads in the columns of the Petty Cash Book, and thus the primary round sum in the hands of the petty cashier is once again restored, the cheque for the last repayment being drawn and cleared at the end of the year, and so covering every item expended in petty cash during that year. A rule should be made that all receipts and payments should pass through the Banking Accounts.

The general and most convenient form of Cash Book is one with a double money column, the inner one for details, the outer one to agree with the totals in the Pass Book, viz.: Payments in on the debit side, and cheques drawn on the credit side. There should also be two single columns, one for ledger folios and the other for voucher numbers ; receipts should be entered in the Cash Book before an acknowledgment is given, and payments as they are made. It is very important that this book should always be closely written up. It is well too to number the Cheque Book consecutively, and enter, in the Cash Book, the number of each cheque against the amount ; this often is of great assistance in tracing a cheque where there is no other voucher for the payment.

In writing up the Cash Book, be careful always to state clearly and fully the name of the Ledger Account, and short particulars of the receipt or payment, and to observe uniformity of dates as regards debits and credits.

In some cases, the debit side of the Cash Book is written up continuously, without any break whatever, and the credit side also ; but this course cannot be recommended, as the date on one page should not be later than the first entry on the next page. Frequent reference should be made to the Pass Book, so as to enter from it, in order of date, any small charges, as also any receipts or payments passed in direct.

I do not advocate the plan of frequently bringing down the balance of the Cash Book ; on the contrary, I prefer that for these accounts they should only be balanced once a year, and that at the end of it : thus gross totals on both sides are preserved, and these prove useful in many ways. The Cash Book should be regularly agreed, say once a week, or at any rate not less than once a month, with the Pass Book, and any differences at once set right.

The Cash Book being written up, the balance should be agreed at the end of the financial year, and a statement recording all differences at that date with the bank Pass Book

should be entered therein, such as country cheques not credited and cheques issued for payment not presented. In many cases, an effort is made to get all cheques cleared within the year, and so make the Cash Book balance exactly tally with that of the Pass Book and cash in hand, or where there is a difference to show the same in the financial statement.

The next thing is to post the Ledger from the Cash Book daily, and to transfer the totals of the ledger balances to the account entitled " Receipts and Payments," a transcript of which, when complete at the end of the year, will as previously mentioned, form the financial statement.

If, however, B form, viz., " Income and Expenditure," is adopted, further closing entries have to be made through the Journal : for instance, if certain items of income are still due at the end of the year, they must be credited to the account, and a per contra Debit Account opened, or a balance brought down in the account, which will become a Balance Sheet item. Should, on the other hand, certain income be received, pertaining to the next year, this might be kept out of the Income Account, and a Credit Account opened for it, or a balance brought down in the account, which in its turn will become a Balance Sheet item.

In the same way with expenditure, outstanding liabilities must all be brought in as a charge by creating Credit Accounts, and should any proportion of expenditure pertaining to the following year have been paid in the then year, it must be kept out of the Expenditure Accounts, and a Debit Account opened for it : in both of these cases these amounts become Balance Sheet items. Where, however, the plan is adopted of at once crediting tradesmen or manufacturers (by personal accounts in the ledger) when goods are supplied, debiting at the same time the impersonal Expenditure Accounts, the necessity for the foregoing is in a measure obviated, as thus the bulk of the liabilities are brought into the accounts, as incurred ; this course, entailing very little extra trouble, can certainly be recommended for many, and I think, obvious reasons. Depreciation too affecting furniture, lease of premises, &c., must also be brought into account : the cost or reduced amount (after deduction of depreciation of former years), a Balance Sheet item, being reduced by credit entries for further depreciation, and per contra the depreciation thus written off being charged to expenditure.

There will then be two sets of balances, viz. :—

    I. Income and Expenditure Balances.

    II. Balance Sheet Balances.

No. I. will be grouped, under their respective heads, in the Income and Expenditure Account ; the balance (either excess of income over expenditure or vice versâ) being carried to the Balance Sheet, to the credit or debit of Capital Account, as the case may be.

No. II. will be grouped under convenient headings, and will form the liabilities on the debit side of the Balance Sheet, and the assets on the credit side of the Balance Sheet, the balance of cash (presuming the cash is not posted in the Ledger, a now almost obsolete practice) being also taken into account in the Balance Sheet.

Although it may not be usual to print these details in the accounts, the written copy of both Nos. I. and II. should contain, in the margin, all ledger folios or references to any schedule or subsidiary lists, for the purpose of ready identification.

I have purposely hurried somewhat over the last few paragraphs, as many of the points affecting them can, I think, be better dealt with in the second part of these remarks, viz., the Audit of the foregoing accounts, and which I am now coming to.

The first duty of an Auditor is to ask for a copy of any Charter of Incorporation, Act of Parliament, Bye Laws, or Rules, relating to the Society whose accounts he is auditing, and to read and master all details of the same affecting the accounts ; so that while auditing he may observe any special provisions therein made. For example, the following is the wording of a bye-law of an institution to which I am Auditor. "98. The Weekly Board shall annually, during the " month of December, appoint a professional Auditor, who " shall receive such remuneration as they shall from time to " time determine, and who shall audit the accounts of the " . . . and for that purpose he shall require and receive " from the trustees, and treasurers, and bankers, and solicitor, " and superintendent and secretary, and collector, all such " information as he shall consider necessary, and shall lay a " statement of accounts, so audited, before the Weekly Board, " which shall be held next after such audit shall be com- " pleted, and the same shall be laid by the superintendent and " secretary before the next Quarterly Court."

Such a bye-law practically throws responsibility upon the Auditor, but I consider it is one that he should not hesitate to assume, it being a step in the right direction. My own experience of it is, that it has worked thoroughly well, with-out once causing the slightest friction whatever; one thing it certainly must do, and that is to put an Auditor upon his mettle. I am sure you all desire this to be the case.

The Auditor should further procure a list of all books in use relating to the accounts, both general and subsidiary, bearing in mind that when once he has thus taken cognizance of them, he is to an extent responsible concerning them; one of the objects of his audit being to trace everything from original and reliable sources, especially as regards receipts, to satisfy himself that no item of income has been overlooked and left out of the accounts. Where it is hardly necessary for him to check, at each audit, the whole of the subsidiary books, he should check at one time one, and at another time others of them, reserving to himself which they shall be.

We will now assume that we have before us an A form, " Receipts and Payments " to audit. This, as I mentioned at the outset, is simply an abstract of the Cash Book; we there-fore begin with this book, the first operation being to vouch, so far as possible, every item on both sides. We start with the debit side, " Receipts." This commences, in the case of an Institution previously established, with cash at the beginning of the year at bank and in hand, being the same amount as the previous account left off with; this can be readily checked. If the Imprest System is adopted, the cash in hand will in-clude the round sum of petty cash already referred to. It used to be said that the receipts side was more difficult to vouch by reason of the possibility of errors of omission, than the payments side with errors of commission, but the thing is certainly not impossible. At the outset let me urge the importance of insisting, before commencing the audit, that everything be in ink, and that full dates be invariably entered. It is very unsatisfactory to come across pencil casts not inked in, or a succession of pages where the year and sometimes the month even have been omitted. The Auditor should tick everything in ink, adopting a uniform tick which he can always distinguish as being his own. It is essential to vouch every item, and in so doing exhaust every entry in counterfoil and other Receipt Books, for instance, in the case of a collector's counterfoil books. These should be filled up in the office, and delivered to him duly signed and ready for issue; he is then made responsible for every one of these receipts which have printed consecutive numbers on them. It is necessary to check each one of these through his Receipt Book into the Cash Book, and a simple India rubber stamp comes in very useful for identification. Any receipts cancelled should be left in the counterfoil book, for the Auditor to finally obliterate with his stamp.

At each quarter, half-year, or year, as the case may be, new counterfoil books will be issued to the collector, but the auditor must watch the old ones for receipts still left in (subscribers sometimes being dilatory in paying up, through absence abroad or other causes), and only release these books one by one as the receipts are finally exhausted, or the outstanding ones cancelled, as being considered to be by that time obsolete. In the event of the collector having to either increase or decrease the amount of his receipt, he must also alter the counterfoil accordingly; and as it is usual in the annual reports to publish the names of the subscribers and donors, or the numbers of the receipts and the amounts of their subscriptions and donations, there is little danger of irregularities in this respect. These amounts should be added and the totals agreed with the entries in the Annual Accounts. Donations are vouched from another counterfoil book, but these are only filled in as they occur in order of date, the numbers being consecutive.

*(To be continued in our next issue.)*

## CHARTERED ACCOUNTANTS' STUDENTS' SOCIETY OF LONDON.

### THE PREPARATION AND AUDIT OF INCOME AND EXPENDITURE ACCOUNTS.

By Mr. G. Van de Linde, F.C.A., F.S.S.

*(Continued from our last issue).*

Dividends are usually vouched from the Pass Book, as being collected by the bank direct, or in the case of a Charity, in some instances by the Charity Commissioners, who invariably collect and pay over the full amount free of Income Tax. But when the Charity has been credited direct, it has generally been the practice to deduct the tax in the first instance, leaving the Charity the onus of recovering it afterwards; and it has been the duty of the Auditor to watch this, and see the repayment has been made and duly entered.

However, on proper application being made to the Inland Revenue Office, Charities which can be dealt with by the Charity Commissioners, are *per se* in a position to obtain an order to be made exempt from Income Tax, and so get credit at once direct for the full amount of dividend so far at all events as stocks (Government, Colonial and Corporation) inscribed at the Bank of England, are concerned, and I rather think this facility may be extended to other banks inscribing stocks, if indeed it does not already exist in one or two instances that have been named to me. This involves a little trouble at first, but when once put right, the advantages therefrom fully compensate: it must be a convenience to at once get credit for the full sum, and to be able to record the same in one clean transaction; and being thus placed on an equality in this respect with the Charity Commissioners' Fund, while still maintaining control over the principal. Any change of trustees should be at once communicated to the Inland Revenue Office, in order that they may notify the bank to continue to exempt the account as thus changed. In making application to the Inland Revenue Office, care should be taken to ask for a full order of exemption, and to cover variations in the amounts of the stock, otherwise the order would lapse on any such change. I think the words of the order run that the stock in question shall be exempt now and for any future time.

As regards the total amount to be received from dividends, there should be no difficulty in agreeing this from the securities held; of course, where purchases or sales of stock have been made during the period, the fluctuations of interest can also be readily arrived at.

The Auditor should see the brokers' contract notes, and ascertain for himself whether the transactions have been *cum* or *ex* dividend.

There are other sources of revenue such as rents, grants, legacies, classes, lectures, patients' payments, sales of waste materials, miscellaneous receipts, &c. &c., but these can all be vouched from counterfoil and other books of record, in the same way; the final result being that every entry in such books for the year should be thus exhausted, and stamped or ticked by the Auditor, and the Cash Book also ticked throughout on the debit side.

In vouching the "Payments" or credit side of the Cash Book, the Auditor should be equally particular, and obtain a voucher for every item. These should all be prepared for him in regular consecutive order, and numbered as per Cash Book. I fear as a rule a little too much haste has hitherto been practised in going through these vouchers: the Auditor should carefully examine them one by one, before stamping and passing them; and see that they either belong to the current year, or if for a former year, that they have not been previously paid; and in fact, that every one of them is a *bona fide* receipt, as far as he can judge; for often laxity or undue haste are apt to prevail in this latter respect; this should not be countenanced. It may happen that occasionally a voucher is not forthcoming; the Auditor should satisfy himself as to the reason, and as a last recourse accept the endorsement on the cheque as a voucher (all cheques being issued to "order") with the invoice, where available, as collateral evidence; but he should endeavour to prevent a recurrence of the omission, and ask for an original and complete voucher in every instance.

In addition to the vouchers, the tradesmen's books and original invoices should also be produced, in regular order, for easy reference. It is important that in vouching, the Auditor should satisfy himself that not only is the receipt in order, but that the account itself is a proper one and that the Institution has received value for the same: such invoice or account is usually initialled by the department, and passed by the committee. In an instance before me, a slip worded as follows is attached to it, and duly signed by a responsible employé before being, with the cheque, submitted for payment. "I certify upon honour that the above-men-"tioned goods were ordered for the use of the establishment, "and were disposed of in that way———."

In most cases it is the custom to attach the receipt to the invoice, and treat the whole as *one* voucher; but where (in B form) personal and impersonal accounts are kept, and transfers from one to the other made through the Journal, they had best be kept separate, and thus the Journal entry is checked through the invoice, and the Cash Book entry through the receipt.

Salaries and wages are often detailed in a book: where this is so the Auditor should go through each line, and see that each recipient has properly signed for his or her respective amount, with a receipt stamp affixed for amounts of £2 and upwards, and where the mark + only is affixed he should see that it is properly witnessed. Where receipts are not yet given, the cash for same should be produced and noted, to be disposed of at the next audit; small bank charges can be vouched from the Pass Book, but the bank, as a rule, issues a slip for each of such debits, and these should be kept and produced as vouchers, like the rest, in numerical order. As regards Charities, I have been informed at the Inland Revenue Office, that there is no statutory exemption as to non-affixing receipt stamps to any vouchers, but that it is not the practice of the board to take proceedings where the receipts are for *voluntary payments*, but that if the Charity give the collector a receipt, this must bear a penny stamp as being his legal quittance; on the other hand, receipts for all payments of £2 and upwards that the Charity make, must bear the penny stamp, and that signatures in a book for nurses' or other wages or salaries, &c.. are in no wise exempt, for although the Charity may supply the receipt stamp, it is really incumbent upon the recipient of the money to furnish the same. I mention this point specially, because I have been asked for information in one or two instances upon the subject, difficulty having been experienced as to knowing what to do. The Auditor will come periodically (weekly, monthly, or quarterly) to certain items of payments made through the Petty Cash Book. This book must also be vouched exactly in the same way as the Cash Book itself, and a separate set of vouchers kept classified in numerical order.

Everything on both sides of the Cash Book being fully checked, the cash balances remain to be verified and agreed. As regards the Pass Book balance, a visit to the bank is recommended: with proper credentials, no difficulty now exists to the Auditor inspecting the account in their Ledger, and while doing so, it is useful to record the same on the audit notes, together with the folio of the Bank Ledger. This, too, is a fitting time to examine all securities of every nature, either by personally seeing the stock and other certificates, or in the case of inscribed stocks, by letters and lists certified from the various banks, stating that the respective stocks are duly in the name of the Institution, or of the proper parties as trustees for them, and in the latter case, an acknowledgment of the trust should be signed by them, and carefully kept in a place of safety. In vouching securities, some little practice and care are needed, for what at first sight would appear to be a proper certificate of stock often turns out to be merely a receipt for consideration money, as in the case of transfers of consols and other securities at the Bank of England, or of receipts for original payments on allotment of stock, and which, with certain inscribed stocks, are not required to be produced on sale or transfer: being really of no value, beyond that of record of the original transaction.

I would, at this stage, ask your very careful attention to this part of the audit, for in view of recent deplorable occurrences, Auditors cannot be too particular in this respect, and the importance of the work that they thus undertake is great and constantly on the increase.

While verifying securities, the Auditor should have them *en bloc* before him, and not piecemeal; and he should not allow any of them to go from his control until he has verified them *all*. In the case of bonds to bearer and stock certificates, these the Auditor will actually examine for himself; but as regards inscribed stocks, he should send in lists to the various banks for verification: and I would now draw your attention to this subject, which is daily growing in importance.

I will here classify inscribed stocks under two categories, viz.:

> I. Those for which no certificate whatever is issued, and the transfer for which can only be made in the register and signed by the transferor or his attorney.
>
> II. Those for which a certificate is issued, and which is transferred by deed.

As regards this second category, I only refer, for present purposes, to such stocks as come under the Colonial Stock Act [40 and 41 Vict. ch. 59] of 1877.

The following is, as near as I can get it, a complete list of inscribed stocks at present in existence, but the number of them is constantly increasing.

CATEGORY No. 1 (No Stock Certificates; transfer only in register), inscribed at Bank of England:

3 per-cent. Consols.
2¾ per cent. Annuities.
2¼ per cent. Annuities.
New 3½ per cent. Annuities.
New 3 per cent. Annuities.
Reduced 3 per cent. Annuities.
Annuities for 30 years.
Annuities for terms of years.
Metropolitan Board of Works 3½ per cent. Stock.
Metropolitan Board of Works 3 per cent. Stock.
Bank Stock.
Liverpool 3½ per cent. Stock.
Birmingham 3½ per cent. Stock.

Swansea 3½ per cent. Stock.
Hull 3½ per cent. Stock.
Wolverhampton 3½ per cent. Stock.
Nottingham 3 per cent. Stock.
New Zealand 4 per cent. Consolidated Stock.
New South Wales 4 per cent. Stock.
New South Wales 3¾ per cent. Stock.
Queensland 4 per cent. Stock (1915 and 1924).
India 4 per cent. Stock.
India 3½ per cent. Stock.
India 3 per cent. Stock.
India 4½ per cent. Rupee Loan.
India 4 per cent. Rupee Loan.
East India 4 per cent. Transfer Loan Stock.
Red Sea and India Telegraph Annuity.
Eastern Bengal Railway " A " Annuity.
Eastern Bengal Railway " B " Annuity.
Inscribed at London and Westminster Bank Limited :
Reading 3½ per cent. Stock.
Cape of Good Hope 4 per cent. Loan (issue of 1883).
Victorian Government Stocks.
    4 per cent. Railway Loan, 1881.
    4 per cent. Redemption Loan, 1882.
    4 per cent. Loan, 1883.
Inscribed at London and County Banking Company Limited :
Croydon 3½ per cent. Stock.
Inscribed at National Provincial Bank of England, Limited :
Portsmouth 3½ per cent. Stock.
CATEGORY No. 2 (Stock Certificates :* transfer by deed).
Inscribed at Messrs. Glyn, Mills, Currie & Co.

Canadian 5 per cent. Stock
Canadian 4 per cent. Stock
Canadian 3½ per cent. Stock

* Prior to 1 July, 1878, no Certificates were issued, but subsequent to that date certificates have been issued on every transfer, and these have to be surrendered on transfer.

South Australia 4 per cent. Inscribed Stock
    (two loans).
Inscribed at Messrs. Baring Brothers and Co. :
Cape of Good Hope 4 per cent. Stock (issue of 1882).
Inscribed at the office of the Crown Agents to Colonies,
    Downing Street :
Natal 4 per cent. Stock.
Regarding category No. 2, the Colonial Stock Act (40 and 41 Vict. ch. 59) of 1877, already referred to, provides under clause 4, as follows : " Colonial stock, to which this Act " applies, while inscribed in a register kept in the United " Kingdom, shall be transferred as follows.

    " I. The transfer shall be made only in the register, " and shall be signed by the transferor, or if he is " absent by his attorney thereunto, lawfully authorized " by some writing executed under his hand and seal, " and attested.

    " II. The transferee may, if he thinks fit, under- " write his acceptance of the transfer," &c., &c.

It should be mentioned that as regards the Canadian stock, it was created before the passing of the above Act, under a special Act of Parliament, and that it is administered under the provisions of that special Act, but this is not so with regard to the other stocks enumerated under category No. 2, and opinions are divided as to whether or not they conform with the spirit of the Act, if not with the letter of it, and as to whether it is safer and preferable to hold a certificate or none at all, and to transfer on a deed and surrender of the certificate, or simply and only on the register. One other thing has to be guarded against, and that is the improper issue of duplicate certificates. Recent deplorable events make it necessary for me just to refer to this point.

It is usual with all the Institutions coming under the scope of these remarks, to register their securities in two or three names, but limited to four (no trust being recognized, except in one or two Government accounts of a special nature), but

I think it right to point out that joint stock companies can register securities under the name and seal of the company, and that the same can only be operated upon under seal, and that Institutions, not for profit, duly incorporated, can register securities under their name and seal in the same way. This course would appear to commend itself as offering additional security, and besides, when once thus registered necessitating no further steps on the change of trustees by death or other causes. This is the case with colleges which each has its seal, which must be affixed in due form to all powers of attorney, transfers, and other documents of a like nature ; and therefore the transfers by corporations must always be by power of attorney, the same bearing the seal of the corporation.

The importance of the subject must be the excuse for the time that has been taken in bringing it under your notice, that when verifying securities you may know what to pass at once, and what not to without verification.

Reverting, then, to form A (" Receipts and Payments "), the Cash Book having been duly vouched, the entries in the Ledger should be checked, and care taken to see that they have been posted to the proper account. All the books should be cast, seeing that every entry has been duly ticked and dealt with ; the ledger balances closed by being transferred to the " Receipts and Payments " account, and the annual statement drawn up therefrom. This should be compared with the statements for previous years, and important variations in amounts, on the respective heads and sub-heads, noted and understood.

Totals should not be lumped together in one sum, but details given under the respective sub-heads. For instance, on total disbursements of, say £20,000, it is hardly proper to lump in three single lines, items of disbursements for over £5,100, £5,300, and £2,000 respectively ; whereas, the bulk of the items, both of receipts and expenditure, is set out in amounts raging from £3 15s. 0d. upwards, as was, in fact, stated in an account lately brought under my notice.

It only remains now for the Auditor to affix and sign his certificate, to make the statement complete. With the present altered state of things, the old stereotyped phrase of " Examined and found correct," would hardly be sufficient.

I do not wish to add to the discussion that has already prevailed on this knotty subject, beyond recommending what I am in the habit of myself adopting, namely, that the certificate should state concisely, but clearly, to what extent the Auditor has carried his audit ; a few lines suffice for this, and I take it this would be more satisfactory, both to his clients and himself. The Auditor's certificate, too, is a convenient medium for recording any special feature in the accounts, as also for what, in his opinion, is an omission or irregularity, and which he has been unable to get set right. Such cases are happily of rare occurrence, but the Auditor should be prepared to cope with them if they arise ; in fact, I was only the other day told of an instance where the Executive while publishing the accounts duly certified, omitted from the certificate an adverse rider. On this coming to the Auditor's notice, and his calling their attention to it, they had to withdraw all the copies from circulation (for these had already gone out) and to have reprinted and to reissue fresh copies containing the certificate in its entirety.

Before closing, I must just say a few words regarding form B (" Income and Expenditure Account," with balance-sheet attached), and they need only to be brief, for I have already, and to a great extent, foreshadowed the differences between the latter and form A. I shall, therefore, deal in generalities, and shall be happy to explain verbally any point that may not be quite plain to all.

Form B of account provides for every item, both of income and expenditure, pertaining to the financial year being included therein. It is, therefore, the duty of the Auditor to see that this has been done ; in fact, he could not conscientiously to his clients or to himself, sanction their issuing such an account, which would be both incorrect and misleading.

He should have no difficulty in making them see this

clearly, for in addition to its having the effect of making the income and expenditure account incorrect and misleading, it would have a similar effect upon the balance-sheet, by withholding from it certain outstanding liabilities (or possibly, but not probably, assets), whereas the balance-sheet, as indeed is often printed below its title, is a statement of "liabilities and assets."

I have already indicated in the early part of this lecture how these outstanding items are incorporated in the books,

either by entering them in at date as a liability incurred, or by a subsequent Journal entry on closing the books; and in the same way, other charges for depreciation, &c., &c. As regards depreciation, I rather refer to that on furniture, lease of premises, books and periodicals for sale (then become out of date), &c., for which the amounts are gradually written off, through the income and expenditure, but it just occurs to me to refer to the securities held, and which often form a principal asset. These are generally of a non-fluctuating

## PRO FORMA.

### THE ST. STEPHEN'S FREE HOSPITAL.—31st DECEMBER, 1885.

| Ledger Folio. | Name of Account. | Trial Ledger Balances. Debits. | Expenditure. | Balance Sheet. |
|---|---|---|---|---|
| | | £ s. d. | £ s. d. | £ s. d. |
| | Provisions— | | | |
| 40 | Meat .. .. | 800 9 6 | | |
| 45 | Bread, Flour, &c. | 890 15 0 | 3,130 11 0 | .. .. .. |
| 50 | Milk .. .. | 539 5 0 | | |
| 55-70 | &c. &c. (detail) | 900 1 6 | | |
| 75 | Washing .. .. | 114 2 0 | 114 2 0 | .. .. .. |
| 78 | Lighting & Gas | 121 7 0 | 121 7 0 | .. .. .. |
| 80 | Insurance (6 years) .. | 30 6 0 | 5 1 0 | 25 5 0 |
| 82 | Rates & Taxes | 16 2 0 | 16 2 0 | .. .. .. |
| 84 | Officers' Salaries— Detail .. .. | 502 5 0 | 502 5 0 | .. .. .. |
| 90 | Wages— Detail .. .. | 900 2 0 | 900 2 0 | .. .. .. |
| | Medical and Surgical Expenses .. .. | | | |
| 95 | Instruments and Repairs | 430 2 2 | | |
| 100 | Drugs .. .. | 750 0 2 | 2,000 4 5 | .. .. .. |
| 101-120 | &c. &c. .. .. | 820 3 1 | | |
| 125 | Collector's Poundage .. | 15 0 6 | 15 0 6 | .. .. .. |
| 130 | Sundries— Funerals .. | 50 2 0 | | |
| | Charcoal .. | 20 1 6 | 125 5 0 | .. .. .. |
| | &c. &c. (detail) | 55 1 6 | | |
| 185 | Sundry Debtors for Rent .. | 50 2 6 | .. .. .. .. | 50 2 6 |
| 205 | Hospital and Land, Cost & Fittings.. | 5,400 2 6 | 400 2 6 | 5,000 0 0 |
| 210 | Investments— Detail .. .. | 30,000 0 0 | .. .. .. .. | 30,000 0 0 |
| | Cash— | | | |
| C B 75 | At Bank .. | 370 2 7 | | |
| 215 | In hand (Imprest) .. .. | 20 0 0 | .. .. .. .. | 390 2 7 |
| | | £42,795 12 6 | 7,330 2 5 | 35,465 10 1 |
| 250 | Balance of Income over Expenditure for 1885, carried to Capital Account. Balance Sheet per contra .. | .. .. .. .. | 130 0 1 | .. .. .. |
| | | | £7,460 2 6 | £35,465 10 1 |

| Ledger Folio. | Name of Account. | Trial Ledger Balances. Credits. | Income. | Balance Sheet. |
|---|---|---|---|---|
| | | £ s. d. | £ s. d. | £ s. d. |
| | Subscriptions— | | | |
| 1 | Annual .. .. | 2,000 0 0 | 2,200 0 0 | 200 0 0 |
| 5 | Life .. .. | 400 0 0 | | |
| 10 | Donations .. | 2,100 0 0 | 2,100 0 0 | .. .. |
| 15 | Dividends on Stock— Detail .. .. | 600 0 0 | 600 0 0 | .. .. |
| 18 | Rents from Sundry Tenants | 400 0 0 | 400 0 0 | .. .. |
| 21 | Sermons— Detail .. .. | 349 7 6 | 349 7 6 | .. .. |
| 24 | Grants— Detail .. .. | 750 12 6 | 750 12 6 | .. .. |
| 27 | Legacies— Detail .. .. | 900 0 0 | 900 0 0 | .. .. |
| 30 | Outside Alms Boxes .. Detail—Gold, Silver, Copper .. .. | 54 0 6 | 54 0 6 | .. .. |
| | Produce of Sale— | | | |
| 32 | Kitchen Stuff | 23 2 6 | 45 19 6 | |
| 34 | Rags & Waste Paper.. .. | 22 17 0 | | |
| 36 | St. Katherine's Hospital— Board of Nurses .. .. | 50 0 0 | 50 0 0 | .. .. |
| 38 | Patients'. Payments .. .. | 10 2 6 | 10 2 6 | .. .. |
| | Sundry Creditors— | | | |
| 150-180 | Tradesmen in detail .. .. | 439 17 6 | .. .. | 439 17 6 |
| 200 | Capital Account | 34,695 12 6 | .. .. | 34,695 12 6 |
| | | £42,795 12 6 | 7,460 2 6 | 35,335 10 0 |
| 200 | Capital Account Balance as above .. .. | 34,695 12 6 | | |
| | Excess of Income over Expenditure for 1885, transferred as per contra .. .. | 130 0 1 | .. .. | 130 0 1 |
| | Total Amount of Capital Account at 31st Dec., 1885 .. | £34,825 12 7 | | |
| | | | £7,460 2 6 | £35,465 10 1 |

NOTE.—The details given in the Trial Ledger Balances must also be given, both in the Income and Expenditure Account, and in the Balance Sheet. In cases where Marginal Ledger Folios are given it implies that they apply to other Ledger Accounts, of which the total amount for present purposes is only extended, but these also require detailing in the accounts; the totals of the heads of accounts being extended in the outer column, and details of the sub-heads given in the inner column.

In stating both the Income and Expenditure Account and the Balance Sheet, the figures, as shown above will be reversed; the debits becoming credits and the credits becoming debits.

nature, and cost value can therefore, as a rule, be maintained, but they should be kept at such an averagely low figure as not to get above market value ; and should they do so, to a certain extent, permanently, they should be writtten down ; but this could hardly be called an ordinary item of expenditure, because the Institution is not supposed to speculate, and therefore the depreciation could, I think, fairly be written off direct to the debit of capital account, without passing at all through the income and expenditure account, or affecting its reserve.   Under special cases they might be written up too in the same way, by crediting capital account direct with the enhanced value, which should be kept at such a moderate figure as not likely to have to be again reduced.

I have already referred to the necessity, when the Ledger Trial Balances are taken out, of adjusting what are income and expenditure items, and what are balance-sheet ones ; and, as I have already stated, the Journal must be brought into requisition to effect this.   As a guide to the final result the following *pro forma* sketch may be found useful as apportioning the respective amounts.

The foregoing remarks may, I think, be applied to other annual accounts generally, and not specially referred to herein, for the same principle pervades throughout.

I trust I have made myself clear.   My desire has been to impress you with the fact, that however simple the subject may be, it involves important issues, and that you should be alive to the same, as also to the responsibility attaching thereto.   You may occasionally have difficulties to contend with, but if you efficiently do your duty, conscientiously and fearlessly, without allowing any feeling of self or pique to come in, you cannot fail to succeed in the end.   Respect yourself, and others will respect you also.   A Latin and a French motto occur to me to close with ; they are : " *Suaviter in modo fortiter in re*," *and* " *Noblesse oblige.*"

## MANCHESTER ACCOUNTANTS' STUDENTS' SOCIETY.

### SOME SAFEGUARDS AGAINST FRAUD.

#### By Mr. Henry M. Ashworth, A.C.A.

At the Thirty-fifth Ordinary Meeting of the above Society Mr. Ashworth read the following lecture :—The paper which I have to read to you this evening is on "Some Safeguards Against Fraud," and the title so far as it is restricted to *some* safeguards has been chosen advisedly.

It would not be possible within the limits of a paper of this nature to deal with any but general safeguards. Particular businesses and particular methods of conducting business require, and sometimes have, their own particular checks to guard against misstatements in account, clerical or fraudulent.

The suggestions which I shall have to make in the course of this paper are, then, of a general character, and such as will arise in the transactions of an ordinary house of business.

I may say here, that I do not purpose in the course of this paper to enter at all into the question of frauds, in what we may term the mechanical part of bookkeeping, fraudulent entries, erroneous additions, &c.

The paper will be quite long enough without going into that branch of frauds, and, indeed, I understand that it has already been the subject of a paper read before a students' society, I think, in another town. I have not seen the paper myself, but probably some gentlemen here may have done so.

The most important as it is certainly the most effective safeguard against fraud is that the books of any business concern should be kept in such a way as will admit of their being balanced, that is their mechanical accuracy tested, what by common usage is called double entry. Any method which does not provide for, and require the proof of the clerical work by a balance of the books is not book-keeping, but simply a series of memoranda, depending entirely upon the carefulness and correctness of the clerks for its reliability, and offering to anyone in a position of trust the greatest opportunities for peculation attended by the minimum amount of risk.

With double entry the case is very different, amounts cannot be written off without showing them to the debit of some nominal account, and to drop a balance would simply mean that the books would refuse to be a party to such an irregularity, and would demand the restoration of the missing amount.

There are two species of fraud which we have to provide safeguards against.

It is evident that if one man is defrauding another, the capital or profits of the man who is defrauded are being reduced, but it depends upon the nature of the fraud whether that reduction shows itself as a present one or not.

If the fraud arises say in the passing of invoices for goods which have not been received, or in sending goods out of stock without invoicing, then it is evident that the loss is a present one, and on a stocktaking the stock would be smaller, and consequently the profit less by so much as had been improperly appropriated, if on the other hand the fraud is the common one of collecting accounts, and failing to pay over the whole of the moneys received, making up present short payments out of future collections—lading and teeming as it is somewhat descriptively called, then the loss is not one which would show itself in paper, because the debtors in the balance sheet would be the amount at which they appeared in the books, and not at the amount actually remaining due, and this is why so many of these frauds when discovered are found to have been continued for a long time past, the capital according to the balance sheet not having been affected by them. The difference to the individual engaged in the perpetration of these frauds, between the two kinds is that in the first named each fraud stands so to speak upon its own responsibility, and is independent of any other, whereas in the second case they all form a string and require to be kept going in order to prevent discovery. I do not know a short phrase to define exactly the difference between these two kinds of fraud. The first one might be described as a fraud concluded, and the second as a fraud to be continued. Of course, it does not follow that the loss occasioned by frauds of the first mentioned class should necessarily be a debit to the profit and loss account for the particular period in which they have been effected. The stock or purchases might be manipulated to cover any such portion as it was desirable to uphold as an asset and to deal with in the future.

In considering stocks and purchases I shall have a remark or two as to the prevention of frauds of this character. The foregoing remarks apply of course more particularly to double entry, as already explained the necessity of having to account for all the balances only exists where the accuracy of the books is tested. In what is known as single entry there is not provision for this, and consequently balances can be passed over, entries of cash made in the ledger to square accounts, and indeed any vagaries which the fancy of the operator may lead him to, with only the risk of their being accidentally discovered, not as in double entry the knowledge that in the inevitable nature of things the entries must come to light.

In relation to purchases we have to be satisfied upon three points.

1. That we get the right quantity of goods.

2. That we pay the right price for them.

3. That we don't pay for them more than once.

Goods as they are received should be entered in a book called perhaps the "Goods Inwards Book." The entry into the stock book, if one be kept, should be made from here.

Stock books are not kept so frequently as they ought to be and might be. We frequently come across cases where the keeping of a stock book to check and agree with the actual stock would be a matter of no difficulty and very great satisfaction, but the book is not kept and the usual stocktaking is relied upon sometimes with considerable doubt as to its correctness. The goods having been debited to the stock from the Goods Inwards Book, the invoice received along with the goods should be passed and initialled by the buyer, and if he adopt the invariable plan of putting his pen through the entry in the Goods Inwards Book or on the face of it, making some distinct mark when he passes the invoice he will protect himself against the probability of passing an invoice twice over for the same goods. The price of the goods of course he should also check by reference to his Order Book.

The invoice having been passed by the purchasing department, then passes to the counting house for payment. Here the invoice is examined to see that the calculations are correct, and that it bears the initial of the buyer certifying the correctness of the quantities, it is then passed through the invoice or purchase book and gets finally to the credit of the seller. The possibility of an invoice being passed and paid twice is so great, that I prefer to have some check against it in the counting house as well as in the department. I am convinced that mistakes in this particular occur a very great deal oftener than is generally believed. There are so many ways in which it may happen, and correctness is dependent to such a large extent upon the carefulness of the clerks through whose hands the invoices pass. I have seen a corrected invoice pasted side by side with the invoice it was intended to correct and both carried out into the money column and posted to the credit of a personal account, a duplicate invoice presumably obtained in place of the original supposed to be lost, sometimes turns up in the same way. A quarterly account say will have the same item for the beginning of the one account as appeared at the end of the previous account. Of course, these mistakes should not occur, but there is no prevention except carefulness, and no cure except accidental discovery, or by some system of ready reference between the invoices of the same creditor.

The plan which theoretically I like the best, and which under some circumstances would work very well, is to keep the invoices of one creditor all together; either keep them in covers, or cases, attaching each fresh invoice as it is passed and entered through the invoice analysis book, or keep them in a guard book reserving one page for each account, the invoices would then follow each other in sequence, and if any item appeared a second time it would be at once discovered, one advantage of keeping the invoices in this latter way would be that each account would form its own personal account, if needful, and the cash and discount might be posted to a debit column, rendering ledger personal accounts unnecessary.

If it should be preferred to keep the invoices upon the more general plan, and to paste them into a guard book in the order of date, the best safeguard against the passing of an invoice, or portion of an invoice twice over, is to have each invoice numbered, and to have an index giving the name of the creditor, and the numbers of his invoices; when the invoice of any creditor is being pasted into the guard book, the index will refer to the previous number or numbers, and the invoices may be referred to, this plan is dependent for its value upon the care with which the index is kept, but it can be checked by comparing it from time to time, with the entries to the credit of the personal account in the ledger. When postings are made direct from the guard book to the ledger account, the reference might be made to the previous invoices by the folios or numbers, appearing in the ledger, but even in this case, I think the index will be found to be more satisfactory and work better. For one reason the invoice will be examined before it is allowed to go into the guard book, and if found to be wrong will be put aside, but if the ledger folio be relied upon to show the reference to previous invoices, the invoice under examination will be in the guard book, or invoice book, and we all know that a mistake which has passed its initial stage unchallenged very frequently goes forward with an air of perfect *bona fides* to the end.

I have dealt at some length with this question of invoices because of its great importance, and of the fact that it allows of an attempt at fraud, which looks very like a mistake if discovered, and can be so explained, and if not discovered, is an actual present gain, not involving "lading and teeming" or having to be provided for, at some future time.

The scope of this paper is rather to show how frauds may be prevented than how they may be effected. I remember a case which happened some time ago in illustration of the danger of a loose method of passing invoices. A clerk being in position to do so was in the habit of passing duplicate invoices, and then after payment of both had been made, used to call upon the person to explain that by an oversight, a certain invoice had been passed twice over, and ask for a return of the amount improperly paid which of course he did not account for to his employers.

More than that it is especially dangerous, because as before explained the full amount appropriated by this means need not be a charge against the profit and loss account for the half year or year as the case may be, which might arouse suspicion and enquiry, but can be spread over as long a period as desirable, by increasing the stock, or by keeping back invoices for goods which have passed into stock.

The precautions against this are to have the stock books compared as to quantities with the day books, to see that all the goods represented as leaving stock, have been charged to somebody, and that all goods so charged are deducted from the book stock, and also that the goods entered to the debit of the stock, are all represented by invoices, which are passed for payment, and that the stock is debited with all goods invoiced, this should be done by some one outside the department, because, of course, its value as a check, if done by the staff, it is intended to check, will be nil. Great care should be exercised to see that invoices are passed for all goods received immediately previous to stock-taking, and included therein, this may be done by tracing the goods received by means of the Goods Inward Book for what is considered a sufficient period before the stock-taking, and seeing that invoices have been passed for each lot. Apart from the opportunity that the possible manipulation of stock and invoices, gives for an actual fraud, it very frequently affords an opportunity for what is almost a fraud, that is misrepresentation on the part of the head of a department in making his return of his trading, the temptation to benefit the closing period in the hope that the future will adjust it is often too great for an anxious buyer to resist, and the means of doing it are so simple, and yet ordinarily so difficult to prove, say a fortnight afterwards when the stock has undergone changes, that in a large number of cases it is not discovered.

In relation to sales, or goods sent out, we require to be satisfied upon three points :—

1st. That the full quantities of goods sent out are invoiced.

2nd. That the price is correct.

3rd. That the goods get into account and are paid for.

The ordinary method and the safest one from a book-keeping point of view, where there is more than one department, is for each department to keep a separate rough day book of its own. This book is frequently made with the thin paper tissue, alternately with the ordinary paper, so that by the use of the stencil and carbon paper, a copy of the details of the sale may be sent into the counting house, to be incorporated with the other slips, (if any), from other departments, to form the invoice. The entry in the day book is made in the counting house, the departmental rough day books should be examined to see that they agree both as to quantities and amounts with the general day book. The stock books should be credited with the quantities appearing in the rough day books, so that every precaution may be taken that all that is removed out of stock is duly invoiced. The details of the invoice being separately calculated by the department, and by the counting house, there is little chance of any mistake in extensions.

Delivery notes should accompany all goods and the counterfoil should bear the signature of the person receiving them, whether carter, carrier, messenger, or principal. If the parcel of goods be composed of purchases from more than one department, then the departmental notes should be fastened together, and a reference made upon them, to the delivery note, the idea being to connect the entries in the stock books, with an actual delivery of those goods to some person. I have known a case of fraud which would have been detected at the outset, if this had been done.

In the rendering of statements there are several important safeguards against fraud, which but for these precautions, might take place. Statements should be sent direct to the customer by post, or delivered, it does not matter which, but it is better that they should not be delivered by the person who is afterwards to collect the account, nor speaking theoretically, should the person who is to collect the account prepare the statement. To send statements to travellers for them to deliver to their customers is bad, to accompany the statements as prepared in the counting house, and this is frequently done, by a number of blank statement forms in case of any alteration being required, is worse.

Many a fraud has been discovered by the accident of sending a statement direct to a customer, which in the ordinary course of things, would have been handed to the traveller, or collector, and by him, of course, altered in accordance with his own private information, and many a fraud, and series of frauds, have remained, for what has afterwards seemed an incredibly long time undiscovered, simply because the traveller or collector, has always managed cleverly to stand between the bookkeeping and the customer.

Whenever the travellers collect an account the receipt thereof should always be confirmed by the house immediately on receipt of his cash sheet, and notice that it will always be done should be printed on the face of the invoices and statements, so that customers may expect to receive the advice, of course, the advice may be by postcard.

There is a plan, which I think, is calculated to prevent, or to make an early discovery of frauds of this nature, and that is for firms to issue a short printed circular to all their customers, at stated times, informing the debtor that the balance due from him according to their books, on such a day, say the 31st. December, was so much. As this circular, to be of value, should be sent to everybody who is a debtor on the date of its issue, even to one to whom the goods were supplied only the day previous, it is necessary to add that the notice is not a request for payment, but merely sent out in accordance with their usual custom, and that if any difference appears between the debtor's account, and the amount in the circular, they would be glad to have immediate notice thereof. This plan is especially valuable where there are a great number of small accounts, and also in those cases where for any sufficient reason it is considered indispensable to send the statement through the hands of a traveller, or collector. Some banks adopt the same plan with regard to their customers, sending out a circular at the end of the year, intimating that the balance was so much, to the debtor or creditor as may be. Building and other societies do it with loan holders, by giving initials and amounts. Limited companies and others, also with their loan holders, should do something of the kind, and it would be well if the custom were established and recognised, so that investors would expect to receive the circular, and would enquire about it, in any case where it was not received. These circulars, of course, ought to be sent out in the case of limited companies, under the direct supervision of the auditors, and in case of private firms, under the supervision of the principals, or of the auditors, otherwise their value is very considerably reduced. After each settlement up to a point with a customer, the bookkeeper should be careful to see that the account in his ledgers is square up to that point, that the last item or items, represent the balance remaining due, and that there is no legacy of a difference unadjusted, carried forward from some time, often many months before. He should see that the items which are due have been included in the settlement, and that the items remaining unpaid, are not due, or that there is some reason for their being unpaid.

I remember, some time ago, a case bearing upon this point ; a collector had been lading and teeming, and had carried it on for some time, success having made him careless, he, in squaring up an account to a point, the money represented, which he had of course received some time previously, paid items say two, three, and four, but overlooked that item No. 1 was not paid. Communication with the customers, on what was taken to be merely an oversight, elicited the fact, that they had paid not only items one to four, but items five to eight as well, so that although it may not be one of the principal safeguards, in fact, used as a check against a man who is careful, of every point, may not come to anything at all, still it is worth bearing in mind, if it does nothing else, it certainly keeps the knowledge of the state of customers' accounts alive. Everyone having charge of the books of a business ought to keep close watch upon the book debts, and see that they do not get in arrear without proper reason. Whenever a sale is made, the date when payment is due is known, and under that date in a diary or some book which can be used in the same way, and used for this purpose solely, then should appear the name of the customer, and the amount of his debt. Then if the day passes, and the debt be not paid, there is a reminder of the fact in the diary, and further application or pressure can be used. Moreover apart from its usefulness as a safeguard against amounts being received and not accounted for, it is frequently valuable for financial purposes, because in every business it is occasionally necessary to be able to estimate how much money, &c., ought to be collected by a certain day.

As a safeguard against fraud the plan of giving collectors a small receipt form to be gummed into the invoice or statement is worthy of mention, it has this advantage, that the receipts being in book form each with its counterfoil, whenever a receipt is given the counterfoil must be filled up, and if a receipt were used improperly it would be necessary to invent some entry for the counterfoil at obviously considerable danger, as the counterfoil in the receipt book will supply the details for the entry to the debit of the cash book. The small receipts of which I am now speaking have a fault to my mind, at least all that I have seen have, they are too small, and they are mostly coloured a deep red, which renders the writing upon the face of them almost unreadable, of course, there should be something distinctive about them, but that may be in design, and need not necessarily be in colour, or have the effect complained of.

Now, as to one very important safeguard against fraud— that is the treatment of cash received and paid. At the outset to my mind all moneys received from any and every source, ought to be paid to the bank. I would make this a hard and fast rule, and if the practice were general, it would simplify account keeping, and especially the onerous and responsible duties of the cashier to a very large extent. Moreover, it would have this advantage, no money could then remain in hand to lose its identity, and every sum would be capable of being ear-marked. To be guilty of something

like a paradox, a cashier should be a man who does not keep the cash. Collectors might often pay their receipts direct into the bank, and simply produce to the cashier a statement of his receipts verified by his collecting book, or his counterfoil receipt book. In the case of corporations this is frequently done, each collector pays the money received by him over to the bank, and informs the treasurer how much he has paid, and on what account. It is not of any very great importance whether the receipts of, say a house in the Manchester trade, pass through the hands of the cashier or not, provided that they do get to the bank eventually. I should like to see receipts and payments made more of a distinct and separate matter even to the extent of keeping the record of them in separate books.

Receipts and payments are two entirely different transactions, and need not appear in the same book any more than we would show purchases and sales in one book, debiting the stock account with purchases and crediting it with sales. The analogy is complete. We receive money and we receive goods, the money or goods requires to be put to the credit of somebody's account, and goes to the debit of stock, stock in the case of money being the banker, we pay money as we sell goods, and that goes to the debit of an account, and to the credit of the banker. This means, of course, that all moneys received go to the banker, and all moneys paid come from the banker, that is my principle.

Cash receipts and payments are now usually kept in the one book, but that is because there is nearly always a balance in hand, but in a large concern I should think the balance of convenience would be on the side of having a debit cash book, and a credit cash book. Let us see how this would work. We have a cash book for receipts ; on the left hand side, there is the column for date, name, ledger, folio, discounts, allowances (if there is a column needed), net amount received, and then a total column for the payment into the bank. The items comprising the bank debit will follow each other in the net amounts column, and will simply require a line to be ruled under the last item, and the amount extended. There is then the right hand page which can either be used in the same way, or as it frequently happens that there are several sales ledgers in a large business it can be used for the purpose of analysing the cash and discounts amongst the different ledgers so as to balance each ledger separately ; or again it is frequently desirable in cases where two or more businesses are carried on under one system of Bookkeeping, to have a ready method of calculating the interest to be debited to each business upon the capital employed by it, and the interest calculations upon the amounts received on account of the different businesses may be shown in the cash book in the same way that bankers do, for the payments of course, a credit cash book will be required on the same principle as the debit cash book except that the details column will not be wanted, because separate cheques are drawn for each payment. All payments except petty cash payments should be by cheque to order unless they are crossed for the credit of the payee. Cheques to bearer, and coin should never be paid in respect of business accounts. Cheques for wages, &c., should be drawn for the precise amount, if it can be ascertained, and if it cannot, the balance remaining over should be returned and credited to wages account.

Bankers usually caution their customers by notice printed inside the pass book, or outside the cheque book to keep the cheques in a safe place, and not to give away a blank cheque, both being necessary precautions. The plan of writing on the face of the cheque a maximum amount as under £10, under £60, &c., is also good. To guard against blank cheques being taken for improper uses, principals signing cheques should initial the corner of the counterfoil, then in case any cheque should be spoiled in the preparation it will be shown to him and cancelled.

For small general expenses, which have to be paid in cash, provision can be made by letting a sum of say £10, £20, or

£50, whatever is found to be required, remain in hand, to the debit of sundry expenses or petty cash account, then once a week or month, let the account be made up showing how much has been spent, and draw a cheque for that sum, thus making the sum in hand up to the original £10, £20, or £50. Out of this sum, if any exceptional circumstances arise, of course payment of such business accounts might be made, but the advantage of making all payments by cheque has only to become known to make the practice much more general than it is now. The tendency, too, is for firms in business, even in a small way, to keep a banker's account, and although some years ago it was different, we hardly ever hear now the application for cash on the ground of not being able to use a cheque.

If the cashier is allowed in any case to keep money in hand more than is sufficient for general current expenses, he should keep a daily record of how the balance appearing according to the cash book is comprised, and it is a good plan, too, in order to square his accounts at the end of the year, or whenever a stocktaking is made and a balance-sheet prepared, to pay into the bank on that day the whole of the cash in hand so as to leave his cash book perfectly clean.

In making payments out of petty cash, care should be taken to guard against paying an item twice over. This would arise, say if the amount were entered through the invoice book to the credit of a personal account in the ordinary way, and if the same item were paid out of petty cash and charged direct to the nominal account.

I mention this because I have known it happen in cases where the petty cash account or general expenses account was allowed to include somewhat heavy items.

I saw, some time ago, a letter in one of the Manchester papers, the *City News* I think, suggesting, having regard to the number of frauds which had been brought to light just about that time, that the system of payment through bankers should be introduced, that is, that each firm should announce the name of its bankers, and that payments should be made to the bankers for credit of the payee. The idea is a good one, so far as it goes, though I doubt if it is likely to be adopted generally. It is, perhaps, a little bit cumbersome, and saddles the firm paying the money with the trouble of protecting, not itself, but the firm to whom the money is owing. I don't think it has been tried, but it seems to me that there might be a plan of payment by transfer, which would be even better than the method of paying through bankers, something on the principle of the clearing house. This would not render it necessary for the firm to announce the name of its bankers, but merely to print on its stationery a number by which it would be known at the transfer office, in the same way that they now print the telephone number. In that case a number of firms, being members of this circle, would send to each other, i.e., the creditors would send to the debtors a statement of accounts due for payment by a certain date. The debtor, finding this to be correct, would advise the creditor that he had so found it, and, having in his hands by the day fixed for payment, a certain number of accounts which he had to pay, and a certain number of other accounts which he had to receive, which would by this time have been acknowledged by the debtors as correct, would simply pay into the transfer office by cheque, on his own bankers, the amount of the difference between those two, or, if the debts due to him were in excess of the amount to be received by him, he would pass through his bankers a draft on the transfer office for the difference.

I have now gone over at somewhat greater length than I originally intended some of the principal safeguards that men in business can use to prevent frauds of which, some times, we seem to have quite an epidemic. I quite believe that these frauds in ninety per cent. of the cases are the result of loose bookkeeping, or of having failed to take advantage of the most obvious means of checking the accounts of the defaulters.

If I had to give an opinion as to what was the greatest safeguard against fraud, I should say balance your books, and the next greatest is to have them regularly examined by a competent professional man. If this were done then the species of fraud which is effected by means of fraudulent entries and erroneous additions, debits with no credits, and credits with no corresponding debit, would be either entirely impossible, or attended with such difficulty as to be practically prevented. Moreover, the accountant moves in a mysterious way, and the fact of the books undergoing an examination of which the bookkeeper does not know the full extent, or depth, has often no doubt a deterrent effect. An accountant by reason of his acquaintance with many forms of books and knowledge of the requirements of special businesses, is able, not merely to point out the best and safest way of keeping the accounts of a business, but also to detect the weak place, and opportunities for fraud, in the method of keeping books, which he may be called in to examine ; and in all cases his first recommendation should be that the system of balancing be introduced, if the books are not so kept already. I think the danger of dealing, in the way of examination, with books not kept so as to balance, is so great, that I would refuse (but here I speak with deference in the presence of accountants) in practice to certify any accounts unless the clerical correctness thereof was proved.

It is not, of course, possible for either double entry or auditors, or both, to prevent frauds of all kinds, if a servant receive a cheque, and having got the proceeds, takes the first train to London, and thence anywhere he can get to, no bookkeeping of any kind can touch a fraud like this. But still accounts well kept and balanced and properly audited will supply the most effective check that can be devised, against continuous or systematic frauds. It is much more general now than formerly for commercial houses to have their books regularly audited by accountants and the practice is, I believe, steadily growing.

I am afraid that my paper has been rather long, it is certainly longer than I meant it to be, but I hope that some portions of it may have been of interest, and may be useful to the younger members of your society.

A vote of thanks to the lecturer, proposed by Mr. Guthrie, seconded by Mr. Boardman, and supported by Mr. Henry Lunt and Mr. Pollitt was heartily accorded.

A general discussion then ensued in which, besides the gentlemen named above, Messrs. Grierson, Abbott, Brewis, Walkden, R. M. Mather, C. R. Wainwright, and the President took part.

Mr. ASHWORTH acknowledged the vote of thanks, replied to various points raised in the discussion, and a very satisfactory meeting closed about 8 p.m. with the usual compliment to the Chairman.

## Letters to the Editor.

#### ACCOUNTANTS' CERTIFICATES.

*To the Editor of The Accountant.*

SIR,— Looking to the great importance of the above subject at the present time, it is to be hoped that the Council of the Institute will take this question into their serious consideration, with the view of endeavouring to remedy the abuses which often arise in connection with the formation of Limited Companies.

Trading Companies are now frequently brought before the public simply on the faith of the Accountants' Certificate, and unless some prompt measures are taken, it seems likely that the way in which these certificates are sometimes given, will have as bad an effect on the profession generally as the abuses which used to occur under the Bankruptcy Act of 1869.

I am, Sir,

Your obedient Servant,

WILLIAM HENRY FOX.

AUSTIN FRIARS, LONDON.

*14th July,* 1887.

## " THE AUDIT AUCTION."

The trick resorted to by ostriches when closely pressed by their pursuers, of burying their heads in the sand, apparently under the impression that by shutting their own eyes no one can see them, has amused generations of schoolboys. But there are some " children of a larger growth " who, forgetful of lessons the moral of which is patent to boys, think that the vain artifice of the ostrich may be successfully tried in actual business, and in regard to business affairs. In another part of our columns will be found extracts from the newspaper reports of the meeting of a certain public company, the heading of which, as of these remarks, is borrowed from a leading financial organ of the city. We will do our contemporary the justice to say that its heading, if sarcastic, is a perfectly true description of the proceedings. It would be affectation more contemptible than the stupidity of the ostrich, for chartered accountants to pretend for a moment that the " auction " in question is not very damaging to professional accountants. It has been publicly commented on. It would be only bare justice to other members of the Institute if Mr. T. W. READ, F.C.A., and Messrs. KELLAS, JOHNSTONE & NASMYTH, at once made any explanation they have to offer in extenuation of the fact that, in the absence of contradiction, their names, and the credit of the body to which they belong, have been dragged in the mire in this fashion? In business affairs we do not believe in hair-splitting or logic-chopping. A man must live, and he is worse than an infidel if he does not work for himself and those who rely on him ; and to lay down fine rules for conduct in all the varying circumstances of business, is beyond the editor of a journal or any other man. But looking at things broadly, taking a not too narrow view of business and the method in which it should be conducted, the effect of a perusal of the report in question must be to create disgust not in the minds of accountants *solely*—that is the smallest item for consideration—but in the minds of business men, who must think that if one chartered accountant asks £100 for what another says he will do for £40, one of the pair must be a peculiar individual ; and when later on the man who originally asked £100 is willing to take £40, the peculiarity gets more marked. We are aware that the shareholders who proposed the respective auditors may not have had express authority. But silence gives consent. We are not aware that either accountant has disavowed the discreditable business, and the language of the shareholders in question, does not sound like the language of unauthorised, or uninspired agents.

Mr. ANYON is not a chartered accountant. Mr. ANYON *ignores* the Institute of Chartered Accountants. Having regard to his compact and concise way of saying what he has to say, it is amazing to read that some of those present told him in effect and roundly, not to waste their time with his fanfaronade. Really, we might overlook the execrable result of the company's trading operations, but this latter incident fills us with foreboding as to the future of this promising concern.

## "AUDITED AND FOUND CORRECT."

The following correspondence on Auditors' Certificates has recently been addressed to a contemporary. Considerations of space obliges us to defer comment until a subsequent issue :—

SIR,—Can you tell me how far shareholders and investors can rely upon the above words when attached to the accounts of a public company ?

I have before me the balance-sheet of————Limited, " for the year ending September 30. 1887 " (I presume the document is meant to be the balance-sheet at September 30, 1887), which is as follows :—

Dr.                 *Capital and Liabilities.*

Nominal capital of the company—30,000
  shares of £10 each.....................£300,000  0  0

To subscribed capital :—
  30,000 shares at £7 per share paid.........£210,000  0  0
  Preference stock..........£100,000  0  0
  Interest thereon to date ..    1,780 17  0
                                            ————————  101,780 17  0

Calls received in advance
  on ordinary shares......  £6,750  0  0
  Interest thereon to date ..    94  6  4
                                            ————————  6,844  6  4

Mortgage debentures  ....  £91,600  0  0
  Interest thereon to date ..   761 17  7
                                            ————————  92,361 17  7

————————mortgage ac-
  count ................  £7,000  0  0
  Interest thereon to date ..   140  0  0
                                            ————————  7,140  0  0

Special reserve fund :—
  Securities at market price of September
   30, 1887 ........................  14,094 15  4
Reserve fund .........................  10,000  0  0
Sundry creditors .....................  28,497  7  7
Profit and loss account :—
  Balance after making
   provision for bad and
   doubtful debts  ......  £19,481 19  9
  Balance brought forward
   from last year........   148 13 10
                                            ————————  £19,630 13  7
                                                      _____
                                                      £490,349 17  5

Cr.                 *Property and Assets.*
By land, buildings, machinery,
  fixtures, tools, &c., as per
  Mr.————————valua-
  tion  at  September 30,
  1887 ..................£185,150  5  5
Stock of worked and un-
  worked materials as per
  Mr.————————valua-
  tion  at  September  30,
  1887 ..................  141,607  1  4

Farm  stock,  as  per  Mr.
  ————— —————valua-
  tion at September 30, 1887   1,178  1  0
                                            ————————  £327,935  7  9
Trustees of special reserve fund—amount at
  September 30, 1887....................  14,094 15  4
Sundry debtors  .........................  143,591 18 11
Cash and bills in hand ..................  4,727 15  5
                                                      _____
                                                      £490,349 17  5

Now, on the face of this balance-sheet, which is certified by Mr.————(chartered accountant) as having been "audited and found correct," the net profit on the year's trading appears to be £19,481 19s. 9d., which on the paid up capital of £210,000 is equivalent to a dividend of over 9¼ per cent—a very fair return on the trading. Attached to the balance-sheet there is, however, a statement bearing the mysterious heading of " Appropriation of Profit Account," from which it appears that the said profit of £19,481 19s 9d. is subject to the following deductions, viz :—

|  | £ | s. | d. |
|---|---|---|---|
| Interest paid on Preference Stock, debentures &c.................................... | 8,619 | 16 | 5 |
| Interest credited on Preference Stock, &c., at 30th September, 1887................... | 1,780 | 17 | 0 |
| Interest credited on calls paid in advance, 30th September, 1887..................... | 94 | 6 | 4 |
| Interest credited on debentures at 30th September, 1887 ....................... | 761 | 17 | 7 |
| Interest credited on———— ————mortgage at 30th September, 1887 .............. | 140 | 0 | 0 |
|  | £11,396 | 17 | 4 |

This makes the actual net profit for the year £8,085 2s. 5d. instead of the £19,481 19s, 9d. shown in the balance sheet. But this is not all ; for from the year's profit an interim dividend was paid to the shareholders on June 14, 1887, amounting to £5 250, thus the unappropriated profit from the year's trading was at the date of the balance-sheet £2,835 2s. 5d., which, together with £148 13s. 10d. carried forward from the previous year, made £2,983 16s. 3d. to the credit of profit and loss account at September 30, 1887, and this surely should have stood in the published balance-sheet, instead of £19,630 13s. 7d. shown therein.

Taking this view, and seeing that the interest and interim dividend had already been paid or provided for in the accounts, I cannot understand how the asset side of the balance-sheet, and the liabilities plus the profit remaining on September 30, 1887, can be made to balance. To me, as an outsider, it looks as if the assets had been overstated to the extent of £16,646 17s. 4d., or the liabilities understated to the same amount.

Unless you, Mr. Editor, can throw some light upon the matter, the shareholders should at once call upon the auditor to explain by what process the accounts were " found correct."

Undoubtedly, the shareholders have great cause of complaint against the auditor for appending his certificate to a balance-sheet so meagre and misleading. Some excuse may be made for the absence of a trading and profit and loss accounts, but in addition to the points which I have already raised, the directors and auditor should be asked to explain : (1) Why is the contingent liability on bills receivable under discount not shown in the balance sheet ? (2) Where is the reserve for bad and doubtful debts shown in the balance sheet ? (3) Of the item sundry creditors, what proportion represents cash, and what proportion represents trade accounts ? (4) Does the item, sundry debtors, include consignments to agents and others ; if so, at what price have these consignments been taken ? I think there ought to have been a special entry for " Stock consigned to agents and others taken at cost price ;" because, if taken at selling price, the company takes credit for a profit not yet earned. (5) Has the auditor verified the existence and valuation of the reserve fund investments ? No mention of this is made in his certificate or report. (6)

Does the wording of the auditor's certificate and report meet the requirements of the articles of association? Without this information before them, the shareholders cannot possibly know the position of the company, nor the value of their property, and upon this depends the justification of the directors in paying the dividend in December last, even small as it was, and though the accounts had been "audited and found correct" by a chartered accountant—I am, sir, yours, &c., 　　　　　　　　　　　　　　　　　　　T. P.

---

Sir,—Your correspondent, " T. P." in his strictures, in your issue of February 25th last, on———————— Limited, balance-sheet is rather hypercritical. What substantial difference can there be between saying "balance-sheet for the year ending September 30. 1887," and " the balance-sheet at September 30, 1887." The balance-sheet which he criticises does not show, as he states, the net profit as £19,481 19s. 9d., but shows that sum as the balance of the profit and loss account, which sum is afterwards, in the appropriation of profit account, reduced by the payment of interest to a net profit. The balance-sheet and appropriation of profit account should be read as one statement, the first part showing the profit made before interest is deducted, and the second showing the net profit after interest is charged. It is easy to make a muddle of anything if a person only takes half a statement for his purpose and overlooks the other half. The net result, as shown in the balance-sheet, at the foot of which is my signature, is perfectly correct.

Any extension of the balance-sheet cannot be objectionable to an auditor; but it is not always wise to expose the inner working of a business to competitors' eyes. The plan followed has been upheld by the shareholders when the subject has been mentioned at the general meetings.

The special reserve fund is in the hands of trustees, who are responsible parties, and who can refuse the auditor, if they please, access to any examination of the securities; but these securities are seen by me each year. I suppose Mr. " T. P." will be inclined to censure me in this case for exceeding my duty.

Your correspondent may, however, take my assurance that all the points suggested by him have had the fullest consideration in the preparation of the balance-sheet, and I have no doubt that he would be quite satisfied with the extent to which his suggestions have by anticipation been met, his views being shared by the board of directors to perhaps a fuller extent than in most cases.

If your correspondent be a shareholder he had no need to ask the question: Does the wording of the auditors' certificate meet the requirements of the articles of association? A reference to his copy of the articles would have shown him that the certificate met the requirements of the articles.

The term " audited and found correct " may be relied on where the accounts are so signed by a respectable accountant.—I am, Sir, yours, &c.,

Auditors' Certificates. THE correspondence taken from the columns of a contemporary, which we reprinted in our last, will do more than half-a-dozen discussions towards the solution of the question of auditors' certificates. " Audited and found correct," is evidently not satisfactory to many of the public, and seems peculiarly open to criticism. Mr. WELTON once stated, that he thought certificates should be put in a narrative form, stating concisely what the extent of the audit had been, thus enabling shareholders to form their own opinion as to whether the audit was sufficient, or whether it should be made more stringent and exhaustive. This seems the best policy to pursue, and the practice of making certificates more specific will, it is hoped, increase. It seems necessary to repeat a warning previously given in these columns. The Institute as such, should not, we conceive, take upon itself, as it has been urged it should do, the serious responsibility of settling " what would constitute a thorough audit of every class of company," and of permitting, much less encouraging, members to word their certificate "audited in accordance with the form prescribed by the Institute of Chartered Accountants." But what would be most impolitic and unwise for the Institute as such, to do, may be laudable in its members in their private capacities to effect ; and it is in this way that the present unsatisfactory state of the matter can be remedied.

———

# THE
# INSTITUTE OF CHARTERED ACCOUN-
# TANTS IN ENGLAND & WALES.

## THE AUTUMNAL MEETING.

The second Provincial Autumnal Meeting of the Institute was held at Birmingham, on the 18th, 19th, and 20th insts., with a very good attendance of members from all parts of the United Kingdom. The success of the meeting will be best gathered by a perusal of the following report, a part of which, owing to its great length, we are compelled to hold over until our next issue.

### THE RECEPTION.

Mr. WALTER N. FISHER, F.C.A., the President of the Local Society, opened the proceedings, he said :—Gentlemen, I am very sorry to have to open our business with two apologies—the one the absence of our Mayor, Alderman POLLACK, who, unfortunately, is detained in London until the middle of the day ; but his Worship has promised to be with us this afternoon in time to dine with the members of the Institute to-night. In the absence of the Mayor, I have much pleasure in introducing to you this morning the Mayor-Elect, Mr. Alderman BARROW (applause), who has been good enough to take the Mayor's place, and to welcome the Institute to Birmingham. (Cheers.) My second apology is on behalf of our esteemed President, Mr. DELOITTE, who, I regret to say, is absent in consequence of indisposition. I am also equally pleased to mention that our President has sent down his address, which will be read to you by the Vice-President, Mr. SAFFERY, who will preside at these meetings in the place of Mr. DELOITTE. I have very much pleasure, therefore, in introducing to the members, Mr. Alderman BARROW, Mayor-Elect. (Applause.)

Mr. ALDERMAN BARROW (who was received with cheers) said : Gentlemen, I am very sorry that the Mayor is not here to-day, because I am sure he would have given an abler, but not a more cordial, welcome than I do to this Institute. We must all feel the very important position which the Chartered Accountants of this country occupy with regard to the commercial classes, and to the community in general. I think we all welcomed the foundation of your Institute, and I think your Institute has done wisely by putting what we should call in Birmingham the "Hall Mark" on those who have the ability and can be relied upon to conduct the very delicate responsibilities which your profession so well and ably conduct. It may be asked why there should be any public recognition of a body like this, which may be regarded as a professional body ? But the fact is you are engaged in this conference in promoting good public work. (Applause.) I thought some years ago when the condition of commercial affairs was very unfavourable, and when great numbers of concerns were going into liquidation, that it was the time of harvest for chartered accountants. (Laughter.) I remember expressing that opinion to one of the first accountants in Birmingham, but I was soon convinced that bad times and small profits were certainly not favourable to chartered accountants (applause), for it is very hard in bad times, and with unprosperous balance sheets to get full fees from clients. In fact, the prosperity of the country is as necessary in the interests of accountants as of anyone else. A chief reason why you are welcomed here is that you are going to discuss matters concerning the prosperity of the commercial classes, and of the country generally, and I think there is no other body in the country that can do that so ably as you can. I see that in Manchester two years ago you discussed the question of Corporation Accounts. I have read the Paper, and the discussion upon it, and I believe that we have followed out in Birmingham nearly all the recommendations of that paper; and you will find in our very elaborate Blue Book that all the statistics deemed desirable are therein recorded. (Applause.) I may say, on behalf of the Corporation, that we shall be very glad to present copies of this Blue Book that all the statistics deemed desirable are (Hear, hear.) I believe you will find it a model of accounts; but at the same time we, in Birmingham, are always open to criticism, and we shall be very glad if the Institute of Chartered Accountants can give us advice how they can even be kept much better than they have been. But there is one subject which, it seems to me, is even of more vital importance than that of Corporation Accounts, which you are going to discuss, and that is the Companies' Acts—the Acts relating to Joint Stock and Limited Liability Companies. I was rather disappointed when I saw the programme of these meetings to think that the subject was not going to be discussed. I am glad it is, for it is one of the most difficult problems of the present time, and there is no body of men so capable of discussing this matter as you are. You have many of you been behind the scenes, and you will be able to advise the Legislature what alterations should be made in the law to prevent the immense loss arising to the public through companies being improperly formed. I suppose the loss to the public in respect of bubble companies has been something enormous. I do not know that I have seen the statistics, but it must have amounted, I should say, to many hundred millions, and one feels that it is not only the shareholders who have suffered by the formation of those companies, but the commercial interest of the whole community has also suffered. These companies have brought a class of competition to bear which has been very unfortunate for other concerns, and I say it is not only shareholders, but, it seems to me, the creditors also suffer by the present law—the law that gives the power, I was going to say, to those companies to deceive their creditors by making a show of assets which really have no existence. Well, I am sure you will be able to show the Government what guarantees ought to be enacted to prevent the formation of bubble companies, and also the very false and misleading statements which are made in the formation of many Joint Stock Limited Companies. I have no doubt you can tell us many unblushing frauds which have been perpetrated by the formation of these companies, and I may say, on behalf of the Mayor, that we very cordially welcome you to Birmingham, and if there are any prominent institutions you would be glad to see we shall be happy in every way to facilitate your doing so. I say this because we feel this Conference is of public interest, and for the public benefit, and therefore the Mayor of Birmingham bids me cordially welcome you to Birmingham, and into our Council House. (Loud cheers.)

Mr. FISHER: Gentlemen, it is my pleasing duty, as President of the local Society, to propose "that the best thanks of this meeting be given to Mr. Alderman Barrow, the Mayor Elect, for his courteous and kind reception of the members of our Institute," and I am sure you will agree with me that this resolution is one richly deserved. Mr. Alderman Barrow, a worthy citizen, and a highly respected member of our Town Council, has taken great interest in our profession, and the address which he has just given us, I think you will

agree with me, is both interesting and at the same time exceptionally kind; because it places before us, as the Chartered Accountants of England and Wales, what a lay Alderman may think in regard to some of the duties of our profession. I have very much pleasure, therefore, in moving the vote of thanks I have read and will call on Mr. Waterhouse to second it. (Applause.)

Mr. E. WATERHOUSE: I have much pleasure in seconding the resolution which has been proposed by Mr. Fisher. I think we all ought to be very grateful to the great public officers of such a huge Corporation as Birmingham for their kind reception on such an occasion. We ought, I think, also to be especially thankful to Alderman Barrow for the very kind and encouraging words he has addressed to us in his opening remarks. I beg, therefore, to second the proposition. (Applause.)

The resolution was then put, and carried by acclamation.

Mr. ALDERMAN BARROW: I am very much obliged to you, gentlemen, for thanking me for the very small duty that I have performed. I can only regret again that the Mayor himself is not in the chair. (Cheers.)

Mr. FISHER: I have very much pleasure now in introducing to the meeting our Vice-President, Mr. J. J. Saffery, (Cheers.)

Mr. SAFFERY then took the chair, and said: Gentlemen, I exceedingly regret that this, the first opportunity I have of speaking to you is as an apologist, and as a *locum tenens*. You have already heard of the unavoidable absence of our worthy President, Mr. Deloitte, and perhaps I may add to the remarks Mr. Fisher has already made that Mr. Deloitte up to yesterday hoped to have occupied this chair. However, he then sent for me, and said he had been suffering for some days past from a very severe cold, and he was advised by his medical man and by his family that he should not venture to come down to Birmingham. Mr. Deloitte, as you all know, is a man well advanced in years. He is, I believe, the oldest member in the profession. I am sure that will weigh with us in pardoning his absence, and in fact we are quite sure he is doing the right thing in preserving his health. Gentlemen, when sending for me, he asked if I would read his address to you. I think it is not quite the address he would have delivered himself. I believe he would have amplified it very much if he had been present, but as that is impossible he has reduced to writing certain remarks he had to make which I will now read to you:—

## THE PRESIDENT'S ADDRESS.

GENTLEMEN: I have much pleasure on behalf of the Council and Members of this Institute, in returning their sincere thanks to his Worship, the Mayor of Birmingham, for our very kind and cordial reception, and for having placed this noble Council Chamber at our disposal.

The members must be highly gratified and proud that the Mayor of so large and important a Town as Birmingham has received them so graciously; which is, no doubt, attributable to the respect and esteem with which our Members in this vicinity are regarded.

I will now, gentlemen, if you please, refer to our own Hall and Offices, and congratulate the Members upon having acquired for a term of 999 years a suitable site for our Hall and Offices, situated in a most central position in the City of London, quiet and isolated, and the spacious and imposing buildings will belong exclusively to the Institute. I think there can be no doubt that when these buildings are erected they will have the effect of increasing the importance of the Institute in the estimation of the public, and be to the advantage of the Members.

I should very much have liked to have submitted to this Meeting a plan of the elevation, but after careful consideration it has been decided to submit the preparation of the plans and designs to six of the leading architects, who have been allowed to the 30th of November to deliver to the Secretary their respective plans, and I sincerely hope we may succeed in securing a structure of which the Members may be justly proud.

The next subject to which I will allude may be interesting to us all, it is the progress and prospects of the profession. I have had 56 years' experience in the profession, and during that period have watched its progress carefully and anxiously, and I have no hesitation in expressing a strong opinion that during that time the duties entrusted to professional accountants have very extensively increased, and that the profession is still rising in the estimation of the public, and the business continuing to increase. In my early recollection there were very few professional accountants of any importance in the City of London, and their business was comparatively limited. Since then the vast expansion of the commerce of the country, the increased confidence, *and the appreciation by the public of the services of the profession,* (together with the business arising under the Joint Stock Companies Acts), have placed us in a very enhanced position, which has resulted in a considerable augmentation of our duties.

Joint Stock Companies have for some years formed a considerable branch of professional practice, in requiring assistance in their promotion, in organising their books, in supervising and auditing their Accounts, preparing and verifying their Balance Sheets periodically, and, in cases of failures, winding up their affairs. During the years 1862 to 1886, 26,513 Companies have been registered in the United Kingdom, with a nominal Share Capital of £2975,288,275—the importance of this branch of the profession will therefore be evident. The profession may now reckon as clients, English and Foreign Railways, Telegraph Companies, Banks, Insurance Companies, and Joint Stock Companies, transacting every description of business at home and abroad, and it has been engaged upon a vast volume of business for the commercial and financial world and the public generally. I therefore, by way of encouragement, assure the younger Members of the Institute that there is a great field open to them, and they have only to use intelligence and perseverance, and pay the greatest attention to every case entrusted to them, whether large or small, to insure success.

The business arising from Joint Stock Companies has become so important a branch of the profession that the Council have considered it desirable to appoint a committee to watch any legislation on the subject, for the protection of the public and the profession. A Bill was introduced into Parliament during the last Session, entitled "An Act to amend the Companies' Act, 1862." This Bill was not intended to consolidate and amend the various Acts relating to Joint Stock Companies, but principally to avoid the promotion of fraudulent Companies, which it was proposed to effect by a provisional, and subsequently, a complete registration. The conditions imposed by this Bill before complete registration appear to be so onerous that it is feared few directors (if any) will be found willing to undertake such serious responsibilities. Experience has proved that Joint Stock Companies have very materially assisted in developing the commerce and trade of the country. Many large concerns have been converted into Limited Companies, and although it is very desirable to avoid fraudulent Companies being promoted, care should be taken that the restrictions do not entail such obligations on directors that will altogether prevent the establishment of such undertakings. A full report has been made by the Committee of the Institute to their Council upon this Bill. Two further bills were also introduced into Parliament entitled Companies Acts Consolidation and Amendment 1887 and 1888, and read first time, which propose the Consolidation and Amendment of the Companies Acts. These bills require very serious consideration and care, and full reports have been made by your Committee to the Council thereon, and will have due attention if they are again brought forward in the House.

The employment of accountants in connection with Bankruptcy cases under the present regulations is not so general as it was formerly, but these cases have been in olden times valuable to many members as introductory to the legal, commercial and financial community, and as a nucleus to a connection available for other matters. It may, perhaps, not be out of place on this occasion to urge members to be prompt in furnishing the Board of Trade with the required returns to avoid giving them unnecessary trouble.

I feel I should fail in my duty if I omitted upon this occasion to direct the attention of the members to the Chartered Accountants' Benevolent Association, which has been formed with the object of affording relief to necessitous persons, who are, or have been, members of the Institute of Chartered Accountants in England and Wales, whether subscribers to the Association or not; and of the necessitous widows and children of deceased persons, who have been Members of the Institute, and in the event of the death of a person, who is, or has been, a Member of the Institute, without leaving widow or child, the relief of necessitous relatives or others dependent on him for support; preference in all cases being given to subscribers and donors. There are about 1,600 members of the Institute, and I regret that not above 15% have become subscribers. I do hope that every member, whether in practice or otherwise, will subscribe at least one guinea per annum towards the fund for this purpose, and I earnestly appeal for further subscriptions. The income available for the purposes of the Association is confined to annual subscriptions and the dividends arising from the investment of Life Donations. Annual subscriptions are therefore very urgently needed.

I have briefly alluded to these various topics, being anxious to avoid being tedious, and I beg to thank you, gentlemen, for your kind attention.

---

The VICE-PRESIDENT.—That is the written address of the President, Mr. Deloitte, but, as I said before, had he been here I have no doubt he would have enlarged very much upon it. (Applause.) I have very much pleasure now in rising to propose a vote of thanks to the President for his address which he handed to me to read. I will therefore move " that the best thanks of this meeting be given to Mr. W. W. Deloitte, F.C.A., for his able and interesting address." (Cheers.)

Mr. J. C. BOLTON: Mr. Vice-President, I feel very much honoured in being selected to second the vote of thanks to Mr. Deloitte for the address that he purposed to have given this day. I suppose it is partly on account of my being one of the oldest members present in this room. Really one hardly knows who has done best, the one who has put this paper together, or the gentleman who has read it, and one might almost say "if I were not Diogenes I would be Alexander." When we listened to the address we could feel that it was but the heads of what would have been given if we had had the good fortune to have had Mr. Deloitte well and with us. We should then have heard more of the points he has brought before us in his address. Mr. Deloitte has touched upon several important matters, but it is left, I suppose, to the gentlemen who are to favour us with papers as to what shall come out of the address. For instance, he referred to Joint Stock Companies and to the Joint Stock Companies Acts, and a committee that we have upon that important and interesting subject, which has been so ably referred to by our friend, Mr. Alderman Barrow, who has just left the chair. Then there are the importance and progress of our Society, and how best it shall be carried on so as to make us, chartered accountants, one of the powers of the country; because with such an enormous business it follows of necessity that we can only be in our infancy, and that the time will come when the audit of accounts will be part of the scheme of every well-established company. Then in regard to Bankruptcy and Local Government Bills, so much might be added to the address, that I feel sure that it is more like the headings of what Mr. Deloitte wished to say to us than the address itself. I have very much pleasure now in seconding the vote of thanks to Mr. Deloitte for his address. (Applause.)

The CHAIRMAN: I should like to add a rider to express our extreme regret at Mr. Deloitte's absence. (Applause.)

The resolution was then put and very cordially received.

The CHAIRMAN: Mr. Bolton has already said that Mr. Deloitte suggests several points, which may be worthy of our consideration and discussion, but I think it may be wise that we should avoid as much as possible trenching on matters that will be brought before us more prominently in the papers and addresses that will be given. (Hear, hear.) I should therefore suggest that there is one point which emanates from Mr. Deloitte's paper which we might possibly consider with benefit to ourselves, that is, the question of certificates to be given by Accountants in various capacities. I think that might take three forms—Certificates to be given on promotion of companies; Certificates as to audit; and Certificates which I think are likely to be required in future as shadowed forth in the Bill introduced by the Lord Chancellor last year—I mean certificates or reports upon companies that have failed. I think we all feel the importance—the growing and immense importance—of the certificates that have been given, that are being given, and that will have to be given, upon companies that are formed from private concerns. (Applause.) How much may hinge on a false word or highly-coloured certificate we little know. My own feeling is that an accountant's certificate should be based on facts and nothing else. I do not think he should allow his imagination to run riot, and I do not think it is his province to colour or suggest what may happen to the company which is about to be formed. (Applause.) I have seen the importance of this, and it has been brought under my notice on many occasions, and I do not think it is within the province of an accountant to say or suggest that by a certain increase of capital or the enlargement of machinery or other suggested alterations certain results may be attained which the future alone can show. (Applause.) I think he should confine his certificate to facts, leaving to the judgment of those about to invest as to how that capital which is asked for should be employed for their benefit. (Applause.) I have seen very inflated certificates, and I think we should be very watchful to guard against the dangers of the little word "if"—"If such and such a thing should take place there is no reason why so and so should not follow." Then the next form of certificate I think we may have to consider opens up a very wide question, viz., the auditor's certificate —where we are to begin, where we are to leave off, what we are supposed to embrace; what is necessary to be checked; and what is not necessary to be checked. Some may consider it is necessary always to check matters which, in many instances it is simply impossible to do. (Applause). As to checking securities I think there can be no two opinions. And there are an immense number of other matters worthy of our careful and thoughtful consideration. If we have time, and it should suggest itself as being advisable, there is a clause in the Bill introduced by the Lord Chancellor of this year, in which he shadowed forth that, if the Bill came up again, in every company which goes into liquidation the liquidator shall issue a report dealing, I presume, with the causes of failure, so that the liquidator will have to do his duty. He must not hide anything, he must tell the truth, and I hope and believe we shall all do so. But his examination will have to be exhaustive. He will have to know where to put his finger upon blots here and there. Now all this is important, and I have this morning suggested this for our consideration, and will now invite any remarks which may be made upon these or any other subject mentioned in the President's address. (Hear. hear.) We have only the President's address to deal with this morning which will leave us free to have a discussion on what I have suggested, not only for our own benefit but for the benefit of the public generally. I do want all to be benefitted by what may be said. (Applause.)

Mr. J. C. BOLTON, F.C.A. (London): Mr. Chairman, I understand you shadowed forth to us three subjects for discussion this morning. (The Chairman: "One subject under three heads.") Certificates on the formation of private firms into Joint Stock companies, the character of the audit given, and the certificates as to the cause of failure. Now, Sir, I am disposed to join issue with you to a limited extent, as to the certificate to be given upon limited concerns. I understood you to lay down as a hard and fast line that we who may be called upon to give such certificates are to say exactly what the results have been in the past, and then to stop. Now it seems to me as if we should be doing an insufficient amount of work were we to do so. As, for instance, taking businesses that are already in existence, you have there got a certain fixed staff that cannot be dispensed with, and the result of the expense of that fixed staff upon a limited business and upon a business of say double the amount, must be very considerable indeed. Take a manufacturing business, there you have a certain fixed staff, if you are employing a hundred hands, and if you employ two or three hundred hands an immense difference must arise in the net profits of the business. And the result of the business may be shown by the books which have already been kept to have been greatly restricted by the want of working capital, so that it may be absolutely unable to carry orders out for the want of space, and of working capital. Now, taking a case that has come under my own observation during the last few weeks, that is of a large gold mine, they have at the present time 30 heads of stamps, and the expense per ton is $15, because of the limited amount of work that can be done with the 30 heads, compared with what could be done with the large quantity of ore in sight if we had more stamps. We have made careful calculation what the result would be with double the number of heads, and we find that it will immediately reduce the cost per ton from $15 to $10. Is it not within our province, and should we not be doing a legitimate and proper duty if we pointed out to people that by doubling the number of stamps in this case they would immediately reduce their working expenses by one-third? It seems to me we should be doing what is right, and if we abstained from giving that information we should err on the wrong side, and be, in point of fact, over cautious. With regard to certificates while the business is going on, and the amount of work that is done, I shall be very glad indeed,—although I am over 60 years of age,—to be taught; for I cannot see in many businesses how it is possible for the whole of the work to be audited; when one bears in mind that a bank like Coutts' at the West end of London, resolved to have a thorough and complete audit of their own books, and for many years past only found that to be practicable by having all the accounts kept twice over, so that the accounts that are kept by one set of clerks for the work of the bank, are kept by another set of clerks quite independently as for the audit of the bank. How would it be possible for any of us, who are so fortunate as to be appointed auditors for such an institution, to audit every item? We must accept certain results, and only audit a part of the work. Wherever the whole audit can be taken I apprehend it is our duty to do so. With regard to the inspection of securities,—that, without any exception whatever, I apprehend ought to be done by every auditor, (applause),—an auditor has not done his work unless he is able to see the securities he is inspecting, and to say they are intact. With regard to the third certificate,— that after failure—I think, if it were generally known that an able and independent chartered accountant would come in as auditor, and make a fair and exhaustive report of what had led up to the failure, we should have fewer Joint Stock Companies than there are, while others that were formed would be carried on in a much more careful manner. I am very much obliged to you for listening to my remarks. I think somebody must open the discussion, and I, therefore, took it upon myself to do so. (Applause.)

Mr. J. MATHER, F.C.A. (Manchester): The fundamental maxim with accountants is that time is money, and we must not set a bad example of wasting time in our transactions by having too long pauses, and that must be my excuse for rising at this juncture. Then just a word with regard to the interesting point which you, Sir, have started for us this morning,—the certificates of accountants—in relation to the three matters that you referred to. I will only refer to two of those points, and in doing so I must say I endorse the remarks of Mr. Bolton, and regret that I cannot entirely follow the lead of so eminent an authority as our Vice-president on that point, because a matter of expedience occurred to my own mind in listening to those remarks. If we are not to certify when new capital is introduced into a business, that it may have the effect of increasing the profits of that business, we may decline to certify to a matter of fact. Now, the Vice-president recommended restricting our certificates to matters of fact, and with that I quite agree. I think matters of mere prognostication and mere inference are outside the limit of accountants' certificates. (Applause.) But,—as now explained by Mr. Bolton—the question of future prospects or results that may be expected to flow from the introduction of new capital into a business, may be to a certain extent a question of fact. A case which occurred to my own mind was that of a long and old-established business which had been conducted successfully, but had declined because the capital had become insufficient to do justice to the business. It could be shown that by paying cash for all purchases which had hitherto been paid for by bills of two, three, or four months—those bills possibly dating forward to some extent—a saving in discount alone could be effected to the extent of £1,000 a year. (Hear, hear.) In such a case, I think, the auditor is warranted in saying he finds from an investigation of the business that the introduction of a certain amount of capital—say the amount proposed—would have the effect of increasing the profit earning capacity of the business. On the very important matter, as to how far the postings and details should be checked in giving an audit certificate, I do not think it should go forth that we recognise it as no part of our duty to check postings. I agree that there are circumstances in certain cases where it is impracticable, and where it may be quite unnecessary, but I think a normal audit should be understood to include the checking of everything. (Applause.) Therefore, when postings are checked sufficiently to ensure their correctness—in such a case it may be a matter of arrangement that the auditor dispenses with the checking of the postings, and it may be understood. But I do not think it should be understood that the auditor dispenses with the checking of postings without the sanction and concurrence of those for whom he is auditing. You see in the case of private businesses and banks they may have as much check or as little as they like. It entirely rests with them. They may say, "we will pay for so much, and do not recognise any more." But in the case of a public company the shareholders rely entirely upon the auditors, and where the auditors find it unnecessary or impracticable to check the postings I think it should be known. My only point is, that as a matter of ordinary routine we assume that we shall have to check postings, but, that in exceptional cases and where there is an understanding on the subject, it may be unnecessary. (Applause.)

Mr. G. B. MONKHOUSE, F.C.A., (London): In the remarks you have made you have provided sufficient matter for two or three days' discussion if it is gone into very exhaustively. But one or two ideas have been thrown out, and I should like to say a few words just upon two of the heads. First, as to certificates upon the formation of companies, I think we all agree with the main lines you lay down—that it is the duty of the accountant to deal with facts. Mr. Bolton and Mr. Mather have referred to the fact that it may be within our province to carry it a little further than you do—although I am not quite sure how far you would carry it, as

you did not place the matter at any great length before us. But I think there are circumstances—such as those Mr. Bolton has referred to, or others—where it may come within an accountant's province to refer to the future, but not as a matter of opinion. I quite agree that we should not give our opinions. It is very difficult to say how far you should lend your sanction to statements as to the future. I think there are circumstances other than those mentioned by Mr. Bolton where it is not only legitimate but your duty to do so. But wherever you leave the absolute region of facts the certificate should be so clear that the veriest dunce can understand what it means. And by making the certificate so clear that it is the record of absolute facts, I think you keep within safe lines. In some cases there are exceptional circumstances which it is desirable should be referred to in your certificate. As regards the audit certificate, you see whenever we begin to speak about audit certificates and audits, there is the question of the principles of the audit, and the question of the details of work done to the satisfaction of the proprietors of a business. In the audit of a Joint Stock Company's accounts, the two important things that you have to audit, and which I venture to think most of the public think you more or less confine yourselves to, are, first of all, to certify that the balance sheet really and truly represents the position of the company, and does not conceal anything; and that it states everything, so that people may clearly understand the position of the auditor's certificate. If the balance sheet is not perfectly clear, or if there are any exceptional circumstances in connection with it, which should be brought to the notice of the shareholders, I think, sir, it is the duty of the auditor to supplement that balance sheet by some words in his certificate, which will bring before the shareholders what he thinks is the true position of the concern. In a great many companies it is now more the custom to state the details on the balance sheet, and the position of the liabilities and assets, so that the shareholders may clearly understand them, without the necessity for an explanation in the auditor's certificate. But, if this is not done, I think it is his duty, and a most important part of his duty, to supplement the matter. The second important part of his audit is the certificate that the profits earned, and the dividend proposed to be declared, have been truly and really earned. That, of course, embraces everything in connection with the matter. And there again if he has the slightest doubt in his mind, or if there are circumstances in the preparation of the Profit and Loss Account which he thinks should be clearly explained to the shareholders, I think, although he may not have an actual doubt, yet still if there are such exceptional circumstances, there again he should clearly state them in his certificate. But as regards the detailed portion of the audit, I think every audit will have to be dealt with more or less upon its own merits, without laying down particular details. (Hear, hear.) It is practically impossible to talk about carrying out the checking of details of large companies. The larger the company, the less proportionate work in detail the auditor does, or could possibly do. Of course the principle involved is the same in large and small concerns, only in large it is more important. There is the principle, which is always to be followed, but after that it must be left in each case to the auditor himself to determine what he should do. I think that it must rest with the auditor, and that upon himself must be the responsibility as to what he will consider a complete audit. If in some companies there is a special committee appointed to confer with the auditor, as to what he shall, or shall not, do, it rests with him to determine what shall be the proper audit of the company. But I do think, where he has not gone into all the details, and checked all the postings, as the second speaker referred to, where he has not made what he calls a very detailed audit, it is part of his duty as auditor to see that, what I should call the internal check of the office is upon the best basis that he can suggest. (Applause.) That strikes me as one of the first duties of the auditor, especially with the large companies, where he knows it is actually impossible, not simply because he may only have a small fee given him, because I do not recognize that position at all, but where it is actually impossible he can exercise the detailed supervision. Because, even if he were given a fee commensurate with exercising such supervision, the effect of his clerks being there every day would materially interfere with the work of the office. One of the first things, when he is appointed to a large company, where he must make a detailed audit, is to sit down and take a note of all the books there, and the purposes those books serve ; noting who keeps the separate books, and what kind of checks there are upon all the transactions, especially upon all payments of money. (Hear, hear.) If he finds he can suggest improvements it is, I think, the first part of his duty to do so, to suggest that the internal check is not sufficient, or can be amended. And having suggested, and got that check into operation, it will then be a part of his yearly or half-yearly duty to see that the internal checks are kept up so far as he can. That is an efficient audit so far as it can be done by a professional man. About the third certificate, we have not come to that, but I quite see it is a probable part of our duties in the future. The experience that accountants have gained in connection with the audit of companies, I think, will quite fit us for investigating, and reporting upon the causes of their failure, especially in connection with the general experience we have. I do not know that really we can get much further upon the third point, but when it comes we shall have to talk about it. (Applause.)

Mr. A. MURRAY, F.C.A. (Manchester) : Some very valuable and important points have been raised on the interesting discussion which has just been opened. Mr. Monkhouse—the last speaker—has gone into the subject so exhaustively that there is little more perhaps to be said as to our certificates, but one must all feel the great responsibility which attaches to us in giving certificates, not only in connection with the initiation of companies, but the audit of them. Sometimes I have shrunk from being associated with companies, feeling the great responsibility in having one's name upon the prospectus, and I think it ought to be more generally understood that in being named as auditors of a company on the prospectus, we really do not take any responsibility in connection with the formation of a company. I am afraid sometimes friends of ours may be apt to say.—" Seeing your name upon the prospectus we have taken it as a guarantee that the foundation of the company in every respect is without objection." As regards the audit of companies—I do not propose to refer to the audit of private concerns, but that of companies only—we must take the responsibility, and I think it must be left to ourselves to settle what course we should take in regard to the details of the audit. For instance, we must not follow the same course on each occasion ; but if desirable make a change so that we may, in time, extend the audit to the whole work in connection with the Company. Take the case of railway companies. We cannot there deal with details ; we must be content with the internal audit, and to a great extent merely satisfy ourselves as far as we can as to results. Take the case of a bank, what are we to do there ? We must limit our examination very much to the balance sheet. We must be careful, of course, as to the examination of the securities, and the whole of the bills by enumeration ; but as to going into the details of the work for the half-year or the year, except the profit, on most matters it is impossible. We must see that proper provision is made for bad and doubtful debts, so far as we are able to judge, but even there again we cannot always say that the accounts are all good, and we must take them as good so long as they are operative. As to the bills we are not in a position to judge of the names upon those bills, and, even if we were to express an opinion on the accounts, and upon the wisdom of advances, or the amount of discount to any particular customer, we should have to be very careful not to interfere with the management. We must stick to our own province,

and not take upon ourselves the responsibility of advising, except so far as we have very reliable information of the position of any firm whom we may suppose is being trusted to a larger extent than is desirable.

Mr. W. H. NAIRNE, F.C.A. (Manchester) said : With respect to the certificates of accountants as to companies in formation—of course it was most essential that whatever certificate an accountant gave should be thoroughly honest. To be honest, it should certainly mention facts, but it should not omit the facts which would have considerable influence in determining the resolution of intending shareholders. To give an illustration it might be that looking back upon some few years business of a private concern—say 3 or 4 or 5 years —you could point to an average profit, but the last of those years might have shown a loss. It might be that owing to exceptional circumstances there was an average profit, and even a consecutive profit on all the years, or that the last year or couple of years the profits exceeded those of the previous years. All these cases might be stated in order to induce the public to take shares. But notwithstanding the profits might have been earned in the manner described, special circumstances probably existed which ought to be made known. To take a manufacturing concern, where the prices of raw material had been exceptionally low for the past two or three years, there might have been profits earned over and above what there had been in previous years, notwithstanding the fact that the turnover of the concern was gradually and steadily decreasing. If, in making the examination, an accountant became aware of facts he himself would certainly take into account in estimating the probable success of the concern in the future, he (Mr. Nairne) thought the accountant did not fulfil his duty unless he made known those facts. (Applause.) With respect to the certificate attached to the balance sheet of a company, he had found it a convenience himself—in certifying the balance sheet—to make reference to a separate report. It was frequently very inconvenient for any man in certifying some profit and loss, or trading account, or balance sheet, to place all he wished the shareholders to know in the certificate on the face of the balance sheet ; and therefore he thought it was frequently necessary to make a separate report. That was contemplated in the original Companies' Act of 1862. He did not think it necessary to say all they had done in the audit, but it frequently was necessary to say what they had done. There were the very wildest opinions in the minds of even experienced business men as to what an audit comprehended. In one instance he had known it was thought not only absolutely necessary, as a matter of course, and as a sine quâ non, that every invoice for goods received had been checked, but that the prices and calculations had also been passed by the auditor. (Laughter.) And when he expressed a doubt as to that being anything like a common opinion he was scouted. It so happened that a person then present spoke of one auditor whose custom it was to make that check, and he (Mr. Nairne) was instructed in future, at the result even of increased fees, that it must be done, and he was quite willing, of course, to do it. (Laughter.) He thought audits should be supplemented by a report giving the facts in order to make them clear to the lay mind. With respect to the third class of certificates, the public would be great gainers by such certificates or such reports being issued on failure of companies. There was one difficulty in the way, in that the liquidator in a company was appointed, or his appointment brought about, by the directors, or those who were most interested in concealing the causes of failure ; and it behoved an accountant, in this, as well as any other position, to feel the full weight of his responsibility, and to determine that nothing which was required to be known in order to form a true opinion as to the failure should be kept back. He thought that no responsible public accountant, nor any member of the Institute, would fail in that regard.

Mr. F. WHINNEY said : He did not propose to speak

then as to forms of certificates, as that formed part of the address he would make to them in the afternoon. But there were one or two remarks, which did not fall within the compass of that address, and those were about accountants giving certificates as to the profits of a business, and indicating not merely what those profits had been, but what they would be in future. He thought an accountant's function was almost entirely limited as to the ascertaining of facts, at least so far as regarded the examination of the accounts, and he believed it would be very unwise indeed if they were to prophecy. (Applause.) The value of an accountant's report depended upon the facts which he set out, and which were believed by the public, and if he incorporated in the certificate of facts something like prophecy the public would attach very likely considerable weight to that prophecy, and they might be misled. That would be a misfortune, because it would throw doubt upon the certificate of facts. If anything was wanted of a prophetical nature, that must be done either by the promoter or vendor. Something had been said about its being the duty of the auditor to check the postings. He ventured to say it was not, and that it was impossible. In the case of a railway company, or of a bank, if they were to check the postings the audit of one balance sheet would not be done before the next was wanted, and how much nearer would they be. They might find all the postings correct, and the balance sheet might not be worth the paper it was written on. They might find the postings of all the amounts of the securities perfectly correct, but it did not follow that because the postings were correct, the values of the securities were correct. He did not say that they were not to check the postings ; but his meaning was this, that it was not necessary, and it was waste of time, to check all the postings of all the books. It was impossible to lay down any precise or definite rule by which all audits should be conducted. (Applause.) Each audit had to stand on its own basis. All the auditors had to do, was to examine the accounts, and find out whether, in their opinion, they were true and correct statements of the position of the company.

Mr. DAVID CHADWICK said : With regard to the certificates of profits of a trading concern, an accountant should only certify as to the facts ; because if he certified that the profit of a concern for a certain number of years had been a certain amount, he was not called upon to say " If you increase that output, 10 per cent. or 20 per cent., the profit will be proportionately increased." The public could easily do that for themselves. Besides, if he did that, he thought he would be called upon to take into consideration whether there was a demand for the increased output, and whether that increased output did not over supply the market with the particular manufacture. With regard to auditors' certificates, they, as professional accountants, should be a little more particular, and when they certified the profits of trading concerns, they should confine themselves, as far as practicable, to a statement of facts. The public wanted to know the value of auditors' certificates, and they had a right to ask, and they were continually asking this. For instance, the assets, consols, or anything else, were taken at the market price ; but the principal asset in a trading concern was the value of its property, machinery and plant. To what extent then was the auditor called upon to estimate the depreciation of the plant ? Whether they took an old cotton-mill, or a colliery, or an iron works, they all knew to what a fearful extent depreciation affected them. When they certified a balance sheet as correct, they should certify the value of the assets in the shape of plant and machinery, which might have suffered greatly in depreciation, as they might do the value of investments in another department. Another matter was that the profit depended upon whether the plant and stock were taken at a fair valuation, and whether proper depreciation was taken into account. The prosperity of the concern depended upon that. If accountants recommended strongly that in every case, where practicable, there should be

a Profit and Loss Account, as well as a balance sheet, then the public would know the extent of the trading, and of the profit. If, therefore, Profit and Loss Accounts were attached to every balance sheet, it would be a great advantage indeed. One word in regard to the new Act of Parliament ; he took a large interest in introducing a Bill in 1867, and if that had passed he believed it would have remedied a great many grievances. He believed the Bill settled by the Institute of Chartered Accountants was the best Bill in the interests of the public that could be devised. He thought the Lord Chancellor's Bill would be an instalment, and do a large amount of good. He did not believe it would ultimately injure the profession, but he believed it would rather increase the value of the audit ; he thought they should support any Bill that was an instalment to prevent either promoters or vendors or anybody else overstating their case. (Applause.)

THE CHAIRMAN : I am afraid the time has now expired. I think in my opening remarks I said we should confine ourselves in our certificates to facts. Mr. Bolton asked if I meant to stop there. I cannot see why we should venture our opinions. Let the vendors or the promoters speak as to the future. It is not our duty to do so. If a company is to be launched, let us do our part, and let them do theirs: they are the promoters. Mr. Monkhouse, I think, said the larger the company the less the auditors had to do ; but I think he qualified it afterwards. I think the word " proportionately " was wanted there. I do not know that there is any other matter I need refer to. I consider the discussion has been very beneficial. (Applause.)

The members then adjourned for luncheon to the Grand Hotel, at the invitation of the Local Society.

## SOME REMARKS ON THE COMPANIES' ACTS.

THE CHAIRMAN on re-assembling said I have much pleasure in calling upon Mr. WHINNEY for his address.

Mr. FREDERICK WHINNEY, F.C.A., after a few remarks as to the reception they had met with, and as to the subject he had chosen being too vast for a single address, said :—

" And now, Gentlemen, there is one fact one can mention which goes without saying, that in these days there has been a great increase in the number of companies, and that, in consequence to a large extent of the principle of limited liability. The question has been raised in several quarters as to whether that principle is, or is not, a sound and good one, but I think it is much too late to discuss that question. My own belief is that most of the complaints we have lately had have emanated from shareholders who have been hit by calls in companies which have come to grief. Again, complaints have been made, I think, to Lord SALISBURY, by a deputation of cotton spinners, who complained that many small companies have been started under the limited liability which undersold them, the legitimate cotton spinners. That may be perfectly true. There has been a good deal of that kind of business done, but it is an evil which cures itself, for people get tired of taking shares in companies which come to grief. Beyond this I do not think there are many complaints as to the inception or carrying on of companies ; at any rate to a very extensive degree. The Chambers of Commerce have, however, been stirring, and at a meeting of the Associated Chambers held at Cardiff last September, this resolution was passed :—" That no Companies' Bill will be satisfactory which does not provide better securities than now exist against the formation of fraudulent companies, and unless it provides for the winding up of insolvent limited companies in the local Courts of Bankruptcy, and by the same procedure as of private firms." There may be no objection to that resolution except that it provides for the winding up of insolvent limited companies in the local Courts of Bankruptcy in the manner and by the same procedure as for private firms. I have looked through the discussion which took place before the resolution was passed, and I cannot find there are any good suggestions for the better management of companies in future, or for winding them up, except that you should go to the Court of Bankruptcy. Now, a short time ago at a meeting of the Institute of Bankers in London,—a very important meeting too—there was a debate on an address delivered by Lord BRAMWELL. I do not find, however, that there were many important suggestions as to alterations which might be made in the law, nor that there was any very great complaint, except complaints that there had been fraud in the inception of companies, and that they had not been properly carried on. There were one or two practical suggestions, but at a meeting of some of the most prominent men in the City of London I repeat that the complaints as to the working of the Companies' Acts were very few. As to the resolution by the Associated Chambers of Commerce that insolvent limited companies should be wound up in the Court of Bankruptcy some questions might arise as to what is an insolvent limited company. I do not know that it would do much good to discuss this, but I may remind the meeting that it is not every company that winds up which is insolvent. Some companies wind up, and there is a distribution of assets amongst the shareholders, and is it contended that all these companies have to go into the Bankruptcy Court? I myself do not see the necessity for it. But to come back from the region of the Chambers of Commerce and the Bankers' Institute, to that which one hears commonly as to the complaints in connection with companies, I think they resolve themselves principally into these : That the promotion has been wrong; that the directors are men of straw and know nothing about their duties; that the prospectus has been fraudulent; that improper prices have been paid for the business or properties purchased; that there is want of control over the directors, and that there is an undue competition by limited companies underselling traders and then failing. I propose to deal with some of those subjects in the course of my remarks, but in doing so I have had to consider what should be laid down so as to give a company a fair chance of success. I think we should say a company must be honestly and ably managed; and if it is wound up it must be honestly and ably wound up. Now comes the question as to how you can secure that a company shall be dealt with in the course of its existence in such a manner, and I have no drastic measures to lay before you. I think it is impossible in the very nature of things to do so. I consider it impossible to lay down any legislative enactments which will deal successfully in detail with the management, inception, and perhaps the winding up of these companies. We must not have that which at the Banker's Institute was designated as "grandmotherly legislation." We must not have anything which will interfere with freedom of contract. We must not have anything which will incite people to say '' we did not exercise our own judgment, in giving into this company, but relied upon the report of the Government Inspector." But what you do want, I think, is to provide that the prospectus in the first instance shall contain several particulars—particulars which are occasionally to be found in the articles of association, but which would be brought home to the notice of the shareholders, if they are inserted, not simply in the articles of association but also in the prospectus. I may add that this subject was considered closely in our Institute. Well, now, with reference to the promoters. Promoters have a bad name, but I do not think there is any absolute reason why they should. I do not see any reason why the business of promoting companies should not be honestly and respectably conducted. (Hear, hear.) That it has been abused up to the present time is, I think, patent to any accountant who has had any experience whatever in winding up companies. I think with reference to promoters it should be enacted that the remuneration of the promoter should be set forth not only in the articles of association but in the prospectus. I can recollect perfectly well when it used to be set forth in the articles, and if it is inserted in the prospectus, notice would be given to all shareholders, as most men would look at the prospectus before applying for shares. If it is placed on the face of the prospectus that Mr. A. B., who is a promoter, and who defrays the expenses up to allotment, is to be paid a certain sum for that, I do not think there is any reason whatever to complain of such a statement. A man would take shares with the statement on the face of the prospectus, and would know perfectly well what he was doing, and it would be for him to decide whether the remuneration is extreme or insufficient. I go somewhat farther, and I would enact that beyond that—beyond the remuneration payable to the promoter—he should not receive any further pay or remuneration whatever. His business should be simply that of promoting companies, and we should then get rid, I think, of almost all those bargains between the vendor and promoter, and between promoter and directors, by which the promoter swallows up large sums of money, which are never disclosed to the shareholders until the company is wound up. Now, I do not know that there is anything further to provide with reference to promoters. One word upon a subject which we discussed to some extent this morning, a subject which is closely connected with the inception of companies—that is accountant's certificates. As you know, it is the fashion now to call in accountants to verify what the profits have been of certain businesses which it is proposed to turn into companies. Great stress is laid—and, I think, justly so—upon the report of the accountant. I will say no more about that, than simply give you my opinion that an accountant's certificate as to the profits of a business should be set forth in perfect fairness and honesty. Everything which he states should be a fact. If he sets forth anything else, or if he begins to gloss over any facts, his reports would be most mischievous. (Applause.) Another thing that accountants would have to bear in mind with reference to those certificates, is that they are eloquent not only by what they say, but also by their silence (applause.) The men who are accustomed to look at accountants' certificates say, '' We expected to find so and so and there is not a word said about it.'' Naturally that would create suspicion; therefore the accountant's certificate should be as full as it reasonably can be. Now, with reference to directors. Of course, it is a most important thing that you should have able and honest directors. The difficulty is how to get them. Well, now, various remedies have been proposed. It has been suggested, and it was laid down in the Lord Chancellor's Bill, that they should hold a certain proportion of the capital. I do not believe in a certain proportion. I think what the Lord Chancellor wished was that the directors should hold one-fifth of the capital applied for. Now, there is one company which came out lately in which I believe the capital has been applied for 29 times over, making a total of £87,000,000. If the directors therefore held one-fifth of that capital, it would be £17,400,000 which is very much larger than the whole of the capital, so that a provision of that kind would be absurd. But what I think would be sufficient is that it should be compulsory to state in the prospectus the amount of shares which each director takes (applause), and that each director shall be bound to pay for those shares out of his own money (renewed applause). People would then be able to judge whether the directors— those gentlemen who are advertised as directors of the company, have a stake in that company. If I choose to take shares in a company where I know there are five directors holding one share each, if I think those directors are exceedingly good men, why should I not be able to do so? Of course, I am taking an extreme case, but it is for the public to judge when applying for shares as to whether the directors have a substantial holding in the concern. It has been suggested that directors should pay up in full on their shares, instead of paying the calls. I really cannot see anything in that. I do not see any reason why directors should pay up in full, in preference to the other shareholders.

I think myself it would be a decent check on the directors that they should have the same liability as the other shareholders (applause). Well, now, we are familiar with directors being qualified by vendors and promoters. I think I should enact this that if they were so qualified the prospectus should be deemed to be false and fraudulent (applause). What the public are entitled to ask is that at any rate directors should testify their *bonâ fides* and appreciation of the prospects of the concern, by subscribing their own money and taking shares in it. Again, I think the remuneration of the directors should be set out on the face of the prospectus (hear, hear). Of course, if it is to be left to a meeting of shareholders to fix, so let it be stated, but I think if those regulations were followed, that is to say, that a man is bound to take shares in a company as a director, if it disclosed the fees of the directors, and shown that he is bound to invest his own money in the concern, you would then get rid of a large number of persons who simply seek a seat on the direction for income, without knowing anything whatever of the duties they have to perform, or the work they have to manage. Now, with reference to the allotment of shares; it has been proposed to legislate that a certain proportion of shares should be allotted. Well, that is rather a dangerous proposition, because it is a very easy thing to run up the number to be allotted. It has been done over and over again, and an allotment has taken place very often with a view to enable the promoter to finger his promotion money. But I think it would be sufficient if the articles of association and the prospectus stated in every case the number of shares to be allotted, and the quantity of allotment money to be paid before the company commenced operations. If the prescribed number is not subscribed for, then the money should be returned without deduction, if that is the bargain, or with the deduction of so much for expenses, according to the way in which it is stated in the prospectus. On the other hand, people should have the materials for judging whether the limit of shares to be reached, before the allotment takes place, is sufficient to enable the company to carry on business. That limit would give them the means of judging whether, with that allotment of shares, a company would be likely to be successful. But you cannot get any Government to provide caution for persons who are about to take shares. They must take care of themselves. The same provision—that is to say a restriction upon the allotment unless a certain number be subscribed—should prevail in the case of debentures. I know a case where an advertisement was issued asking for subscriptions for debentures to pay off charges on real estate, something like £80,000 was wanted, and £30,000 odd was subscribed. The charges were not paid off, and the debenture-holders instead of finding they had a charge on real property to secure their debentures, found that the original mortgages upon the real property were still in front of them, and that they were left with something like an unsecured claim against the company. Of course, every prospectus inviting application for shares on debentures should be filed within a specified time. If these conditions were complied with, I think you would get rid of all necessity for provisional registration, which is provided in the Bill of the Lord Chancellor. I do not see the necessity for it. People must have the proper information set forth in the prospectus to enable them to form a judgment, and then they must form that judgment for themselves. As far as the management of companies goes, we should have an honest and able Board of Directors. As to the control of those directors, you have the annual meetings of the company, and the extraordinary meetings whenever you get a number of shareholders to enable you to summon one. I do not know that you can specify anything else. Shareholders must manage their own affairs, and if the directors do not do their duty they must turn them out. The legislature cannot interfere. But there is one power provided in the Companies' Act of 1862, which, I think, has scarcely ever been used—the power of the Board of Trade to appoint Inspectors to inquire into the affairs of companies, under sections 56 to 61 of the 1862 Act. I think on the application of one-fifth of the shares the Board of Trade can appoint Inspectors and give all the requisite authority to make reports, &c. We hear a great deal about rows in companies, and turning out of directors and committees of investigation, but, I believe, no case is known of any application having been granted by the Board of Trade with the view of inspecting the affairs of a company, though this power could be used in case of need. One other material necessity for a company being carried on properly is good auditors. They act as checks on the directors, and at the same time they may be of great assistance to them. I shall have to consider by and bye the position of auditors, and I will defer any further remarks until I come to that, with this proviso, that I think if auditors have to make any objection to items in the accounts their objections should be sent to the shareholders before the meeting takes place, with the reply that the directors have to make, so that when the shareholders meet, to discuss the items objected to, they may have the matter before them. I do not know that I need say anything about complaint of competition between limited liability companies. If people will throw away their money in unsound trading I do not know any power on earth which is to prevent it. Now we come to the creditor side of the question, and one wants to see whether there should be any further provisions for the protection of the creditors. I think it should be made compulsory on all companies to send a copy of the balance sheet to the Registrar of Joint Stock Companies. I do not think it is necessary that a copy of the Trading Account, or the Profit and Loss Account, should be sent. There is such a thing as competition in trade, and it may not be desirable for a company to disclose everything connected with it. But I really do not see any reason why all companies who are asking the public or their creditors to trust them, should not give the creditors the opportunity of examining their affairs and ascertaining whether the company is, or is not, worthy to be trusted. There is one evil which has cropped up in connection with companies, and that is a charge on the undertaking. I think you must all know that any company can, by the insertion of a few words, charge the whole of its undertaking in favour of any creditor, and that there is no necessity to register that undertaking at the Joint Stock Companies Registration Office, and but a very small penalty on the directors if they do not enter it in their register of mortgages, and that though a non-entry of the charge does not invalidate it. I should like to see the charge on an undertaking, as such, abolished. (Applause.) I think when a company is obliged to give a mortgage upon its current bankers' balance, which is involved in a charge on the undertaking, the sooner that company shuts up the better for everybody. I would modify the charge upon stock-in-trade by saying it should be registered under the Bills of Sale Act, just the same as an ordinary trader's charge on his stock-in-trade. I would abolish the charge on the undertaking so far as it relates to book debts, unless notice were given to the debtors that they have been so charged. If that were done it would have the effect very probably of shutting up the company, and I do not think that is an evil which is to be deplored, because if a company gets into such a position that the shareholders will not raise more capital, but that directors are compelled to charge the book debts the sooner the company is brought to an end the better. As to winding up, there has been some suggestions that you should be able to wind up a company, or get a winding up order more easily than at present, but I do not think there is much in that point. A suggestion has been made—of course, by some gentlemen who are not practical—that as soon as a company has lost three-fourths, say, of its capital, it shall be bound to wind up. Well, we know perfectly well that it is almost an impossibility for directors to know the precise day when the three-fourths of the capital is lost. Take a case in point. How can directors know whether the large quantity of debts which gather round a bank when it is badly managed, are doubtful or bad. It is almost an impossibility to say that of the £300,000 of debts which represent say the whole of the capital three-fourths are bad. The difficulty is to ascertain that they are bad, and anyone who has practical experience in that matter must see it is almost an impossibility. Take the case of a going concern which has a large quantity of machinery. The machinery and plant of a going concern are worth a great deal more than they are to break up. Are the directors to value that business for the purpose of winding-up, at the going-price or at the breaking-up price, if they have to determine the value in order to comply with this clause by which it is proposed to say they shall wind up when three-fourths of the capital is lost. That is an unworkable proposition, made by gentlemen who have had no practical experience, and do not know really what it means. The Lord Chancellor, in his Bill, suggested that the liquidator in every case where there was fraud in the inception or management of a company should make a report. Before that enactment passes the House, I wish the House would be good enough to define fraud. It is a very wide word, and it is easily and lightly talked about, and yet it is very difficult to define. What one man might consider to be fraud, another man would not, and before you order the liquidator to make that report they should have some guide as to what fraud means. I am not sure that it is altogether a wise proposition in another aspect. A company fails, and it can only pay 15s. in the £. Why should the money of the creditors be wasted in attempting to find out whether the directors have, or have not, committed fraud? The creditors themselves may not like to have the money spent for that purpose, and surely they ought to have some voice in the matter. I do not think, therefore, that the suggestion is altogether workable. Then there is a great desire in the minds of the public—almost at the bottom of the complaints about the Companies' Acts that winding-up should take place in the local County Courts. I do not know how you, gentlemen, in the country look upon that. Probably you may approve of it. It is part of a large question, that is, the decentralisation of the Law Courts. I, for one, think companies are best wound up in that Court which understands winding-up, where there are judges and officials who know perfectly well what are the questions to come before the Court in connection with the winding-up, and who are able to deal with those questions. (Applause.) At the present time I do not think the County Court judges know very much about company winding-up, and as for the suggestion that companies should be wound up in the same way as the estate of a bankrupt, the suggestion emanates from those who know very little about it. Winding-up a company means winding-up a partnership: it means also the ascertainment of the liability of the directors. There is also an instance where the company can be carried on and re-constituted, but there is no such thing in the case of a bankruptcy. There is the question as to whether directors are liable for malfeasance, but no such thing in the case of a bankruptcy. You get another question in bankruptcy as to whether a man is entitled to his discharge, but you do not get that in the case of a company. Just look at the magnitude of the interests involved. There is one case on record where there was an action brought against a director for just half-a-million for dividends improperly paid out of capital, and money paid away improperly, it was alleged, for which he was liable. Is that the kind of case you would discuss in a county court? I could give many cases connected with companies involving sometimes millions— at any rate, hundreds of thousands of pounds—which require the very best intellects you can find to solve them, with as much satisfaction to the parties as they can reasonably expect. Then we are told that the court of bankruptcy is a proper place to wind-up companies. But I do not know whether it is in the recollection of many of you gentlemen— it is within mine—that the court of bankruptcy was charged with the winding-up of limited companies, and it had the

winding-up for two or three years, when it was taken away from it. They had had experience in the matter, and I suppose it was not because the experiment was successful that they took the companies away again. It must have been, I suppose, that the winding-up was not done so satisfactorily as elsewhere. I am sure it was not—from what I myself recollect. But you must not forget this— that the winding-up of companies never can be an agreeable process to any parties connected with them, except perhaps those who are doing it. Shareholders are compelled to pay calls, and they do not like it. They have been hit, or entrapped into taking shares, and they consider it very hard to have to pay calls. Litigation is commenced, and if litigation is not commenced by the liquidator, it may be commenced against him, and there is no power I know of which can prevent anybody who fancies he has rights suing a trustee or liquidator. And shareholders and creditors do not sufficiently recognise that the affairs of such companies are almost always in a state of embranglement, and that litigation is almost also a necessary consequence, and he is the best liquidator or trustee who avoids that, and who can smooth away difficulties. (Applause). The suggestion is made that it would be very desirable to have publicity. Well, publicity to a great extent is a good thing. It is suggested that directors should pass an examination. I go as far as this, that it should be the duty of directors in every failed company to bring into court a statement of affairs, and that at their own expense. That is a provision and penalty which is imposed by the French law upon all the directors of failed companies, and I think it is a very useful one. To that extent I would penalize directors; but has anyone ever thought of what is the meaning of a director passing an examination? The company fails; the director has to file accounts and go and be examined. Suppose he does not go, what is to happen? Is he to be committed to jail for contempt of court? And supposing he does go what is to happen?—is he to pass an examination? He will not get a discharge. There may be something in it, but my impression is that that, happily, to a great extent, can be obtained by providing that a liquidator should come in and report on every case, who shall give a short succinct history of the establishment of the company, and, if possible, the way in which it has been carried on; and that, I think, might be done without much difficulty. If that report disclosed a very disastrous and wrong state of things, it would be a matter for the Public Prosecutor to take up. I think in that way, that is to say, by providing for a report to the public prosecutor you might meet gross and flagrant cases of fraud. People complain of the delays in Chancery. Chancery is no more perfect in its administration than any other court, or any other institution on the face of the earth. There are delays everywhere, and evils to be found, and I dare say we all think we can suggest some improvements in that matter. Whether with a multitude of doctors we would get anything like safety I do not know, but speaking from experience I know if I want to get things through in the Court of Chancery, by sticking to them myself, and making a stir, I can manage to get them through in a tolerably short time. Now there is one important question in winding up, and it is a matter, I think, in which you will agree that accountants are very much interested, not only as liquidators, but as auditors. I mean the liability of directors for payment of dividends out of capital, in cases where the assets are insufficient to pay the creditors. Directors are trustees or *quasi*-trustees of the assets of a company. Those assets in limited companies should be available for the payment of creditors, and those assets must not be returned to shareholders, that is to say, if they are paid out of profits, of course, they belong to the shareholders, but if out of capital, it is improper, and the money must be kept back. So far as I have found there is no legislation on this point, except under the Land Clauses Consolidation Act, which applies to companies which have private Acts of Parliament, and there it is enacted that a company shall not make any dividend whereby their capital shall be reduced. The only other place in which I can find anything like attempted legislation on the subject is in Table A of the 1862 Act. Section 73, says:—" No dividend shall be payable, except out of the profits arising from the business of the company." Table A, you as now know, is not compulsory. No company is bound to adopt Table A. We find that very few companies do, and therefore they contract themselves out of that table, and it is simply supposed to be a blank. But the question has been very much debated, and it has come before the Law Courts on several occasions as to the liability of directors. It has been suggested in the first instance that directors are responsible for any dividend which is paid out of capital. That does not mean—and it cannot mean—that directors are liable to repay the creditors or liquidators any amount of dividend which is proved ultimately to have been paid out of capital. If that were so no board of directors would be safe in paying any dividend. In the case of a bank they would have to wind up the concern every year in order to ascertain whether the profits were made. It would be the same with every trading company, you, therefore, must come to something like a reasonable interpretation of that, and the reasonable interpretation of that is best found in what is laid down by Mr. Justice Kay, in the case of *The Oxford Benefit Building Society* where he states it is now settled that directors who *improperly* pay dividends out of capital are liable to repay such dividends personally on the company being wound up. Now the whole gist of that depends on the word "improperly," on which there has been a great deal of discussion, and I think there will be a great deal more, because there are several very curious questions in connection with the improper payment of capital amongst shareholders. I have had this suggested to me. We will assume a company trades in houses. A house at the beginning of a profit account is valued at £1000. At the end of the profit account it is valued by competent valuers at £1,500 and during the six months the company has succeeded in borrowing £1,200 on it. Is not the company justified in saying that at any rate to the extent of £200 that house is worth more, and are they not justified in saying that is profit? That is one instance. There is another —about ground rents. Take a field laid out for building purposes and part of which is sold. The houses and the rest of the field are valued. If you value it at the same rate as the ground rents which have been created and sold you make an enormous profit, and are the directors justified in assuming that profit has been made and dividing it? Again, there is an instance, which is laid down in Buckley. A shipping company has a capital of £300,000, invested in ten ships, worth £30,000 each. During the year 1885 they made a profit upon their trading of £10,000, but the same year they lost one of their vessels, which was not insured. May they divide the profit of £10,000, or must they apply that £10,000 in partly recouping the loss of capital by one of the vessels sinking? Mr. Buckley says he thinks you are not bound to recoup; but that is one of the questions which will have to be raised, and there are many other questions of that kind which will have to be discussed some of day.

Now the only reasonable and safe suggestion I can make with reference to the calculation of profits, is that the profits of a company should be an account of transactions completed, and paid for, and an account of transactions entered into, which, the directors have fair and reasonable grounds for believing, will be paid for. (Applause.) I think if you keep within these lines you are safe, and if you travel outside you are apt to get into difficulties. I will ask you to pay careful attention to a case which I am going to endeavour to enforce upon you personally. Some articles of association make use of the expression—"dividends shall be paid out of realized profits," and others "out of

net profits." I am not quite certain what net profits should be. I am familiar with the ordinary acceptation of the term, and if I follow the lines I have laid down, I shall know what net profits mean. But when I come to "realized profits," I am at sea directly. There is a well-known case, that of *The Oxford Benefit Building Society*, which was before Mr. Justice Kay. The articles provided that no dividend should be paid except out of the realized profits. Mr. Justice Kay, in his judgment, said : " Realized profits must have (there) its ordinary commercial meaning, which, if not equivalent to reduced to actual cash in hand, must at least be rendered tangible for the purposes of division." I do not know if any gentleman present can tell me what is meant by "rendered tangible for division." Realized profits, in the meaning of Mr. Justice Kay, mean something like having the money in your hands to pay dividends, and he further said : " He cannot accede to its meaning no more than ' real profits honestly earned.' " Railway companies— and I think the very largest – have been known to borrow money for the purpose of paying their dividends, and I do not know that anybody would say that is improper. But whether the borrowing by a railway means " profits tangible for the purpose of divisions " or not I do not know. I must confess it is a very difficult thing. It is extremely difficult to find out what is the meaning of what are "realized profits." I want you to bear that in mind, because I wish to show you that you are interested in finding out the meaning. I have told you that in the same case the judge says it is settled that directors who improperly pay dividends out of capital are liable to repay such dividends personally upon the company being wound up. Now that is rather a serious case, and I am afraid you will find it so. There is another case called *The Leeds Benefit Building Society*, which came before Mr. Justice Stirling. That was a case where directors were sued to be held liable for the same thing. Mr. Justice Stirling says in his judgment— "The law, as regards the payment of dividends out of capital, is perhaps not yet completely settled." Of course, you must, please, understand in any remarks I am making with reference to the decision of these judges, that I make them with the most profound respect. They are able to comprehend law better than I can. It is not my business ; and I would not venture to trouble you with these remarks except that I think you will find it is absolutely necessary you should know something about the matter. And further you will be obliged to act and interpret this law, or find out what it is, and that very often without any reference to a lawyer. I may say that I feel with Mr. Justice Stirling, that the law is not completely settled. He further says— "Directors who make such payments, either with actual knowledge that the capital of the Company is being misappropriated, or with knowledge of the facts which establish the misappropriation, are liable for a breach of trust." In both cases the judges agree it is a breach of trust for which the directors are liable. Well, the case which came before Mr. Justice Stirling, is not only remarkable for laying down the law with reference to the liability of directors for the payment of dividend out of capital, but it goes very much further and it lays down this, that the auditors of the company who audit the company's balance sheet are also liable for the money so paid away, and that brings the matter very very near home to us (laughter). In other words it means this, that we gentlemen, who act as auditors, may be made responsible in case of the winding up of a company—may be made responsible for any dividend, that has been improperly paid out of capital. Well, some gentlemen will say: "That is a very hard thing, I only get 10 or 20, or 40 or 50 guineas for auditing the accounts of the company. I might make a mistake, or I might be weak, or I might do this, that, or the other, and I should be hit for a sum of money which might entirely ruin me." This judgment has been given, and you might be entirely ruined and therefore, I have asked your very serious attention to this case. And not only for that purpose, but because this case—and something which is said in regard to *The Oxford Building Society*—throws some light upon the way in which judges look upon the performance of an auditor's audit. I will read you the head-note in this case. The head-note, as I suppose you know—is a *resumé* of the case prepared by a reporter and it is condensed. He condenses the case very much, and brings before you principally the most important salient points—"Held that it was the duty of the auditor in auditing the accounts of the company not to confine himself to verifying the arithmetical accuracy of the balance sheet, but to enquire into its special accuracy and to ascertain if it contained the particulars specified in the articles of association, and was properly drawn up so as to contain a true and accurate representation of the state of the company's affairs." Now, gentlemen, that is about the very first intimation we have had from the bench as to what is the duty of an auditor, and I say I agree with the principle laid down. (Applause). Now, then follows something with which, I think, I do not agree as to directors instructing auditors. Mr. Justice Stirling says, the directors—

"failed properly to instruct the auditor, or at all events to require him to report on the accounts and balance sheets in the mode prescribed by the articles."

And after some further remarks his Lordship continued—

"Each one of them (the directors) says that he was ignorant of the mode in which the balance sheets were prepared and of the inaccuracies contained in them, and that he trusted entirely to the secretary and manager and the auditor. I see no reason to doubt these statements. Still the fact remains that they did not require either that Crabtree (secretary and manager) should present the accounts, or that Locking (the auditor) should report on them in the form and manner prescribed by the Articles of Association."

I will read a further extract from this.

"*Locking*, the auditor, also appears to me to have been guilty of a breach of duty to the company. He has, however, pleaded the *Statute of Limitations* by way of defence, and the Plaintiff, without arguing the question, has admitted the validity of the plea, which will cover all the accounts except those for the years 1878-1879, and 1879-1880. In each of those years Locking certified that the accounts were a true copy of those shewn in the books of the company. That certificate would naturally be understood to mean that the books of the company shewed (taking for example the certificate for the year 1879) that on the 30th of April, 1879, the company was entitled to "money's lent" to the amount of £29,515 15s. This was not in accordance with the fact; the accounts in this respect did not truly represent the state of the company's affairs, and it was a breach of duty on *Locking's* part to certify as he did with reference to them. The payment of the dividends, directors' fees, and bonuses to the manager actually paid in those years appears to be the natural and immediate consequence of such breach of duty; and I hold Locking liable for damages to the amount of the moneys so paid."

I think I may take it that the directors have no power whatever to require the auditor to report in any particular manner. The auditor is totally independent of the directors. His work is to check their accounts and not to take his instructions from them, and I think in that case Mr. Justice Stirling has misapprehended the position of the auditor. Again, Mr. Justice Stirling referred to the standard laid down by the Judge in *The Oxford Benefit Building Society* and says the directors can if they think proper instruct the auditor or at all events require him to report on the accounts and balance sheet in the mode prescribed by the articles. I do not think they have any right to instruct the auditor who is perfectly independent. Now, his judgment as far as the auditor goes is contained in this case. Now, gentlemen, I have ventured to bring this case before you. I think it is almost the only case of late years and it is one which at any rate shows that if a company winds up with which we are connected as auditors we may have incurred very serious responsibility. But I venture to think the learned judge who decided that case has not carefully considered what an auditor is. He is the agent of the shareholders for the purpose of checking and verifying the accounts of the directors (applause). The accounts are prepared by the directors; no matter whether they are prepared by the manager or secretary, or if an accountant is called in they are still the accounts of the directors, the accounts which the directors give of their stewardship. It is they who say the profits amount to so and so. It is they who submit these accounts to the shareholders, and it is they who suggest the division—and in many cases pay the dividends which turn out to be paid out of capital. Why from the fact that the auditor has said these accounts were right,—why he should be made responsible for what is a breach of duty or trust on the part of directors, I cannot exactly see. I think this case is one which requires to be thoroughly thrashed out, and if it happens to any member of the Institute to be placed in a similar position, I cannot help thinking it would be our duty, in justice to ourselves, and our fellow-members to have the case fought out perhaps to the very highest court. (Cheers). I do not see any reason why we should be placed under such a very serious responsibility. I say it with all proper respect, and I am bound to do so though the arguments or the conclusions which are arrived at by Mr. Justice Stirling are such as I cannot follow. The case was not appealed, and it may not have been appealed for this reason, that the auditor may not have had the money to enable him to do so, or there may have been other reasons. But I think if we are to be subject to this terrible responsibility, we ought, at any rate to have the luxury of knowing the reason why, and we ought to know whether we are liable or not,—whether it will prove that we are to be hit in this fashion or not. I think that the moral of this case is certainly this : that it is the duty of directors to prepare honest accounts—not to catch at setting down as profits something which may be turned into profits in the future; they had far better under-do their profits than over-do them. And if they follow that line, which I suggested some time ago,—the line of simply making their profits mean an account of the transactions completed, and paid for, and an account of transactions entered into, and which they have reasonable grounds for believing will be completed and paid for—then I think they will be safe. The only safety in my mind for auditors, is that they should exercise all reasonable care in examining the accounts of any company, such an amount of care as will satisfy and enable them to sign a certificate that the balance-sheet which they have audited does, in their opinion, set forth a true and correct account of the position of the company according to the books. I know perfectly well that a proper auditor must go further, and see that the books themselves do correspond with facts. I think if an auditor takes reasonable care to enable him to give a certificate such as that, he very likely will not come to any grief at all; but it does show the importance of an auditor acting honestly and independently. I have ventured to bring this before you, because I think it is the most important thing which has happened during the past year, with reference to our profession. It is a matter which involves our interests very much indeed, and it is a matter which, I hope, will receive at your hands a full and complete discussion. (Applause.) I have the reports of these cases here, if any gentleman would like to look at them, and I must ask you to pardon my having brought these law matters before you, for in a matter of this kind, we, to a certain extent, are obliged to advise ourselves. (Applause.)

Mr. E. GUTHRIE—The address we have just listened to I think is the most complete, opportune, and appropriate that we could possibly have at the present time. Mr. Whinney has taken us over the whole ground—the present positions and prospects of the mercantile affairs of the country as influenced by the Companies Acts, referring very completely to the points which need amending, and to the probable direction of legislation. Touching these particular Acts reminds me of the superstition there seems to be in the British mind against tinkering with legislation, which is just what I desire to see, for if we had had the tinkering of legislation in the case of the Bankruptcy Act, we might have had perfect bankruptcy legislation; instead of that, our Parliament takes upon itself—instead of giving us gentle reforms—to give us periodically great revolutionary measures. In time the difficulties and imperfections are developed, and we find although we have cured some evils, we have created opportunities for fresh ones. That is the great danger we are under now in relation to the Companies Acts. Just as half-a-dozen small clauses on the 1869 Bankruptcy Act might have given us something like a perfect bankruptcy measure. I think a Bill of half-a-dozen new clauses with the consolidation of the present Acts would have sufficed to give us a sound and perfect Companies Act such as we could wish to have. Undoubtedly we do not want consolidation and two or three reforms. There is a very weak place in connection with the promotion of Companies. The great evil to be met is the prevention of the deception of the public. The public undoubtedly are deceived, and in a great many cases deceived very grievously, and indeed, principally by the suppression of facts—the omission from the prospectus of statements which would influence people, who otherwise apply, not to invest their money, is one of the chief remedies desired. Mr. Whinney has pointed out that the contemplated bill was intended to provide that all points which would influence people in taking shares should appear on the face of the prospectus. Now, the bill which is at present in Parliament, and which probably will be dropped in the Autumn season, contemplates a full and complete disclosure of all persons occupying any interested position, and I think with that we all agree. That is one of the weaknesses of the present acts which one feels, and which I think a few effective clauses might be sufficient to give practical protection against. Another and principal feature in the bill, which has passed the House of Lords, is the statement on the face of the prospectus to be issued as to the amount upon which an allotment may be made. That, I think, in the matter of small companies, is one of the most material weaknesses of present legislation. (Applause). Vendors and promoters interested largely in the getting up of companies, are often tempted and able to persuade the directors to go to an allotment on an altogether inadequate amount of money (hear, hear) to attempt to work the company with which must inevitably lead to difficulties and which difficulties prevent the getting in of any additional capital. That is another one of the few points on which the present Companies' Acts are weak and need remedying. Turning to another feature—that of debentures. Mr. Whinney puts his finger on one of the greatest abuses in connection with companies at the present day. It is possible in a legal way to carry out the issuing of debentures over an undertaking which practically give, and do in fact give, a preference to a new set of creditors. Very often even a preference of that sort is given to existing creditors, who, unable to get their money, are willing to take debentures in satisfaction thereof. I have seen that done, and I daresay we have all seen it done, and have been in the position of liquidators in cases where morally it has been a substantial fraud. The ordinary innocent trader supplies the goods from day to day, having been permitted to send in his goods up to the last day of working, and all at once he finds the whole assets of the company have been alienated in favour of people who have taken up debentures over the undertaking. It is possible he will find alienated not only the stock-in-trade, but the real estate, the plant and machinery, and the book-debts, and I know myself of a case where even the uncalled capital was also pledged, effecting what I have no hesitation in saying was morally a palpable fraud, leaving the ordinary and unsecured creditors with a dividend of nothing in the £. That is another of the abuses capable of being remedied by a single clause. I do not propose to carry you over all the points on which I agree with Mr. Whinney; that would be a work of supererogation,

but there is a controversy open as to the publication of Balance sheets. I am not at all certain whether it is right, advisable, or fair, that the balance sheets of limited companies should be filed with the registrar of joint stock companies. I am certainly of opinion it would not be right that the trading account and the profit and loss account should be so filed, and I am not prepared to admit that it would be fair or wise to compel the publication of the balance sheet either. I do not think it would be fair to compel that on the part of limited companies unless it were applied to all traders. If companies are to file their balance sheets, I do not see why all persons in trade should not be placed under the same obligation. Those who have to give credit are as much at the mercy of private traders as limited companies. The practical claim as a creditor is limited by the capital of the private trader, or the private firm, just as his position of safety is limited by the capital of the limited company. It may be a proper general question for consideration whether all persons in trade should not be bound to register their capital, and show their position, but I am not prepared to admit that limited companies should be bound to file their balance sheets. I am not quite certain, but I think in France people in trade are bound to announce their capital, whether they do it honestly or not I do not know. But all persons trading as firms, I think, in France have to register the amount of their capital. I do not say it gives them the benefit of limited liability to the amount registered, but they have got to do it. One strong objection to compulsory registration of the balance sheet of a company is that there are throughout the country an immense number of companies which are called in common language " private limiteds," but with which to all intents and purposes, the public are not in any way concerned. A great number of the cotton spinning mills in Lancashire are what are called " private limiteds." They are placed under the Limited Liability Acts for private rather than public purposes, for partnership considerations, and considerations of death, so that the estate of individuals having a large amount of capital invested in a non-realisable form unless it were placed under some regulations of that kind would lead probably to the liquidation of the concern under very disastrous conditions indeed. I think that it is a legitimate use to make of the Limited Liability Acts. It certainly was not the original motive of them, but I think it is a very proper use to make of them, and I do not think those special private concerns should be forced to place their affairs under the eye of the public any more than the next door Mill, where they have continued as a private firm. With respect to the position of auditors, I do not think we ought to shirk reasonable responsibility and liabilities, but under some of what has been stated from the bench, which has been produced by Mr. Whinney, I think we are threatened with responsibility beyond that which we ought legitimately to expect to take. There is one feature in connection with the appointment of auditors which is certainly, perhaps, a cause of very great weakness, and that is the mode of their appointment. (Hear, hear.) Mr. Whinney has given us the theory of the position of an auditor. He has pointed out that the shareholders, in general meetings, are his employers and masters, and that he has to report to them, having no regard whatever to the opinion or opposition of the board. Now, probably in five cases out of ten, if not in nine cases out of ten, the special nomination to the position of auditor is by the directors, or at their instigation, (hear, hear.) and, whether rightly or wrongly, there is naturally a respect paid to the desires and views of directors. They have an influence, and unless the auditor is a man of singular moral strength of character and ability in his profession, he may, by reason of that weakness, very easily be the instrument of doing a great wrong to the proprietary. Nevertheless it is an unfortunate feature that the boards of directors should have the particular initiatory work of giving the public accountant the position which he is only very glad to obtain. Directors will sometimes go so far—and I have seen it in my own case, and have shrunk under the reading of the words—they will go so far as to say "the directors recommend the re-appointment of A. B. as auditor," and theoretically, nothing could be more improper than that directors should make such nominations. (Applause). These are just the points I desire to put before you, for I see the Chairman looking very properly at his watch, and I quite agree we should be very brief in our remarks. (Applause).

THE CHAIRMAN : I am sorry to have to close the discussion, but we all know that appointments have been made for us and we are bound to close punctually to the minute at half-past four.

MR. WHINNEY : If anyone would like to refer to the reports of the cases of *The Oxford Benefit Building Society* and *The Leeds Benefit Building Society*, he will find the reports in the hands of the secretary. The books belong to the Institute, and I have given them in his charge. I think you will find the Leeds case, will well repay perusal.

MR. JACKSON, F.C.A.,(London): It has been entrusted to me to move a vote of thanks to Mr. Whinney, for his paper, and in the following perfunctory words :—" That the best thanks of this meeting be presented to Mr. Frederick Whinney, for his able and interesting paper." (Applause). I call the words "perfunctory," because they would apply to a much less interesting paper. It is one of the most valuable contributions we have ever listened to, because it comes from a mass of reading covering both sides of a public question, Mr. Whinney having been the auditor of companies which live, and also the remover of the remains of those companies which are deceased (laughter), I am therefore certain that there is wisdom to be found in most of the suggestions which he has put forward as regards the Amendment of the Companies' Acts. I entirely agree with the last speaker in thinking the case does not demand any drastic measure, or Act of Parliament reconstituting the Companies' Acts, and I do think in the main they cause little real and justifiable objection on the part of the public. Everybody who has lost money in companies grumbling, and I have heard grumbling from persons who have lost their money by private traders. You may provide all sorts of safe-guards, but the public and investors will never use them. I will merely give an instance why I think amongst other reasons that a balance sheet should not be filed. The theory would be to give constructive notice to any person who was about to supply goods to a company, as to the position of the concern ; but under the Companies' Act he has power to go to the company's register, and find out who the members are, and whether the shares are paid-up. He can thus draw his own inference. There is nothing analogous to that in the case of private individuals, and I therefore think these creditors are sufficiently protected. And from my own experience in regard to certain companies in my office, I never recollect any person who was about to give credit to a company, coming to inspect the register. The only person who came we found was getting up another company, and he was going to circularise the shareholders. I never remember a proposed creditor coming and looking at the register, and I do not think that causing a company to file its balance-sheet is required in the interest of the trader, nor do I think that a great many of the proposals made in the Lord Chancellor's Bill for their protection would serve their purpose. The individual public must to a large extent protect themselves. (Applause.)

MR. J. S. HARMOOD BANNER, F.C.A. (Liverpool): I have had the honour to be asked to second this vote of thanks. I think if we had no other reason to be thankful to Mr. Whinney and grateful to him for his services to the society, the address he has given to us to-day would have rendered us truly grateful to him with the right to acknowledge him as our chief—and as a man who has done more in our interest than any other person who has been in the society (Applause). The remarks which he has made throughout, I think, will show that what the worthy alderman stated in receiving us is true : we ought to give some suggestions in the interest of creditors and though the end of the paper was full of those matters which appertained to the very serious responsibility which has now come upon us in consequence of this recent decision, the first part of the paper showed clearly how creditors as well as shareholders would be protected. In my own mind there was only one thing, I was not quite certain of. Whether Mr. Whinney had considered in reference to this question, and that was just as to whether there should not be as in the case of those chartered banks he spoke of, and of almost every other bank at present, a reserve liability in the case of all shares of public companies, such reserve liability to be used if the company goes into liquidation and to be collectable by the liquidator only for the purpose of existing creditors. I merely mention this because one or two leading financial papers have been discussing it at some length. The banks have adopted it, and it occurred to me as regards the interests of creditors that is a point of very considerable importance. I venture again to call your attention to the very splendid paper we have heard read to us by Mr. Whinney, and to second the vote of thanks. (Applause.)

The resolution was put and carried by acclamation.

MR. WHINNEY (who was received with cheers): Mr. Vice-President and gentlemen, it is some little reward for the labour and pains I have bestowed in this address that I find it meets with your approbation. In one respect I have to apologise. I have taken up so much time with this paper that I am afraid I have left little room for discussion. I should be glad indeed if the discussion could be continued two or three hours, or relegated to some future occasion, but the more important subject of the dinner is looming at the moment in the immediate future, and therefore we must adjourn. In reference to Mr. Banner's suggestions as to reserve liability, the subject has been running through my head, and I am by no means certain it is not an idea which ought to be carried out. I did not discuss it. The subject is too vast to be dealt with in one address. I can only apologise to you for having crammed so much matter in. Mr. Banner is perfectly correct when he says that the first part of the address was devoted to the interests of the public. The second part of the address was rather a domestic matter for ourselves, but it was a part of the subject in which I think we are quite as much or more interested than in the first part. I can only say that I am very pleased indeed that I have been able to give you some food for thought, and it has given me great pleasure to address such an enthusiastic and complete meeting as we have had to-day. (Cheers).

The sitting was then adjourned.

## CHARTERED ACCOUNTANTS STUDENTS' SOCIETY OF EDINBURGH.

### ON AUDITING COMMERCIAL AND COMPANY BOOKS.

#### By Mr. George Johnston Hutton.
*Accountant, Edinburgh.*

In his prefatory remarks to the following paper, read at a meeting of this Society, Mr. Hutton says his aim "was above all to be practical, but it was impossible in the limits originally prescribed to include therein everything connected with the subject. Some points which some may consider of importance may have been omitted; it is thought, however, that the main points taken up are sufficient to suggest what further work should be done by an auditor" :—

What a vast place of business the world is now becoming! Every country seems to be tumbling out its wares and its goods to the outside of its windows and its doors that they may be seen, and, by means of the telegraph and the telephone, is shouting to the ends of the earth that its prices are so and so, and indeed a great deal cheaper than any one's else. Moreover, it sits in its back-parlour, and, counting up its wealth, it launches out anew on some fresh startling scheme to the green envy and violent irritation of its neighbour. Every day thousands of ships are ploughing away through the seas, carrying to and fro the produce of toiling millions. Throughout all the earth the din of business and the noise of the toilers are becoming ever more and more heard the more you sit down to listen to them. A few hundred years ago Venice and Amsterdam were commercial centres in their day, and were accounted splendidly rich and influential; but what were they to the London or New York of to-day? What a volume of trade there is throughout the whole world flowing in and out of these and other great cities, the value of which is simply incalculable! The volume is such that it might indeed fitly be likened to an ocean rather than a river. In the midst of so much wealth, so much noise, so much eager buying and selling, is there not a splendid opportunity for fraud and dishonesty? The deed will be done before it can be noticed, and the robber will escape with impunity. What remedy for this? How can we protect ourselves, cries the whole community, against such insidious enemies?

It is only in comparatively late years that the profession of an auditor has risen in public estimation, but within that time it has risen very rapidly, and now the office of an auditor is one of distinction and desire. An auditor stands as the one reliable man, so to speak, amidst all. *He* is trusted, *he* is believed as no other man in the whole mass of business in the world is trusted and believed.

Thus saith the world unto every auditor, "Is this state of affairs true?" and he, putting his hand to the document, replies, "It is no sham; it is no lie; it is truth." That document is then looked upon by all mankind as irrefragable. It is a fixed fact for all time, and the world frames its actions for ever in accordance therewith.

Woe be to the auditor who knowingly subscribes to a lie! He of all men will never be forgotten—he chose to pose on his height as a man of virtue and truth; but he attempted in the sight of all to deceive, and he fell, never to occupy such an honoured height again; to the end of life he is discredited.

In the days of Diogenes, it seems to have been a wearisome matter to find an honest man, and the grim old philosopher seems to have been bitterly hopeless as to his success. Let us hope that nowadays honesty is not so rare. Indeed, I am strongly of opinion that it is not, seeing the numbers of accountants who now stand forth to the world as men who can be relied upon in telling the truth as to a state of business affairs.

Ye are auditors, or wish to be—how then will you conduct your audit in order to attain to a true statement of affairs?

What follows is an humble attempt to show a practical method by means of which such a desirable end may be arrived at.

In an audit you have got (first) to see what the accounts before you say, and (second) to consider whether they tell the whole truth.

First, then, how are you to satisfy yourself as to what the accounts say? This will necessitate a large amount of detail work, portions of which are highly disagreeable to apprentices as being irksome and laborious, but which nevertheless are of the greatest importance—such as summing pay sheets and long ledger accounts, or posting journals and cash books. Yet I would impress upon apprentices that such work is very important, for in many cases frauds are only detected by means of checking weary lengths of summations and volumes of postings. I would further remind apprentices that it is *not* because such work is unimportant that they get it to do, but because it is comparatively easy work. Wherefore, comfort one another with these words.

Strictly speaking, every single transaction made during the period under review should be examined, and an experienced auditor always satisfies himself that practically he does examine every transaction. Now, if what I say is to be beneficial, I wish to show how such thorough examination can be made.

We are all aware that the four principal books kept by a merchant, in which all entries of transactions are made for the first time, are—

1. The Invoice Book, or Purchase Day Book, in which all purchases are entered as they occur.
2. The Sales Day Book, in which all sales are entered as they occur.
3. The Cash Book.
4. The Bill Book.

There are a few other subsidiary books, which are of minor importance. If we know how to grasp the larger books, we shall know how to master these smaller ones. I shall therefore confine my attention principally to these four larger books, for through them we may say almost every transaction of the business passes. Almost nothing enters the ledger but from them, except it be transfer entries from one ledger account to another. If, then, we are satisfied that every entry in these four books is correct, and that such entry has been correctly posted to its last resting place in the ledger, we may assure ourselves that, so far as the actual transactions have taken place, we are able to make a report, either favourable or unfavourable. How then are we to get at such a desirable standpoint in our audit?

### THE PURCHASE DAY BOOK.

Let us take up first the Purchase Day Book. Here we enquire at the outset who has the authority to make purchases; are the invoices certified by managers of departments that the goods have been received; who gives authority for accounts being paid; and who pays the accounts? Our enquiries may not always be thrown into such form as I have formulated them, nevertheless we ought always to obtain the information, the more especially if it falls to our lot to audit the books of a large commercial concern. It is quite clear that there are many opportunities for fraud in connection with the purchases made for a business, unless precautions are taken. Has it not often happened that where no supervision was made in regard to purchasing, payments have been made for purchases which never took place? It has also been the case that goods got and paid for during one month, have been paid for again during some succeeding month, the accounts for the goods having been discharged by the cashier, or other official forging the signature. All this has taken place through there being no proper system in force for sanctioning the payment of accounts. It is not only undesirable, but improper, that in a large establishment the same official should have the power both of authorising payment and of making payment. It is true, in some houses, a partner has this power, and perhaps less can be said against the arrangement in that case. I would, however, remind you that a partner has long ere this defrauded his co-partners. It is the duty of an auditor to point out such precautions; and in cases of the audit of limited companies' books it would be his duty to insist upon such precautions being taken, because the auditor is an officer appointed directly by the shareholders. Unless the invoices are certified by managers of departments, what guarantee is there that the goods were ever received into stock? Moreover, the invoice being certified by the manager will prevent it being used again by a fraudulent official for a double payment of the account.

Having then satisfied ourselves that what is in the purchase day book has entered it under some authority, we have the book summed. It should then be compared with the invoices, but this would be in some cases an enormous labour. If such a system, however, in reference to the invoices, is in use, as I have pointed out, it is perhaps only necessary to make a general comparison of invoices so certified, with the invoice book, because it is quite possible to have another check upon the total sum of the purchases. In this way; if some official or partner has the duty of sanctioning payment of the accounts, he no doubt will satisfy himself that the invoice is certified, and he will keep some record of all accounts he authorised to be paid, and then he will hand over the account to be paid to the cashier, whom I presume to be a separate official from the party *authorising* payment. If then the record kept by the party authorising payment agrees with the total in the invoice book, say month by month, we may have some confidence that the invoice book is correct. He will then see that the totals of the book are carried by means of the journal (if such a book be in use) into the proper accounts in the ledger, and our examination of the book is at an end.

### THE SALES DAY BOOK.

Turning now to the Sales Day Book, we enquire what there is to instruct it; and if the business is a general one, dealing with many kinds of merchandise, we are met with serious difficulty. Where the business is all of one kind, such as of iron or cotton, where the quantities sold should correspond with the quantities purchased or received, after taking into account the stocks on hand, we have not much difficulty in satisfying ourselves how the whole goods are disposed of. But in a large miscellaneous business, as a store of any kind, or large retail establishment, it is evident such a check cannot be obtained without extremely minute detail. In such business, however, it is usual that money is not paid to the shopman or party selling, or if so, only after the note of goods sold has been initialled by the supervisor or by the cash clerk. These notes of sales are filed by the cash clerk and recorded by him, the total of which record should agree with his cash in hand. By such a method, or some such adapted to the requirements of each business, if efficiently carried out, the cash sales, even of a large miscellaneous business, may be said to be sufficiently instructed. Without some such system there would be great opportunity for robbery, for it is in cash sales more readily than in credit sales that theft will take place. Indeed, with credit sales the auditor should feel confident that if such methods of procedure as he approves of are carried out, there should be no room for theft, and he might suggest something on the lines of the following method:—

All the orders having been entered into the order book, the orders are then made up from that book, and an outvoice prepared and certified by the despatching department with a number corresponding to the order in the order book. The outvoice is then sent to the counting house, where it is entered in the sales day book, and having been copied into a press copy book, it is finally despatched to the customer.

Thus every entry in the sales day book will be instructed by a copy of the certified outvoice in the press copy book, and also by the entry in the order book.

If the sales day book has been correctly kept in some such fashion as this, all we may find necessary to do will be to test the entries in the book, here and there, with the order book and with the press copy book, so satisfying ourselves generally that it is correct; and after we have seen the book summed, and that the totals are carried into the ledger, our intercourse with it for the meantime is finished.

If, however, as I have already stated, the sales consist of one species of merchandise, it is most probable you will be able to see whether the total quantities sold account for the whole stocks in hand at the commencement, *plus* the new goods procured during the period. Moreover, as it is most likely that contracts will have been entered into for the larger sales, such contracts should be examined to instruct the sales made and the prices received for them. If we have some such evidence as that laid before us, we may rest assured that the method in use for recording all sales transactions is a reliable one.

*(To be Continued.)*

# The Accountant.

A MEDIUM OF COMMUNICATION BETWEEN ACCOUNTANTS IN ALL PARTS OF THE UNITED KINGDOM.

VOL. XV.—NEW SERIES.—No. 781.          SATURDAY, NOVEMBER 23, 1889.

## The Accountant,

NOVEMBER 23, 1889.

### ON AUDITING COMMERCIAL AND COMPANY BOOKS.

IN our last issue was concluded the report of a lecture on the above, which we have no doubt has been read with interest and advantage by our subscribers in general, and by South Britons with a natural feeling of curiosity as to the ideas and practices prevalent north of the Tweed on what always has been, and probably always will be, the chief branch of the work of professional accountants. The paper is able and instructive. It is written with the thoughtfulness and the literary exactness which we instinctively expect Scotchmen to possess; containing also, here and there, idioms not wholly familiar to the average Englishman. Evidently intended to deal with the subject in a general way, the few isolated and specific references it contains to manufacturing concerns, and to what we presume to be ordinary building societies or mortgage companies, rather impairs the unity of the paper, and perhaps its power of resistance to criticism. For Mr. HUTTON must know we do criticise each other, and sometimes ourselves, in England, and though the Caledonian debater, like the Caledonian heckler, is not to be lightly engaged or faced; discussion is always good whichever side prevails. And we are of those who try at least to get at and acknowledge the best views and the best practices, even if we have not always held or supported them; and in this spirit we propose to take up a few points that strike us in Mr. HUTTON's paper.

The remarks on the Purchase Book do not impress us very greatly. For efficacy, in the prevention of fraud for practicability in our daily work, and in the average run of audits, no lecturer, either before or since, has, in our opinion, improved or

99

even reached the standard of the remarks made on this subject before the Manchester Students, by Mr. H. M. ASHWORTH.* The one weakness in the routine work of examining the invoices, (which has often a soporific effect on assistants) is that accounts may be twice credited, and the entry of the second credit used fraudulently. Mr. ASHWORTH's suggestion, shortly stated, was to index the invoices of each seller, so that they could all be examined consecutively, and this plan is being very frequently adopted. The mere apprehension which such a mode of audit would inspire should, in most cases, deter any contemplated frauds. Whilst we do not undervalue, we do not over-estimate the point so often insisted on of scrutinising the invoices to see that they bear the initials of the storekeeper or other official. He would be a poor sort of a rogue who could not get over that difficulty. Mr. HUTTON might have uttered a warning against accepting invoices drawn on plain paper—a common practice where the audit commences soon after the closing date, and before statements or invoices have been rendered for the purchases made towards the end of the period. Sometimes, however, the ingenuity of the rogue beats the sagacity of the auditor even on the latter's own ground. In Yorkshire a year or two ago, a fraudulent officer of a company got the bill-heads of certain tradesmen printed; but for fraud effected by that means an auditor can no more be blamed than the Courts of Justice can prevent being imposed upon by perjury.

English accountants must note as a curious circumstance that as far as his remarks on the Cash Book indicate, Mr. HUTTON does not appear familiar with the convenience and the advantage of the plan of having a bank column in the Cash Book instead of the old and cumbrous Ledger account system. Moreover, the illustration which he uses as the reason why the Bank Pass Book should be examined in detail with the bank account in the books, is neither particularly happy nor particularly conclusive. The particular method of fraud which Mr. HUTTON wishes to guard against is the work more of a stupid than a clever rogue; at least the English rogues we have known, personally or by reputation, are better artists than the Scotch species, if Mr. HUTTON's illustration is a fair sample of their work. It would not be necessary to

*The Accountant, No. 552, p. 7, Manchester Transactions, 1884, p. 167.
†The Accountant, 1887, p. 112.

check the bank account with the Bank Pass Book to find out an irregularity of the kind mentioned. It would come out in the natural course of a routine audit, if the audit clerks did their work properly; as so clearly laid down by Mr. GODDARD at Newcastle some time ago.† The chief value we ascribe to the detailed checking of the Bank Pass Book is that it stops the little ways cashiers sometimes get into of keeping heavy sums in hand for months, and lodging it 10 days before the audit, so that the *balance* in the end appears right. It is convenient to know the trick sometimes; chief clerks in chambers do not universally understand it. "The Revenue Account," Mr. HUTTON says, "must include *all* earnings and expenditure for the year—not simply such earnings as have been received. With such excellently correct views, it is rather sad to notice that Mr. HUTTON's practice, if his *pro formâ* accounts are to be taken to mean what they say, is not in accordance therewith.

GROSS REVENUE ACCOUNT.

*Expenditure* | *Receipts. (sic.)*

is rather a curious way of giving effect to the opinion that a Revenue Account should include *all* earnings, not simply such as have been *received*. Going further into the Revenue Account (which, by the way, should precede the balance sheet) we feel rather chary of making specific criticism, because it might hardly be fair to pin Mr. HUTTON down as if he were prescribing a form for any particular business. But this much we will say, if the Revenue Account is given as a model for manufacturing concerns, it is not a good model. No spinner, whether his staple be cotton, silk, wool or flax, arrives at his "gross" profit by taking the purchases and sales and the stock at the commencement and the close of the period. In fact, we hardly understand what the meaning of "gross" profit is when it is used in connection with manufacturing concerns. If a merchant's or a trader's accounts are under review, it is most useful to show the difference which is here called gross profit; that is supposing the goods are sold in the state in which they are bought, and that no manufacturing process is needed. An auditor's duty and his liability in regard to stock is a big question, and one we could not deal with in our present space. The remarks on "Wages" are not very strong, neither are those on depreciation. In speaking of Income Tax charged to net Revenue, Mr. HUTTON, we trust, does not overlook the fact that he intends to deduct tax from the dividends and interest paid to share and debenture holders and mortgagees; the wording of these latter items in the net Revenue Account, if made explicit, might prevent misapprehensions as to whether the *full* dividends and interest were being charged as well as Income Tax. When Mr. HUTTON says Goodwill does not often *appear* in accounts, (as an asset we presume) we hope he does not forget, as those who read his remarks may do, that appearances are very often, and in late years especially, deceitful. We doubt, if amongst the hundreds of joint stock companies that have been floated in the late excitement, a single instance could be found where Goodwill was not an item, and in many cases to an enormous extent. We doubt if, in one case out of every twenty, an auditor in England checks the opening entries in the share ledgers with the original letters of application, or even with the allotment sheets. As in nearly all cases, the preparation of the application and allotment sheets, and the opening of the books is performed by chartered accountants. Even where the auditor to the company has not done this work, we do not think it is usual to go behind the allotment sheets; and in large companies it would be almost impracticable to do so. What should be done with regard to transfers is rather debateable. It is not, we think, the rule to examine the transfer deeds, but remembering the operations of such persons as REDPATH, ROBSON, and others of the same stamp, but of later date, who have made this ground classic, the certificates returned should certainly be checked with the new ones given out. We heard some time ago of a few cases of ordinary companies where an additional fee was paid the auditors in consideration of their examining the transfer deeds, and Mr. VAN DE LINDE in his paper on " Company Work," 15 *Accountant* 98, refers to the growing practice with railway and other large companies of treating the checking of the issue of new certificates, and the verification of the share registers generally, as outside the ordinary audit, paying an additional fee for the work. In England the simple but effectual precaution of issuing to all transferors a notice of transfers lodged, is generally, almost universally, followed, and constitutes a safeguard to some extent. We always think the transfer book itself should be initialled by a director; or that it should give the reference to the minute book, where the sanction of the transfer may be found. Beyond what has been already said, the *pro formâ* balance sheet and accounts call for no remark, except it may be, as to the balance sheet, that, as a rule, accrued rent, wages, income tax, &c., are usually shown; some matters could hardly fall under the designation " Sundry creditors on open accounts." Though it makes no difference in the end, we think it would be preferable if the items of debit to net Revenue Account were stated in their right, and not as is the fact, in their wrong order. A dividend on ordinary shares does not take precedence of interest on debentures; and interest on debentures probably ranks after, not before, interest on mortgages. No further points strike us on the paper, which we have read with much interest

## MANCHESTER ACCOUNTANTS STUDENTS' SOCIETY.

### AN ADDRESS.

### By W. H. Nairne, Esq., F.C.A.

At a meeting of the above Society, held on the 9th October, 1889, the President, Mr. W. H. Nairne, F.C.A., delivered the following address :—

Following the precedents set by previous occupants of this chair, it becomes my duty to read an address to you, on this the opening night of the session. Most, if not all, duties have their painful and their pleasurable sides ; and the pain and the pleasure are sometimes so inextricably mixed, that it would be difficult to decide where the one ends, and the other begins. Commonly speaking, we may say that the painful part of a duty commences when we first try to realise what it is we have undertaken to do, and have to cast about for the means to be employed in its accomplishment. Then it is that the diffident man, the man who is not of those classed as "fools (who) rush in where angels fear to tread," begins to realise to some extent his own deficiencies ; and this process is somewhat painful and humiliating : it has, however, its compensating benefit, inasmuch as it produces an educational effect ; for we make a distinct advance in learning when we become convinced of our absolute or comparative ignorance of a given subject. Then arises the necessity for exertion in order to acquire the means requisite for the performance of the work set before us : in this process of exertion, the calibre of a man is tested ; and where the too confident man, who over-rates his own powers, fails at the outset, becomes discouraged, disgusted, and retires ; the diffident man, often becomes aware (in the process of exertion) of the existence of latent powers within himself, of which he was not before conscious, is encouraged to greater effort, and succeeds. It is in this exercise of his mental or moral strength, in order to grapple with and overcome the obstacles to the attainment of his object, that the sensation of *pleasure* commences, and which increases until the moment of complete success.

These thoughts were suggested to me, when I reflected that my acceptance of the honorable position of president of this Society involved, in the first place, the preparation of an address to you, and in the second place an increased share of moral responsibility for the well-being and success of the Society. When I remembered who were the gentlemen who had preceded me, their acknowledged eminence in the profession, and the efficient manner in which they had discharged the duties of the office, my natural tendency to shrink from positions challenging notice and criticism, which has been intensified by the private nature of my own work as an accountant, made me almost regret that I had yielded to the persuasions of your late president, Mr. Halliday ; whose practical and unobtrusive manner of presiding over your meetings is fresh in your memories. I was, however, encouraged by the consideration that this is, after all, a Society of Students, in every sense a mutual improvement society, whose meetings we attend in the hope of learning something from the experience of others, and with a modest desire to reciprocate by imparting to others something of what we have acquired in our own experience.

It is in this light I wish to be regarded by you this evening, and indeed on all future occasions, as one of you, willing and wishful to learn by intercourse with you, and with the desire to give to any who may need it the benefit of such experience as I have gained in a somewhat lengthy, though quiet and retired practice.

I do not propose on this occasion, to deal in detail with any specific branch of accountancy. I prefer, and (I trust it will not be considered inappropriate to the occasion), to take a wider view, and to endeavour as far as lies in my power, to make my address applicable to the circumstances, and comprehensible to the minds of the youngest and most inexperienced members of our Society ; while I hope that what I may say may find a response in the minds of my older and more experienced hearers. I hope no one will accuse me of intentional plagiarism, if I should state truths which have been more ably and forcibly enunciated before. It is not the lot of many men to say something altogether new ; the utmost that ordinary persons like myself can hope to do, is to say what has been said before in a somewhat different way.

Our Society from its very nature, must continually renew its youth ; and it is not unreasonable to suppose, that at the beginning of a new session, we have present among us a few *new* members, and a sprinkling of *old* ones, whose professional appetites have not been so thoroughly satiated, as to turn away with nausea at everything homely, (and, may I say, wholesome) ; but who are perhaps secretly hoping to find that they have not joined the profession, and this Society, so late in the day as to be unable to understand its vocabulary ; and who will welcome a comparatively youthful, and absolutely inexperienced president, whose own hope of success lies in the remembrance, that the ablest and the cleverest have had a beginning. This must form a plea for patience and forbearance on the part of those learned and experienced gentlemen whose presence here this evening I consider a proof of their goodwill to the Society.

I have chosen to say a few words to you on the honour or dignity of the profession, on its scope and usefulness, and its applicability to some of the needs of society.

We may measure the honour or dignity of any position by the nature and extent of its responsibilities, by the opportunities for influencing or benefiting others, and by the moral qualities and mental acquirements necessary to be possessed by its occupant. Measured by these standards I propose to show that the honour and dignity, attaching to the practice of public accountancy in its various branches, is worthy of our aspirations. Before proceeding to do this, it may be well, and may disarm criticism to which I might otherwise lay myself open, to make it clear that I do not overrate the importance of the profession to which I have the pleasure to belong. From the point of view of the nature of its responsibilities, I am willing to place the profession of a Chartered Accountant below several other vocations which I have in my mind, but which it is unnecessary to specify.

It is incumbent on me, however, to refer generally to the numerous classes of producers, makers, and distributors, whose labour and enterprise, whose varied and conflicting interests, during their lives, and the interests of whose representatives after their decease, furnish the material which finds us employment. It is, in fact, the extent and importance of such interests, entrusted to accountants, which has called into being the Institute of Chartered Accountants, and this, and kindred societies of students affiliated to the parent Institute ; with the object of providing a body of men specially trained for their work.

I will now endeavour to show that Chartered Accountants may claim a definite place in the economy of the world. If I may, without appearing invidious, make a comparison, our position is somewhat analagous to that of the legal profession : as a corporate body we are a younger brother of that profession, and as such, we must out of respect to the law of primogeniture take a subordinate place. Some of our more enthusiastic members might be disposed to say that we occupy, not a subordinate, but an equal position with the legal profession. I should agree with them from the point of view of mere usefulness in the every day work of commercial life: and I think most lawyers would admit this; but when I regard the nature of the responsibilities attaching to the profession of law, I am constrained to admit that to lawyers (classing solicitors and advocates together) are confided interests much more important than any the value of which can be ascertained in money. This I take to be the chief difference between the two professions in their relations to those engaged in other walks of life: that, whereas the accountant's aid is sought only on matters in which his client is pecuniarily interested, the lawyer is consulted on almost every conceivable matter affecting his client's rights, privileges, liberties or interests (pecuniary or otherwise). Moreover from the ranks of the legal profession are chosen the judges, men of the highest attainments, than whose responsibility none is greater; for on the exercise of their authority and influence depend in a measure not only the most important interests, but the liberties, and even the lives of men and women.

There are, however, in their respective relations to the commercial life of the world, several points of resemblance between lawyers and accountants. Negatively, they are neither of them producers, makers, or distributors, in the sense of providing for the absolute wants of men; that is, they do not directly feed, clothe, or house them; nor even, as part of their usual avocations, do they risk their capital in, or employ themselves in supervising, the production, manufacture or distribution of necessities.

They are both in fact (in common with other professions which might be named) products of a complex civilisation—experts, whose existence has become a necessity to the producers, manufacturers and distributors, who require lawyers and accountants to regulate and record their various transactions with each other, to unravel the complications arising out of such transactions, to reconcile their differences, to be their advocates or supports in their disputes, to protect them from injustice, and (not to weary you) generally to do for them either periodically or as special circumstances render necessary, those things within the scope of a lawyer's or accountant's knowledge and practice, which from their absorption in their own daily round of work and anxiety they are unable or indisposed to do for themselves. Such inability or indisposition induces (and indeed in some cases compels) them, to turn for guidance or assistance to an expert, and thus they become the clients of the lawyer or accountant, or as frequently happens, of both.

In this association of their labours on behalf of their client is engendered between the man of law and the man of figures mutual respect and esteem; I may say for myself, that some of my most pleasant professional reminiscences are associated with labour of this kind. It may be either the lawyer or the accountant who is first approached by the client, but whichever it is, the one often finds it necessary or prudent to recommend that the services of the other be procured. I should weary you, and should fail, were I to attempt to detail the many and various occasions on which lawyers and accountants become co-workers on behalf of their clients. But in reviewing some of the work of an accountant, it becomes necessary to refer to events which involve his honourable association with lawyers; when, although their labours are essentially different in their nature; the one being describable as literary, and the other mathematical; they are directed to one end, the interest of their client; the two find frequent necessity for consultation together; and the results of their several and joint labours are frequently contained in one legal instrument.

In such labours it often happens that the accountant takes the principal part (if measured by the time occupied) by reason of the nature of his work, which frequently involves minute investigation of details. For example, a man contemplates investing his money in some business, in which case the accountant is usefully employed in an enquiry into the financial stability of the person, firm, or company, by whom such business is carried on; and into

the nature of the security offered. This being done, the lawyer prepares the agreement or deed to be executed by the parties, and in doing so has regard to the accountant's report. Or, a partnership may be projected, when the accountant may be required on behalf of one or other of the parties or their solicitors, to ascertain from the books of a business already established, the past profits and present capital of the owner of the business; facts which influence the terms of the partnership deed, which is to be drawn by the solicitor. Although not always recognised by solicitors, an accountant's experience is valuable in connection with the framing of the financial articles of a partnership agreement.

I am glad to record a graceful recognition of this fact by solicitors in more than one case, where they have submitted to me the draft articles of their own proposed partnerships. I remember an instance of a loan to a firm, on which there was to be paid a minimum interest of four per cent. per annum, with a share of net profits, if any; but it was found impossible to ascertain from the deed executed by the lender and borrower, whether in calculating the net profits, the minimum interest was to be taken into account; that is, whether the lender was to be entitled to only a share of net profits, when they exceeded four per cent., or was to have his minimum interest, *plus* a share of net profits. I think it is not too much to say that if the draft of this deed had been submitted to a qualified accountant, he would have suggested a clearer definition of the term "Net Profits."

It is not uncommon, and it is consistent with common sense, and the interests of their clients, for solicitors to submit draft articles of partnership to an accountant, who is already, or is to become, the auditor of a firm; or is to examine the accounts on behalf of one or more of the partners. There arise disputes between partners; many of which (arising out of a misunderstanding on matters of account), it is within the accountant's province to settle or compromise with or without the aid of a solicitor. After a time, it becomes necessary to re-arrange the terms of a partnership, and prepare a fresh agreement; or it may be that a dissolution is decided upon; in either of which cases, the accountant is often the most clearly cognisant of, and the best exponent of, the intentions of the parties; and by the preparation of clear and definite statements, facilitates the labour of the solicitor in giving legal and binding effect to such intentions. A dissolution may take place under various conditions. One partner may wish to retire, and this may involve not only the ascertaining of the amount of capital and profits to which he is entitled, but the value of his interest in the goodwill; the period to be allowed for payment of the sum found to be due to him; and the security to be given by the continuing partner. Again, partners may wish to apportion their assets and liabilities, and to carry on the same kind of business separately; in which case, very delicate negotiations have sometimes to be carried through between the parties. Or, they may desire to discontinue business, to dispose of it, (if it has any value), and wind up their partnership affairs. In all these cases, while it is expedient to employ a lawyer in order that the obligations undertaken may be legally binding, that no unfair advantage may be obtained by the one party over the other, and that they may neither of them suffer the consequences of slovenly and irregular arrangements; it is also expedient, prudent, and in many cases absolutely necessary, to call in an accountant: whose special training and experience fits him for the several duties of ascertaining the respective shares of the partners in the capital of the partnership, the carrying on of negoiations, the apportionment of values, and the realisation of outstanding assets and liabilities.

To take another instance, and now a very common one. A firm may determine for various reasons to convert their concern into a joint stock company, with a view to limiting their liability to the amount of their capital, to giving certain of their employées a share in the business, or to facilitate the sale or disposal by gift or bequest, of their interest therein.

In such a case, it is necessary to have recourse to a lawyer for the purpose of conveying the property, and for the drawing of the memorandum and articles of association ; and an accountant is generally required in connection with the re-arrangement of the books. consequent upon the re-valuation of assets, the adjustment and closing of the capital accounts of the partners, and the allotment of shares in place of a portion or the whole, of the amount of such capital.

The instance I have just mentioned is the case of a conversion of a concern into a company, with only, or little more than, the minimum number of members required by the companies' Acts, and the share capital in which is held largely by the original owners.

I will now take a more important and complicated case, namely, that of an absolute sale of a business undertaking to one or more persons ; with a view of its being formed into what is known as a public company, the shares in which are offered for public subscription. The purchasers almost invariably instruct an accountant to make a searching examination into the accounts of the business for several years back, partly with a view of ascertaining the value of the visible property and assets offered for sale. by an enquiry into their cost, age, probable depreciation, &c.; but chiefly with the object of getting at the net profits of the concern, after making due provision for maintenance and renewal of plant, losses by bad debts, &c.: for it is a recognised principle that the value of a commercial undertaking is the capitalised value of its net income ; the number of years' purchase adopted in such capitalisation, depending upon the value of money, the nature of the undertaking, and the probability of the amount of its income being respectively maintained, increased, or decreased. The excess of such capitalised value over the structual value of the plant, and the floating assets, constitutes the *goodwill*, which rises in value in proportion as the probable duration of the income approaches permanency.

An accountant engaged in such work has a great responsibility ; he represents directly those from whom he has received his instructions ; but beyond them, he is acting indirectly on behalf of a large number of unknown persons, who may become shareholders in the projected company; his duty to them is a very real and responsible one ; for he is aware that his certificate will probably form part of the prospectus, and will be largely instrumental in deciding possible investors as to whether, and to what extent, they will risk their money in the undertaking. He has, so to speak the whole community for a client; and apart from the risk of having to appear as a defendant in a suit for damages, instituted by one or more disappointed shareholders, if he wilfully or carelessly makes any misstatement. he is bound as a man of principle and honour, and out of respect to the profession to which he belongs, to so frame his report or certificate, that its meaning shall not be ambiguous ; but that it shall be a plain statement of the facts necessary to enable a careful investor to form an opinion upon the prospects of the undertaking. It should conceal nothing which it is essential to take into account in forming such an opinion; in short, it should contain such information as he would consider necessary to give to one of his own clients, or to have regard to himself, were he contemplating taking shares in the undertaking.

This should be done without fear or favour, and without regard to the effect it may have in confirming or cancelling the provisional agreement which is usually entered into between the vendors and promoters.

The accountant engaged by the promoters of a Company, is usually retained as the first auditor of such company and his name appears on the prospectus in that capacity ; this is an additional reason (if one is required) why he should be careful and painstaking in his investigation and report ; for intending shareholders know that as auditor he he will, from the commencement of the company's operations, stand in a fiduciary relation to each one of them ; and they naturally conclude that such relationship is retrospective ; that it extends back to the date of his certificate. This must be so, for I cannot conceive a more unenviable position than that of an auditor, who should find it his duty to inform the shareholders of essential facts which he was previously aware of, but omitted from his report set forth in the prospectus.

I am afraid I am digressing, but I cannot refrain from taking this opportunity to make my position clear in reference to a point which arose in the discussion of an excellent paper by Mr. MATHER, on the "Ethics of Accountancy," read at one of the meetings of the Manchester Society of Chartered Accountants.

The point raised was the need for exercising great prudence in allowing our names to appear on the prospectuses of projected companies. I am afraid that my remarks on that occasion were misunderstood, at least by our esteemed vice-president; for I remember that Mr. WADE in his speech, took very high ground; and Mr. MATHER, in replying to the remarks which had been made, referred to Mr. WADE and myself as representing the two extremes of opinion on this subject; and as Mr. WADE was at the top, I was necessarily at the bottom ; from which it would follow that I was disposed to allow great latitude in this matter. Now, I agree with Mr. WADE, and others who spoke on that occasion, that the presence of the names of well-known firms of accountants on the prospectus of a company may possibly influence people to place more confidence in the representations made therein.

Therefore I hold that a Chartered Accountant should not lightly, and without some enquiry into the circumstances, and characters of the promoters, permit his name to appear on a prospectus. But it would be very difficult to define the nature and extent of the precautions to be taken on all occasions when a request is made to us to allow our names so to appear.

What I wished to convey in my remarks, on the occasion I have referred to was : That the duties of an auditor commence *after* the company has been established, *after* the share capital has been subscribed, and usually *after* a considerable amount of ordinary business has been transacted ; and therefore, that the fact of his name appearing on the prospectus should not be taken as implying that he accepts any sort of responsibility for the probable success of the Company ; not even such a responsibility as would be implied in a certificate as to the past profits of the business.

The responsibilities of an auditor to the shareholders in a joint stock company are numerous and onerous enough, without his needlessly accepting more; and I think it is well that the public should clearly understand that such responsibilities do not (strictly speaking) commence until he makes his examination of the accounts, and places his name at the foot of a report to the shareholders.

To return, however, to our projected company. If the promoters, as representing the future shareholders, find it expedient to call in an accountant ; the vendors also, if well advised, employ an accountant; who anticipates the requirements of the promoters ; and by making himself thoroughly acquainted with the accounts and past working of the business, can render valuable assitance to the vendors in arriving at the true value of the undertaking proposed to be transferred ; and in the negotiations as to price and other conditions, is eminently qualified by his training and experience to maintain and promote the interests of his clients. His position may become one of considerable anxiety : for he is frequently entrusted with great discretionary power in the negotiations with the intending purchasers ; in the carrying out of which, he finds ample scope and opportunity for care and vigilance, and for mingled firmness and tact. The price being agreed upon, the lawyer, (who has probably been consulted at the outset, and been advising and assisting in the negociations), prepares a provisional agreement between the vendors and purchasers, which is the basis of the conveyance ultimately required. Here, again, we have the association of the lawyer and accountant; for, while the lawyer's special skill is necessary to give clear and unmistakable expression to the intentions of the parties, and a valid title to the property purchased, he requires the accountant to supply him with particulars and values of the various classes of property and assets, to be transferred; and as the accountant is the person usually responsible for the opening of the books of the company, and for the apportionment and settlement of accounts between the parties, it is consistent with prudence that the drafts of the agreement and conveyance or other legal instruments necessary to vest the property in the company, should be submitted to him; in fact, it may be said, without derogating in the slightest degree from the importance of the labours of the solicitor and counsel in drawing and settling a conveyance, that such conveyance is much less likely to be the cause of future misunderstandings, disputes, and disagreements, if it has been submitted to the accountant, and been passed by him as conveying to his mind the intentions of the contracting parties.

One of the most important branches of accountancy, and one in which almost all Chartered Accountants are more or less engaged, is that of Auditing.

It is hardly necessary to say anything as to the value of an audit conscientiously performed by a qualified person. If any proof were necessary, it could be amply supplied from the records of any firm of accountants who have been in practice a few years. Any one of them, were they free to mention their professional experiences, could give numerous specific instances of the detection of fraud, the stoppage of irregularities, the prevention of loss, of the imprudent and extravagant expenditure checked in time, and of positive gain to their clients from following their suggestions.

Many of us, were we not bound in honour to keep silence, could relate incidents of almost dramatic interest, arising out of such prosaic work as the examination of figures. But in addition to the beneficial results of an audit, illustrated by some striking incident which fixes them on the mind; there are the undeniable benefits which arise from the systematic arrangement and regular performance of work, which the periodical supervision of an auditor is calculated to ensure. It is said that: "that nation is the happiest which has no history." Paraphrasing this, I might say that the most efficiently conducted commercial establishment is that which has no records of a sensational kind.

Permit me to give a further illustration. It is not uncommon for a man who has passed the meridian of life, and whose experience has taught him to regard with favour the system of payments by results, to make an arrangement with his doctor, by which he is to pay him a certain sum per annum during his life. Such a man would be considered unreasonable, were he, after receiving regular medical treatment for a time, to suggest, as a reason for discontinuing the contract, that he did not experience any acute bodily suffering. Apply this to the commercial man and his auditor, *verbum sat sapienti.* The value of an audit is, however, largely recognised by the commercial public, and is becoming increasingly so.

If our profession had to stand or fall on this branch of work alone, it would have a good reason for existence. If in connection with this subject, we consider the nature and extent of our responsibilities, of which we are constantly reminded in the course of a year; the almost endless variety of businesses which come under our review, embracing nearly every kind of industry or trade; manufacturers, merchants, shippers, municipal corporations, with their numerous departments, banks, insurance companies, building societies, charitable, social, and educational institutions, &c., each of these having its own special features or peculiarities, to which we have to adapt and apply a set of general principles; or, if we try and calculate the immense amount of capital invested in the undertakings with which we are professionally connected; or try to realise the almost implicit faith and trust reposed in our ability and honour by the large number of shareholders in joint-stock companies, members of building societies, depositors in saving banks, &c.; or that which, perhaps, we prize most, the friendly trust and confidence of those clients with whom we are brought into more personal intercourse; we must be impressed with the fact that we belong to an honourable and useful profession, which is worthy of our best efforts.

As the result of an audit, the accountant is frequently called upon to make special investigations and reports These often require greater effort of mind than an audit pure and simple, as every audit necessarily comprises a considerable amount of routine. Such investigations, arising out of special circumstances, are more interesting to the accountant, as he finds therein a larger field for his abilities, knowledge, and experience, and important consequences frequently follow upon his report. I have in mind a case where the property of a private firm had been purchased and was being worked by a limited company; finding in the course of his audit that the facts differed from his instructions, the accountant made further inquiries; with the result that he discovered that whereas the purchasers had been under the impression that they had bought the property and assets for £20,000, they had actually made themselves liable for a mortgage of £7,000, making the cost £27,000. The vendors, on being appealed to, declared that they had sold the "business" for £20,000. It was in fact a misunderstanding and was compromised. Here was a case for the employment of an accountant in the negotiations, and in an examination of the draft of the contract executed by the parties.

Another instance will illustrate the benefit to be derived from a thorough audit. A certain old-established Building Society had for years been audited in a perfunctory manner at a fee which shall be nameless, but which, although diminutive, was certainly in excess of the value of the work performed; which consisted in an examination of a summary of receipts and payments, and a comparison of same with the bank pass book. The result of the first complete audit was, that although the actual profits for the year amounted to thousands of pounds, they were almost if not entirely absorbed in making up a deficiency which had been accumulating for years; caused by an erroneous system of arriving at the amount of the dividends which had been annually declared. Many instances might be given of irregular methods, or the absence of any method, of making up the accounts of building societies; the results of which to shareholders and loanholders, have been most mischievous: and this quite apart from the losses which have been caused by reckless competition for borrowers, and the serious depreciation in the value of property; from which last-named cause many comparatively well-managed societies have suffered heavily.

Accountants have found most useful and responsible work in the assisting officials of building societies in their re-organisation, and in doing so, have met with most remarkable and almost ridiculous instances of inequitable division of profits; usually in favour of the advanced or borrowing members. In some cases, such mode of division was authorised by the wording of the rules, the effects of which could not possibly have been understood by the ignorant and confiding unadvanced member; these effects being hidden for a time by the unsound basis (often innocently adopted) on which the accounts were made up.

There is a class of work on which accountants are becoming more frequently employed; namely, the preparation of Profit and Loss Accounts for the purposes of Income

Tax returns, or appeals against assessments; in connection with which I have reason to believe they are welcomed by the Inland Revenue Officials, from whom (I may say for myself) I have received uniformily courteous treatment, and who have at times a thankless office to perform in firmly administering laws wh a they cannot but acknowledge cause hardships in individual cases. One very simple mistake which is not unfrequently made by persons who are by no means anxious to pay more tax than they are compelled, is, after paying tax under Schedule A, in respect of property belonging to them, which they occupy for the purposes of their business; they do not deduct the amount of the assessment in making their return under Schedule D, in respect of the profits of such business.

There are other kinds of work performed by accountants which, will readily suggest themselves to your minds, but of which I must omit any lengthened description, as my time for the preparation of this address, and your patience in listening to it, have both their respective limits. I need only mention a few of them to suggest a crowd of ideas in the minds of those engaged in them for example: Bankruptcies and Liquidations, which formerly occupied so much of the time and energies of many accountants, and the more important of which are still conducted by some of the most experienced members of our Institute. My own experience in this branch has been very limited, so I am not competent to discuss the subject in detail; but I am able to form some idea of the arduous labours, anxieties, and onerous responsibilities of those who have made this branch of accountancy the principal part of their practice.

Trust Accounts. This is a branch of the profession in which most of us are engaged in a greater or less degree; and there is no part of our work more varied and interesting requiring more knowledge and experience, more care and vigilance, than that which we have to perform in connection with trust accounts.

I might go on to refer to the very responsible work we often find ourselves engaged upon in connection with the various kinds of litigation in which our clients become involved; and might take you through the various stages of investigations of accounts, covering long periods, and made difficult by the scarcity of information, of reports, setting out the results of such investigations; and the subsequent evidence presented in the form of affidavits, or given in the witness box, when the accuracy of our labour is put to the test; but I refrain.

I think I have said enough to prove that in choosing the profession of a Chartered Accountant, a young man is entering upon a laborious, useful, and responsible occupation: one in which he will have frequent opportunities for the exercise of those sterling qualities of mind and heart and will, which are necessary for the due performance of duty and the achievement of success in every walk of life.

## CHARTERED ACCOUNTANTS STUDENTS' SOCIETY OF LONDON.

### AUDITING.

#### BY MR. C. R. TREVOR, F.C.A.

When asked by your secretary to prepare a paper for your Society, the subject of Auditing was suggested to me as one which had not been recently taken up, and which was more needed than any other. I found, however, on looking over the records of the Society since its formation in 1883 that you have had no less than five Lectures on Auditing and Auditors, viz.:—

By Mr. PIXLEY, on Auditing, July, 1883
   ,, CHADWICK ,, Auditors, Oct., 1883
   ,, WELTON ,, Bank Auditing, Sep. 1884
   ,, BOLTON ,, The First Auditing of a Company's Accounts, December, 1885
   ,, FISHER ,, Bank Audits, Dec. 1887.

All these papers have entered very fully into the subjects they have dealt with; they contain very important and practical thought and suggestion, and leave little to be added by any one coming after them. Mr. PIXLEY, I observe, considers Auditing the mainstay of our professional work, and regards all the other departments of work which we are called upon to undertake as offshoots of this. Without expressing an entire agreement with this view, I maintain that we can scarcely over-estimate the importance to members of our Students' Societies of a thorough acquaintance with the principles on which a complete and systematic audit must be founded, and with the many points which have been found by experience to be essential to a practical mastery of its details.

At the same time I agree entirely with the remarks of our esteemed President of the Institute, Mr. SAFFERY, in regarding Book-keeping as the basis of our work, and a thorough knowledge of its general principles and practical development as essential to personal success or enduring confidence. It is the groundwork of Auditing, and a defective or incomplete education in its principles is certain to produce muddling, unintelligent, and floundering work in prosecuting an Audit, with the probable result that needless time is spent upon trivialities, whilst errors in principle may escape detection, and devices by which irregularity or fraud are concealed are in danger of passing unnoticed. Therefore, the first qualification of an auditor must be thoroughness in the principles and practice of book-keeping. It is well that this is fully recognised in the foremost place given to Book-keeping in the scheme of examinations of the Institute, and in the ability and care which have been bestowed upon the questions set in the Intermediate and Final Examinations. I believe that an ill-grounded book-keeper is pretty sure to show his defects in those examinations, and to receive the disappointing record "failed to satisfy the examiners."

It is beyond the scope of my paper to discuss other qualifications which should be possessed by competent auditors, or persons who accept and undertake such duties. That these have been greatly under-estimated is evident on a consideration of the grounds on which auditors of Companies, Building Societies, Public Bodies, and Philanthropic Institutions, have been chosen or appointed by reason simply of membership, or leisure, or general education or character, but without any reference to the special work to be done, and the need of special training, experience and fitness for such work. Mr. ERNEST COOPER has ably set forth the grounds on which Chartered Accountants as a body may reasonably claim to be possessed of the special qualifications and fitness which such responsible duties call into exercise.

The necessity of a higher standard of qualification for the position of Auditors than that hitherto formed by public opinion has been forcibly demonstrated from time to time by unexpected disclosures of irregularities, frauds, defalcations, &c., in the accounts of institutions supposed to be under the guard of auditors duly appointed according to the rules or statutes governing their appointment. The commercial public are being gradually awakened to the conviction that a system which allows of such results must be inherently imperfect and fallacious, and that the notion which has commonly prevailed that anyone who can add up columns of figures is competent to fulfil the duties of an auditor is one which ought to be set aside as fruitful in mischievous results, and dangerous to public interests. There are without doubt indications of a sounder public opinion on the importance and necessity of audits, and the necessity once being granted, the conviction that to be of any use, they must be carried out in a thorough, comprehensive and efficient manner, is certain to follow. The next step must be the demonstration that there are to be found amongst the ranks of Chartered Accountants those whose character, training and experience fit them for the special work, enable them to undertake the responsibilities with advantage to the interests involved, and entitle them to the confidence of the public.

To prove the existence of such a class, and to assert its title to public confidence, as well as to maintain a standard of efficiency and honourable conduct, is the object of the Institute of Chartered Accountants in England and Wales.

To assist in educating for the work, in elevating the standard of efficiency, and in strengthening the ranks of the Institute, I take to be the aim and scope of this Society.

In order that it may be educational in its character, there must be not only papers or lectures which are addressed to the experience of the honorary members on subjects open to enlargement by discussion, but also papers designed for the help and instruction of the younger class of members, who may be called beginners or learners. The latter I have in view this evening, and, therefore, I must ask the indulgence of others who may be present whilst I take the more humble place of treating the subject of Auditing in a somewhat elementary manner.

A consideration of what has already been said and written on this subject in the Lectures to this Society, to which I have referred, as well as in several Lectures to other Students' Societies, leads me to feel the hopelessness of endeavouring to bring forward anything new, or to throw new light on what has gone before, and still more to feel that I can, after my best endeavours, only be far behind those who have so ably preceded me.

Enough has been written on the history of the use of the term "Auditor" and the changes through which its meaning and application have passed. I take it that it is now sufficiently understood in its present usage. The several Acts of Parliament by which the appointment of Auditors of Companies of various classes is regulated have also been sufficiently dwelt upon, and any student needing information on these may be referred to Mr. PIXLEY's useful work on "Auditors: their duties and responsibilities."

I propose this evening to localise my remarks as far as possible by dividing them under three heads:—

1st.—The *subject* of the audit—that is, what is to be audited; and
2nd.—The *object* or scope of the audit.
3rd.—The *manner* in which it is to be performed.

*First.—The subject of the audit*, by which I mean the constitution or organisation of the company, partnership, business, or undertaking whose affairs have to be inquired into. Here we shall have to consider for whose protection, or in whose interest the audit is to be made, and we shall find: *First*, companies under special Acts of Parliament in which the auditor must acquaint himself with the clauses or regulations relating to his duties, and the powers which are given to him. In some of these such as gas and water companies, railway and canal companies, and insurance companies special forms of accounts are provided, and the books must necessarily be so framed as to work up to these. The Companies Act of 1862, sec. 44, provides a summarised form of statement of liabilities and assets which must be exhibited for the information of the public by the first Mondays in February and August in each year, by every limited banking company, insurance company, and deposit, provident or benefit society. This, however, is so very crude a form that it has no effect on the arrangement of the accounts or the course of the audit. For companies generally registered under the Act of 1862, the well-known schedule comprised in Table A. contains a form of balance-sheet in which the property and liabilities are arranged under heads very fully described, and the balance-sheet is to be set out in this form "or as near thereto as circumstances admit." The adoption of Table A. is, however, optional, and as companies of any importance almost invariably provide articles of their own, within the limits of the Act generally, the form may be regarded as a dead letter: except in so far as it operates suggestively in the division of heads in the balance-sheet. It is moreover so encumbered with needless titles and words that its adoption entire would destroy the symmetry of a balance-sheet. The next attempt to provide forms of account by Act of Parliament was made in the Regulation of Railways Act, 1868, the first schedule to which contains a very complete series of forms—14 in number—showing a great improvement on the form of 1862, and evidently the result of experience in the working of railways and their accounts. The complete information contained in these forms has without doubt contributed greatly to the protection and assistance of the great body of British railway shareholders. Next we come to the Life Assurance Companies Act, 1870, which contains forms of account comprised in the first four schedules. to the Act, which every life assurance company is obliged to adopt and deposit yearly with the Board of Trade within nine months from the date to which they are made up. The Act is binding only upon companies doing business in life assurance, either alone, or in combination with other kinds of insurance. It is somewhat remarkable considering the events which led to the passing of this Act, viz.: the failure of some very large life assurance companies, that the necessity of the appointment of auditors was not recognised and provided for at the same time. It is unfortunate that the principles governing the construction of such accounts generally are violated in the forms by the reversal of the sides of the revenue accounts, the revenue being debited with receipts, and credited with payments. Other insurance companies, not bound by the regulations of the Act, have generally followed the example, so that we have the inconsistency of assurance companies generally presenting their accounts in the opposite mode to those of trading companies, and to the forms provided for railway and gas companies. A Manchester assurance company, not bound by the Act, has taken the bold course (it appears under the advice of its auditors) of presenting its accounts in the opposite form and in harmony with commercial usage, which step has been strongly condemned by *The Review*, and defended with much vigor and ability by the auditors, a well-known and highly respected Manchester firm (*vide The Accountant*, September 7th, 1889.)

Next we have the forms of accounts prescribed for gasworks in Schedule B to the Gasworks Clauses Act, 1871. The Act of 1847 was a very important one in the interest of the public by reason of its limiting the profit to be taken by shareholders or proprietors of gas undertakings having exclusive privileges of supply, to a uniform and continued dividend of 10 per cent., and a reserve fund equal to one-tenth of the nominal capital of the undertaking. That Act provided that a yearly account in abstract of the total receipts and expenditure, duly audited and certified by the chairman and also by the auditors, *if any*, should be trans-

mitted to the clerk of the peace for the county, and be open for public inspection. This left the form of account open to the discretion of the proprietors, so long as it answered to the definition. For the further protection of the public as consumers of gas, the Act of 1871 provided the forms now referred to—9 in number—which, on examination, will be found to be very lucid and complete, although containing more detail than would generally be considered to be necessary, or advisable, in the accounts of trading companies. The principle of their construction, however, is that a monopoly is not to be entirely for the benefit of the proprietors, but that the public must have opportunities of judging and testing the measure of its profits and the mode in which they are ascertained.

The Waterworks Clauses Act, 1847, has provisions in the same words as regards the annual account in abstract to be supplied to the clerk of the peace, but it does not appear that any forms of account similar to those of the Gasworks Act, 1871 have been made applicable to these undertakings, except that certain water undertakings are required to forward yearly accounts to the Board of Trade in such form, and containing such particulars, as may from time to time be prescribed by that Board.

The Banking Companies Act, 1879, requires every banking company registered as a limited company since that date to have its accounts audited by one or more auditors, who are to be elected by the members in annual general meeting. It also directs the terms of the certificate to be given by the auditors, and the manner in which the accounts shall be signed, but provides no forms of accounts.

The Friendly Societies Act, 1875, provides forms of accounts to be audited by one of the public auditors appointed for the purposes of the Act by the Treasury, or by two or more auditors appointed by the Society. This is a somewhat special class of work which does not come to accountants generally, unless they have obtained the appointment of the Treasury, and I do not propose to refer further to the manner of audit. It seems highly important that societies of this description should be subject to more thorough and efficient audit than they usually obtain at the hands of the auditors of their own appointment, but until the members of the Societies are alive to the importance of it in their own interests, or Parliament makes such audit compulsory, it is not likely that the officers will go out of their way to seek it, or to pay even the modest fees which are asked by accountants holding the Treasury appointment.

Companies generally registered under the Acts 1862 to 1887 usually embody in their articles clauses relating to the audit of accounts in similar terms to those in Table A, which provide that the appointment of auditors (after the first appointment) shall be made by the shareholders, that the auditor shall have a list of books delivered to him, and shall at all reasonable times have access to them, and that he shall make a report in which he shall state whether in his opinion the balance-sheet is a full and fair balance-sheet, containing the required particulars and drawn up so as to exhibit a true and correct view of the state of the company's affairs. In all which provisions, the auditor is regarded as the representative and protector of the shareholders.

The audit of the accounts of corporations is, as regards the real work and value of an audit, at present very much of an open question, owing to the provisions of most Local Acts under which elective auditors are the only recognised guardians of the public or ratepayers' interest, and as these are not usually chosen on account of their special fitness, the appointment has frequently been of little use. This is, however, one of the directions in which the public attention is becoming fixed upon the necessity of fitness for the work, and whilst the office of elective auditor is being more frequently taken by persons suitably qualified, corporations themselves are more generally disposed to employ accountants in their own interest. It is to be regretted that in the passing of the Local Government Act, the importance of trained auditors was not recognised, and that consequently the audit of the accounts of County Councils has been relegated to the auditors of the Local Government Board, who are seldom trained accountants.

A large field of auditing work is in the accounts of private partnerships, and one likely to be extended. The advantage of audit is frequently only recognised as a *remedy* after the necessity has been enforced by some proof of the consequences of lack of oversight, but it may be strongly urged that a great element of value of an audit is as a *preventive*, by removing the temptation to frauds which is frequently engendered by the ease with which irregularities remain without detection or observation. A sound audit tends to keep cashiers, book-keepers and collectors up to the moral tone of honesty, and also tends to remove suspicion by partners of each other, and to leave them more at liberty to devote their energies to the common good, in the assurance that the interests of all are being cared for by an audit in which they all have confidence In such cases the auditor is the judge or arbiter as well as the protector of the interest of each partner. This is more specially manifest in the case of dormant partners where one or more active partners are left with the conduct of the business. In such cases, the articles of partnership should be freely opened to the auditor, in order that he may see how far the mode of keeping the capital accounts accords therewith as regards drawings, interest, and division of profits. In the more frequent cases in which the drawing of the profit and loss account and capital accounts is left with the auditor, these articles form the basis on which he has to raise the superstructure. In the formation of a partnership or the introduction of a new partner, a perusal of the proposed articles by the intended or continuing auditor may often be of great advantage in having the mode of dealing with the accounts clearly stated and every point in connection therewith adequately provided for.

*Second.—The object or scope of the Audit.*

Assuming that by the art of book-keeping, completely and correctly worked out, a perfect picture of a merchant's affairs is produced, which can be readily grasped and understood, and which displays its artistic character by its simplicity and clearness and truthfulness to nature, the object of an audit must be to test the picture in every one of its parts, by dissection and ultimate reproduction, and so to beautify the whole by additional strength, light and colour. With this view, we must first find the component parts by going down to the foundation, tracing them from their origin and then proving that the manner in which they have been put together is true to nature, that there has been no dislocation or forced connection, but that the proportions are just and the combinations harmonious.

Literally we must first enquire for all the books used in the business or undertaking, prepare a list of them, unless Table A in the case of companies has been complied with and the auditor supplied with the list as provided by Sec. 93. Having obtained the list and ascertained that it purports to be complete, we next examine the books cursorily to ascertain their character and mode of entry, and how they work into each other and form the necessary sequence of records. Difference of opinion may arise here, as to where the auditor's work begins. I have seen it stated that he must begin at the order book, trace the fulfilment of each order, and proper charging and calculation of each item of sale, and on the other side trace each purchase and examine the invoice. This I contend is not auditor's work, unless he be specially instructed and paid for doing it It is the work of the office staff, and merchants or manufacturers who do not make this a part of daily routine run great risks. If the auditor be expected to do it, to be of any use, he ought to be in daily attendance. Think of the folly of sending out invoices or charges unchecked, and having to find out and remedy any errors after a lapse of months, or of

paying accounts without check. An auditor should certainly satisfy himself that proper checks of this sort has been used, and if not, point out their necessity and importance.

I remember once being told by a foreign shipping merchant that he expected an auditor to examine every one of the letters received and copies of those sent, and that every order received should be traced through the books, and goods invoiced to the firm should be traced by the invoices of goods outwards. This would really be an investigation rather than an audit. Such steps would be very necessary for evidence in a police court investigation, and as the result of an office having fallen into a chaotic condition, but surely merchants should not have to be dependent upon auditors for such work as this, unless they make the audit a weekly or monthly business and are willing to pay accordingly.

The auditor's work properly begins where the book-keeping begins, that is with the sales and purchases at the point of their entering into the ledgers. As a general rule all the postings to the ledgers should be called over, unless the very numerous character of the transactions be such as to render it practically impossible, and in such case, the parts to be dispensed with, should be only those affecting the sales and the payments therefor. The purchases and payments on account thereof must be checked for an audit to be of any value whatever. Whether the purchases are entered in an analysis book or carried into analysis columns in the invoice guard book, the original invoices should always be examined and any absence of check marks be noted and enquired into, or any irregularity in the form of invoice, as, for instance, an invoice on a written instead of a printed form, or a statement used as an invoice, or especially an invoice made out in the office, and not having emanated from the vendor of the goods, or an invoice made out to a manager, or any other person than the firm or company.

The cash book entries must be proved as far as possible on the receipt side by counterfoils of receipt books, and completely on the payment side by vouchers of payment, to which I will again refer later. I have found it in many cases preferable to go through the vouching before checking the postings from the cash books to the ledgers; in other cases to leave the vouching until after. As the audit which I am now supposing is that of a manufacturing or trading business or partnership, I need not refer to all the books likely to be in use, and I will only briefly allude to the journal, which for such business is seldom in use, as the transactions being generally of one kind, they can be more conveniently, and with less risk of error, posted direct to the personal ledgers, and in their analysed totals to the nominal accounts. I have before expressed the opinion that in the transactions of importing and exporting merchants, and shipping and shipowning firms or companies, the journal is a most important and essential book, and the construction and narration of the entries affords one of the best tests of a book-keeper's intelligence and capabilities. In the accounts of companies, it is necessary for opening capital, casual and closing entries, and therefore I think it should not receive the unmerited abuse to which it has often been subjected. It is most useful in shortening the ledger postings in businesses having many departments, by collating the transfers from one department to others. In dealing with the accounts of a company there are other books which require the auditor's attention, viz.: Those which record the subscription and division of capital and the issue and transfer of shares, such as application and allotment book, shareholders' ledger, register of calls, register of transfers, register of mortgages, share certificate book. These should be proved by the original applications and transfers, and compared with the aggregate amounts of capital and calls in the capital, nominal, or private ledger, as the case may be. The certificates issued, as represented by the counterfoils, should be compared with the register of transfers, and it should be ascertained that certificates, cancelled by such transfers and new issues, have been given up,

It is frequently recommended in books on companies' accounts, and especially by registration agents, that a numerical register of members and shares held should be kept, in which there is to be a line for each share and the name and address of the holder entered opposite to the number; also when a transfer takes place, the name and address of the new holder. I consider this a great and needless waste of time and of no practical use, as the requirements of Sec. 30 of Act 1862, can be fully satisfied by the shareholders' ledger with the aid of the annual summary entered up yearly, or which can be entered up more frequently, say quarterly, so that a list of present shareholders of recent date may be at hand. I observe that in MR. VAN DE LINDE's lecture on "Company Work," Schedule X., the book which he there entitles the "Shareholders' Address Book or Alphabetical Register of Shareholders," corresponds entirely with the form of the "Annual Summary" required to be filed yearly, and he does not recommend any other book or register as being necessary.

Before passing from the scope of an audit, some reference must be made to that of a bank, as its conditions differ so greatly from trading or other companies. It is, of course, impossible in a half yearly audit to check and vouch the daily receipts and payments through customers' accounts, or the daily postings of totals from the bank cash books to the account entitled "Current Accounts" in the nominal ledger; but the general double entry balance must be as certainly proved as in a trader's books by means of the various accounts in the nominal ledger into which all the transactions flow in their totalised forms, and by this means the total correctness of the postings is inferentially proved. A bank's audit really resolves itself into an audit of the balance-sheet, in which great importance attaches to the examination of cash, bills, investments and securities. An audit is greatly strengthened by the extent to which customers' pass books can be examined, or the confirmations obtained.

In the audit of a savings bank, this is of special importance, as the chief source of frauds in such institutions has been the knowledge that a manager or clerk who can manipulate the pass books without check has the power to screen his transactions for at least a considerable time. In large and well-managed institutions, the internal checks adopted render this manipulation well-nigh impossible, or at least possible only by a system of collusion which frequent changes of clerks from one post to another may effectually defeat. An auditor's occasional visit for the purpose of examining with the ledgers all pass books brought in operates in a salutary way in preventing collusion and also in establishing confidence on the part of managers and depositors.

*Third.—The manner in which the audit is to be performed.*

Under this head my remarks must be brief and general, or I shall have encroached too long on your time and patience.

In the first instance, obtain a firm grasp of the system pursued, and of the mode in which different kinds of transactions pass through the books, and consider within yourself in what manner, omissions, irregularities, or frauds might most easily slip in or lie concealed. See how returns, *allowances, discounts,* or *overcharges* are treated, and what check there is upon them, or proof that they are genuine. If they appear to be allowed to pass without check or confirmation, attention should be called to the point, the usual or regular discounts ascertained, and any excess specially noted for further enquiry. Ascertain that the returns book is entered in the place in which the actual returns are received, and not allowed to lie in the office for casual entry in order to balance an account, which balance might have been really paid and appropriated. Allowances and overcharges should be proved by letters or other evidence of actual credit and approval. The practice of having an audit book for each audit is highly important, with

columns for the initials of each person who has performed the work, and made himself responsible for its having been correctly and thoroughly done. By this means, much labour is saved on a second audit and thorough continuity secured. It is an auditor's duty to take nothing for granted, and to allow no confidence of character, or general appearance of neatness or good order to turn him aside from thorough examination. The cash book comes first as the chief object of scrutiny, in which every available means must be used to check the receipts. The practice of paying all receipts into the bank on or about the day of receipt is very useful in proving the correctness of the sums entered on the debit, and any irregularity in following out this practice, if laid down for adoption, should be carefully traced through. Counterfoil receipt books should be carefully examined, any discrepancy in date noted for enquiry, and if blanks occur, full explanations capable of proof should be given. If there be found in the counterfoils entries of receipts from firms which are known to be in the habit of sending their own forms, or receipts for dividends in bankruptcy or company liquidations, suspicion would at once arise that the actual receipt forms had been used for other purposes than those recorded on the counterfoil. As a matter of course, the bank passbook must be examined in detail with the Bank columns in the cash book and the payments compared with the withdrawals from the book, as any payment made without a corresponding withdrawal would point to some irregularity in dealing with receipts. I assume that it will be considered a part of the auditor's duty to examine the cash in hand; whether the balance be large or small, and in doing so, to see that all cheques or Post Office orders produced as a part of the balance have been entered as receipts, and that all cheques drawn, as appearing by the cheque book, have been entered to debit. It is advisable to have the bank passbook direct from the bank on the day of balancing, and to see that cheques issued are all out of one book, and if more than one book be in use, to know the reason and authority for such a course, and to examine carefully the second book. Also to see that all payments to petty cash, disbursements, or any subsiduary books are accounted for to date, by debits in the corresponding books. Where partners are absent or not in the habit of paying particular attention to the amounts charged against them, difficulty may arise in obtaining proof of debits to their drawing accounts. Attention should be called to this, and the partners asked to initial the amounts received by them, or bills paid on their account, in a book or books to be kept for the purpose. Much has been said and written on the subject of wages books as vouchers for the amounts entered as paid under that head, as they may so easily become the source of irrregularity, carelessness, or the beginnings of frauds. We have, no doubt, heard of names having been kept on the wage list after the persons have left or died, or have been dismissed, and the sums entered as paid have been appropriated by foremen or clerks who have had the making up of the list left under their control without check, and have also had the money passing through their hands. The mode of making up and paying should, therefore, have the attention of auditors, who might assist the principals by suggesting salutary checks. For instance, time books or piece work books should form the foundation from which the pay sheets are made up, and the keeping of these should be in different hands from those who enter up the pay sheets. The latter again should be distinct from the paying department, which should do the paying exclusively, after the sheets have gone through independent check and revision by persons not concerned in the time-keeping or paying, and their initials should be found on the sheets or in the books. In the calling of the books, I think it advisable to call the whole of the debit side of the cash book first, before proceeding with the credit side, as an assistance in detecting any wrong-sided postings. In checking additions, never pass the totals in pencil, as inexperienced bookkeepers may be under temptation to correct errors or introduce new entries, or strike out erroneous ones by altering the pencil figures, congratulating themselves that their alterations are still in time. In extracting or checking the trial balance, it is needless to say, be careful not to allow unticked entries to escape notice. In large b...nesses, the books should be balanced in sections, a little arrangement by the auditor or accountant in framing the books or at the first audit may easily accomplish this by means of a general account of debtors or creditors to which the monthly totals of sales, purchases, cash received, and cash paid can be posted, which would give the final balance to be found in detail from the debtors' or creditors' ledgers. An intermediate trial balance between the periods of auditing or stock-taking or balancing either by the bookkeeping staff or by the auditors, is much to be recommended for securing early discovery of errors, and bringing under notice casual differences in accounts which might otherwise remain unobserved for a longer period, also it has the advantage of expediting the work to be done after the closing of the books for the periodical audit and balancing. A balance book should be used for this purpose with two or more sets of debit and credit columns to save the re-copying of names.

It is manifest that an auditor can only trace what is contained in the books, and he cannot divine what ought to be there, but has been purposely or fraudulently kept back. This suggests the necessity of looking carefully to the debts standing in the books as owing to the business, and noting any of long date for special enquiry and proof that they are still owing. How is this to be accomplished? The sending by the auditor of statements of account to all the debtors and asking them to confirm the correctness or point out promptly any difference or omission by communication direct to the auditor, is a course which is as yet not sufficiently recognised to prevent its implying suspicion. Is there any reason why this should not be generally done? If it became usual, commercial houses would look for it as a matter of course, and it would tend to promote greater regularity in the adjustment and balancing of accounts, as well as closing a door to fraud, which is now a temptation to it. A still better plan has been suggested, viz.:—that the auditor should issue a circular to each debtor giving the dates and amounts of the payments credited during the half-yearly period, and asking to be informed of any difference. This, however, would not be a complete check, unless the circular were also sent to those who stood as debtors and had paid nothing.

The responsibilities of auditors in relation to the stock-taking of a company's business have frequently been discussed, and no general rules can be laid down which would be applicable in every case. If the stocks are of such a nature as to be capable of being tabulated in ledger stock books so that the incoming and outgoing can be checked by inward and outward invoices, such a record is highly valuable and should be strongly recommended, and it would then be part of the auditor's duty to see that the actual stock-taking corresponded with the book-stock. Where such cannot be done, the auditor can generally only see by inspection of the stock books that the quantities are probable and reasonable, that the prices of goods existing in the form in which they were purchased agree with the invoices, and that the prices of manufactured goods correspond in a reasonable way with sale prices, after allowing a margin for expenses of sale and delivery and for profit, so as to ensure that unearned profit is not anticipated. Especially it behoves an auditor to ascertain who is responsible for the taking and pricing of the stocks and for correctness in the calculations, and to see that such responsibility is acknowledged and certified in writing or by initials. If arithmetical correctness be not clearly admitted, let the auditor have the calculations into money checked by his staff. Where it is possible, this should in the case of a company invariably be done.

The auditor has certainly a responsibility in regard to deductions for depreciation of wasting assets, and although the recent judgment of the Appeal Court in the case of the *Neuchâtel Asphalte Co.* sets aside the necessity for making provision for such waste before estimating or declaring a dividend, an auditor cannot, by reason of such decision, relieve himself from the responsibility of making it plain to shareholders that such waste has occurred and that the recoupment of capital by reason thereof has not been provided for. A course suggested lately from a highly mathematical city north of the Cheviots, that depreciation may properly be taken out of profits when such have accrued, but may be treated as a matter of indifference where there are no profits, has rather astonished me. It is true that depreciation is only an arbitrary or approximate way of attaining to a yearly valuation, yet it is in my opinion a sounder mode of attaining the result than a complete yearly valuation would be, as such valuation must be to some extent affected by temporary causes, such as increased or diminished cost of building or value of metals or machinery operating at the time, but fluctuating from year to year. Now depreciation at a fixed percentage ignores all such fluctuations, and represents, if correctly and continuously applied, the reduced value arising from wear and tear and the operation of ordinary causes. It is sometimes argued that depreciation should be treated as an equalisation of the cost of repairs and renewals. The latter, I admit, but not the former, for if repairs are charged against depreciation, the reserve for renewals and ultimate replacement would be seriously interfered with and might be entirely absorbed. It may in many cases be found advisable to adopt some similar course to equalise the cost of repairs, naturally variable, but in such cases it should be done by an extra and independent percentage.

Before reaching the close of the audit, as represented by the certificate, I must refer to the construction of the trading and profit and loss accounts—assuming that the preparation of these is entrusted to the auditor. Such accounts may very usefully be divided or sectioned according to the nature of the business. If manufacturing, group the debit items so as to show the cost of materials and labour in one total for comparison with the produce, by which the gross profit will appear and may be carried down to form the credit item for the next stage, which would have on the debit the various items, comprising cost of sale in one group, and in another those which form the standing expenses such as rents, taxes, insurance, office and management salaries, audit, and depreciation of plant, etc., the deduction of which from the credit would give the nett profit to be carried to the credit of profit and loss account. On the debit of the last named account would appear interests on loans, debentures, or mortgages, directors' fees, (if a company) bad debts actually incurred (or preferably, a percentage reserve to cover and equalise them) income tax paid or reserved, and any other special item, leaving the final balance as profit divisible by way of dividend or credit to capital accounts. I should propose to reduce all these divisions to their relative proportions to the total produce, taking that as 100, after the following manner :—

| Dr. | | | Cr. | |
|---|---|---|---|---|
| To Cost of Materials and Labour .. .. .. | 64·50 | | By Produce of Manufacture represented by Sales, after deducting Stock at Jan. 1st and crediting Stock at June 30th .. .. .. | 100·00 |
| Gross Profit .. .. | 35·50 | | | |
| | 100·00 | | | |
| To Cost of Selling in Agency, Advertising, Travelling, Discounts, &c | 15·00 | | | |
| To Standing Charges, Management, &c. .. | 15·00 | | | |
| Net Profit .. .. | 5·50 | | | |
| | 100·00 | | | 100·00 |

| Dr. | | | Cr. | | |
|---|---|---|---|---|---|
| To Interest, &c. | .. .. | 2·50 | By Net Profit | .. .. | 5·50 |
| To Bad Debts | .. .. | 50 | | | |
| Balance available for Distribution or Reserve Fund | .. .. | 2·50 | | | |
| | | 5·50 | | | 5·50 |

For statistical purposes, the *separate* items may be reduced to percentages, and would thus afford very instructive tests of the cause of increased or diminished profit. Other denominators may be used, as for instance in iron or mining, the cost per ton of produce under each head, or in textile manufactures, the cost per lb. of yarn spun or cloth manufactured.

Were I dealing in this paper especially with the accounts of a banking, financial or trust company, much would have to be said on the inspection of securities, but as my supposed audit is not of that special character, a few words must suffice. The securities of such institutions divide themselves into three classes :—

 1st.—Those representing investments or property held.

 2nd.—Those deposited by customers for safe custody, and collection of coupons.

 3rd.—Deeds, shares, guarantees or policies held as security for advances or overdrafts.

The verifying of these is one of the most important duties of an auditor and should be done with the greatest care, and in a methodical manner. The same remark would also apply to the inspection of the deeds representing mortgages held by a building society or loan company.

The form of certificate to be given by an auditor has given rise to much discussion, and must vary greatly according to the nature and circumstances of the company, partnership or other organisation. It is important that it should convey in definite terms what has been done, without implying a general responsibility for matters which an auditor can only testify to as found in the books. A private audit may very properly be closed by a full report on the state of the books and on any matters which have been taken on the authority of managers or others, such as the value of stocks, work in process, debts owing, &c., so as to direct attention to the need of any fuller enquiry, and to avoid responsibility being attributed to a greater extent than the means of knowledge justify. Such a report may also call attention to the need and mode of applying any checks which are wanting, and may suggest any improvements in the arrangement of the books or accounts. In a Company's audit, it may sometimes be found needful to make a special report, if matters have arisen in which the auditor has not been satisfied with the information or explanations given, or has differed from the directors in the mode of treatment of any items of expenditure, or in depreciation being insufficiently or not at all provided for, or if he considers that there ought to be a greater reserve for bad debts, or discount than has been made. An auditor incurs great responsibility in issuing such a report, as the publication of it may injure the company, and the shareholders, in whose interest and for whose protection he is acting. Therefore every endeavour and representation should be made in order to prevent such necessity, but if it be unavoidable, the auditor's duty is plain.

Certificates to bank audits are frequently very vague and quite insufficient to justify the confidence of shareholders in the completeness of the audit, or the correctness of the accounts. Instances of such certificates have been the occasion of very unfavourable comment respecting the value of bank and other audits, to the prejudice of professional auditors.

I quote the following as being in my opinion something of a model for such certificates :—

"In accordance with the provisions of the Companies' "Act 1879, we have examined the details of the total figures "contained in the above balance sheet, with the books and "other accounts of the company. We have counted in "detail the bills, notes, cash and stamps on hand. We "have had produced to us the securities for investments, "government and other stocks, and have carefully enquired "into all accounts for loans and advances made by the "company.

"We therefore certify that the above is a full and fair "balance sheet properly drawn up so as to exhibit a true "and correct state of the affairs of the company as shown "by their books."

In conclusion, I must express my sense of the incompleteness of the paper which I have submitted to you, arising partly from the impossibility of dealing in one evening with everything which ought to be comprised in an audit, and partly from the desire which has actuated me to avoid repeating that which has been previously said and written on the subject.

Auditing is so large and important a subject that to do justice to it, it should be specialised, and each branch treated of and studied separately. Much useful work has been done in this subject in papers which have been published, and I advise students to read and digest carefully these special papers, as in them, the details of work have been systematically explained. I refer to such as :—

Mr. F. R. GODDARD'S on "Defalcations and how to prevent them, 1887."

Mr. HOWARD SMITH'S  „  "Vouchers, 1887."

Mr. E. H. FLETCHER'S  „  "Method and Form in Bookkeeping, 1886.

Mr. G. VAN DE LINDE'S  „  "The Preparation and Audit of Income and Expenditure accounts, 1885."

besides those mentioned at the outset of my remarks.

All of these have been published in the *Accountants' Journal*, which I would recommend each of you to take and to peruse regularly, and to have the monthly numbers bound for ready reference.

# The Accountant.

A MEDIUM OF COMMUNICATION BETWEEN ACCOUNTANTS IN ALL PARTS OF THE UNITED KINGDOM.

VOL. XV.—NEW SERIES.—No. 785.　　　　　SATURDAY, DECEMBER 21, 1889.

## The Accountant,

### DECEMBER 21, 1889.

## AUDITING.

Professional education has been so splendidly
carried out of late that general lectures are nearly
played out, and general lecturers find their occupation almost gone.   The thorough, systematic, and
continuous attention devoted during the past six
or seven years to the public discussion of such
general subjects as Book-keeping, Auditing, Company Law, Bankruptcy Law, and the like, has made
it almost impossible for the writer of a paper on
such subjects to achieve anything like a fair measure
of success, unless he deals with bank, colliery,
building society, or any other distinct type of
accounts as a specialist, or unless he concentrates
his remarks to a separate part of a general subject ;
such as the extent and the manner in which
stocks ought to be examined and tested ; the best
means of so arranging the routine of an audit as
to prevent in the ordinary course the commission
of well-known and common forms of fraud, or any
other matter of a similar kind.   But a fresh generation of students arises every five years at least,
to whom old and tried lessons have to be repeated ;
moreover, there is nothing haphazard about the
arrangement of the London lectures, a fact which
those who manage the affairs of other student
societies should take cognisance of. We can predict,
without knowing it to be the fact, that the course of
the year's operations of the London Students'
Society is carefully reviewed in perspective, and that,
as the result of reflection, it was decided that the
lecture, which we reported in our last, was required,
and, being required, was obtained.  It is a good
lecture, and as part of a year's work it will appear
to even better advantage when seen as part of a
whole in its place in the Transactions and side by
side with contributions dealing with subjects of a

special kind. Mr. TREVOR says nothing new, nor indeed could he be expected to do, but he arranges in a clear and attractive form a good deal of sound matter, and he corrects some unsound views which the members may have contracted from erroneous teaching in the past. As Mr. TREVOR has now a special interest in the matter, we take advantage of his remarks on the importance of book-keeping, to repeat a suggestion made more than once in these columns, that it should not form part of the Final Examination, but should, if possible, be made of even more importance than it now is in the Intermediate. The encomiums passed on the form of accounts prescribed for railways are well deserved. Any professional accountant who has ever read the accounts of the frauds perpetrated on railway companies forty or more years ago, when railway enterprise was in its infancy, might be excused for supposing that the use and meaning of simple multiplication tables were at that time unknown by the investing classes in England, much less the principles of book-keeping. In those days—the *good old times* some wags call them—a managing director thought nothing of pocketing two or three thousand new shares and realising £40,000 or £50,000 on them; if he, or any brother director, found himself short of pocket money at a holiday season, a cheque for ten, twenty or even forty thousand pounds would be drawn and charged to *works;* and if a company earned—as one did—about £6,000, it was supplemented by a transfer of £97,000 charged to capital, making a fund available for dividend of £103,000, and so on. In truth, the state of the accounts of our great railways in 1840-58, can scarcely be conceived by us of the present day. When, in 1857, Mr. DELOITTE was called in to unravel REDPATH's frauds on the Great Northern Railway, it was found that the registers had never been adjusted for 11 years. REDPATH had issued a quarter of a million of fictitious stock, on which the company had regularly paid dividend; but the wonder is not that he did it, but why he was so moderate, because an odd million more or less, would, apparently, never have been found out in the ordinary routine of the office work. The defect in principle in railway accounts at present is, that they do not provide that a proper charge for depreciation should be made. This defect once, and not so long ago, brought the Lancashire and Yorkshire very low; in fact, in this respect

we depend on the honesty of the directors—are practically at their mercy; and there is not the slightest reason why it should be so. We agree with Mr. TREVOR's opinion as to the point where the auditor's work begins; but in connection with it, we may record our impression that many frauds are carried out because accountants, or their clerks rather, are utterly ignorant of the work which precedes the entries in the Sales, Cash and other Books, and as ignorance is said to be bliss, there is "fear that this blissful state of things will not soon or easily pass away." Another reason why frauds are so frequently carried out successfully is to be found in that kind of "audit" which consists in seeing that a balance sheet apparently agrees with the books. The balance sheet may be correct enough, but the company may have been robbed of £10,000 or £20,000. An examination and verification of the balance sheet is, of course, all that can be done in some cases, notably banks; but if this can truly be called an *audit*, it is quite clear that some new term must be invented for use in those cases—the vast majority throughout the provinces, and, we think, in Scotland — where every posting is checked, every payment vouched, and the books examined throughout. There is absolutely nothing to prevent a bookkeeper from putting £10,000, or any smaller or larger sum, in his pocket, and still making his books balance perfectly; the mere checking of his trial balance with the balances brought down in his books would disclose nothing; and we know of a case where the postings of books that actually balanced, were regularly checked, and failed to disclose the fact that one of the book-keepers and cashiers had been systematically and ingeniously robbing for years. The most careful office arrangements should be made where the work is not thoroughly done; the auditor should regularly see that the arrangements are in force, and he should clearly put on record the fact that he does not check the postings (or whatever the omitted portion may be), and is not responsible for any irregularity that may arise from such omission. We doubt considerably if the practice of issuing notices to customers of commercial houses, stating the balances to their debit or credit, much less showing their transactions, will ever become universal; and if it ever does become general, that fact will condemn it, for the simple reason that every counting house would want an extra staff of clerks to deal with the work;

on a small scale, it would resemble the rush
attending the floating of a company.  The thing
has been tried in the North of England and failed.
We doubt whether, in most cases, securities deposited by customers for safe custody, are examined
by the auditor.  The form of certificate given by
Mr. TREVOR strikes us as excellent, and as a great
improvement on many forms commonly used.
Nothing else occurs to us on the paper.  We are
always glad to read the publicly expressed opinion,
as to hear the private utterances, of its author—
they are, invariably, the result of great experience
and reflection.

Audits of
Building
Societies.

Public opinion is being very slowly educated to the necessity of an audit of these and kindred societies' accounts. Notwithstanding recommendations of select committees, and newspaper articles, directors and shareholders still continue to live in fools' paradises, and begrudge the small fee which in many instances would have saved them thousands of pounds. *The Times* writing on the Cardiff Building Society frauds, says :—

"But where were the auditors all this time? It is inconceivable that the society, which seems to be one of the principal in Cardiff—a city of important building societies—should have been without these highly necessary officials. If they existed, and were in the habit of comparing the cash book with the ledger, they could hardly have failed to detect ROBBINS' misappropriations in the first year in which they commenced, not to speak of the nine years which followed. We are certainly tempted to conclude that their audit, if one was ever held, was a purely formal affair, and that the directors never took the trouble to see that it was anything else. It consisted, probably enough, of a cursory examination of the totals of the ledger, without any attempt to check the items continuously. Such was the nature of the audit in the case of the Cardiff Savings Bank ; such it was in the notorious Macclesfield Savings Bank case, upon which we recently commented ; and such it would seem to have been here. Auditors of building and friendly societies—where there are auditors at all—are, as a rule, wretchedly paid, and more often than not bring no special skill to the performance of their duties. But they might not be so ready to accept an office to which they are unable to do justice, or, if they accepted it, their attention might be stimulated, if they were aware of the legal liabilities to which an incompetent or reckless auditor exposes himself. These scandals in the management of building and friendly societies are becoming too frequent not to necessitate the intervention of the Legislature. Although a Government audit may be inadvisable, as encouraging a belief in the existence of a Government guarantee, it may be found possible to insist upon the employment of competent auditors."

Chartered Accountants do not in the slightest degree desire to shirk their liabilities, but they must be proportionately paid for their services.

## Letters to the Editor.

### AUDITORS' CERTIFICATES.

*(To the Editor of The Accountant.)*

SIR.—Looking through the pages of some volumes of your paper I came across a letter of WILLIAM H. FOX in issue of 16 July, 1887, pointing out the advisability of the Council of the Institute taking into consideration the subject of Auditors' Certificates. Though a careful reader, I see nothing done since.

In signing certificates we tread on dangerous ground. The vendors are the only persons who know the true prospects and peculiarities of the business, and if too sanguine will put too high a price on the concern.

I would state that no Certificate should be signed in the following cases:—

   1st. If the business be not an increasing one.

   2nd. If proposed Directors do not take a substantial interest in the Company's Capital.

   3rd. If the vendor's price for goodwill exceeds three years' net profits.

I also wish to add that an accountant will err on the safe side if he does not add Interest on Bills Discountable to the Profits.

A great many companies have been formed. It is too much to hope that no harm has been done, unknowingly perhaps. In the future accountants should be very careful by thorough probing, sounding, and investigating, to save to the public their investments and to themselves their

REPUTATION.

22 *April*, 1890.

**Westhead's Limited.— Auditors and Stocks.** In his remarks at the half-yearly meeting of the shareholders of this company, the chairman said, "In the December balance-sheet there was a clerical error amounting to £1,746 8s. 11d. This error was made by one of our clerks, a man who had been over twenty years in our service, and who had for many years performed the duties wherein he made the mistake, namely, the final abstracting of the department stock-book accounts into one general sheet, which sheet was signed and given to the accountants as being correct. The clerk omitted to deduct the amount of depreciation allowed in the millinery and ribbon departments from the gross stock, thus causing a false increase in the assets of the sum named. This was found out by Mr. Thomson on the examination of the trading accounts when completed in April. This amount of £1,746 8s. 11d. has also been charged to profit and loss account." In reply to a shareholder, the chairman is reported to have further stated that "the auditors could not have found out the mistake except by going through every department of the concern." Possibly the chairman's remarks are not fully reported, for, while discussions as to the extent of an auditor's responsibility in relation to quantities and values of stock are frequent and legitimate, it is unpleasant to read the discovery of an error such as the one above described, is to be placed outside the sphere of his duties.

---

## CERTIFICATES.

### By Mr. G. B. Monkhouse, F.C.A.

I propose to deal with two kinds of Certificates given by Chartered Accountants; first the certificates given by them as auditors in certifying the yearly accounts of Joint Stock Companies; and second the certificates given by them as to the profits and accounts of private firms, or private joint stock companies, upon their conversion into joint stock companies with a public issue of debentures or share capital.

I do not propose to criticise or deal with any particular Certificate that may have been given, nor do I propose to formulate or suggest any special or uniform Certificate to be given under all circumstances, for this would not be possible ; but it will be my endeavour to treat the subject on broad and general lines, dealing with the questions of principle involved, and some of the special points which require the accountant's attention in framing and giving his Certificate, in the hope that a consideration of these important questions, and the discussion which I trust will take place following the reading of this paper, may be useful and helpful to all of us, and that in this way additional light may be thrown upon some of the difficult points involved.

*First as to Auditors' Certificates, and their duties and responsibility, or liability.*

I do not propose to discuss how much or how little detail work in the examination of the accounts an auditor should undertake before he gives his Certificate, as this must depend upon circumstances; but it is his duty to do so much as will enable him to certify that the Balance Sheet or accounts submitted to the shareholders truly and correctly show the position of the Company's affairs, and involved in this that the profit claimed to have been made is correct (or the loss as the case may be), and in whatever form the auditor gives his Certificate, or signs the accounts, unless he states anything to the contrary, the shareholders properly understand that he is certifying this. It is, I think, desirable that the Certificate should be definite, clear, and comprehensive. Let us generally examine a few of the ordinary forms of Certificate given and see how far they comply with the suggested requirements.

1.—" Audited and certified."

This Certificate has the merit of brevity, and I think may be termed definite and comprehensive, perhaps too comprehensive ; but is it clear what accounts have been audited ? is it meant that the whole of the accounts for the year have been audited, or only the Balance Sheet? that is comparing the detail balances composing the summary or abstract of balances appearing in the Balance Sheet with the books of the Company ? I cannot think this is a desirable Certificate either from the shareholders' or accountants' point of view. It does not give the shareholders sufficient information as to what the accountant has done or is really certifying, and puts a vague and unnecessary responsibility upon the auditor, for it is difficult to say, in this instance at any rate, what " audited " does mean, or what is " certified."

2.—" Audited and found correct."

This is very little different from No. 1. The question may be asked what has been " found correct," ? the whole accounts for the year, or only that the balances in the Balance Sheet agree with the books?

3.—" Examined and found correct."

The main difference from Nos. 1 and 2 here is the use of the word " examined " instead of " audited," but the same question arises again, viz : " what has been examined ? " the accounts for the year, or only that the balances in the Balance Sheet agree with the books?"

4.—" Examined and approved."

This form appears to me very vague, and it is rather difficult to know what is meant by the words here used. " What has been approved ? the mere form of the Balance Sheet ? " " or is it meant that the auditor approves of the principle on which the assets have been valued and so approves the profit shown ? "

5.—" Examined the above Balance Sheet with the books and found it to be in agreement therewith."

This Certificate is fairly clear and definite, and no doubt it may be desirable or necessary sometimes to give a Certificate somewhat on these lines, but for an ordinary audit Certificate it is not sufficiently comprehensive, and does not go far enough.

6.—" We have examined the Books and Accounts for the year ending 31st December, 1890, and find the same correct."

No distinct reference is here made as to whether the Balance Sheet to which the above Certificate is attached has been examined with the books and correctly shows the position of the Company's affairs.

In order further to show the need of more uniformity in the form of Certificates and the desirability of our sometimes exercising greater thought and care in their preparation, I give below without further remark the following additional specimens of Certificates which I have taken at random from various Balance Sheets, one Balance Sheet being simply signed by the Auditor without any certificate or remark.

7.—" Audited."

8.—" Audited the above accounts and found the same to be correct."

9.—" We certify that these accounts have been examined and found correct."

10.—" Examined with the books and found correct."

11.—" We beg to report we have audited the accounts of your Company for the year ending 31st December, 1877, and have signed the Balance Sheet."

12.—" We have examined the above accounts with the Books and Vouchers of the Company and find them to exhibit a true statement of the Company's affairs."

13.—" We have compared the above statements with the Company's books and vouchers, and have found them in accordance therewith. We do not value the assets, but have examined the securities and investments, or receipts for same, and have found them as described in the Books."

14.—" Examined and confirmed."

15.—" We have examined the entries in the Ledger from which these balances result, and we hereby certify that they are correctly extracted."

16.—" We have examined the above Accounts and certify them to be correct."

17.—" I have examined the Books and Accounts for the half-year ending 31st December, 1880, and find the same correct."

18.—" Examined with Books and Vouchers and found correct."

19.—" I have examined these Accounts with the Books and vouchers of the company and found them in conformity therewith."

20.—" This Balance Sheet is correctly stated so as to give an accurate view of the affairs of the —— Company."

21.—" I hereby certify that I have compared the items in the above statement with the Banker's Pass Books of the Company, and find the same to be a correct record of the Company's transactions and position."

22.—" We have audited the accounts of your Company for the year ended 31st December, 1889, and certify that the above Balance Sheet correctly shows the position of the Company's affairs as shown by the Books."

23.—" We have examined the above Balance Sheet and certify that it correctly shows the position of the Company's affairs."

24.—" We have audited your Books for the year ending 31st March, 1888, and certify that the Balance Sheet which bears our signatures correctly sets forth the position of Company at that date as shown by the Books. So far as we have been able to ascertain, all liabilities of the Company have been included, but we have no reliable means of judging as to values of the debts and properties appearing on Balance Sheet."

I think, also, it would be very desirable that more uniformity should exist as regards the form of accounts published; and in default of legislation on this subject I think the Stock Exchange Committee might usefully devote themselves to this point by declining to grant a quotation to Companies which by their Articles are not compelled to publish a Balance Sheet and Profit and Loss Account. I do not include in the latter a Trading Account.

Bearing indirectly upon this point I would direct your attention to the phrase often used in Articles of Association in referring to the accounts to be submitted to the shareholders, viz:—" Statement of Income and Expenditure," and would suggest the desirability of accountants endeavouring to get this phrase altered to " Profit and Loss Account " in the Articles of Association. Whenever I have mentioned this suggestion to solicitors engaged in drawing up Articles of Association I have always found that they appreciate the suggestion and make the alteration.

Perhaps we have all of us felt more or less the difficulty of altering or changing the form of Certificates we commenced to give years since, when we had not had so much experience, or could not avail ourselves of the experience of others to the extent we can now ; but I think it is desirable that we should every now and then overhaul our work, see what work we are doing generally in audits, and consider the form of our Certificates.

I further propose to consider the forms of Certificates given, or references made to Auditors' Certificates, in three Acts of Parliament, from which I think we may obtain valuable assistance in the consideration of this subject.

1.—THE COMPANIES' ACT, 1879, being an Act to amend the law in respect to the liability of members of Banking and other Joint Stock Companies and for other purpo es.

Section 7 refers to the audit of the accounts of Banking Companies, and sub-section 6 states that—

" The auditor or auditors shall make a report to the members on the accounts examined by him or them, and on every Balance Sheet laid before the Company in general meeting during his or their tenure of office ; and in every such report shall state whether in his or their opinion, the Balance Sheet referred to in the report is a full and fair Balance Sheet properly drawn up, so as to exhibit a true and correct view of the state of the Company's affairs, as shown by the books of the Company, and such report shall be read before the Company in general meeting."

Subject to one remark, this Certificate in many respects appears to me difficult to improve upon. I think so far as it goes it fairly fulfils the conditions I commenced by saying a Certificate should fulfil. It is clear, definite, and comprehensive and it can be enlarged at the auditor's discretion. I would, however, like to direct your attention to the words " a full and fair Balance Sheet." You will readily see that there may be considerable difference of opinion as to what constitutes " a full Balance Sheet," and unfortunately we have no experience, or very little, as to what view the Judges under certain circumstances would take of this matter. It can never have been intended that, to comply with this requirement, all the balances should be set forth in the Balance Sheet or Statement. This would be practically impossible and generally most undesirable in the interests of the company. The custom generally followed is to group the accounts under convenient headings so as to bring the Balance Sheet into a moderate compass, and make it clear and intelligible to the shareholders; and if the auditor sees that this is done and takes all proper steps to ascertain whether all liabilities have been included, he will, in my opinion, have fulfilled the intention of Parliament, and will truthfully be able to state that the Balance Sheet is, in his opinion, "full and fair."

2.—THE COMPANIES ACT, 1862.—Section 1. The following is an extract from Table " A," Article 94.

" The auditors shall make a report to the members upon the Balance Sheet and Accounts, and in every such report they shall state whether, in their opinion, the Balance Sheet is a full and fair Balance Sheet containing the particulars required by these regulations, and properly drawn up so as to exhibit a true and correct view of the state of the company's affairs, and, in case they have called for explanations or information from the Directors whether such explanations or information has been given by the directors, and whether they have been satisfactory; and such report shall be read, together with the report of the directors, at the ordinary meeting."

The report herein referred to generally follows the Banking Certificate, excepting the inclusion of the words " containing the particulars required by these regulations," and the omission of the words " as shown by the books of the company," I cannot but think that this is from every point of view an important and unfortunate omission; for it is, of course possible to draw up a Balance Sheet without introducing into the books all the items included in the Balance Sheet; but as very few companies are under Table " A " the auditor in any Certificate he gives can add the words. At the same time the auditor of course must make proper enquiries and ascertain as far as possible that all assets and liabilities have been included in the books. It does not appear to me to be necessary for the auditor to refer in his report to his having asked the directors for explanations or information unless the answers have been unsatisfactory, or explanations refused, or information withheld.

3.—THE RAILWAY COMPANIES ACT, 1867.—Section 30 provides that—

" No dividend shall be declared by a company until the auditors have certified that the half-yearly accounts proposed to be issued contain a full and true statement of the financial condition of the company, and that the dividend proposed to be declared on any shares is *bonâ fide* due thereon after charging the Revenue of the half-year with all expenses which ought to be paid thereout in the judgment of the auditors."

This Certificate appears to fulfil the three requirements previously referred to, and should be followed in certifying Railway Accounts. You will, however, notice that it contains the word "full" the same as the Banking Certificate.

There are more or less direct references to auditors and their Certificates in the four following Acts of Parliament, but I do not propose to further refer to them as they do not appear to help us in considering the subject, viz :—

(1.) THE METROPOLIS WATER ACT, 1871.
(2.) THE GAS WORKS CLAUSES, 1847.—Clause 38.
(3.) THE FRIENDLY SOCIETIES ACT, 1875.—Clause 1.
(4.) THE INDUSTRIAL AND PROVIDENT SOCIETIES ACT, 1876.—Clause 1.

In deciding what form his Certificate or Report should take, the auditor will, to a great extent, have to be guided by the manner in which the Balance Sheet and accounts are stated, and whether there are any special items not in his opinion sufficiently clearly stated, or matters which he thinks require further explanation. The clearer the auditor can get the accounts stated in the Balance Sheet and accounts submitted to the shareholders the more definite can he make his Certificate and the fewer remarks he will find it necessary to make. I would here lay great stress upon the importance of getting the Balance Sheet drawn up so as to show on the face of it not only the true position, but the basis on which it has been drawn up. The auditor must also, of course, have regard to the Articles of Association in the framing of his Certificate; as some Articles define to some extent the form his Certificate must take. If the Balance Sheet does not show clearly how the difficult question of depreciation has, or has not, been dealt with, it may be desirable that the auditor should refer to this in his report. In cases where there are large cash or bank balances, or where there are large investments or securities held, it might be advisable to state in the Report that they have been verified and examined; this can do no harm, and will show the shareholders that this important matter has had the auditor's attention.

If the provision for bad and doubtful debts appears quite inadequate, or the stocks appear to be taken on a wrong basis, or expenditure is charged to Capital Expenditure Account, which should, in the opinion of the auditor, properly have been charged to Profit and Loss, this should be mentioned in the Report; and if there are any large extraordinary, or special profits included in the profits and not disclosed in the accounts, the auditor may find it necessary to refer thereto in his Report; or if a dividend guaranteed by the vendor has not, in the auditor's opinion, been properly dealt with he should state this. I do not pretend that the above cases by any means exhaust all the special matters which may have to be dealt with by the auditor in his Report, I only give them as examples.

As regards the auditor's responsibility or liability, whatever form his Certificate may take, the auditor is, of course, liable if he signs false or incorrect accounts knowingly, and probably also to a greater or less degree according to the circumstances for gross negligence in cases where reasonable care has not been exercised, and it is questionable how far the auditor would be protected by the addition in his Certificate of the words " as shown by the Books of the Company " if there was a serious omission from the Accounts of any item or items, or errors of principle made, which the auditor should under the circumstances, have detected.

It is a question for consideration whether in the Certificate, it is desirable to state " we have audited " or " we have examined." There appears a certain amount of doubt as to what is meant, or involved, when the former expression is used; and unfortunately we have very little to guide us as to this, either in Acts of Parliament, or decisions of the Judges. In the forms submitted below as specimens for Certificates for consideration, the latter form " we have examined " is adopted.

(1.)—" We have examined the foregoing Balance Sheet with the books of the Company, and in our opinion it is a full and fair Balance Sheet properly drawn up, so as to exhibit a true and correct view of the state of the Company's affairs, as shown by the books of the Company."

(2.)—" We have examined the foregoing Balance Sheet with the books of the Company, and in our opinion it correctly exhibits the position of the Company's affairs, as shown by the books of the Company."

(3.)—" We have examined the foregoing Balance Sheet with the London Books of your Company and the certified accounts received from the mines, and in our opinion it correctly represents the position of the Company's affairs, as shown by the books of the Company."

Optional or dependent upon circumstances.

" We have verified the correctness of the Banker's Balances."

" Certificates have been produced to us for the investments specified in the Balance Sheet."

" The Trading Stocks have been included at the valuations of your officials."

" No provision has been made for Depreciation, but all maintenance repairs and renewals have been charged to Profit and Loss Account."

" The question of provision for Depreciation is, we understand, proposed to be dealt with by the Directors in their Report."

"Provision for Depreciation of the plant and machinery has been included at the amount fixed (or approved) by Mr.———the expert valuer, consulted by the Directors."

,, The assets, freehold and leasehold land and buildings, machinery and fixed plant are included at the valuation of Messrs.                 of
                              ."

" The assets, freehold and leasehold land, buildings, machinery, and fixed plant, are included at the original purchase price, plus the further additional expenditure."

" A provision of—per cent. has been made to meet doubtful debts, and this your Managing Director considers ample."

" All accrued interest and charges appear to have been provided for."

If the Auditor's Certificate is too long to attach to the foot of the Balance Sheet, the accounts might be sent in signed " Examined and certified as per Report," and the Report sent in as a separate document, but if the Report contains any important qualifications with reference to the Balance Sheet or any statement with reference to the accounts which the auditor deems very important to bring before the shareholders, it might be desirable instead of signing " as per Report" to use the words " subject to Report."

If, in addition to the Certificate or Report to the shareholders, the auditor has sent in a detailed report to the directors referring to anything in connection with the accounts beyond mere matters of detail, it might sometimes be advisable to say in the Report to the shareholders " we have reported fully to the directors upon details connected with the audit and accounts," or something to this effect.

The above are only given as examples of a few of the special references which it may be necessary to put in a Certificate.

I do not wish it to be supposed that I am attempting to lay down rules which must never be departed from, for each particular case must be considered as it arises, and dealt with according to the circumstances; but before leaving this point I must remind you that there is one important factor which must always to a greater or less degree regulate the amount of investigation which the auditor can bestow on any accounts, and that is, to him, the important question of the amount of the fee. It is not to be supposed that the auditor can work for nothing, or give the benefit of his knowledge and experience to shareholders and others unless he is properly paid for it; and I feel sure that in many cases in which the accounts are published and signed by an auditor, that one of two things must have happened, viz :—

(a.)—Either the auditor has not examined the accounts to anything like the proper degree necessary to certify their accuracy, or

(b.)—He has made a serious loss by so doing for the very inadequate fee which the shareholders vote him at the meeting, and this I expect is what often occurs.

This question of auditors' fees is, perhaps, as important to the shareholders as it is to the auditor, and I am glad to have an opportunity of referring to it, for I do not think that shareholders as a body understand the position that the auditor holds; the value of his experience, or the responsibility involved in his office; for the object of many of them seems to be nothing else but cutting down the auditor's fees, and they moreover often seem to imagine that the auditor is in some way responsible if the company in which they have embarked their capital proves a failure, even though it be a hitherto unprospected mine, or completely untried patent.

In cases where the auditor, in consequence of the inadequate fee voted him, or in consequence of his instructions having been limited to making a partial audit, or for any other reason has not made such a thorough examination

of the accounts as he considers necessary or desirable, he should, in giving his Certificate, be careful to let the firm or shareholders see that his examination of the accounts has been more or less limited.

*I now come to the second division of my subject, viz : Certificates given by Chartered Accountants as to the Profits and Accounts of private firms, or private Joint Stock Companies upon their conversion into Joint Stock Companies, with a public issue of Debentures or Share Capital.*

This department of our work has developed very rapidly during the last few years, and I think will still further develope as the tendency of the age is for private firms to convert their businesses into Joint Stock Companies; such companies often being formed by the combination of several businesses. It is most responsible work, as the public now invest in such enterprises greatly on the faith of the accountant's certificate as to the profits and position of the accounts instead of solely relying upon a valuation of the assets; though the latter is often a most valuable adjunct to the certificates of profits. There is, however, one important difference between the certificate of profits and valuation. The latter, however carefully made by experienced valuers, is to a great extent only a matter of opinion; whereas the certificate deals specially with facts which, by a skilled accountant, can be accurately ascertained; but in the result certified there is no doubt sometimes involved a certain amount of opinion as to the question of depreciation, provision for bad and doubtful debts, &c.

Before the Certificate can be given, the accountant should satisfy himself among other things on the following points :—

That all the additions to the Capital Expenditure Account appear to be *bonâ fide* additions, and none of them of the nature of repairs or renewals, &c., and that all the latter are charged to Profit and Loss Account.

That the stock-in-trade appears to have been taken upon a correct basis, and it is always desirable where possible to get the stock sheets signed by one or more of the officials who are responsible for the same.

That there is a sufficient provision for bad and doubtful debts; and here again it is often desirable to get the managing director or other officials to certify that in their opinion the debts are good trade debts, or that the provision made for doubtful debts is sufficient.

That all necessary adjustments of income and expenditure between the years under examination have been duly made, including the provision at the beginning and end of the year, for outstanding accounts, accrued liabilities, &c.

As to whether it is desirable for the accountant to deal with the question of depreciation of plant, &c., or whether this forms part of his duty, I believe there may be some difference of opinion; but clearly there are cases where this question of provision for depreciation should be dealt with; in fact, I think we may go so far as to say, that notwithstanding the apparent uncertainty of the law, some provision is generally desirable or necessary, either for the ordinary wear and tear which has taken place, or to meet extraordinary repairs or renewals which have often to be incurred at certain periods; and the accountant here requires to make use of all his experience and knowledge of the subject. I would suggest that if he finds much difficulty in dealing with the question, he should call in the aid of an expert or professional valuer and take his opinion; and where this has been done refer to the same in the Certificate. I cannot but think that it would often be desirable to call in such assistance in dealing with this most difficult question, which is so much a matter of opinion and not an ascertained fact.

The important decision in the case of *Lee* v. *The*

*Neuchâtel Asphalte Co., Limited*, which has been so often referred to, leaves us in a certain amount of doubt as to what " Wasting Assets " are included in this decision. It, therefore, appears desirable that in dealing with this question of depreciation the accountant should be careful to see that the accounts, or his report, are clear as to how it has been dealt with.

Next as to what the Certificate should, or should not, contain, or what should, or should not, be certified.

There should be no ambiguity about the Certificate or the phrases used in it. It should be made so clear that every one who reads can understand it, and be in no doubt whatever as to the position, or how the accounts referred to have been dealt with.

The accountant, of course, should not knowingly include anything in his Certificate calculated to mislead or deceive ; nor on the other hand exclude anything from his Certificate, the absence of which would be calculated to do so.

As to whether the accountant should insist on giving each year's profits separately where the average, or averages, of a series of years is put forward, must be entirely a matter of judgment in each case. In cases where the business is a seriously declining one, as regards either profits or sales, it will be a serious question for the accountant to consider whether he should certify the average of profits of a series of years without showing the fact.

In a combination of several businesses where the profits are included for different periods this should be clearly stated ; and, although it may not be necessary, or even desirable, to state the profit of each business, it might be advisable to specify the period for which the profits were included opposite each business ; and where the accounts of some only of the several businesses proposed to be amalgamated have been investigated, and the average rate of profit on the production of these taken and applied to the production of the remainder, it appears desirable that those so taken should be specified.

I need scarcely say it is not proper to include in an average of profits for a period of years—one or more years—where a loss has been made, without making a distinct reference to the fact ; whether the amount of such loss is specified or not ; nor is it proper in the case of a combination of several businesses where one of the businesses has been carried on at a loss, to certify the average of profits without clearly stating that one of the businesses has been carried on at a loss for one or more years as the case may be, and I think the business which has been carried on at a loss should be named and the amount of loss stated with the reason for such loss if it can be satisfactorily explained.

I think that it is desirable that the Certificate should show how the question of management charges, such as partners' drawings for services, or directors' salaries or fees, have been dealt with. If any are included it may be advisable to mention the amount. Where several businesses are proposed to be amalgamated, it is a question whether the best plan is not to write back, *i.e.*, recredit to Profit and Loss Account the whole account so charged, mentioning the amount, and thus leaving this charge possibly amongst others to be dealt with in the prospectus before the profit is used in the appropriation for dividend.

There are one or two other matters which it appears desirable we should consider as to whether they should be referred to in the Certificate or not, as sometimes reference is made to them, and in other Certificates no reference is made.

1st.—Interest on Capital.

In private firms this is an entry which is sometimes passed to the debit of Profit and Loss Account before profits are divided as it appears to me for two reasons.

  (*a.*) To see whether the business is earning a rate of interest which makes it worth while carrying it on, and

  (*b*) In order to adjust the position as between the partners where their drawings and capital are unequal.

It does not appear to me that this interest is a proper charge against the profits as far as the certificate of profits is concerned.

2nd.—Interest on Loans and Borrowed Money.

This stands in a little different position possibly to interest on capital ; at the same time if the company is going to acquire the business free of all incumbrance there will be no interest on borrowed money chargeable against the profits, excepting the interest on mortgages, or debentures created by the new company, and this interest is always allowed for before the profits are dealt with for dividends.

3rd.—Rent charge for freehold which the company will acquire in the purchase.

This, again, although a proper charge against the profits in the past, in cases where the firm paid such rent, is not a charge which the company will have to meet in the future in cases where they acquire the freehold ; but as regards both this and the interest on loans, it appears desirable we should consider whether, under such circumstances, as the above, it is necessary for us to refer in the Certificate to the fact of our having written back these charges, and to state that the profits are exclusive of interest and rent. In cases where large profits have been made in the past, from some very exceptional business which is not very likely to occur again in the future, the accountant will have to consider whether he should not make a reference to the fact in his Certificate.

It must be remembered that whatever is not referred to in the Certificate is by the public properly taken for granted to be correct, or not considered by the accountant necessary to be referred to, or brought to their notice.

Now I come to a most difficult matter, viz. :—the dealing with estimates, either referring to the past or future. Much as we may dislike to include the result of estimates in our Certificate, or incorporate them with ascertained facts, there are cases in dealing with past profits where this cannot be avoided. For instance, where two businesses, hitherto worked more or less together and the results kept in one set of books, have to be separated and the profits of each ascertained ; where two or more businesses are to be combined and the profits of one cannot be accurately certified. In these and in other cases where estimates of an important nature with reference to past profits are included in the results certified, it is desirable that the fact should be clearly referred to in the Certificate or Report ; and I would suggest that it would generally be a good plan to set out the profit of those businesses that can be accurately certified, and then add the profit of the business or businesses which cannot be so accurately certified, or in which the question of estimate has had to be introduced, and show how the estimate has been arrived at. The adoption of this straightforward way of dealing with the matter will, in my opinion, go far to neutralise the weakness of having to include any estimates, and will help to give the public confidence in the Certificate.

As to the question of accountants estimating the future profits of the proposed company and including such estimates in the Certificate or Report, I cannot but think this is a most dangerous and exceedingly undesirable thing for the Accountant to do. There is, in the first place, the risk of weakening the position of the facts included in his Certificate ; and it appears to me the responsibility of certifying the past profits and having the same used in the prospectus in connection with the dividend that may be expected by the Shareholders of the proposed company in the future, is quiet sufficient responsibility, without making himself directly responsible for the forecast of the future profits. It is possible that in the changes and developements of the future the public may demand that accountants should in some way deal with the question as to the profits that may be expected from the business, but this time has not yet come yet, and I do not think it is desirable that we should endeavour to anticipate it.

Sometimes it may be desirable that the accountant should give a detailed report in addition to his Certificate. If this report is in any way in further explanation of the results certified in his certificate, or the basis adopted by him in ascertaining such results, it is desirable such detailed report, whether intended to be printed or referred to in the prospectus or not, should be referred to in his Certificate, as he cannot be too careful that everything in connection with his work not only is, but appears, straightforward.

There is one thing the accountant must not lose sight of that is to see that extracts and all references direct or indirect made in the prospectus to his Certificate and the results therein certified, whether such Certificate is printed in the prospectus or not, are true and not calculated to mislead, I do not think it is sufficient for him to say " I have signed my certificate and there is an end of it so far as my responsibility is concerned," and it does not appear to me a bad plan for the accountant to refrain from actually signing his certificate until he sees the references made to it, or the results certified therein, in the final prospectus.

I have, I feel, imperfectly dealt with this important subject, but I hope the members here present will supply my deficiencies by their contributions in the shape of suggestions or remarks made in the course of the discussion, which I trust will now take place.

The PRESIDENT, at the close of the paper, invited discussion upon it. He hoped the remarks would be made as concise as possible, so as to give the members an opportunity of saying all they had to say upon it.

Mr. GIBSON said, he wished shortly to refer to the first part of Mr. Monkhouse's paper, in dealing with the question of auditors' certificates, and the qualifications which Mr. Monkhouse thought necessary to introduce into every certificate that the balance sheet was correct, " as shown by the books of the company." He thought the words quoted required their special consideration before they were endorsed, as properly entering into an auditor's certificate (applause), because as looked at from the public point of view it tended to very much depreciate the value of the audit. (Hear, hear.) The public were very apt to regard it as reducing the auditor's function pretty much to the question of extracting balances and making additions. Now, he held it to be the auditor's duty, as representing the shareholders, to see that the books did properly represent the position of the company—(applause)—and that he should take special care to satisfy himself that the books were bonâ fide in every respect, and having done that he could leave out of his certificate the words of limitation. The auditor represented the shareholders, who could not themselves be satisfied that the books represented the position of the company, and it was his duty, as their representative, first of all and primarily, to satisfy himself of their bonâ fide character, exactly in the same manner as if he were advising a client as to the purchase of a business in a private sense. Subject to that, he would suggest that the second of the forms which Mr. Monkhouse gave, admirably supplied a form of certificate which, he considered, should be as closely adhered to as possible—"We have examined the foregoing Balance Sheet with the books of the company, and in our opinion it correctly exhibits the position of the company's affairs." He would suggest that the words "as shown by the books of the company," were redundant. and tended only to weaken the effect on the public mind. (Applause.)

Mr. J. BLACKHAM, F.C.A., said, that it occurred to him that the extract given from the Companies Act of 1862 very clearly laid down what the certificate should be. (Hear, Hear.) He would impress upon his brother-accountants throughout the country, that in all their certificates they should disclose the work they did for companies or private concerns, and should be careful in no case to mislead the public, for

if they did so, they would find that the confidence they were anxious to see reposed in them would disappear. He also saw that Mr. Monkhouse referred to cases where the auditor, in consequence of the inadequate fee which was voted to him, did not make such a thorough examination of the accounts as was considered necessary and desirable, He should, in that case, when giving his certificate, be careful to say that his examination of the accounts had been more or less limited.

Mr. T. BOWDEN, F.C.A. said that Mr. Monkhouse had stated very clearly two forms of certificate—the one in the case of reporting to a private body, and the other in the case of a public company. In the one case there 'were no rules or regulations laid down; while in the other case accountants were compelled to use certain phrases and words. He considered that in the case, not only relating to private firms, but also relating to public companies, there should be a report. He believed that the report referred to in the Companies Act meant something more than simply quoting certain words. It might be considered that it was unnecessary to do more than quote from the Act, and intimate that in the opinion of the auditor the balance sheet was a fair and full one, as shown by the books of the company. He, however, thought it was the intention of the legislature to go beyond that, so that there should be a fuller report. He himself was of opinion that it was impossible in a simple certificate to report fully and fairly upon the affairs of either a private individual or those of a company. He considered in the case, particularly of depreciation—and many other vexed questions, which must necessarily arise, and in regard to which there was not an agreement of opinion either amongst commercial men or any legal body—he considered in such cases they should be careful to set out as fully as possible the basis on which the profit and loss was arrived at, and which, of course, was incorporated in the balance sheet. A balance sheet might be full and contain everything that was set out in the books, and yet might be very far, even in the auditor's opinion, from being correct. Therefore, he would echo the words of the Mayor that morning —he being a man of very wide experience in the district, and engaged in a great many kinds of commerce—when he emphasised the importance of having a full report upon companies' accounts whenever they came before the accountant. With these remarks he would not detain the meeting longer, as he hoped there would be a great many speakers to follow. (Applause.)

Mr. F. WHINNEY, F.C.A., said, that the first thing the members ought to do was to congratulate themselves upon having heard Mr. Monkhouse's excellent paper. (Applause.) Of course, there were one or two things in the paper with which he did not agree. He would first impress upon them that the paper certainly was only a matter of opinion, and he did that because in the Companies' Act, 1867, the words were introduced in the form of certificate, or that part which laid down what the certificate should be—that the auditors were to certify that " in their opinion " a balance sheet was a full and fair statement of the affairs of the company. If they would consider the matter for a moment, they would see that it could only be a question of opinion whether debts were good or doubtful; whether the proper reserve had been made for debts which might be doubtful and bad; whether the stock in trade was there, and many such things must be purely matters of opinion. But the auditor, in giving his opinion, was bound to do so to the best of his ability, and it was incumbent upon him to exercise a reasonable and diligent care. When he had done that he had stated his opinion that the balance-sheet was a full and fair one, and unless he did so, he would probably be held responsible. In one case auditors were held responsible because they had not exercised a proper amount of care, namely, in the case of the Leeds Building Society, which was a leading case. They would no doubt see at once that they could not certify as to what was the amount of debts. Some of these might have been received, and the money put into the pockets of the men who received them ; and there were a variety of other things making it absolutely impossible to certify as to the exact fact that the balance-sheet was full and fair, and correctly represented the state of the company. What they could do was to certify that in their opinion it was so, and in arriving at that opinion, they were bound to take all the precautions they could, and to exercise the greatest possible care. Now, Mr. Monkhouse said it was very desirable that there should be legislation upon the subject. Well, perhaps it was very desirable ; but, in his opinion, it was an impossibility ever to get any form which would fit all circumstances. They might lay down something like a broad basis, similar to that laid down in the Companies' Banking Act, but the form must be varied from time to time. With reference to the form itself, it said that in the opinion of the auditors the balance sheet was full and fair according to the books of the Company. Now, the books themselves might be all wrong. (Hear, hear.) They might have books saying that the cash in hand at the bank was a very large sum, and yet it might not be there, so that it was actually necessary to count the money or to get the account certified in the best way they could. He had had that very objection taken. A certificate was given that a balance sheet was full and fair, and correctly represented the position of the company as set forth in the books, but a shareholder said that was not sufficient. But they ought to do a great deal more than that, and satisfy themselves of the absolute correctness of a great many items by actually handling those items ; so that although the form might be "according to the books of the company," they might amend it by saying, "We have investigated these books, and we believe them to be correct." There was one small matter which he would throw out for consideration, and which arose out of a remark made by Mr. Monkhouse, when he suggested to solicitors in drawing up articles of association that the phrase "Statement of income and expenditure" should be altered to "Profit and loss account." That was a very good suggestion, and he was going to suggest something else—accountants might be consulted from time to time about Articles of Association, and it would be well to bear in mind that it was desirable to provide in the Articles that notice should be given of the intention to appoint A.B. or C.D. as auditor. If that were not done, the following might happen : the present auditors of a company might be open for re-election, as was usually provided in Articles of Association, but a rush might be made at the meeting; someone might get up, and propose that some other person should be elected ; and in the case of a bank that would be very serious. There might be a rush made at the meeting, which was, generally speaking, not numerously attended, and anyone might be put in as auditor, unless the directors made a resolute stand. He, therefore, suggested that they should endeavour to carry this out as far as they possibly could. One word with reference to the fees. Mr. Monkhouse said that the amount of fees should always in a greater or less degree regulate the amount of the investigation. He was afraid that Mr. Monkhouse would find that the smallness of the fees would be no excuse if the work was negligently done. The fee was a very small one in the case of the Leeds Benefit Building Society, but the judge held that that was no excuse, and made the auditor responsible. If a man was employed to do work, and he did it badly, it was no answer to say that he was not paid a sufficient fee ; he must be responsible for the way in which he did his work. Speaking generally, so far as the first part of the subject went on Certificates, there was little difference between the ideas of Mr. Monkhouse, and the remarks which he (the speaker) had made. But with reference to certificates for turning businesses into joint stock companies, he would like to say one or two words. Mr. Monkhouse said that in cases where the businesses were seriously declining, as regards the profits or sales, it would be a question for the accountant to consider whether he should certify the average of

profits over a series of years without stating that fact. He, the speaker, thought when an accountant took up a declining business to certify the average of profits as being a certain figure—when the last two years showed that that did not exist, he would be held responsible. Then there was another thing. Mr. Monkhouse said :—

" In cases where large profits have been made in the past, from some very exceptional business which is not very likely to occur again in the future, the accountant will have to consider whether he should not make a reference to the fact in his Certificate,"

He (the speaker) considered that that should be done. An accountant would not be doing his duty if he did not state that a certain amount of profit arose in that way from something which was not likely to occur again. In fact, the accountant, in making a Certificate for the sale of the business of a company, ought to place before the intending purchasers such information as would enable them to judge fully and fairly whether the business was worth the sum asked for it. The accountant ought to be perfectly straightforward, and honest about the matter, and if that were done Certificates would acquire a greater value than they had at present, and be considered thoroughly reliable by the general public. (Applause.)

Mr. ROBERT MELLORS, F.C.A., thought that the members were very greatly indebted to Mr. Monkhouse for bringing this important subject forward. Mr. Monkhouse had shown in his twenty-four specimens of certificates how exceedingly varied their practice was, and the great want of uniformity there was amongst auditors. The suggestions he would make was, that the Council of the Institute should take this question up, and make some recommendations to the members generally as to what the form of certificate should be. (Hear, hear.)

Mr. E. M. CARTER, A.C.A., remarked that there was one question which frequently affected auditors before they gave their certificate on a balance sheet. It was this. Supposing they satisfied themselves that the liabilities and the assets, as stated in the balance sheet, were correct, did their duties go any further ? Were auditors supposed to find out frauds which had been committed ? The public seemed to expect this, and he was very interested to hear what the gentlemen present thought of the subject.

Mr. T. A. WELTON, F.C.A., thought the task such a course would involve was one which was beyond human power, and in a very great number of audits it could not possibly be done. He thought the suggestion made by Mr. Gibson with regard to one of Mr. Monkhouse's pattern certificates was not amiss. He agreed with Mr. Whinney that the books to a great extent must be depended upon and that they could only form an opinion after having used their utmost care and judgment in ascertaining whether they were bonâ fide. He thought, however, that the word "opinion" would sufficiently cover that. If the certificate was of a narrative character it told the shareholders something of what the auditor had done, though it did not usually disclose all that he had done. It was a good thing that the public should not over-estimate what the auditor had done, but should see that it was his opinion only, and that he had counted and examined those things only which were susceptible of being counted and examined. Therefore, he would strongly advocate the making of such a certificate, which did not go beyond what it was in the power of auditors to do. With regard to the accounts and certificate, which ought to be given in the case of a new company being projected, he entirely agreed with what Mr. Whinney had said, and he would press another point a little more strongly ; which was that the inclusion of any kind of estimate in the certificate seemed to be so wrong that he would like to eject from the Institute every accountant who published such a certificate. (Laughter.) The province of an accountant was to declare facts and not to make estimates. If estimates had to be made they ought to be in the prospectus. There was a case not very long ago in which a company was stated to be launched, principally on the faith of the auditor's certificate as to a rate of profit that it was alleged was then being earned, and not upon the past actual earnings. This he considered such a blot on the profession that until it was wiped away in some manner he should not be happy. (Applause.)

Mr. G. W. KNOX, F.C.A., felt sure that the members would join in congratulation that a paper like this had been brought before the meeting. Like those who had preceded him, there were one or two points which had struck him as he had followed the paper, which was one he would have desired to read over a second time before criticising. One or two points, however, had occurred to him, one being with regard to the first class of certificate. He thought that together with the books of the company should be mentioned its vouchers. He considered that in the case of an audit of a concern specially relating to cash payments being vouched, the public looked for some reference in the certificate to the vouchers of the company being produced and audited. He quite thought with Mr. Whinney that the certificate should state the opinion of the auditor, but Mr. Monkhouse, in the three forms he had drawn up, in each case supposed that the words " in our opinion" were used, and probably he, Mr. Whinney and himself (the speaker) were at one on that point. Mr. Monkhouse said that " in cases where there were large cash or bank balances, or where there are large investments or securities held, it might be advisable to state in the report that they have been verified and examined." He thought that that ought to be a part of the certificate that they had been examined, and the auditor should certify that he had found the securities in order. With reference to the fee relating to the auditor's work he was rather sorry that Mr. Monkhouse had referred to that in his paper, because he considered that if beforehand the auditor felt that the fee was insufficient for the work, he should not undertake it. (Applause.) If, on the other hand, the auditor found, after starting the work, that the fee was an insufficient one, he should continue his audit just the same as if he had a sufficient fee. The work of an auditor should not be regulated by the fee. With regard to the second class of certificates, he quite agreed with Mr. Monkhouse, and those who had followed him, as to the undesirability of prophesying. Accountants could not do it, and ought not to do it. He did not quite understand how Mr. Monkhouse arrived at the profits of businesses where the books had not been properly kept, or how he took the average of the business where the books had been properly kept. It might be that he had not read the sentence correctly, but it read as follows :—" Where the accounts for only a few of the several businesses proposed to be amalgamated have been investigated, and the average of these taken, as representing the remainder, it appears desirable that these so taken should be specified." He did not quite understand how the average of these businesses which had been investigated could be taken as showing the profits of the businesses which had not been investigated. Mr. Monkhouse had referred to interest on capital ; and under sub-section B. he said— " it does not appear to me that this interest has anything to do with the profits." He fancied that Mr. Monkhouse had in his mind simply the interest chargeable on partners' drawings, but if he looked at it a little more carefully it was only given as a reason where the interest on capital had been charged to the debit of profit and loss before arriving at what was considered profit. He did not believe that Mr. Monkhouse thought any more than he did that the interest on partners' capital had anything to do with the profit of the business.

Mr. MONKHOUSE: You think the interest on capital or drawings has nothing to do with profits?

Mr. KNOX said he did not know. He thought it had to do with profits. The partners might in another form of account take it as a debit on profit and loss. He considered it was

really a payment out of the profit though taken in the form of a charge. There was just one more point on which he should like to dwell. On the last page Mr. Monkhouse said, it does not appear to me a bad plan for the accountant to refrain from actually signing his certificate until he sees the references made to it, or the result certified therein in the final prospectus. Presumably Mr. Monkhouse referred to the financial papers. (Laughter.)

Mr. MONKHOUSE : If you look, you will see it refers to the prospectus.

Mr. KNOX. He says, " Or the results certified therein in the final prospectus." He did not quite understand what Mr. Monkhouse meant by that, and perhaps he would explain it a little later on.

Mr. WELTON thought that Mr. Monkhouse had alluded to the circumstance that sometimes a board of directors would introduce into the prospectus a garbled edition of the auditor's certificate, in which case the auditor was, of course, aggrieved. He always made it a rule to stipulate that his certificate should be fully placed before the public, and in that case any comments the directors might like to make upon it in the prospectus they were at liberty to make.

Mr. KNOX said that he would end as he had begun, by congratulating Mr. Monkhouse, and thanking him for the paper he had so kindly placed before the meeting.

Mr. ADAM MURRAY, F.C.A., said, they had had the privilege that morning of listening to a very valuable paper, which was well deserving of much consideration at their hands. He had noted a few points which he should like to remark upon. He was glad to see that Mr. Monkhouse referred to the question of uniformity of Balance Sheets, or rather the want of uniformity in Balance Sheets, and Profit and Loss Accounts. This, he thought, was a very important point in connection with Certificates, and was one to which they might very well direct their attention. Mr. Monkhouse gave one instance of the great want of uniformity in the case of Bank Balance Sheets and Profit and Loss Accounts. There was an infinite variety of ways in which Bank Balance Sheets, and Profit and Loss Accounts were presented. Some Profit and Loss Accounts, for instance, included on the credit side the gross amount of profits without deduction of rebate on bills. The rebate at the beginning of the period was included in the profits, but that at the end was not charged. Now, they all knew that the rebate was as much a charge on Profit and Loss Account as the interest due to depositors, and that was only one instance with regard to these Balance Sheets. Again, sometimes the gross profits were included on the liabilities' side without any deduction for expenses of management, these expenses being treated under the head of assets, on the assets' side of the account. This was the case with several of the London and Country Banks. With regard to the wording of the Certificate, he had always taken the same view as that expressed by Mr. Gibson. It seemed to him that the words "As shown by the books of the Company," had a meaning which might bear a double construction, such as that the books might not contain all they ought to contain. The Balance Sheet was limited in that respect to the books, while the books ought possibly to contain entries which were not in them. With regard to the phrase in the Certificate that it was only "an opinion, " that was an expression which he thought might be left out altogether. Mr. Monkhouse spoke of the " provisions for depreciation." Sometimes the words used were "the reserve for depreciation," but he considered that a better term than either was, " charge for depreciation." Depreciation, he apprehended, was not a provision or a reserve, but an actual writing down of something. As to the question of interest, which Mr. Knox had referred to, he understood Mr. Monkhouse to mean that in certifying the profits on the transfer of a business to a company, interest would not be a proper deduction from profits, because in the transfer to the company it would be understood that capital would be provided to such an amount that there would not be any borrowed money or advances from bankers on which interest would be payable.

Therefore, in considering accounts for the transfer from a private concern to a company he had made it a rule always to exclude interest. Another item of "charge for rent" it seemed to him would be a proper trade charge. These were the only points he had to refer to. (Applause).

A MEMBER said that the word "opinion" was a term which should seldom be used. Accountants were not like lawyers, they did not give opinions.

Mr. W. C. JACKSON, F.C.A., remarked that Mr. Monkhouse's paper was a very important one. It was divided into two parts, one part it seemed to him being of much wider application than the other. It was not given to everyone of them to be called upon to examine the accounts of a number of concerns which were going to be turned into public companies, but it was probably within the experience of every person present that he had many balance sheets in the course of the year to sign. The question of the certificate was, therefore, of very great importance to them. There was one thing he wished that Mr. Monkhouse had referred to, and which he had not observed any of the speakers had made reference to. It was that in the formation of a company such as Mr. Monkhouse spoke of, namely, the taking over of one or more businesses, every accountant should hold himself very independent, and see that he was not paid by the vendor or vendors of those companies. In his opinion, no auditor ought to make a report except to the directors of the new company, to whom he was responsible, and by whom alone he should be paid. Not only were accountants human—so that it was possible some of them with the best intentions might be biassed by the fact that they had been paid by persons whose profit it was to sell their businesses—but, in addition to that, unless the public knew that the accountant was wholly independent, his certificate lost a great deal of its force. With regard to the first part of the paper, he would entirely express divergence from the gentleman who last spoke. To his mind the words "In our opinion," "In my opinion," mentioned in several examples, were the very centre of the whole thing auditors should stick to. (Applause.) It seemed to him that to simply certify that they had done so much work without reference to its application, was to place them in the position of superior clerks, without giving their constituents any advantage from that experience which they had gathered in other places. To his mind it was the *opinion* of the auditor, which was the most valuable thing to his client, and the member of their profession who should say that in his opinion accounts were correct, expressed in that opinion everything else. No Chartered Accountant who did his duty would dare to give his opinion that he was certifying full and fair accounts, unless he had done all the minor things included in making a true balance sheet. Therefore he entirely diverged from the last speaker. There was another matter which he would like to refer to. He was only one member of the Council, but he would be very much astonished if the Council dared to take the responsibility upon themselves of laying down anything like a common form of Certificate. He could see but one, and that was contained in the words—"In our opinion." If they said this honestly, everything else was covered, and shareholders got the benefit of their experience, as well as their adding up of the figures. He was very glad to see that Mr. Monkhouse had cut away the ground from these old-fashioned Certificates of "Audited and found correct." He remembered the time when he thought after he put his name to the foot of a Certificate, which said "Audited and found correct," or "according to the books" that he was clear of all responsibility. But all of them now knew that an accountant's responsibility was very much greater; and he agreed with Mr. Monkhouse, that vague phrases ought to be rejected, and that no other form should be adopted except that intimated in the Act, including the words "In our opinion." He had never yet seen a better Certificate than that devised in the early days, when Table A. was formed. Whoever drafted that particular portion of the Act,

was a man, to his mind, of great prescience, for although he drafted a schedule, which he then could not see the working of, the fulness of time showed that the phrase in Table A. was the very best which could be adopted. People were often ready to abuse persons who drew up Acts of Parliament loosely, but whoever drafted that clause, 28 years ago was a man of excellent foresight. (Applause.)

Mr. O. BERRY, A.C.A., said he would have liked an expression of opinion from Mr. Monkhouse as to how far an accountant was responsible for having prepared a balance sheet, setting forth certain things which appeared in the books, and were fully borne out by statements, invoices and documents, but which, after all, were fraudulent. Again, what was Mr. Monkhouse's opinion of a balance sheet signed by an accountant, without any remark whatever? Did he vouch for the full correctness of it in all its details?

(The meeting then adjourned for luncheon at the County Hotel—on the invitation of the Northern Institute of Chartered Accountants — Councillor Thomas Bowden, F.C.A., presiding.)

On re-assembling, the discussion was continued by

Mr. W. F. HARRIS, A.C.A., who considered it was desirable that the Certificate should state the period covered by the Audit.

Mr. R. F. MILLER, F.C.A., thought it would be well that Chartered Accountants who were to make the audit of companies should have some voice in devising the Articles of Association relating to the accounts and the audit. He considered that it should be made compulsory that the auditors' reports should be circulated with the accounts.

Mr. C. K. WORSFOLD, F.C.A., said, one matter which required attention was the appointment of the auditor. Nominally the auditor was appointed by the shareholders, but practically in many cases he was simply the nominee of the directors, who held proxies enough to carry the appointment of any officer of the kind. This did not seem to secure the neutrality and independence of the auditor, and there should be no mistake about his being positively appointed by the shareholders of the society whose accounts he had to audit. (Applause.) He did not know what course might be suggested for adoption, whether one security might not be that of requiring the appointment of auditor to be made absolutely by the shareholders, independently of any proxies which the directors might hold for other matters. Certainly the auditor was the go-between in the case of the directors and the shareholders. It was essential, and at the root of the whole matter, that the auditors should be independent men and independently appointed. (Applause.)

Mr. MONKHOUSE said, in replying to the various criticisms, that he wished to say in the first instance that his special object in writing this paper, and coming before them that day was to draw the members instead of drawing himself, and he was not at all sorry that there had been criticisms on certain portions of the paper. He had tried to drive into as small a compass as he could some very important matters connected with the subject. Therefore he had not been able to explain his reasons as he otherwise should have done, nor did he think it advisable that in a paper on a subject like that, that he should go into as much detail as he could otherwise have done; he was, therefore, not at all surprised that in one or two cases his meaning had been a little misapprehended. He would, as rapidly as he could, glance through a few of the remarks and criticisms which had been made on the paper. Mr. Gibson, the first speaker, took up specially the point, "As shown by the books of the company," which had been referred to by several speakers. Now, these words were used in Acts of Parliament referring to the certificate. He did not mean to say that that certificate should not be altered on certain points, and amplified under certain circumstances, but that certificate was really fulfilling the conditions that he laid down as his opinion, and which had been with one exception carried out in Table A. Now, looking at that point

" As shown by the books of the company," what could a man certify that he did not see? It was all very well saying that these words added or created an impression in the public mind that the auditor had done the work very mechanically, and not gone beyond it. But after all, their reputation was at stake in the matter, and surely now the public had got to understand that Chartered Accountants generally did pledge themselves that the account was a true representation so far as they could ascertain it of the position of the company. But if they referred to his paper they would find he particularly pointed out that it was not sufficient precaution as regards responsibility or liability, that the auditor should say that the books of the company showed it. The auditor, who verified the accounts, held himself forth to the world as a Chartered Accountant, who was able, competent and willing to undertake certain duties for the payment of a fee, and whatever words he used there, was a moral, and to a certain extent, a legal responsibility upon him. It was his duty not only to certify that all this was in the books, but it was also, in his opinion, his duty to see so far as he could, that the books did contain all that they ought to contain with reference to the transaction. He could not go further than that. (Applause). There was an undoubted responsibility upon the auditor to do something more than simply certify that the balance agreed with the books. He could not quite agree with one or two of the speakers, who had considered that " As shown by the books of the company," was an improper phrase to use as regarded their certificates. The phrase was used in the Act of Parliament and also in connection with one of the greatest classes of companies, namely, the banks of this country. He certainly personally would not feel inclined to do away with the phrase. If they did away with this, and signed the balance sheet, also doing away with the phrase "in my opinion" he could not tell them what their responsibility was. In his paper he had said—and he repeated it—that they must make clear what they had done. Although he had given two or three specimens of certificates for consideration, he did not say that he considered these the only kind of certificates which should be given. He thought it was desirable in many cases to do something more than follow the words of the Act of Parliament; as Mr. Welton had said it might be desirable enter into a narrative of what had been done. Of course that narrative must be more or less limited. They could not carry it to any extent, but with regard to the words " In our opinion," he stood by those words, that were in the Act. (Applause). Mr. Blackham had spoken as to the limit of the audit. In his own experience he had had firms coming to him, and even limited companies, and saying, " We know that a thorough audit of this would involve a great deal of time, and a large amount of money. There is no time for that, and besides we do not want it. What we want you to do is a certain thing." Well, he did not see why a firm coming to an auditor should not say, " We don't want a thorough audit of the whole accounts, or going into every item and vouching everything in great detail, but we want you to put a balance sheet before us and certify that it is correct in principle. On these lines we want you to come in as arbitrator between the partners, and define what our position is. If an auditor was appointed in the ordinary way without any limitation, he must take the responsibility, and do his duty, no matter if he had to lose any amount of money by it. (Applause.) He now came to Mr. Whinney's remarks, and he thought that Mr. Whinney had made a little mistake as to what he (the speaker), meant, Mr. Whinney said he differed from him in one instance. Now, with all respect to Mr. Whinney, he believed that Mr, Whinney really agreed with him. He thought, however, that they would be able to read between the lines, and that when he said it was a matter for consideration they would see so far as he personally was concerned, which way his doubts inclined. Mr. Whinney had talked about the words " full and fair," and that the books might be wrong. That was true, but it really came under what he had referred to, namely,

that the auditor was bound to see everything was there to the best of his experience and knowledge. He quite agreed that in the case of industrial companies it would be very difficult to lay down a uniform balance sheet, the same as in the case of banks, railways, or insurance companies, but he did think it would be very desirable for the shareholders and the public, and very helpful to them as auditors, if they could have more uniformity. He only said " more uniformity." for he did not think that any one of them could suggest a uniform balance sheet for all trading companies. Mr. Whinney also referred to articles of association, and about providing for notice being given for the appointment of auditors. He was glad of this, because he had often suggested such a course, and had been able to get it introduced. He hoped that accountants as far as they could would endeavour to have a clause inserted to that effect. Mr. Whinney, he believed stated he differed from him as to the statement that it would be a question for the Accountant to consider whether he should certify the average profits of a series of years without showing the fact in cases where the business was a seriously declining one. He was glad to find that he personally thoroughly agreed with Mr. Whinney, that under the circumstances stated, the facts should be shown.

Mr. WHINNEY: You mean it is a question for your consideration,

Mr. MONKHOUSE said, he meant it as a question for them to consider generally, because there had been cases where it had not been thoroughly attended to. Mr. Carter had referred to fraud and defalcation, but he thought that Mr. Carter had been answered by the Mayor that morning. The Mayor had referred to the matter exceedingly clearly and fairly. Of course, private firms, as well as joint stock companies, expected that the audit was going to help them in getting the accounts properly stated as between themselves as partners. And as to the detection of fraud, and he believed that a proper audit did so help them. To begin with, there was the moral effect of the audit, and further than that there was the experience that they, as auditors, had gained in the past. (Applause.) He was glad that the Mayor that morning had alluded specially to the fact, and had stated that the commercial public did not expect that auditors should always be able to protect them against fraud and defalcation. (Applause.) He thought that was a full and a fair admission for a commercial man to make. At the same time it was perfectly true; and if any man expected that an auditor, because he was a Chartered Accountant, and called in for the purposes of auditing, could protect him under all circumstances against fraud, he would be much disappointed. The auditor could only use reasonable care and judgment, making use, at the same time, of all the experience he had gained. With regard to the question of estimates, there were two kinds of estimates referred to; one was estimates in connection with past profits, and the other, estimates in connection with future profits. As regards the latter, or the forecasting of profits, he thought that he had defined that clearly. So far as his own opinion was concerned, he considered it dangerous and undesirable. He believed that in a great many cases accountants had improperly and unwisely gone into estimates of the future, which they had no business to do, and in regard to anything of that sort he thoroughly agreed that it was a most dangerous principle to adopt. (Applause.) With regard to the estimates of the past, he did not think that he had quite apprehended what one or two speakers had meant, because he defied them to give a certificate as regards the past, in any large combinations of businesses, where the question of estimate did not enter. But he did say that where anything in the nature of an estimate occurred, if the accountant had to certify, let him state clearly and boldly, and fully on what basis he had made his estimate. No accountant could give an ordinary audit certificate of any important company without being concerned with estimates such as what depreciation should be taken off &c. In such questions, they must use their experience and the knowledge they had gained in the practice of the profession. As to the provision for bad and doubtful debts, supposing they had £50,000 of debts appearing on the balance sheet, and they made a provision for loss on these, what was that but an estimate? It was a matter of opinion in regard to which they must use their judgment and knowledge in arriving at the proper amount which should be fixed. The only thing was to be careful, and especially in cases where they had to give a certificate, that whatever they did should be shown as clearly as possible, and then they had done their duty. (Applause.) Mr. Knox had said that he would like the words, " The vouchers of the company " added to the certificate. Well, in some respects he did not differ from Mr. Knox, but he was not quite sure whether it was desirable that they should use those words. Mr. Knox had no doubt hit on something of great importance in connection with certificates given on the floating of companies, namely, how the question of interest on capital should be treated. The question of interest on capital had nothing whatever to do with profits (Hear, hear.) He had heard it stated more than once, by accountants, that before they could show the profits, they should deduct interest on capital. How could that be? Supposing it was a limited company, ought they to deduct the dividend paid, and supposing the interest on capital paid was 10 per cent., and they found that only 10 per cent was made they would have to certify that no profits had been earned He could not think that that was right. With regard to the question of the period covered by the audit, he did not see any objection, if it could be worked in properly, to refer to the period covered. With regard to the report being published he did not think they could insist upon that but if the Legislature chose to insist upon it they could do so. At the same time, they should take care that their report, was brought to the shareholders' notice. With regard to articles of association, he thought that the suggestion made by Mr. Miller a very good one, and one which many of them did carry out. He would not take up the time of the meeting any further, but would merely thank them for the kind manner in which they had listened to his paper, and the kindly criticisms that had been made upon it. (Applause.)

Mr. W. N. Fisher, F.C.A., proposed, " that the thanks of this meeting be presented to Mr. G. B. Monkhouse for his able paper on Certificates." Although it might be impossible for them to agree with all that Mr. Monkhouse brought forward he believed they would agree in this, that they were indebted to him, both for the time and labour he had bestowed on his paper, and for the excellent manner in which he had brought it forward. Whatever Certificates might be issued in the future, the opinion of the meeting generally was that they should be true, out-spoken, and should deal with facts. (Cheers). The public should be informed that accountants dealt with facts. He knew nothing more interesting to the profession than the question of Accountants' Certificates, and he only regretted that they had not had a much larger attendance, not only to listen to the paper which had been read, and the papers which would follow, but also to respond to the exceptionally kind and genial hospitality which had been exhibited by Mr. Bowden and the members of the Northern Institute. (Applause). Those who had listened to the paper that day would have discovered that there was an enormous amount of force and knowledge thrown into it, which could not fail to bring good results both to the profession and to the public at large. (Applause).

Mr. T. G. Shuttleworth, F.C.A., seconded the resolution. As Mr. Fisher had said, the subject was one of very great extent beside being of the utmost importance. In Mr. Monkhouse's paper there was one paragraph which would commend itself to everyone present. It was as follows :— " The accountant, of course, should not knowingly include anything in his certificate calculated to mislead or deceive ; nor on the other hand, exclude anything from his certificate, the absence of which would be calculated to do so. (Applause.)

# The Accountant.

A MEDIUM OF COMMUNICATION BETWEEN ACCOUNTANTS IN ALL PARTS OF THE WORLD.

VOL. XVI.—NEW SERIES.—No. 830.          SATURDAY, NOVEMBER 1, 1890.

## The Accountant,

### NOVEMBER 1, 1890.

### CERTIFICATES.

There can be no doubt that the audit and investigation of books and accounts of all descriptions, as the result of which Certificates can be given, is the most legitimate as well as the most important section of Accountancy practice, and we, therefore, hail the discussion of Mr. MONKHOUSE'S paper at the Autumnal Meeting on this subject with satisfaction. The subject was discussed in all its bearings, and opinions of every shade were freely expressed, the point in common being the high standard which the Chartered Accountant is now taking in connection with all such matters.

As was emphatically pointed out by several speakers, the public now expect more than a mere extracting of balances and verifying of the figures in the books has taken place, before a Chartered Accountant feels himself at liberty to give a Certificate upon the general position and profits of a commercial undertaking.

Every audit may be broadly divided into two great branches—the actual facts investigated and verified; and the second and most important part, the proper determination of questions which are more or less matters of opinion, where the result of experience and sound judgment comes into play. After all, as was pointed out by Mr. JACKSON, what the public really go upon in a Certificate now-a-days is the expression of opinion upon the accounts under notice by an expert in whom they have confidence, both on account of his being a member of the Institute of Chartered Accountants, and possibly of his known professional reputation. As a rule the public does not pay much attention to—and possibly would not appreciate—a long recapitulation of the specific work done by the Accountant in the particular instance under notice. The general public does not understand which portion of the work done in each particular case is of vital importance and which is not, and trusts to the Accountant to look after its interests in that respect. Indeed it may be said that his opinion is the Accountant's stock-in-trade, and its value depends upon the soundness of his judgment and business acumen, and the extent of his experience. He is an expert, and, like any other expert, if his opinion is proved to be fallacious and his judgment unreliable, then his reputation and practice naturally suffer, though his *bonâ fides* may be unimpeached.

As regards the phrase "according to the books," the use of which was objected to by some members *in toto*, we think in almost all cases it is advisable to retain it. How can the Accountant in general arrive at any facts at all if there are no books for him to refer to, or arrive at the correctness of accounts presented to him without comparing them with the books? It is quite true that he should not go by the books, and the books only, in ascertaining the facts and forming his opinion upon the debateable points, but the accounts if they are to be passed at all should be in accordance with the books and *à fortiori* the books should be in accordance with the facts, and this we consider the Accountant should state, both with a view of showing that the books are in his opinion correct, and also that he has examined them. The accounts indeed should be in accordance with the books and with the facts as well.

A separate report in every case in addition to the Certificate we think (disagreeing with Mr. BOWDEN), is unnecessary, for where an Accountant is satisfied as to the accuracy and fulness of accounts, he can give an ordinary short Certificate to that effect. It is only when the Accountant is not satisfied, or where there are some special circumstances, the mention of which would entail the occupying of too much space in the Certificate that a separate report becomes necessary.

Mr. MONKHOUSE's remark as to the advisability of taking (in an amalgamation of businesses) the average percentage of profits in the ascertained cases to apply to the remainder is not very distinctly stated ; but in his reply to his critics we are glad to see he specifically disavows such a mode of procedure, the dangers of which was disastrously exemplified in a noted case which we recently commented upon.

Estimates as to future profits were very generally condemned by the various speakers, for, of course, the Accountant's business is to deal with facts, and simply give his statement of what events he considers have happened in the past. Upon this statement, of course, it is perfectly open to the promoters or directors to base any financial estimate if they choose, so long as it is distinctly declared to be their own, and not in any way vouched for by the Accountant.

As to the question of how much and what sort of work the Accountant should do, referring to the amount of his fee, Mr. MONKHOUSE's strictures on this subject were, we think, rather too guarded, and the sense of the meeting was shown in no uncertain voice that a very high ground should be maintained in this matter by members of the profession, and that the question of remuneration should in no case enter into the consideration of the Chartered Accountant in connection with the thoroughness of his work. If he considers he is underpaid he has a very simple remedy—he can decline to do the work—and the more frequently and consistently this principle is adhered to, the more the profession at large will rise in public consideration, and the better it will be for the individual members in the long run. It is a question for the Council to consider whether some general uniform forms of accounts might not well be recommended by the Institute for the use of members, for although there is an infinite variety in accounts consequent on the constantly increasing complexity of business affairs yet we think it would be of advantage if the Institute were at all events to give some indication of the lines upon which it considers, after mature consideration, Certificates should run and forms of account be stated.

*(To be continued.)*

### CERTIFICATES.—*Continued.*

THERE was one point raised by Mr. BERRY which Mr. MONKHOUSE does not appear to have referred to in his reply—the question of what is to be inferred from the mere signing of a Balance Sheet by an Auditor without any remark whatever. This is, we fancy, a most unusual course to take, but the commercial public would certainly take the common sense view, and consider that the Auditor, by appending his signature, declared that he had not only compared the accounts in qnestion with the books, but also considered them correct to the best of his knowledge from the means at his disposal. We are also disposed to think that if an Auditor signs accounts in this manner, which he either knew, or ought to have known, were incorrect, the law would hold him responsible, looking at the view taken by the Judges in some recent cases, notably that of the *Leeds Building Society.* If we are not to infer that the Auditor considers the accounts as correct, then what earthly reason has he for appending his signature at all ?

We now propose to give a few typical specimens of Certificates which we have made acquaintance with in recent practice, commenting upon them as we go along, and which are principally examples to be avoided.

In the first place, for a good example of a Certificate of the prophetic order, and in general of what a Chartered Accountant's Certificate should *not* give, commend us to the following, published in the prospectus of a company a few months ago.

---

ACCOUNTANT'S REPORT.

........1890.

DEAR SIR,

I have examined your already audited accounts, and find that the business has been progressive and shews a gross profit of over sixty-seven per cent (67 per cent) on the cost of production, and that the net profit upon the average capital employed has exceeded twenty-five per cent (25 per cent) and with increased capital, which will allow of new steam machinery to be used, and also the extending of the business, there is no reason why the same per centage should not be fully maintained.

I understand that it is the intention of the Company to sell the patent rights in foreign countries, and if this is done, in my opinion taking into consideration the increased business being done each year, and the net profit thereon, the patents and business are fully worth the amount asked by you, and as you are handing over a certified freehold of 13,000 square feet on which good workshops are erected, and are prepared to take half the purchase money in deferred shares and only receive in absolute cash £5,500, it is evident that the greatest faith is placed by you in the success of the Company, and more especially as you have agreed to devote your time and energy in its development.

I am, dear Sir,

Yours truly,

(Signed)————

*Chartered Accountant.*

It seems to us that not only is prophecy indulged in here, but that the Accountant has encroached upon the valuer's functions ; and even then he does not venture to give a decided opinion in figures as a valuer would do. Part of the Certificate is pure surplusage, for what in the name of common sense does it matter to the outside public how financial questions are arranged with the vendor regarding his purchase money ? It is also very incomplete in the information it affords, none being given which would really be of any value to an intending investor. In this respect it shares these defects with the following three Certificates.

"I have examined the books and accounts of Mr. A. B.'s business for the years 1888 and 1889, and, after charging the entire sum expended during the two years in advertising, but excluding interest on capital, I estimate the net profits upon the capital employed to be as follows :—

Yearly average for the two years was 10 per cent.

For the year 1889 15½ per cent."

The vital question of course here, as in the former specimen, is what was the amount of the capital employed, and why were the actual net profits for a series of years not given.

The next is a Certificate given in connection with the flotation of a brewery.

"We certify that the net earnings of the trading for the twelve months preceding the date upon which the stock was last taken in the respective businesses, amount to the sum of £46,777, which would be sufficient to pay debenture interest, the preference dividend, 10 per cent. on the ordinary shares, and leave a surplus of £2,177."

There is no reason given why the examination of the books should be confined to one year only, and there is no information to show when the stock was last taken in the respective businesses, so that it is impossible from the Certificate to ascertain what particular 12 months' trading is referred to, or indeed whether the examination of the accounts has in all cases been made for the same 12 months. In other Certificates in connection with the same class of business the actual sales and sales of ales and beer are given, and the exact profits for several years in detail.  In this case, like that previously quoted, no valuation is given, although the purchase price was over £600,000, so that it is impossible to say how much proportion of this may have been for goodwill, and what amount was for the properties themselves.  A waiver clause as to contracts was inserted, so that it is impossible for a puzzled investor to find out for himself.

The following Certificate of the Birkbeck Building Society is given as among the incomplete forms ; no date being given, and no mention whatever made as to whether the Auditors have examined any books except the Pass Book, which seem to us a material omissions.

" The foregoing accounts together with the vouchers have been examined by us and found to be correct.  We also find that the balance in the Bankers' Pass Book corresponds with that shown above.  We have inspected the bonds and securities above set out, the amount stated in the Table of Assets representing the actual cost.  We have also examined the mortgage securities, which appear to us correct, and to agree with the several amounts thereby secured to the society."

The next Certificate, that of the Prudential Society, also seems to us to be incomplete, and indicates only a partial examination, and moreover does not disclose whether the Auditors have made an examination of all the entries included in the accounts or the books.

" We have examined the cash transactions, receipts, and payments, affecting the accounts of the assets and investments for the year ended December 31st, 1889, and we find the same in good order and properly vouched.  We have also examined the deeds and securities, certificates, &c., representing the assets and investments set out in the above account, and we certify that they were in possession and safe custody as on December 31st, 1889."

*(To be continued.)*

# The Accountant.

A MEDIUM OF COMMUNICATION BETWEEN ACCOUNTANTS IN ALL PARTS OF THE WORLD.

VOL. XVI.—NEW SERIES.—No. 832.          SATURDAY, NOVEMBER 15, 1890.

## The Accountant.

### NOVEMBER 15, 1890.

### CERTIFICATES.—*Continued.*

Whether it is necessary or advisable to give a narrative of the work actually done depends on the circumstances, but the following Certificate of the accounts of a Savings Bank is a case in which we do not think much has been gained by giving so much detail of the work done. As a thorough audit of a Savings Bank can only be effected by calling in all Pass Books of depositors, we do not see much use in this relation of the work done.

I beg to report that I have completed the audit of the accounts of your Institution for the year ending 20th November, 1886. The following is a summary of the work performed in respect of the audit, viz :—

1. Verification of the totals of cash received and paid.
2. Verification that said totals have been posted to the correct Accounts in the General Ledger.
3. Examination in detail of the Treasurer's Pass Book (Messrs. Robarts, Lubbock & Co.) with the books of the Institution.
4. Comparison of the Extracted List of Balances due to the depositors with the Ledgers.
5. Verification of the Total Amount due to the depositors.

6. Production of all vouchers, including the certificate from the Commissioners for the Reduction of the National Debt, which showed due to your Institution £1,322,490 5s. 0d., and also the Treasurer's Certificate, which showed in their hands £5,297 4s. 5d."

Here are one or two examples of qualified Certificates, which should be given as sparingly as possible, for if they contain any material qualification they are rendered of little or no value to those investors who can read between the lines.

"I have compared the above balance sheet with the books and vouchers of the company, and, subject to the value of the stock, lease, plant, &c., being as stated, certify the same to be correct."

This shows that the Accountant either was not satisfied with the figures put down for these items, or had no information upon the subject, which he should certainly have insisted upon, if necessary. The Certificate seems to us in its present form absolutely worthless.

The following Certificate was the form used for the first two years of the existence of a company whose chief asset consisted of patents.

"We have examined the above accounts with the books and vouchers of the company in London, and with the returns from the branches, and subject to a proper reserve being made for depreciation of patents, we are of opinion that they are respectively full and fair accounts properly drawn up so as to show a true and correct view of the company's affairs."

In the third year it was found necessary to write off nearly £50,000 from the cost of these patents, and the Certificate for the third year was in the following terms. The italics are ours.

"We have examined the above accounts with the books and vouchers in London, and with the statements received from the branches, and subject to a provision, if any be necessary, against the disputed claim of the late Technical Director, *and to the adjustment of the undiscovered difference in balancing,* we are of opinion that they are full and fair accounts properly drawn up so as to show a full and correct view of the company's affairs."

We have spoken of those investors who can read between the lines, but the danger of these qualified Certificates is to investors who can not, and who do not realize the full importance of these qualifications. Take the last instance: The mention of the undiscovered error in balancing (about £240) renders the accuracy of the accounts null and void, as of course this difference might be caused by errors of very serious amount on both sides, though this fact might not be appreciated by the general public.

Incidentally here arises a question in wording.

We do not think accountants as a rule realize the importance which the little conjunction "and" makes between the so frequently used phrase "Correct and in accordance with the Books," and— "Correct in accordance with the Books." The first is a much more absolute statement than the second,

for it definitely states the accounts to be correct, supplementing this information by the mention of the fact that the accounts agree with the Books, whereas the other only affirms that so far as the Books go the accounts are correct, but limits the statement to that fact.

We find that eminent authority, Mr. F. B. PALMER, Q.C., considers a certificate of the latter class "of little or no value." He also says:—

"Shareholders generally assume that the duties of an auditor are well defined, whereas the contrary is the fact. It is also assumed that their duties are easily discharged, and accordingly that a small remuneration is sufficient compensation, and further, that the form of the auditor's certificate is immaterial. In the result auditors generally take care that their labours shall be proportioned to their remuneration; and shelter, or attempt to shelter, themselves under an empty certificate. But how far such a course really does shelter the auditor may be a question."

This must surely have been written some years ago.

The next Certificate (of an Australian Mine) is a very guarded one, and does not say anything as to the correctness in principle, or otherwise, of the accounts, and as we have pointed out before, we consider the Certificate should give either more or less information.

"We have examined the above accounts with the books and vouchers of the company in London, and the accounts of the vouchers received from the manager at the mines, and the above accounts are made out in accordance therewith."

As regards the question of setting forth a separate report in addition to the Certificate, the next specimen is a good example.

"We have attached our signatures to the accounts to the 31st December, 1888.

A complete and detailed retrospective audit of the accounts for the year 1888 has been effected by Mr. D., of the firm of Messrs. C. D. & Co. The income has been checked, the outgoings properly vouched, and the outstanding balances verified.

The directors having given effect to their consideration of the values at which properties held as securities are maintained in the books, have assured us that, in their judgment, no further depreciation of such values is necessary.

The amount of the defalcations since the Quinquennial Valuation of 1884 is set out on the face of the accounts.

Investments in Government Stocks and Railway Debentures are taken at prices considerably below the market value at the date of closing the accounts.

We have assured ourselves that all deeds and certificates are in existence, and in the safe custody of the solicitor or bankers.

We have not examined the calculations of the Actuary made in relation to the Quinquennial Bonus to be declared as at December 31st, 1888."

As we have already remarked, we do not see much advantage in a separate report unless any special circumstances arise.

Next we will mention one or two accounts which have absolutely no Certificate appended to them at all.

The Medical and Clerical Assurance Company's accounts have no Certificate whatever attached to their accounts, and apparently no Auditor, as he does not sign the Balance Sheet. Of course the Life Insurance Company's Acts do not insist upon an auditor being appointed, but we think this is nearly the only Insurance Company which does not provide for a periodical audit and Certificate.

Again, in the prospectus of another concern, (Guinness Son and Company, Limited,) now lying before us, we have been unable to find any Certificate whatever, but simply a cash statement that the profits for the three months ending . . . were £ ; : and no information given as to who audited the books, or whether they were audited at all, although the other particulars of the business are pretty fully set forth. However the shareholders have not suffered in this case, for the dividends paid since the formation of the Company we understand have been actually more than was anticipated.

Lastly, the Accountant if he is sure of his facts should state them plainly and unmistakeably, and in no uncertain tone. The following Certificate is one given by a Scottish firm of Accountants.

We have, as requested, examined the books of Messrs. A. B. & Co., Engineers and Contractors, London and Paisley, with the view of ascertaining the amount of profit earned by the company, and we have to report as follows :—

The average annual profits earned during the five years ending 31st December, 1889, may, in our opinion, be stated at £9,950; and the average for the last three years of that period at £12,500.

In bringing out the average for the last three years, we have included £4,000, which we consider to be a moderate estimate of the profit likely to be derived from a contract, the accounts of which were not closed at 31st December, 1889.

It has to be kept in view :—First, That a considerable sum may have to be set aside out of future profits to provide for the gradual extinction of the amount standing at the debits of patents, the value put upon the patents in Messrs. Smith's report being £61,500; and second, That a charge will be brought against the limited company which the old firm had not to meet, viz : a charge for direction and general management.

This may be the ordinary style of certifying to profits in Scotland, but, owing no doubt to the wavering manner in which the Certificate was couched, only 20 per cent. of the Capital was subscribed by the public. We believe that in this case the Accountants erred on the side of caution, and that the profits are really as a matter of fact considerably greater than the amount shown in the Certificate !

## CERTIFICATES.

*(To the Editor of The Accountant.)*

SIR,—In the leader on " Certificates," in your last issue, you refer to the remarks made by Mr. JACKSON at the late Autumnal Meeting, in the discussion which followed the reading of Mr. MONKHOUSE's paper, on the words " in my opinion," which were called forth in reply to the remarks which I made on the subject, and which, in the two lines you give them in the report, do not accurately represent what I did state.

You also state that " An Accountant's opinion is his Stock-in-Trade," that " he is an expert, and, like all experts, if his opinion is proved to be fallacious or his judgment unreliable, his reputation and practice naturally suffer, though his *bonâ fides* be unimpeachable."

Will you be good enough to allow me to refer to what I did state at the Newcastle Meeting, and to refer shortly to the general question, and in doing so you will understand that I am not speaking " *ex Cathedra*," but rather with the object of inviting a discussion on this important subject from others more competent to deal with it than I can possibly do.

The proposition I put forward was that the words, " in my opinion " were words which I considered should be seldom used by Accountants ; that lawyers gave *opinions*, and when it turned out that they were wrong—as I need hardly remark they often are—the law did not hold them accountable for the result of the advice, although it may have caused great wrong and injury ; that our position as " experts " brought in to examine and report on the trading accounts of a firm about being turned into a limited company was analogous to a solicitor being employed to investigate the title of premises or land about being sold, and that where a solicitor would be held liable for gross negligence, so would an Accountant in a like case be held responsible.

I think Mr. MONKHOUSE puts this question of " opinion " in a proper light in his paper when referring to the fact that the public attach more importance to the Auditor's Certificate than the valuer's report. " There is, however, one important difference between the Certificate of profits and valuation. The latter, however carefully made by experienced valuers, is to a great extent only a matter of opinion, whereas the certificate deals specially with facts which by a skilled Accountant can be accurately ascertained, but in the result certified, there is no doubt sometimes involved a certain amount of opinion as to the question of depreciation, provision for bad and doubtful debts, &c.," and Mr. WELTON in his remarks, when discussing Mr. MONKHOUSE's paper, stated that " the province of an accountant was to declare facts and not to make estimates."

Now, we are all familiar with the dictum laid down by Mr. Justice Stirling in the *Leeds Benefit Building Case* as to the duties of auditors ; and Mr. WHINNEY at the Birmingham Meeting frankly admitted the principle laid down in that case, and in the course of his remarks, when dealing with the learned judge's decision so far as it related to auditors, made the followed remarks which I think strongly bear on the question of Certificates. He said: "the only safety, in my mind, for auditors is that they should exercise all reasonable care in examining the accounts of any company, such an amount of ca   as will satisfy and enable them to sign a Certificate that the balance sheet which they have audited does, in their opinion, set forth a true and correct opinion of the position of the company according to the books," and he adds, "I know perfectly well that a proper audit must go further and see that the books do correspond with facts."

In my opinion, and you will please note that I only give it as an opinion, which according to Webster is "a mental conviction of the truth of some statement founded on a low degree of probable evidence," the public have a right to expect more from us in our Certificates than an opinion.

We should not forget that we obtained our Charter on the grounds, amongst others, that our functions are of "great and increasing importance, and that it would be to the public benefit if we were incorporated in one body," and we have fresh in our minds the admirable address of the Mayor of Newcastle whose diagnosis of our future is so well expressed in the following extract which I take from his address: "Just in proportion as we assert our independence, and show by our report that the public can depend upon us, just as much will we grow in the confidence of the Public."

I will not attempt to improve upon what the Mayor of Newcastle has so well expressed, but I will say that the sooner the members of the Institute of Chartered Accountants teach unscrupulous promoters and others that our duty to the public precludes us from being made catspaws of, and that when these gentlemen require the assistance of some person to play the part of the confidence trick man for them, they will have to apply elsewhere for assistance.

One would have expected that the time had long since passed when the hackneyed saying that "An accountant was a person employed to bring round the balance, whichever side his employer required it" held good. In your second leader on the Bread Union, you very properly refer to the Auditors' Certificate, and as you have called on the gentlemen in question for an explanation as to the part they have played in the matter, I will refrain from expressing an opinion on their Certificate, but you will allow me to refer to the letter signed "Onlooker" with reference to the Certificate given by a leading firm of Birmingham accountants at the time of the floating of Ingall, Parsons, Clive & Co., Limited. I cannot think that "Onlooker" has done any good to the firm in question by his reference to this matter in your columns. We cannot shut our eyes to the fact that, to use the words of a member of the firm who gave the Certificate *re* Ingall, Parsons & Co., "Intending investors look to see if there is an experienced firm of Chartered Accountants connected with the Company," and it is an equally well known fact that when a member of the Institute, or for that matter any practising accountant, makes a slip inadvertently, or otherwise, the odium and discredit come on us all.

It is, therefore, much to be regretted, that the accountants did not, before they signed the Certificate of this company, consider what was due to themselves, to the members of their profession, and to the public.

I am,

Yours truly,

EDWARD KEVANS.

*Dublin, 4th November,* 1890.

---

[We had no desire to limit our correspondent's remarks at the Autumnal Meeting to two lines, but our reporter, although a very able man, was unable to do justice to our correspondent's Hibernian eloquence.—ED. *Accountant.*]

## THE INDEPENDENCE OF AUDITORS.

IN our last issue but one we gave an instance where auditors very rightly objected to proceedings which they did not think the directors of a company were justified in adopting, and we now are in a position to give the details of a still more flagrant case where auditors most properly have taken a firm stand and adhered to their position. The issues raised are between Messrs. LANGTON, HOLMES, & McCRINDLE, a well-known firm of public auditors in Melbourne, and the directors of the Anglo-Australian Bank (Limited), whose accounts are audited by that firm. The paper we quote from states that they have by their action "justifiably repudiated the notion often held by directors of companies that the functions of auditors are confined to merely vouching the arithmetical accuracy of the entries in a statement of accounts, and that there has been by far too much subserviency in this view of the duties of auditors shown by the profession in Australia." The case between the auditors and the directors has been recently placed before the shareholders, and it appears that Messrs. LANGTON & Co. were requested to give "a certificate of the clerical accuracy of the books." Had they merely done so, however, they would have ignored the spirit of the Articles of Association, which set forth that the auditors "shall make a report to the members upon the balance sheet and accounts, and in every such report shall state.whether, in their opinion, the balance sheet is a full and fair balance sheet, containing the particulars required by the regulations of the company, properly drawn up so as to exhibit a true and correct view of the company's affairs," etc. The article, however does not add the clause in Table A as to explanations from directors.

The points upon which the disagreement occurs are as follows:—

In the first place the paid-up capital in the accounts to September 30, 1890, submitted to the auditors, was stated as £100,317; but of this two shareholders held no less than £90,230, made up as follows:—

A.  8,180 shares paid up to £5 ...... £40,900.
B. 39,464 shares paid up to £1 5s..... £49,330.

There appears to be no dispute as to these amounts, but Messrs. LANGTON & Co. proceed to say that A.'s shares were originally held by C. as 42,360 shares paid up to £1, but only £5,000 was ever paid upon them, the balance being placed to the debit of C. in his current account. These 42,360 shares were then transferred to A., and, after allowing for several small transfers, are now represented by the 8,180 shares paid up to £5,

above-mentioned. But beyond the £5,000 already referred to, no other money has ever been paid to the company on account of these shares, the debit to C.'s current account having been transferred to that of A., where it now stands at £37,060 2s. In the face of these facts Messrs. LANGTON & Co. cannot recognise these shares as having been paid up to £5, nor can they see their way to recognise the 39,464 shares of B. as paid up to £1 5s., seeing that there is a debt due to the company of £33,538 8s. 9d., unless it can be shown that for this advance the company holds substantial security. The directors' explanation of these facts is as follows:—" It is a part of the bank's business, as defined in its Memorandum of Association, to make advances *on all descriptions of shares*. In the case of B.'s shares, the shares *were fully paid up at the time of issue*, and no advance was made against them for 14 months after their issue. To challenge the bank's right, as they virtually do, to make advances on shares is, in their opinion, to go behind, and attempt to override, its Memorandum of Association. The same remarks apply to A.'s shares, the only difference being one of time, the advance being made sooner in the latter case than in the former. The bank's vouchers prove that the shares were genuinely and *bonâ fide paid up*, and the advances made by the bank were subsequent acts."

So far as B.'s shares are concerned, the two statements are reconcilable; but with regard to A.'s shares they do not correspond, the technical question being, whether the shares held by A. were only partially paid on account, the balance being treated in current account, or, whether they were actually paid up, and afterwards advanced against. In any event, it is to be surmised that the "paid up" capital of the company is made up as follows:—

|  | Debit in Current Account. | | | Amount clear from Advances. | | | Total. |
|---|---|---|---|---|---|---|---|
|  | £ | s. | d. | £ | s. | d. | £ |
| A.'s shares .... | 37,060 | 2 | 0 | 3,839 | 18 | 0 | 40,900 |
| B.'s shares .... | 33,538 | 8 | 9 | 15,791 | 11 | 3 | 49,330 |
| Other shares (assumed not to be under advances) ...... | — | — | — | 10,087 | 0 | 0 | 10,087 |
|  | £70,598 | 10 | 9 | £29,718 | 9 | 3 | £100,317 |

so that out of a paid-up capital of £100,317

there is only an unencumbered balance of less than £30,000. The company may be within their right in making such advances, but it seems very far from prudent to advance so large a proportion of the paid-up capital to members holding nine-tenths of the stock. Such advances cannot be satisfactory to the depositors and debenture-holders of the company who, at the last balance of the books, stood at £110,339, and the auditors were fully justified in objecting to the share capital item appearing without proper explanation. It may be thought remarkable that the directors should lend on the security of the shares of their own company ; but they allege in support of this policy that they are empowered under the Memorandum to advance money without any security whatever, for among the objects for which the company was established is " (8) to lend money without taking security." Under such circumstances it is only fair that depositors should be distinctly informed that they are asked to lend money to an institution which has power to re-lend it without taking security, thus abolishing the most valuable safeguard to which the depositor is entitled.

The second point raised concerns the balance at the company's bankers,—£8,405 9s. 7d., on 30th September,—and it is alleged that, with the exception of £68 14s. 5d., it was made up by paying in cheques on two current accounts in the company itself on 30th September, which were retired the next morning by the company's cheque upon its bank. As, however, the bank gave a certificate to the effect that on the 30th September the balance was £8,405 9s. 7d. it is possible that the directors may be in the right from a technical point of view.

Messrs. LANGTON & Co.'s third objection— one of considerable importance to auditors—is that the amount of the freehold property of the company—£329,113 2s. 8d.—included interest, £22,034 14s. 4d., written up during the year, and therefore they declared that " unless this addition of interest to the amount of the assets can be sustained by clear evidence of an equivalent increase of value we shall not be able to certify to its correctness." To this the directors reply that "the question of charging properties with interest is entirely one of policy. The directors

have exercised a wise discretion in charging properties with interest, in one case only charging 3 per cent., in another 6 per cent., and in a third 10 per cent." The directors then go on to point out that the value of many of these properties has been greatly enhanced by various circumstances, such as the erection of railway stations, etc. As a matter of fact, we understand the real property market in Melbourne has been very depressed for some time, and from motives of policy, the more advisable course would be to write down the property even from its cost price. However this may be, even if the property in question has really improved in value, that is no proper pretext for the increment being added in the books, and credited to Profit and Loss, as evidently it has been done. We do not gather whether Messrs. LANGTON & Co. definitely object to such a course, as we should have expected, or have merely taken exception on the ground that they are not sufficiently assured as to the reliability of the increase of value. Nor do we clearly understand the Profit and Loss Account, for we find that in the year the nett profit was £9,141 1s. 6d.; but the interest written up on the property is shown to be £22,034 14s. 4d. for the year. In the accounts of all institutions which deal in real property the fullest details should be given for the protection of the investing public, and we fail to see why, if it is wrong here to take into account a profit not yet realised, it should be justifiable in Australia.

There is, finally, a small point to which the auditors raise objection, and that is the inclusion of 109 shares on which it appears that no money has been paid ; that, therefore, Messrs. LANGTON & Co. have declined to recognise these shares as having been legally issued. The other side affirm that the shares were given in lieu of commission, and if they were issued as fully paid up, in the ordinary way, we do not see how this can be objected to. However we are, at all events, glad to see our professional brethren in Australia standing out firmly against what they consider to be errors of fact or of principle, and in the case of the Anglo-Australian Bank there is evidently a great deal which wants very careful looking into. We notice that in its advertisement the bank is stated to be prohibited from dealing in land, freehold property, stocks or shares, of any kind whatever. How these statements are reconcilable with some of the facts to which we have made reference in our preceding remarks, it is rather difficult to imagine.

# The PROFESSION in SCOTLAND

## FRAUD AND ERROR IN BOOKS AND ACCOUNTS.

A Paper read before the Chartered Accountants Students'
Society of Edinburgh, by Mr. T. WATSON SIME, C.A.
7th April, 1892.

THE study of the weaknesses and imperfections to which
mankind are prone is, doubtless, to the metaphysically-
inclined, a very interesting one, but, to common minds, a
theme of rather a painful nature. In justification of my
choice of such an unpleasant subject for this evening's paper,
I would submit that I know of no topic of more general
interest to accountants than the one I have selected, as to it,
more than any other, our profession owes its very inception.

Public Accountants no doubt lived and practised prior to
the year 1800, but, in Scotland at any rate, their functions
would seem to have been limited to investigations in connection with Court of Session Remits and to inpromissions
as factors on landed and other estates. Accountancy may
therefore be regarded as almost entirely a nineteenth century
growth—which is only natural, considering the vast development which in modern times has characterised the commercial interests of our country. More especially is this
seen to be the case when we consider the great expansion
which has taken place in the joint stock enterprise of the
country during the last three decades—an expansion which
has incalculably extended the sphere of the accountant. The
greater the commercial activity, the more is opportunity
afforded to the fraudulently inclined, and, I may add, the
greater the necessity for those opportunities being check-
mated. It will be profitable, therefore, for us to consider for
a short time some of the methods by which fraud and error
have been perpetrated, and some remedies which in certain
cases should be adopted as preventives.

My subject would appear to divide itself into two heads,
but, at the outset, I do not propose drawing any broad line
of demarcation between Fraud and Error, my reason being
that my remarks will in most cases apply almost with equal
force to both. In practice you will find that often an error
in books and accounts looks very like a fraud, while, on the
other hand, a fraud can be made to very closely resemble an
error. The close of my paper I intend devoting to the consideration of some common clerical errors which an accountant frequently meets with in practice. I should further
premise that my remarks are intended to apply, not only to
audits (the primary function of which I hold to be the
detection of Fraud and Error), but to special investigations
where fraud is suspected, and indeed to all cases where books
and accounts come under the examination of an accountant.
The same procedure cannot of course be followed in every
case, but the general principles may well be borne in mind.

The concerns which come under an accountant's observation
may for my purpose be divided into five great classes.

(1) Railway, Shipping, and kindred companies.

(2) Banks, Insurance and similar offices.

(3) Building, Investment and Friendly Societies.

(4) Charitable Institutions and Clubs.

(5) Manufacturing and Trading concerns.

The first four of these I shall dismiss with very few remarks for the reasons (first) that the financial organization of any one of these classes might very well form the subject of a whole evening's discussion, and (second) that my personal experience, like that of, I daresay, many of us here has been confined in a great measure to the fifth class. A sixth class I might have added, viz., the Accounts of Factors and Trust Estates, but I do not propose to touch upon these, as they have on previous occasions been under your consideration. In the large concerns which I have mentioned, next to a well arranged system of books and accounts, I would place the desirability of, at frequent intervals, so interchanging the duties of the subordinate officials that any irregularity on the part of one might lead to its detection by his successor. Of late years, we have been startled by the enormous frauds perpetrated by officials of savings banks, frauds which have brought financial disaster to many a home. The Cardiff Savings Bank was a notable example. For upwards of 30 years, about £1,000 annually was embezzled by the very simple method of debiting false amounts to the accounts of depositors. Had the pass books in this case been examined periodically by an independent person, the continuance of these frauds could never have happened. No doubt, in the cases of large savings banks and building societies, it is difficult, if not impossible, for all depositors' pass books to be called in and examined, but this difficulty could in a great measure be obviated by an auditor attending at uncertain intervals and examining such books as might be handed in during the course of business. In concluding this portion of my subject, it is manifest that the discovery of frauds of a limited amount, must in the cases of railways, banks, and similar concerns of great magnitude, be left practically in the hands of the inside staff.

I shall now deal with the Books and Accounts of Manufacturing and Trading Companies, or, with what is very common, a combination of the two. I think that you will agree that this class alone affords ample food for study and reflection, as, all along the line, from the office boy to the manager, fraud is too frequent an occurrence.

The first and most important remedy for fraud and error in commercial concerns which I have to suggest is the adoption in every case of a good and simple method of book-keeping, and no system deserves these adjectives which is not based upon the principles of double entry. It is extraordinary (although true) that in these days of advanced education, so many concerns (some of considerable importance) will persist in adhering to the old system, if system it can be called, of single entry. Single entry might aptly be called the "accountant's provider," as the facilities it affords for fraud and error have been, and still are, the source of considerable business to our profession. It is true that no system of bookkeeping, however perfect, will completely prevent the occurrence of fraud, but single entry positively invites it. The reason for such defective knowledge of the correct principles of bookkeeping among the majority of business men is not far to seek, and

may be traced at once to the imperfect instruction on the subject given in schools. The ordinary Text Books in use are not practical, and few of the instructors possess the requisite practical knowledge of their subject. Most youths leave school with altogether erroneous notions about bookkeeping, notions which take several years of after-training to dispel. As a remedy, I would suggest that the study of the subject should not be commenced until a more mature age than is usually the case has been attained, and it seems to me that it is altogether a subject more fitted to the Commercial Colleges which are gradually being instituted in our large towns. As accountants, we need not fear that a better knowledge of the subject on the part of business men will be detrimental to the advancement of our profession, for I feel sure that many of us recognize the fact that clients who thoroughly realise the advantages of an accountant's services, and understand the principles of his work, are more likely to seek our aid. Besides, in these days of keen competition in trade and cutting of prices, it is more than ever necessary for commercial concerns to have their books based upon a sound and useful system.

Single entry affords so many loopholes for fraud and error that, without a most exhaustive analysis and examination of the whole of the transactions during the period dealt with, one can never feel safe in submitting results attained by this method. One of the most common devices for fraud in this system is the collection and appropriation of customers' accounts; and cases have occurred where thousands of pounds have been embezzled, the amounts being credited properly in the ledgers but religiously excluded from the Cash Book.

It is, however, to books kept by double entry that I more particularly invite your attention to-night, and the two chief points for our consideration in beginning an investigation are

(1) The existence of any special motives to commit fraud on the part of the officials with whom we are brought in contact.

(2) The means by which such frauds are likely to be effected.

In regard to the first, we may find that the cashier or manager has a direct interest in the success of the business, and in such an event our scrutiny cannot be too searching. Or it may be that a principal has an interest to serve, and frauds by a partner to the detriment of his co-partners are by no means uncommon.

Our first duty should be to obtain and record a list of all books kept in the particular concern ; and this is more important than might be imagined, as there have been cases where certain books have been purposely withheld from the accountant's scrutiny.

Naturally, we commence with the Cash Department, as in it frauds are more likely to occur. Beginning with the receipt side of the Cash Book (always the more difficult to verify) our object should be to ascertain that every sum received by the cashier has been duly accounted for. In many businesses this is a most difficult task. Cases are frequent where a cashier either omits altogether to debit himself with cash received, or where the amount so received is short entered. In the majority of cases subsequent sums received are applied to conceal earlier defalcations : a process which, in England, is known by the term of *Lading and Teeming.* How are we to check or prevent such occurrences ? The plan adopted by many firms, of issuing acknowledgments of cash paid to them from counterfoil receipt books numbered consecutively, is no doubt a good one, and should be more generally followed ; but this system is open to the following defects, viz. :

  (1) The cashier may enter in the counterfoil a smaller amount than that actually received.

  (2) He may give a discharge upon another document, and appropriate the amount.

  (3) Many firms, in remitting money, send their own form of of receipt, which they insist upon getting discharged.

  (4) Some firms pay all accounts by cheque without taking formal acknowledgments, and writing upon the face of the cheque, which is usually crossed " not negotiable," that it is in payment of account to a certain date.

  (5) Cases have been known where dishonest cashiers have had receipt books specially printed which they, of course, concealed from knowledge.

Wherever these counterfoil receipt books are used, I think that an accountant should compare them with the Cash Book entries, and when dates are found to disagree he should be upon the alert. He will, of course, note carefully the number of the last counterfoil examined by him, and endeavour to ascertain that all books got from the stationer are accounted for. It goes without saying that firms using counterfoil receipt forms should, for their own safety, insert a printed note on their invoices and accounts that no other description of receipt is valid. An English case decided that where a customer paid his account to a collector and, in disregard of such intimation, accepted from him a plain receipt, he was liable to make a second payment of the debt. Many firms of accountants have adopted the practice of issuing to all debtors appearing in the books postcards stating the amount appearing at their debit and requesting, where discrepancies occur, that the customers should communicate with them direct. In practice, I think, this is found not altogether satisfactory, as many people object to be troubled with such communications. I have seen it tried, but, on the whole, I think that such notices should emanate from the office of the client rather than that of the accountant. If done at all, it is obvious that the bookkeeper himself should on no account be entrusted either with the despatch of the notice or with the replies received. Another weak point in the system is that it does not guard against transactions settled prior to the date of balance. Some English accountants go the length of sending to customers statements specifying the dates and amounts of cash credited in their Ledger Accounts, but I fear that, north of the Tweed, at any rate, the fees which we are allowed would not justify such an Herculean task.

On the whole, therefore, as regards sums received from debtors, accountants are in a great measure at the mercy of the cashier. One comfort is that, sooner or later, such embezzlements are usually found out ; and, in my subsequent remarks upon Sales Ledgers, I shall suggest points which frequently lead to their detection.

Receipts of sundry amounts, such as the proceeds of old plant or materials sold, are as a rule easily verified, although here again we are met with the difficulty of ascertaining that *all* sums so received are accounted for. The partners, if a private concern, and the Minute Books, if a limited company, should assist us in this.

The remainder of the receipt side of the Cash Book will to a great extent be made up of the cheques drawn upon the firm's bankers. Here fraud is frequently carried out. After ascertaining who have power to operate on the bank account, we should satisfy ourselves that all cheques issued during the period under review are duly debited. As a rule it will only be necessary to reconcile the totals of the cheques entered with those shown in the Bank Pass Book, a comparison in detail either with the pass book or the original counterfoils not being required. It is advantageous, however, to compare with the Cash Book the counterfoils of cheques issued, for, say a week before the balance, as cases have been known where a cashier, in order to reduce his cash balance to such an amount as he could instantly produce, has entered the payment of the money under its proper date, but omitted to debit himself until after the balance with the issue of the cheque. A cashier who had the power might, of course, issue such cheques from another book than the one submitted to the accountant, a fact which a reconciliation of the bank account would not disclose, but a scrutiny of the payments made during the two last days of the period would generally in cases of large payments reveal such an expedient. Before taking up the credit side of the Cash Book I would like to express my strong disapproval of the system adopted by some firms of passing all bill transactions through the Cash Book. Such a plan is not only confusing but may tend to conceal frauds on the part of the cashier. Unless where cash is actually affected, bill transactions should be recorded only in the Bill Books or Journal.

Taking now the payment side of the Cash Book, the heaviest disbursements of a mining or manufacturing concern are found to be the wages paid to employés, and probably more frauds have been perpetrated in this department than in any other. The pay sheets should of course be called for, and, no matter how lengthy they may be, and how particularly they may be certified, an accountant should not part with them until the summations have been found to be correct. This duty is of course strikingly apparent in small concerns, where one man is entrusted, not only with the preparation of the sheets, but the actual payment to the men ; but even in large concerns where these functions are performed by independent parties (as they always should be) it has been repeatedly found that the figures have been tampered with by the cashier after undergoing the scrutiny of the managers. The ways by which these sheets can be manipulated are manifold. Sometimes the totals are found to be short of the amounts entered in the Cash Book. In other cases, the sheets are found to be systematically oversummed ; while again "dummy" men may be inserted, or the calculations of the details of the pay may be overstated. Where collusion happens between a cashier and works manager, frauds of this kind are almost incapable of detection. Unless specially directed to do so, an accountant can do little more than check occasional calculations, while the comparison of the sheets with the original Time and Work Books is too lengthy a task for him to attempt. I would recommend the appending to the sheets of a certificate giving *in words* the total amount paid, and that each person certifying the sheets should indicate plainly his function in regard thereto. Initials only should never be accepted. The sheets should be scrutinized generally to ascertain that no wages or salaries are entered which also appear as separate payments in the Cash Book. Where advances are made on account of the pay, you should see that such advances are regularly deducted from the next pay. Any sum standing at the debit of the Advances Account at the date of the balance should be carefully compared with the book showing the details.

The lodgments in bank next invite our attention, and we should carefully compare the dates and amounts of the payments with the bank Pass Book, regarding sharply any instances where the Pass Book entry is of much later date than that in the Cash Book. We shall then be in a position to reconcile the balance appearing in the Pass Book with that in the firm's Ledger, and here the suggestion occurs to me that in no case should we be content with the production, by the cashier himself, of an apparently certified Pass Book or even with a formal certificate. Bankers, if applied to by the accountant, are always ready to supply independent certificates, and instances have been known where cashiers have for their own purposes fabricated Pass Books.

A peculiar case once came under my observation. It was found that, on the last day of the balance of a mining company's books, certain calls in arrears by shareholders were entered as received, and the amount paid into bank. The date of the lodgment in the bank Pass Book was, however, found to be several days subsequent to that in the Cash Book, and, on enquiry, it was discovered that this plan had been adopted with the innocent, though mistaken, intention to suppress the fact that certain officials of the company, who were also shareholders, had been unable to meet their calls at the proper time. While on the subject of calls in arrear, I may express the desirability of the accountant communicating direct with any shareholders appearing in this position, in order to verify the fact.

Receipts for staff salaries paid should be obtained and examined, and it is of assistance to the accountant, in ascertaining that no official has been overpaid, where these salaries are debited, not to the Expenses Account, but to personal accounts opened for each individual, that these individuals should periodically be credited by Journal entry with the salary due to them.

With the routine observed in satisfying ourselves as to the accuracy of general cash payments, you are, no doubt, all thoroughly conversant. A few remarks as to the checking of vouchers will not, however, be amiss. We ought, of course, to guard against over-statements of amounts, and

should see that the discharges on the vouchers agree accurately with the cash entries. All vouchers should be so cancelled that they cannot again be produced, and this should be done by initialling them in coloured ink, or by the use of a rubber audit stamp. Pencil, whether red or otherwise, should never be used for this purpose. Personally, for reasons after-stated, I am in favour of using a rubber stamp fitted with movable dates, and bearing upon it the use to which it is put. The audit marks should always cover to some extent the discharge upon a voucher. Frequently, in satisfying ourselves as to vouchers, we are handicapped by the slovenly methods used by many business men in discharging accounts paid to them. In rare instances do we find that the amount of the payment is expressed in words on the receipt, a want that sometimes leads to additional items being afterwards added to the account by the cashier wherever a blank space enables him to do so. Sometimes you will have produced to you a bundle of invoices tacked together, the items of which are carried and added to one of them, and a discharge adhibited which does not specify the total amount paid. Such vouchers afford a ready means for fraud. Again, forged receipts may be submitted to, and passed by, us, and against such contingencies we are, in a measure, obliged to trust that time will show the truth. Wherever, for lack of time, you accept as evidence of a payment the retired cheque by which it has been paid, note the details carefully in your Memorandum Book, and at your next audit see that the missing receipt or a duplicate of it is produced and cancelled. Duplicate receipts should be regarded with a jealous eye. If by any chance you should initial or mark vouchers for payments made after the period, take a careful note of all such, and on no account be persuaded to tick the Cash Book entries until the proper time comes round. I have already alluded to the advantages of counterfoil receipt forms; and, in concluding this portion of my subject, I have to commend the system which many business houses, particularly in London, have adopted, of lodging all sums received in bank, and of making all payments by cheques upon their bankers. Were this more generally adopted, the field for fraud would be vastly curtailed. Our duties in such a case would involve our satisfying ourselves that our clients adhere rigidly to the system, and safeguard themselves as far as possible. Much lies in their own hands. In particular, they should be careful to cross to their own bankers all cheques endorsed by them in the course of business. In issuing cheques they should see that no room is left for the subsequent increase of the amount, and their marking—as, " not negotiable "—should be more frequently attended to. A good plan is the crossing of cheques with a note of the cash limit they cover. The Petty Cash Book should then have our careful attention; and, considering the large amounts annually expended by some firms in petty cash, this Book often meets with less scrutiny than it deserves. In particular, you should see that no payments have been included which are also charged separately in the principal Cash Book. Vouchers should also be required for all sums capable of being so verified.

The accuracy of the Cash Balance should next be tested;

and trading firms or companies would do well to follow the practice of insurance offices and other concerns, who make it a rule to lodge in bank all cash on hand at the date of balance. In some cases this cannot, of course, be done, but where large cash balances are kept in hand, either the accountant or a principal should verify the cash by actual production on the day of the balance. It is manifest that these regular verifications are not entirely sufficient, as a cashier might, and often does, arrange to have his cash in order for the occasion. I do not urge the accountant to take upon himself the duties of a detective, but it is frequently salutary for the cash to be verified at irregular intervals, when visits of this kind are quite unlooked for. In verifying the cash, you should see that all cheques and bills forming part of the cash balance have been duly entered in the books. A strictly honest cashier of business habits will invite, rather than condemn, the fullest investigation. Our remaining duties, so far as the Cash Department is concerned, consist of testing the summations and postings of the Cash Book. It may be added that the keeping of scroll Cash Books should be discouraged as far as possible.

The Sales Books next demand our scrutiny, and here we are confronted with the task of ascertaining that all goods sold have been accounted for—in some businesses almost an impossibility. In small businesses this difficulty is frequently enhanced by the fact that one person has, practically, the control of the concern, and in such a case our scrutiny of all the transactions is almost imperative. In large concerns, where one department acts as a check upon another, we feel tolerably safe. Sometimes we shall require to ascertain from the press copies or despatch books that the goods are passed to the Sales Books, and occasionally we may have to examine Railway and other Carriage Accounts with the same object. Doubtless, where Stock Books are kept, or where stocks are capable of reconciliation, any large leakage could be detected ; but in many businesses, such as chemical manufactures, oil works, and others which will readily occur to you, the stocks are not an absolute check. Cost Sheets, carefully prepared, aid us to some extent. The accountant should, if possible, ascertain that goods credited as sold towards the end of the period have actually gone out of stock.

Passing to the Purchase Books, we should, in the first place, ascertain who have power to order goods, and what means are used to see that the goods are actually got in, and that the checked invoices are duly passed to the debit of the business and the credit of the parties supplying the goods. In particular, we should guard against the possibility of the same invoice being passed twice, for it occasionally happens that goods are twice paid for ; while, on the other hand, payments have been made for goods which were never received. It is recorded that a clerk was in the habit of passing duplicate invoices and, after payment of both had been made, used to call upon the person to explain that by an oversight this had happened. The overpaid amount was in good faith refunded, but somehow the money never found its way back to the clerk's employers. Of course, where an employé conspires with either a customer or a creditor for

the purpose of defrauding his firm, peculation may pass undetected for a long time. Happily, such instances are not frequent, though the scope is almost unlimited. I would here refer to the baneful practice which some manufacturing and mining businesses that are newly established have of passing from their Cash Books straight to the debit of the Capital Accounts, sums paid for the erection of buildings and purchase of plant. Personal Accounts should always be reared in such cases. In one instance in my own experience, where heavy payments had been made extending over many months, a dishonest secretary entered one or two large sums twice over, producing as vouchers the second time invoices bearing a forged discharge. This would have been more readily detected had these amounts been first passed to the credit of Personal Accounts in the Purchase Ledger. In examining invoices, you should see that they are initialled or certified by responsible parties, and what precisely they certify. Invoices written by a bookkeeper himself should rarely, if ever, be passed, and the accountant should see that the official form of the party supplying the goods is used. It would be a distinct advantage were the practice more often followed, to print upon such forms the word "Invoice," as there would then be less danger of our afterwards being presented with an account falsely converted into a receipt. It follows, of course, that on receiving payment of goods so invoiced, the recipient should decline to discharge the "invoice" form. On the whole, traders are too careless in such matters, and they have often but themselves to blame. As in the case of cash vouchers, I would recommend the accountant to so mark invoices that they may not be produced to him a second time, and I am in favour of devoting a special stamp to this purpose. If time should permit after the close of my paper, I shall tell you of a case which justifies my advice on this point. The invoices for, say, the last month of the period under review, should be carefully examined, as we can sometimes thus guard against the omission to enter the last goods got in from the knowledge we acquire as to the frequency of their supply.

Both the Sales and the Purchases Books should, of course, be carefully summed, and in one way or another we should satisfy ourselves that the whole of the transactions recorded find their way to the Ledgers. In small concerns, especially where controlled by one man, I think we should not be satisfied until every item is compared to the Ledgers.

The Ledgers being the focus of the whole system, require a high degree of attention. At the outset, we must satisfy ourselves that the commencing balances are in order, and it is most important, I urge, that, at each succeeding examination, we should find by comparison with the trial balance sheets retained by us that none of these balances have been tampered with since our previous investigation. Where possible (although it cannot be done in many cases) the books should be examined in the accountant's own office. In checking postings, some prefer to exhaust every Ledger account by calling from the Ledgers outwards. This has its advantages, but is in large concerns inadvisable, as the constant reference to the other books, would, I consider, waste much valuable time. Wherever, in cases of outside investigation, Ledger postings cannot be taken up and disposed of at a sitting, our first duties should be to check off the balances at the beginning of the period, and record in a private statement the balances at the close, which we have to verify.  This obviates the risk of the books being tampered with during the interval—an occurrence not unknown.  In examining debtors' accounts, you should be on the watch for any anomalies, such as payments credited for goods supplied at a later date than items left unsettled.  You should also regard critically the age of the various balances and the course of payments.  Debts written off require to be watched carefully, and we should satisfy ourselves that they are really bad, and that track of them is not entirely lost.

Where Aggregate Sales and Purchases Accoun's are kept in the General Ledger, it may be unnecessary to check the details of the postings to the Sales and Purchases Ledgers, but we ought of course to satisfy ourselves that the various balances in these Ledgers correspond in total with the balances on the Aggregate Accounts.  We should also run over the names in the Sales Ledgers to ascertain that no goods got by partners are included.  The question of checking the details of Ledger postings is altogether a vexed one, but I know of no better method of satisfying ourselves that everything has been included, and also of discovering a discrepancy in the books, than the now ancient plan proposed by Jones, of reconciling the debit and credit totals of the Subsidiary Books with those of the Ledgers.  You will be wise to keep the Book-keeper as much as possible in the dark as concerns the routine of your audit, and to make variations therein from time to time.  I find it a good plan myself to adopt a different form of check mark at each succeeding audit.  It is unnecessary to add that all entries should carefully be examined, and any left unticked noted.  This in my opinion is one of the most important matters to attend to in investigations, as it is a complete preventive against entries being made in Ledgers without the intervention of the proper subsidiary books.

The question of clerical errors is a vast one, and one which I have time to hardly more than touch.  Common errors arise in some of the following ways :—

Under- or over-castings of totals.

Transposition of sums in posting from one book to another, or in carrying forward the totals of pages.  Pounds are often carried forward as shillings and shillings as pence.

The carrying down of the total of a Ledger Account instead of the Balance, or the omission to carry down anything at all.

Sometimes, great trouble is caused through the indistinctness of figures, and wherever doubt is possible the accountant should write the proper amount alongside, or rule out and re-insert the figures.

The type of the old Scottish bookkeeper, who added up the year of our Lord among the pounds, is not so uncommon as might be supposed, and I have myself seen before now the number of the street included in a similar way, where the heading of the Ledger Account was in too close proximity to the entries.  Sometimes a blot over the amount does the

mischief, but two of the most uncommon errors that ever came under my notice arose as follows :—

A small difference was found on balancing the books of an extensive company, and after much search it was found that it arose through a slovenly habit the cashier had of elongating the ticks placed by him in the money columns to signify blanks, these ticks having been mistaken for the number 11.

Great labour was involved by a discrepancy which occurred in the balance of another concern, and which seemed for a time to defy detection.  At last, it was found that it arose through the thin kind of paper used in a ledger, a bold 1 on a certain page showing through to the other side, and being included a second time in the additions.

We should always bear in mind that a small discrepancy may extend upon investigation to errors of thousands of pounds, and may thus merely be the balance of many errors.

In concluding my paper, I am conscious that I have submitted nothing novel for your consideration, but I trust that my remarks, however crude, may be means of stimulating more attention to what is a highly important subject.

## The Duties of Auditors.

WE reprint from the *Daily Chronicle* the following article on this subject which appears in that paper of the 30th ult. :—

WE are glad to see that our remarks upon the evidence of the Chartered Accountants of the "Balfour Bubbles," calling the attention of the Institute of Chartered Accountants to the apparent uselessness of the audits they presented, has elicited the letter we print elsewhere. The Council of the Institute remark that, inasmuch as the conduct of the accountants is still before the Court, it would be unbecoming in them to express an opinion. The Council knows its own business best, but since the Registrar has expressed such extremely frank opinions, this hesitation seems somewhat unduly scrupulous. When an accountant, for instance, signs a report which practically declares that the securities held by a company are what they profess to be, but does not look over these in detail, on the ground that there are a very large number of them, and he has not sufficient time to do so, there can be only one opinion upon his fitness for the post. The Council points out that "an auditor has no concern with the administrative management of a company except so far as to see that its operations have been within its statutory powers." We would add to this, perhaps, for the sake of clearness only, that it is also an auditor's duty to see that the public is not deceived. Yet there were a great many Chartered Accountants auditing the affairs of the Liberator Society, and the public was grossly deceived. We cannot help thinking, and we should greatly like the opinion of the Council of the Institute of Chartered Accountants upon this point, that if among all the accountants there had been one man sufficiently capable, painstaking, and fearless, the ghastly swindle would have been instantly exposed, and a large portion of the thrifty public saved from the alternative of starvation or common charity. The Secretary of the Institute declares that "an auditor will fail in his duty if he does not use reasonable care to satisfy himself as to the propriety of the figures contained in the books and Balance Sheet. His certificate, unless he expressly raises objection or limits the application of his words, must be taken to imply that the figures of the Balance Sheet as audited present, in his opinion, a true view of the position of the affairs of the company." Nothing could be fairer or more honest than this, and if the Institute deals in the spirit of this declaration with the Liberator auditors, the interests of the public will be better watched in future. The fact is that the Institute of Chartered Accountants must take some action at once in self-defence. The very name of "Chartered Accountant" is under a cloud, and unless something is done to reinstate it in public estimation, investors will prefer to have accounts examined by somebody less technical and more trustworthy.

## Auditing.

*The Building Societies Gazette* for August last has an article on auditing, suggested by the Liberator Building Society's failure which, being the antipodes of the view usually entertained by our contemporaries, is of sufficient interest to reproduce. It says:—"We have no hesitation in saying at once, for the evidence has gone quite far enough to justify our view, that the auditors of the Liberator Building Society took a very easy view of their duties, and were less than just to their own reputation as accountants and to the shareholders and members in whose interests they were appointed to act. At the same time we are bound to say that, while the evidence has disclosed the fact that in the case of this society the auditors did too little, there is a disposition on the part of the public generally, and especially on the part of Mr. Registrar Emden, to expect too much. An auditor should neither be expected to be satisfied with the mere superficial examination necessary to prove that the books balance, nor on the other hand should it be required of him that he should review the policy of the directors and be personally responsible for the good government and stability of the society whose accounts he may be called upon to inspect. Between these two extremes the auditor's duty lies, and it is absurd to suppose that the certificate of an auditor that the accounts represent the state of affairs can or ought to convey any guarantee that the assets are, beyond all doubt, of the value set down. There has recently been a good deal of nonsense talked about the duties of an auditor. The vulgar notion appears to be that he should be a sort of censor of the directors' proceedings, and that nothing in the way of business should be done that does not commend itself to his judgment. He must, in fact, be a man of very superior intelligence and business capacity, of conspicuous honesty and integrity, a lawyer that he may the better inspect the title deeds and see that there is no flaw in them to impair the society's title, a valuer that he may satisfy himself that the property is worth the advances; and if there be any other virtues or capabilities that may be wanting in the Board of Directors individually and collectively it is expected that the auditor will have them all oozing out of him and ready for use at the shortest notice! Never was a more unthinking demand. Shareholders are content to pay an auditor one, two, five, or twenty guineas, according to the size of the society, but they in no case pay him for one-tenth part of the time that would be necessary to do what, when things go wrong, they think he ought to have done, nor for one-hundredth of the qualities that they vainly look to find in mortal man. What, then, are the duties of an auditor? It is not easy to define them or to limit them, and it is better that they should not be either defined or limited. Let the shareholders pay their auditors a fee that will enable them to devote as much time as may be necessary to thoroughly examine and sift the accounts, and let them appoint trustworthy men for the purpose. The auditor on his part should keep his eyes and his ears open, and should immediately report to the members anything which in his opinion is being done to their detriment. Such 'cooking' of the accounts as has been discovered by the Official Receiver in this case might and ought to have been detected by the auditors. The members of a society and the public at large will never be satisfied with an audit that is limited to the elementary calculation that twice two are four; but they ought not to look for too much. The directors are, when all is said, the persons in whom the members have reposed their confidence, and it is cowardly when that confidence has been betrayed to make the auditor the 'whipping boy.'"

## Birmingham
## Chartered Accountant Students' Society.

A CRITICISM OF THE OPINIONS OF SOME CHAR-
TERED ACCOUNTANTS ON THE ROUTINE
WORK OF AN AUDIT.

### By Mr. Eric M. Carter, F.C.A.

At a meeting of the above Society held on the 5th Dec.,
1893, Mr. Eric M. Carter delivered the following lecture:—

The routine work of an audit is, I think, a subject of peculiar importance to accountants' students. As beginners they
have to do a great deal of it, and they should form an accurate idea of the nature and objects of their work. Nothing
helps us so much to form our own opinions as to hear the
opinions of others who have had experience. Unfortunately
there are serious differences of opinion in our profession as
to what are the responsibilities of auditors, and consequently
there are just as great, if not greater, differences of opinion as
to what work he should do. Still, I think you will find that
an examination and comparison of these very differences
will in itself be of use.

The question first arises as to how far it is possible to lay
down general rules. It may bo argued that circumstances
differ so much that it is not possible. This, I think, is only
true to a limited extent. In practice, an accountant when
he arranges the work of an audit has in his mind a general
scheme, such as he is accustomed to adopt, and he looks out
for any special circumstances which would render necessary
a modification of his general plan or any addition to it. Such
a general scheme is evidently in the minds of all those who
have written on the subject, and it is the best general scheme
we should endeavour to arrive at, as well as a clear idea of
the circumstances which render a modification of it necessary or desirable. It is only by freely discussing the ques-

tion that we can make auditing more systematic and
scientific, and then, perhaps, it can be more clearly settled
where an auditor's duties begin and where they end.   Anyhow, the more our present differences are discussed the
sooner they will disappear.   I do not mean to say that
auditing is altogether an exact science ; there are, as has
often been pointed out, matters of opinion and principle on
which two auditors of equal capacity may hold different
views.   For instance, there may be two opinions of the
value of a book debt, but it is mostly a question of fact
whether the book debt exists or not.   It is in the verification
of facts that routine work is to a great extent concerned,
and it is here, I think, that a more general understanding is
needed.

In reviewing the opinions of different accountants, attention should more particularly be given to the writings of
those who hold a leading position among us.   Three members of the Council have written on the routine work of an
audit with some minuteness, namely, Mr. F. W. Pixley, Mr.
C. R. Trevor, and Mr. David Chadwick.   Besides these
members of the Council I may mention Mr. L. R. Dicksee,
who has written a useful book on auditing, and there are
papers by Mr. F. R. Goddard, and other accountants, to
which I shall have to refer several times.   For convenience of reference I have prepared a list of the books and
papers I mention in my lecture.

Auditing covers a wide ground, but in dealing with the
subject most writers seem to have laid down rules applicable
to manufacturing limited companies.   I think it is best to
confine ourselves to these because an auditor's duties, as set
forth in articles of association, are generally very similar to
those in Table A., and there are usually no special instructions to modify or amplify our work, such as there would be
with a private firm, and the audit of banks or of the
accounts of public bodies would be quite different.

I propose to lay before you the opinions of various writers,
first on the objects and general scope of an audit, and then
I will set side by side their views more in detail on the different parts of the routine work.   Having done this, I will
later on attempt to make a few criticisms and suggestions.
To begin with, I will give some extracts from the audit
clauses of Table A.   The following are the most important :—

(Art. 83.)   Once at the least in every year the accounts of
the company shall be examined, and the correctness of the
Balance Sheet ascertained, by one or more auditor or
auditors.

(Art. 84.)   The first auditors shall be appointed by the
directors ; subsequent auditors shall be appointed by the
company in general meeting.

(Art. 88.)   The remuneration of the first auditors shall be
fixed by the directors ; that of subsequent auditors shall be
fixed by the company in general meeting.

(Art. 92.)   Every auditor shall be supplied with a copy of
the Balance Sheet, and it shall be his duty to examine the
same, with the accounts and vouchers relating thereto.

(Art. 94.)   The auditors shall make a report to the members upon the Balance Sheet and accounts, and in every

such report they shall state whether, in their opinion, the
Balance Sheet is a full and fair Balance Sheet, containing
the particulars required by these regulations, and properly
drawn up so as to exhibit a true and correct view of the state
of the company's affairs.

The Council of the Institute last June expressed the following opinion :—

" The Council desire to point out that an auditor has no
" concern with the administrative management of a com-
" pany, except so far as to see that its operations have been
" within its statutory powers.   The duties of auditors must
" necessarily, to a greater or less extent, vary with every
" class of business and with the constitution of the com-
" panies whose accounts are under review ; but an auditor
" will fail in his duty if he does not use reasonable care,
" such as the circumstances of the case may allow or render
" necessary, to satisfy himself as to the propriety of the
" figures contained in the books and Balance Sheet."

Mr. Whinney, in an able lecture on Auditing, goes rather
fully into the objects of an audit and an auditor's responsibilities.   He says that it is not an auditor's duty to interfere in the management of an undertaking, and he thinks
that the *Leeds Estates Company* case clearly lays down
" that, if auditors are negligent, they have to suffer for it.
" If, from the result of their negligence and want of skill,
" dividends are improperly paid out of capital, then the
" auditors are liable for damage caused by their breach of
" duty.   It is their duty to see that the accounts are true
" and correct."   Whether the auditor is only the agent of
the shareholders for certain specified purposes, or whether
he is to some extent an officer appointed to certify the
accounts in the general interest, Mr. Whinney thinks, has
not clearly been decided ; and he thinks that legislation is
needed to define an auditor's position.   Mr. Whinney says,
in regard to detailed checking work : " Of course, you have
" to go through the usual routine of auditing—checking
" cash with the vouchers, checking postings and cash
" balances, and verifying bills of exchange, etc.   That, I
" think, you are all tolerably acquainted with."   And that,
unfortunately, is all he says on the subject of routine work.

In 1892, after Mr. Whinney's lecture, Mr. C. R. Trevor,
speaking in reference to the province of an auditor to a
limited company, pointed out that he has nothing to do
with directorial management, though, of course, friendly
comment to directors, even in a letter, was important and
very useful ; but it would be out of place in an auditor's certificate to call the propriety of management in question.
Mr. Trevor, it will be found later on, attaches much importance to detailed work.   His idea as to the point at which an
auditor's duties begin can, to some extent, be gathered from
the following extract from his lecture : —

" Difference of opinion may arise as to where the auditor's
" work begins.   I have seen it stated that he must begin at
" the Order Book, trace the fulfilment of each order, and
" proper charging and calculation of each item of sale, and
" on the other side, trace each purchase, and examine the
" invoice.   This, I contend, is not auditor's work unless he
" be specially instructed and paid for doing it.   It is the
" work of the office staff ; and merchants or manufacturers

" who do not make this a part of daily routine run great
" risks. If the auditor be expected to do it, to be of any use
" he ought to be in daily attendance. . . . . An
" auditor should certainly satisfy himself that proper checks
" of this sort have been used, and if not, point out their
" necessity and importance. The auditor's work properly
" begins where the bookkeeping begins, that is, with the
" sales and purchases at the point of their entering in the
" ledgers."

Mr. Trevor, you will notice, tries to draw a distinction
between the work of an office staff and the work of an
auditor, and although he does not say clearly where the
checking work of the office staff ends and where that of the
auditor begins, the admission that such a distinction exists
at all is important; but it is a pity he does not tell us more
accurately where he thinks an auditor's work should really
begin, or else the principles which guide him in deciding the
question.

Mr. Pixley, in his book, describes an auditor of a limited
company as the representative of the shareholders, whose
duty it is to ascertain that the funds of the company have
been properly accounted for, that such of them as have been
expended have been applied in the manner indicated in the
accounts, and generally that the accounts are accurate in
every respect. Mr. Pixley says: " A thorough and efficient
" audit should embrace an examination of all the transac-
" tions of a company."

And again: " It would be no answer for an auditor to a
" body of shareholders to say he had not thought it neces-
" sary to check any item in particular. The shareholders
" would have a perfect right to reply, 'It is your duty to
" 'check everything.' "

However, so far as I can judge from his writings, Mr.
Pixley does not think that, as a rule, an audit includes so
much routine as most other writers think necessary, and I
expect that Mr. Pixley's views are shared by many other
leading London firms. Mr. Pixley maintains that " It is
" not the practice for auditors of a public company to call
" over the postings, their correctness is usually taken for
" granted; but the auditor must be entirely guided by his
" experience as to what he may take for granted; in fact,
" anything he does take for granted is at his own peril."

Mr. Pixley also describes most routine work as mechanical.
Mr. Pixley says :—

" I should myself very much like it to be settled by
" the Institute of Chartered Accountants what would
" constitute a thorough audit of every class of company,
" and for all auditors' certificates to be in this form:
" 'Audited in accordance with the forms prescribed by the
" 'Institute of Chartered Accountants.' "

Mr. Pixley's views, it will be seen, are most contradictory. In one place he says: "A thorough and efficient
" audit should embrace an examination of all the transac-
" tions of a company "; and he admits it is the auditor's
" duty to check everything." But yet he says elsewhere
that " it is not the practice for auditors of public companies
" to call over postings, their correctness is usually taken for
" granted "; but " everything he does take for granted is at

" his own peril." Can anything be more unsatisfactory? It
is equivalent to saying that it is an auditor's duty to do certain work, but he usually neglects his duty at his own peril.
Instead of admitting that it is an auditor's " duty to check
" everything," it would have been more reasonable of Mr.
Pixley to have said that " it is an auditor's duty to check or
" see that some qualified person checks everything affecting
" the Balance Sheet." This would have been much more in
harmony with his description of the actual work of an
audit. At the same time I think our thanks are due to Mr.
Pixley for his candour in admitting that an auditor cannot
do the vast amount of detailed work which other accountants describe as essential; and though some of his reason-
ings appear to me to be weak, still I think that most of h
conclusions as to the actual work an auditor should do are
of real value.

Mr. Chadwick says that the main necessity of auditing
" is to secure absolute honesty in the case of all persons who
" touch or have control over other people's money or goods."
He gives a list of the particular duties of an auditor, which I
will discuss in detail later on. The value of this list, however, is small, as Mr. Chadwick admits that it has only been
" as far as practicable " carried out by his firm; and he does
not even hint at how he decides on what is practicable and
what is not. Mr. Chadwick expresses doubt as to whether
or not an auditor may omit part of the work if the audit fee
is fixed at too low an amount to be remunerative.

As regards other writers, including Fellows, Associates, and
students, some say that the detection of fraud is the chief
object of an audit rather than errors in accounts, and some
set out very full schemes of work, and some find fault with
the inadequacy of audit fees; but the chief point to notice is
the enormous amount of detail in most of their schemes.
So comprehensive, indeed, are some, that in large companies
it would be necessary for the auditor, if he acted up to them,
to keep one, two, or more clerks engaged permanently
throughout the year on a single audit, and the amount of
the audit fees—as far as my experience goes—would generally
not be enough to pay the clerks at artizans' rates of wages,
to say nothing of the principals' time. I cannot help thinking that many of these writers must have described audits
such as they would like them to be, rather than what is
really practicable; but this you will be better able to
judge after I have gone more into the details of their
schemes.

In the opinions I have quoted, it strikes me as remarkable
that though we have to look to articles of association for our
instructions, yet hardly any reference is made to them by
most writers, and where Table A is quoted, no attempt is
made to show how the exact words therein defining an
auditor's duty are in harmony with their own opinions. The
fact is, that the audit clauses in Table A are brief, and, unfortunately, the cases affecting the question are, as Mr.
Whinney has pointed out, not clear, and contradict each
other. But, though Table A is not explicit, there is one important point in it which seems to have been often overlooked, and as the audit clauses of most articles of association are very similar to those in Table A, it is worth while
saying a few words on the subject.

I think that Table A defines very clearly the object of an auditor's examination of the books and accounts to be the verification of the Balance Sheet; it is as to the Balance Sheet that he has to report, and this, I think, is the auditor's first and chief duty. Notwithstanding this, some of the opinions I have quoted are to the effect that it is an auditor's duty to detect and prevent theft, and some put this forward as an auditor's first duty, although there are many thefts and errors which, if detected, would not alter the Balance Sheet.

It should be noted, however, that the Council of the Institute and Mr. Whinney speak only of the verification of the Balance Sheet as an auditor's duty, unless, indeed, when the Council says that an auditor should "see that a com- "pany's operations have been within its statutory powers," they include the detection of theft by its officials. The question then arises—Is the auditor bound to go into such details as will ensure that theft and error are not taking place in wages, petty cash, cash sales, or the receipt and dispatch of goods? Or are these matters dependent on the proper organisation of the concern? I will refer to this later on.

Again, another question of greater importance is as to the extent to which an auditor's examination should be carried. Should the amount of his work depend on the fee? Or should it depend on what he considers to be the requirements of the case? If the latter, is it to be understood that an auditor is bound to himself make good any defects in the system of check carried out by a company's staff over whom he has no control, except in an indirect way through the goodwill of the directors? The latter is an unreasonable and unfair responsibility to throw on an auditor, and yet it is one which there seems to be a strong disposition to impose on us, and we, to tell the truth, are too ready to accept it.

I will now take the separate parts of the routine work of an audit, and compare the different views which have been expressed respecting them more in detail.

First, as to vouchers for payments. No one disputes the necessity of examining them, but there are different opinions as to the nature and utility of the work. Mr. Pixley describes the work as "mechanical," and again as a "most "childish operation." No other writer, however, holds such an opinion, some entering into details of vouching with considerable minuteness; and Mr. John Gourlay goes so far as to describe it as of "paramount importance." Two writers think that the auditor should not only see vouchers for each payment, but that he should also make sure that each payment is authorised by duly qualified persons.

The next point to consider is the verification of the cash received. Mr. Pixley in his book, speaking of the Cash Book, says that "the debit or income side should be checked "with the most independent source the auditor can find "available—for example, the counterfoils of receipts." But, apparently, he only considers it necessary if he suspects fraud.

Mr. Trevor says, "The Cash Book entries must be proved "as far as possible on the receipt side by counterfoils of

"receipt books." Mr. Trevor therefore considers this a necessary part of an audit wherever counterfoil receipts are used.

Mr. Chadwick makes no reference to checking the received side of the Cash Book.

Mr. Goddard does not think it always necessary for the auditor to compare cash received items with counterfoil receipts, but thinks he should see that it is done by someone, and he should examine them for the last few days before the audit and counting the cash.

Mr. G. P. Norton says nothing about counterfoil receipts, but he thinks that someone other than the cashier should send out the monthly statements.

Mr. Howard S. Smith, in a useful lecture on "Vouchers," seems to think that counterfoil receipts are of dubious value as a check; he looks on a careful examination of outstanding accounts as important, and recommends a reference to rental books for rents, and to correspondence in case of old balances, allowances, or bad debts, and proposes that auditors should send circulars to customers with copies of their accounts for confirmation. I imagine, however, that Mr. Smith does not look on these as part of the ordinary work of an audit, but rather as special work to be done if making an investigation.

Mr. Gourlay thinks that the proper system is to send an intimation by post, under the eye of the auditor, addressed to each creditor and debtor stating the position of his account and asking if the amount corresponds with his books, it, of course, being essential that the auditor sees all the replies. Mr. Gourlay, however, does not say to what extent he does this himself or whether he ever does it.

A question connected with the two preceding ones is, the comparison of the Bank Pass Book with the Cash Book or Bank Account. Here we still find great divergence of opinion.

Mr. Pixley says: "It is not, of course, necessary to check "the Cash Book with the Bankers' Pass Book in detail, as a "rule; but, as I have said before, what might be unnecessary "in twenty cases, might be on the twenty-first."

Mr. Trevor says: "As a matter of course, the Bank Pass "Book must be examined in detail with the bank columns "in the Cash Book, and the payments compared with the "withdrawals from the book."

Mr. Chadwick, Mr. Goddard, Mr. Norton, and Mr. Dicksee all think that the Bank Pass Book should be compared in detail with the Cash Book, and the two latter would also compare the details of a certain number of pay-in slips.

Having referred to the verification of the entries in the Cash Book, I will now quote some opinions on the verification of the Purchases Day Book.

Mr. Pixley says that: "As a rule, it is not usual to " . . . . . compare entries from the original invoices; "but if the auditor has the slightest doubt in his own mind "that everything is not perfectly straightforward and "correct, he should, at any rate, take some test cases."

Mr. Chadwick says that, as far as practicable, an auditor should "Examine all the Day Books, and see that the

" proper returns of purchases and sales . . . . . are
" made by each department, and that the bought . . .
books are properly entered up, and that the invoices are
properly checked as to quantities and prices ; obtain a de-
" claration, or otherwise satisfy yourself, that every liability
" of the year is brought into account."

Mr. Dicksee does not make much reference to the examination of invoices.  Speaking of hotel accounts, he says :
" Under ordinary circumstances, it is not usual to carry
" the investigation behind the Day Book."

Mr. Gourlay is in favour of stock account books, which,
he thinks, should be examined by a clerk from another department in order to verify the Day Books.

Messrs. Trevor, Norton, Goddard, Sisson, and Stacey, say
that invoices should be compared with the Purchase Day
Book.

Mr. Bourne, in his prize essay, goes further, in thinking
that the auditor should make sure that the goods have been
*bonâ fide* ordered by reference to the counterfoil Order
Book, or the press copies of orders, and he should satisfy
himself that the goods have been received by reference to
the Stock Account Book, if one is kept.

Next, as to the verification of the entries in the Sales Day
Book.

Mr. Pixley and Mr. Trevor say nothing particular on the
subject.  Mr. Chadwick says no more than I have already
quoted under the preceding head.

Mr. H. S. Smith, speaking of the check upon sales, says :
" From the accounts kept by manufacturers in this district,
" we can usually do little more than compare the trading
" accounts of successive periods, make allowance for special
" circumstances affecting the cost of production, &c., and
" draw general conclusions as to the things being all right, or
" as to there being a screw loose somewhere."

Mr. Goddard, Mr. Bourne, Mr. Stacey, and Mr. Sisson
think that the tissue Copy Invoice Book should be checked
through with the Day Book.  Mr. Goddard also thinks that
Cost Books, if kept, should be compared with the Sales
Book, and also the Order Book.    Mr. Gourlay would have
Stock Account Books, if kept, compared by the auditor with
the Sales Book.  Mr. Sisson agrees with Mr. Goddard as
to a Cost Book, and he further thinks that the Warehouse or
Delivery Book, as well as the Order Book, should sometimes
be compared.

I will now read to you various opinions on the question of
checking postings to Ledgers.  This is often the heaviest
part of an audit, so it is worth while for us to pay the greatest
attention to it.  Every one thinks that all the postings to
Nominal Ledgers should be checked.  As to the postings to
Personal Ledgers, Mr. Pixley in his lecture on Auditing says
" In the case of a thorough audit the books should balance
" exactly, and in order to do this, it is *frequently* necessary
" for the auditor to call over the postings from the Cash Book,
" Day Book, Invoice Book, and Journal to the Ledger, for
" the purpose of discovering where the error lies."  " In no
" case, however, is this necessary in the audit of a company's
" accounts, unless the auditor is employed by the directors
" to prepare the accounts, as he may require that the books
" be correctly balanced before they are placed in his hands."

Again he says, "As already stated, it is not the practice for
" auditors of a public company to call over the postings, their
" correctness is usually taken for granted, but the auditor
" must be entirely guided by his experience as to what he
" may take for granted, in fact anything he does take for
" granted is at his own peril."

In the discussion on the lecture Mr. W. Harris, A.C.A.,
said that he did not think the postings ought to be, as a
matter of practice, or usually were, taken as correct and in
order if the books had been balanced.

Mr. C. R. Trevor says " As a general rule all the postings
" to the Ledgers should be called over unless the very
" numerous character of the transactions be such as to ren-
" der it practically impossible, and in such case the parts to be
" dispensed with should be only those affecting the sales and
" the payments, therefor.  The purchases and payments on
" account, therefore, must be checked for an audit to be of
" any value whatever."

Mr. Dicksee quotes with approval Mr. Slocombe's opinion
that " there are some cases wherein an audit, to be efficient,
" should comprehend an examination of every entry in the
" books ; there are others, more numerous, wherein the accu-
" racy of the accounts may be verified by tests which render
" the checking of every posting unnecessary.  Speaking
" generally, the Cash Book, which is in truth the root and
" foundation of all, should be exhaustively examined, both
" as to receipts and payments, and checked into the Ledgers
" and other books of account under review."

Mr. Goddard thinks that all postings to Ledgers should be
checked, and gives as a reason an instance of how a cashier
might enter during an audit an item of cash to the credit of
a Ledger Account, although not debited in the Cash Book,
inserting a contra item in a Nominal Account, and putting
the auditor's tick to both.  Mr. Goddard recommends that
the auditors should, as a rule, call back the postings from
the Ledgers to the Day Books and Cash Book, in order to
prevent such a fraud.  (*Note.*—The ordinary way of checking
the Personal Ledgers would not discover it, but proper checking of the Nominal Account should.)  Mr. Goddard speaks
of the checking of postings to Ledgers as " a very important
portion of audit work."  Mr. Goddard also states that " In
" no counting-house should the duties of cashier and Ledger
" clerk be combined."

Mr. G. P. Norton says " that the postings to all Ledger
" Accounts should be called over and ticked " from the
separate books of entry, and he finds it more convenient and
surer to call back from the Ledgers to the separate books of
entry, instead of *vice versâ.*

Mr. Chadwick says that " The postings in the Personal
" Ledgers must be checked from the Bought and Sold Day
" Books and the Cash Book, and also from the Bill Books
" and Journal."

Mr. J. A. Sisson is inclined to think that an auditor need
not check postings to Purchase and Sales Ledgers if the
books balance, and remarks that this would give us time for
other important work.

In Mr. Retchford's prize essay (1892) on " Other methods
" of Proving Ledgers and Accounts than by detail check-

" ing," he seems to think that the balancing does away with the necessity for detailed checking.

Mr. Bardsley, however, in his prize essay on the same subject, says: " It must be clearly understood at the outset " that any such method can only be adopted by an auditor " as supplementary to, and not as a substitute for, detail " checking."

Later on, I will be rash enough to state my own opinions on the question of checking postings.

As to additions, Mr. Dicksee says: " In all cases it is de- " sirable, although it is not always practicable, that all the " additions should be checked. In every case, however, the " additions of the Private Ledger, Nominal Ledger, Cash " Book, and Wages Book will require to be verified."

Mr. G. P. Norton thinks that all additions should be checked.

Mr. Retchford says: " All the additions of the Ledgers " must, of course, be checked."

Mr. Goddard thinks that all additions should be checked, and the Cash Book additions should be checked, both at the interim audits, and again at the final audit for the year.

In regard to the Wages Books, I find the following opinions :—

Mr. Trevor seems to think that the auditor's duties in re- gard to the Wages Books consist rather in advising as to methods of check, and in seeing that the books are properly initialled when comparing with the Cash Book, but it is not his business to go behind the Wages Book in the audit.

Mr. Chadwick thinks that " The auditor should, in regard " to the payment of wages, note any unusual items . . ."

Mr. G. P. Norton seems to think that the auditor's duties are limited to checking additions, and seeing that the system of making-up and paying wages is so organised as to ensure proper checks.

Mr. Goddard thinks that the auditor should check the additions of the Wages Books, and see that they are signed by works' manager, time-keeper, and pay clerk.

Mr. Stacey thinks that all additions should be checked, and some of the extensions.

Very similar opinions seem to be held in regard to Stock Books as to Wages Books.

Mr. Pixley says: " The auditor is not, of course, respon- " sible for the accuracy of the stock-in-hand, but should " inquire into the method on which the stock has been " taken."

Mr. Whinney says very much the same thing.

Mr. G. P. Norton thinks that the auditor should ascertain that the stock has been carefully taken down, calculated, and checked, but he says nothing about the auditor doing any checking.

Mr. Chadwick thinks that an auditor should " see that " all Stock Sheets are duly signed . . . ," but nothing is said as to detailed checking.

Mr. Trevor says: " If the stocks are of such a nature as " to be capable of being tabulated in Ledger Stock Books, " such record . . . should be strongly recommended, ' and it would then be part of the auditor's duty to " see .that .the actual stocktaking corresponded with the " Stock Book." " If arithmetical corrections be not clearly " admitted [i.e., by the staff], let the auditor have the cal- " culations into money checked by his staff. Where it is " possible this should, in the case of a company, invariably " be done."

The different opinions on an auditor's work on Share Books, and other matters, I have not time now to speak of.

I have now laid before you, as fully as the time at my disposal permits, and as fairly as I am able, the opinions of several accountants on the routine work of an audit, and I expect you will agree with me in thinking that there is good reason for serious reflection. Auditing is the most impor- tant and responsible part of an accountant's work, and yet, though our profession is supposed to have passed the stage of infancy, there are still really startling differences of opinion in regard to the right way to conduct an audit. It is true that a few of the opinions are those of students, who cannot be considered authorities on these questions, but they have been awarded prizes for those opinions, and taking only the opinions of members of the Council and one or two other accountants of high standing, we find that they differ from and contradict each other in a truly astonishing manner. These questions are, however, of the utmost im- portance to us, and this is my excuse for venturing at all on such a difficult subject.

I have already made a few comments on the general aspects of an audit, and before going into details of the opinions I have quoted, we must have some sort of general definition of the object and scope of an audit. Articles of association dealing with the audit are, as I have already said, generally very similar to those in Table A., and the chief point in these is that the auditor has to " verify the Balance Sheet with the accounts and vouchers relating thereto," and he has to give a certificate as to the Balance Sheet. I will assume, then, that the object of an auditor's examination, as far as routine work is concerned, is to enable him to express an opinion on the correctness of the Balance Sheet. This must be his first and paramount duty. Anything else is of minor importance, and, I think, would be rather a matter of special arrangement, which I need not discuss. I have shown you that many accountants think this is too meagre a definition, that he should also discover where losses may or do occur through careless clerks or defects in the system of bookkeeping, or theft of all sorts by officials. These, I maintain, are not the legal duties of auditors as defined in Table A, they are matters of in- ternal organisation, and if an auditor were really made responsible for them it would be a burden greater than he could bear ; it would involve a surveillance over all those who are connected with the despatch and receipt of goods, and who make up and pay the wages, as well as over anyone else through whose hands money passes, and it would be necessary to make an exhaustive examination of all the books, and this without any direct control over the organi- sation. Such a state of things is clearly impossible. At the same time many errors of this sort can be, and should be, discovered by the auditor in the course of his proper work, and directors, as a rule, fully appreciate the value of suggestions from an auditor for imposing proper checks and safeguards, but this is a very different thing to making the auditor responsible.    I may mention that Mr. Justice Vaughan Williams has given it as his opinion that it is not the duty of an auditor to consider the honesty of the officers of a company (see *The Accountant*, 24th December, 1892); though it is not very clear what he meant by this.    Rightly or wrongly, then, I will define an auditor's duty to be the verification of the Balance Sheet, and let us now proceed to examine in detail some of the opinions I have read to you.

A weakness in these opinions is that in each case the conditions which the auditor has to deal with are an almost unknown quantity.    To avoid making this mistake myself, and to have a proper basis for discussion, I will take as a typical office staff one which is composed of a cashier, who enters up the Cash Book and posts up the Private Ledger, but has nothing to do with the Day Books, and does not post up the Personal Ledgers; and besides him, let us suppose that there is at least one competent ledger clerk, who posts up the Ledgers, and at least one invoice clerk, who is responsible for the invoices, and the invoice and ledger clerks between them enter up and check the purchases and sales Day Books, but do not handle money. These clerks are supposed to be under the direction of a manager, who would not himself touch the books.    We will further assume that the books are balanced, and that a rough Balance Sheet and Trade Account are handed to the auditor by the manager.

With conditions such as these, let us first enquire how far the checking of postings to the personal accounts in the Ledgers from Day Books and Cash Books help us to verify the Balance Sheet.    I take this part of an audit because it is often the heaviest.    Turning to the opinions I have quoted, you will see that while some think that all postings should be checked under all circumstances, others think that they need not be checked at all if the books balance, and between these extremes we find Mr. Trevor, who thinks that all postings to the Purchase Ledgers should, under all circumstances, be checked both from Cash Book and from Day Book, but that the Sales Ledger postings, if very numerous, need not all be checked.    Though how the mere number of entries affects the question Mr. Trevor does not explain, and I cannot imagine, unless indeed he means that where there are many entries there is a check in the number of different persons employed, but this does not necessarily follow, and anyhow it is a question of system and checks, not number of entries.    Or, perhaps, he thinks it is a question of fees.    Mr. Slocombe, as quoted by Mr. Dicksee, thinks that the Cash Book is the important book which must invariably be completely compared with the Ledgers, while the Day Book postings need not always be checked.    None of these gentlemen give definite reasons for the faiths which are in them, except Mr. Goddard, who suggested a rather improbable fraud as a reason for checking everything.

Assuming that everyone agrees that all Nominal Ledger postings should be checked, then, if the books are kept in such a way as to enable the bookkeeper to balance the Sales Ledgers and Purchase Ledgers each by themselves, which is easily done with a Transfer Book and a Cash Book ruled with special columns for the Sales Ledger and Purchase Ledger entries respectively, the result is that we can have two general accounts which show the whole of the Sales Ledger accounts collectively, and the whole of the Purchase Ledger accounts collectively, and no entry not in the Day Books, Cash Book, or Transfer Book can be entered in the Personal Ledgers without making the Ledger balances disagree with the general account balance, unless a contra entry or error in Ledger additions is made to balance it.

I am afraid that I may not have explained myself very clearly—but taking the Sales Ledgers first, it really comes to this, that by separating all Sales Ledger items in the Day Books, Cash Book, and Transfer Book, we are able to carry the totals of these to an account in the Nominal Ledger, which, in this way, becomes a summary of all the accounts in the Sales Ledgers, and the balance of this account is equal to the total of all the Sales Ledgers balances; and assuming entries in the Day Books, Cash Book, and Transfer Book to be correct, if we check their additions and see that their totals are properly carried to the General Sales Account, then we can tell to a certainty that the total of the balances in the Sales Ledgers is correct, and if we do not check the detailed postings, the only error we cannot be sure about is whether some balances are overstated, and other balances understated to an equal amount. The chance that such an error could occur accidentally is extremely remote, and if it did occur, the amount would certainly be small and would soon be discovered, and, anyhow, would make no practical difference to the value of the debtors in the Balance Sheet: so, I think, that without fear of contradiction, I may say that the auditor need not check the postings to the Sales Ledgers for the sake of discovering accidental errors.

Then, as to intentional errors.    They might be of three sorts: First, intentional errors made by a ledger clerk to conceal other errors which he may be too lazy to search for; secondly, errors to conceal theft; thirdly, errors made to falsify the Balance Sheet by making the debts look better than they really are; no one, as a rule, would have any motive for this last sort of error except the manager.    The first would almost certainly be found out by the manager when he goes through the balances.    The auditor should, however, satisfy himself that the manager, or some other qualified person does go through the balances, and, if possible he should go through them with such person himself.    An error of this sort could only be small in amount, and most probably would not affect the value of the debtors in the Balance Sheet, so its discovery is outside the auditor's duty just as much as similar accidental errors.    As regards the second and third sorts of intentional errors in postings, errors to conceal theft, and to conceal bad and doubtful debts, only the cashier or manager would have any object in making them, so that they could not well be effected with a staff such as I describe without collusion with the Ledger clerk, and collusion is a thing which an auditor cannot be expected to discover.    If he were expected to do so his work would be endless.    I venture, then, to assert that, under the conditions I have named. it is not necessary for the auditor to check postings, though I think that it is a good plan to test the correctness of part of them.

If the Sales Ledgers, Purchases Ledgers, and Nominal Ledgers, were not balanced separately the same arguments would apply, except that instead of the total of the debtors being an unalterable amount it would be possible to understate debtors and creditors equally, or overstate them equally, in the Balance Sheet, which, of course, makes no difference to profits and would not matter much, because, as I have already said, the amount could only be small.

I will next attempt to show how the situation would be altered if the cashier were to post up the Ledgers, assuming always that the auditor has satisfied himself that he could rely on the correctness of the Purchases and Sales Day Books and Returns Books. In such circumstances, a cashier might use the postings into the Sales Ledgers to conceal theft by not entering in the Cash Book cash received in payment of an account, and yet entering the amount to the credit of the account in the Sales Ledger, so as to prevent the manager and auditor from noticing that the company has not received payment for the account. To hide this, he would have to make a debit entry direct to some other Sales Ledger Account, or if the Sales Ledgers are not balanced separately, then a debit to a Purchase Ledger or Nominal Ledger Account would, if not detected, equally conceal the omission of the entry in the Cash Book. The Nominal Ledger entries, however, I assume are all checked, and if great care is used no fictitious amount could be interpolated among them; so this brings back the fictitious balancing entry to the Sales Ledger or Purchase Ledger. This system of false entries can be further elaborated, but it is seldom made use of by a dishonest cashier who, as a rule, prefers to hold back cash received until such time as there may be a risk of it being noticed, when he enters it in the Cash Book at the later date and posts it in the ordinary way. A similar fraud could be concealed in the Purchase Ledger postings, by omitting to post a false payment entered in the Cash Book, a voucher for which might be fraudulently obtained by getting a duplicate voucher from some firm or by some other device which might not be detected in that "childish and mechanical operation" which Mr. Pixley calls vouching. I do not know of any other way in which a cashier could hide theft under cover of false postings or omission to post to Personal Ledgers, although I possibly need correcting on this point, if not, the question now arises as to whether it is an auditor's duty to check the postings merely to discover such deceptions. They are different from the errors of ledger clerks previously described, in that they affect the Balance Sheet, for there would be debit balances in the Sales Ledger not representing real debits, so it comes within the duties of an auditor to use reasonable diligence to discover them; how this is to be done depends on circumstances. If the manager is so well up in the financial part of the business that he knows the state of the Purchases and Sales Ledgers Accounts, there is little likelihood of the cashier going wrong, and if the manager will give a certificate that they are correct,

perhaps the auditor might be satisfied with testing the correctness of only part of the postings; but, as a rule, I think that if the cashier posts the Personal Ledgers, the auditor should check a considerable part of the postings into them, and, under some circumstances, he should check the whole.

It will frequently happen that although it may not be the duty of the cashier or manager to post up the Personal Ledgers, yet they may do so occasionally, or may have a certain indirect control over the Ledgers and Day Books. This is a factor which must be duly considered in deciding what part of the posting should be checked.

The advantage of omitting the checking of postings when practicable is, that an auditor's time would often be better spent in trying to detect or prevent the original fraud of the cashier, than in doing a large amount of routine checking of postings. Let him understand the system adopted. Does the manager open letters; and, if so, does he make a list of cheques received? Is all cash received paid into the bank? Are all payments made by cheque? On what evidence would a director sign a cheque? Are all cheques entered on the minutes? Would the cashier or manager have any opportunity of altering the Day Books or Returns Books? Could the manager alter dates, or otherwise tamper with the Ledgers? Having mastered the system, the auditor should think of the different tests and checks he might apply, varying these from time to time; and, assuming that such work is done, I maintain that it is not, as a rule, necessary to check postings more than I have indicated.

Supporters of complete checking will, I expect, say that this is all very well; but, in checking everything, an auditor has other objects in view than to catch a careless clerk or dishonest cashier, for it gives him a knowledge of the details of the transactions of a company such as he otherwise could not obtain. This, however, I emphatically deny. What is the usual plan adopted for checking postings? The senior clerk takes the Ledgers, and the junior calls from the Day Books and Cash Book. In this way, the senior does not see the Day Books at all, and the brief moment a Ledger Account is open before him seldom gives time to study the account or notice any peculiarities. If an auditor were to devote a few hours to the examination of Day Books, working back here and there to the Order Book, Delivery Book, Invoices, and Correspondence, and thereby gaining a knowledge of the system; and again, by lengthening his examination of the Ledger Accounts when checking out the balances, always noticing the handwriting, and inquiring into the causes of alterations and erasures, he would then learn infinitely more about the working and accounts of a company than weeks of detailed checking of postings would teach him.

Closely connected with the question of checking postings is that of checking additions. The additions of the Personal Ledgers are affected by exactly the same considerations as the postings into those ledgers; where it is unnecessary to check the one it is unnecessary to check the other. The necessity for the auditor to check the Day Books and Returns Books additions depends to a great extent on which of the office staff make them and check them. If they are made and checked carefully, and if they cannot be tampered with by the cashier or manager, then perhaps it is only necessary to do a part as a test, but it should be remembered how important the totals of Purchases and Sales are. If we are sure that we have the whole and no more of the Sales and of the Purchases in the Nominal Ledger, then all the cash received and no more than the cash paid must be accounted for by the cashier in the long run ; and it goes a long way to confirm the correctness of the debtors and creditors in the Balance Sheet—that is if all Nominal Ledger entries are properly checked and verified. As a matter of extra precaution I am inclined to think that the Day Books and Returns Books additions should be entirely checked, but if the Sales Ledgers and Purchases Ledgers are separately balanced in the way I have already described, perhaps test checking would be enough; but I confess that I have not quite made up my mind on the subject. The Cash Book additions, I think, should almost always be checked ; there are various reasons, but there is not time to go into them now. It is a good plan to check the Cash Book additions directly the posting has been done, to prevent the cashier from manipulating the figures. The Nominal Ledger additions should of course be checked.

I should much like to speak about the value of other routine work—to see whether we should, with Mr. Pixley, look at vouching as a "mechanical and most childish operation," or, with Mr. Gourlay, as of "paramount importance"; whether we should "of course" agree the bank account in detail with the Bank Pass Book, or whether "of course" it is unnecessary to do so ; whether the auditor should, or should not, compare the Purchase Day Book entries with the original invoices, and the Sales Day Book entries with the tissue copy Invoice Book and Delivery Book, or Stock Books, or Cost Books. These and many other questions are of the greatest possible interest to us, and if I had time I would say something about them, but I abstain, as I want to make a few concluding remarks about matters of more general importance. At the same time, I hope that the way I have worked out the questions of checking postings and additions will suggest to you how to approach other questions connected with audit work. The great thing is to think out carefully your exact object in doing any particular work, and then consider whether you can best attain your object in that or some simpler and more reliable way.

An auditor's position, as I have described it, is undoubtedly an anomalous one. I have assumed that we can rely on the checks which happen to exist in the organisation of an office if they appear to us sufficient, but where they are absent we have to try to make them good ourselves as far as we are able, for the purpose of verifying the Balance Sheet; thus, work may be thrown on us which ordinarily should be done by a company's own staff. We have no power to dictate to the staff as to their work, yet we can hardly report to the shareholders on defects in the system of bookkeeping, and though directors who control the administration are generally ready enough to adopt all reasonable suggestions, such is not quite always the case. I can think of instances n which it has taken years to get directors to agree to

changes of real importance. In this district it is frequently left to the auditor to balance the books himself, and he is even required sometimes to write up the Private Ledger ; this, perhaps, explains why accountants in the Midlands often check all postings when nothing whatever is gained by doing so. I think that the less an auditor does of the actual balancing and writing up of the books the better ; first of all, there is no one to check the auditor; then, again, it tends to make him put aside the critical attitude he should always adopt, and it gives an erroneous idea of his functions.

Most routine checking can be better done by an office staff than by an auditor who pays only occasional visits, and it is more economical, because an auditor should be an expert, and he expects to be paid accordingly. There is a proverb which says "do not set a race horse to cart stones." It would clearly be an expensive plan and would spoil the race horse. In the same way an endless amount of routine work tends to destroy the activity and alertness of an auditor's mind.

An ideal state of things would be an office organisation which has a complete system in itself of proving and checking, so that the auditor would only have to see that this system is kept up, to enable him to get at reliable facts ; he could then give more time to matters of estimate, principle, and opinion. Such a state of things is not often attainable at present, but it would be a great advantage to have some definite rule laid down, so that an auditor may with authority say what checking work properly belongs to the office staff. I am sure, as I have said before, that it is unsatisfactory for an auditor to be looked on as a sort of supplementary clerk, whose duty it is to do any checking which it happens to be nobody else's business to perform. In this respect the Local Government Board auditors have a great advantage over us, possessing as they do the power of surcharge, and having the Local Government Board at their backs they are able to insist on their directions being carried out in a way that is absolutely impossible for us.

The question as to the grounds which justify an auditor in using tests instead of checking everything is a difficult one. Suppose that a fraud were undiscovered through a part only of certain work being checked as a test instead of the whole, would the auditor be responsible ? The answer, I think, will depend on the reasonableness of the tests applied. The public, I am sure, do not expect an auditor to go through every minute detail of all the books of a company. The usual fees he receives clearly indicate this, and tests made unexpectedly are often more valuable than the most complete system of routine audit could possibly be. If the comparatively useless mechanical checking recommended by writers I have quoted were to be partly discontinued, we should have more time, not only to inquire into questions of principle and opinion, but also to test the reliability of the foundations of the system of bookkeeping, and that these foundations need closer examination than many of us, including myself, have given them in the past, I have not the shadow of a doubt.

Mr. Whinney and others have spoken of the necessity for legislation in order to define an auditor's position and responsibilities. It has to be decided whether it is an auditor's sole duty to verify the Balance Sheet on behalf of the shareholders or whether it is something more. If the Council of the Institute cannot obtain legislation, then I think it becomes their own duty to define our position. This, however, is only part of what the Council might do. I agree with Mr. Pixley in thinking that the Council should decide what would constitute a thorough audit in different classes of companies. This would be a valuable guide to us. We could then go to the directors of a company, and, with the authority of the Council of the Institute to support us, we could tell them that certain checking work should be done by their own staff and not by the auditor, and they would be themselves to blame if frauds remained undiscovered through their neglect to adopt such checks. I do not suggest this merely to take work off the auditor's shoulders, but in order to free him from unsuitable work that he may make himself of greater use in other directions. Who can now say that an auditor is not justified in cutting his work according to his fee? At present, there is no limit to the amount of work an auditor may or may not do. Given a skilled auditor, the degree of certainty with which he can satisfy himself on matters of fact is dependent on hardly any other consideration than internal checks and the length of time taken on the audit; though I admit that with a company which has not adequate checks on its staff, it might be necessary for the auditor to be permanently attached to the place if it were really his duty to step into the breach. On the other hand, if a company has in its own organisation sufficient checks, then the auditor may be able in a very short time to satisfy himself on questions of fact, and thus be free to devote himself more thoroughly to questions of estimate, principle, and opinion.

It seems to me that merely to state the present position of auditors is to condemn it, and unless something is done soon to improve matters our Institute will not have justified its existence. If the Institute do not take the question up, the profession will continue in a state of uncomfortable uncertainty, until in the course of years, it may be by costly litigation, some sort of understanding will be arrived at, but surely this would be an unsatisfactory way of settling the question, and so I sincerely trust that the Council of the Institute will bestir themselves, and do what is their clear duty.

----

LIST OF BOOKS AND PAPERS referred to in Lecture.

----

" Auditors: Their Duties and Responsibilities," 2nd Edition, 1881; by Francis W. Pixley, F.C.A. (Published by *Effingham Wilson.*)

" Auditing," a Paper read to the London Accountants Students' Society, 25th September, 1883, by David Chadwick, F.C.A. (*The Accountant*, 29th Sept., 1883.)

" Auditing," a Paper read to the London Accountants Students' Society, 8th May, 1883, by F. W. Pixley, F.C.A. (*The Accountant*, 26th May, 1883.)

" The First Audit of a Joint Stock Company's Accounts," a Paper read to the London Accountants Students' Society, by J. C. Bolton, F.C.A. (*The Accountant*, 12th Dec., 1885.)

" Defalcations, and how to prevent them," a Paper read to the Northern Institute of Chartered Accountants' Students' Society, 13th January, 1887, by F. R. Goddard, F.C.A. (*The Accountant*, 1887, p. 112.)

" Auditing," a Paper read to the Northern Institute of Chartered Accountants, by J. A. Sisson, A.C.A. (now F.C.A.) (*The Accountant*, 1887, p. 125.)

Essay on " Auditing," awarded a prize by the Liverpool Accountants Students' Association, by J. H. Bourne (now A.C.A.) (*The Accountant*, 1887, p. 330.)

Essay on " Auditing," awarded a junior prize by the Liverpool Accountants Students' Association, by W. E. Stacey (now A.C.A.) (*The Accountant*, 1887, p. 345.)

" Auditing," a Paper read to the London Accountants Students' Society, 25th October, 1887, by F. W. Pixley, F.C.A. (*The Accountant*, 1887, p. 676.)

" Vouchers," a Paper read to the Birmingham Accountant Students' Society, 22nd November, 1887, by Howard S. Smith, F.C.A. (*The Accountant*, 1888, p. 25.)

" Auditing," a Paper read to the London Accountants Students' Society, 6th November, 1889, by C. R. Trevor, F.C.A. (*The Accountant*, 1889, p. 658.)

" A Talk about Accountants' Work," a Paper read to the Glasgow Institute Accountants' Debating Society, by John Gourlay, C.A. (*The Accountant*, 1890, p. 17.)

" The Audit of a Manufacturer's Accounts," a Paper read to the Leeds and District Students' Association, by G. P. Norton, A.C.A. (*The Accountant*, 1890, p. 619.)

" Auditing: A Practical Manual for Auditors;" 1892; by Lawrence R. Dicksee, F.C.A. (Published by Gee & Co.)

" Audits and Certificates," a Paper read to the London Accountants Students' Society, 4th May, 1892, by Fredk. Whinney, F.C.A. (*The Accountant*, 1892, p. 404.)

Essays on " Other Methods of Proving Ledgers and Accounts than by Detail Checking," awarded prizes by the Manchester Accountants Students' Society, by A. W. Retchford, A.C.A., and J. H. Bardsley. (*The Accountant*, 1892, p. 629.)

## THE VALUE OF AN AUDIT.

### II.

PURSUING this subject, we may go further than we went in our last article, and express our conviction that it is not only impracticable for the Legislature to formulate a system of audit which would prove effective upon all occasions, but that such a system could not, in our opinion, be prepared, even as the result of a conference of the most experienced auditors of the day.   Auditing is not (as many appear to think) an exact science, but rather in the nature of a fine art ; and if this proposition be but admitted, we at once find an explanation of the very diverse methods which appear to be adopted by different auditors of experience.   The fact is—and it cannot be too widely understood—that no two audits are precisely alike in all particulars, and that, consequently, the systems upon which the accounts· of any two undertakings are to be audited can never be precisely identical.

The explanation of the apparently conflicting opinions of various members of the profession is— we take it—that, even when speaking in generalities, each. is speaking from his own particular experience, which in most cases is naturally of a more or less restricted nature.   We question very much whether, as a matter of fact, any accountant who has written upon the subject invariably follows the rules which he has laid down as a general guide for others.   In the nature of things, a general guide can only be of general application, and for particular instances it must be supplemented by the discretion of those seeking to apply the general rules.   It is this fact that makes auditing at once one of the most responsible and the most difficult of professions, and if this were only generally appreciated shareholders would understand better the extreme importance of appointing as auditors only those who, by their previous training and experience, had acquired the discretion necessary to enable them to intelligently adapt a general system of auditing to the particular requirements of any individual case.

As is usual when a discussion of this nature arises, we find that one or more of those joining in the discussion are in favour of the appointment of Government auditors—a proposition which they usually supplement with the somewhat impracticable one of a Government responsibility. It seems desirable that those seeking to convert others to this opinion should first enquire at somewhat greater length what would probably be the position of affairs if their scheme could be actually carried into effect. To a certain extent it is, of course, difficult to foresee the precise lines upon which the Government would work if they were called upon to undertake the duty of universal auditor in addition to their already numerous functions, but the following results might be fairly anticipated.

The staff appointed to perform the work on behalf of the Government would either be recruited from the ranks of Chartered Accountants, or from clerks in Chartered Accountants' offices, or from other sources—in which latter case the official staff would possess but little, if any, previous training to qualify them for their duties. Thus, at the outset, the staff would not be better qualified than those already available as auditors, while, on the other hand, it might be very much less qualified. It may further be mentioned in passing (but as we have already pointed out this danger at considerable length, we do not now enter into it in detail) that the enormous increase in the number of permanent appointments at the disposal of the Government of the day would be a source of danger to the efficiency of the service from which, until recent years, the country was comparatively free.

Having then obtained a staff of auditors of more or less experience and ability, the Government, if it proceeded upon its usual lines, would proceed to lay down a stereotyped system of audit for different classes of concerns (perhaps roughly classifying different industries and applying a different system to each), while the staff would be required in every instance to exactly carry out the letter of their instructions. Under these circumstances, the system employed would in every single case be found, as a matter of fact, to require the performance of certain duties which would really be superfluous, while, on the other hand, various points which, in each particular concern, really require special attention would be passed over unnoticed. Consequently in each case the audit would be defective as regards its routine work.

Then, with regard to that portion of each audit which does not consist of routine work, and which is ordinarily performed either by the principal himself or under his direct superintendence, those who have experience in such matters would understand (although it is, perhaps, hopeless to expect that the general public could be made to understand) that these higher duties, upon which the real value of an effective audit absolutely depends, are altogether too subtle to be reduced to any sort of system; consequently, it is but too probable that they would be altogether overlooked in a Government audit. At first, when the official auditors were fresh from their individual practices, and still retained their individual personality, these questions would doubtless receive consideration, even if they formed no part of the routine duty of an official auditor; but this state of affairs could not be expected to last. The rank and file of Government officials are not, and are not expected to be, anything higher than intelligent machines; and it is in the highest degree probable that, from whatever source official auditors were in the first instance obtained, they would soon acquire the ideas and manners of other officials, and altogether cease to exercise that vigilant and intelligent discretion without which no effective audit can possibly be made.

Yet, again, we might go on to show that the cry for an official audit is based upon a condition of affairs which would certainly not be guarded against by the proposed remedy.

The serious losses which have of late been inflicted upon shareholders have been due primarily to the incompetence and recklessness of directors, and also, to a considerable extent, to causes for which no person or class of persons can be considered directly responsible. In but few instances can it be argued with any show of plausibility that a more thorough system of audit would materially have affected the ultimate result; and consequently the question to which attention should be most directed appears to be, not the duties and liabilities of auditors, but rather the duties and liabilities of directors. We have not yet seen the proposition advanced by any capitalist that the Government should provide a staff of official directors with a collateral responsibility for the funds which they are entrusted to administer; but, in all seriousness, we think it would be more possible for the official system to produce a competent director than a competent auditor.

For our own part we consider that the class most to. blame for the present state of financial depression is the investing class.  To a great extent they.directly encourage fraud by the greed with which they snap up shares in any impracticable concern which may pretend to offer them a higher rate of interest than can ever be legitimately expected, or which appears to offer facilities for a profitable gamble on the Stock Exchange; while, on the other hand, even when they place their money in a concern which, under proper management, might be fairly expected to afford a remunerative return, they not only display the utmost apathy as to the conduct of the management (provided only the market price of shares is sufficiently maintained to allow speculation therein to be conducted with advantage), but, moreover, cases are not infrequent in which they have exhibited the utmost resentment when an auditor has exhibited sufficient independence to presume to differ from those who are recklessly squandering the resources of the company.  To speak quite plainly—a large number of shareholders in a certain class of company care nothing for the continued prosperity of the company, but care everything for the market price of its shares during the few months they may happen to be upon the register.  Thus the interest of the speculator takes the place of the proprietor's interest in his investment, and there remains not a single soul, unless it be the auditor, who cares a cent what may happen to the company after he has parted with his holding.

The remedy for the evil appears to be in the exhibition of greater intelligence (and, shall we say, greater honesty of purpose?) on the part of shareholders and directors in the concerns of the company.  If these things could but be assured we should no longer have the spectacle of shareholders and directors seeking cover for their own recklessness and greed behind the responsibility of an auditor, whose duties they had hitherto sought to reduce to the most perfunctory level, but whom they now seek to clothe with the responsibility for their own deficiencies..

## The Value of an Audit.

THE correspondence under this head is still being desultorily maintained in the *Pall Mall Gazette*, and we accordingly reproduce the following :—

### REPORT TO INDEPENDENT AUTHORITY.—A PLEA FOR PRACTICALITY.

#### To the Editor of the Pall Mall Gazette.

SIR,—In perusing the correspondence that has appeared in the *Pall Mall Gazette* upon the value of an audit the conclusion has been forced upon me that an audit is frequently rendered inoperative from the want of power which an auditor has.

An auditor discovers certain irregularities in the accounts that are submitted to him, or in his opinion they are calculated to convey a wrong idea of the company's position ; what means are there by which he can compel the directors to present a fair balance sheet to the shareholders ? He can refuse his certificate, and I believe occasionally an auditor has sent a report to the shareholders direct ; but as either course very often has the effect of his not being re-elected, he prefers to give a qualified certificate by which he commits himself to nothing.

Would not the simplest way to render an audit efficient be to make the auditor report to some official (say, the Registrar of Joint Stock Companies) who should have power to decide the matter and take any action that might be necessary ? Should an auditor fail to report any patent irregularity (such as writing up the value of an asset), I think he should be liable to refund the fees he has received, or even to a heavier punishment.

As to the value of the assets, it is only with the floating assets that the question of what they will realize has to be considered so long as the company is a going concern, and I think an auditor in the course of his audit should find sufficient evidence to satisfy himself that these are not unduly overvalued.

Yours truly,

*January* 31.     EFFICIENT.

---

SIR,—In regard of the question, "The Duties of an Auditor," it strikes me that your correspondents are beating round the fence, and don't approach the great need. An auditor, be he ever so able, is to a great extent, by his training and pursuit, little more than a first-class clerk. He may be a fine mathematical or classical scholar, his pastime may be the study of electricity or billiards ; but as for real actual business —the practical knowledge of a manufacturer, merchant, banker, or tradesman—where is he ? He cannot understand the spirit of enterprise, sometimes called speculation, for what is all commerce but that ? Everything imported— coffee, tea, sugar ; everything manufactured, grown, or dug from the bowels of the earth, is a speculation on a future market. Individuals and companies dealing in securities are speculators for a rise. Now the auditor goes from the books of a bankrupt shop in Bond Street to a broken-down company in Broad Street. Can his advice, his valuations be of good ? All he can do faithfully and truly is to compare the books with the balance-sheet and certify the same to be correct or incorrect.

What is wanted (many of your correspondents mistake one for the other) is not an audit, but an inspection such as of a large banking corporation, where the inspector walks into the office and takes possession of everything, knows generally, from his training, a good deal about the classes of securities, and, after finding them correct in detail, hands them back to the proper officers in charge ; then calls for their opinion of each, or, if bills of exchange, of the names. After that, from the knowledge he has or obtains in addition, he estimates everything and reports the result, how or why obtained, value, marketability, &c., in a report to his directors. An inspection of any company is practicable, by the obtaining of one or two persons conversant with the class of business undertaken, probably among the shareholders—or say a shareholder and an outsider. Any way, the appointed persons must upon entering listen to no one, but take possession of everything down to " petty cash," if such an abomination be allowed. The inspections at first would perhaps show the need of a broom, but kept up and performed at intervals would prevent disaster, ruin, and misdoing.—Yours truly,

*New Travellers' Club, W., Jan.* 30.     F. G. R.

# The Accountant

## THE ORGAN OF CHARTERED ACCOUNTANTS THROUGHOUT THE WORLD.

### (Awarded Silver Medal, Esposizione Italo-Americana, Genova 1892).

VOL. XX.—NEW SERIES.—No. 1005.　　　　　SATURDAY, MARCH 10, 1894.

## Leading Articles.

### THE VALUE OF AN AUDIT.

THE letter of Mr. FREDERICK HOVENDEN, which we reprint in another column of the present issue from *The Pall Mall Gazette* of the 3rd inst., is chiefly conspicuous for its extreme bitterness ; and if we were to regard Mr. HOVENDEN's case as adequately expressed by him, it would, probably, be considered undeserving of notice, for it is obvious that one so strongly opinionated is not likely to be convinced by any verbal arguments. On the other hand, the question that has been raised is of no little importance both to the profession and the public, on account of the extreme differences of opinion that are prevalent among both, and we therefore cannot afford to decline to discuss the present condition of affairs.

In the first place, then, we must protest against the action of our contemporary in making a very careful selection from among the points raised in our articles of the 27th January and 3rd February last (ignoring altogether our article on the 10th ult.), and describing that selection as being representative of the general opinion of the profession. The extracts quoted gave no adequate idea of our own views, while the comments of our contemporary would appear to imply that all Chartered Accountants were of the same opinion—an assertion which we should be loth to make.

At the same time our views are sufficiently representative to be entitled to something more than the scant courtesy afforded them by Mr. HOVENDEN, and we venture to think that they are sufficiently reasonable to require a little more argument upon the part of our opponent before they can be considered as finally disposed of. Most people, moreover, would look for a higher ideal than the Post Office affords as an example of a model public department. Mr. HOVENDEN must be singularly ill-informed. There is scarcely a week passes without voluminous correspondence appearing either in the London or provincial press respecting the Post Office, and a correspondence was raging for weeks a short time back in the *Glasgow Herald* on the ineptitude of this public department. We ourselves could contribute one or two spicy items, but that our space is too valuable to devote to such matters. Then as regards the celerity with which Government officials act, *Truth* seems to have a very poor opinion, as witness that journal's remarks *re* the London and General Bank. Probably Mr. HOVENDEN is an antiquarian, in which case the ways of Government officials would have much to commend them; but in discussing, as the Board of Trade does, company concerns for 1892 in its document issued a fortnight back, Mr. HOVENDEN can scarcely say that this department's "expedition and accuracy are actually marvellous."

The spasmodic manner in which the present correspondence has appeared in *The Pall Mall Gazette* raises the presumption that our contemporary is not sufficiently whole-hearted in the matter to afford the space necessary for its adequate consideration. If Mr. HOVENDEN really wishes to ventilate the subject freely (and is not merely actuated by a desire to throw mud at an honourable profession) we invite him to continue the discussion in these columns, promising him at the same time a fair hearing.

In the meantime we may remind him that there is no point raised in his letter of the 3rd inst. which has not been already considered in our previous articles upon the matter; we therefore think that it is for him to make the next move. We would suggest that any discussion which may take place would be more profitable if conducted upon somewhat more definite lines than those hitherto adopted, and we accordingly throw out the following headings as a suggestion of what, we take it, Mr. HOVENDEN desires to prove:

(1) That a more effective system of audit than that now usual would prove beneficial to the investing classes.

This requires to be dealt with somewhat precisely, showing that (a) ineffective audits are now general; (b) that the audit *per se* is at fault; (c) that a more effective audit is practically possible; (d) define "effective audit."

(2) That there are in the ranks of professional accountants no firms or individuals who can be relied upon to carry out an "effective audit." And

(3) That the Government could undertake to carry out an "effective audit" at a scale of fees within the means of companies to pay; and that such work, if undertaken by the Government, would necessarily be "effective."

Note here that Government would never undertake to be responsible for its own errors; also realize (and allow for) the fact that, as has been repeatedly proved, Government auditors are *not* infallible.

This we take to be a short statement of the case that Mr. HOVENDEN wishes to prove; and, if it will afford him any convenience, our columns are open to him for that purpose.

## The Value of an Audit.

BEING SOME FURTHER CORRESPONDENCE FROM *The Pall Mall Gazette.*

*To the Editor of the Pall Mall Gazette.*

SIR,—Since the able article in your newspaper of January 17th last, on the above very important subject, there have been published by you numerous letters giving all shades of opinion, and I venture to think the time has now arrived when we may form a deduction or judgment from the published letters.

None of the writers touches upon the all powerful issue raised by you. What is the value of an audit as safeguarding the investing public, especially with respect to the assets represented in figures being a true statement as to values? We may now confidently affirm that for such a purpose the value of an audit is not worth the paper it is written on.

Various writers have criticised my suggestion of a Government audit and valuation, the chief objections, coming from accountants, being — that it is not expedient to call in Government for such work ; that, in fact, Government is not capable. My reply is : When Government is called upon to do real honest commercial work it has shown itself quite capable. The Post Office work is a full answer as to competency, and I think I may venture to assert that there is not an institution, private or public, so ably conducted as our Post Office. Moreover, there is as little red-tapeism displayed in its management as can possibly be, and its expedition and accuracy are actually marvellous.

Failing the remedy suggested by me comes the power of the Chartered Accountants to consolidate themselves into a corporation for the purpose of auditing, so that shareholders could elect the corporation as the auditing body. No doubt this would be a wise step. The *Accountant* newspaper, as foreshadowed in your issue of the 26th ult., has published the correspondence from your newspaper, and the editor has inserted two very weak articles on the question. Evidently the paper courted the ventilation of the important issue. Not one letter has appeared, and the question is dropped. The fact is, the Chartered Accountants know their audit is an absolute failure, and the less said about it the better. But do they think by shirking investigation or suppressing publicity they are likely to stamp out enquiry? No, sir, your article has spread too far and sunk too deeply for such a result to take place.

It must be remembered that Accountants probably live more upon rotten institutions than upon healthy financial ventures. Why then should they move to remedy the present condition of things? They are quite content as things are. They say to Messrs. Swindler, Defaulter, & Co. : " Go on, and when things come to a crisis let the poor shareholders call us in to wind up. We can take care of ourselves. The shareholders must and do pay. It is most profitable work, and the more of it the better for the Accountant." But is it wise for the community to allow this condition of things to continue ? Most certainly not.

Why do not the Chartered Accountants concentrate their powers and form such an institution that the investing public can reliably employ it and feel confident in its full audit? Probably it is the individuals' petty jealousy which prevents any such combination. The firm A. B. and Co. think they can get more in the free fight for the plunder under the present conditions than they would obtain as part of a strong and reliable institution. It is a pity this is so ; it is this want of cohesion amongst us which is doing so much mischief at the present time.

Let us consider how things are now managed. The public are always taken in detail ; from the nature of things there cannot be any joint action. The rotten financier knows this full well. Here is an illustration of a common mode of procedure. A company is floated. A director, Mr. C., is going to perpetrate a fraud upon the community. He purchases a property or commodity, and pays for it say £1,000. The transaction is not in his own name, but in the name of D. D. sells the property on the recommendation of C., who is on the board, for say £10,000. The profit is divided between C. and D. Proper vouchers are given: An auditor has been appointed at the instigation of the board, through a shareholder being put up to nominate him. This is generally the way. Proper vouchers being tendered to the auditor, they are inspected and passed, and a something is inserted in the balance sheet to the asset side of the accounts, as valued at £10,000, when the intrinsic value in the market is only £1,000. All is in order, and then at the end of the financial year comes the certificate :—

> "We have examined the above balance-sheet with the books and vouchers of the company, and find the same in conformity therewith."

I am using the actual words of the first company balance-sheet which comes to my hand. It is signed by a most respectable firm of Accountants. What a farce the words make of the audit!

There is another important point to be dealt with. Continuing the transactions of the above company at the annual meeting, the same firm of auditors are re-elected with a miserable remuneration of twenty guineas per annum. This is not a large company. Nominal capital £1,000,000, shares £10, of which £2 is paid. The liabilities are £800,000 odd, including reserve fund, and of course there is a similar, but somewhat larger amount, represented as assets. The revenue is £50,000 odd. Now, I ask, what can a firm of Accountants do to safeguard the shareholders in investigating such accounts, ranging over one year, for the meagre sum of twenty guineas? To believe that they can afford to give adequate audit, such as will safeguard the proprietors, for such a sum is simply impossible. The audit is a farce. It is worse than useless—it is terribly misleading. Let us do away with such absolute rottenness. But how to do it is the question.

Practically' I am as adverse to applying to Government as any one can be, but after mature thought and years of observation I am of opinion that such audit and valuation can only be efficiently done by such a central authority.

Let the Chartered Accountants effect the remedy if they can, by consolidating themselves, so that the investing public, instead of taking the lead from the directors, can have a body which shareholders can independently and confidently elect. This will be an improvement upon the present condition of things.

The Accountant newspaper in its issue of February 3 states that in the event of Government electing to do this important work of auditing and valuing, the auditors would have to be drawn or recruited from the ranks of the Chartered Accountants. Yes, this must be so; but then The Accountant adds :—

> "The rank and file of Government officials are not, and are not expected to be, anything higher than intelligent machines; and it is in the highest degree probable that, from whatever source official auditors were in the first instance obtained, they would soon acquire the ideas and manners of other officials, and altogether cease to exercise that vigilant and intelligent discretion without which no effective audit can possibly be made."

This is a doubtful compliment to Government officials, and a still more doubtful compliment to Chartered Accountants. But when these observations are considered in face of the form of the certificate quoted above, I must frankly confess I fail to see the point.

Yours truly,<br>FREDERICK HOVENDEN.

---

SIR,—Regarding the letter in your issue of this date, under the heading "The Value of an Audit," may I ask, as one of the public, what is the new and up-to-date definition of the term "audit"? When a company issues its, say, half-yearly balance sheet duly certified, is it not (to coin an expression) for "moneys in action"—that is to say, simply a verification of receipts and expenditure and amount of capital subscribed. Beyond this I never personally believed a Chartered Accountant pretended to go. But if, as your correspondent says, all accountants should form themselves into corporations (save the word) to assess in their audit the value of the particular company as a going concern, where would such an Augean labour end?

Fancy the companies now quoted in the Stock Exchange list being duly *valued* each half-year, no matter in what place or what the nature of their business. Why, all the accountants existing would fail in such a task—leaving out the multiplicity of cross-purposing and what not that must of a need ensue. No, sir. The remedy lies with the shareholders. It is a platitude to repeat, but cannot be told too often. If it is a risky, not to say shady, venture in which they embark, the fault is with themselves. If a sound undertaking the directors are nearly always men who can well be trusted to safeguard their interests without the intermeddling of corporations of accountants and such-like bodies.

I remain, sir, yours obediently,

March 3.                    F. T.

## The Value of an Audit.

ANOTHER SUGGESTION.

(*From the Pall Mall Gazette.*)

Sir,—With reference to the controversy on auditors and
their certificates which has been appearing in your valuable
journal, there is not the slightest doubt that auditors'
certificates have been in several cases a simple farce, and
have conveyed little or nothing to the shareholders—misleading not only in what they have said, but most especially
in what they have left unsaid.

The fact is, sir, that auditors are far too much under the
influence of the board of directors, and, though nominally
elected by the shareholders, they are utterly out of touch
with them, and in most cases don't even as much as know
one of the shareholders whom they are supposed to
represent.

We are all aware of the regular farce that takes place at
each meeting when the retiring auditors Messrs. Blank and
Blank offer themselves for re-election and are invariably
duly elected, after which the shareholders neither see nor
hear more of them till the next annual or half-yearly meeting as the case may be, when the same farce is gone
through.

I think we should hear less of scandalous audits if auditors
were placed in a more independent position by being verita-
bly appointed by the shareholders themselves at a specially
convened meeting, quite apart from the directors, and took
their instructions from a duly appointed committee, whom
it would be their place to meet and report to fully, verbally
as well as in writing, and receive their remuneration from
such committee, which could be done by the directors lodging the amount before the commencement of each audit.

The auditor would thereby be at once put in direct touch
with the shareholders he represents, and the secrecy which
has hitherto been the bane of audits would have some
chance of being abolished, and we should also stand a
chance of being spared the disgraceful spectacle of companies like the Liberator and its kindred institutions, companies like the vast Trust companies distributing dividends
in the dark till just on the point of toppling over, and frantic
efforts of committees of investigation endeavouring to
discover where the fault lies when, alas, too late!—I am
sir, your obedient servant,

*March 7.*                                ACCOUNTANT.

## THE VALUE OF AN AUDIT.

### (*To the Editor of The Accountant.*)

SIR,—I have taken a week to carefully consider your personal article on my letter to *The Pall Mall Gazette* on the above subject.

You say my letter is " conspicuous for its extreme bitterness." Yes, this is so. But have I not good reason for this? I am a sufferer, although comparatively to a small degree, in the present grave crisis. I find friends and neighbours—men who have been doing their work in life conscientiously, observing all the amenities of life, almost ruined by the present system. I see the object for thrift absolutely undermined. What is the cause of this misery ? An over-confidence in their fellow creatures, which confidence has been abused. The factor which has produced this unhappy condition of things is the want of an efficient audit. I reply therefore : Have I not good cause, under these circumstances, for being bitter, and in using my best endeavours to condemn such a system ?

Then you say I am " strongly opinionated." Well, I deprecate speaking of myself in such a case, but it is necessary for me to do so, in order to get that attention from accountants which I hope my opinions deserve.

For twenty of the best years of my life I helped to conduct a large business, with a very varied staff—manufacturers, warehousemen, clerks—a business full of petty detail. Our accounts were on the Italian method of double entry, and by means of weekly, monthly, and annual, trial balances we uniformly succeeded in obtaining a mathematically accurate balance at the end of the financial term within a few hours, often in a few minutes. To successfully conduct such an institution, I think you will agree, involves experience, and experience gives strong opinions, hence I may be pardoned if I feel and write as you say in " so strongly opinionated " manner. This experience is exceptional ; few auditors have had such a training, because I had to do with commodities as well as with accounts. So I think that under these circumstances the word " opinionated," in the sense it is used, is questionable. This however does not matter, because my letter, out of the profession, is appreciated.

Now I want to draw the attention of accountants to the mode adopted in a well-organised commercial, but large firm, at the annual stock-taking. Of course the partners could not be masters of the whole of the detail. To do so would require a super-human power. The practical question arises : How is it possible for the principals (who are the shareholders as well as directors) to effect a valuation which shall properly safeguard the financial condition of the firm ? This is the problem for auditors at the present moment. In the case I cite (and I speak from experience) the result is obtained in the following manner : When each department has taken down its stock the stock-books are brought to one of the partners, and he takes them one after the other, and selects one or more items from each page for the purpose of proof. He has the commodities produced; he counts, weighs, or measures them (or has this done in his presence), and thus by the law of average he can ascertain the value of the assets of the firm. It is remarkable how accurate this works out on the average, and with a little practice how readily one " spots " the possible weak points. This valuing is the all-important factor in conducting any commercial institution, private or public. Now, it is this element which is wanting in our present system of audit, and which makes the value of an audit by the professional accountant practically a failure. What the partners do in the illustration given, the accountants can do, if they will to do so, for shareholders generally. It will sufficiently safeguard the shareholders, but it involves some degree of technical knowledge ; hence there must be added to the pure accountantship the knowledge of valuing. This demands a staff of valuers. Of course, this valuing cannot be carried out in every case, but in most cases it can be done. When it is impossible, the absence of such valuation should be noted in the audit certificate. In practice, the cost will not be excessive, and it will be well to the interest of shareholders to pay this extra cost, and they will willingly pay for such adequate audit.

You intimate that I may be " actuated by a desire to throw mud at an honourable profession." You make a mistake. I am the last to do such a thing. I have now shown you enough to prove that I respect your fundamental principles, but they are imperfect. I have friends in the profession ; I have the highest esteem for the greater number of the individuals ; but it was necessary I should speak in the strongest manner against an incomplete and pernicious system, or, perhaps better expressed, want of system—a condition of things which is rearing in our midst a number of well-dressed and *well-educated* thieves ; a condition producing misery of the direst description. Had I not written in the terms of my letter you would not have invited me to discuss the matter in your columns.

The letter published in your issue of the 17th inst., signed " Accountant," speaks nearly the whole truth. " There is not the slightest doubt that auditors' cer-" tificates have been in several instances a simple " farce, and have conveyed little or nothing to the " shareholders ; misleading, not only in what they have " said, but especially in what they have left unsaid " (this latter should have been printed in capitals). " Auditors are far too much under the influence of the " board of directors, and though nominally elected by " shareholders they are utterly out of touch with them." This is a great confession from one of your own body, but it is understated, the words " in many cases " should read " in most cases." Hence the gravity of the present situation. How can an audit be independent in such a condition of things ? It is impossible. A servant cannot speak against his employer. The evidence in the discussion in *The Pall Mall Gazette* clearly showed that if the servant do so he is discharged. The remedy suggested by " Accountant " I feel sure is not practical. I believe there is only one remedy which can save the profession. If agreeable

to accountants, I will, on an intimation from you, make an effort to enunciate a scheme—which will, of course, be faulty in its first inception. I believe it will sufficiently and permanently give the remedy for the present defective and intolerable position of affairs, and will raise the office of auditor from its present comparatively low condition to perhaps one of the most powerful in the world. But it means individual self-sacrifice, not to a large degree, but one of a character which I fear accountants will object to. Here will be the test. Are accountants men of large views, regarding their profession as a factor in our common prosperity, or are they men who look at their profession *solely* as a means of existence, regarding gain as the *one* object, and utterly indifferent if that gain is obtained through individual and national prosperity or through individual and national adversity and misery ? I offer here no opinion as to the result, but if I am to be heard in your columns this question will be the true test, and will show of what stuff an accountant is made.

I am, sir,

Yours obediently,

FREDERICK HOVENDEN.

*West Dulwich, March 19th, 1894.*

———

(From *The Pall Mall Gazette*).

Sir,—I have read with much interest your correspondent " Accountant's " letter, and thoroughly endorse his views, and think that it is quite time that shareholders in limited companies should be allowed to appoint an independent auditor to inquire into and report to them from time to time their opinion on all matters relating to the working and general management of the concerns they are interested in.

If this suggestion had been acted upon in the Liberator and other large societies, it would have saved many an aching heart and empty cupboard.

Yours, &c.,

SHAREHOLDER.

*Earlsfield, March 16.*

———

ANOTHER SUGGESTION.

(From *The Pall Mall Gazette*.)

Sir,—To ensure an efficient audit the following plan may deserve consideration :—

Let two auditors be appointed, both Chartered Accountants ; or two firms of Chartered Accountants.

Let them audit the accounts year by year alternately, not working together, but conferring whenever they may see fit

with each other, and each certifying only his own Balance
Sheet.

By that means the shareholders would have a better
security against errors of judgment or laxity of method on
the part of an individual auditor.

None but experts in accountancy should undertake or be
entrusted with an important audit ; but whenever desired a
shareholder might be appointed to act in conjunction with
them, as is sometimes the case at present.

Your obedient servant,

S., F.C.A.

*March 19.*

# The Accountant

## THE ORGAN OF CHARTERED ACCOUNTANTS THROUGHOUT THE WORLD.

**(Awarded Silver Medal, Esposizione Italo-Americana, Genova 1892).**

VOL. XX.—NEW SERIES.—No. 1008.              SATURDAY, MARCH 31, 1894.

## Leading Articles.

### THE VALUE OF AN AUDIT.

WE are gratified to find that Mr. FREDERICK HOVENDEN has availed himself of our invitation to continue this discussion in our columns; but we regret to notice that he has not thought fit to approach the subject from the lines indicated by us as being the most likely to end in the deduction of any definite conclusion.

The greater part of the letter appearing in our last issue is either in the nature of personal explanation, or else a mere repetition of opinions that have already been enunciated, but which have not yet been supported by the arguments necessary to carry conviction to the unbiassed mind. So far as the personal explanations go, they are interesting—and even necessary to a proper comprehension of Mr. HOVENDEN's present attitude—but we can only regard the repetition of the *ipse dixit* of an anonymous writer styling himself "Accountant" (with the ingenious substitution of "most" for "many") as a distinct example of that frame of mind which we have designated as "a desire to throw mud." Mr. HOVENDEN must be well aware that such assertions are not arguments, and there is nothing in his personal explanation to show that he has any experience upon which to found any reliable opinion upon the manner in which " most " audits are conducted.

There is very little to take hold of in the letter appearing in our last issue; but, upon the only occasion upon which Mr. HOVENDEN commits himself to a definite statement as to the mode in which an audit is conducted, we at once find him lacking in practical acquaintance with the subject upon which he professes to enlighten us.  It may very possibly be news to Mr. HOVENDEN, but the fact remains that the system of " testing " by means of a detailed examination of various items selected from the whole is perfectly well known to every qualified auditor and very generally acted upon.  At the same time, no auditor of any experience would care to assert that such tests had any affinity to " the law of average."  That certain selected items are correct may raise a strong presumption as to the correctness of the whole, but it certainly does not *prove* the correctness of the whole by the law of averages, because it leaves the question as to whether *all* the items are of a similar nature to those selected for detailed examination absolutely *in statu quo*.  An audit conducted upon such lines, and with no further safeguards, would indeed be of very questionable value.

Having invited Mr. HOVENDEN to continue this discussion in our columns, we have no desire to tie his hands by unduly restricting the scope of his observations; but it seems to us that, if we are to arrive at any tangible result, he must either accept or combat those principles that we have already laid down in our previous articles (which, for that purpose, we respectfully commend to his consideration), for it must be obvious that so long as his replies to our arguments are in the nature of reiterated assertions, we are not very likely to arrive very much nearer to the object of the present discussion.

We are therefore compelled to ask Mr. HOVENDEN (if he wishes to continue) either to accept our offer upon the conditions in which it was made, or else to show cause why he should not do so.  We have tabulated his assertions, and we have asked that they should be supported by something like proof before they are used as premises from which deductions may be drawn.  It must be admitted that in this respect we are asking for nothing but what is fair and reasonable.  We are quite willing to hear any suggestion that Mr. HOVENDEN may have to make for the improvement of auditing generally and the accountancy profession in particular, but what we are still waiting for is some sort of a proof that either (except in certain exceptional and isolated cases) is in such a shocking state as would appear to be suggested.

## Audits and Certificates.

THE following advertisement appears in *The Pall Mall Gazette* of the 21st inst. :—

To the MEMBERS of the several LOCAL CHAMBERS of COMMERCE forming "The ASSOCIATION of CHAMBERS of COMMERCE of the UNITED KINGDOM."

GENTLEMEN,

AS a shareholder in several limited liability companies, I am dissatisfied with the wording and the inefficient character of the auditors' certificates appended to their periodical balance-sheets. These certificates do not, in my opinion, accord with the intention of the Legislature as expressed in "The Companies Act, 1862," and its First Schedule (Table A). Unfortunately, in my judgment, the adoption of Table A was not made compulsory on all companies registered under the Act, whilst at the same time giving power to vary certain of the clauses by special resolution.

In a letter, dated November 17, 1893, I brought the subject of auditors' certificates under the consideration of the Council of the Institute of Chartered Accountants for England and Wales, and I regret that I was not successful in inducing the Council to give support to my views on this question.

I have since, therefore, requested permission to address the Right Honourable the Lord Chancellor on the subject, in a letter, dated 20th January, 1894, and I have advocated the extension of the operation of the whole of the clauses relating to "dividends," "accounts," and "audit," contained in Table A (revised if necessary), but more particularly clauses 93 and 94, to all companies registered under the Act.

On the 3rd February, 1894, I placed a copy of my said letter before the Right Honourable the President of the Board of Trade ; and on the 21st February I placed a copy of my letter before the President of "The London Chamber of Commerce."

I cannot see any reason why the auditor of every limited liability company should not be compelled by Act of Parliament to state on the balance-sheet before appending his signature to it, whether, in his opinion, "the balance-sheet is a full and fair balance-sheet, containing the particulars required by the articles of association, and properly drawn up so as to exhibit a true and correct view of the state of the company's affairs." (*Vide* Clause 94 at foot.)

Indeed, I would go further, and suggest that the balance-sheet of every trading limited liability Company should be accompanied by clearly stated "Profit and Loss Account," which should also be duly approved and certified by the Auditor.

I append copies of Clauses 93 and 94, and I respectfully ask your earnest consideration of this letter, and if you approve my views, as herein expressed, I ask for the support of your respective Chambers of Commerce in my effort to bring under the operations of those clauses every company registered under "The Companies Act, 1862."

I am, Gentlemen,
Your most obedient servant,
JOHN G. BARRY, F.C.A. .

87, Cannon-street, London, E.C.
15th March, 1894.

Clause 93.—" Every auditor shall have a list delivered to him of all books kept by the company, and shall at all reasonable times have access to the books and accounts of the company. He may, at the expense of the company, employ accountants or other persons to assist him in investigating such accounts, and he may in relation to such accounts examine the directors or any other officer of the company."

Clause 94.—" The Auditors shall make a Report to the members upon the balance-sheet and accounts, and in every such report they shall state whether, in their opinion, the balance-sheet is a full and fair balance-sheet, containing the particulars required by these Regulations, and properly drawn up so as to exhibit a true and correct view of the state of the company's affairs, and in case they have called for explanations or information from the Directors, whether such explanations or information have been given by the Directors, and whether they have been satisfactory ; and such report shall be read, together with the Report of the Directors, at the Ordinary Meeting."

*Audits and Certificates.* To many of our readers it is probable that the line of action taken by Mr. John G. Barry, F.C.A. will appear singular—to say the least of it. We have no particular fault to find with most of his suggestions (indeed, we have recently advocated all the more important ones in these columns); but there is something a little presumptive in the idea' that any individual member of the Institute should take so much upon his shoulders, and one is involuntarily reminded of the proverb that some people " rush in " where others " fear to tread." It may be added that many will not be disposed to regret that Mr. Barry " was not successful in inducing the Council to give support to his views on this question." An accountant is obviously not the right person to express any deliberate opinion as to whether or not the articles of association of a company have been conformed to; while it is obvious that no stereotyped form of certificate would be universally applicable. We believe that these two points are the only ones upon which the Council of the Institute were consulted by Mr. Barry.

---

## THE VALUE OF AN AUDIT.
*(To the Editor of The Accountant.)*

SIR,—In your article of March 10th last, on the above, you state: " The question that has been raised " is of no little importance both to the profession and " the public, on account of the extreme differences of " opinion that are prevalent among both, and we can- " not afford to decline to discuss the present condition " of affairs." This is practically a confession from the professional auditors. If the present audit were sufficient to safeguard the investor from fraud how could such a doubtful " condition of affairs " exist? Yet, in face of the notoriously unsatisfactory condition of things, you ask me to enter on a controversy " whether the audit *per se* is at fault." I really must decline to " flog a dead horse ": life is too short to waste time on such useless work. Moreover, the circular letter of Mr. John G. Barry, F.C.A., contained in your issue of the 31st ult., and who writes " as a shareholder in several limited liability companies" as well as a Fellow of the Chartered Accountants, sufficiently establishes the fact that, in many cases, the professional audit as at present carried out does not safeguard the investing public, because the audit lacks the very important factor—the assets are not certified as representing intrinsic values. Under the present system this is really no part of the auditor's business.

It is no news to me (as you intimate) "that the "system of 'testing' by a detailed examination of "various items selected from the whole is perfectly "well known to every qualified auditor," but it is news to me when you say this mode is "very generally acted upon." As far as my experience goes the meagre fee paid to an auditor is not sufficient to cover such a test. If Chartered Accountants profess to give two pounds' worth of labour for a sovereign then I am very gratified to find they are such patriots. This is, indeed, news to me and to the investing public also, and the quicker you let this information be known the better. But it will be asked in reply : " How about the late dreadful frauds perpetrated on the investing community if accountants do 'test' the value of assets by such detailed examination ?" It is this very issue which has been debated in *The Pall Mall Gazette*, and in which Chartered Accountants have joined by name, and not, as you object, as the *ipse dixit* of an anonymous writer styling himself "Accountant." All agreed the evil was a defective audit. I say the issue has been debated with the unanimous verdict of "incompetency against the present system." To go over the ground again I do not think " is fair and reasonable," as you suggest.

What is required to be done is to see if some common action can be taken by Chartered Accountants in order to remove the present known defects. Now, I have ventured to offer to draw up a scheme essentially from the investor's point of view, but with such consideration of detail which my experience and common sense dictate will in the main be acceptable to the profession of public auditors. Let the past be buried; it is to the present and the future we have to look. I assert the present system is a premium in many cases for fraud, and you and the accountants know it. Then alter the system. Any new system must be so perfect and complete as to nip those frauds in the bud.

I do not quite understand by your article of the 31st ult. that the consideration of such a scheme will be acceptable to accountants, hence I am reluctant to enter upon a thankless work until I feel sure that my efforts will be appreciated and reasonably considered.

The scheme will require much thought, and I am anxious to make it complete.

You ask in your leader if I am an antiquarian. No, I have no sympathy with the past. I am giving, and

have been giving for years, my best powers to study what are known as "fundamental problems." They are intensely interesting and instructive, and I believe, from the necessities of our condition, they must come to the front in civilized life. Amongst these problems, there are two which are now pressing on the commercial community. One may be expressed thus : What is the value of a sovereign and a shilling ? This brings the question of Bimetallism to the front. I have endeavoured (I am told successfully) to *simplify* and solve this problem in my brief essay, " The A.B.C. of International Bimetallism." The second is " What is the value of an Audit ?" and I do hope, with the help of the Chartered Accountants, to assist in making the latter a real safeguard to the investing public. The question of currency is really part of the second question. I wonder how many Chartered Accountants have fairly thought over the former important issue, one which so intimately connects the successful operations of the profession of accountants.

Yours truly,

FREDERICK HOVENDEN.

*West Dulwich, S.E., April 3rd*, 1894.

_____

## THE VALUE OF AN AUDIT.

IF we wished, for any reason, to avoid the fullest possible discussion of this question, the letter from Mr. HOVENDEN, which appeared in our last issue, would certainly afford us an excellent excuse for doing so. No fair-minded spectator would consider it unreasonable if we were to decline altogether to deal with an antagonist who so persistently refuses to come up to the scratch ; but as we are still hopeful that Mr. HOVENDEN may have something to say, and as we would very much sooner have the question dealt with in these columns than in those of one of our contemporaries, who might possibly refuse to give a fair hearing to our side of the matter, we again return to the weary task of trying to direct this discussion into something approaching a definite and tangible form.

In our issue of the 10th ult. we suggested that Mr. HOVENDEN should advance some proof of his previous assertions, which we classified as follows : (1) There is urgent need of a more effective system of auditing ; (2) professional audits are worthless, as at present conducted ; (3) an official audit would supply the existing need. We are gratified to notice that Mr. HOVENDEN appears to have recognised the absurdity of seeking help from officialism, for neither of his last two letters mentions this view of the matter at all ; but we think he might have had the grace to acknowledge that our arguments against the further extension of officialism are irrefutable.

With reference to the first two assertions, we understand Mr. HOVENDEN to maintain that they have already been substantiated, (a) by our admission that differences of opinion exist in the profession as to the mode in which an audit should be conducted, and as to the limit of an auditor's responsibility ; (b) by the statements made recently by Mr. JOHN G. BARRY, F.C.A. ; (c) by the discussion which lately appeared in *The Pall Mall Gazette*.

That there should be any difference of opinion among professional accountants concerning a matter that has never yet been properly defined either by Legislature or by Court of Law may at first sight appear to be unfortunate ; and, doubtless, these differences are a source of inconvenience and of undue responsibility to accountants themselves, but we have already shown that the general public would not be benefited (although the profession might) by a cast-iron set of regulations and definitions. We considered this point in the article appearing in our issue of the 27th January last, but perhaps Mr. HOVENDEN's memory does not carry him back so far as this. What we wish to emphasise now, however, is that there is not, and never has been, any such difference of opinion as need call for comment upon the part of outsiders. Every reputable accountant fully realises the legitimate extent of his responsibilities, and no legislation that may be passed is likely to add to these responsibilities.

With reference to the manifesto of Mr. J. G. BARRY, F.C.A., and to his further communication, which we reprint in another column of the present issue, we are thereby enabled to "better understand" the position he has taken up. We now gather that the "views" which the Council of the Institute did not see their way to accept were that there was something radically wrong with the preparation and audit of the accounts of the Trustees', Executors', &c., Corporation. Doubtless, the Council considered that any complaint upon these matters would be best made—in the first place—at a general meeting of the Corporation, and it is not at all surprising that they should have declined to discuss the question with Mr. BARRY until the recent meeting had been held. It may be added that at the adjourned meeting, held on the 10th inst., the former auditors were re-elected, and we have not been able to learn that Mr. BARRY or any other shareholder thought it necessary to dissent from this resolution; it, therefore, looks very much as though they knew that there was no reasonable fault to be found with the former audits. For our own part we see nothing in the accounts for 1892, nor in the auditor's certificate, to which exception can reasonably be taken. Turning from the particular to the general, the suggested improvements bear a very close resemblance to some that were made by ourselves in a recent issue, and we, therefore, need hardly pause to consider them again at the present time. It is important to remember that a company may make heavy losses from many other reasons besides a defective audit; nobody is so unreasonable as to assert that an increase in the death-rate, in times of epidemic, is any argument against the ability of the medical profession.

Coming now to the *Pall Mall* correspondence (and allowing Mr. HOVENDEN's twisting of "Accountant's" words to slide, as being of no very great importance either way), it becomes necessary for us to speak somewhat explicitly.

The question was originally started by a leading article in our contemporary. A second article (of a decidedly modified character) commented upon the reply published in our issue of 27th January, and *no reply whatever* was vouchsafed to the article in our issue of the 3rd February. The correspondence dragged on in a desultory manner for some weeks afterwards, but our second article has never yet been challenged. Our contemporary has not even issued a further article closing the discussion. We therefore maintain that our contemporary has tacitly admitted the justice of our contentions, and we must be excused if we (always respectfully) express the opinion that the opinions of our contemporary's correspondents are, for the most part, without any very weighty significance. Any tyro can write a letter to a daily newspaper, but the insertion of such a letter does not entitle it to the respect of experts. If the honest truth is to be told, very little sense was to be found in most of the letters upon this subject that appeared in the columns of our contemporary, and it is absurd to suppose that it would really have affected the question even if "all agreed the evil was a defective audit"—which, as a matter of fact, they did not do. We are never likely to get him very much nearer to the real point at issue, however, if Mr. HOVENDEN's present attitude is continued; we therefore suggest (by way of a compromise) that he may take it that accountants are quite willing to learn anything about auditing that he feels able and willing to teach them, and that any communication he may be disposed to make will be treated with all the consideration that it deserves. Whether it will be "appreciated and reasonably considered" will naturally depend upon its intrinsic merits.

## VALUE OF AN AUDIT.

*(To the Editor of The Accountant.)*

SIR,—With reference to the correspondence which has recently been appearing in your issues as to the value of an audit, perhaps I may be allowed to ventilate the opinion that an audit is *per se* simply valueless as a means of detecting fraud, if such fraud is initiated and carried through by a person blessed with even a very small average modicum of common sense. That, however, an audit may possibly prove valuable I should not for a moment hesitate to admit, but the value is an indirect rather than a direct one, and consists simply in the fact that by employing an accountant of experience and tact a company can secure to itself through him that system of account-keeping best suited to the requirements of the particular business and most aptly fitted for the detection of fraud. With such a system properly inaugurated and thoroughly and efficiently carried through, the possibility of a fraud being successfully manipulated is reduced to a minimum. With the inauguration of such a system, judiciously arranged, the value of an audit begins, and with the efficient carrying through and enforcement of the system the value ends. Here, then, the value of an audit begins, and here also it ends.

It is true that an audit often acts as a deterrent because the officials of the company do not know to what extent the audit may be carried, and consequently are uncertain of their position, but as this uncertainty is essentially the product of ignorance on the part of the employees, and in no way forms part of the *system* of the audit nor in any way results through any merit in the audit, it seems to me no value should be claimed in this respect by the auditor as a resultant of *his* work or of the audit he has carried through.

It seems to me that the sooner the profession recognise the true state of affairs, and not attach a fictitious value to work which any average schoolboy can see contains no merit in itself, the better will it be for the profession. Let them raise themselves from the lethargy of their position, and see to it that in future all audits be done not perfunctorily as at present but through the medium of a system, the adoption of which may give confidence to the employer, satisfaction to the employees, and status to the auditor.

Yours faithfully,<br>J. McL.

*London, April 10th, 1894.*

---

### AUDITS AND CERTIFICATES.
*(To the Editor of The Accountant.)*

Sir,—I beg to thank you for placing before your readers in your issue of the 31st ult. my letter addressed to " The members of Chambers of Commerce," which was advertised in *The Pall Mall Gazette* of the 21st March, and previously in other papers.

As in your editorial notes you criticise my independent action in this matter, I trust for the information of your readers you will do me the favour of publishing in your columns my letter to the Council of the Institute dated 17th November last, a copy of which I beg now to forward to you for that purpose. Your readers will then the better understand my position.

In the note in your issue of the 31st ult. you state : " The profession has views of its own on this question." I shall be very glad if the publication of my letter should result in these views being placed before the public in some practical form. I inferred from Mr. Howgrave's reply to my letter, and I shall regret if I did so in error, that the Council of the Institute had no practical views on the subject.

The point I am agitating to secure—and in doing so I have no objection to my action being considered "singular "—is that the auditor of every limited liability company shall be compelled by Act of Parliament to certify on the Balance Sheet which he signs, using the words approved by the Legislature and so expressed in the first schedule of the Companies Act 1862, that, in his opinion, " the Balance Sheet is a full and fair Balance Sheet, containing the particulars required by the articles of association, and properly drawn up so as to exhibit a true and correct view of the state of the company's affairs." The words in the Act of Parliament are : " These regulations," instead of " The articles of association," the meaning being the same.

This does not involve, if you will permit me to say so, a " stereotyped form of certificate," as you assume in your editorial note of the 7th inst., for it is obvious that the auditor can write in his certificate any additional words he may think necessary. But I think it does involve that, if the auditor is of opinion that the Balance Sheet is not " a full and fair Balance Sheet," he will not sign it, and surely it will not be disputed that such a result will be to the advantage of investing shareholders and in the public interest.

I desire to add, also in my capacity of a shareholder, that the auditor's remuneration should be proportionate to the responsibility of the position in which the Legislature intended to place him under the Act of 1862. I recently wrote the secretary of a company in which I am shareholder, that the sum debited in that company's accounts as " Auditor's Fee " ought, in my opinion, to have been three or four times the amount.

I am, Sir,<br>Your very obedient Servant,<br>JOHN G. BARRY, F.C.A.

*London, 10th April, 1894.*

## WHAT IS AN AUDIT?

THE article appearing in the *Westminster Gazette* of the 13th inst., which we reproduce in another column of the present issue, will attract the attention of our readers, not only on account of the importance attaching to the question, but also because the writer appears to have a more practical knowledge of his subject than is usually the case when professional or technical matters are discussed in the columns of one of our daily contemporaries.

We do not attach very much value to the views of the " distinguished amateur," as to what an audit should be, for they are obviously too hazy to be of any practical utility (however suitable they may have been to the precise occasion upon which they were uttered); but our contemporary has, undoubtedly, performed a great public service in calling attention to the remarkable statement of Sir GEORGE RUSSELL, M.P., to the effect that "directors need not concern themselves with accounts certified to by auditors." This statement is by no means an isolated one of the manner in which the auditor is too often made the scapegoat upon whom is visited all the sins of omission and commission perpetrated by careless or dishonest directors.

Did it never occur to Sir GEORGE RUSSELL that the accounts submitted to the shareholders of a company are the accounts of the directors, not of the auditors? and, did it never occur to him to enquire why the directors are supposed to sign such accounts before they are submitted to the shareholders? Possibly Sir GEORGE has never troubled himself to think the matter fairly and squarely out; in which case it will, doubtless, be news to him to hear that it is the directors, and not the auditors, who are required by law to submit true accounts to the shareholders.

Even if we were to admit (which we do not for one moment) that the auditors were "the servants of the directors," the position of affairs would not be altered; for an employer is liable at law for the acts and defaults of his servants.

Our contemporary very fairly says that an auditor "would need to be endowed with a superhuman faculty of appraising securities in all parts of the globe, and he would have to combine in his own person the entire knowledge of the whole City," if he aspired to fulfil all the manifold functions that have been ascribed to him by various impractical scribblers. Still it seems a fair question to ask Chartered Accountants precisely what force, in their opinion, an audit should carry; and —at the risk of appearing tedious to those who have already studied all that has recently appeared in these columns upon this very subject—we propose to once more express, as concisely as possible, our views concerning what a professional audit may reasonably be expected to imply.

In a letter that appeared in our last issue, a certain "J. McL." points out that a professional audit properly conducted secures *inter alia* the adoption of the best possible system of accounts, "most aptly fitted for the detection of fraud." Incidentally also, the audit acts as a deterrent.

So far our correspondent is talking sound commonsense; but the concluding paragraphs of his letter sufficiently indicate that, while anxious to instruct others, he is himself unacquainted with the *modus operandi* of the leading firms of Chartered Accountants, and accordingly we must look elsewhere for a solution to the question raised by our contemporary.

The general opinion among the profession appears to be in accord with that so ably expressed upon several occasions by Mr. FREDERICK WHINNEY, F.C.A., viz., that while there are many points that an auditor cannot positively certify as facts, he is required to review all points in the light of his experience as an expert in accounts and a business man, and to criticise the accounts in the same way that each shareholder might do for himself, had he the auditor's experience and facilities of acquiring information.

The fact is generally lost sight of, and yet it is of paramount importance, that it is the *accounts* that the auditor is called upon to criticise, not the general policy of the directors.

The following paragraphs from DICKSEE's *Auditing* form an appropriate conclusion to the present article :—

"When addressing the Autumnal Meeting of the Institute of Chartered Accountants in 1888, Mr. FREDERICK WHINNEY, F.C.A., expressed himself as follows: 'I know perfectly well that a proper Auditor must go further (than comparing the published accounts with the books), and see that the books themselves do correspond with the books,' and this view appears to be endorsed by the legal decisions to be considered later on. As to how far it is possible for this standard to be carried into practice, there is perhaps some room for the elasticity of individual opinion, but the general statement is absolutely unassailable.

"In actual practice, however, the question naturally arises: How is the Auditor to ascertain the actual facts? To which it may be replied: In the same manner as a jury —*by sifting evidence*. The chief evidence is, of course, the books (and it may be remarked, incidentally, that it is clearly the Auditor's duty to see that the accounts he certifies, in addition to being correct, are in accordance with the books), but the books must not be considered the sole source of evidence; the fact that a statement appears in the books is *primâ facie* evidence only, and must be verified, not only by internal cross-examination, but also by reliable and independent evidence.

"The result of such an investigation will be that the auditor has proved to himself that certain statements represent absolutely indisputable facts, and that certain other statements, *in his opinion*, appear to represent facts. Beyond this—not being omniscient—he cannot go, and should never attempt to go.  Let him therefore certify that he has thoroughly examined the accounts, that they are in accordance with the books, and are, in his opinion, correctly stated : he will then be occupying a logical, manly, position far more in keeping with the dignity of his profession than that afforded by the most skilful of word-juggling."

## AMATEUR AUDITORS.

A T a time like the present, when so many complaints are being made as to the manner in which some audits are conducted, and when such disastrous results have so frequently attended an injudicious selection of auditors, it seems strange that any insurance company should be so far behind the times as to render it possible for the following to be an extract from the report of the proceedings of its last general meeting.

" Mr. Hawks proposed the re-appointment of the retiring auditor, Mr. R. J. Pead.

Mr. Garnet seconded the motion.

Mr. Coles suggested the advisability of having a Chartered Accountant to act with the auditors on a future occasion.

The Chairman replied that under the deed the auditor must be a policy-holder and a proprietor to the extent of £1,000.

The resolution was then agreed to.

Mr. Pead in returning thanks for his re-appointment said, that in dealing with the voluminous figures connected with the company he had often misgivings as to whether he had the requisite qualifications for the post of auditor of an important institution like the Eagle.  He, however, had a very able and experienced colleague in Mr. Woods ; but if in the future it was found desirable to have a Chartered Accountant as auditor he was willing to give way."

It will be seen from the above, which we reproduce from *The Insurance World* of the 11th inst., that the auditor in question was re-elected in spite of the fact that he " often had misgivings as to whether he had the requisite qualifications for the post of auditor." We do not wish to say anything upon our own authority as to what the qualifications of Mr. PEAD may be, for we must admit that we are absolutely without information upon this matter, but we should have thought that the Eagle Insurance Company might have done better than re-elect an auditor who admits that he is doubtful whether he is capable of carrying out the duties of his office, and we may further suggest that if the chairman is right in his state-ment that, under their deed of settlement, the Eagle Insurance Company are obliged to elect their auditor from among those of their policy-hoiders who may also happen to hold stock to the extent of £1,000, the sooner such a provision is altered the better it will be for the Company in question.

## THE VALUE OF AN AUDIT.

*(To the Editor of The Accountant.)*

Sir,—I am sorry that I cannot respond to your request. The fact is, I do not care to enter on a controversy with an editor who regards me as "an antagonist who so persistently refuses to come up to the scratch," neither do I profess to " teach " auditors, as you sarcastically suggest. All I have undertaken is, in a very grave crisis, to give some help to get matters right. So I have decided altogether to decline your invitation. I have drafted a scheme, as promised : I think it has a value, even if it is only as a starting point, but I now put it aside, as I am sure, whether it has merits or not, it cannot be fairly considered with the spirit you have disclosed.

Of course, I cannot put my suggestion, which is one solely interesting to the professional auditor, in any other newspaper than the recognised organ of the Chartered Accountants, so I must be content in rejecting the professional auditor and see what can be done in other quarters.

In the meantime my views are like seeds set in the ground—they may germinate or not, all depends upon the favourable external conditions, but when I find that " Oldham shareholders " are seeing the issue, and the public are being gradually educated to the true position of affairs, as illustrated in your report on the audit of " The New Zealand Loan and Mercantile Agency " (extracted from *The Telegraph* newspaper), I think I can well afford to wait events, giving from time to time the little help I may be able in order to advance a better condition of things. I now much doubt if the reform, which must come, will be brought about through Chartered Accountants.

I must correct your error when you say I " have dropped the official audit idea." Failing the Chartered Accountants doing the right thing, I believe that is the alternative. I would have much preferred that the accountants had taken the proper initial steps. I have a great distaste to an appeal to Governments to do work which can be done by other means, but in this case it would seem there is no alternative.

I am, yours obediently,

FREDK. HOVENDEN.

*West Dulwich, April 19th, 1894.*

[The late arrival of Mr. Hovenden's letter precludes our reply thereto in this issue, but we shall have something to say in our next. In the meantime we must express our regret that Mr. Hovenden has decided to wipe out the professional auditor, but it will not for a moment be inferred by those who have carefully followed this matter that we have attempted to stifle our correspondent's views ; on the contrary, we stated in our last issue that accountants were " quite willing to learn anything about auditing " Mr. Hovenden " felt able and willing to teach them." As our correspondent had drawn wholesale conclusions from one or two isolated cases we thought, and still think, he should prove the existence of widespread disease before seeking to apply drastic remedies.—*Ed. Acct.*]

## What is an Audit?

THE *Westminster Gazette* has taken up the question of Audit, and in a recent issue, under the above head, says:—

IF the proceedings in the case of the New Zealand Loan Company do not open the eyes of the investing public in many directions, it will not be the fault of the learned Judge who is presiding with so much acuteness and spirit. There are many points which will demand full discussion when the public examination is over. Meanwhile, it may be well to emphasise one point to which Mr. Justice Vaughan Williams specially directed the attention of the public. The question is one which was raised in these columns during the public examination into the Balfour Companies, and which is of vital importance to the investing public. What is the value of an audit? The form in which the question has come up most prominently in the present investigations is as follows:—

"Sir James admitted that the balance sheet of 1891 was misleading, inasmuch as £393,000 New Zealand Land Company shares were included under 'advances on wool, produce, current account, etc.,' and not under 'stock and share investments.' Witness thought the responsibility rested in this and other matters with the auditors.

"His Lordship said that this did not seem to be the opinion generally held, and he hoped the Institute of Chartered Accountants would note what the witness had said."

We reserve for some future occasion any remarks on this particular case. It is the general question which for the moment we wish to raise. What is the responsibility of auditors? When a shareholder sees the certificate of an eminent auditor at the bottom of a balance sheet, what value should he attach to it? Is it worth everything, or anything, or nothing? The most sweeping and satisfactory description of an auditor's duties which we have ever seen is that given by a distinguished amateur in the business, the Reverend Dr. Dawson Burns. Here is the passage; it occurs in a speech in which that philanthropic financier once returned thanks for "the auditors":—

"What is an auditor? He ought to be very much like a watch-dog: very careful to listen for any suspicious sound; able to bark and, perhaps, even to bite if necessary. The peculiarity of his position is this, that whereas the watch-dog has to watch those outside, he has to watch those who are inside. He has to take care that those who manage the accounts do their business properly."

If this were a correct description of an auditor's functions, then an auditor's certificate would be worth everything, and Sir George Russell, M.P., who said that "directors need not concern themselves with accounts certified to by auditors," would be well justified. But does the Institute of Chartered Accountants agree? And, if not, what exactly is the usual audit worth?

Now, no one demands that a Chartered Accountant shall do impossibilities. If we believed some directors we should suppose that it was the auditor's business to value the securities, to control the policy, to determine the dividend, and prepare the balance sheet—in short, to relieve the board of every matter that presented the smallest difficulty. If that were so, the auditor would need to be endowed with a superhuman faculty of appraising securities in all parts of the globe, and he would have to combine in his own person the entire knowledge of the whole City. That is obviously unreasonable. The auditor cannot be expected to know other people's business better than they know it themselves. But what we may reasonably ask of the Chartered Accountants is to know precisely what force, in their opinion, an audit should carry. Whether it is little or much is a comparatively minor point, so long as we know where we stand. For the danger of the present situation is that, while the director trusts the auditor and the auditor the director, the shareholders' interest falls to the ground between the two stools. We should like also to point out to the Institute of Chartered Accountants that in a great many cases the ground is cut away from their feet by the very directors who may presently shield themselves under the auditor's opinion. There is a very significant passage upon this subject in the last report of the Inspector-General in Bankruptcy:—

" Although Table A of the Companies Act, 1862, provides for a regular audit of the company's accounts, and prescribes that the auditor shall report to the shareholders whether, in his opinion, the published balance sheet is a full and fair balance sheet. . . . and 'properly drawn up so as to exhibit a true and correct view of the state of the company's affairs,' this provision may be and frequently is evaded or modified by the articles of association, and audit certificates are not unfrequent which merely state that 'the balance sheet has been compared with the books of the company and found correct.' Persons giving credit to a company on the faith of such an audit may subsequently find that the position of the company is entirely different from that set out in its published accounts, although these may accurately represent the entries in its books."

Now this is a matter which touches the Chartered Accountants, as a profession, very closely. For if they acquiesce in this form of audit it means that they will be reduced from the position of accountants to that of counting clerks, with this further drawback, that the public will wholly misunderstand their position, and hold them responsible for matters of which *ex hypothesi* they know nothing. It is not for us to advise them upon professional policy, but we may fairly ask, as representing the public, that they should accurately define in which capacity they elect to serve.

These are not questions of any merely personal or particular import. They go to the root of joint-stock enterprise. A sense of security is the very soul of legitimate and profitable business in this kind. If audits mean nothing, then it were far better to abolish the legal necessity for them altogether. A false sense of security is far worse than none; and there would be something to be said for a system of complete freedom of trade and absence of control in joint-stock enterprise. For a system of legal control which is a delusion and a snare, there is nothing to be said. We have gone too far in the direction of control to go back at this time of day to a system of unrestricted licence to defraud or mislead. But if so, nothing is more urgent than to stop up the loopholes and increase the stringency of the law.

Mr. Mundella should, therefore, take prompt steps to bring his great experience to bear upon the preparation of a Bill for amending the Law of Public Companies.

---

(*To the Editor of the Westminster Gazette.*)

SIR,—I have read with much pleasure your able leader

entitled " What is an Audit?" and that which strikes me as being particularly pleasing is the recognition by you that a Chartered Accountant is not endowed with a superhuman faculty of appraising securities.

You ask most pertinently, " When a shareholder sees the certificate of an eminent auditor at the bottom of a balance sheet, what value should he attach to it? Is it worth everything, or anything, or nothing?"

To give a general answer to this question is clearly impossible. Each case must stand upon its merits, and upon the merits of the auditor who certifies, and on the wording of his certificate; and from these causes arise the unpleasant surprises which astonish investors and shake faith in the value of the work performed by Chartered Accountants in their capacity of auditors of joint-stock companies. That this should be so is, to say the least, unsatisfactory. The auditor's certificate ought undoubtedly to be a candid expression of opinion as to whether or not a true state of the company's affairs is disclosed in the balance sheet. Mere checking of the books with the balance sheet is, as you say, clerk's work, but when an expression of opinion is involved, then arises the value of the services of the expert.

Now, it stands to reason that it is only fair, both to the expert auditor and the shareholders, that the auditor should be placed in a position where he is free to use his unbiassed judgment, and I contend that under the present system of appointment auditors do not occupy the position of independence which this involves. True it is that the auditor is the agent of the shareholders, appointed by them in general meeting to check the accounts of the directors' stewardship, but it is equally true that the directors are also shareholders; and as a rule they and their friends constitute large voting power in the company, with the result that the auditor, instead of being in the independent position of a free agent, finds that he is under an obligation to the very men over whom he has been set as a watch; and in the event of a collapse, more often than not he is appointed liquidator, either under " voluntary " or " supervision " winding-up proceedings.

It is difficult, in the space which I hope you will allot me, to do more than foreshadow a remedy for this state of things. I maintain that the free and candid opinion of an expert is not only desirable but absolutely necessary. No amount of Government auditing will ever give us this; we, Chartered Accountants, must have our hands strengthened; and until our position as auditors has an official position given to it by law, the deplorable abuses so well known to us will not cease to exist. We cannot serve God and Mammon.

I am, sir,

Your obedient servant,

W.

*London, E.C., April 13.*

---

To the Editor of the Westminster Gazette.

SIR,—The question, " What is an Audit?" raised by you is

undoubtedly of great importance, but I submit Mr. Justice Vaughan Williams is wrong in saying it is a question to be dealt with by the Institute of Chartered Accountants.

The principle of admitting into an account moneys accrued due but not received has been sanctioned by Parliament in the Schedules to the Life Assurance Act, and constitutes the essential difference between a revenue account and a cash account.

The principle is also clearly admitted in the accounts of the Metropolitan Water Companies and Gas Companies annually presented to Parliament.

In the summary of Life Assurance Companies' Accounts for the year 1887 (p. 265, No. 37 of the year 1888) the item for outstanding interest figures for the sum of £1,656,956, and I submit unhesitatingly that no proper valuation, as required by the Life Assurance Act, could be made of a Life Assurance Company if the item, outstanding interest, were omitted.

I particularise this item because around it, if I mistake not, the main contention has arisen both in the Liberator and the New Zealand inquiries.

Whether sums outstanding for interest, or due to a company, are proper to be carried into the profit and loss account, and afterwards inserted in the balance sheet as an asset depends—emphatically depends—on an intimate and detailed knowledge of the operations of the company and the solvency or otherwise of its debtors. Such knowledge, I submit, can reside only in the breasts of the directors and officers of the company, and the duty of an auditor, however much he may be Chartered, must necessarily end when he has satisfied himself that the directors have examined, and in turn satisfied themselves that the assets are what they profess to be—*i.e.*, property realisable and available to meet the liabilities of the concern as represented in the balance sheet.

And having admitted accrued income as an asset, it is obviously necessary to make provision for possible losses, and here again the question arises, who but the directors and officers of the company, daily dealing with its affairs, can have knowledge sufficiently minute and intimate to settle the amount which should be set aside for this purpose?

The directors, not the auditors, are under the statutes penally responsible if the facts are mis-stated.

But few auditors are really independent, nor will they be until they are irremovable. An auditor differing from his board of directors, if the board be a strong one, is liable not to be reappointed by the shareholders if his action is likely to reduce the dividend or affect the market price of the shares. It then becomes a question of confidence in the board or in the auditors. And, unfortunately, too frequently the auditor, to save his bread and cheese, gives way, and protects himself by giving a cautious certificate and writing a letter of protest to the recalcitrant board of directors.

I venture to think it is to this aspect of the case the attention of the judge and the public should be directed, and not to the fact that items are included in the balance sheet which have not been received.

Dr. Dawson Burns has very accurately described the auditor's true function as that of a " watch-dog, careful to listen to any suspicious sound, able to bark, and perhaps even to bite, if necessary." But I have heard of such things as watch-dogs being drugged, and it is even possible that an auditor may be misinformed and led astray by the officers of a company, and against them he has, so far as I know, no remedy. I enclose my card for your information, but not at present for publication, and I think I shall be justified in signing myself as

AN ADMITTED AUTHORITY.

April 13.

---

*To the Editor of the Westminster Gazette.*

SIR,—The letter of your correspondent, " An Admitted Authority," is certainly an interesting and valuable contribution to the discussion of the question, " What is an Audit ? " but I am inclined to think that the true solution will be found more nearly to approach the views expressed in your article than those urged by your correspondent. Admitting, for the sake of argument, that, " an intimate and detailed knowledge of the operations of the company and the solvency or otherwise of its debtors," is essential to a satisfactory audit ; it must be borne in mind, as your correspondent remarks, that " the directors, not the auditors, are, under the statutes, responsible " for the facts stated in the balance sheet, and that the Auditors' duty, according to the statutes, is to report " whether, *in their opinion*, the balance sheet exhibits a true and correct view of the state of the company's affairs." It is certainly to be regretted if the plain, but difficult, duty of expressing an opinion on the crucial point in a balance sheet, the directors' valuation of the assets, has been avoided. Whether the opinion of the auditor is worth anything or not, is a perfectly distinct question, and I submit that the shareholders have it in their power to appoint as auditors those whose opinion they may think of some value. With great respect I beg to differ from your correspondent on the subject of the " dependence " of auditors. The ability and independence of Chartered Accountants is recognised by the ever-increasing demand upon their services and advice, and the experience of your correspondent must have been singularly unfortunate in this respect. Nor do I agree with him that the existing condition of things would be improved by making the auditors " irremoveable." Security against the appointment of incompetent auditors, and provision as to the scope and presentation of their report to the shareholders, are no doubt needed, and I believe that public opinion will come to see that the path of safety lies in that direction rather than in the establishment of a public auditor.

Yours obediently.

Signed)    ALEX. W. PAYNE, F.S.S.

# The Accountant

## THE ORGAN OF CHARTERED ACCOUNTANTS THROUGHOUT THE WORLD.

### (Awarded Silver Medal, Esposizione Italo-Americana, Genova 1892).

VOL. XX.—NEW SERIES.—No. 1012.     SATURDAY, APRIL 28, 1894.

## Leading Articles.

### THE VALUE OF AN AUDIT?

THAT what we have said in the course of our discussion upon this subject should suggest to Mr. HOVENDEN the idea that we are wishful to stifle any criticism with which he may be disposed to favour us is the last thing that we desire ; and we venture to think that any such conclusion is the last that will be drawn from our remarks by anyone who views the circumstances dispassionately.

Let us review the facts of the case. At the beginning of the year the *Pall Mall Gazette* started a discussion upon " The Value of an Audit," stating that " some reform in the present system of auditing accounts is not only desirable but essential," and asking " how the existing evils are to be remedied?" Mr. HOVENDEN followed up the matter by writing to the *Pall Mall* on the 17th January last, saying, " The answering of this question has occupied my mind for over a quarter of a century. I conceive there is *only one* remedy, viz., let the Government have an audit and valuing department. . . ." Reviewing the discussion at the time, we pointed out (1) that auditors are, at the present time, liable for any loss directly occasioned by their negligence (*vide The Leeds Estate Building and Investment Society, Lim., v. Shepherd*, L. J. Notes, 1887, p. 130);

(2) That no case had been made out against the efficiency of audits by professional accountants generally; (3) That no advantage could possibly be expected from an official audit that could not be better obtained by an audit by a competent professional accountant; and (4) That the real need of the day was the exhibition of greater intelligence, and perhaps even greater honesty, upon the part of shareholders and directors. We devoted three articles to the consideration of these matters, and after their publication our contemporary let the matter drop.

Shortly afterwards Mr. HOVENDEN wrote another letter to the *Pall Mall Gazette*, which our contemporary inserted early in March (nearly a month after its receipt), which—while mentioning our articles upon the subject—added nothing to Mr. HOVENDEN's previously expressed opinions beyond the remarkable statement that " There is not an institution, public or private, so ably conducted as our Post Office." It occurred to us that our contemporary was getting about tired of the discussion, and, accordingly, in our issue of the 10th March last, we stated that we should be pleased to afford Mr. HOVENDEN any reasonable amount of space in our pages if he really had anything more to say upon the subject. We reminded him (*vide* page 214) that we dissented from three assertions that he had advanced, and suggested that he should, in the first place, deal with them as follows :—

(1) That a more effective system of audit than that now usual would prove beneficial to the investing classes.

This requires to be dealt with somewhat precisely, showing that (*a*) ineffective audits are now general: (*b*) that the audit *per se* is at fault; (*c*) that a more effective audit is practically possible; (*d*) define " effective audit."

(2) That there are in the ranks of professional accountants no firms or individuals who can be relied upon to carry out an " effective audit." And

(3) That the Government could undertake to carry out an " effective audit" at a scale of fees within the means of companies to pay; and that such work, if undertaken by the Government, would necessarily be " effective."

Note here that Government would never undertake to be responsible for its own errors; also realize (and allow for) the fact that, as has been repeatedly proved, Government auditors are *not* infallible.

We then went on to say that this appeared to us to be a short statement of the case that Mr. HOVENDEN wished to prove; and that, if it would afford him any convenience, our columns were open to him for that purpose.

Since that date we have been favoured with three letters from Mr. HOVENDEN, occupying about six columns in all, none of which have advanced us an inch nearer to the points upon which we invited him to address us; and we submit that it is hardly remarkable therefore that our patience should be somewhat exhausted, and that we should describe Mr. HOVENDEN as " an adversary who so persistently refuses to come up to the scratch." Whether Mr. HOVENDEN " cares to enter on a controversy with an editor who so regards him " is, of course, a matter upon which we must leave him to please himself, but he can hardly suggest that the rebuke is not well deserved.

It must be admitted by all impartial observers that Mr. HOVENDEN has failed to make out the case which he entered upon our lists in order to establish, but it is not easy to perceive the connection between his failure to make out a case against Chartered Accountants *en masse* and his present attitude. Are professional accountants to be thrown over and replaced by official auditors, because *we* have not the grace to accept unquestioned the isolated views of Mr. HOVENDEN ? Or does that gentleman really think that our influence with the profession is so enormous that we could prejudice our readers against whatever intrinsic m˵rits his suggestions might possess ? The latter suggestion is a delicate compliment to ourselves, but it does not say much for Mr. HOVENDEN's opinion of the profession generally. The whole thing is too absurd. If Mr. HOVENDEN thinks he has a scheme that is worth anything, in the name of goodness let him produce it, instead of merely talking about it. For our own part we have promised him fair play, and we have given him more—forbearance. Has Mr. HOVENDEN any scheme to offer at all, or has he gone back to his original idea that " there is *only one* remedy ?"

Anent this question, we reprinted in our last issue some correspondence upon this subject which appeared in *The Westminster Gazette* after our leading article had been written. There is but little in it, however, that we have not already dealt with, but we must take exception to some of the remarks made by " An Admitted Authority " (?)

In the first place, we cannot admit that the auditor is not to be expected to have an opinion of his own, for the purport of his certificate should clearly be that he is of opinion that the accounts are correctly stated.  And secondly, we altogether dissent from the assertion that " few auditors are really independent " : this assertion has been frequently made of late (usually by anonymous critics), but it has never been substantiated, and is undoubtedly altogether misleading.  One aspect of the question which is unfortunately invariably overlooked in this outcry as to the value of an audit is the proportion that the failures and scandals we have experienced lately bear to the concerns which are flourishing and well-conducted.  The annual percentage of companies in liquidation is (including reconstructions) only about 6¾ per cent. of the total number carrying on business, while the number in which any complaint (justifiable or otherwise) has been made concerning the mode of audit is certainly less than one per cent., and in these cases the audit has, in a great many instances, been the work of irresponsible and incompetent amateurs.

## MR. F. WHINNEY, F.C.A., ON AUDITS AND CERTIFICATES.

Mr. Fredk. Whinney recently gave an address in his capacity of President to the Birmingham Chartered Accountants Students' Society on this subject. In the course of his remarks he said that an auditor's certificate should not be hastily given or without a proper examination of all the matters it purported to deal with. It should be based upon information obtained by the exercise of all reasonable and necessary care. In that he thought they would find the keystone to the whole

difficulties of an auditor.   Ignorance of commercial
transactions, of bookkeeping, want of skill in the examination of accounts, and insufficient remuneration were
no excuse whatever for a certificate which was inaccurate.   That had been  expressly decided  in courts of
law.    At the same time it was true the duties imposed
on auditors were not perfectly clear.  He thought they
might lay down as a principle that no auditor should
sign any Balance Sheet unless he believed it was true,
and he must take all reasonable means to  satisfy himself that it was true.   He thought it was desirable that
the public should really understand something of the
position and responsibilities of an auditor.  If they did
he thought they would see that it was very desirable,
in appointing an auditor, to have a man who really
knew what he was about, and was capable of judging
whether accounts were really true or not.   A Balance
Sheet should, as far as it was able to ascertain, correctly and faithfully represent what were the assets of
a concern.   Balance Sheets which were bad generally
erred in the assets being stated at an excessive amount.
He thought he could give them two or three hints so as
to enable them to exercise the requisite reasonable
care.   In the first place, as an auditor he should insist
upon books being kept by double-entry : then they
should be careful to check Balance Sheets out from the
books.   The checking out of Balance Sheets taught an
auditor a good deal of what had been done in the working
of the company whose affairs he was examining.  He
did not mean a mechanical checking, but a thorough
examination, which frequently enabled him to detect
anything wrong in the accounts.  An auditor should be
sure that figures represented facts, because the whole
object of an audit was to ascertain whether figures were
facts. Those few words represented the whole duty of
an audit.   It was necessary to be alive to the slightest
trace of fraud in the accounts; but he did not mean to
say that in checking accounts they were to suspect
everybody, and fancy every entry they saw was fraud.
They would, in conducting audits, occasionally come
across something that they did not like, and if a company was going to the bad there was sure to be something they would not like.    But in such circumstances
it was even better to insist upon their certificate being
a true  representation of the facts than that egregious
errors should be passed over.  If they had to deal with
something that was clearly wrong, his advice was,
" Don't pass it."  He was not speaking of very small
things covered by contingent funds, but anything that
was clearly and flagrantly wrong.   He was quite sure
that good auditors, men who had the courage of their
opinions, were of very great use in a company ; and
lirectors and officers who wished to do their duty did
  ot take offence at suggestions made by auditors if
   y looked upon them as safeguards.

## Liverpool Chartered Accountants Students' Association.

### AN AUDITOR'S DUTIES.

#### By Mr. J. MERRETT WADE, F.C.A.

(Being a paper read at a recent meeting of this Society.)

WHILST public companies and corporations in their regulations often define generally what their auditor's duties are, these definitions are sometimes vague, and the auditor is left very much to himself to decide what his duties are. Consequently, in many cases, especially where the auditors are honorary or non-professional, their ideas as to their duties vary very much.

On the other hand, there can be no doubt but that the public are growing more exacting than they formerly were. They expect more and more from their auditors. Directors themselves often confer with them, and defer more frequently to their advice as to the way in which accounts are to be stated, and shareholders now-a-days are often more satisfied by a specific statement from the auditor than by the report and accounts of the directors themselves.

These facts are very pleasing to an auditor for more reasons than one. They add dignity to his position, they minister to his vanity, and they enable him to attach an increased value to his services. But, on the other hand, they undoubtedly increase his responsibility.

An auditor is expected to do a great deal more than he formerly did.

He is often supposed to know more about a company's affairs than he ought reasonably to be expected to know. The Law Courts have attached responsibilities to him, and punished him for sins of omission as well as of commission ; and he has even been expected to act as a sort of general critic of the acts and accounts of the directors and managers of a company.

These facts all make it very desirable that some more general and explicit definition of an auditor's duties should be laid down than at present exists.

The nearest approach to anything of the sort is found in the form of articles of association recommended by the Limited Liability Acts; but these articles are not compulsory, and are often not adopted. In default of anything more explicit they may, I think, be taken as the nearest approach to a definition of an auditor's duties which we have. Auditors are here directed to report whether, in their opinion, the Balance Sheet is full and fair, containing the particulars required and properly drawn up, so as to exhibit a true and correct view of the state of the company's affairs, and also to report the result of any explanations called for.

For this purpose the books and accounts of the concern are placed at their disposal, and they can even examine the directors and managers as to the same.

Before they can sign such a report they must, of course, check and examine the books and accounts, satisfy themselves as best they can as to the actual existence of the assets and liabilities. and, in fact, go through all the usual routine of an audit, the details of which I will not trouble you with.

Two things, however, may be gathered from the foregoing. The first point is this—

That it is not the duty of the auditor to comment upon or criticise the management and conduct of a concern by the directors and managers.

He may think they have managed it unwisely or extravagantly, that they have bought and sold just when they shouldn't, but all this is no business of his as auditor, and he has no right to interfere with it. It is his duty to see that the result of such management is fairly and honestly set forth in the accounts he signs, so far as accounts are capable of setting the same forth, and here his duty ends. He is not an expert in the management of businesses, but only in accounts, and when the shareholders get a full and fair account before them of the state of the company's affairs—and the auditor is responsible for this—it is then the shareholders' duty to decide for themselves whether the persons they have appointed to manage their own affairs have acted wisely or otherwise.

I think it well to point out to you where auditors should draw the line in this respect, because if they cross it directors and managers will, very properly, think they are interfering unduly with them in the performance of their duties, and because, as I have already hinted, shareholders are getting very exacting in this respect. Often when a certain policy which, at the time, was not understood or not noticed by shareholders turns out unfortunate, they are apt not only to condemn the directors—which is within their rights—but to enquire : Why did not the auditors tell us of this at the time ?

Now, this is outside the auditor's functions—who has no authority to interfere in the management at all—and he should at all times avoid and disassociate himself from any responsibility in connection therewith. If he does interfere the chances are he knows less about the matter than the directors and managers themselves, and will only end by getting himself into hot water all round. Of course, if an auditor is actually consulted upon matters of business outside the actual routine of his duties it becomes a different matter, and he should then use his own judgment and experience as to the advice he gives.

The powers of directors and managers are usually defined, and if, in the auditor's opinion, they exceed their duties and do things they have no right to do, and which, according to the company's constitution, are consequently illegal, the question arises as to what is his duty in relation thereto. This may depend very much upon the particular circumstances of the case.

If, for instance, the accounts themselves do not disclose the irregularity, it seems to me that the auditor is bound to call attention to it, because if he passes the accounts as correct shareholders will be apt to assume that the transactions themselves of which an account is given are also correct.

If, on the other hand, the transactions are disclosed on the face of the accounts then the accounts themselves are correct, although they disclose transactions which are irregular ; and if the auditor is satisfied as to the accounts I do not know that there is any legal obligation upon him to discuss the nature of the transactions which they disclose.

It must, however, be borne in mind that shareholders may not be so alive to the fact that transactions so disclosed are irregular as the auditor is, and as they often place great reliance upon the auditor's certificate, instead of examining the accounts for themselves, a moral obligation may be thrown upon him to tell them plainly that he thinks the particular transactions in question are irregular, and why.

This is a very serious thing to do, but it is one of the things the public are more and more trusting auditors to see to, and if they accept the responsibility they at the same time increase their usefulness to shareholders, and their value financially ought to increase likewise. Cases, however, sometimes arise in which transactions takes place which, though irregular, are undoubtedly beneficial, and if disclosed, perhaps the less said about them the better. In these cases the auditor must judge for himself where his legal and his moral responsibility begins and ends.

I have called your attention to an auditor's duty with regard to the management of a concern generally, principally because a great deal has been said in the press lately with regard to the audits of some large concerns where gigantic frauds have been perpetrated. And this brings me to the second point—and, in fact, it is the principal one I wished to bring before you—that is, with regard to fraud.

Now an auditor is not a detective. There is nothing in the Limited Liability Acts or elsewhere, so far as I am aware of, which points to him in this capacity.

He cannot possibly be at the company's office all the time and watch each transaction. To do so he would require to keep a staff there almost as large as that of the concern itself, and to be remunerated accordingly. This is impracticable and absurd. He can therefore at the best only dog the footsteps of the thief, and sooner or later overtake him.

Of the many frauds which unfortunately take place from time to time perhaps the detection of only a few is due directly to the auditors, and the question is sometimes asked " Of what use are auditors as a protection from fraud if they don't stop or find out these things ?"

Even if frauds do take place in spite of audits and are not always first found out by auditors, it is very desirable that accountants should impress the public with these undoubted facts : that an efficient audit makes thieving much more difficult, and its cloaking up by any systematic falsification of accounts for any length of time almost impossible, and that the more systematic way in which books have to be kept and written up in consequence of an audit renders an early discovery—whoever may happen to be the discoverer—much more certain.

How many young men get into difficulties and are sorely tempted to rob their employers in the hope of being able to make it right again afterwards if they could see their way to do so by falsifying their accounts, with a fair chance of not being found out, and are prevented from yielding to the temptation by the knowledge that an auditor comes after them.

" Prevention is better than cure," and I venture to say, after a considerable experience, that I believe an efficient audit prevents more robberies taking place than is the number of these which do take place when no such audit exists.

Surely, this alone is a great boon to the public.

Again, the difficulty of thieving without the certainty of discovery almost immediately following is enormously increased. Many ways of cooking accounts so as to hide defalcations which might be resorted to with comparative impunity without a check, become useless in the presence of an audit, and a man must therefore be very clever and very unscrupulous before he attempts to hide his delinquencies from an auditor. Surely, it is a great protection to the public to know that an audit places so many obstacles in the way of fraud.

Again, even if the auditor is not the first to discover the theft, the regular system of check introduced and the fact that the books have to be kept well posted up to date to enable the audit to proceed, often lead to its early discovery by someone. And, again, it is almost impossible for any systematic fraud to take place, and be hidden in the books for any very lengthy period without it being ultimately discovered by a careful auditor, whereas in his absence it might be carried on for years.

It is very important that all these considerations should be impressed upon the public when frauds take place in spite of audits and auditors, and perhaps are not discovered by them in the first instance.

It is somewhat disappointing to an accountant who is as careful as he can be over his audits to find that, in spite of his care, frauds take place—now here and now there—and someone else is first to find them out ; especially if, when too late, he finds that if he had only done something which he didn't do and which, perhaps, he was under no obligation to do, he would have been the first " in at the death."

There is, however, no "royal road " to the discovery of theft, and he can only resolve to be more careful than ever in the future and to profit by each new experience, and console himself with the general considerations I have just set forth.

No doubt, when the question is asked of an auditor, " Why didn't you stop or find out this fraud ?" he mostly has a good defence and can show that it was through no fault of his. Yet, although this may be so, and although I have said he is not a detective, as a matter of fact, if he is the means of detecting a fraud he gains more credit than he would by proving that in half-a-dozen other cases it was no fault of his that he didn't find them out also.

The public do look to an auditor not only as one who satisfies them that acccounts are correct, but also as an important means for the prevention and for the detection also, as far as possible, of fraud ; and whether he likes the task or not the fact remains that the more succesful he can become as a means of preventing and of assisting to detect fraud the more valuable he will become to the public and, as a consequence, to himself also.

This all leads to the conclusion that, whilst the first duty of an auditor is to satisfy himself as to the accuracy and fairness of the books and accounts he examines, there is subsidiary to this, and it should always be borne in mind during the progress of his examination, the fact that possibly the very books and accounts which appear so correct may have been manipulated and altered in some ingenious way or other, so as to hide a theft or a system of fraud, or to misrepresent the true position of affairs, which is almost as bad.

If I have brought you to realise the importance of this, my principal object in these remarks is accomplished.

It is not of much use asking me " What particular course would you, as the result of your experience, recommend us to follow ? "

I confess that I have no patent for the discovery of thieves.

I can only offer a few general suggestions, and the first that occurs to me is this. Don't make up your mind that the staff in any particular office are honest, and say to yourself, " Here, at any rate, things are all right. I feel satisfied that I can take so-and-so's word as to that," but in every case where it is possible to verify verbal statements by actual evidence, go to the evidence itself.

Too often when things go wrong it is in places and with people we were the last to suspect, and I have come to the painful conclusion that if an auditor wishes to do his duty completely he had better do his work under the assumption that every one without exception whose work he has to check may possibly be a thief in disguise. Several other suggestions with regard to the details of an audit occur to me.

Be careful to verify the cash balance occasionally. I had a case where the cash balance shown in the Balance Sheet produced was very large, somewhere about £1,000, I think. This was a month or two after the date of the balance. I asked the reason, and the reply was that most of it was cash which had come in after bank hours, and would probably be paid in next day.

This was in a shipping office where a good deal of cash does come in from time to time, and the explanation was not improbable. I wasn't satisfied, and therefore asked for the Cash Book, so that I could trace the transactions subsequent to the balance.

I was told that the fair Cash Book wasn't written up, and then asked for the rough Cash Book. This was objected to as unusual, and that it was very rough and partly in pencil, &c. &c. I insisted and, as I began to suspect, found no trace of the money having been paid into the bank next day nor any other day, but the cash balance continued large. I then insisted upon the additions being made to date, and upon verifying that day's cash balance.

This was of course objected to, so I at once went to the principals, told them something was wrong, and insisted on the matter being cleared up at once, and we found a deficiency of about £800.

The many opportunities which exist for stealing large sums of cash in Liverpool are much greater than in London, owing to the antiquated system which exists here in many businesses of paying large accounts in cash in order to avoid bank commission on cheques.

I do not know to what extent it exists in other large towns, nor whether the bankers here are more to blame than the public, but I understand that in London it is almost unknown, and nearly everything there is settled by cheque. It is about time the provinces followed the example of the Capital in this respect. It has been followed in some trades here already to the manifest advantage of all parties, and has removed a temptation from the path of many tempted ones, and the sooner the rest of the community follow it the better for all.

Even the petty cash is worth attention. On one occasion I found it was £2 or £3 short. It was a. small matter, but instead of admitting that he had borrowed it the cashier tried to put me off with improbable explanations. I felt that he was untrustworthy and warned his principals. They wouldn't hear of it, and said the matter was too trifling to take notice of. Six months later they thought differently when they found the cash several hundred pounds short, and said they wished they had taken my advice.

Bank balances should be verified by direct application to the bank wherever possible. The mere comparison of the Ledger Account with the bank pass book is not sufficient. I have taken pass books to the bank, and they have pointed to red ink initial, as evidence that the book had been examined, but I have still asked them to compare it. I have reason to be careful on this point, for years ago I was examining the accounts of a private trust estate.

The banker's pass book was quite in order, and agreed with the Ledger, and I passed the accounts. Shortly afterwards defalcations were discovered, and we found that, after the pass book had been made up and balanced at the bank, the cashier had by means of very skilful erasures and the insertion of other figures, made it appear that he had paid in several hundred pounds, which had, in fact, gone into his own pocket.

The alterations had been so beautifully done that no ordinary inspection would have led to their detection.

The artist got five years, but I always regret that I didn't take that book to the bank to be verified. I would have had the credit of catching the thief instead of somebody else.

Another thing I would suggest to you is, always to object to erasures in books. If wrong figures have been inserted they should be ruled out, and the correct figures inserted above. If erasures are allowed they can be made after the auditor has ticked and passed the figures, which would at once make his check valueless, besides which they could be made use of to hide all sorts of frauds and cooked balances.

A common way of stealing is to receive money and not enter it in the Cash Book at all. The debt, although paid, thus appears in the Ledger as still outstanding. This process is repeated, and when the earlier debts begin to look suspicious, subsequent receipts are entered as on account of the earlier debts, and thus the ball is kept rolling. It must be very difficult for the thief to keep the game up long, for he has to give receipts, and the counterfoils have to be carefully manipulated on every occasion, or surely the auditor would be down upon him at once.

This shows that it is desirable to scrutinize counterfoils carefully, and to go over the outstanding book debts at each balance, and see whether they represent balances more than usually overdue, and if so to enquire as to why extra credit has been given.

Then, again, the discounts and allowances taken off both debtor and creditor accounts should be looked to. They may include sums which have gone into the wrong person's pocket.

Of course forgery is resorted to to cover numerous robberies, and it may be impossible for an auditor to detect this at the time, but this shows the necessity for great care when going over the final balances.

In the case of assets, for which securities exist, the latter should be inspected, their real value ascertained, and nothing should appear at greater than its real value unless the reason is given; for instance, the words "at cost price" might, in some cases, justify investments held which were not stock manufactured, or dealt in by the company.

Stock sheets, signed by some responsible official, should be produced for the latter. Book debts should be scrutinized in the manner already indicated, and especial care should be devoted to debts due from directors, managers, or other officials, which should be stated separately from trade debts.

On the other side, care should be taken to ascertain whether all liabilities up to the date of the account have been included. For this purpose, when going through the invoices, and checking them with the journals or day books, care should be taken especially in the cases of firms with whom regular running accounts are kept, to see that invoices have not been kept back, or burked for any particular month or other period.

Then, again, it should be seen that things go to their right account.

That things belonging to revenue do not go to capital, and vice versa.

That proper depreciation has been provided, etc., etc.

These matters, however, belong to the details of auditing, with which I did not intend to deal on this occasion.

My main object has been to call your attention to the growing importance of auditing, to the views of the public upon the subject, to the duties of auditors generally, and to the detection of fraud in connection therewith; and this I have endeavoured briefly to do.

## Auditors and Joint=Stock Companies.

*The Scotsman* of the 6th inst. has a contributed article on this subject which we reproduce, as follows:—" In the course of the investigations which have been dragging their weary length during recent months in the English Bankruptcy Courts, not the least interesting and instructive feature has been the public examination, among other officials of the companies in liquidation, of the auditors under whose sanction and upon whose certificate many of the misleading accounts had been issued to the public by the companies involved. The strenuous efforts made by these gentlemen, including some of the most prominent members of their profession in England, to justify themsel under the pungent criticisms of the Court and the Official Receivers cannot have formed very pleasant reading either for their professional brethren or for the investing public ; and the matter seems to call for more than passing notice. No sort of explanations which may be made after the event can remove the fact that great frauds have been perpetrated on shareholders and creditors alike without these having been discovered or at least exposed by the auditors until it was too late ; and it becomes necessary to ask whether, and in what way, the regulations applicable to auditors should be altered so as to make any recurrence of this state of affairs impossible in the future. Now, to arrive at a proper conclusion on this question it is necessary to bear in mind the position which the auditor of a public company occupies. He is a necessary consequence of the adoption of the principle of joint-stock trading. It being impossible for each of the partners or shareholders to examine the accounts showing the results of the company's working, they appoint a professional auditor for the purpose of safeguarding their interests, and particularly of exercising proper supervision over the actings of the managing partners, the directors. The auditor thus occupies an intermediary position between the shareholders and the directors ; in the matter of the accounts he is the agent of the shareholders, and to a certain extent he has power to bind them. In him also is placed the reliance of parties transacting with the company, as they are largely guided in these transactions by the accounts issued by the company, and docquetted by him as correct. It will thus be seen that the auditor's duties are of the highest importance, and the public are entitled to ask that the check imposed through his appointment shall be real and efficient. That in many cases it has not fulfilled these conditions is only too apparent, and the reason is not far to seek. The position and reputation of the auditors who have been found in default enables us to clear out of the way any question in the general case of fraud, so far as they are concerned. There can be no doubt that the examination which the auditors had thought fit to make did not disclose, in many cases, the frauds which have since been brought to light by the Official Receivers, and for this the shareholders, in a large proportion of companies, quite as much as the auditors, are to blame. Competition in this field, as in all others, has had its inevitable effect, and too often shareholders, in order to reduce expenditure and increase profit, have exercised a pressure in the matter of the remuneration of auditors which has proved a most unwise economy. That reduced fees should mean inefficient work is, of course, no excuse for the auditor ; but it supplies an explanation of his failure to detect in many cases frauds which have cost shareholders and creditors many times the amount of the saving effected by the reduction of his salary. In point of fact, that salary, instead of being a fair remuneration for work done, has rather formed a premium paid to him by the company for the risk incurred by him in appending his docquet to accounts of whose accuracy he was not absolutely assured. Such a state of affairs, of course, removes entirely the advantage and utility of the auditor's examination, and serious as the result may be, he is, perhaps, not entirely to blame should he judge as to the efficiency of the examination desired by the amount of the remuneration fixed by the shareholders by whom and in whose interests he is appointed. It is a matter for the shareholders themselves whether a thorough or a perfunctory examination is required, and their fixing an inadequate fee may very well be looked upon by the auditor as a tacit hint that an inadequate examination will be quite satisfactory, apart altogether from the consideration of the risk which he incurs should it afterwards appear that he has neglected to observe the provisions on the subject contained in the articles of association.

It is by no means, however, satisfactory in the interests of the public that a check which is practically the only one imposed for the protection of shareholders and creditors should be thus efficient or non-efficient merely as the conscientiousness of the auditor or the cupidity of the shareholders may direct; and the Legislature having, in the Directors' Liability Act of 1890, acknowledged and approved of the principle of State interference for the protection of the public in this department, there does not appear to be any good reason why this principle should not be extended, and auditors be made liable for the consequences of their neglect. The draft of the Act referred to, as originally submitted to Parliament, contained, as is well known, a provision which would have had this effect, but which, after much debate, was ultimately struck out. The clause referred to provided that if any person in any prospectus, Balance Sheet, or notice, made any false statement which caused damage to any person, the Court might, in case of winding-up, order such person to pay a sum of money by way of damages. As will be seen, such a clause, if passed, would have rendered not only auditors, but directors and other officials, liable for their misconduct or negligence; and it certainly seems a pity, in view of the revelations which have been made since 1890, that the clause as drafted was not incorporated in the Bill. There would appear to be little doubt that, if it were now introduced, it would be allowed to go through without much opposition.

It is outwith the scope of this article to discuss the effect of such a provision as regards directors and other officials, but as regards auditors, there seems little that can be urged against it. Unless they are willing to accept such a provision, there does not appear to be much that can be said in favour of their existence at all. They are appointed for the express purpose of detecting false statements, if there be any, in the accounts of the company, and if they fail to do so, there is no good reason why they should not abide the consequences. The clause quoted above appears to have been conceived in the most reasonable terms, the whole power in the matter being left in the discretion of the Court, a provision which would permit of the facts and circumstances of each case being separately considered. In the interests of the profession themselves, it would appear to be a desirable enactment. The foolish acceptance of appointments on terms however meagre would become impossible, in view of the risks involved in granting a docquet except after due inquiry; and to the public there would be the assurance, which has all along been absent, and which recent events have proved to be all too necessary, of the audit being full and satisfactory, and one upon which, without dubiety, reliance might be placed.

On reassembling on the Friday, Mr. THEODORE GREGORY, F.C.A. (President of the Manchester Society of Chartered Accountants), read a paper on

## THE RESPONSIBILITIES OF AUDITORS.

THE subject chosen for this paper is one which would require a treatise if it were proposed to consider it exhaustively. That, however, is far from my intention. The duties and responsibilities of auditors have been repeatedly discussed during the past twelve months, both by the press and by the public, and it has seemed to me that a conference such as this would be incomplete were it to be allowed to pass over without any expression of opinion on matters of such importance to the profession by those who are so intimately acquainted with the facts. At the request of the Council of the Manchester Society of Chartered Accountants, I undertook to write this short paper; but it is intended to be suggestive rather than dogmatic; to elicit opinion rather than to pronounce judgment.

In many respects the discussion that has taken place has been of advantage to the profession. It has drawn attention to the value of a properly conducted audit, and to the importance of the auditor being properly qualified, and no one here who has been in practice for the last fifteen years can doubt that the standard of efficiency has been raised very considerably during that period, especially when regard is had to the large increase in the number in the profession; while it is equally evident that much of the progress is due to the formation of the Institute of Chartered Accountants, and to the efforts of those local societies and students' societies which have sprung up in the principal industrial centres.

Very widely differing opinions are held as to the responsibility of auditors; and in this, as in other matters, much depends upon the point of view. The non-professional auditor appears to be sometimes satisfied by merely checking the castings of the balance sheet, and accepting the assurance of the secretary or cashier that everything is in perfect order (as in the case of the West London and General Permanent Building Society, where one of the auditors admitted that he did not make any examination of the Accounts, but trusted entirely to the honesty of the officials to do their work); while, on the other hand, the indignant shareholder would widen the responsibility of the auditor to an unlimited extent, demanding that he should undertake duties for the performance of which he would need, as has been pithily said, " to be endowed with a superhuman faculty of appraising securities in all parts of the globe, and to combine in his own person the entire knowledge of the whole city."

It should be clearly understood that Chartered Accountants

have no desire to evade responsibility; far from it; they fully appreciate the fact that theirs is a responsible position. If they were not prepared to accept responsibility, there would be little reason for their existence. It was in consequence of their recognition of the responsible nature of their duties that steps were taken some fifteen years ago by leading members of the profession to obtain a royal charter, one object of which was to ensure that those entering the profession subsequently should not only have a theoretical knowledge of certain subjects, tested by a preliminary, an intermediate, and a final examination, but should also have some years' practical experience in an accountant's office; and when, by the granting of a charter, the Institute of Chartered Accountants in England and Wales came into existence, disciplinary powers were obtained enabling the Council of the Institute to deal with any cases of professional misconduct which might arise among the members, and in other ways to maintain a high standard both of character and efficiency.

But though they are prepared to accept responsibility, it would clearly be an advantage that their responsibility as auditors should be defined, and the question at once arises by whom is it to be defined? There would appear to be an impression that the Institute of Chartered Accountants has laid down rules as to the way in which an auditor should perform his duties, and this view appears to receive countenance from some recent remarks which have fallen from the judicial bench. Although we must cordially recognise the compliment paid to the Institute by this appreciation of their efforts to increase the efficiency of the profession, it may be desirable, in order to remove any misapprehension caused by these remarks, to say at once that the Institute of Chartered Accountants in its corporate capacity has abstained from laying down any rules as to the manner in which an audit should be conducted, or as to the duties which an auditor should perform. It is a question worth considering whether the public would gain anything even if it were possible for the duties of an auditor to be strictly defined, as his investigation could then be more easily evaded; and if he had performed the prescribed duties, and yet had failed to discover malpractices which were in existence, it is doubtful if he would be liable for any loss occasioned by his neglect. So far as the details of an audit are concerned, each accountant decides for himself what plan he will adopt in each audit he undertakes, and though there may be substantial agreement in the main lines of enquiry adopted by accountants, these are varied according to the class of accounts to be audited, and according to the plan resolved on by the accountant who is conducting the audit as being the best adapted to that particular case. It is a question of custom rather than of rules, and whether the right course was adopted in any given case could only be ascertained by a comparison of what would be done by other accountants in similar cases, with the possibility of finding that different accountants took different views.

I have known a solicitor, when puzzled with a question of personal liability, ask "Can he be sued for it?" If we apply this method to the auditor, and enquire whether he can be sued for negligence in auditing, we very soon find that he has incurred a responsibility of a definite kind, and that if negligence on his part can be proved, damages can be recovered. The leading case on this point is that of the *Leeds Estate Building and Investment Company, Lim. v. Shepherd*, tried in 1887, before Mr. Justice Stirling, in the Chancery Division. Shareholders do not always remember, when criticising the conduct of an auditor who has come under their displeasure, that he has to be guided by the articles of association of the company whose accounts he is auditing, and that these articles not unfrequently limit his action. It should therefore be pointed out that in this case of the *Leeds Estate Company v. Shepherd*, Mr. Justice Stirling held that the auditors really entered into a contract by reason of the articles of association, and that it was the duty of the auditor to ascertain that the Balance Sheet contained the particulars required by the articles, and that it was drawn up so as to contain a true and correct representation of the company's affairs. Although primarily applicable to the case of the *Leeds Estate Company*, Mr. Justice Vaughan Williams is of opinion that the judgment does not apply to that case only, but that Mr. Justice Stirling was laying down general propositions. It is, therefore, worth our while to understand what the facts were in this first action for damages brought against an auditor.

The Leeds Estate Building and Investment Company, Lim., was registered under the Act of 1862 with special articles of association. By articles 79 and 80 the directors were authorised to declare a dividend upon such estimates of accounts as they might see proper to recommend, but no dividend was to be payable except out of profits. Articles 86 to 89 provided that the directors should cause true accounts to be kept, and should lay before the company once in every year a statement of the income and expenditure; and also a Balance Sheet in the form prescribed by Table B of the Companies Act 1862, or as near thereto as circumstances would permit. Then followed twelve articles relating to the auditing of the accounts, and providing that the auditor or auditors should examine the Balance Sheet with the accounts and vouchers, and should state in their report whether, in their opinion, the Balance Sheet was a full and fair Balance Sheet, containing the particulars required by the articles, and properly drawn up so as to exhibit a true and correct view of the company's affairs. The company carried on business for thirteen years, made no profit during the whole period except in one year, and went into voluntary liquidation in 1882. Dividends of 5 per cent. and upwards had been paid every year, and an action was finally brought by the company in liquidation against the directors, the manager, and the auditor of the company, to make them liable in respect of certain sums paid out of capital for dividends, and for fees and bonuses to the directors and manager respectively, which would not have been paid had there been no dividend. It appeared that the Balance Sheets were false and misleading, and contained fictitious items; and were framed with a view to the declaration of a dividend. They were prepared by the manager and examined by the auditor. In examining the Balance Sheets the auditor was not furnished with a copy of the articles, and he did not comply with their provisions. No account of income and expenditure was prepared, and the auditor's certificate was usually to the effect that he had examined the accounts and found them to be a true copy of those shown in the books of the company. The directors did not investigate the accounts, but trusted entirely to the manager and the auditor.

The result of the trial was that the directors were ordered to make good the sums paid out of capital; but it is with the auditor we are more particularly concerned. At the time of his original appointment he was a clerk in a bank, and received at first a fee of five guineas, and ultimately, a fee of 12 guineas per annum. In holding him liable in damages (along with the secretary) to the amount of the dividends paid out of capital, together with the fees and bonuses paid to the directors and manager, subject to the Statute of Limitations, Mr. Justice Stirling made the following weighty remarks: " It was, in my opinion, the duty of an auditor not to confine himself merely to the task of verifying the arithmetical accuracy of the Balance Sheet, but to enquire into its substantial accuracy, and to ascertain that it contained the particulars specified in the articles of association (and consequently a proper income and expenditure account), and was properly drawn up so as to contain a true and correct representation of the state of the company's affairs. It was no excuse that the auditor had not seen the articles of association, when he knew of their existence."

" To see that the Balance Sheet is a true and correct representation of the company's affairs." Here we have a very concise description of the duties of an auditor of a limited company, and one that we have no reason to complain of. That is a judicial definition of an auditor's duties.

Mr. Frederick Whinney, in a recent address to the Birmingham Chartered Accountants Students' Society, gave a still more concise description of the object of an audit. He said that the whole duty of an audit was " to ascertain whether figures were facts." That is an accountant's definition of an auditor's duties.

It will be observed that both authorities refer to the examination of the Balance Sheet, and not to its preparation, which is no part of an auditor's duty.

It has been stated by an influential financial paper " that the prevalent view among accountants as to an auditor's duty is that it consists solely in a call-over check of the figures put before him." I have given you the view taken by a representative accountant, one who worthily occupied for four successive years the office of President of this Institute, and who has deservedly great influence in the profession. It is evident that he takes a much more extended view of his duty. Take also, the views expressed at the Autumnal meeting of this Institute at Newcastle-on-Tyne four years ago, and you will find that speaker after speaker in the long and interesting discussion on Auditors' Certificates emphasised the importance of not merely seeing that the Balance Sheet agreed with the books of the company, but of being satisfied also that the books properly represented the position of the company. Another point was emphasised in that discussion, namely, that the work of the auditor should not be regulated

by the fee: that if the auditor felt beforehand that the fee was insufficient for the work, he should not undertake it. If, on the other hand, the auditor found, after starting the work, that the fee was an insufficient one, he should continue his audit just the same as if he had a sufficient fee.

It is evident, therefore, that Chartered Accountants are prepared to accept the responsibility as defined by Mr. Justice Stirling, of certifying as to the substantial accuracy of the Balance Sheet, and if it be charged against them that their certificates " suggest a lot and mean nothing," and that " the common form of certificate that ' the foregoing accounts agree with the books of the company, &c.,' does not, and is not intended to express any opinion as to the accuracy or otherwise of those books," I say in reply that the leading members of the profession have set their faces against any such practice as is suggested, and that if there is attached to a certificate of the nature referred to the signature of a Chartered Accountant with a reputation to lose, it should be evidence not only that the Balance Sheet agrees with the books, but also that in his opinion the books do properly represent the position of the company. If they do not, he should say so.

I believe that it will be to the advantage of auditors to magnify their office, and for members of this Institute to show the public that their certificates can be relied on; that it is not with them a case of simply adding up figures and fulfilling the letter only of the law, but that they form an independent judgment on the facts put before them, and express their opinion in unmistakable terms. If the members stand by each other, and they have the Institute behind them, it can be done, to the great advantage ultimately both of the public and the profession.

The Institute has been so frequently called on of late to make a pronouncement on the duties and responsibilities of auditors that it is evident the only communication made by the Council of the Institute to the press on the subject of auditing has been lost sight of, for it answered in anticipation many enquiries that have since been made. The letter is dated June 30th 1893, and was addressed to The Times and other newspapers; it is signed by Mr. Howgrave as Secretary of the Institute. After referring to the proceedings relating to the Liberator Building Society and kindred companies, it proceeds as follows:—" To prevent misapprehension on " the part of the public, the Council desire to point out that " an auditor has no concern with the administrative " management of a company, except so far as to see that its " operations have been within its statutory powers. The " duties of auditors must necessarily, to a greater or less " extent, vary with every class of business and with the " constitution of the companies whose accounts are under " review, but an auditor will fail in his duty if he does not " use reasonable care, such as the circumstances of the case " may allow or render necessary, to satisfy himself as to the " propriety of the figures contained in the books and Balance " Sheet. His certificate, unless he expressly raises objection " or limits the application of his words, must be taken to " imply that the figures of the Balance Sheet as audited " present, in his opinion, a true view of the position of the " affairs of the company."

That, I presume, may be taken as the well-considered and authoritative judgment of the Council.

Public opinion has been excited with reference to a few notorious companies, and conclusions adverse to the conduct of auditors have been formed from a too limited view of the facts. From the outcry that has been raised it might be thought that a large proportion of companies audited by Chartered Accountants had gone into liquidation, and that they had been wound up through some default on the part of the auditors. If regard be had to the number of companies whose accounts are audited I believe it will be found that those about which complaint has been made do not amount to one per cent. of the whole number, and many of these have not been audited by Chartered Accountants. I do not wish to underrate the importance of the interests involved in even a few companies, but, at the same time, their importance should not be unduly magnified. It is not proposed to abolish the police because thefts and burglaries occur in spite of their best efforts to prevent them, for it is recognised that but for those efforts the number of crimes would be vastly greater; and it is well to remember that, although fraud is not invariably prevented or discovered by the auditor, still there are few Chartered Accountants who have been some years in practice who cannot recall many cases where, in the course of an audit, fraud has been discovered; some, before much pecuniary loss has resulted, others, where the loss has been considerable—though the public hears little about them, because those most concerned have not proclaimed them from the housetops. The statement that fraud is prevented by the periodical examination of the books of a company or firm is often greeted with a scornful and incredulous shrug of the shoulders; but we have not heard that the police have discontinued patrolling the streets at night because a few burglars escape their vigilance, and the demand for the services of competent auditors has increased rather than diminished.

Even with regard to the accountants who were auditors of this small percentage of limited companies, and who are condemned for not having foreseen the crash, and taken the very heavy responsibility of making such a report as would have brought the business to a much earlier termination, there are two considerations to be borne in mind. First, that it is easy to be wise after the event. Facts look very different when suspicions are aroused (and still more so after liquidation has taken place) from what they do when there is every outward appearance of prosperity. Second, that an auditor must have evidence of an extremely convincing character to justify him in taking steps which will bring certain ruin on thousands, rather than allow the business to be carried on for some time longer with the probability of its difficulties proving to be of a temporary nature only.

Here let me pause for a moment to remark that the responsibility of auditors generally crops up in connection with companies rather than with private firms. This may, possibly, arise from the fact that, although the duties of accountants as auditors for private firms are of a very responsible nature, and this class of business reaches large proportions, the auditors are usually instructed by the proprietor of the concern, who is intimately acquainted with all its details and ramifications, and can, therefore, form a fairly accurate idea whether the business is financially sound: so that the audit is less onerous than when auditors are representing the interests of shareholders scattered all over the country, who know absolutely nothing of the business in which they have invested. If these distant shareholders supported and appreciated the services rendered to them, they have it in their power to place the auditor in such an independent position, with regard to the directors, that he would be the master of the situation so far as the accounts are concerned; but, so long as a dividend is paid, the shareholders usually support the directors and not the auditor when an acute difference of opinion arises; and the only result to the auditor is that he is not re-elected; both directors and shareholders, perhaps, expressing the opinion that he is too inquisitorial and is exceeding his powers. Possibly, the time may come when the Council of the Institute will take action to support Chartered Accountants who are not re-elected in consequence of the tone of their report, and, after due enquiry into the circumstances and being satisfied that the auditor has done his duty and done it with discretion, may take such steps as will effectually prevent any other Chartered Accountant accepting the vacant appointment. At other times, the shareholders regard the auditor's report with supreme indifference; as in an instance mentioned by a Chartered Accountant where, although attention was called on the face of a Balance Sheet to the existence of a separate report, no shareholder for three or four years in succession asked to see it.

I am tempted to enlarge on the duty of shareholders, for it might almost be said that auditors are what shareholders make them, but I must not further tax your patience. I will, therefore, only add that if shareholders were aware of how much the accounts of a company depended on the articles of association they would study the articles more than they do.

No auditor can afford to omit a careful perusal of the report of the proceedings against the auditors of the London and General Bank, Lim., especially the comments and questions of the judge; but, as Captain Cuttle would say, " the bearing of these remarks lies in the application of them"; and, as the case is still *sub judice*, I have only made a passing reference to it.

On the question of the criminal liability of auditors, much useful information is contained in the report of a case tried at the Manchester Assizes in March of the present year, in which the auditor of the Lancaster Building Society was charged with conspiring with the secretary to defraud the company by means of false Balance Sheets. The auditor, who was a bank manager, was acquitted. A detailed report will be found in *The Accountant* of March 31st.

At present there are very few decided cases to refer to bearing on the responsibility of auditors. Possibly, we shall have more material to judge from in the near future.

In conclusion, I would remark that it is impossible for an auditor to check in detail, in a few days, work which it has taken a large staff twelve months to do. An audit is really an examination by an expert in accounts resembling the diagnosis of a skilled physician. His wide experience and knowledge of affairs enable him by a careful examination to form an opinion as to the financial soundness of the business, and to say whether the Balance Sheet gives a truthful account of the state of the constitution. The expert may be mistaken, for he is neither omniscient nor infallible. Many a man has been told by a physician that he has not six months to live, and yet has survived for a score of years; but eminent physicians still have a large practice, and rightly so. Much depends on the experience, the judgment, and the character of the expert you have called in. He observes how the books are kept, suggests precautions against fraud, points out in what way the accounts can be arranged so that the working of the business can be facilitated and its operations controlled, and forms an opinion whether the liabilities are stated at too little or the assets put down at too much. Subsequent visits enable him to keep the accounts on right lines, if his advice be followed. If through negligence on his part loss is sustained, he is liable for damages. If he is not merely negligent but is guilty of wilfully shutting his eyes to the truth; if when the truth lay under his hand he abstained from finding it out, not from mere negligence, but from the wilful determination not to inquire then he may be liable to imprisonment. If he has been auditor of a company, and it is wound up, he may as an officer of the company, be examined as to the manner in which he performed his duties, and unless he has full notes of his audit to which he can refer, and an able counsel, it may go hardly with him. If through want of care on his part a dividend has been paid out of capital, he may have to refund as damages 50 or 100 times the amount of the modest fee he has been paid. If, owing to any report of his, a dividend has not been paid, and alarm is in consequence occasioned amongst the shareholders or customers, and the company comes to a premature end, he runs the risk of being sued for damages for having by his report caused the suspension of a concern which was perfectly sound. He is between Scylla and Charybdis, and needs a clear brain and a stout heart, for the responsibility of auditors is a reality; but so far as the members of the Institute of Chartered Accountants are concerned, I think I may safely say that they intend to face that responsibility, and to perform the duty that is laid upon them without fear and without favour.

---

Mr. FREDERICK WHINNEY, F.C.A. (London), proposed a vote of thanks to Mr. Gregory for the very able and interesting paper which he had just read. He need scarcely remind them how very important it was that the duties of an auditor should be properly performed. The public knew very little, indeed, of what an auditor's duties were, and what an auditor's certificate should be. He did not propose to address them at any length upon the subject, but he would simply say that, so far as he could see, it was an auditor's business to determine not merely the figures, but to see that those figures represented what he believed to be facts; and in making his certificate he was bound to exercise a reasonable care. If he were negligent in his work, then he would be responsible. What reasonable care he must use was a matter he must decide for himself, and if he decided it wrongly he might be liable to a judicial decision to the effect that he had not exercised the reasonable care he ought to have given. Mr. Gregory had spoken about legal definitions of audits. At the present time there had been two decisions as to audits and the responsibilities of auditors—the Leeds Building Society and the Oxford Building Society; but counsel learned in the law, and who held a very good position, had intimated their doubts as to whether or not the judgments, so far as related to the responsibility of an auditor in regard to the improper payment of dividends out of capital, could be upheld. He could not help thinking that the Institute should take up, and fight through to the House of Lords, if necessary, any case which again raised that point. The paper was one which would commend itself to them all, and which ought also to reach the outside public. He had, therefore, great pleasure in moving a hearty vote of thanks to Mr. Gregory for his able and interesting paper. (Applause.)

Mr. HUDSON SMITH, F.C.A. (Bristol), in seconding the resolution said they were very much indebted to Mr. Gregory for the thoughtful and able paper he had read, and he was cer-

tain they would all be happy to read it when they had copies of it put in their hands. (Applause.)

Mr. CHARLES BEEVERS, F.C.A. (Leeds), remarked that the case which had been emphasized by Mr. Gregory—that of the Leeds Society—was one in which he was interested. The Auditor of that Society, as stated in the paper, was a banker's clerk, a middle-aged man, and probably quite competent to perform his duties properly if he had consulted the Articles. He did not know why that gentleman resigned, but the directors appointed him (Mr. Beevers) in his place. At the audit he (the speaker) discovered that the Balance Sheet for some time had been improperly prepared and he refused to certify the one he was engaged upon. The directors held a meeting at which he was present, and pointed out to him that if the dividend was not paid there would be a run upon the society by the depositors, which would bring it down. He still refused to sign, and the Balance Sheet was issued by the directors with the recommendation for the payment of the dividend, but without an auditor's certificate. The shareholders met and he attended the meeting, and when the Balance Sheet was put before the meeting, and the dividend proposed, he informed them that the figures were false, that no dividend had been earned, and that if paid it would have to be paid out of capital. They would be surprised to hear, notwithstanding all this, that the shareholders passed it. (Laughter.) He was re-elected auditor, but he declined to accept the office—(applause)—and within a few months after that the crash came, and a liquidator was appointed. The rest they knew from the public papers, but there was a remarkable sequel to the case—his costs were about £25, but he never got paid. (Laughter.) He thought the meeting would be pleased to learn that the auditor in the case he had referred to was not a Chartered Accountant, but it was through the efforts of a Chartered Accountant that the disclosures were brought about. (Applause.)

Mr. BLACKBURN said that he had noticed in that morning's paper a report of their meeting of the day before which contained a statement which ought to be corrected. The sentence he would draw attention to was, that it was an auditor's duty to require the assets to be written down to the value they would have on the market if sold. The value of assets was a crucial point in any Balance Sheet, and he did not think the statement ought to go out to the public in that form, because it was not stated whether a going concern or not was intended. The difference between selling a going concern and a forced sale would be immense.

Mr. W. F. TERRY, A.C.A. (Liverpool) said that he followed the remarks relative to the point, and the words "as a going concern" were distinctly stated.

Mr. S. RALPHS, A.C.A. (Stockport) remarked that Mr. Whinney, in proposing a vote of thanks to Mr. Gregory, had used words indicating that it was the duty of an auditor to ascertain whether figures were facts. There was involved in those words perhaps the most serious responsibility which could devolve upon an auditor. It was a responsibility which troubled his mind considerably, because in his own practice and experience for him to be able to certify that figures represented facts in every item of the Balance Sheet would require an experience he did not think it was possible for any one to obtain in the ordinary operations of human life. He had had a large experience for the last thirty years in auditing the books of private concerns and public companies, in the district twenty-five miles round Manchester, embracing such concerns as the following:— Colliery companies, copper mining and smelting works, iron forging and iron founding, steam boiler works, English timber merchants, builder and contractor, cotton spinning and manufactures, chemical manufacturers, newspaper printing and publishing company limited, building society, wine and spirit merchants, &c. For him to be able to say that the whole of the assets set down in any Balance Sheet were of the actual value stated would be utterly impossible. Mr. Waterhouse had read a paper the day before, and had referred to the question of stock bearing a very important part in the matter of dividends. It would have come within the experience of most of them that dividends had occasionally been paid on the faith of the value of the stock, which value subsequently had been proved to have been very seriously impaired, and disaster ultimately resulted. Supposing Mr. Waterhouse had to deal with a large wine and spirit merchant's accounts, and assuming the stock contained 50,000 or 100,000 bottles of champagne, which were put down at all sorts of prices from 45s. to 150s., how would he be able to say that they represented that value. (Laughter.) He, the speaker, was not a champagne drinker, and he could not speak from experience, but he should imagine that any gentleman who tried to sample 10,000 bottles would have curious ideas at the end of it. (Laughter.) He had to do with a hatting concern, and possibly he might be able to form an idea of the value of a felt hat when he saw it in a finished state. But was he expected to be able to form an idea of all the various items used in the process, from the bale of raw wool and the packet of fur, down to the trimmings and all the various articles used—yet all these were involved in the valuation of stock, and the question of stock was a most serious one in regard to assets. (Applause.) That was a point which, he thought, required elucidating by the chiefs of the profession. He did not claim to have a tithe of the experience of some of the gentlemen around him, but it was a matter which, more than once, had very seriously troubled him. It had fallen to his lot on several occasions to refuse to sign Balance Sheets, and he believed he had more than once lost an audit in consequence of doing so. (Applause.) Whilst saying without egotism he, personally, would not sign a Balance Sheet if he thought it was not right to do so, they all knew it was a very difficult position for any ordinary human being to be placed in. (Applause.)

Mr. ALLEN EDWARDS, F.C.A. (Birmingham) would like the opinion of the Council, as to whether it was or was not contrary to public policy for the names of auditors to be inserted in the prospectuses of companies. On the one hand the public might have more confidence in a prospectus when they saw the names of a responsible firm of accountants as auditors; but on consideration, it seemed to him, that the principle was hardly correct, because, an auditor was supposed to receive his mandate, not from the promoters or directors of a company, but from the shareholders. If, therefore, the auditor received his mandate from the directors, he received it from those whom he was supposed to check and watch. Therefore, it was a very fair subject for the Council to consider, as to whether they would not in the future deprecate the members of this Institute allowing their names to appear upon the published prospectuses of companies.

MR. R. CASSON, A.C.A. (Ulverston), said that one of the last speakers had brought before them a very important part of the Auditor's duty. He knew from his own experience that, in dealing with stocks in trade of which they had little practical knowledge, they were to some extent in the hands of the managers of such businesses. At the present moment he was acting as liquidator for a small manufacturing concern where so recently as last June the stock was returned at some £1,400, and which he would now be glad to dispose of for £200. Another point which had not been touched upon was the question as to assets in the form of book debts. They would find a certain amount of book debts debited to various customers all over the country, and except from the period during which the accounts had been in existence they had no knowledge as to whether a large majority of them were good or otherwise. It might be that where a long credit—say six months—was given, the customer might be practically solvent when he gave the order; but perhaps, before the account became due, he might be insolvent and unable to pay it. Therefore, neither the auditor nor any one could say what would be a proper sum to take for the book debts.

He thought there was considerable difficulty in ascertaining really whether figures were facts. He had experienced that difficulty many a time in a small way, and if Mr. Whinney could point out a general system by which they could make figures facts it would be of great benefit to everybody.

Mr. GERARD VAN DE LINDE, F.C.A. (London), had only one remark to make on this very interesting and excellent paper. He would call attention to the remark which ran " Unless he has full notes of his audit to which he can refer, and an able counsel, it may go hardly with him." He was sure Mr. Gregory would not go to the full length about the notes, putting down everything. If queries had arisen, and those points were examined and explained at the time, he did not think they should load their Note Book with them, otherwise the Note Book would become a Journal.

Mr. F. TAYLOR, A.C.A. (Birmingham), took some interest in what had been said as to that part of the assets which represented stock. He considered that a Chartered Accountant could not take upon himself to possess those omnipotent powers which auctioneers and valuers seemed to claim. They could not be presumed to attempt to value certain assets. He knew very little of the value of various things, and could only see where the stock appeared to be carried out in the stock books on a proper basis, and to some extent he was in the hands of the valuer. Accountants could not be held responsible for that, and therefore they ought not to trouble themselves with the responsibility in every case of valuation. He would venture to suggest another wording for a certificate. They might say somewhat in the language of the liturgy of the Church of England— " We have not left undone those things we ought to have done, and we have not done those things we ought not to have done." (Laughter.)

A MEMBER said that most of them must feel the absolute impossibility of making themselves responsible for the accuracy of the stock. In certificates which he had made he had in cases inserted some such words as these, " This certificate is made subject to the accuracy of the stock, which is certified as correct by So and So." Having done that, he had absolved himself from all responsibility, and had not left undone one of those things he ought to have done.

Another MEMBER said, with regard to the stock, it had been suggested that it should be taken by a specialist. That required the consideration of the Council. He was interested in several concerns where it was difficult to ascertain the exact values of stock. They all knew that officials of companies were very apt to value stocks at a high figure, and it was difficult for accountants to check the valuations of officials. He thought it would be very much better if stocktaking could be done by some expert, and that the accountant might say that this expert's certificate was in proper form. With regard to other assets set out in the Balance Sheet, if the accountant had any doubt as to their value, an expert should be called in periodically. It would be better in a going concern if the assets could be re-valued, say every five or six years. There was no doubt very grave difficulty in valuing the assets of a going concern. He knew many cases where the assets had been bought when prices were inflated, and probably in times of depreciation if they were re-valued there would be considerable loss, and it was questionable whether for a period any profit could be paid by such companies. He had simply made these remarks that the points might be considered, and probably by their next annual meeting they might have some discussion on those matters.

Mr. A. NIXON, F.C.A. (Manchester) said there was one point on which they ought to make themselves clear, and that was with regard to the words " Examined and found correct," on the Balance Sheet. He believed the outside public now attached considerable importance to that point. They relied upon Accountants, as professional men, being satisfied that the stocks were of the value stated in the Balance Sheet, and yet they learned that morning that they were not able to do these things. Therefore, it ought to be made clear that they did not take the responsibility of that, and to get rid of this the plan would be to have the stocks certified by responsible people before they were submitted to the shareholders. (Applause.) He thought the Council might make some statement for the guidance of the Members, as to the means of letting the outside public know that they did not care to say " examined and found correct" when they had any doubts in their minds as to the value of the assets.

Mr. W. H. Fox, F.C.A. (London) remarked that the last speaker had referred to the verification of the stock list by some official as if it were some new idea, but surely it was quite an old one. (Hear, hear.) Mention had been made that the appointment of the Auditor by the promoters was not satisfactory. Of course, an auditor might sometimes be appointed by promoters, and sometimes on the recommendation of directors, but surely it was not suggested that in either case the auditor would not do his duty towards the shareholders. (Applause.)

Mr. W. F. Terry, A.C.A. (Liverpool), thought that the introduction of the names of eminent firms into a prospectus was very likely to influence people in taking shares. Without mentioning any names, were those of some eminent firms in Liverpool attached to any particular prospectus, no man would consider that that would bias them in regard to their own action, but he did maintain it would have a very important effect on the minds of the people to whom the prospectus went. That was therefore a matter well worthy of consideration. With regard to the certificate of assets, it had been said that they ought not to take the responsibilities upon themselves they were not fitted for, and that by taking all the responsibilities upon themselves they might bring themselves and the profession into ridicule. The last speaker had said that a previous speaker referred to the matter as if it were his own original idea, but he did not think he had intended them to assume that the idea was his own. It had been mooted already in *The Accountant* some time ago, and he saw at that time a very important article in a Liverpool paper under the head of " Auditors and their responsibilities." He replied to that article, saying that auditors very often put their names to Balance Sheets containing stocks and valuation of which they had little knowledge, and suggested it would be very much better if other courses were adopted. Where there was a stock of which they had no knowledge, they should require a proper certificate by someone who had that knowledge. The right value of the property was a very important matter. He quite agreed that it was necessary to have assets taken in a Balance Sheet at their proper value, but he would not permit the valuing of assets at their value without allowing for depreciation. It would be better if assets were treated in the Balance Sheet by the certificate commencing to say " We put in the value of these not for sale as a going concern at so-and-so," putting so much for stocks. Then there were other things. There was the question of deeds, which would be more properly supervised by a solicitor, and his certificate given in some cases. A gentleman had said that it was his practice to make a remark against those debtors who had been long outstanding. He would give one illustration in regard to that. Some five or six years ago he was called upon to audit the accounts of a tradesman in Liverpool, whom a gentleman proposed to join, and put in £1,000 or £2,000. The tradesman said that his affairs were in a flourishing condition, that his assets consisted principally of book debts. He, the speaker, first of all checked the books and the Balance Sheet, and found it right. He then turned his attention to the book debts and found that several debtors had not paid anything for a considerable time. He therefore made a brief note of each of them, and the result was that the matter did not go through. (Applause.) The tradesman said that his Balance Sheet showed such and such book debts, but at the same time it was clear that some of these were of little value if the debtors had paid nothing for the twelve months previously.

Mr. Adam Murray, F.C.A. (Manchester), said that in listen-

ing to Mr. Gregory's paper they must all have appreciated the points raised by him, and he thought a few of them were well worthy of comment, even if only of approval. He was sure they would all agree as to Mr. Gregory's view in desiring to widen the responsibility of the members of the profession, and also his desire to magnify their office. These were views they had frequently heard not only among themselves but from the public, and some of them might remember that on the occasion when they were received by the Mayor of Newcastle four years ago, he spoke very strongly on that point—that they ought to make themselves responsible and not limit their responsibility in any way. A distinction seemed to have been drawn between the preparation of the Balance Sheet and the certificate of audit. He had not been able to follow the difference, because it seemed to him that if they approved a Balance Sheet they adopted it. He thought Mr. Gregory had also said something as to their action being limited by Articles of Association, but he did not quite remember any case in his own experience where that was so. As to criminal liability, there was one very important case in Lancashire—that of the Northern Counties of England Fire Insurance—where the Directors and Auditor were charged with conspiracy, and where he thought one or two of them were imprisoned. That was before 1880, and the granting of the Charter. As to the case of an auditor not being re-elected, he was concerned in a matter many years ago where he refused to certify to a Balance Sheet, and it was sent out without any certificate. His objection was that there had been exchange of bills and financial operations which were unstable, and which might have gone on to a greater extent than they did. The result was that in three months the company lost many thousands of pounds. As to the examination of auditors in Court, he thought they had not much to fear from the cross-examination or the comments of judges, whether they had made notes or not, if nothing was brought home to them in proof of negligence. In important audits, of course, they would make notes of anything special, but in ordinary cases he apprehended they did not make lengthy notes where there was nothing seeming to call for any special attention. As to Mr. Allen Edwards' point about auditors having their names on prospectuses, he thought a distinction might be drawn between the case of businesses which had been transferred, and where accountants gave a certificate of the results of the business, and were perfectly satisfied and willing to be auditors of the new company. It was for accountants individually to see for themselves whether they chose to take the responsibility of their names being on the prospectuses of new companies which were somewhat speculative. At the same time, there was no need that the names should be on the prospectus, for the appointment might be made by the shareholders at the statutory meeting.

Mr. T. Smith, A.C.A. (Hereford), remarked that a gentleman on the opposite side of the room had stated that during the past 15 years he had been experiencing a very great difficulty in certifying as to figures being facts, and dealing with the question of values. Might he be allowed, as one who had been in practice for 44 years, to say that he had never certified figures unless they had been facts, and he had never acted as a valuer.

Mr. Frederick Whinney, F.C.A. (London), said that exception had been taken to the phrase that " figures should represent facts," but surely no one would venture to say that figures should represent the opposite of facts. In giving a certificate they had to deal with figures most of which represented facts. Some of these facts could be certified at once, if they were facts. They did not intend that figures should be fictions. As to valuations, there were certain things on which one could form an opinion, and certain things on which one could not very well do so. They might take the stock in trade, and ascertain whether it was in accordance with the stock list, but even there they could not stop, because they must see whether the stock had been taken on the same lines at the end of the account as at the beginning. They must to a certain extent form an opinion as to value. It should be remembered that an auditor's certificate was an expression of opinion

(Applause.) They would permit him perhaps to call their attention to the only form of certificate he believed laid down by Act of Parliament. That was in the Bank Act of 1879, and the provision was shortly this: "The auditors shall make a report and state whether or not in their opinion the Balance Sheet is full and fair, and correctly represents the position of the company according to the books." The duty of an auditor was to give his opinion as to whether or not accounts were correct, and he could not do that if he allowed figures to represent fiction. (Applause.)

Mr. DAVID CHADWICK, F.C.A. (London), said that thirty years ago, as an accountant largely connected with Sheffield, he persuaded all interested that in the case of a certificate of stock an expert opinion should be called in. He was then acting as auditor for Sir John Brown, of Sheffield, for Mr. Cammell, and others, who all agreed that it was impossible for an auditor to certify that a Balance Sheet was correct, when the valuation of assets was out of his line altogether. He held that an auditor was to a large extent responsible when he put his name to the formula "Audited and found correct." It really meant that the valuation on which the Balance Sheet was made had been correctly done. Now what he ventured to ask was that the accountants there assembled should consider the whole question as to whether they should not rigidly revise their certificates, and whether they ought not to require in every case, where they had not the means of ascertaining the facts, the aid of an expert, whether a stockbroker, an ironmaster, a manufacturer, a cotton spinner, or a shipbuilder. He had ventured to put these views forward when he was President—he was almost afraid to say how long ago—of the Manchester Institute of Accountants, before the Institute was established. He would like them to take the matter up, and to show that accountants were not afraid or ashamed of the responsibility of the certificate which they gave. (Applause.)

The PRESIDENT was sure that they had had a most interesting discussion upon the question of Audits. There was one thing at all events they all had admitted—viz. that audits involved a very great and serious responsibility, and he hoped the public at large would not only be made aware that these responsibilities existed but that accountants were prepared to undertake them. He trusted, however, that the results of the ample discussion they had had would cause them, if possible, to be even more guarded in the future in the mode in which audits were conducted. He would not trouble them further, except to say that be would commend to their serious consideration whether, where they found one of their professional brethren, whom they believed to have done his duty, had been rejected from his office by the directors and shareholders, any other member of the Institute should accept the post?

The vote of thanks was then put to the meeting and unanimously carried.

Mr. GREGORY returned thanks, and said he was very gratified that his paper had led to such a useful discussion. With regard to audit notes, what he had in his mind was the desirability of making notes of the queries which occurred in going through the audit and clearing them up afterwards. Mr. Murray had referred to limitation by Articles of Association, but he thought he had in his mind when he used that phrase the distinction drawn between profits earned and realized in the Articles of Association. In a case which had occupied a good deal of prominence in the Courts lately—that against the *Westminster Gazette*—a great deal turned on the question whether profits had been earned or realized. In that case they had not been realized, but there was a specific article giving an interpretation of the phrase. As to the question of the stock, he wished to emphasize what Mr. Whinney had said. The certificate was the opinion of the auditor, and one could not always call in an expert. (Hear, hear.) The auditor could take the best means of ascertaining that the stock had been taken by experienced people and on a proper basis. (Hear, hear.)

A paper on "Consulting Chartered Accountants" was read by Mr. Francis W. Pixley, F.C.A., and contained suggestions of considerable originality. It was submitted by Mr. Pixley for the consideration of the profession only.

A cordial vote of thanks was accorded to him on the motion of Mr. J. J. Saffery, F.C.A., seconded by Mr. J. Hudson Smith, F.C.A.

The PRESIDENT said his official duties were now at an end, but before quitting the chair he felt that they ought to pass a vote of thanks for the handsome reception given them by their brethren in Liverpool. (Cheers.) Mr. Harmood-Banner deserved their utmost thanks for the time he had given and the courtesy he had displayed. (Cheers.) Then thanks were also due to Mr. Jackson, the Hon. Secretary, and to Mr. James S. Holt, one of the most genial and hardworking of men he had ever had the pleasure of knowing. (Applause.) Their friend Mr. Mounsey also had been constantly at their disposal, and had done very much to assist them in the duties they had had to discharge. He would therefore propose, "That this Autumnal Meeting of the Members of the Institute of Chartered Accountants in England and Wales desires to place upon record its hearty thanks to the Liverpool Society of Chartered Accountants, to its President, Mr. J. S. Harmood-Banner, to its Hon. Secretary, Mr. Jackson, to Mr. James S. Holt and Mr. W. E. Mounsey, Junr., the Hon. Secretaries of the Reception and Entertainment Committees, and to Mr. Finney, the Chairman of the Dinner Committee, for the cordial invitation given to it, and the admirable arrangements made for its convenience, comfort and entertainment." (Loud cheers.)

The VICE-PRESIDENT seconded the resolution, and said he had had the privilege of attending all the Autumnal Meetings held since the granting of the Charter in 1880. He felt sure that the meeting they were now holding had been as successful, if not more so, than any of the gatherings they had hitherto held. As they grew in numbers the Autumnal Meetings must naturally increase in size, and the greater was the responsibility and work thrown upon the local committees. The Liverpool Society had done its work in such a way that it would be difficult for another town to come up to it, and certainly impossible to excel it. (Applause.)

The motion was put and carried by acclamation.

Mr. HARMOOD-BANNER, in replying, said he was almost overwhelmed by the manner in which the vote of thanks had been received. They had endeavoured to do their best, and he hoped they would forgive any shortcomings. They in Liverpool would remain wiser men for the visit, and he hoped that those who went away would also appreciate the papers that had been read. He hoped also that the public would value what had been said and done. (Applause.)

Mr. T. W. REED, F.C.A. (Liverpool), moved "That the best thanks of this meeting be given to Mr. C. Fitch Kemp for his able and courteous conduct in the chair." (Cheers.)

The resolution was seconded by Mr. R. S. BLEASE, F.C.A. (Liverpool), and cordially received.

The PRESIDENT, in reply, tendered his warm and grateful thanks for the reception that had been given to the resolution just passed. He felt, in coming there, thoroughly conscious of the responsibilities and duties connected with occupying the presidential chair, and that if he were rewarded by the assurance of the members present that he had done his duty properly and well it would be a source of great satisfaction to him. One thing he would say, namely, that he had been most earnestly supported by every member of the Institute. All the advice of those who had occupied the chair in the past had been at his disposal; whilst he had been supported in the chair in a manner which he should never forget. He had made the acquaintance of many brother members of the profession, which would, he hoped, form a bond of union between them as long as life might last. He could assure them that if he could be, in any future part of his career, of service to any member of the Institute it would be his pleasure and pride to tender them his best services. (Cheers.) He would also like to place on record their high appreciation of the courtesy they had received from the Lord Mayor of

Liverpool, and for the convenience and comfort of the chamber in which they had met. (Applause.)

The proceedings then terminated.

---

In the afternoon parties were personally conducted over the steamship "Lucania" (Cunard Line), and over the grain warehouses at Waterloo Dock, a number of members having previously taken train for Northwich to view the Salt Union Company's mines. All expressed themselves very pleased and highly entertained.

---

### THE TRIP TO MANCHESTER.

On Saturday a great number of the members present availed themselves of the arrangements made to proceed on the Manchester Ship Canal to Manchester. A special train took the members to Warrington, whence they embarked on the steamship "Magnetic," kindly placed at the disposal of the members of the Institute by Messrs. Ismay, Imrie & Co., and made the voyage up the Canal from that point. The members on leaving the steamer proceeded to the Grand Hotel, Aytoun Street, and there partook of an excellent luncheon, on the invitation of the Manchester Society of Chartered Accountants, Mr. Theo. Gregory, F.C.A., presiding.

After a most substantial repast the President (Mr. Gregory) proposed the Queen, and this toast having been duly honoured,

Mr. ALDERMAN CLAY proposed "Success to the Institute of Chartered Accountants." The Society, he said, was a very important one. He found that their Charter was granted by the Privy Council in 1880, while their roll of Membership now exceeded 2,000. At the same time he believed the general public did not know very much about the Institute. He looked, however, upon them personally as being one of the most influential and important bodies that existed in this country, to whom many widows and orphans were largely indebted for their care, ability, and trustworthiness in examining and testing the accounts of public companies. The Institute had been established on a thoroughly sound basis, and he trusted they would maintain the position they had gained as reliable scrutineers of public and private accounts. (Applause.) In fact, he wished that all public companies would open their books to the members of this Institute, and pay them for audits in a proper manner. His experience was that auditors were often poorly compensated for their work. (Applause.) An efficient audit of the accounts of the Manchester Corporation was worth double the money paid for it. He would therefore appeal to the members of the Institute to be earnest in their work and to remember the grave responsibility that rested on their shoulders. (Cheers.)

Mr. C. FITCH KEMP (the President) replied. He thanked Mr. Alderman Clay for the manner in which he had proposed the toast, and the Manchester Ship Canal Company for the trip along that great waterway. Referring to the Ship Canal he said that London people had assisted very considerably in its completion. He did not think his metropolitan friends anticipated very early or very large dividends from the undertaking. They wished well, however, to the enterprise, and while hoping it would benefit Manchester, they did not believe it would injure the prosperity of the great city of Liverpool. (Applause.) As Chartered Accountants he believed the public looked to them with confidence. In this Institute the public had a body of trained and educated gentlemen, who were conscious of their responsibilities, and who were prepared to discharge them faithfully and in a manner which was satisfactory to the public. (Applause.) The public might therefore rest assured that their interests would be safeguarded. Chartered Accountants were all bound together by ties of sympathy and regard; they were all qualified men, and he hoped to live to see their important public position still more widely recognised. (Cheers.)

Mr. G. VAN DE LINDE then proposed "Success to the Manchester Ship Canal."

Mr. J. K. BYTHELL, who replied, said that Chartered Accountants were closely allied with underwriters. He had no doubt that some of them had heard that the Canal was not navigable for large ships, but they had seen for themselves that day that such a statement was not correct. It was a perfectly safe and navigable canal, and there was no need to charge extra premiums on vessels coming to Manchester. He, as the chairman of the company, recognised the uphill task they had before them. It was not an easy matter to divert traffic from its accustomed routes, but they were all working with the conviction that they would succeed with their endeavours at last. They all knew there was no royal road to learning, and certainly there was no royal road to securing full traffic along the Manchester Ship Canal. At the same time, they had the unshaken belief that in time they would achieve the success which they all desired. (Applause.)

Mr. C. FITCH-KEMP next proposed the health of Mr. Theodore Gregory, the Chairman of the Manchester Society of Chartered Accountants, which was drunk with enthusiasm, and Mr. Gregory having suitably replied, the proceedings terminated.

*The Value of an Audit.* We reprint below, from the columns of *The Western Press*, an article that bears able tribute to the advantages that may reasonably be expected to accrue from the appointment of a professional auditor. The suggestion that Chartered

Accountants might " draw up a statement of the duties that belong to an audit " has been frequently shown in these columns to be impracticable, and, moreover, it was not suggested that this point should be considered by a Royal Commission. The suggestion made was that a Commission should take evidence upon such questions as the meaning of " Reserve Fund," etc. ; and, if found practicable, prescribe form of Balance Sheets for general use.

#### "AUDITED AND FOUND CORRECT."

The subjects discussed at the Conference of the Institute of Chartered Accountants yesterday are of concern to everyone who has anything to invest. After the Liberator crash, the ethics of auditing were much discussed, and the language used by a reverend gentleman who had been auditor of one of the unfortunate companies was naturally criticised very severely. For he had told the shareholders who relied upon him that he was the watchdog who would guard their interests, and when they found that their interests had not been watched, they were much incensed. But now that so much time has elapsed that controversies concerning the Balfour group have begun to cool, it may not be out of place to suggest that the shareholders themselves, who appointed a clerical auditor, when they might have appointed a professional one, were most to blame. Wisdom will not have been gained by experience if, as the result of recent disasters, investors who have money in concerns that are more or less speculative, and that are under the control of men of considerable business capacity, do not insist that the accounts shall be audited by a member of a recognised and honourable profession who has given proofs of capacity and guarantees for integrity. The amateur auditor is often the unconscious ally, or, in other words, the blind dupe, of the dishonest director, and after the law has done its best to protect the public against dishonest enterprises, the investors may nullify these efforts for their own protection by omitting to select as auditors men who are thoroughly competent of undertaking a very serious and responsible position. The auditor is supposed to be, and he should be, a guarantee to the shareholder that the statements issued by the directors are correct. The remark was made at Liverpool yesterday that it was immaterial whether he is appointed by the directors or not, and that is obviously so when he is a man of high character. But at the same time it is better in most cases for the theory to be adhered to by which the auditor is the caretaker of the interests of the shareholders, many of whom, as a gentleman at Liverpool remarked yesterday, are people having but little knowledge of business. It would be interesting to learn if it were possible, how many, or rather how few, of the average investors in joint stock undertakings give any sort of study to the Balance Sheets with which they are favoured. Many men who have the capacity have not the time to do more than hastily scan the columns that are nothing more than a source of bewilderment to the non-business investor, and all alike regard the signature of the auditor as an endorsement of the statements issued by the directors. This idea exists even when it should not exist. Men who know the value of the time of a first-rate accountant are often amazed at the smallness of the remuneration which some companies offer their auditor. They are not, apparently, ready to pay for the time and the skill that a thorough investigation of all the details of the Balance Sheet would demand, and there are many shareholders who have not

yet realised that an inadequate fee to the official who is expected to exercise a check upon directorial Balance Sheets may be a disastrous form of false economy.

What is the audit shareholders have a right to expect ? Mr. Fitch Kemp, the President of the Institute of Chartered Accountants, laid it down yesterday as a doctrine that no Chartered Accountant is justified in attaching his name to a Balance Sheet unless he is reasonably satisfied that such Balance Sheet conveys to the shareholders a true and accurate statement of the position of the company, and that if he feels in doubt he should not sign the Balance Sheet without bringing the doubtful matter before the shareholders. This is taking a very high standard. No investor could possibly ask for more than this, but it is certain that many auditors do not attain to this counsel of perfection. If they all agreed to do so, however, many reports would be less glowing than they are, and some dividends would be less—to the ultimate advantage of the shareholders. But the question certainly arises whether it is the duty of the auditor to carry the doubts of which Mr. Fitch Kemp spoke to the region of directorial policy. It may be conceded that it is the duty of an auditor of a bank, for instance, to satisfy himself that the reserve capital is invested in the securities mentioned, and that all the documents that have been submitted to him are faithfully described in the statement issued to the shareholders. But is it possible for him to test the usual declaration, " after making allowance for bad and doubtful debts ? " Is it his business to investigate every advance or security, and to form an opinion as to the wisdom of the management in allowing credit ? Have the shareholders any right to expect that he will check and criticise the policy of the Board, as distinguished from testifying that so far as documents are concerned, the statements of the directors are correct ? These are questions which have, no doubt, often given anxiety to conscientious auditors, and the evidence that has been given in some notable cases of financial failure shows that some auditors have not taken the view of their duties which is held by Mr. Fitch Kemp. It is not a light matter for an auditor, coming into a place of business once in six months, to set his opinion of the value of securities against that of managers and directors who are presumably honest and capable ; and it is absolutely impossible to lay down any hard and fast rule which is capable of adoption in all circumstances. Still, experience has shown that the tendency of auditors should be towards strictness rather than leniency, and the fact that the auditor is known to be a particular man, who will not be easily satisfied, and who will not be afraid of being disagreeable upon occasion, will often have the effect of inducing greater caution on the part of directors as to the statement which will have to be passed by the auditor before it is issued to the shareholders. Indeed, many shareholders may be to-day living in blissful ignorance of the fact that their interests have been safeguarded by auditors who have induced directors to take a less optimistic view of investments and resources. A series of commercial disasters may have some benefit, after all. They make directors more careful in their statements, and they make auditors more sceptical as to the figures they are asked to pass. What should be the form of words adopted by auditors is a matter of no little importance, and the present tendency is to depart from the bold simplicity of "audited and found correct," to adopt—for the security of the auditor as well as for the benefit of the investor—a long sentence narrating all that the auditor has done. It was suggested yesterday that a Royal Commission should be appointed to examine the question of Balance Sheets; but this hardly seems necessary. The Chartered Accountants might surely draw up a statement of the duties that belong to an audit that will really safeguard the interests of investors, and it should be possible to give the public a guarantee that an audit of this kind is ensured, when it is conducted by a Chartered Accountant. Many companies would doubtless have to increase the amount they vote for an audit, but there should be little reluctance to pay adequately for the satisfaction of knowing that—save for the possible exploits of knavery by dishonest directors, who might deceive the most careful auditor—the statements that have been audited can be relied upon.

———

# The Accountant

### THE ORGAN OF CHARTERED ACCOUNTANTS THROUGHOUT THE WORLD.

#### (Awarded Silver Medal, Esposizione Italo-Americana, Genova 1892.)

VOL. XX.—NEW SERIES.—No. 1042.   SATURDAY, NOVEMBER 24, 1894.

## Leading Articles.

### THE RESPONSIBILITIES OF AUDITORS.

PERHAPS the most important paper read during the course of the Institute's recent gathering at Liverpool is that by Mr. THEODORE GREGORY, F.C.A., upon the above subject. Certainly, it would be difficult to choose a topic of more vital interest at once to the profession and the public ; and it is further to be admitted that Mr. GREGORY's treatment of his subject is such that, for this reason alone, his paper is entitled to very careful consideration.

Commencing at the outset with the statement that his remarks were intended to be suggestive rather than dogmatic, and to elicit opinion rather than to pronounce judgment, Mr. GREGORY proceeds to define the present relative positions of the profession and public in a manner to which few can take exception. He points out that, although Chartered Accountants are prepared to accept responsibility, and, indeed, are prepared to magnify their responsibilities, yet it would clearly be an advantage to them could these responsibilities be defined in a practical manner. Still, as he points out, it is very questionable whether any definition of these responsibilities that could possibly be arrived at would not, as a matter of fact, leave the public in a worse position than now ; for, at the present time, it would seem that auditors are responsible under the common law for *any* negligence that can be proved against them, and are liable in damages for such losses as can be proved to be a direct result of this negligence; while, on the other hand, if it were merely provided that an auditor should be liable in the event of his not performing certain specified duties, it would seem to follow naturally that so long as he performed those duties, no matter how inadequate they might be, under the particular circumstances of the case he would be free from all liability, whatever the consequences or losses that ensued.

It is, perhaps, desirable here to turn for a moment from Mr. GREGORY's paper itself to the discussion which followed it, and to the question that was raised with respect to the legality of the decisions in the *Oxford* and *Leeds* cases. Mr. GREGORY, in the course of his paper, stated that "Mr. Justice VAUGHAN WILLIAMS is of opinion that the judgment (in the *Leeds* case) does not apply to that case only, but that Mr. Justice STIRLING was laying down general propositions." We do not ourselves remember when Mr. Justice WILLIAMS expressed this opinion, but, doubtless, Mr. GREGORY is prepared with his authority; and it may well be suggested that if three such sound lawyers as Lord Justice KAY, Mr. Justice STIRLING, and Mr. Justice VAUGHAN WILLIAMS are of the same opinion upon this question, one may well hesitate before accepting counsel's opinion to the contrary.

It is well that particular attention should be drawn to the somewhat misleading nature of certain remarks that fell from Mr. Justice VAUGHAN WILLIAMS, in the case of the public examination of certain of the officials of the New Zealand Loan and Mercantile Agency, Lim. As Mr. GREGORY rightly points out, it would certainly seem to the outsider, from his Lordship's remarks, that the Institute in its corporate capacity had laid down distinct rules as to what were, and what were not, the proper methods of conducting an audit. Of course, Chartered Accountants know very well that this is not the case, but the outside public is, probably, not so well informed upon such matters ; and they might well

have supposed that the Council of the Institute had formulated a series of rules for the guidance of auditors. The only document published by the Council which in any way answers to this description is the letter, dated the 30th June 1893, sent by the Secretary of the Institute to the various newspapers, which Mr. GREGORY reproduced in his paper; and it will be seen that this letter contains very little that concerns the duties of an auditor which is not of a negative character ; its main object being to show the limits of an auditor's duties, rather than their exact extent or nature.

The possibility of ever laying down any positive rules that will be found to be of general application is a question which has already been freely discussed in these columns, and we think the general opinion of the profession is that it would be impossible to settle this matter upon such lines that any directions laid down would invariably answer under such various circumstances as would naturally arise from time to time. It remains to be seen, however, whether the Committee recently appointed by the Board of Trade will accept this view as final, or whether they will attempt to achieve something in this direction. Could any practical solution be arrived at, the result—as we have pointed out—would hardly fail to benefit the profession, inasmuch as the effect would be to replace a practically unlimited and indefinable liability by a limited and definite one; but, as we have also frequently stated before, we question whether it would be possible to devise a scheme under which any codification of the law relating to this question would not leave loopholes for escape that would place the investing public in an even more unfortunate position than that which they at present occupy. It seems to us— and we think that the view is one that is adopted by many men of large experience in the matter— that in the vast majority of cases the system of auditing the accounts of public companies by means of professional auditors is one that leaves little to be desired, and which could be made as perfect as any human institution is likely to be were shareholders of companies more interested in, and more alive to, the permanent welfare of the companies whose shares they hold. The indifference of shareholders to the continued prosperity of the company is a matter concerning which probably every accountant has occasionally had personal experience, and if statistics could be taken it would no doubt be found that the number of Chartered Accountants who had lost an audit through a strict adherence to what they considered to be the plain duties of their office was far in excess of the number who, by any neglect of theirs, had, either directly or indirectly, contributed to the loss of a company's assets. The ease with which, under the present system, directors can get rid of an auditor whom they find "inconvenient" is well known to most members of the profession, and is a matter which we have frequently had occasion to comment upon in these columns. We are very gratified to see that Mr. GREGORY advocates as a preventive a course which we have frequently urged, namely, that the Institute should take such action as would render it impossible for any company to obtain another Chartered Accountant as auditor after it had already displaced one for merely doing his duty. Mr. KEMP, in the discussion which followed Mr. GREGORY'S paper, put this another way, and suggested that members *individually* should adopt this view of the matter; but we are inclined to think that the time has come for some more definite action. Naturally the Council is indisposed to interfere lightly with the freedom of individual members, but it is at least a question to be considered whether the adoption of such a line of action as this would not prove more effective than a dozen Royal Commissions to enquire into, and recommend legislation with regard to, the duties of auditors. Several influential members of the press appear to have been much struck with this idea, which apparently comes upon them with all the force of novelty, and it is certainly worthy of enquiry whether the time has not now come for some definite move to be made in this direction by the Institute in its corporate capacity.

Were it to be a result of the recent meeting at Liverpool that in future, directors who found it convenient to get rid of an auditor whose opinions upon various matters were less " easy " than their own were, would find it impossible to replace that auditor by any other member of the Institute of Chartered Accountants, we think that the strongest possible move would have been made in favour of a more satisfactory conduct of audits for the future, seeing that the position of the auditor would be then so strengthened that his independence of action, as well as of thought, would be practically assured in all cases. On the other hand, directors would naturally be more disposed to patiently and reasonably consider any objections that the auditor might have to suggest, were they aware that there was a possibility of their finding themselves in so awkward a position as to be obliged to confess to the shareholders that they had searched the membership of the Institute in vain for a Chartered Accountant who was prepared to audit their accounts. Were such a condition of affairs accomplished, the recent gathering of the Institute at Liverpool would, undoubtedly, form a most important landmark in the history of the profession.

# The Accountant

## THE ORGAN OF CHARTERED ACCOUNTANTS THROUGHOUT THE WORLD.

### (Awarded Silver Medal, Esposizione Italo-Americana, Genova 1892.)

Vol. XXI.—New Series.—No. 1063.　　　　　Saturday, April 20, 1895.

## Leading Articles.

### DIRECTORS *v.* AUDITORS.

THE SOUTH BRISBANE GAS AND LIGHT COMPANY, LIM.

IN our issue of the 20th January 1894, we drew attention to certain facts in connection with this company which seemed to be of general interest to the profession. It will be remembered that the position of affairs then was that one of the auditors, Mr. ROBERT FORREST, F.S.A.A., had declined to sign the Balance Sheet on account of certain transactions to which he had taken exception, and which were fully recorded in the circular issued by him to the shareholders, which we reprinted in our issue of the 20th January 1894. It seemed to us at the time—and, indeed, we wrote to that effect—that certain of the transactions to which Mr. FORREST took exception were hardly of sufficient importance to merit the attention which he so specially directed to them; and we further ventured to express a doubt as to whether the main point of difference between him and the directors, namely, the question as to the necessity for providing depreciation before arriving at the profits, was one which could be decided off-hand in Mr. FORREST's favour. On the other hand, we did not hesitate to state our view that Mr. FORREST had done the only possible thing for him to do, under the circumstances, in taking special steps to acquaint the shareholders with the precise reasons that induced him to decline to certify the accounts submitted for his inspection.

We have now received particulars of all that has since occurred with respect to the matters that we then referred to, and it would certainly seem as though subsequent events have amply justified the somewhat exceptional course taken by Mr. FORREST eighteen months ago. Among other papers, there is now before us a copy of a circular addressed, under the company's heading, to certain of the larger shareholders, suggesting that steps should be forthwith taken with a view to altering the company's articles of association, so as to afford greater voting power to the large shareholders. In order to make clear the significance of this proposal it is necessary to call attention to the fact that Article 60 of the company's articles of association provides that " no member holding less than ten shares shall vote; every member holding ten shares and less than fifty shall have one vote; every member holding fifty shares and less than 100 shares two votes," and so on, an extra vote being given for each additional 100 shares, " no member to have more than five votes." The reason stated in the circular as the necessity for such an alteration is on account of " some trouble having been experienced at general meetings caused by persons who had secured proxies to vote for themselves as auditors interfering in the election of directors,"

and it was suggested in this circular that, with a view to remedying the possibility of the recurrence of such a position of affairs, the larger shareholders should " temporarily increase their voting power " by transferring some of their shares to one or more friends or relations for a time. " Thus," continued the circular in question, " you hold 10,747 shares, and are only entitled to " five votes. If you retain 400 shares, and transfer " the remainder to or between twenty-six of your " trusted friends and relations, you will secure " 129 votes in all, and can have the shares re- " transferred to yourself when the articles have " been altered. I enclose blank forms of transfer." So that there may be no mystery about the authorship of these remarkable circulars, we may state at once that Mr. HELLICAR, a director of the company, admitted having sent out a number, and that he has stated at a meeting of the company that others were sent out by a Mr. COLLINS, who, we believe, was at that time also a director of the company. It seems unnecessary for us to discuss at the present time the general question of the best possible incidence of voting power in the case of a large public company. This is a matter which the Legislature has, as we think wisely, left to be settled by the proprietors of each separate company in such a manner as they may think best, and it may be taken that no general rule could be laid down which would be equally desirable in all conceivable cases; but we think that our readers will all agree in regarding the suggestion contained in the circular we have quoted above as being more than questionable, and indeed, this circular has been described in a local paper as " an infamous document," with what appears to us to be considerable justification. It is, as we have already said, open to any company to make whatever regulations it may think fit with regard to the voting power of its proprietors, but it is questionable procedure for the proprietors of any company to make bogus transers for the purpose of artificially disturbing the incidence of voting power; and particularly is such a course of action discreditable when the object is not to promote the general well-being of the company as a whole, but rather to provide the existing board of directors with proxies for the purpose of enabling them to carry through transactions, some of which at least have most rightly been called in question by the company's auditor. Indeed, it is, we think, more than likely that one of the reasons which prompted the issue of these circulars was the hope of employing the increased voting power so afforded for the purpose of replacing Mr. FORREST by an auditor whose views were more in accordance with the views then held by the existing board of directors.

From the report of the ninth annual meeting of the South Brisbane Gas Company, however, which was held on the 21st February last, it would seem as though the general body of creditors had not been disposed to fall in with the views of the directors, for we find that whereas the directors were successful in obtaining the proxies of 98 shareholders, Mr. FORREST attended the meeting with 136 shareholders' proxies, and the result naturally was that the two retiring directors, namely, Mr. HELLICAR, the admitted author of some of the circulars in question, and Mr. PORTER, a director whose relation with some of the company's transactions had already been somewhat unfavourably criticised by Mr. FORREST, were not re-elected. In their stead were elected Mr. ROBERT FORREST himself and another gentleman, who, like him, stood pledged to those reforms which Mr. FORREST, as auditor, had already called attention to as being absolutely imperative, while the two auditors elected were also appointed on the strength of the proxies held by Mr. FORREST.

We may note in passing, however, that apparently only one of the retiring auditors was eligible for re-election, and it also seems as though Mr. FORREST had ceased to become one of the company's auditors before the date of the last meeting; and this condition of affairs suggests that the company's articles of association place a limit upon the time during which any one auditor can continue in office. If this be so, we recommend this article to Mr. FORREST and his supporters as being one of the next things which urgently claim their consideration, and it seems unnecessary in our columns to seriously argue the advantages which would accrue from its repeal.

In conclusion, we may add to our congratulations to Mr. FORREST, for the determined stand that he has made against the directors in this instance, our undisguised surprise of the success that has attended his efforts. Such cases as this are by no means uncommon in the profession, but it is rarely, if ever, that the stand of an auditor against the directors is attended with such unqualified success. To the casual observer it may, perhaps, appear that Mr. FORREST's nomination of himself as a candidate for a seat upon the board raises the suggestion of self-interest, but such a question as this is one which we cannot possibly judge upon with the very insufficient information at present before us; although, so far as such evidence goes, it clearly seems to be altogether in his favour. The facts which attract our attention, however, are that, in this case, an auditor who was dissatisfied with the transactions recorded in the accounts he was called upon to certify refused to sign such accounts, and stated to the shareholders in detail his grounds for refusal; and that when the directors endeavoured by fair means and foul to frustrate his attempt, he sufficiently carried the war into the enemy's camp to turn the balance entirely to his own advantage to such an extent that, at the present time, there does not remain upon the board of the South Brisbane Gas and Light Company a single director who sat there during the period covered by the accounts to which he had first objected. This is a victory of which any auditor might well feel proud, and we must heartily congratulate Mr. FORREST upon the success that has attended his efforts.

## Auditors.

OF late a great deal of attention, says the *Bullionist*, has been concentrated on auditors and their certificates, and we are glad to see that there is a tendency towards a decided change in the matter. At one time bank balance-sheets had appended to them an auditor's certificate bald in the extreme—one which meant anything or nothing. But since, on several occasions, very strong opinions have been expressed in the Courts as to the absurdity of any value being attached to such certificates, the tendency has been to make them far more explicit. There can be no question that an enormous responsibility rests on the shoulders of gentlemen undertaking to audit accounts, and they should be made clearly to understand that if they take in hand the work, at the same time they undertake the responsibility. Let us give an example. A few years ago the accounts of a certain bank in London were audited by a distinguished firm of accountants twice each year—on the 30th June and the 31st December. On each of these occasions they attended with the staff and two other gentlemen elected by the shareholders as auditors. They all proceeded to the Board-room, where on side tables, &c., were placed in order brown paper packages containing the deeds of property and the bonds on which the bank had advanced money to its customers at the head office and branches. One of the managers and a clerk were also present. The books in which the bills discounted were listed were taken in hand by some of the auditors' staff, and they at once proceeded to check them back with the actual bills. So far, so good. The chief auditor then took a seat at the head of the table, and had placed before him books in which were recorded the customers' names, the amount of the advance, and particulars of the securities on which the money was lent. The other gentlemen sat round ready to examine the security. A name would be read out and the amount of the loan standing against that name, then the clerk would produce the parcel of deeds and hand them to his manager. An auditor would then open and overhaul them, and if all were found to be in order the amount would be passed. The clerk would then tie up the parcel again, and the auditor who had examined the deeds would initial it. Note this carefully. If when a name was called and the amount of the advance was found to be the same as on the previous audit day, the clerk would look on the parcel for the auditors' initials, and in nine cases out of ten the auditors would then pass the parcel as correct without even untying the string. Consequently, with a large number of standing loans parcels could be despatched with great rapidity by this process, at once novel and labour-saving. Yet the shareholders were under the happy impression that every deed was scrutinized each half-year with an eagle eye. What prevented fraud here? How did the auditors know the parcel contained what it purported to do? As a point of fact, it might have been opened again and again during the half-year and the contents added to or taken from. We have been assured by a bank official that, to his own certain knowledge, on several occasions mistakes like this have occurred, and been repeated half-year after half-year. Can this be called auditing accounts? What is a certificate worth if the securities have only been overhauled in the manner specified above?

Take another case. Another big firm of auditors. Another big bank. Do bank shareholders actually believe that each time a balance-sheet is sent to them, with the customary few lines below by way of certificate, that all the securities have been carefully gone into? Do they imagine that because some well-known firm sign such certificate that that is a guarantee that all the securities are safe and right? If so, they are wofully mistaken. In this second instance, the firm of auditors compared the amount of the loan with the securities as entered in the books of the bank, and on that gave their certificate. That requires a little further explanation. Some of the auditors' staff would attend the bank during the half-year and go over the securities themselves, and see if they were duly and properly entered in the books, which would then be initialled. When the actual audit came on, if the security books were turned to and the entry found duly initialled, the auditors would be satisfied. Of course everyone can see that the bank officials, had they been so disposed, could easily have given up the security or taken it away without making any record in the books. How could the auditors discover this?

We have only given one or two instances; we could easily multiply them were it necessary, but where there is enough it is unnecessary to add more. There is no question that in many cases an audit, in the sense in which it is generally understood, is little more than a farce, and under existing arrangements it must continue to be so. We do not say anything against auditors as a class; but what we maintain is that they should be made to clearly comprehend that their work does not begin and end with the act of auditing. They are part and parcel of the company itself. They are officials, therefore they continue their responsibility. That being so, they must understand that if they certify a balance-sheet is right they are responsible for its being right in every particular.

We have said on previous occasions that we shall be glad when the time comes for Government to appoint auditors, not only for banks, but for public companies of all kinds. There would then be a far greater measure of security. Let there be an adequate staff, and pay unexpected visits at irregular intervals to the different institutions. This should not in any degree interfere with the usual half-yearly audit of the banker. Let him go on as before, by all means, but let him clearly understand that at any moment the Government official may drop in and ask for his securities for examination. Had such plan been adopted long ago many of the big building society frauds of recent years would have been prevented. It would perhaps cause considerable inconvenience to the banker to be suddenly disturbed by the advent of a Government auditor, but he would find that his shareholders and customers would be better pleased and satisfied.

One more point. An auditor should be allowed a very strong voice in the matter of old accounts—practically dormant—insufficiently covered by the security held, and should have the power of insisting that adequate amounts should be written off as the securities depreciated. Do auditors do this? It would be interesting to see the books of some of our large banks and note the advances made and the value of the security held.

# The Accountant

### THE ORGAN OF CHARTERED ACCOUNTANTS THROUGHOUT THE WORLD.

#### (Awarded Silver Medal, Esposizione Italo-Americana, Genova 1892.)

Vol. XXI.—New Series.—No. 1082.　　　　Saturday, August 31, 1895.

## Leading Articles.

### DIRECTORS *v.* AUDITORS.

WE have had occasion during the last few
months to call attention to one or two
instances of auditors being blamed for confining
the scope of their investigation to the mere
verification of the accuracy of the bookkeeping
and of the questions of principle connected with the
preparation of accounts; and, on the other hand,
there have been cases (of which, perhaps, the
most notorious for the moment is the *Grand Junction
Waterworks* case) in which auditors have been
blamed for setting up their views in opposition to
those entertained by the directors as to the precise
amount of information that should be contained
in the accounts submitted to the shareholders.  A
case of a much more satisfactory nature, which
lies somewhat between these two, has recently
come to our notice, and the result has been so
unusual that upon this ground alone it is worthy
of a record in these pages.  The facts are as
follow :

John Bland & Co., Lim., is a company
registered under the Companies Acts, which for
some years past has been in the habit of presenting accounts showing a satisfactory result, and of
declaring dividends somewhat in excess of the
dividends usually earned by industrial undertakings.  The business carried on is that of
timber merchants.  In spite, however, of the
apparently satisfactory state of affairs the undertaking does not appear to have commanded any
great measure of confidence locally, inasmuch as
shares were transferred at a price which enabled
the purchaser to realize what appeared to be a

very handsome return upon the purchase money. Whether the auditors have gone more fully into the company's affairs during the past year, or whether their present attitude is merely the culmination of a view that they had formed upon previous occasions, and had hesitated to act upon until more complete evidence was before them, or, again, whether the circumstances which have contributed to their present action have only arisen in the course of the last year, is a matter upon which we are not in a position to speculate; but the fact remains that when they came to audit the accounts for the year ended 30th April last they found the position to be one of such exceptional nature as to necessitate their specially reporting to the shareholders in the following terms:

### AUDITORS' REPORT.

44 Gresham Street,
95 Colmore Row, Birmingham,
20th June 1895.

To the Shareholders of John Bland & Co., Lim.,
Rotunda Buildings, Cardiff.

We regret to have to report that this year we are unable to certify the Balance Sheet in the form usually adopted and required by the articles of association, for the following reasons:

The assets include some large debts due to the company from businesses, &c., in which your managing director is directly interested, and which are to a certain extent guaranteed by him. At our request the attention of the shareholders was, we understand, drawn to these accounts by the chairman at the last general meeting.

These debts have since then increased, and are in a less satisfactory condition than they were last year. Under the circumstances we feel that it is impossible for us to sign the accounts until the position and value of these debts is more correctly ascertained, and the attention of the shareholders more specifically drawn to them.

The result of the trading is also subject to the adjustment of an account showing this year a large debit balance, which in its present form we are unable to pass.

Under these circumstances we cannot certify that the balance shown to the credit of profit and loss is available for dividend, and have recommended the directors not to pay any dividend until the position of the accounts referred to is more definitely ascertained.

We may add that we think the system of writing down the Purchase of Business Account should be continued, and that a portion of any balance remaining to the credit of profit and loss in any year should be applied in reduction of such account.

We are, gentlemen, yours faithfully,

PRICE, WATERHOUSE & Co.,
BAYFIELD & BAYFIELD,
Chartered Accountants, Auditors.

In addition to this special report the published accounts were only conditionally certified as follows:

We have examined the above accounts with books and vouchers of the company, and find the same to agree therewith, but they are subject to our report to the shareholders of this day's date, and, for the reasons stated in that report, we are unable to give this certificate in the form required by the articles of association.

PRICE, WATERHOUSE & Co.,
44 Gresham Street, E.C.
BAYFIELD & BAYFIELD,
95 Colmore Row, Birmingham.
Chartered Accountants, Auditors.

20th June 1895.

It will be seen that, in this particular instance, the auditors have thought it desirable to go beyond the limitations which have been put upon the scope of an auditor's investigation by some authorities, and have expressed their doubt as to whether certain debts due to the company were, or were not good debts, and further have taken it upon themselves to call especial attention to the fact that these debts were due from other companies in which the managing director of JOHN BLAND & Co., Lim., was more or less concerned.

The company was of course a trading company and not a banking company, and consequently these disclosures would not, in the ordinary course of events, be attended with such disastrous consequences as might result from a similar disclosure in the case of a banking company; but at the same time it is difficult to see in what respect such a circumstance as this would materially affect the question of the auditor's duties, and it is indisputable that the auditors of the company which we are now considering had at least to face the contingency of being blamed for directly causing a serious fall in the market value of the shares. Had their action been unjustifiable, this might perhaps have been attended by serious consequences. It is, however, particularly satisfactory to notice that, at the general meeting of the company at which the accounts were presented, the shareholders unconditionally supported the attitude taken by the auditors, and further that the board as a whole also supported them, and even went so far as to announce that the managing director had sent in his resignation.

It will thus be seen that the shareholders and directors of JOHN BLAND & Co., Lim., are to be congratulated upon the possession of a larger amount of common sense and business ability than that possessed by the shareholders and directors of many other companies; but we are tempted to wonder whether an equally satisfactory result would have been arrived at, had it so happened that the auditors of the company had been firms whose ability and integrity had been less absolutely unchallengeable. The mere fact that in this particular instance the auditors were encouraged in making the stand that they did does not alter the fact that by so doing they placed themselves, and in a measure their reputation, absolutely at the mercy of the shareholders. It must be remembered that the shareholders might reasonably be supposed to be controlled by the board of directors, whose management was undoubtedly more or less implicated by the auditors' report, and the mere fact that upon this particular occasion the result was satisfactory to all concerned in no respect alters the unsatisfactory position that auditors usually occupy; namely, that in the event of their making themselves unpleasant to the directors, the latter will as a rule not scruple to use their influence for the purpose of securing the election of a different firm of auditors in the future. This is a matter which, in spite of the successful issue of the auditors' action in the case of JOHN BLAND & Co., Lim., still requires the attention of the Legislature at an early date; but in the meantime it is most satisfactory to notice that at least some firms of auditors are accepting the enlarged field of responsibility which we have always maintained must be adopted by the profession if it wishes to retain its influence upon the commercial and investing communities.

## Liabilities of Auditors.

### The Kingston Cotton Mill Case.

WE have already, in our issues of the 21st and 28th ultimo, dealt with the general nature of Mr. Justice VAUGHAN WILLIAMS' recent decision in this matter and with its actual legal effect, but it still remains for us to consider his lordship's judgment from the point of view of business men and of professional accountants.

Our readers will have gathered that the charges of misfeasance came under two headings, namely, mis-statement as to the value of the mill, and mis-statement as to the value of the stock-in-trade. With regard to the first, it will be remembered that in the case of a business of this kind the mill and machinery come under the head of " fixed " or " permanent " assets, and the respondents accordingly claimed protection under the decision of the Court of Appeal in *Lee v. Neuchatel Asphalte Company, Lim.*, and in *Verner v. Commercial and General Trust, Lim.* Curiously enough, the case of *Wilmer v. McNamara & Co., Lim.*, which certainly is more to the point, inasmuch as, like the present case, it dealt with an industrial undertaking, was not quoted; but Mr. Justice VAUGHAN WILLIAMS appears to have come to the conclusion that the cases cited were binding upon him, and he, therefore, decided this point in favour of the respondents. This seems to dispose of a question, which we raised some little time ago, as to whether the decisions in the *Neuchatel* case and the *Commercial and General Trust* case amounted to anything more than a refusal on the part of the Court to interfere with the decision of the directors and of the company, while the company itself is in a position to pay outside creditors even after the proposed dividend has been distributed; and we should have thought it by no means followed that the Court was necessarily bound to afterwards hold that such a course of action in itself was justifiable, even although the ultimate result might be that creditors were defrauded. We confess that we cannot see any reason why the Court should necessarily consider itself obliged to uphold a line of action merely because it has on a previous occasion, and under altogether different circumstances, declined to interfere. One would have thought that there might have been a middle course, in which the Court would virtually have said that the directors and the company in general meeting must decide those points for themselves, and at their own risk, in the event of subsequent occurrences showing that such a course was unwise, or perhaps even dishonest. In the *Kingston Cotton Mill* case there was of course no question of dishonesty, and the dividends which it is alleged were improperly paid do not amount to a figure which would materially affect the creditors in the liquidation either one way or the other,

Still the principle remains the same, and the actual effect is that if these dividends had not been paid there would have been more for creditors, and we cannot but think that this decision of Mr. Justice VAUGHAN WILLIAMS—that respondents to a misfeasance summons in respect of dividends alleged to have been paid out of capital are entitled to the benefit of the decisions given by the Court of Appeal in the case of perfectly solvent companies—is going beyond what was actually contemplated by the Court of Appeal when they gave those decisions. On the other hand, it is perhaps satisfactory to note that even the respondent to a misfeasance summons is entitled to some consideration.

Nevertheless, the recent judgment brings us back very forcibly to the extreme importance of a more accurate and scientific settlement of the all-important question as to what are profits available for dividend.

The other question, as to the inaccuracy of the stock-in-trade, is perhaps of even more immediate interest. It will be remembered that the value of the stock was accepted upon the statements of the manager, which of later years had been verified by a certificate given by him. These statements were accepted by both the directors and the auditors without further enquiry, and appear to have been wilfully falsified by the manager. Mr. Justice VAUGHAN WILLIAMS has now decided that the directors were not guilty of negligence in assuming the correctness of the manager's statement, but that the auditors ought to have adopted means for independently verifying these statements, and were accordingly responsible under the "misfeasance" section of the 1890 Act.

Taking the case of the directors first, their position should be, and no doubt is in a large number of cases, that of persons who on account of their knowledge of the trade are authorised to carry on the business of the company; some, at least, would be expected to have a *special* knowledge of the business carried on, and such special knowledge might very advantageously be utilised in such matters as checking the stock. Further, one would certainly have thought that any "practical" director upon the board might reasonably have been expected to

notice that the stock of this company was gradually, but materially, increasing in amount from year to year. Nevertheless, his lordship appears to have come to the conclusion that it was no part of the directors' duty to go into this matter for themselves, and accordingly he has dismissed the summons as against them. It will be interesting to know whether the Official Receiver proposes to appeal against this decision, as doubtless he would have done had the judgment with respect to the auditors been against him. In the meantime, the directors are to be congratulated upon having got out of what undoubtedly was a very dangerous position for them.

Turning to the case of the auditors, we cannot but think that the judgment has been framed upon some misconception of the actual state of the case. The correct valuation of a stock-in-trade is a matter which requires expert knowledge, and it is a matter upon which the opinion of an expert in accounts is practically valueless. If, therefore, it is held that directors—who presumably have some special knowledge of the business carried on by the company—are not responsible for the valuation placed upon the stock-in-trade, by all laws of logic one would have thought that *à fortiori* the auditors were not responsible, and we have searched Mr. Justice VAUGHAN WILLIAMS' judgment in vain for any convincing argument to the contrary effect. It is true that the evidence of Mr. ROWE, an assistant-examiner in the department of the Official Receiver, is to the effect that a detailed scrutiny of the figures would have shown a discrepancy in the quantity of the stock on hand; but, on the other hand, if respondents are to be allowed to give evidence at all, it would seem to be only fair that their evidence should receive due weight, and the evidence of both Mr. PEASEGOOD and of Mr. PICKERING is to the effect that every reasonable precaution was taken. Without going so far as to say that the auditors could not have discovered the falsification of the stock from the books of the company had their suspicions been aroused, we think it may safely be asserted that no such detailed investigation as that conducted by Mr. ROWE—when, by reason of the stoppage of a company, which may have failed with immense liabilities, every facility and every incentive to examine minutely would e present—could reasonably be expected from auditors under ordinary circumstances. The point is especially worthy of note, inasmuch as the Official Receiver has had upwards of a year in which to make his investigation, while in the nature of things it is essential that an audit should be completed in a few weeks. Again, the fact that in this case the auditors were supplied with a certificate as to the valuation placed upon the stock, which had been approved by the board of directors, is surely entitled to some consideration.

Without desiring in the least to be disrespectful to the Court, we may, perhaps, be allowed to express the opinion that the policy now being pursued in respect of the liabilities of auditors is an unpractical one, which is calculated to deter honest and competent men from undertaking such appointments rather than a policy which would increase the efficiency with which audits are conducted, and we must protest most strongly against the manner in which recent decisions have been based one upon another, each *extending* and *generalising* the facts of the previous decision. We have always advocated the expediency of auditors being held responsible for a clear neglect of their duties, and when any neglect has been proved we have never suggested that the auditor should be allowed the advantage of any technicalities which might appear to improve his position ; but we cannot view with satisfaction the present policy of the Courts, which appears to be to stretch all previous decisions (which necessarily have been given in view of all the circumstances of that particular case) into general decisions to the effect that an auditor will always be liable, if he leaves undone what the defendant of a previous case perhaps also left undone, but upon which that previous case in no way actually hinged.

In the decision which we are now considering Mr. Justice VAUGHAN WILLIAMS has undoubtedly gone far beyond any previous judgment relating to the liabilities of auditors, and he has virtually decided that even when the correct valuation of assets depends upon the evidence of experts the auditor is not entitled to accept such valuation as correct, even when he states in his certificate the authority of such valuation. There may, in this particular case, be reasons why the auditor might reasonably have been expected to go behind the valuations that were submitted to him, but at the rate at which we are now progressing it seems pretty clear that when the next case comes on for hearing it will be assumed as a matter of course that the Court has already decided the general point upon the lines which we have just stated. The position would be sufficiently impossible for auditors, if they were conscious that this liability was shared by them with the board of directors ; but we have now a clear decision upon the part of the Court that the directors are justified in depending upon the auditor for the correctness of what, after all, are their accounts, and their accounts alone, and we think it likely that, until the matter is placed upon a more satisfactory footing, many auditors will expressly decline to incur any responsibility in connection with the accounts of any company whatever.

In the meantime it is clearly essential, in the interests of the profession, that the case should be taken into the Court of Appeal, so that, even if the judgment is not to be varied, some more satisfactory reasons may be obtained for the decision arrived at, which may afford auditors some specific indication as to what is expected from them in respect of their verification of the accounts rendered to a company by its directors. At the present time, as *The Times* aptly states in its issue of the 31st ultimo, " the auditor is ' between the " ' devil and the deep sea '; on the one hand, his " insistence upon proper accounts and a full " disclosure of losses often seems ' masterful " ' domination ' to a well-meaning, but nervous, " board," and is punished - as was recently the case of the late auditors . of the New Zealand Mercantile Agency Co., Lim.—by removal. On the other hand, if they adopt the view that they are justified in accepting without further verification statements which (according to this latest decision) a board of directors would be perfectly justified in accepting, they are liable—like the late auditors of the Kingston Cotton Mill Co., Lim.—to find themselves mulcted in damages for misfeasance. It is impossible for the profession to allow matters to remain in this state, and the sooner a move is made with a view to obtaining a better understanding of the position, the more satisfactory will it be, not only for auditors and directors, but also for the general public.

Our contemporary, *The Law Journal*, has a few sensible remarks fringing on this question, which we reproduce in another column under the head, "Dividends and Wasting Securities."

## The Kingston Mills Judgment.
## Liabilities of Auditors.

*(To the Editor of The Accountant.)*

Sir,—Can you give me a little space on this subject? Without stopping to discuss the merits of the case upon which the judgment itself is based, the decision unquestionably creates a most grave and perilous outlook for auditors in relation to stocks and stock values generally. Unhappily, the judgment sets up no exact and certain standard or principle of action. If the law will only tell us in clear and exact terms what we are to do, then we will do it. The practice, I need hardly say, in all good offices, has been to check, as far as it seemed possible to do so, the correctness of the stock and its valuation, but when this has been done, it now appears that we are still exposed to the risk of ruinous litigation in order to have it determined whether or not "reasonable care" has been exercised in accepting such valuation. The gravity of the judgment does not consist in its relation to the facts of the *Kingston Mills* case, or even to the stock values of cotton mills generally, but in its application to unknown eventualities of all kinds, and to circumstances, judicial and otherwise, which it passes the wit of man to provide against. Is it not possible to do something to protect ourselves absolutely against such a narrow definition of "reasonable care" as might mean utter ruin, both professionally and financially, to the unhappy auditor involved? I am not a lawyer, but to keep myself clear of risk, I now need, as it seems to me, to be skilled accountant, lawyer, and High Court judge, all in one.

May I put two questions to you, sir, and the profession generally? My first is:—Can an auditor protect himself absolutely by his certificate? In case some such addition as this were made to the usual certificate, would it avail, viz.:—

" No responsibility is assumed under this certificate " for the quantity and value of the stock-in-trade, the " value thereof set forth in the Balance Sheet being the " amount at which it appears in the company's Stock " Book."

When the Court says an auditor must take "reasonable care" to satisfy himself that the stock values are correct, can such auditor, by explaining to the shareholders how he has obtained the stock values, and by disclaiming any responsibility therefor, really rid himself of responsibility? In other words, can an auditor by rejecting responsibility in this way, avoid a responsibility which the Court says really attaches to him?

My next question is this:—Can an auditor be protected by such a wording of the shareholders' resolution appointing him as would amount to a direction that the stock and stock values should be accepted by him as supplied by the company's officials responsible for the taking and valuation of such stock?

If either or both of these courses would serve then, I think, the Council of the Institute should take the highest legal opinion as to the exact form of the certificate or resolution, and publish them for the benefit of the members. I need hardly say that the farthest thought from my mind is to make it easy for any auditor to do wrong, or to neglect his duty; but, rather, when we have to the best of our judgment honestly done all that seems to be necessary, then to have that protection against undefined and uncertain risks which, surely, even auditors have a right to ask for.

I am,

Yours, &c.,

*December* 1895.     LANCASHIRE C.A.

## The  Liability  of  Auditors.
### The  Kingston  Cotton  Mill  Case.

WE have been asked by several Chartered Accountants to print copies of the accounts issued by the Kingston Cotton Mill Company, and we have been favoured by the auditors (Messrs. PICKERING, PEASEGOOD & Co.) with the accounts for that purpose for the years 1889, 1890, 1891 and 1892. The following is a copy of the Trade Account for the first-named year:—

### TRADE  ACCOUNT  FOR  YEAR  1889.

| | £ s d | | £ s |
|---|---|---|---|
| To Stock-in-Trade, 31st December 1888 .. .. .. | 21,775 17 6 | By Yarn and Packing, *less* discount .. .. .. .. | 119,727 12 |
| „ Cotton .. .. .. .. .. .. | 92,454 16 7 | „ Waste .. .. .. .. .. .. .. | 862 7 |
| „ Coal.. .. .. .. .. .. | 2,200 11 1 | | |
| „ Oil .. .. .. .. .. .. | 358 11 4 | | |
| „ Tallow .. .. .. .. .. | 100 16 10 | | |
| „ Paper .. .. .. .. .. | 444 10 5 | | |
| „ Brushes .. .. .. .. .. | 65 5 0 | | |
| „ Starch .. .. .. .. .. | 40 5 0 | | |
| „ Water .. .. .. .. .. | 44 8 10 | | |
| „ Printing and Stationery .. .. .. | 32 11 11 | | |
| „ Gas .. .. .. .. .. .. | 182 19 1 | | |
| „ Wages and Salaries .. .. .. | 22,084 1 6 | | |
| „ Miscellaneous Expenditure .. .. .. | 358 14 1 | | |
| „ Rates and Taxes .. .. .. | 563 0 7 | | |
| „ Insurance .. .. .. .. .. | 359 6 1 | | |
| „ Commission .. .. .. .. | 711 9 1 | | |
| „ Dyeing .. .. .. .. .. | 106 3 7 | | |
| „ Skips .. .. .. .. .. | 10 8 9 | | |
| „ Twines Account .. .. .. .. | 449 4 7 | | |
| „ Rents Account .. .. .. .. | 13 10 0 | | |
| WEAR AND TEAR— | | Stock-in-Trade, 31st December 1889 .. .. .. .. | 29,760 3 |
| To Repairs—Machinery .. .. ..£1,497 11 3 | | | |
| „    „    Engines and Boilers .. .. 159 3 1 | | | |
| „    „    Buildings .. .. .. 244 15 1 | | | |
| „    „    Card Clothing .. .. 249 16 6 | | | |
| „    „    Roller Leather, &c... .. 378 8 4 | | | |
| „    „    Bobbins and Skewers .. 141 3 5 | | | |
| „    „    Strapping and Laces .. 402 9 5 | | | |
| „    „    Tinners .. .. .. 138 14 0 | | | |
| | 3,212 1 1 | | |
| | 145,568 12 11 | | |
| Trade Profit (1889) .. .. .. .. .. .. | 4,781 10 2 | | |
| | £150,350 3 1 | | £150,350 3 |

It will be seen that this account is not divided to sections, and therefore does not show any-ing that might be said to represent the amount gross profit; the balance of the account being escribed as "trade profit," which is carried to rofit and Loss Account, against which are ebited "interest on loans," and two items mounting to £743 for "new machinery." In e following years Profit and Loss Account is ly debited with interest and dividends, while e unappropriated balance of each year's Profit d Loss Account is credited to Reserve Fund. the last year, namely 1892, the balance of the rofit and Loss Account was not sufficient to pay terest and preference dividend, a sum of 2,817 was therefore drawn from " Reserve Fund ccount," to make up the required amount, and further sum of £1,481 was also drawn from this count for "new machinery," &c. We think unnecessary to reprint the Trade Account each separate year, as they are all cast in e same form, but have constructed " Goods ccounts" for each of the four years under scussion.

Assuming, which we believe was the case, that e auditor did as we contend he should be allowed do, viz., rely on an expert's certificate of stock, hich was held to be sufficient to justify the pproval of the directors, the question that we are out to enter upon does not arise. But as the oint is mentioned in Mr. Justice VAUGHAN VILLIAMS' judgment (although, as we think, rongly), it is perhaps worth while to consider hat, if anything, it would have been open for e auditors to do in the way of testing the

accuracy of the figures submitted to them.

It is possible to roughly test the accuracy of the stock-in-trade by comparing the percentage of gross profits earned in different years. This plan is well known among traders, who—in the event of the percentage of gross profit falling—would naturally suspect a leakage, such as theft of stock itself; and although, of course, the com-parison of the percentages of profits earned in different periods is necessarily a matter which has to be considered in conjunction with the condition of the market during the different periods, it is one that is well deserving of attention under all ordinary circumstances. It is, however, very important to remember this limitation, and not to apply the test without, at the same time, taking into account all such modifying conditions as the changes in the market may necessitate. In pro-ceeding to apply the test to the accounts which now lie before us, the question arises as to whether for this particular purpose it is best to compare the percentages of true gross profits—that is, actual cost of produc-tion in the different years—or whether we should not arrive at a better test by keeping entirely to the percentage of profit shown by an account stating on one side the goods purchased and the opening stock, and upon the other side the goods sold and the closing stock. We think that if we restrict our comparison to these items, many disturbing influences arising from the varying costs of wages and sundry commodities will be removed, and accordingly we have constructed the following " Goods Accounts" for the four years in question :—

| Dr. | GOODS ACCOUNT FOR THE YEAR 1889. | | | | | Cr. |
|---|---|---|---|---|---|---|

| | £ s d | | £ s d |
|---|---|---|---|
| Stock in Trade, 31 Dec. 1888 .. .. .. .. 21,775 17 6 | | By Yarn and Packing, *less* Discount .. .. .. .. 119,727 12 1 | |
| Cotton .. .. .. .. .. .. .. .. 92,454 16 7 | | „ Waste .. .. .. .. .. .. .. 862 7 10 | |
| Gross Profit .. .. .. .. .. .. 36,119 9 0 | | „ Stock in Trade, 31st Dec. 1889 .. .. .. 29,760 3 2 | |
| | £150,350 3 1 | | £150,350 3 1 |

GOODS ACCOUNT FOR THE YEAR 1890.

| | £ s d | | £ s d |
|---|---|---|---|
| Stock in Trade, 31st Dec. 1889 .. .. .. 29,760 3 2 | | By Yarn and Packing, *less* Discount .. .. .. 122,694 5 0 | |
| Cotton .. .. .. .. .. .. .. .. 101,950 9 11 | | „ Waste .. .. .. .. .. .. .. 1,255 8 9 | |
| Gross Profit .. .. .. .. .. .. 36,721 11 5 | | „ Stock in Trade, 31st Dec. 1890 .. .. .. 44,482 10 9 | |
| | £168,432 4 6 | | £168,432 4 6 |

GOODS ACCOUNT FOR THE YEAR 1891.

| | £ s d | | £ s d |
|---|---|---|---|
| To Stock in Trade, 31st Dec. 1890 | 44,482 10 9 | By Yarn and Packing, *less* Discount | 106,382 6 4 |
| „ Cotton | 77,565 4 0 | „ Waste | 797 18 0 |
| „ Gross Profit | 39,050 14 8 | „ Stock in Trade, 31st Dec. 1891 | 53,918 5 1 |
| | £161,098 9 5 | | £161,098 9 5 |

GOODS ACCOUNT FOR THE YEAR 1892.

| | £ s d | | £ s d |
|---|---|---|---|
| To Stock in Trade, 31st Dec. 1891 | 53,918 5 1 | By Yarn and Packing, *less* Discount | 91,694 2 5 |
| „ Cotton | 63,467 18 6 | „ Waste | 698 14 8 |
| „ Gross Profit | 35,972 19 0 | „ Stock in Trade, 31st Dec. 1892 | 60,966 5 6 |
| | £153,359 2 7 | | £153,359 2 7 |

It will be found that the percentage of so-called gross profit upon the sales of each year is as follows :—

| 1889 ... | ... | 29·95 per cent. |
|---|---|---|
| 1890 ... | ... | 29·62 „ |
| 1891 ... | ... | 36·43 „ |
| 1892 ... | ... | 38·93 „ |

It will thus be seen that there is no practical difference between the percentage of profit shown on the first two years' accounts ; but, that, in the year 1891 the percentage increases nearly 25 per cent., and, in 1892, it increases yet another 4 per cent. Probably the rise in the rate of profit for the year 1891 is the only one that really called for serious attention upon the part of the auditors ; but in this connection it must be noted that the variations are considerably modified, if we add to the debit side of our account the expenditure upon wages. The percentages then become as follows :—

| 1889 ... | ... | 11·64 per cent. |
|---|---|---|
| 1890 ... | ... | 10·97 „ |
| L891 ... | ... | 13·74 „ |
| 1892 ... | ... | 12·77 „ |

It will be seen that here, again, the greatest difference is between the years 1890 and 1891, when there is a difference of 2·77 per cent., or, roughly speaking, an advance in the rate of profit of 25 per cent.; so that, even if the calculation were made with the addition of the wages, there is a variation in the percentage of profit earned to call for enquiry. It will be seen that the addition of the item of wages has the effect of reducing the rate of profit for 1892 below that for 1891; whereas, without wages, the rate of profit goes on increasing.

It is only fair to add at this point, however, that the evidence produced at the hearing of the summons does not seem to have gone very fully into the matter from this point of view ; and we do not know that anyone would be justified in saying, in view of the evidence, that the point which we are now calling attention to did not at the time engage the attention of the auditors, and was not satisfactorily explained to them. If any explanations were advanced to the auditors which did, in their judgment, sufficiently account for the material alteration in the percentage of profits, we think it must be admitted that they did as much in the way of scrutiny as could reasonably have been expected from them. It may be that an Examiner of the Official Receiver's Department was able, in the course of two years, to go into the question of the quantities of stock in detail, and construct accounts which showed that the *quantities* shown upon the various stock sheets must have been incorrect ; but it is needless to say that an auditor can scarcely be expected to perform, in the ordinary course, such a detailed examination as the Official Receiver may consider expedient *after* the happening of events which put an entirely different complexion upon the whole matter. Among other matters, in this connection, it would be interesting to know whether the suspicions of any official in the Official Receiver's Department were aroused upon this particular point until after JACKSON had confessed that he had been systematically falsifying the stock.

We now come to the other two points arising out of a perusal of these accounts which may help to throw some light upon the effect of Mr. Justice VAUGHAN WILLIAMS' recent decision. It will be remembered that the value attached in the Balance Sheet to the "mills, machinery, etc.," was decided in favour of the respondents. This item appears at the same amount in each of the four Balance Sheets before us, and is stated to be "as per Construction Account." No depreciation was written off at any time, but, as the Trade Accounts show, repairs were all charged up against profits, and renewals were not added to the value of the property. The effect of his lordship's decision in this respect, therefore, appears to be that the Double Account System may properly be applied to the "fixed" or "permanent" assets of a commercial undertaking. The only point to be noted in passing is that, so far as the evidence goes, it would appear that the property was never worth anything like the amount at which it stood, and that so long as repairs were duly executed and never charged up to Capital, the value of such property would probably be approximately the same at the date when the company went into liquidation as it was at the date when the company acquired it. Perhaps, however, the most important point of all in this portion of the decision is that his lordship appears to have felt constrained to admit the correctness of the principle adopted by the directors in this case, for it can hardly be said that the words "as per Construction Account" would convey a clear meaning as to the precise procedure adopted, when it has already been held by a higher Court that the expression that certain assets are "subject to realisation" is *without* any clear meaning that ordinary shareholders might be expected to understand.

The second point of note in connection with the Balance Sheet is the manner in which the stock-in-trade is stated. The wording in all four Balance Sheets is identical, namely, "stock-in-trade as per manager's certificate," the amounts for the four years being £29,760, £44,482, £53,918, and £60,966 respectively; while on the 31st December 1888 the stock was stated at £21,775. It will thus be seen that in the course of four years the stock-in-trade had increased almost threefold, although as a matter of fact the sales had been steadily decreasing since the year 1890, and were some 25 per cent. less in 1892 than they were in 1889. This would be another point which (as stated during the hearing of the case, and in his lordship's judgment) would naturally suggest enquiry upon the part of the auditor, but for all we know to the contrary such enquiry may have been made and satisfactorily answered.

Going back to the manner in which the stock is stated in the Balance Sheet, it will be seen that the authority for the figure at which each year's stock is put is duly stated as being the "manager's "certificate," while the auditor's certificate in each case has been "examined with the books "and found correct." It is of course important to remember that stock-in-trade, being a floating asset, must always be taken at a rate not higher than its market-value at the time; but it does appear to us that an auditor ought not to be held liable for the valuation of assets, particularly when the accounts clearly state by whom such valuation has actually been made, and especially when every information was given to the shareholders as to the source of the valuation adopted. We should have thought that if they chose to allow the accounts to pass upon such a basis, the auditor would be held harmless in any event.

In this particular company it does certainly appear, upon the face of it, that there was some surprising difference between the results of the year 1890 and the year 1891 which called for careful enquiry upon the part of the auditor, but what we feel about the case as a whole is that unless this decision is reversed on appeal—or at least upheld upon very different grounds—there is a very serious danger that it will be taken as a matter of course that it has already been decided that the auditor is responsible for the accuracy of the valuation placed upon the stock-in-trade of a company, even in cases where that valuation has been made by persons far better qualified to make it than the auditor, and where the authority for the valuation adopted is clearly stated in the accounts of the company. This, of course, is a very serious position in the interests of the profession, and we trust that steps will speedily be taken to arrive at a more reasonable conclusion upon the matter.

# The Accountant

## THE ORGAN OF CHARTERED ACCOUNTANTS THROUGHOUT THE WORLD.

### (Awarded Silver Medal, Esposizione Italo-Americana, Genova 1892.)

VOL. XXII.—NEW SERIES.—NO. 1102.                    SATURDAY, JANUARY 18, 1896.

## Leading Articles.

### The Valuation of Fixed Assets.
### The Kingston Cotton Mill Case.

WHILE the details of this decision are still fresh in the minds of our readers we would like to call attention to an aspect of the case which appears to us to be deserving of the most careful consideration on the part, not only of accountants, but also of lawyers.

As stated in our last issue, the effect of Mr. Justice VAUGHAN WILLIAMS' judgment with regard to the valuation of the fixed assets appears to be to sanction beyond all question of future dispute (provided, of course, the decision is upheld upon appeal) the principle that the Double Account-System is applicable to trading companies. It has already been pointed out in the columns of *The Law Journal* that the case of *Lee v. Neuchatel Asphalte Company, Lim.*, did not go to this length, for, in that case, the evidence showed that, although the property was of a wasting nature, there had, in point of fact, been no depreciation—but rather appreciation—

during the period covered by the accounts that were challenged ; and the Lords Justices of Appeal expressly declared that they did not intend their decision to be taken as a statement that it would not, in the future, be necessary to provide depreciation against the assets of the company before declaring the dividends out of current profits. As our contemporary points out, if the decision of the Court of Appeal went further than this, it would indeed be " difficult to reconcile it with *Trevor v. " Whitworth* and with the policy of the Companies " Acts." The same general remarks apply to the other case cited in support of Mr. Justice VAUGHAN WILLIAMS' view, namely, *Verner v. Commercial and General Investment Trust, Lim.*, for, in this case also, it was expressly stated that the judgment given was not to be taken as necessarily applying to any ordinary commercial company. Indeed, the only case upon record, so far as we know, that could possibly be mentioned in support of the view now advanced by Mr. Justice VAUGHAN WILLIAMS is that of *Wilmer v. McNamara and Co., Lim.*, which was decided last year. And even this case did not go so far as the *Kingston Cotton Mill* decision, seeing that all it amounted to was that the Judge was not prepared to state that the sum which had been set aside for depreciation of leasehold premises was insufficient for the purpose. Our readers will doubtless agree that there is a vast difference between dictating the precise *manner* in which depreciation is to be spread over a period of years, and deciding in general terms that *no* depreciation at all need be provided.

Even in the case of the decisions, which we have already quoted, considerable discussion arose as to the desirability of such a policy being pursued by the Courts ; and it was repeatedly pointed out that there appeared to be a growing tendency to ignore the existence of the provisions of the Companies Acts which require a company which has incurred losses to reduce its capital before proceeding to distribute dividends out of current profits ; and all that has hitherto been advanced in this direction applies in a far greater degree to Mr. Justice VAUGHAN WILLIAMS' decision in the *Kingston Cotton Mill* case.

The effect of his lordship's most recent judgment is to make the statutory provisions in respect of the reduction of a company's capital nugatory—except, perhaps, in so far as such reduction might still be necessary, where a company wishes to write off losses upon Revenue Account in order to distribute dividends ; but we very much doubt whether even this distinction can be maintained, for it is difficult to conceive what are really losses upon Revenue Account if the principle be once admitted that depreciation actually incurred is not chargeable against Revenue.

For the sake of distinguishing clearly between the *Kingston Cotton Mill* case and its predecessors, it seems desirable to point out that no evidence whatever was produced in the former case to suggest that, in point of fact, no depreciation of the property had occurred since it had been acquired by the company. If this judgment is to be upheld, we think it will prove a source of danger in sanctioning—and even encouraging—the distribution of dividends out of the capital, or at least the distribution of dividends out of current earnings after the capital is no longer intact. If this be indeed the practical effect of the decision, it is obvious that not only the provisions with regard to the reduction of a company's capital, but also the enactments with regard to the issuing of shares at a discount and the issuing of bonus shares, are avoided, and the whole policy of the Companies Acts —which attempts to safeguard the interests of creditors by insuring that at least shareholders shall not be receiving dividends except where value exists for the amount of paid-up capital issued—becomes absolutely inoperative.

It may or may not be legally possible that the obvious intentions of the Legislature should be thus disregarded, but we cannot believe that it is sound law that on the one hand the Courts should be increasing the stringency with which they view allotments of shares which can only, by some stretch of imagination, be said to have been issued at a discount, while on the other hand every benefit that might possibly have been derived from such procedure is being nullified by the establishment of a proposition to the effect that when once a company has started it is lawful for it to distribute in the form of dividends what every accountant knows are not true profits, and this, even when it is further ascertained that the capital adventured in the business is no longer intact.

# The Accountant

## THE ORGAN OF CHARTERED ACCOUNTANTS THROUGHOUT THE WORLD.

### (Awarded Silver Medal, Esposizione Italo-American, Genova 1892.)

Vol. XXII.—New Series.—No. 1103.                    Saturday, January 25, 1896.

### Leading Articles.

#### The Valuation of Stock-in-Trade.

#### The Kingston Cotton Mill Case.

WE are pleased to see that our comments upon the judgment in this case have already produced some correspondence, and we trust that before the matter drops out of immediate discussion we shall be favoured with the views of others of our readers. In the meantime, it will doubtless prove of interest if we proceed to consider the opinions that have already been advanced by them in respect of the judgment itself, and the comments thereon which have already appeared in these columns.

The letter from " W." deals with the first part of Mr. Justice VAUGHAN WILLIAMS' decision, which, it will be remembered, was confined to the question as to whether or not the directors were justified in including their " fixed " assets in successive Balance Sheets at cost price, even after they had direct evidence to the effect that the value of such assets was considerably less than the figure stated in the accounts. Our correspondent states that "the Judge felt that he was " bound to follow *Lee v. Neuchâtel* and *Verner's* and " *McNamara's* cases, but still he does not seem at " all to take away the liability which might arise " under certain circumstances." We think—that our correspondent is mistaken in supposing that the *McNamara* case was referred to ; indeed, we have already pointed out in these columns that it is strange that this case should not have been cited, seeing that it is very much more in a line with the *Kingston Cotton Mill* case than either of the other two decisions referred to. We confess that we do not quite understand the drift of the atter part of the sentence which we have quoted. f it is not improper for directors to state their ixed assets at cost when they have before them . valuation made upon their own instructions which comes out at a very much lower figure, it is lifficult to say under what "circumstances" the " liability would arise for the issue of a Balance " Sheet which did not properly set out the facts " as they were known."

Turning now to the question of the valuation of tock, which, after all, is by far the most important oint in this judgment, we think that "Enquirer" s mistaken in saying that our "general view " appears to be that the auditors were justified in " accepting the certificate of the manager and not " going behind his figures in any way." In the irst place, there is always a broad distinction etween what an auditor ought to do if he wishes o be of the utmost use to his clients, and what it s reasonable that he should be held legally esponsible for omitting to do. We have always dvocated a very high standard of what *ought* to e done, but, on the other hand, we are certainly ot prepared to say that it necessarily follows that he auditor has been negligent because this igh standard has not been acted up to. Then, gain, it appears to us that the scrutiny of the tock Books, which would be performed by any rdinary auditor, would be confined at the most o the checking of the calculations, the comparing f the prices with the invoices, and an enquiry as o the general principles upon which the valua- ion had been made. No ordinary scrutiny of he Stock Books themselves would reveal the act that the *quantities* were wrongly stated, and, as ur readers are aware, it was the quantities, and ot the prices, which were falsified in the case which we are now discussing. It is, of course, rue that the managing director of a company is ot, strictly speaking, an independent expert, but nasmuch as the choice of the expert employed is ot under the control of the auditor, we do not see vhy the latter should be blamed for any defici- ncy in that expert's work, particularly if (as in he case before us) the shareholders are clearly nformed as to whose valuation has been adopted. The circumstance that the expert employed was ersonally interested in the result would, of course, aturally induce an ordinarily careful auditor to

be more than usually particular in his scrutiny of the figures, but we do not see any reason why he should be held responsible for fraud upon the part of a person appointed by the directors to make a valuation of the stock, unless an ordinary examina- tion of the accounts would have sufficed to reveal that fraud.

This, indeed, is the view of the matter adopted by Mr. Justice VAUGHAN WILLIAMS, and his decision would, doubtless, have been different, but for the fact that, in his opinion, a proper examina- tion of the accounts would have revealed the fraud. We, upon the other hand, are more than doubtful whether any examination that could reasonably have been expected from the auditor in this case would have had that effect. In our last issue we dealt at some length with a rough system of check by means of comparing the per- centages of gross profits, which might have aroused enquiry under such circumstances as those which accompanied this case; but we were careful to point out that there was nothing to show that there were not other exceptional features connected with the accounts for the years 1890 and 1891 which might, apparently, have explained the marked variation in the per- centages of gross profits. "Transactions of the " nature of re-sales" might, undoubtedly, account for the difference; or extensive operations of a gambling nature would also, doubtless, have that effect ; and we understand that there was a good deal of this sort of thing carried on by the Kingston Cotton Mill Company. Another correspondent, whose letter was not intended for publication, suggests that *waste* might also account for the discrepancy. We think, however, that no ordinary waste could make so vast a difference; although, possibly, a breakdown in machinery, which had the effect of destroying a large parcel of goods, might do so in part. Still—as we are careful to point out— the test is in itself a very valuable one, if applied with intelligence, and it is also one which may be applied even by one who has no technical knowledge of the industry carried on.

The comparison of the relation between the stock and the turnover, which is mentioned in the letter of "Vindex," is also a test which we pointed out in our last issue, and as our correspondent states, its effect when applied to the figures of this case, is perhaps even more suggestive than the gross profit test.  Still, here again, it is possible that some adequate explanation might be afforded, and we do not know that there was no explanation forthcoming in response to the enquiries of the auditors.

It occurs to us that if this decision is to be upheld it can only be justified by allowing auditors in future to nominate their own expert valuers.  It is preposterous that, in matters which are admittedly so technical that an expert valuation is necessary, the auditor should be held responsible for fraud upon the part of the valuer even when he has had no voice in his appointment, and more particularly when it has been clearly stated to the shareholders that the valuation adopted is that of an expert valuer and not that of the auditor.

## Birmingham Chartered Accountant Students' Society.

### An Auditor's Duty in respect of Depreciation.

#### By Mr. O. Holt Caldicott, F.C.A.

At a meeting of the Society held on Tuesday the 5th November 1895, Mr. O. Holt Caldicott delivered the following lecture. Mr. A. J. Cudworth, A.C.A., occupied the chair.

It was formerly assumed that these lectures, arranged by the various societies of accountant students, should have a direct bearing upon the papers which would be set at the ensuing examination; but, since the institution of special classes for giving instruction in legal subjects and book-keeping, there has been a tendency for the lectures to take a wider range, and deal with some subject pertinent to our profession, rather with a view to affording the students food for reflection, than of giving them definite instruction in regard to some branch of our professional work.

It is with this view that I propose to consider an auditor's duty in respect of depreciation; not with the intention of dogmatically laying down hard and fast rules for your guidance, but to put before you some of the difficulties affecting the valuation of assets in a Balance Sheet, in the hope that I shall provoke a good discussion this evening, and that each of you will afterwards revolve the subject in his own mind, with a view to forming a sound judgment upon a very important part of our work.

First of all, I wish you to bear in mind that the term "Depreciation" applies not only to such assets as are of a wasting character through wear and tear or effluxion of time, but to every item on the "Assets" side of a Balance Sheet; so that a consideration of the duties of an auditor in respect to depreciation really involves his duty in dealing with the whole of the values set out upon a Balance Sheet. The auditor's duty is defined by the articles of association of each company; but these are almost invariably based upon the audit clauses of Table A, and, if there is any variation, it is now more frequently in the direction of expanding than of contracting the auditor's responsibility to the shareholders. The clauses which concern us this evening are the following:—

Article 83.—Once, at least, in every year the accounts of the company shall be examined, and the correctness of the Balance Sheet ascertained, by one or more auditor or auditors.

Article 84.—The first auditor shall be appointed by the directors; subsequent auditors shall be appointed by the company in general meeting.

Article 92.—Every auditor shall be supplied with a copy of the Balance Sheet, and it shall be his duty to examine the same with the accounts and vouchers relating thereto.

Article 94.—The auditors shall make a report to the members upon the Balance Sheet and accounts; and in every such report they shall state whether, in their opinion, the Balance Sheet is a full and fair Balance Sheet, containing the particulars required by these regulations, and properly drawn up so as to exhibit a true and correct view of the state of the company's affairs.

These clauses appear to define the auditor's status and duties as follows:—

(a) He is the nominee of the shareholders, and it is his duty to report to them.

(b) He must ascertain the correctness of the Balance Sheet which is supplied to him by means of the accounts and vouchers of the company relating thereto.

(c) His report shall state whether, in his opinion, the Balance Sheet is a full, fair, and truthful representation of the state of the company's affairs.

Gentlemen, I do not think that the duties of any officer could be more clearly defined, and I do not think that a more serious responsibility could very well be thrown upon one man in reference to other men's affairs. The only saving words are "in his opinion," and these words appear to me to have no saving power if the auditor has not taken care that his opinion in reference to the particular Balance Sheet which he certifies is of value, and one which ought to be accepted.

I think that an auditor, in giving a full and clear certificate, must be assumed to say, "I, *speaking as an expert*, say "that, in my opinion, the above Balance Sheet is a full and "fair Balance Sheet, and that after conscientiously check- "ing the figures with the vouchers relating thereto I am "enabled to say that I consider it a truthful statement of "the company's financial position."

I wish to guard myself here against the possibility of being misunderstood. Let us assume that the auditor is of opinion that a company has purchased assets at much more than their real value, but that the board think otherwise; and that these assets appear in the Balance Sheet *explicitly at cost*. I do not think the auditor is guilty of any casuistry if he certifies the Balance Sheet containing these assets "as "a full and fair Balance Sheet, correctly setting forth the "position of the company's affairs," inasmuch as the account states how the value of the asset is arrived at; but this, or any such mental reservation or qualification, is a matter to be very jealously watched, as it has been held that it is the auditor's duty to inform the shareholders, not to put them upon an enquiry.

If the auditor subsequently finds that his suspicion was well grounded, and that the price paid was excessive, he has before him the very difficult question, whether to ask for a re-valuation, which may imply reconstruction, or whether the form of his certificate be altered.

Take the case of a mining property, which may have been bought and sold in all good faith, but which afterwards turns out to be faulty ground. The auditor does not inspect the mine, and can only know what is reported to him of the state of things underground; but assume that he is told that the value of the mine is seriously deteriorated, is he still justified in certifying the Balance Sheet stating this at cost? According to the *Asphalte* case, the Double Account system comes to his rescue here to this extent that the depreciation need not affect immediate profits, but it does affect the value of the shareholders' property. I should like you to consider whether the real value of the mine is a question for the auditor. I think not, as a mining property is always a speculation, and may at any time turn out better or worse than was expected, but if it is known to the auditor to be worse I think he should at least call attention in his certificate to the fact that the property is stated at cost price. Whether he should say more each auditor must decide for himself as circumstances arise, and his decision may be fraught with serious consequences to himself and others. In deciding, he must never forget that he is the nominee and representative of the shareholders, making on their behalf an investigation which it is inconvenient and impracticable for them to make individually for themselves.

After this digression I will return to Table A and its interpretation of an auditor's duties, and ask you to consider more in detail his proper attitude in respect to a valuation of the assets, or in other words "depreciation."

I have already said that I do not use depreciation in the narrow sense in which the word is often employed, that is, a periodical diminution of the alleged value of plant or machinery consequent upon wear and tear, age, or disuse, but in the broader sense of a diminution in value of any asset consequent upon any circumstances whatever.

Now, what are the assets which are usually met with in the Balance Sheet of any commercial, industrial, manufacturing, or mining company. They are:—

Cash in hand or at bank.
Bills of exchange.
Book debts.
Stock-in-trade.
Plant.
Machinery.
Properties, freehold or leasehold.
Investments.
Goodwill.

I propose to view these very shortly in relation to a bank, a building society, a merchant's business, and a manufacturing or mining company. I shall omit "cash," assuming that care has been taken to ascertain that this includes nothing but actual cash, and that any money deposited is in the hands of a sound bank.

Firstly, in relation to a bank. Bills under discount form a very heavy item in a banker's assets, and, if they are all good trade bills, they are amongst the most convertible assets which he can hold; but, when an auditor sits down with a parcel of bills amounting, perhaps, to a total of millions, how is he to know if these bills are good, bad, or doubtful. Only as the banker does,—by observation, enquiry, and experience, ripening in time into something like intuition. Neither banker nor auditor can pronounce upon each separate bill, but he can form a very shrewd opinion which are legitimate trade bills, which are one-legged discounts (that is, bills with only one good name upon them), and which are mere accommodation paper. There are the

means at hand of ascertaining if there is an excessive amount of the paper of any one firm under discount, and there are various tests which will enable an experienced auditor to properly assess the amount of depreciation (if any) required upon a banker's bill case, and in assessing this he claims to give his opinion as an expert.

Customers' balances must be judged by the relation of the advance to the extent of the customers' transactions, by the nature of his business, and by the value and nature of the security deposited to cover the advance.

If an auditor has reason to doubt the ability of a customer or customers, to repay loans to a large amount, it is his duty to report his opinion to the shareholders; and an auditor has lately been cast in damages because he failed to report his opinion, and a dividend was paid, when profits would not have been shown if sufficient depreciation had been written off doubtful accounts.

Bank premises and office furniture are usually insignificant figures compared with the other items in a banker's Balance Sheet, and their depreciation is not likely to be a matter of controversy.

"Investments" is a term which can open its doors very wide; and, in regarding these, it is better to classify them. High-class securities, which are dealt in daily, *may*, if they have gone up since their purchase, and *must*, if they have gone down, be valued at the price of the day; but any unrealisable securities should be steadily written down, and properties in hand should not be written up upon anything but the strongest testimony of increased value.

The above remarks as to investments will apply to any other undertaking as well as to a bank.

I may also deal with "goodwill" as an asset of general application, and I give it as my opinion that if a price has been paid for the goodwill of a business, that amount may justly continue to appear as an asset upon the Balance Sheet. It is stated to be the amount paid, and no one can be deceived. If the business is a prosperous one, the goodwill remains, and if the reverse of prosperous, I see no use in building up a deficiency upon the Profit and Loss Account for the sake of writing off an unreal asset, whose name at once indicates its nature and value.

In the case of the prosperous company, this question of writing off goodwill is quite apart from the prudence of creating reserves against goodwill, or any other asset. My contention is that goodwill is as much an asset and often as saleable an asset as land, buildings, plant, or machinery.

Now let us turn for a moment to a land or building society, whose business is mainly to acquire estates in the neighbourhood of populous centres, with a view of developing them, and selling them in small lots at enhanced prices, for building purposes.

How should you deal, by way of depreciation, with estates which developed slowly, or not at all? Should you consider that the directors were justified in writing up the unsold portions of estates which were selling freely, for the purpose of showing a profit or paying a dividend?

What evidence should you consider sufficient to prove that the unsold portions were of equal value to those which had been sold?

How should you treat outlay in road making, etc., upon estates which proved unmarketable?

I do not propose to answer these questions, which I hope you will presently discuss, as they are all matters with which an auditor must deal.

In a merchant's business you will be chiefly concerned with stock and book debts, and will have to provide for unsaleable stock and irrecoverable book debts. Upon whose judgment shall you rely, your own or the manager's?

A merchant is a person engaged in the distribution of goods, as opposed to a person engaged in production, and the term includes retail as well as wholesale trades.

If you had to deal with an assorted stock, could you divide it into good or bad? I think you should have the requisite knowledge, or an assurance from some independent person who has such knowledge, before signing a certificate that the stock is fairly valued; or, in other words, properly depreciated. Book debts an accountant should be qualified by all his training to assess at or near their true value, and at this value he must insist upon their being stated.

I now come to the class of assets which belong particularly to a manufacturing company,—buildings, plant, machinery, and stock,—and upon each of these there is room for a wide diversity of opinion as to the proper rate of depreciation when things are going badly, but very little when substantial profits are being earned. In good times everyone concerned is disposed to take a cheerful view of things; and, having as much profit as will suffice to pay a good dividend, neither directors nor managers are averse to strengthening their position by writing off liberally from all the assets. But, when profits are scanty, you will find a tendency to review the rates of depreciation, and to claim that certain assets have been written down quite enough for a time. Of course this is not a scientific treatment, but I think an auditor would be scarcely wise who refused to sanction a liberal writing off in good times, or to be a little tender in his dealings with assets during a temporary depression of trade; but this discretion must be very guardedly used, and must never be allowed to grow to a judicial blindness in the case of a company which is going steadily down hill. All buildings, plant, and machinery, used in productive enterprise must be depreciated according to their respective lives, —so many years for an engine-house or pit shaft, so many years for engine or boilers, so many for shafting or banding, so many for a lathe, and, if special machinery is employed which is liable to be superseded by improvements, great care must be taken that costly machines are not kept upon the books at a high price, when they are little better than scrap. New stock should be valued at its cost price where it stands, but any unsaleable stock should at once be reduced to its value for a forced sale. It was not my intention in speaking to you of an auditor's duty in respect to depreciation to give you definite instructions as to what percentages should be written off, but to throw out some hints for your guidance, and to give you a glimpse of the many difficult and intricate questions which arise upon this vital point to the auditor and his clients.

Whatever valuation is put before you, ask yourselves *Quo tendit*? Where it will lead you and others? Always remember that, if a cart is slipping backwards downhill, its pace is terribly accelerated as it gets near the bottom; but keep your head cool, and do not take alarmist views, if the results of one year's trade are disappointing. The audit is too often regarded by shareholders as a mere formality until trouble comes, and then the outcry is "Where was the auditor?" But in good times or bad times never let an audit degenerate into a formality, but qualify yourself to form a sound judgment of the position of every company whose accounts you have to examine, and then speak the truth without fear or favour, ever bearing in mind Polonius' parting words to his son :—

> "This above all: to thine own self be true,
> And it must follow, as the night the day,
> Thou canst not then be false to any man."

Your honorary secretary was pleased to announce this as an important and authoritative address. The subject is very important to us as a profession and to the whole community, as it deals with the accuracy of accounts upon the faith of which enormous sums are invested. Authoritative it is not and cannot be, as no one has yet attempted to lay down hard-and-fast rules for the guidance of an auditor in the performance of his duties. Any little authority my words may have is derived from a varied experience extending over nearly thirty years, and I hope this has enabled me to give you a few useful hints and some food for reflection.

## Company Law Amendment.

### The Position of Auditors.

IN a recent issue of *Engineering* there appeared a long and well-written article upon the subject of Prospective Amendments of the Companies Acts, as conceived in the interests of engineers, manufacturers, and producers generally.

As this article is of some interest, and as, moreover, it is desirable that we should avoid taking too narrow a view of such matters, we have reprinted it in full in another column of the present issue; and we now propose to deal with one or two of the points that appear to be especially worthy of attention, or in need of qualification.

In the first place our contemporary draws attention to the insufficiency of the representation afforded to commerce upon the Departmental Committee appointed by the Board of Trade; but, as this is a matter which we have already considered, it need not now detain us, beyond stating that, from our contemporary's point of view, this appears to have resulted in a very inadequate consideration of the whole matter as regards the interests of commercial men and manufacturers. At the same time, we do not see upon what our contemporary bases the assertion that "the Committee . . . have subordinated "the directors and managers to the authority of "the auditors in all matters of bookkeeping and "of Profit and Loss Accounts and Balance "Sheets." On the contrary, it is expressly stated that the accounts (including the Profit and Loss Account and Balance Sheet) are to be prepared by the company, the auditors' duty being confined to the verification of the same, and the expression of an opinion "as to whether or not the Balance "Sheet and accounts fairly represent the position "of the company, having due regard to the mode "of valuation (of the assets) disclosed in the "accounts." We are not aware that this proposal amounts to any projected alteration of the existing law, but, undoubtedly, the position is more clearly stated than heretofore; and, for our own part, we are at a loss to understand why our contemporary should complain of this.

The same remarks apply to the general provisions as to audit. Our contemporary takes alarm at the heading "Duties of Auditors," which appeared in Table A of the 1862 Act, being replaced in the draft Bill by the heading "Rights "of Auditors." For our own part we are by no means sure that there is any practical distinction between the two headings; but, if there is, surely even our contemporary must admit that auditors in the midst of their manifold liabilities, have at least *some* rights, and that it is desirable that these should be defined by the Legislature. Another point at which our contemporary appears to take exception is the provision that "every auditor " of a company shall have access at all times to " the books and accounts and vouchers of the " company." It is thought that this provision will justify the auditors in requiring the production of the Cost Accounts and estimates, and will afford an occasion for the auditor enquiring into the manner in which these accounts are kept, with a view to placing them upon a more scientific and accurate basis. If the position is viewed calmly, we think it must be admitted in the first place that, inasmuch as Cost Accounts do not, as a rule, form part of the financial system of accounts, the auditor who merely fulfils the duties imposed upon him by the Act will not require to investigate these "side " books " at all; and, that being so, it is hardly to be supposed that he will go to the trouble of examining them unless he is specially paid for the purpose. On the other hand, a company is not likely to specially pay him for the purpose unless it really wishes for his services and advice upon the matter. As to whether or not it is possible for accountants to be of service to their clients in the matter of Engineering Cost Accounts is a point upon which our contemporary's views and our own differ somewhat widely, as our readers will, doubtless, remember; but, we think, it may safely be taken that professional accountants are hardly likely to interfere with Cost Accounts when they are not wished to do so, seeing—as we have already stated—that they are under no statutory liability in relation thereto; moreover, the danger which our contemporary anticipates is materially minimised by reason of the fact that the draft Bill does not propose to give the auditor any authority with regard to the manner in which even the financial books of an undertaking are to be kept.

Another point upon which our contemporary falls foul with the decisions of the Committee is that referring to the valuations of certain assets— for example, goodwill, patents, leases, and concessions. If there were any other practical solution of the difficulty doubtless not a few auditors would like to be relieved from *all* responsibility in connection with this valuation. But, after all, the practical position is this,

that experience has shown that it is necessary that there should be some outside check upon the valuations placed upon these items by directors and managers; and, on the other hand, in the absence of an expensive examination by an independent expert, experience has hitherto failed to point to a better means of checking the directors upon such items than that afforded by the scrutiny of a competent auditor. No one will be disposed to gainsay our contemporary's statement that such valuations are in many cases highly technical, nor will accountants at least assert that they possess the necessary knowledge to enable them to make such valuations for themselves; but there is no inconsistency in this admission of a lack of technical knowledge, and the statement that accountants are by their training qualified to scrutinise the valuations of independent experts when placed before them, and to express an intelligent opinion as to whether or not they appear to be fair and reasonable.

This brings us to our contemporary's next point. Exception is taken to a resolution passed by the Departmental Committee "that it is desirable and " necessary, especially for large companies, that " auditors should be skilled accountants with " staffs of trained clerks, and that it should be " recognised that it is impossible for an auditor " personally to supervise all the details of every " audit." We should like our contemporary to fully face the only alternative schemes. They are as follow:—(1) No audit at all; (2) an audit by amateurs, or accountants in a very small way of practice—which, of course, implies a limited experience; (3) an official audit, which for all practical purposes would mean an audit conducted by the same class of persons as those who are now to be found in the offices of the larger firms of Chartered Accountants. We do not like to suggest that our contemporary would view any of these alternatives with greater favour than the original proposition, but from various observations which are let fall it would almost appear as though the scheme of having no audit at all is the one which finds the greatest favour in our contemporary's eyes.

The attention which is called to the unanimity of opinion on the part of various Chambers of Commerce is somewhat gratuitous. It is, of course, possible that the presence of certain prominent Chartered Accountants among these bodies has its due effect in forming the opinion of the whole, but it is beyond dispute that the majority of the members of every Chamber of Commerce are commercial and not professional men; and, therefore, the resolutions of these bodies are entitled to be looked upon as the opinions of commercial men, rather than views inspired by an interested profession. With regard to the suggestion that, with the increased authority given them by the proposed Act "the supervision and " control of every act of the company will become " centred in the auditors, as representatives of the " financial or banking and investing public," we do not know that it is necessary to take the remark too seriously. Up to a point an increased measure of attention to the suggestions of auditors will, undoubtedly, be an improvement in the interests of all parties concerned, but to suppose that auditors will ever allow themselves to be pushed forward into the position of being responsible for the welfare of a company is to suppose that they are anxious to assume even further responsibilities than those which at present fall to their lot. Of course, if our contemporary really is of opinion that engineers know more about accounts than accountants, and belong to a race apart, whose dealings it is superfluous to enquire into or investigate, there is something consistent in the attitude adopted in the article before us; but, on every other ground, we think it must be admitted that it fails to achieve its apparent purpose, by reason of its case having been overstated. It is interesting to hear what particular classes of manufacturers or merchants may have to say upon so important and widely interesting a matter as company law reform; but we do not think that any serious importance will be attached to most of the views advanced by our contemporary.

## Weekly Notes.

*Elective Auditors' Fees.* We learn from the columns of *The Western Mail* that the elective auditors of Pembroke have joined in the "strike" of elective auditors, which is becoming fairly general, for adequate remuneration. At a recent meeting of

the Town Council a notice from one of the auditors was read stating his intention to sue for the recovery of the balance claimed by him unless the amount was paid at once. The auditor claimed £6 6s. (three days' work at £2 2s. per day), of which the Council had only paid £2 2s. The money was ordered to be paid.

*The Cardiff Elective Auditors.* It will be remembered that in our past issues we have already related how the elective auditors of the borough of Cardiff have recently taken up the standpoint that they are entitled to do as much work upon the audit as they may think necessary, and that they may claim an adequate remuneration for such services as they may have rendered. From a recent issue of *The Western Mail* we gather that a special meeting of the Finance Sub-Committee of the Corporation was held on the 27th ult., when the Town Clerk attended and laid before the Sub-Committee the correspondence which had taken place with the Local Government Board, to whom the Corporation had applied for guidance under these somewhat unusual circumstances. It appears that the Board has now expressed the opinion that the matters referred to were "not within its jurisdiction," and that accordingly no advantage could accrue from its receiving a deputation upon the subject from the Corporation. In the meantime the elective auditors have rendered an account for upwards of £1,200 in respect of their services, and it will be interesting to note how the Corporation proposes to deal with the matter. As we have already stated, our own view is that there is not the least reason why the audit should not be properly paid for, but so soon as the principle of adequate payment is generally recognised we trust that such work will only be undertaken by really competent accountants.

*Duties of* The following interlocutory remarks on
*Auditors.* the duties of auditors, reprinted from the
last issue of the *Law Journal*, are of great interest, and
it is matter of some surprise that they should so long
have remained unobserved :—

### LORD HERSCHELL ON AUDITORS.

Some unreported interlocutory observations of Lord
Herschell in *In re The Kingston Cotton Mills Company*, on
the duties of auditors, are very pertinent: " No doubt," says
that high authority, "auditors have to check the books to see
" that the accounts are correct, but it would be stretching the
" duty of an auditor considerably beyond what is reasonable
" to say that he is to go into all the business of a company so
" as to be able to check the valuation.  In a banking company,
" for instance, are the auditors to take the bills and to estimate
" the character of the people and the standing of the firms
" whose names are on the bills, and to determine whether they
" might turn out not to be good bills ?  Yet the true position
" of the company might depend on that.  An auditor
" may certify the accounts as correct, and be perfectly
" honest in the full discharge of his duty, yet the
" accounts, nevertheless, may not truly represent the
" position of the company.  Is an auditor supposed
" to go through an independent stocktaking of a great
" concern and put his own valuation upon it ?  Most auditors
" would be absolutely incompetent to do anything of the kind ;
" they are thoroughly versed in accounts, but not necessarily
" versed in the valuation of every kind of business." This is
common-sense, and we may well pause for a reply.

Lord Herschell has not yet had before him the
main point raised in the case of the *Kingston Cotton
Mills*, but he was one of the Court which decided
that the auditors of that company were " officers "
within the meaning of section 10 of the Companies
Winding-up Act 1890.  His lordship was bound so
to decide, though he evidently did not relish the
decision.  It was in the course of this discussion
that the remarks chronicled by our contemporary must
have been made.  Lord Herschell is not averse to
making such interlocutory dicta, but as they do not
amount to a decision, they are not binding on any
Court, and, indeed, are not necessarily followed on
subsequent occasions by the Judge who makes them ;
indeed, often the law is stated, without mature reflection, merely to cause counsel to meet the view
enunciated, and so enable the Court to be acquainted
with all the arguments for or against the proposition.
Nevertheless, these dicta show to a certain extent
the bent of Lord Herschell's mind on the Auditor
question; and, as his lordship is a member of the
House of Lords, and may have to review the decisions
already arrived at, his sayings cannot be altogether
neglected.

————

## Manchester Society of Chartered Accountants and Manchester Students' Society.

### "The Present Position of Accountancy in view of Recent Legal Decisions."

AT a joint meeting of these societies held at 65 King Street, Manchester, on Monday the 9th March 1896, Mr. W. H. Nairne, F.C.A., President of the Manchester Society of Chartered Accountants, opened a discussion on "The Present Position of Accountancy in view of Recent "Legal Decisions."

There was a large attendance, including Messrs. Adam Murray, F.C.A., John Mather, F.C.A., Theodore Gregory, F.C.A., William Moss, F.C.A., Ashton-under-Lyne, M. L. Walkden, F.C.A., R. Brutton, A.C.A., J. W. Pollitt, F.C.A., G. E. Haworth, A.C.A., A. A. Gillies, F.C.A., Jno. E. Halliday, F.C.A., E. Williams, F.C.A., S. Peirson, F.C.A., and H. L. Price (Manchester Guardian Society).

The PRESIDENT in opening said : We have met to-night on the suggestion of the executive of the Manchester Chartered Accountants Students' Society, who invited the Manchester Society of Chartered Accountants to devote the joint meeting of this session to a discussion. The Council of the latter society recommended in general terms the subject to be discussed, and appointed a sub-committee to make final arrangements. The sub-committee then requested me, as President of the Society, to open the discussion, the subject of which, as chosen by them, is described in the Syllabus as "The "Present Position of Accountancy in view of Recent Legal "Decisions."

Now, I take it that the "recent legal decisions" here referred to are the judgments given in the cases of

(1) *The London and General Bank, Lim.* ; and
(2) *The Kingston Cotton Mill Company, Lim.*

These two cases are, in some respects, similar ; they are both cases in which the Official Receiver took out a misfeasance summons (under section 10 of the Companies (Winding-up) Act 1890) against the directors and auditors; and in each case it was sought to make the directors and auditors liable to make good sums paid away as dividends which, it was alleged, had not been paid out of profits, but out of capital ; but, while in the case of the *London and General Bank, Lim.* both directors and auditors were held liable, in the case of the *Kingston Cotton Mill Company, Lim.*, only the auditors were held liable to refund the dividends improperly paid. In the case of the *London and General Bank* the summons included a charge of " making " advances on worthless securities "; and, in the *Kingston Mill* case, a large sum (£80,000) was claimed " as compensa- " tion for the loss sustained by the alleged misfeasance "; but, as these charges and claims were not established, I need not refer to them at length on the present occasion.

Both these cases are specially interesting to Chartered Accountants, because they involve questions affecting our duties and responsibilities in one of the most important branches of our professional work, viz., the audit of th accounts of joint stock companies.

They are, in fact, object lessons, illustrating in a practica way our liability for pecuniary loss if we fail to recognise and appreciate our responsibilities, or to perform the duties expected of us.

It follows, from these decisions, that it is very desirable we should know what our duties are, and where our responsibility ends. But is it possible to ascertain authoritatively what *are* the duties which we are expected to perform in auditing and reporting upon the multifarious joint stock companies' accounts which are submitted to us ? The fact is they are not defined, and cannot well *be* defined, to meet every case. As accountants in practice, and as students, we have been lecturing upon and discussing this subject, and the various branches of it, for many years ; several members of our Institute have published books upon it, and the organ of our profession (*The Accountant*) has dealt with it from many points of view. But, having done what we can to inform ourselves in these various ways, we find that in practice we have to rely largely on our individual judgment as to what is necessary to be done in each case, and on our own experience as to the manner of doing it.

It is a fact not sufficiently known or appreciated by shareholders and the public generally, and of which I could give many examples from my own experience, that accountants are frequently confronted with difficult questions as to the nature and extent of the enquiries necessary to be made, the mode of stating accounts, and the matter and manner of their certificates and reports ; and if the effect of these trials is to make the public understand something of the difficulties we have to meet, and the onerous responsibilities resting upon us, we shall have no cause to complain, but rather to congratulate ourselves.

We have further cause for congratulation in so far as these legal decisions do define our duties and responsibilities.

We shall not shrink from any responsibility which is clearly and specifically defined; for responsibility supposes power : and if it be well understood that an auditor is legally responsible for the accuracy of certain items in a joint stock company's Balance Sheet, he must perforce have the necessary powers to satisfy himself of their accuracy, and adequate remuneration for the exercise of such powers. This has been lately exemplified in the case of the Building Societies Act 1894. In that Act, section 2 prescribes the particulars which the annual statement shall contain, and requires the auditor, amongst other things, to certify that such account is "in accordance with law," and that he "has examined the mortgage deeds and other "securities"; and in section 3 public accountants are recognised by the Legislature as the persons best fitted to be the auditors of building societies. Now, for many years prior to the passing of that Act, accountants who were worthy of the name not only recommended but insisted, as a condition of their certifying the accounts, that the annual statement should show the subscriptions in arrear and the amounts owing on properties of which the societies had taken possession—which are the objects aimed at by the first schedule to the Building Societies Act of 1894. It was also customary to certify that the mortgage deeds had been inspected. But the auditor had no power, as he now has, to insist on the accounts being prepared in a specified form which he can certify as being "in accordance with law"; and the time and trouble he took in connection with the form of the accounts and the inspection of securities was not so generally recognised as necessary to be paid for as it now is, when such duties are defined and made obligatory by an Act of Parliament.

We welcome, therefore, any legislative enactment or decision of the Courts which, recognising our profession, imposes on us duties clearly defined, the due performance of which will free us from indefinite responsibility.

In the case of the *London and General Bank, Lim.*, there were three judgments in which we are interested :—

1. That in the Chancery Division, by Mr. Justice Vaughan Williams, in which he found the directors and auditors liable to make good two dividends improperly paid in 1891 and 1892.

2. That in the Court of Appeal, before Lords Justices Lindley, Lopes, and Kay, when they decided the question which had been raised "whether an auditor was an officer " within the summary jurisdiction of the Court under sec- " tion 10 of the Winding-up Act 1890"; and

3. The judgment given in connection with Mr. Theobald's appeal on the main issues, heard by Lords Justices Lindley, Lopes, and Rigby, which relieved Mr. Theobald of liability for the dividend paid in 1891, but confirmed the judgment given by Mr. Justice Vaughan Williams as to his liability for the dividend paid in 1892.

Now, the *London and General Bank* case was a long and intricate one, and the judgments given were lengthy and elaborate ; and I may at once relieve your minds by saying that I do not propose to read even the judgments, though I shall have occasion to refer to and comment upon them. It may be said that the case is now "ancient history," the first judgment having been given in December 1894, but as it was the first case in which it was attempted to apply the 10th section of the Act of 1890 to the case of an auditor, and as the last judgment was given in August last, I concluded that this was one of the "recent decisions" in relation to which I was requested to address you. Moreover, no one can read the arguments and judgments, especially those in the Court of Appeal, without coming to the conclusion that it is necessary to refer to the case in considering " the present position of accountancy."

Before doing so, let me state that the impression I received in first reading this case has been confirmed by a more careful perusal of the arguments and judgments, namely, that it was hardly possible to come to any different conclusion to that arrived at by the judges ; and further, that the real and permanent interests of our profession would not have been promoted by any different conclusion.

The auditor's case was very ably and strenuously argued by his counsel, and while he urged various points on his client's behalf which we as accountants would wish to have put before the Court, and which in a less difficult case would probably be effectual, some of his arguments were such as to convey an impression that an accountant's standard of duty was a low one.

Many of the arguments of counsel, for and against the auditors, and the remarks of the judges, serve to illustrate what I have said as to the difficulty an auditor may experience in deciding what is his duty in special cases.

Taking the case as a whole, I do not think that we as accountants have any cause to regret the decisions which were arrived at, and further some of the remarks made by the Judges in the course of their judgments were in the nature of definitions, or strong expressions of opinion, as to our duties and responsibilities, which may prove useful to us.

Mr. Justice Vaughan Williams commences his judgment with the remark : " This case is one of great importance, " not so much from the magnitude of the amounts involved, " but because it raises questions of the greatest practical " importance as to the duties both of directors and of " auditors."

A question arose in the case whether the interest charged to certain customers was rightly included in the Revenue Account, and it has been thought that Mr. Justice Vaughan Williams was of opinion that profits to be paid away as dividends must have been actually received, and some parts of his judgment would lead to that inference ; but the following remarks are not consistent with such a view of his meaning. He points out that dividends, other than interim dividends, must not be declared on profits merely estimated, and says :—" Because when in the articles it is " intended that the dividend shall be paid out of 'estimated " 'profits,' one finds it expressed in plain terms ; thus " article 99, which deals with the power of directors to " declare interim dividends, runs thus. It is dealing with " power of the directors 'to declare and pay not oftener " ' than twice in each year, out of the estimated profits of " ' the company, such interim dividend, not exceeding six " ' per cent. per annum, as they may think fit.' Lord " Justice Kay in the *Oxford Benefit Building Company's* " case says that 'realised' is the direct converse of " ' estimated,' and that 'realised,' if not equivalent to " actual cash in hand, must at least be cash rendered " tangible for purpose of division. It would seem, there- " fore, that in the present case the dividends are to be paid " out of profits, and it would seem from the case of *Lee v.* " *Neuchâtel Asphalte Company*, that profits are in the case " at all events of a trading or banking company the excess " of the current gains over the working expenses as shown " by a Revenue Account, as distinguished from a Capital " Account. And it would seem from the authority " beginning with *Stringer's* case (reported in L.R. 4, 4 Ch. " App., page 475), and ending with Lord Shand's observa- " tion in *Glasgow Bank v. McKinnon* (19 Scotch Law " Reports, 316 and 9 Court of Sessions Cases, 4th Series " 602), that the profits for the purpose of the Revenue Ac- " count need not be in hand. Lord Shand says, 'It is clear " ' that it is not necessary that there must be cash realised " ' and in the coffers of the bank received expressly on " ' account of interest or profits in order to justify the divi-

" ' dend. To enforce such a rule would be to run counter to " ' ordinary and reasonable usage in cases of commercial " ' companies. In order to ascertain the profits earned and " ' divisible at any time the Balance Sheet must contain a " ' fair statement of the liabilities of the company, in- " ' cluding its paid-up capital ; and, on the other hand, a " ' fair or more properly *bonâ fide* valuation of assets, the " ' balance in favour of the company being profits. These " ' profits may, and must often to a great extent, be repre- " ' sented by obligations of debtors, or secured by direct " ' securities over property. They are not the less profits " ' fairly realised and divisible because they exist in that " ' form, and have not been received in cash.' It is to be " observed that both in *Stringer's* case and in the Scotch " case the Judges were speaking of a profit balance arrived " at by a comparison of the assets' and liabilities' side of a " Balance Sheet, in which the paid-up capital was included " as a liability, and not of profit arrived at in a Revenue " Account by a comparison of the working expenses and the " gains of the financial year ; but the same principle would " seem to apply, and I think, therefore, that it follows from " this that if directors, honestly exercising judgment, treat " in a Revenue Account a debt as a profit earned, though " not received, they could not be said to be paying dividends " out of capital, although the debt should afterwards turn " out a bad debt, and although, in fact, the dividends " should ultimately prove to have been paid out of working " capital."

Here you will notice that the learned Judge appears to be drawing a distinction between the divisible profit shown by a statement of liabilities and assets, and that shown by a Revenue Account or Profit and Loss Account; but I need hardly point out that if in each case profits previously undivided were included, the result would be the same. If interest charged to a customer were thought good enough to be placed to the credit of a Revenue Account, it follows that it would be good enough to be included among the assets as owing by a customer. He appears to have had some doubt as to the reality of the distinction he was making, because he goes on to say that " the same principle " would seem to apply."

At another place he says: " I now propose to consider " whether, although the interest was not paid and the profits " were not realised, the profits were so earned as to justify " the directors in recommending the declaration and pay- " ment of the dividends which were declared and paid, or in " declaring and paying the interim dividends."

And again: " With regard to the interest due from Benham, " who obtained enormous advances on the security of an " unproved will said to have been lost, but which had no " real existence, it is idle to suggest that either the security " or the personal solvency or credit of Benham justified " treating the unreceived interest as profits in each year.

" The same observation applies to Wilkinson.

" In conclusion, it seems to me that whatever may be the " right line to draw as to when profits not received may be " carried to profit for the purpose of the annual Revenue " Account, it is plain that there was no justification for so " doing in the present case."

The last remark was quoted and adopted by Lord Justice Lindley in the Court of Appeal.

The following remark gives some colour to the idea that Mr. Justice Vaughan Williams did deprecate the inclusion in a Revenue Account of unpaid interest as profits. But my view of his meaning is that he deprecated only the inclusion of unpaid interest where the principal debt was of doubtful value :—

" It may be that accountants may justify including year " after year unpaid interest without observation in Revenue " Accounts, and may certify such accounts, but if this is the " rule of accountants, the practical value of an audit is " very little, and I cannot help hoping that a great institu- " tion like the Institute of Chartered Accountants will see " the propriety and expediency of declaring against such a " practice."

I shall be interested to hear whether the Council of the Institute has taken any notice of the remarks I have just read, or of the following, where our Institute is again referred to :—

" I wish also to say, with regard to the form of the " certificates and the form of the Balance Sheets, that the " duty of auditors must necessarily be more or less defined " by the articles of association of the particular company, " and I have already called attention to the fact that the " articles of this company expressly declare that which one " would assume even if there were no express declaration " that the object of the Balance Sheets and Profit and Loss " Account was to inform the shareholders of the financial " state and condition of the company, and to enable them " to judge of the propriety of paying the dividend recom- " mended by the directors, and whatever may be a sufficient " Profit and Loss Account or Revenue Account, whatever " may be a sufficient statement of assets and liabilities to " satisfy the theoretical requirements of the Institute of " Chartered Accountants, it is quite plain that the duties of " these auditors in this particular case was to take care that " the Balance Sheet which bore their name and was " accompanied by their certificate was a Balance Sheet " which should be drawn in such a form and contain such " statements as would give the shareholders the information " necessary to enable them to arrive at a judgment as to the " propriety of declaring and paying the dividend recom- " mended by the directors."

Before leaving Mr. Justice Vaughan Williams' judgment, I may remark that the order was " without prejudice to " any right the directors (and presumably the auditors) " might have to recover from each shareholder the amount " of each dividend paid."

But it is the judgments given in the Court of Appeal by Lords Justices Lindley and Rigby to which I more particu- larly referred as containing definitions, or valuable expres- sions of opinions, as to the duties of auditors. Thus Lord Justice Lindley, in " considering what are the duties of " auditors as respects companies governed by the Companies " Act 1879 and by such articles as those of the London and " General Bank," says : " It is impossible to read section 7 of " the Companies Act 1879 without being struck with the " importance of the enactment that the auditors are to be appointed by the shareholders, and are to report to them directly, and not to, or through, the directors. The object of this enactment is obvious. It evidently is to secure to the shareholders independent and reliable information respecting the true financial position of the company at the time of the audit. The articles of this particular company are even more explicit on this point than the statute itself, and remove any possible ambiguity to which the language of the statute, taken alone, may be open if very narrowly criticised.

" It is no part of an auditor's duty to give advice either to directors or shareholders as to what they ought to do. An auditor has nothing to do with the prudence or impru- dence of making loans with or without security. It is nothing to him whether the business of a company is being conducted prudently or imprudently, profitably or unprofitably ; it is nothing to him whether dividends are properly or improperly declared, provided he discharges his own duty to the shareholders. His business is to ascertain and state the true financial position of the com- pany at the time of the audit, and his duty is confined to that. But then comes the question, How is he to ascer- tain such position ? The answer is, By examining the books of the company. But he does not discharge his duty by doing this without enquiry and without taking any trouble to see that the books of the company themselves show the company's true position. He must take reason- able care to ascertain that they do. Unless he does this, his duty will be worse than a farce. Assuming the books to be so kept as to show the true position of the company, the auditor has to frame a Balance Sheet showing that position according to the books, and to certify that the Balance Sheet presented is correct in that sense. But his first duty is to examine the books, not merely for the pur- pose of ascertaining what they do show, but also for the purpose of satisfying himself that they show the true financial position of the company. This is quite in accor- dance with the decision of Mr. Justice Stirling in *The Leeds Estate Company v. Shephard* in 36 Chancery Division, page 802. An auditor, however, is not bound to do more than exercise reasonable care and skill in making enquiries and investigations. He |is not an insurer; he does not guarantee that the books do correctly show the true posi- tion of the company's affairs; he does not guarantee that his Balance Sheet is accurate according to the books of the company. If he did he would be responsible for an error on his part, even if he were himself deceived, with- out any want of reasonable care on his part—say, by the fraudulent concealment of a book from him. His obliga- tion is not so onerous as this.

"Such I take to be the duty of the auditor ; he must be honest, that is, he must not certify what he does not believe to be true, and he must take reasonable care and skill before he believes that what he certifies is true.

" What is reasonable care in any particular case must depend upon the circumstances of that case. Where there is nothing to excite suspicion very little enquiry will be reasonable and sufficient, and in practice, I believe,

business men select a few cases at haphazard, see that they are right, and assume that others like them are correct also. Where suspicion is aroused more care is obviously necessary, but still an auditor is not bound to exercise more than reasonable care and skill even in a case of suspicion ; and he is perfectly justified in acting on the opinion of an expert where special knowledge is required."

The following is even more important: "A person whose duty it is to convey information to others does not discharge that duty by simply giving them so much information as is calculated to induce them, or some of them, to ask for more. Information and means of information are by no means equivalent terms. Still, there may be circumstances under which information given in the shape of a printed document circulated amongst a large body of shareholders would by its conse- quent publicity be very injurious to their interests, and in such a case I am not prepared to say that an auditor would fail to discharge his duty, if instead of publishing his report in such a way as to ensure publicity, he made a confidential report to the shareholders, and invited their attention to it, and told them where they could see it. The auditor is to make a report to the shareholders, but the mode of doing so, and the form of the report, are not prescribed. If, therefore, Mr. Theobald had laid before the shareholders the Balance Sheet and the Profit and Loss Account, accompanied by a certificate in the form in which he had prepared it, he would, perhaps, have done enough under the peculiar circumstances of the case. I feel, however, the great danger of acting on such a principle, and in order not to be misunderstood, I will add that an auditor who gives shareholders means of informa- tion instead of information in respect of a company's financial position does so at his peril, and runs the very serious risk of being held, judicially, to have failed to dis- charge his duty.

" In this case I have no hesitation in saying that Mr. Theobald did fail to discharge his duty to the shareholders in certifying and laying before them the Balance Sheet of February 1892, without any reference to the report which he laid before the directors, and with no other warning than is conveyed by the words ' The value of the ' assets as shown on the Balance Sheet is dependent upon ' realisation.' "

Then, in allowing Mr. Theobald's appeal as to one of the dividends, he says:—" I am not satisfied that he was then guilty of more than an excusable error of judgment; although now that all the facts are known the error is seen to have been very serious in its consequences."

Lord Justice Rigby refers to, and gives his view of, the words " as shown by the books of the company," which were referred to frequently in the course of the arguments. He says:—" The words ' as shown by the books of the company' seem to me to be introduced to relieve the auditors from any responsibility as to affairs of the company kept out of the books and concealed from them, but not to confine it to a mere statement of the correspondence of the Balance

" Sheet with the entries in the books. Now, a full and fair
" Balance Sheet must be such a Balance Sheet as to convey
" a truthful statement as to the company's position. It
" must not conceal any known cause of weakness in the
" financial position or suggest anything which cannot be
" supported as fairly correct in a business point of view."

He also comments on the insufficiency of the words " de-
" pendent on realisation ":—" In the last-mentioned report
" is contained for the first time a statement, ' The value of
" ' the assets as shown on the Balance Sheet is dependent
" ' on realisation.' Great stress has been laid on this by
" counsel for the appellants. They argue that it was
" sufficient to put members upon enquiry, and that from the
" course taken at the trial they were debarred from giving
" the evidence of experts as to the importance and signifi-
" cation of this. I may at once say that it was the duty of
" the auditors to convey in direct and express terms to the
" members any information which they thought proper to
" be communicated, that the words of the statement are
" perfectly clear in their meaning, but also entirely unim-
" portant, amounting to a mere truism, and that no evidence
" of experts would have been of the slightest use for the
" purpose of giving them a greater importance or significa-
" tion than they possessed in themselves, even if such
" evidence were admissible."

I do not think that in these remarks the Judges put their
conception of our duties on a higher level than the standard
which we have as a body set up for ourselves. But, in my
opinion, the "position of accountants" is, if anything,
improved by these references to their duties in the judgments
of high legal authorities.

So far, I have dealt only with the judgment given on the
main issues affecting the auditors, viz.:—(1) Whether they
were guilty of misfeasance, and (2) whether the misfeasance
occasioned loss to the company. But there remains the
question which was raised, whether an auditor is an officer
of the company.

The question, as put by Lord Justice Lindley in his judgment, was " whether an auditor of this bank can be properly
" regarded as an officer within the meaning of section 10 of
" the Winding-up Act 1890." The insertion of the words
" of this bank " is important, as the articles of association of
the bank were considered in determining the question, and
the decision was limited to that bank and cases like it.

As, however, this was the first time the question was
raised, it may be convenient to read some portions of the
judgments given in this case. He says:—

" The question which has been submitted to us in this case
" is, whether an auditor of this bank can be properly regarded
" as an officer within the meaning of section 10 of the
" Winding-up Act of 1890. That section runs thus : ' Where,
" ' in the course of the winding-up of a company under the
" ' Companies Acts, it appears that any person who has
" ' taken part in the formation or promotion of the company,
" ' or any past or present director, manager, liquidator, or
" ' other officer of the company has misapplied, or retained,
" ' or become liable or accountable for any moneys or
" ' property of the company, or been guilty of any mis-

" ' feasance or breach of trust in relation to the company,
" ' the Court may, on the application of the Official Receiver,
" ' or of the liquidator of the company, or of any creditor or
" ' contributor of the company, examine into the conduct of
" ' such promoter, director, manager, liquidator, or other
" ' officer of the company, and compel him to repay any
" ' moneys or restore any property so misapplied or retained,
" ' or for which he has become liable or accountable, together
" ' with interest after such rate as the Court thinks just, or
" ' to contribute such sums of money to the assets of the
" ' company by way of compensation, in respect of such
" ' misapplication, retainer, misfeasance, or breach of trust
" ' as the Court thinks just.'

" Now, it is urged by Mr. Cohen that the auditor of a
" company is not an officer within the meaning of that
" section. It appears to me that, in order to decide that
" question, we must examine and consider what an auditor
" is, how he is appointed, by whom he is paid, and what his
" duties are. This is a company—a banking company—and
" the auditor is required to be appointed under the Companies
" Act of 1879. This Companies Act of 1879 is one of the
" group of Acts which are usually referred to as the
" Companies Acts from 1862 down to, I think, 1890. Now,
" section 7 of this Companies Act of 1879 runs thus:—
" ' Once at the least in every year the accounts of every
" ' banking company registered after the passing of this Act
" ' as a limited company shall be examined by an auditor or
" ' auditors, who shall be elected annually by the company
" ' in general meeting. A director or officer of the company
" ' shall not be capable of being elected auditor of such
" ' company. An auditor on quitting office shall be re-
" ' eligible. If any casual vacancy occurs in the office of
" ' any auditor, the surviving auditor or auditors (if any)
" ' may act, but if there is no surviving auditor, the directors
" ' shall forthwith call an extraordinary general meeting for
" ' the purpose of supplying the vacancy or vacancies in the
" ' auditorship. Every auditor shall have a list delivered to
" ' him of all books kept by the company, and shall at all
" ' reasonable times have access to the books and accounts
" ' of the company; and any auditor may, in relation to
" ' such books and accounts, examine the directors or any
" ' other officer of the company. Provided that if a banking
" ' company has branch banks beyond the limits of Europe,
" ' it shall be sufficient if the auditor is allowed access to
" ' such copies of and extracts from the books and accounts
" ' of any such branch as may have been transmitted to the
" ' head office of the banking company in the United
" ' Kingdom. The auditor or auditors shall make a report
" ' to the members on the accounts examined by him or
" ' them, and on every Balance Sheet laid before the
" ' company in general meeting during his or their tenure
" ' of office; and in every such report shall state whether,
" ' in his or their opinion, the Balance Sheet referred to in
" ' the report is a full and fair Balance Sheet properly drawn
" ' up, so as to exhibit a true and correct view of the state
" ' of the company's affairs as shown by the books of the
" ' company, and such report shall be read before the
" ' company in general meeting. The remuneration of the

" ' auditor or auditors shall be fixed by the general meeting
" ' appointing such auditor or auditors, and shall be paid by
" ' the company.' And section 8 says ' the auditors shall
" ' sign a Balance Sheet,' and so on. Now, reading that
" section alone, it seems impossible to deny that for some
" purposes and to some extent an auditor is an officer of the
" company. He is appointed by the company, he is paid by
" the company, and his position is described by the section
" as that of an officer of the company. He is not a servant
" of the directors. On the contrary, he is appointed by the
" company to check the directors, and for some purposes,
" and to some extent, it seems to me quite impossible to say
" that he is not an officer of the company."

He then quotes from the articles of the bank as confirming
and amplifying the sections of the Act :—

" Well, so much for the Act. If we pass to the articles of
" this particular company, we shall find there are some which
" are important. On page 6, Article 2, 'Auditors and
" ' Secretary' (this is the definition clause) ' means those
" ' respective officers from time to time of the company.'
" Article 73, on page 23, runs thus : ' Every director, auditor,
" ' manager, secretary, and other officer shall be indemnified
" ' by the company from all losses . . . . .' "

And he concludes thus :—

" I do not think there is anything else in those articles
" which is material. I do not know that those articles carry
" the matter very much further than the section of the Act
" to which I have alluded, and my observations upon the
" articles and that Act are those which I have already made,
" viz., that for some purpose, and to some extent, at all
" events, an auditor is an officer appointed by the company,
" although in no sense a servant of the directors.
" Then it is said—it is not denied in truth—but it is said
" that for all that he is not an officer of the company within
" the meaning of section 10. And it is put in this way, that
" an officer within the meaning of section 10 is an officer
" who, in some way or other, has control over the assets of
" the company. Now, it is quite obvious that this section
" applies to something more than the misapplication of
" assets. Misapplication or retainer or becoming liable or
" accountable for the assets is provided for by the first part
" of the section which I have read ; but, in addition to that,
" there is mention made of misfeasance or breach of trust
" in relation to the company, and, with reference to that,
" provision is made not by the words which authorise the
" Court to compel the person guilty of misfeasance or breach
" of trust to repay any moneys or restore any property, but
" to contribute such sums of money to the assets of the
" company by way of compensation in respect of such mis-
" application, retainer, misfeasance, or breach of trust as
" the Court thinks just."

He then meets the objection that the auditors should be
proceeded against by action, and not by a misfeasance summons. He says :—

" Now, it is said that that is very hard upon persons who
" are auditors, and that if they are guilty of negligence,
" fraud, or misconduct, the proper way is by an action. But
" suppose an action were brought against an auditor upon

" the ground that the accounts had been fraudulently
" audited, how could that be possibly tried by a jury ? It
" would demand and would necessitate a prolonged investi-
" gation of the accounts, and no one who has any experience
" of trial by jury would for a moment pretend that it could
" be so tried, and therefore it must be referred to some other
" tribunal. Therefore the point made by Mr. Cohen that
" you are going to deprive him of his constitutional right
" really does not apply, and it appears to me that the objec-
" tion fails, and therefore we are not prepared to say, and
" cannot say, that the auditor of a company in a case like
" this is not an officer of the company within section 10."

Lord Justice Lopes says :—

" I am of the same opinion. The question is whether an
" auditor, such as the auditor in this case, is an officer within
" the true meaning of section 10. I do not propose to read
" the section again, which has already been read, but it is to
" be observed in respect of this section that it does not
" create any new rights, but it gives a very summary mode
" of procedure in enforcing rights already existing. Now, if
" it were not for the word ' misfeasance ' in section 10, I
" should not have thought that an auditor, such as the
" auditor in the present case, came within the meaning of
" that section."

And then he defines " misfeasance " as a " breach of
duty." Later on he deals with an objection arising out of a
previous case, and he says :—

" Now, there was a case referred to, which is a case *In re*
" *The Liberator Permanent Benefit Building Society*, which
" came before Mr. Justice Cave and Mr. Justice Collins, and
" I find it reported in the 71st volume of the *Law Times*, on
" page 406. That was not a case of an auditor. That was
" the case of a solicitor. It was not the case of a banking
" company but of a building society. And it is true that Mr.
" Justice Cave, in the course of his judgment, says, ' It
" ' seems to me that merely because he was appointed soli-
" ' citor to the society, without more, the solicitor does
" ' not become an officer of the society any more than it has
" ' been held that a banker does if he is appointed banker to
" ' the society, or a broker if he is appointed broker to the
" ' society, or the auditor if he is appointed auditor to the
" ' society.' I do not think that the attention of Mr. Justice
" Cave was drawn to the word ' misfeasance'; but, however
" that may have been, that was not a case of an auditor, but
" the case of a solicitor, that had been decided ; and it may
" be again said that the section of the Act of 1879 which
" relates to the auditor of a banking company, would not
" relate in the same way to a solicitor, and, for anything I
" know (I have not been able to find it out), it does not
" appear that the articles of association, so far as I can see,
" recognise the auditor as an officer. I come, therefore, to
" the conclusion that the auditor of this banking company
" was an officer within the true meaning of section 10 of the
" Companies (Winding-up) Act of 1890."

As further qualifying or limiting this decision, I ought to
read the opening remarks of Lord Justice Kay, who says :—

" I come to the same conclusion, but I wish to guard
" myself against being understood to hold that, in every case

" of a joint stock company, the auditor employed by the
" joint stock company is an officer of the company. I do
" not at present hold that opinion; I can quite conceive
" there may be one or two cases of a joint stock company
" who call in an auditor to make a particular audit, where
" the auditor called in could not be properly treated as an
" officer of the company."

He also deals with some words in the Act and articles
which had been put forward as pointing to an opposite conclusion to that arrived at by the Judges:—

" Section 108 (some comments were made with regard to
" the words and the language of that section) provides that
" no director or officer of the company shall, during his
" continuance in office, be eligible as auditor. It was said
" that that shows plainly that an auditor is not to be an
" officer of the company but somebody who is not an officer.
" I do not read it in that sense. That is a mere copy of the
" language of the Act of 1879, which provides in section 7,
" sub-section 2, that 'a director or officer of the company
" ' shall not be capable of being elected an auditor of such
" ' company.' Here the auditor is treated as an officer of
" the company. They provide also in their articles that the
" auditor shall not hold any other office in the company.
" At the same time I take article 108 not to contradict that
" which has been said in the earlier part of these articles,
" that an auditor of this company is an officer of the com-
" pany, but merely to provide, as the statute provides,
" that while he is an auditor he shall not hold any other
" office in the company. The object of that section is that
" he might not hold some other office the duties of which
" might bias him in his conduct as an auditor; and there-
" fore, to prevent the danger of that, it is provided by the
" statute, and repeated by the articles, that he cannot hold
" at the same time any other office of the company."

I will now deal with *The Kingston Cotton Mill Company,
Lim.* In connection with that case, there were three judgments, two in relation to this question of whether an
auditor is an officer of a company, and the other on the
hearing of the misfeasance summons. Before the hearing
of the misfeasance summons, " the auditors in June last
" took out a summons asking that all further proceedings
" might be stayed as against the auditors, on the ground
" that they were not officers within section 10 of the Act of
" 1890."

The importance of this case was that the previous decision was in the case of *The London and General Bank*,
which was a banking company, under the Companies Act
1879, of which section 7 makes compulsory the audit of
accounts; and, moreover, the articles of that bank referred
to the auditors as "officers," whereas the articles of the
Kingston Cotton Mill Company nowhere so described them.

In the course of his judgment, Mr. Justice Vaughan
Williams made the following remarks, and I wish to call
your attention to them, because the effect of his decision is
so general and far-reaching, that one can scarcely imagine
a company with the usual ordinary provisions as to audit
that would not be included in its definitions. The report
says:—" If there had been no previous decisions as to who

" was an officer of a company, his lordship would not have
" had much hesitation in holding that the auditors of the
" company were officers, having regard to the fact that
" directors were officers. . . .

" Mr. Eady instanced the case of an accountant being
" called in by a committee of shareholders to make a report
" on the financial condition of a company, but it was un-
" necessary to express an opinion as to this, and wiser not
" to do so, having regard to the effects sometimes produced
" by *obiter dicta.* What was the position of an auditor
" appointed under the articles of association, and not merely
" called in if his services happened to be required? An
" auditor under articles like these was called in every year.
" Under the articles the business of the company could not,
" without him, be carried on in any year. Such an auditor
" was not a casual person appointed for that particular
" turn. He had to perform duties without the performance
" of which the company could not go on. Not only had he
" to make a report, without which dividends could not be
" paid or declared, but some of his duties had to be per-
" formed in conjunction with the directors. No doubt he
" was appointed to be a check on the directors, but he and
" they had to do acts without which the business could not
" be carried on. Under these articles the auditors had to
" examine the Balance Sheet with the accounts and
" vouchers. They had free access to the books and accounts,
" and might, in relation to the accounts, examine the
" directors and other officers of the company. Having done
" that, the auditors had to make a report on the Balance
" Sheet and accounts, and to state whether the former was
" a proper one showing the true state of the company's
" affairs, and if they had called for explanations they had to
" state whether satisfactory explanations had been given;
" and this report had to be read at the ordinary meeting of
" shareholders. His lordship wished to say of auditors
" generally that those who had to perform such duties as
" these were officers of the company. His lordship then
" examined at some length the judgments delivered by the
" Lords Justices in *Re London and General Bank*, particu-
" larly the judgment of Lord Justice Kay, who, said his
" lordship, had guarded himself from saying that an auditor
" was in every case an officer of the company. But if an
" auditor had to perform the ordinary duties of the position,
" examining directors if thought necessary, and reporting
" on Balance Sheets to the shareholders, he was an officer of
" the company. Lord Justice Kay had referred to the
" articles of the London and General Bank, which were very
" like the articles in the present case, and his lordship did
" not think Mr. Eady asked him to say that the Companies
" Act 1879 was the ground of the Appeal Court's decision; the
" Lords Justices did not say that. His lordship could not
" see what Mr. Eady could rely on as preventing these
" gentlemen from being officers of the company. They were
" called in to perform the duties of an office created by the
" articles. He said they were paid by fees, but so were the
" directors. He said they were appointed only for a time,
" but so were the directors. Having regard to the articles
" of this company, these particular auditors were officers of

" the company. But his lordship could not stop there.
" They were officers because they had to perform a duty the
" performance of which was required by the articles, a duty
" which they had to perform in conjunction with officers of
" the company, and a duty which, as appeared by the
" articles, would be mainly the basis on which the action of
" the shareholders, with reference to declaring dividends,
" rested."

The auditors appealed, and the appeal was heard by Lord
Herschell and Lords Justices A. L. Smith and Rigby. The
appeal was dismissed, but Lord Herschell, in the course of
his judgment, made some remarks which suggest that possibly these decisions might be reversed if the point were taken
to the House of Lords :—

" Now, a question very similar to this came before the
" Court of Appeal in the case of *In re The London and*
" *General Bank.* The question there was whether the
" auditors of the London and General Bank were officers
" within the meaning of the section in question. This Court
" held that they were, and I can see no substantial distinc-
" tion between that case and the present. I will allude in
" a moment to the distinctions which have been suggested,
" but it seems to me that it would be frittering away the
" case altogether if we were to rest our determination upon
" any of the distinctions which alone can be made in the
" present case. Now, I desire to express no opinion upon
" the question whether *In re The London and General Bank*
" was rightly or wrongly decided. It may be that the
" reasoning in that case is open to criticism. It may be
" that some considerations which bear upon the question
" were not referred to, or had not full effect given to them ;
" on all that I express no opinion at all. I desire to retain
" absolute liberty of action, in case it should hereafter
" become necessary, on the question whether *In re The*
" *London and General Bank* was rightly decided. Now, let
" us see what *In re The London and General Bank* did
" decide. It decided that the auditors appointed in that
" case were officers within the meaning of the section. On
" what grounds ? Under the Act of 1879 certain articles
" contained in Table A to the Act of 1862, which prior to
" that Act companies might either adopt or reject as they
" pleased, became by statute absolutely binding on banking
" companies. That, even if not strictly accurate, is suffi-
" ciently accurate for the purpose of this case. They had to
" appoint auditors, and certain provisions were made applic-
" able to them, which were in substance the provisions of
" Table A so far as auditors are concerned. Now, the London
" and General Bank, besides these, what I may call compul-
" sory articles, had also articles of its own. The reasoning
" in that case was rested largely, I may say mainly, on this
" —that the auditors were by the provisions of the Act of
" 1879, which were made applicable to the bank, made
" officers of the company. The language of those provi-
" sions was dwelt upon as showing that they were officers of
" the company. It is true, and here comes the distinction
" suggested, that in that case they were so denominated in
" an indemnity clause, whereas in the present case they are
" not so denominated. But it would be far too narrow a

" distinction to rest any difference of decision on that
" ground. Therefore, in the present case the articles are in
" substance the same, the auditors are created officers, if
" they are officers in that case, in precisely the same way as
" in the present case. I can see no substantial distinction
" between the two. If misfeasance of officers extended to
" the auditors in the case of the London and General Bank,
" it seems to me that no substantial reason can be given
" why misfeasance of officers should not extend to auditors
" in the present case. I cannot in substance distinguish
" the two cases. But, of course, all that we decide is that,
" in a case identical with *In re The London and General*
" *Bank,* as I take this to be in substance, the auditor is an
" officer. We decide that as bound by the previous decision
" of the Court of Appeal. Beyond that our decision does not
" go. I say this in consequence of some general observations
" made by the learned Judge in the Court below, as to which
" I express no opinion. For these reasons I think that this
" appeal must be dismissed."

I shall not weary you by attempting to carry the discussion
further than the point at which it has been left by the
learned Judges.

I now turn to Mr. Justice Vaughan Williams' judgment in
the case of the *Kingston Cotton Mill Co., Lim.,* whereby the
auditors were held liable for the preference dividends
which had been illegally paid. This differs from the subject
I have just left, inasmuch as it is not so much a legal
question, involving the interpretation of sections of an Act of
Parliament, but more a question of common sense, upon
which any business man is competent to form an opinion.
It is a question on which Chartered Accountants, as professional auditors, are not only specially qualified to offer
opinions, but one in which they have a very real and practical
interest.

Time will not permit me even to refer to several suggestive
remarks made in the course of the case (which is reported in
*The Accountant* of the 28th December last), but I will go at
once to the question of the stock, in which we are most
interested.

This, you will remember, was falsified by the manager (as
he admitted) to a very large extent ; as counsel stated, in one
year £10,000, and in another year £37,000. It was not
suggested that the auditors knew of this, but it was alleged
that they ought to have made such inquiries as would have
resulted in the discovery of these fraudulent statements of
value.

I may remark that although both Judge and counsel made
pertinent remarks as to the extent of the responsibility sought
to be thrown upon auditors by directors when they are
defendants in such a case as this, the judgment nevertheless
appears very lenient to the directors (I do not say unjustly
so) but very severe upon the auditors. It acquits the
directors on the ground that " they acted reasonably in
" accepting the certificate of the manager," that " they paid
" away these dividends in the honest and reasonable belief
" that the necessary profits had been earned," and " that
" the grounds of their belief were the statements of the
" manager, whom they had no reason to suspect." But the

Judge held that "with regard to the stock-in-trade the case "of the auditors is very different from that of the directors," and he gave as his reason that the auditors "certainly were "not entitled to rely upon the manager's certificate if an "ordinary careful examination of the books ought to have "made them suspect that statement."

Here we have it laid down that the certificate of a manager or other officer of a company, as to the quantities and values of stock, must not be accepted by the auditor without testing their accuracy; and the auditor will not be exempt from responsibility, even though it is stated in the Balance Sheet (as was done in this case) that the figures of the stock were in accordance with the manager's certificate. I come to this conclusion from the following defence which was set up by the auditors: "And the auditors say that in "the Balance Sheets and accounts which they certified, the "figures in respect of the stock-in-trade were stated, as the "fact was, to be by the manager's certificate, and that the "auditors had no duty to go behind that certificate, and "showed no want of reasonable skill and care in abstaining "from so doing, once they believed the certificate to be true "and had no ground for suspecting the contrary."

At first sight it appears fair to a superficial observer to state, as a general proposition, that an auditor must be held liable for errors or misstatements in a Balance Sheet which "an ordinary careful examination" would enable him to discover or suspect; but, before the proposition can be accepted, we, as auditors, require to have some definition of what is "an ordinary careful examination." In some cases the examination necessary to test the accuracy of the stock list might be an extremely simple matter, and might occupy only a comparatively short time; while in others it would be exceedingly complex, and practically impossible in the time usually allowed for an audit, owing to the nature and the extent of the business.

Another element which must not be lost sight of is the amount of fee allowed for an audit. It may be said that if an auditor cannot properly perform the duties of his office for the fee attached to it, he should not accept the appointment. In answer to that, an auditor often finds it difficult to estimate the amount of work that may be necessary; but I do not dissent from the proposition that, having accepted the office, he must do his duty, even though it results in pecuniary loss to him. But here, again, we want a definition of his duties. Assume that in one of his audits, in the exercise of his discretion, and for reasons which he considers sufficient, he not only examines the stock list as to extensions and additions, but checks the prices of each considerable lot of goods, as he can do so with a reasonable effort and expenditure of time. In a second case, the prices cannot so easily be checked, or are not of the same importance; but he thinks it advisable to test the quantities; and, being able to do so with facility, he instructs his clerks to make this a special feature of the audit. But, in a third case, he finds that he cannot in the time allowed, or in any reasonable time, or with any degree of certainty, test the values, or the quantities, or either of them; therefore, he determines to inform the shareholders (some of whom, at least,

may be presumed to have some knowledge of the business) that the quantities and prices or bulk values have not been checked by him, but have been supplied by the manager or others. In such a case, has he, or has he not, done his duty? If he has, then he ought not to be held liable if it is afterwards discovered, when the concern has gone into liquidation and a special enquiry into the causes is instituted, that the stock was over-valued, and that dividends have been paid out of capital.

If it be said that he has not done his duty in such a case, it follows that auditors are responsible for the accuracy of stocks, and must therefore be present personally or by a representative when the stocks are taken, and must make minute inquiry into the reasons for the values affixed to them. Even if shareholders were prepared to pay for this, accountants do not claim to know everything, and would be liable to be deceived; therefore, in doubtful and difficult cases, prudent men would decline to undertake the responsibility. In my opinion, it would be better and more equitable that auditors should be held to have discharged their duty if they openly state that they must not be regarded as responsible for this or that item in the Balance Sheet, and thus throw the responsibility on the shareholders to instruct them, or some other experts, to make a special inquiry in cases where it is thought necessary.

I do not know whether I am right in assuming that Mr. Justice Vaughan Williams' decision would have been the same if, instead of its being stated on the Balance Sheet certified by the auditors that the stock was by the manager's certificate, that fact had been expressly stated as part of the auditor's certificate; but I have assumed that they would still have been held responsible.

I have been dealing with the subject generally, and not specially with reference to the *Kingston Cotton Mill Company, Lim.* It may be that in that particular case the facts and circumstances were such as to make it a subject of surprise that suspicion was not aroused.

Personally, I cannot altogether efface from my mind the impression I first received on reading the case—that it was a weak one from the accountant's point of view, that it was not in fact one we should choose as a test case. I refer more especially to the examination of Mr. Peasegood by Mr. Hardy and the Judge with respect to the stock, and to the finding of the Judge that "Mr. Pickering knew that the "value of the mill, machinery, and site was not half the "value mentioned in the Balance Sheet." He gave the auditors, as he said, "the benefit of his decision with respect "to dividends so far as it was based on *Lee v. Neuchatel Co.* "and *Verner's* case," and therefore he did not hold them pecuniarily liable for withholding the fact of the valuation of the mill, &c., but it is probable that he was influenced by it, and by the form of their certificate, as he declined to allow them costs, having regard, as he said, to "the manner "in which the audit was carried out."

But, whatever the merits of this particular case, the important fact we have to consider is that the Judge's decision was based on the ground, as stated by him, "that the "auditors were not entitled to rely on the manager's certifi-

" cate if an ordinary careful examination of the books ought
" to have made them suspect that statement." He then
illustrated what he considered in that case was "an ordinary
" careful examination," thus:—

" Now, it is plain to me that if the auditors had added to
" the stock-in-trade at the beginning of any year the pur-
" chases of raw material in that year and had deducted
" therefrom the sales, they must have seen that the state-
" ment of the stock-in-trade at the end of the year was so
" remarkable as to call for explanation, and they called for
" none.  It is said that it is no part of the duty of an auditor
" to take stock.  I agree it is not; but when it is said that
" it is no part of his duty to test the accuracy of the manager's
" certificate by a comparison of the figures in the books that
" require auditing I cannot agree."

Here the Judge clearly referred to the evidence given by
Mr. Rowe, the Official Receiver's clerk, which was as
follows:—

" Mr. Arthur Francis Rowe (assistant examiner in the
" Official Receiver's department) gave evidence as to the stock
" of cotton and yarn in the company's possession.  He said
" that the investigation of the books showed that in the
" beginning of each year the stock had undoubtedly been
" unduly loaded.  Cross-examined by Mr. Haldane as to the
" system by which he arrived at his conclusions as to the
" inflation of stock, he said he took the initial figures from
" the Stock Journal, and assumed that they were correct, in
" order to ascertain the inflation during the year.  It was a
" process of scrutiny, and for that scrutiny the first figure to
" be got was the figure showing the amount of raw cotton
" purchased.  He got that from the Invoice Guard Book,
" which showed the weights, and the goods sold he got direct
" from the Sales Day Book."

But I submit that such an inquiry as the Official Receiver's
clerk made into the quantities of stocks, purchases, and
sales, was something more than what the Judge described as
" an ordinary careful examination," and moreover it was
made "after the event" (when it is easy to be wise).

But once such an inquiry was thought necessary, it was
comparatively easy in the Kingston Mill case, where I
believe only spinning was carried on, and the raw material
and the finished goods were respectively bought and sold by
weight.  But how, if the company had woven the yarn into
cloth?  I admit it would have been possible to discover the
existence of large errors or misstatements; but the inquiry
would be much more difficult and prolonged.  It would be
necessary to get from a disinterested expert the weight of
cotton yarn (as distinguished from size) in each of the many
classes of pieces made and sold by the company.

It is possible in the case of some merchants to trace and
connect each lot purchased with one or more lots sold, or in
stock, and in one of our audits we actually do this, but it
would not be quite so easy to trace goods bought in the grey,
and then bleached, dyed, or printed, and cut and sold in
varying lengths.  I made such an inquiry once, and succeeded
in tracing in which department the stock had been falsified;
but I should not recommend you to insist on doing that in
all such cases as part of "an ordinary careful examination."

Many other instances will occur to you where it would be
practically impossible, as part of an ordinary audit, to test
the quantities in stock; but it would be still more difficult
to discover an error or wilful misstatement of value where
the quantities given were correct, but low quality goods were
classed as of higher quality.  Nothing short of a careful
examination of the records of production (assuming them to
be properly kept) would enable this to be done—even
approximately.

I do not go so far as to say that Mr. Justice Vaughan
Williams would, in such cases as I have instanced, necessarily decide as he did in the Kingston Mill Company case;
he would probably say that each case must be decided on
its merits.  But, even so, it depends upon the nature and
extent of the enquiry into a stock list, which he or any other
Judge may (after the event) consider to be an " ordinary
" careful examination," whether an auditor is to be mulcted
in damages for misfeasance.  But, if I am right in my
assumption of the scope of this decision, there is the further
hardship than an auditor cannot contract himself out of
this liability for erroneous or fraudulent statements of value
made by the company's officials.  This, to me, is the most
important point, and one to which we should direct our
attention with a view to having it decided authoritatively,
if it is still in doubt.  Mr. Justice Vaughan Williams'
decision would be comparatively innocuous if it were possible
for an auditor to free himself from liability by stating that
he is not responsible for the accuracy of the stock, or to limit
his responsibility by explaining how far, or in what respects,
he had tested the value.

If I am asked how the "position of accountancy" is
affected by the Kingston Mill case, I must reply that I do
not think it will have any very adverse effect.  It has called
public attention to the very heavy responsibilities which rest
upon us, and it will probably result in our duties being
more accurately defined, which, as I have already said, I
regard as a real advantage.

Mr. ADAM MURRAY, F.C.A.: It is very good of you, Mr.
President, to have called upon me, but I should almost have
preferred to listen to what may be said by others.  I am
placed somewhat in a difficulty this evening, as I am now
almost out of practice, although I continue to take an
interest in accountancy questions.  (Hear, hear.)  I am
sure we have all been very pleased to listen to the able
address which the President has been good enough to prepare
for us.  (Applause.)  The two cases, sir, which you have
based your paper upon are very important to us all as
accountants, and I am glad personally that you have taken
the view that they will be very valuable to us, and make us
feel our responsibilities.  You have enunciated the views
which we have had expressed before from time to time, and
very clearly in the able paper by Mr. Gregory which some
of us had the pleasure of listening to in October 1894 at
the autumnal meeting at Liverpool.  (Hear, hear.)  He
then used words somewhat to this effect: " That we must
" recognise and face our responsibility, and that we should
" magnify our office."  That is the view which I have held
myself.  The two cases that you have referred to in your

address to-night, therefore, are useful to us ; and the judgments in connection with them will have a very good effect in regard to the practice of accountants in making us feel our responsibility. (Applause.) We must all have felt some anxiety in consequence of the judgments which were given in those cases, and that we must be exceedingly careful in our audits and not pass anything upon which we may have a doubt. In the case of *The London and General Bank*, it is a little difficult to form an opinion as to the judgment delivered, although generally we seem to have the impression that it was right (hear, hear) ; and that the auditors could scarcely have escaped the view which was taken not only by Mr. Justice Vaughan Williams, but also by the Court of Appeal. As you have said, we felt some uncertainty on the question of interest, if the judge intended to say that no interest carried to the credit of a Profit and Loss Account could be used for the purpose of dividends until it had actually been received. If that were to be the case, and that principle were to be applied to all companies, then it would be impossible to declare a dividend within a reasonable time after the close of the period for which the dividend is declared. (Hear, hear.) A long time would have to be allowed to elapse, and debts would have to be got in, before we could say that the profit, although earned, had actually been realised. The words in the Act of 1879 are not so clear as they might be ; but still we must all feel that the view taken was the right one in considering auditors as officers of a company. The clause would have been much clearer if it had run something in these words : " An auditor shall " not be a person holding any other office in connection " with the company." (Hear, hear.) Then that would have implied that the auditor was an officer of the company. In the case of the *Kingston Mills Company*, one can see great difficulties in connection with the judgment which was given. Suppose there was a change of auditor. How could the new auditor tell anything about the stock at the beginning of the period ? He might be able to make some test at the end of the period ; but if there had been errors, if the stock had been falsified at the commencement, he would scarcely have the means of testing that stock or satisfying himself upon it unless it had been certified by others in such a way as to relieve him from the responsibility of going into that question. (Hear, hear.) He would, of course, have to satisfy himself as well as he could, but still there would be a responsibility which we might have to take, and of which we might not feel the effect for a considerable time. It has been put in a general way that if the auditors had made a careful examination in connection with the stocks they might have found out that the stock at the end of the period had been magnified. Well, it is a little difficult to say unless one saw how the Profit and Loss Account was prepared. From what we have read, taking the stock to begin with and the purchases, I do not know that any accountant could very readily have found out that there were errors in connection with the stock. If it had been put in another way, and said that the Profit and Loss Account had been made up showing the consumption of cotton and of other materials,

then it would have been more easy to make a test of the Profit and Loss Account in that way than by reference to the amount of stock in comparison with the turnover. That I do not think would have helped us very much. However, these two cases lead us to consider our position, and to free ourselves from liability as far as we can. Mr. Whinney has very well said that we must do all that is possible ; but if we are to be responsible for stocks, then our position is a very anxious one. (Hear, hear.) If we are not to be relieved by a statement in the Balance Sheet that the stock has been certified by managers or employees of the company, then I do not know how far our responsibility is to go. (Hear, hear.) We should have a difficulty in some accounts in satisfying ourselves whether stocks were correct or not ; but it seems as if the view was to saddle the auditors with all possible responsibility. Some accountants were very much alarmed by the decision in the *London and General Bank* case, and thought that they must at once give up their bank audits. I was rather surprised myself to hear that view expressed ; because I should think there is about as little anxiety in connection with the audit of the accounts of a bank as with any company. I consider it easier to satisfy oneself in connection with a bank audit than it is with many other audits. There is, of course, a great deal that we can do, and which we should not omit. If we take the accounts of a colliery company, for instance, we might find a large amount of over-paid royalties upheld. Well, we ought not to be content with the mere fact of these royalties having been paid, and a large amount upheld after writing off so much of the royalty as was chargeable against the coal got. We should ask for the certificate of the valuer—either the valuer for the lessors, or the valuer for the company. That point, and many others, we have to be more anxious about ; and, therefore, out of these two cases good, I think, will come to us. I do not know that we are likely to get much from legislation. We have had the report of the Departmental Committee, appointed by the Board of Trade to enquire what amendments might be made in the Companies Acts, but in the draft Bill of that Committee we find that the 10th section of the Act of 1890 is adhered to ; and it does not seem to have been thought that we could have any relief from it. It is a matter of sentiment to some extent. I have not been very anxious about it myself, and have not thought it important whether an auditor would be liable to an action at law or under the misfeasance section. It seems to me that too much was made of the question in considering whether it should not be taken to the House of Lords. We have our lessons to learn in connection with these cases, and I hope we shall profit from them. (Applause.)

Mr. JOHN MATHER, F.C.A.: I would have preferred hearing the views of one or two others before saying what few words I wish to say to-night, but unfortunately I have to leave to keep another appointment, and, therefore, I will say what occurs to me on the subject now. I am sure we cannot fail to feel very grateful to our President for the way in which he has dealt with the subject. (Hear, hear.) I think I may take credit to some extent for having urged that this question should be dealt with, and dealt with by ur President, and I fully expected that we should have it ealt with in a very able and exhaustive manner, and I must ay I have not been disappointed. (Applause.) But the 'resident began by congratulating us that our duties and esponsibilities had been defined by these recent decisions. 'hough I agree with that observation to a certain extent, et we must admit that they have been defined in such a vay as to make us feel that if they do exist to the full ex- ent as defined, the future generations of auditors certainly ught to come into much larger fees than the present one. Laughter.) Now, a good deal was said in these judgments ,bout "reasonable care and skill." Well, that is a very lastic phrase. (Hear, hear.) It is a phrase, I suppose, hat must be ultimately defined by a Judge of the Court in vhich such cases are decided. An auditor may have his wn ideas, and a client may have his own ideas, as to what s "reasonable care and skill," and a Judge on the bench nay have somewhat different ideas from either of them. t is a matter in which we have no certainty, and I suppose t throws the whole question back upon the conscientious egard which an auditor has in respect of the duties which ie undertakes. It certainly warns all persons who enter he profession against what is called "scamping" their vork (hear, hear) ; a thing that is known in other occupa- ions, more or less, but which will not be excused n the profession of an auditor, and young students can- not be too much impressed with that fact. I vas struck by one remark which occurred in a ιuotation which the President read from one of he judgments, that an auditor although he must use reasonable care and skill in ascertaining that the books how the true position of the company, is nevertheless not responsible, not bound to certify that the Balance Sheet shows the position of the company, or states the position of he company as shown by the books, because it is possible hat a book may have been fraudulently withheld from an iuditor, and therefore he is not called upon to certify that the Balance Sheet, which is described as his Balance Sheet (and there I think we may take exception to the phraseology because a Balance Sheet may be prepared by the directors, und then they are responsible for the form of it, I think, within certain limits, but if it is a reasonable disclosure of the position of the company, I suppose the auditor would not be too fastidious as to the exact form—that is to say, within certain reasonable limits), discloses the true state of the company. The auditor is not usually supposed to pre- pare the Balance Sheet, and he is not usually paid for preparing the Balance Sheet—that is, as an auditor. It is accountancy work, which, of course, may be done in some cases by the auditor ; but an auditor's duties, as defined by law, of course do not include the preparation of the Balance Sheet. It is simply the examination of it and the verification of it that he has to look to, and therefore it is not his Balance Sheet in any sense. But I do submit that we ought to consider ourselves bound to certify whether a Balance Sheet is a correct abstract from the books of the company, and whether it discloses the position of the com- pany as shown by the books (hear, hear) ; that being a dis- tinct question from the examination and verification of the

correctness of the books themselves. With regard to the very important question of stocks, I think the President dealt with that matter in a very lucid and a very satisfac- tory manner, but the whole question is left in a state which is certainly unsatisfactory to the profession at present. (Hear, hear.) I gather that the Judge would not go so far as to say that an auditor is in all cases responsible for the correctness of the stock, but that he is responsible in those cases where he might have discovered that it was incorrect by the exercise of reasonable care and skill. Well, I sup- pose we would admit that within those limits the auditor is responsible to endeavour to ascertain whether there is any- thing in the stock sheet which would indicate anything wrong or which might indicate a reason for suspicion ; but there are so many concerns in which an auditor would need to be an expert, where he would need to be a skilled valuer in order to certify the stocks, that it would distinctly im- pose upon an auditor larger and very responsible duties which have not hitherto been supposed to be within those which devolve upon an auditor. (Hear, hear.) If we are to be responsible in all cases for the correctness of the stock I think auditors ought to be at liberty (and the law should be so amended, if possible, that an auditor may be at liberty) to protect himself from any liability upon that point if he makes his certificate perfectly clear and calls attention to the fact that the officials of the company alone are respon- sible for the stock. (Hear, hear.) Of course, we all admit that whether a legal liability or not on the part of the auditor, he, nevertheless, has a moral responsibility for going to a certain extent into the question of the stock so far as to see whether there is anything at all suspicious which requires fuller examination. (Hear, hear.) Then, I think a most desirable thing would be that the Council in London should, if possible, try and get that other point settled one way or the other—whether an auditor is, or is not, an officer of the company. (Hear, hear.) I should take it that if it could be decided that he is not an officer of the company, but only an outside observer who is to protect the interests of the shareholders by watching the officers of the company and checking their figures, that would, perhaps, be the position that we should prefer ; but, whether or not, if it is to be accepted as a fact in future that the auditor is an officer of the company, well, then, we must face the fact and act accordingly ; but to leave it in its present somewhat vague and undefined condition is certainly undesirable. (Hear, hear.) The undoubted effect of these recent decisions, and the discussions which have resulted from them, I suppose will be to exalt the importance of the auditor's pro- fession in the eyes of the public. On the part of some adverse critics it may have had the effect of lowering the character of certain auditors—as individuals—or it may have led to suspicions as to whether auditors' duties are suffi- ciently discharged in certain cases ; but on the whole we may congratulate ourselves that the profession, taken as such, has been held up to the public gaze as having an importance and a dignity that, perhaps, a good many people had not previously thought it possessed. (Applause.)

Mr. THEODORE GREGORY, F.C.A. : If you will allow me to conclude with moving a vote of thanks to the President for the able introduction of this discussion, I will offer a very few words on the paper and on the subject to which it draws attention. The judgment of the greatest man which has been read is the judgment of Lord Justice Lindley. I think that is almost the Magna Charta of the accountant's profession. (Hear, hear.) It distinctly brings out not only what are the liabilities of the auditor, but it brings out also what an auditor is not expected to do, and that is almost more important than the other. Because if one can judge by the various communications which have been made in all sorts of papers, wise and otherwise, during the last two years, an auditor might be expected to do anything; even to the extent of running a business entirely, as well as checking all the transactions and the directors and the managers. But it expressly says that it is not the duty of an auditor to manage a company. The auditor is not expected to guarantee the accuracy of the Balance Sheet, but he is really to examine the Balance Sheet as an expert, in the same way that a physician examines the body of a patient who asks him for his opinion as to his state of health, and he certifies as to the soundness or otherwise of the concern whose Balance Sheet he examines, as shown by that Balance Sheet. He gives an opinion, and the opinion of an expert; but he does not guarantee its correctness any more than the physician guarantees the correctness of the opinion which he has given. (Hear, hear.) If the physician was continually to be giving bad opinions the probability is that his practice would very soon fall off; and if an auditor were continuously found to be making mistakes the probability is that his business would also fall off, and he would not have the opportunity of making mistakes. But still an auditor is human, and I think Lord Justice Lindley's judgment recognises the fact that he is human; but clearly rules that he is to do his best. (Hear, hear.) Well, then, on the question of what is his best comes the further question of what he is to do. He is to use reasonable care. And I think Lord Justice Lindley showed that he was prepared to take a reasonable view as to that, for he said that Mr. Theobald in the *London and General Bank* case had used reasonable care. The only thing in regard to which he found Mr. Theobald in default was in not reporting to the shareholders. If he had conveyed to the shareholders in any way the opinion which he conveyed to the directors, Mr. Theobald would not have been in the unenviable position in which he stands to-day. (Hear, hear.) Mr. Whinney used a phrase two or three years ago to which I had previously called attention, and which still seems to me to put the matter in a very concise way—that an auditor's duty is to certify that figures are facts. The Balance Sheet consists of figures representing the values of certain properties and the liabilities. Well, the auditor has to look into the books and see whether those figures are supported by the facts as disclosed by the books or as they ought to be disclosed by the books. (Hear, hear.) It is impossible with regard to all concerns to give an instance which will appeal to you all. Take the concern of Rylands & Sons, Lim. How in the world could any auditor certify that those stocks are all correct by such an exhaustive analysis as appears to be contemplated by the decision of Mr. Justice

Vaughan Williams in the *Kingston Cotton Mills* case? The thing is impossible. And so one can only conclude that that decision either is not properly understood or else that it is not conclusive. I think that we have more to learn yet as to the responsibility of auditors with regard to the stocks, and I should like to hear the opinion of Lord Justice Lindley on the subject of stocks before being satisfied that the opinion of Mr. Justice Vaughan Williams really lays down the duty of auditors in regard to that matter. (Applause.) As to the question of the position of the auditor as an officer of the company, I doubt whether there is very much to be gained by carrying the matter further. The matter has been decided by the Court of Appeal in two cases —in the *London and General Bank* and in the *Kingston Cotton Mills* case—and I do not think there was the slightest loophole given in either case to justify carrying it further with the hope of obtaining a reversal of that opinion. (Hear, hear.) The opinion being so strongly expressed by the various Judges before whom the cases have come that the auditor is an officer of the company, I do not think it is well for our reputation to endeavour to shirk our responsibility in the matter too much. (Hear, hear.) The best way is to accept the responsibility and endeavour to discharge that responsibility to the best of our power. (Applause.) I have very great pleasure in proposing a vote of thanks to Mr. Nairne, the President, for the very able way in which he has opened this discussion. (Applause.)

Mr. WILLIAM MOSS, F.C.A., Ashton-under-Lyne: I will first take the opportunity of seconding the vote of thanks Mr. Gregory has proposed to our President for the very admirable paper which he has given us this evening, and then, in what I have to say I think I will confine myself to the facts in the *Kingston Mills Company's* case, with which I had, perhaps, a better opportunity of being acquainted than with the other case. And I would say that the decision in that case, as I understand it, was a decision in reference to the facts in that case, and that it was very distinctly stated by the Judge that he did not hold the auditor responsible for anything more than the exercise of reasonable care in overseeing the stock-takings which were presented to him ; and that, unless he had reason, from the books disclosing to him facts which put him upon enquiry, he was not called upon to use more than ordinary care and discretion. And the question arises whether, in this particular case, the auditor had used ordinary care and discretion. (Hear, hear.) You have not read the whole of the cross-examination of the auditor, but it appears to me that he had not. In fact, if I remember rightly, he had not even checked the extension. At all events, in the cross-examination, he could not point out any checks.

The PRESIDENT: He said he had, but it was not apparent on the face of the stocks.

Mr. MOSS : That is so. He said he had checked the extension, but he could not point to any checks at all. Well, I should myself contend that that was not using ordinary care and discretion, particularly if you come to take the facts as they appear in *The Accountant* from the Balance Sheet which was supplied to the Editor of *The Accountant* by the auditor, where the stocks row in this manner: December 31 1888, £21,776; 889, £29,760; 1890, £44,483; 1891, £53,916; 1892, 60,966. Now, the turnover, of course, was practically the ame. That is to say, although the value might be more at ne period than another, the raw material and the manufac- ured article would have the same proportion to each other. s a matter of fact, the turnover in 1889 was £119,000, and n 1892 it was £91,000; and in 1889 the stock was only 29,000, while in 1892 it was £60,900 or £61,000. Now, sir, should contend that, if those were not facts to put an uditor on his enquiry, it is very difficult to conceive such a tate of things as would put an auditor on his enquiry. Applause.) And when you have an auditor who, when he s put on his cross-examination, does not produce a single act, or figure, or note to show that he had asked any uestions whatever with reference to the growth of the tocktakings, I think his case is bad. (Hear, hear.) Now, there is another thing to be taken into account, and hat is this—what brought about this enquiry was the liqui- lation of this company, and this liquidation, I presume, was rought about because somebody wanted money and could ot be paid. Now, that was a state of things that would not rise at once, and it would probably have appeared by a easonable examination of the books that accounts were wing by this company, and had been owing for a consider- ble length of time, that could not be paid; and that was nother fact which I contend should have put the auditor on is inquiry. If the company was being pressed for money, nd if the company could not pay the money, then why was t carrying such an enormous stock? Now, I happen to now something about cotton stocks, and therefore, perhaps, am not as fair a judge on this particular question as some ne who is not so closely identified with the cotton trade as I ave been myself; but there is a year's Balance Sheet, and he turnover for the year is £91,664 in 1892, and the stock is 60,966. It is rather unusual for Balance Sheets to be ublished yearly, but where they are made up for yearly eriods they are often balanced half-yearly or quarterly. The thing would perhaps have been more palpable if the Balance Sheets had been made up at the end of the half- ear. Look at it in this way. If the Balance Sheet ad been made up at the end of the half-year ou would have had a turnover of £46,000, and a tock of £60,000—a most incredible thing in the cotton rade. The cotton trade is not like many other trades. Mr. Murray has already said that Bank Accounts are, perhaps, as asy to be satisfied about at the close of an audit as any usiness there is, but I should say that if you wanted to find nother business that was comparatively easy to check it would be that of a cotton spinning company—spinning only. If you had to deal with the manufactured article and with loth then the matter would be more complicated; but this was a cotton spinning company and the judge dealt with hose facts: and he was trying whether the auditor had lealt with the facts before him with ordinary care and dis- retion. Then there is another matter. It seems to be con- sidered a rather difficult thing by some, to take the weight of otton at the beginning of a period and add to it the purchases, nd then to take the weights of yarn and compare them. Now for a period approaching twenty years I have been very closely connected, as you know, with a large number of otton spinning companies, and during all that time I have never known a cotton spinning company which did not pre- sent these very figures made up quarterly, half-yearly, or annually for the directors. The figures are there, they are asily accessible, and I do not remember a single instance where they have not been available. It might not have been o in the Kingston Mill case, but, as a rule, these figures imply need checking; and having these figures, and having he cotton spinning company's Balance Sheet, such a falsifi- ation as you have referred to would be absolutely impossible. remember a case not very long ago, where the application f such a simple test as this detected an error of 1,000lbs., not a deliberate or intentional error on the part of the directors at

all, but simply a question of starting the mill and the alloca- tion of stock which was in the machinery; and the question of carrying out the capital and adding it to the machinery led to the error of including in the second or third stocktaking after the mill had commenced the stock which had been added to machinery, and in the result the weights showed the discrepancy; that is to say, there was actually more yarn accounted for than they had had cotton, taking into account the waste. Well, then, I think that what this judgment means is that, in such a case as this, where you have the stock growing out of all proportion to the business done—from £21,000 to £60,000, and the turnover in the meantime not increasing at all; when the company is pressed for money, and the auditor is asked what steps he took, and he says that he took the manager's certificate, which might have been right if he had applied every other common-sense test that he could apply, he ought to be held liable, and I think it is a decision which we have no need to fear. (Hear, hear.) If we go about our business in the proper way, and we apply the tests which common-sense says ought to be applied, then I think we have no need to be afraid of the result. (Ap- plause.)

Mr. H. L. PRICE, Manchester Guardian Society: It is rather a difficult thing to decline a personal invitation to say a few words on such a subject, although when I accepted your secretary's courteous invitation to be present, as a stranger, I did not anticipate being called upon to make any remarks. I came merely with the object of listening to what I expected—and I have not been disappointed in my expecta- tions—would be a very interesting and profitable paper from the President. It seems to me that the decisions in relation to auditing, as well as to other subjects that come within the purview of our profession, are at the present time rather in a state of transition or flux, that, in fact, the profession is not old enough to have created a body of legal precedents and decisions upon which it can act in all cases, and therefore I do not look upon these decisions which the President has brought before us to-night as being at all final. I do hope, with Mr. Murray, that the time will come when the Council will upon both these points, see their way to carry the matter to the ultimate Court of Appeal in the House of Lords, so that we may know once and for all, and with absolute definiteness and certainty, what we have to expect. (Hear, hear.) The cases in point, however, do not seem to me to have been sufficiently strong on their merits to have warranted the Council in taking that course with regard to them. I think it must be the feeling of all of us that in both these cases there were faults on the part of each of the auditors of which we cannot acquit them. (Hear, hear.) There was the miserable fault of Mr. Theobald, first in his certificate to the directors stating what was the fact, that he did not recommend a dividend, and then hesitating and halting and withdrawing it, and thus putting himself in the wrong. As to the Kingston Mills case, there were the facts mentioned by Mr. Moss and Mr. Gregory that the auditor did not exercise what we as accountants should call reasonable care in re- gard to the verification of the stock. When I say that the decisions are not final, may I point you just to this apparent contradiction? In the case of the London and General Bank, we have this statement of the Judge, as repeated by Mr. Gregory, that the auditor is not expected to be a valuer. If he is not expected to be a valuer, what then is the meaning of the decision in the Kingston Mills case, which says that if he does not value he shall be held liable? (Hear, hear.) I say that those two statements stand in direct contradiction to each other; and we must, before we can feel certain of our ground, have a decision that decides the difference between them. Then, again, as to the Kingston Mills case The Accountant does point out one very simple test that the auditor omitted and which, in addition to those stated by Mr. Moss, ought to have satisfied any reasonable man of the inaccuracy of the accounts, and that was, the gross profits shown on the Trading Account. I think, if I remember the figures correctly, in one year the gross profits were 25 per cent., and in the following year the man, exaggerating his stock without any discretion, showed a gross profit of 37 per cent. Well, that ought to have led the auditor to put enquiries afoot, either to the directors or to someone, with a view to ascertaining whether they had had such an exceptional year as that their gross profits had, at a bound, gone up 50 per cent. (Hear, hear.) If he had only made that enquiry the whole thing would, no doubt, have come to light, and the reputation of the auditor would have been saved. (Hear, hear.) Personally, I feel very much indebted to the President for the very capital paper to which I have had the pleasure of listening to-night. (Applause.)

Mr. RICHARD BRUTTON, A.C.A.: I should like to add my testimony with regard to the paper that our President has read to-night. I think it is quite due to him. It will come to us, perhaps, in a printed form, and then it will certainly be extremely valuable. (Hear, hear.) The cases to which he has drawn attention are, I think, very useful to us, and will be so in the future; but they do not alter our position with regard to our duties, or to the responsibility which we have always accepted; and I do not know that we shall care to give any more attention to our work than we have done in the past, assuming that we have all of us hitherto done our very best. (Hear, hear.) In regard to the stocks I think there are very few leading accountants, or auditors, who do not go into the question of the stocks very much and to a great extent. I have always conceived that it has been one of our greatest and gravest duties to compare one year with another in regard to the stocks, and to see that the prices are, to a very great extent, somewhat on a par with the sales, and that they are conscientiously taken. I think myself that there is no very great difficulty in dealing with them to such an extent as Mr. Justice Vaughan Williams referred to, and that is to deal with them in a reasonable way. (Hear, hear.) I think that the great value of our President's paper will be in regard to some of the points that he has brought forward. I will not, at this late hour, go through all the notes that I have made, but there are many points which Mr. Nairne went through that are interesting. He referred to what was said in the *London and General Bank* case in regard to interest on doubtful accounts. I think the judge was very strong on the point that interest on doubtful accounts brought to the credit of Profit and Loss Account and paid away as dividend was very injurious and very improper. And I think so too. I think in respect of all banks (so far as I know about banking accounts), in all well-regulated banks, I believe, as soon as an account becomes doubtful in any shape, or there is any symptom of doubt about it, they continue to charge interest on the account, but instead of bringing it into their accounts to the credit of Profit and Loss Account, they put it to an "Interest Suspense Account," we will say, or some account of that kind; and, until that account becomes wholesome again, they do not use it. It is advisable to charge it to the customer for the reason that he might not like it if he was not charged (laughter), for the reason that he might look upon it as an insult. I am quite sure that if we continue to do our duty and work hard we shall retain the respect and the confidence of the public, as I hope we have both now.

The vote of thanks was then unanimously adopted.

The PRESIDENT: I need not say, gentlemen, that it is a sufficient reward to me for any efforts I have made that you should have appreciated those efforts, and I am very much obliged to you for the vote of thanks which you have passed. I do not think you will expect me to reply at any great length, more especially as I do not think the speakers have to any large extent disagreed with the conclusions to which I have come myself. I would just say with regard to Mr. Moss's remarks that I quite agree with him, as I think I showed in the course of my paper, and I also agree with Mr.

Price with regard to the *Bank* case, that both these cases are weak cases, and not such as we should be justified in taking to higher Courts as indicative of our opinion as to the extent of our duties, and therefore we are in a great difficulty in criticising them at all. We cannot but agree, as I said in the course of my paper, with the decisions which were given; but, nevertheless, what we fear, or what I fear, is that these decisions may be carried into other cases, and that conclusions may be drawn from them as matters of principle, and that these judgments may be taken to mean more than the Judges intended them to mean. But still I would say with regard to the *Kingston Mills* case that, as Mr. Moss puts it—and he used the same words which were used by Lord Justice Lindley and which were evidently quoted by Mr. Justice Vaughan Williams afterwards when he commented upon reasonable care and skill being employed—that the questions are, What is reasonable care and skill in cases which are more difficult than the *Kingston Mills* case? and how far are we expected to go and how much is expected of us in the way of discovering these errors? Lord Justice Lindley said of those what we should wish him to say —that we do not guarantee these things. And those are the words I emphasise—that we do not guarantee the correctness, but we are called upon to show that we used reasonable care and skill. But the danger is that different Judges may presume upon these decisions to come to different conclusions as to what is reasonable care and skill in varying cases, and more especially in more complicated cases than the *Kingston Mills* case was. In what Mr. Moss has said he is speaking generally, I take it, of the companies in the Ashton and Oldham district, which are spinning companies, and which deal entirely by weight; but the "reason-"able care and skill," to use Mr. Justice Vaughan Williams' words, if applied to a case where they go no further than the weaving of yarn which they themselves have spun would make the difficulty at once apparent if such a test as that applied by the clerk of the Official Receiver were to be applied, and it could not be done without a very careful examination of the books. And, then, if we go on further to the companies which spin the yarn and then send it out to be dyed and polished as we have instances of in the neighbourhood of Manchester, then the weights become very different. Indeed, I remember in my early business life being connected with a place of that kind, where the counts differed after the yarn had been sent out to be dyed and polished, and 50s. became 55s. or 60s. by some manipulation which I cannot attempt to explain. Each of us, I have no doubt, could from our own experience point to the difficulty of making any such examination as that, unless it were a special one, which would occupy much longer than the ordinary time which an auditor is expected to take when shareholders are clamouring for Balance Sheets, and more especially for dividends.

I do not know that there are any other points it is necessary to refer to, except to that question of interest unpaid. I should like to have read that part of Mr. Justice Vaughan Williams' judgment where he deals with that question; but he certainly did keep harping upon the words " not received " and " not paid," and so on; yet in other parts of his judgment he made it perfectly clear that what he referred to were unrealised or unearned profits: and he went so far as to say that, if directors actually took into the Revenue Account profits which were earned, but which could not be realised, it would be very unfair to hold them responsible for the fact that these customers went bad, and the money was not actually realised. So that I do not think he went so far, or intended to go so far, as to say— though parts of his judgment appear to lead to that conclusion—that, because interest was not actually received, you ought not therefore to declare a dividend and divide the profits, because it would necessarily, I think, come out of the capital until the interest came in.

I thank you very much for the patience with which you have listened to me.   I was afraid that I should weary you by the long extracts, but I felt I could not make the case consecutive or interesting to you unless I referred at some length to the main points or salient features of the judgments on which my remarks were based.

The proceedings then terminated.

# The Duties of Auditors.

## A SYMPOSIUM.

THE publishers of *Practical Accounting*, New York, have forwarded us for publication the following views of American Accountants on the Duties of Auditors:—

In carrying out the suggestion of topical discussions proposed in this journal some time since, we have recently submitted to a number of practising accountants in different portions of the country through correspondence the question: " What are the " duties of an auditor?" The replies which have come to hand answer the question from many different points of view, and a perusal of extracts from what our correspondents have sent us, even though names are suppressed, cannot fail to be of interest to all our readers.

The auditor of one of the largest national organizations in the country writes as follows :

" In general terms it is the duty of an auditor to ascertain what property the firm or company has, and to whom it rightfully belongs, what profits have been made, making sure that they are real and not fictitious, and where they have gone—or if losses have been incurred, to what causes they are attributable.

" In addition to the usual examination of postings and balances, he should make sure that all the entries effecting the return and transfer of stock have been in accordance with legal requirements, and that they have the sanction of the proper officers ; that no entries have been made to the injury of any of the stockholders or parties in interest ; that all disbursements have been made by proper authority, and vouched for by the proper parties ; that the assets are as represented in the books as to quantity and value ; that proper allowances have been made for depreciation, both on plant and book accounts, and that at closing all items accrued, such as interest, insurance dividends, rents, etc., have been taken into account.

" Of course there are many other things which would be required to be looked into and verified in special cases, but in a general way the above are my conceptions of the duty of an auditor."

### TRYING TO ASCERTAIN.

A practising accountant, who has wide experience in New York, and who is, perhaps, better known in his profession than almost any other man to whom we might refer, writes as follows:

" I cannot help being amused at the question, ' What are the ' duties of an auditor?' It is what I have been vainly trying to find out for many years, and yet to make such a statement seems absurd, for I have just gone over a set of books and have styled my examination an audit, in order to make my employers happy. I expect to go over two or three additional sets of books in the course of the next few weeks, and shall similarly describe my work. In fact, I am employed to do this kind of thing right along, and I am called an auditor. I know what is expected of me in each particular case, and I am following lines laid down by myself in each instance : whether what I am doing covers what is known by an audit, or whether I actually perform the duties of an auditor, I know not. I question if the duties of an auditor are anywhere fully defined—if they are I do not know where.

" It seems to me to go without saying that one business of the auditor is to see that there are vouchers for all expenditures for which vouchers are capable of being obtained. It is his duty, as well, to see that the cash stated to be on hand proves with the bank account or with the absolute money. It is also proper to see that the footings of the cash book are correct. All this done,

it would seem that no money has been gotten away with on the side of the payments. Then the question arises, How are the receipts to be checked ? It seems to me that each case proves its own solution, and of necessity must be left very much to the auditor's judgment. The same remark applies, also, whether or not criticism in the conduct of the business is permissible, upon the part of the auditor. Of course, criticism of the enterprise and of the bookkeeping at large comes within his province without argument. It does not seem rational to expect the auditor to go over the entire details of all the work. Such an undertaking is altogether too voluminous, and yet, if this is not done, is the work thoroughly performed ? From what I have written, it is evident, perhaps, that I can perform the duties of an auditor better than I can define the thing itself. My view is, that the auditor should have some system by which he can prove the correctness of the books without the labor of going over each entry."

### A PUBLIC AUDITOR IS AN OFFICER OF GRAVE RESPONSIBILITIES.

A prominent public accountant in Philadelphia, making a specialty of real estate, mining and industrial enterprises, answers as follows :

" The question is, What are the duties of an auditor ? As it pertains to one who is called upon to make examination of matters relating to an accounting, the query is one of such importance to the profession, known as the public accountant, that it admits of deep study and conscientious thought. So different are the views taken by the accountant and the mercantile and legal fraternity that an interesting volume might be published on the subject. An English court of equity has been engaged for a considerable time in the hearing of a case wherein the duties of an auditor has been brought into question ; and *The Accountant*, published in England, has made full reports of the arguments by the learned counsel on both sides ; and the expression given from the bench by the eminent jurists sitting in the case, gives weight to the position taken, that a public auditor is an officer who is clothed with power and grave responsibility. In the United States, the enlarged ideas of progress in all matters makes it incumbent upon all who are interested in this subject (and that means everybody) to seriously and intelligently consider the question in its entirety.

" The first and paramount qualification of an auditor is honesty of purpose, and to this end he should devote his energy, not to a construction intended to elicit favour upon anything which comes to his notice, but to demonstrate facts from the records presented to him, to accomplish which he must be a master of the science of accounts, as well as a correct arithmetician. An auditor makes a grave mistake when he commences his work with a determination of mind that error certainly exists. If perchance as a result of his investigation he discovers error or fraud, it is his duty to clearly establish the proof beyond a question, and make plain statements, which can be clearly understood. If in his investigation he finds a system of accounting which is defective and misleading (through ignorance or intention) it is his duty to call attention to the defect or intent, and mark out a system better calculated to meet the requirement of the parties in interest.

" A public auditor cannot do justice to his profession without performing the duty of acting as a counsellor in the matter of the accounting. It happens in the course of business that a public accountant is called upon to verify a statement taken from account books, his duty in this case being limited by the order of his client that he shall restrict his labor to the arithmetic involved. The office or duty that an auditor owes to the public should cause him to be careful how he accepts that kind of work, as by the reason of the case it is not in a line of duty for a public auditor to have restrictions placed upon him, as his superior knowledge in the matter of accounting makes him the better qualified to judge of the necessity of the case.

"It is expected of a public auditor that his adjustment of the accounts (as to their correctness) shall determine the true condition of affairs as they should be between individuals, partners, heirs, executors, administrators, etc., and *his duties can have no limit* in so far as they are necessary to justice in the accounting."

### A STATEMENT OF PRINCIPLES.

The following extracts from a letter received from one of the leading Chartered Accountants of Ontario will be read with interest :—

"There will, without a doubt, be much difference of opinion among accountants as to the extent and scope of an auditor's duties. Individual views will be shaded in some measure to correspond with individual practice and methods, and it by no means follows that, if one definition be right, others are wrong. In any case, the question cannot, in my opinion, be satisfactorily answered so as to be universally applicable. A few general principles may, however, be stated, and these will be applied in special cases to an extent depending upon the intelligence and judgment of the auditor.

"Firstly, then, an auditor should become thoroughly conversant with, and keep in mental view always, the articles of association or other authority by virtue of which the enterprise has been created and continues to exist, and the specific powers thereby conferred.

"Secondly, an auditor should take nothing for granted, either as to mathematical accuracy of the work under review, or as to the substantial accuracy of details, but should require proof of every transaction capable of being proven.

"Thirdly, an auditor should assure himself that proof of matters involving technical knowledge, such as inventories, valuations and depreciations, upon the accuracy of which his findings may to any extent depend, shall have been prepared and certified to by competent and personally disinterested persons, failing which, he should procure expert assistance.

"Fourthly, an auditor should certify to the facts only as far as he has been able to verify them.

"An auditor may always advise as to the system of accounts followed, and may in certain cases insist upon changes therein. He may not at any time base upon his findings statements as to the future ; his duties end with the present."

### LAWYERS AND AUDITORS CONTRASTED.

The following extract is from a letter that reaches us from a member of the profession in New York City :

"Everybody is of the opinion that the duties of a lawyer are clearly defined and well understood, so I will assume it is so just to save time. So, then, a public auditor and accountant is, in the realm of accounts, about what the lawyer is in the realm of law, with this important difference : that while a competent lawyer would not be considered dishonest if it was known that he withheld or distorted facts in the interests of his clients, a competent public auditor and accountant would be so considered."

### A COMPREHENSIVE STATEMENT

The following letter reaches us from an accountant of wide experience who holds a very important position in one of the most prominent estates of New York City :

"So far as a short letter will answer the purpose, I herein give you my views as to the duties of an auditor. To fulfil these duties he must be a man of no mean qualifications ; he must be a skilful bookkeeper in all its branches, a man not prone to jump to conclusions, and to have the courage of his convictions—must not only know bookkeeping, but have a considerable knowledge of business, and especially of the business the books of which he undertakes to audit—must be versed in commercial law, corporation law and partnership law, not with the intention of supplanting the lawyer, but rather of intelligently working hand in hand with him ; must know systems of valuing assets, so that he can work with those whose duty it is to value them.

"The name Auditor, which is derived from the Latin "audit," he hears, suggests in a general way the duties of the office. It is the auditor's duty to hear, *i.e.*, examine the evidence, whether verbal or written, and sift it out. In this respect he is like the lawyer, without taking sides like the lawyer. His duty is to state the truth, the whole truth, and nothing but the truth. His duties also seem to be of the like kind as those of an arbitrator—he must confine himself strictly to the field of inquiry given him, and if possible he should obtain from those employing him the points his services are required to investigate.

"In general his duty is to testify that the accounts have been accurately kept, and that the moneys mentioned in the Books of Accounts as having been received, to the best of his knowledge, after diligent examination, are all the moneys received, and that the moneys mentioned therein as having been disbursed have been correctly disbursed for the purposes therein mentioned, according to the best of his knowledge, after a careful examination of the same and of the sundry evidences at his command. It may be his duty to report on the outstanding assets—the securities held by the owners of the business in their possession as well as hypothecated—the contingent liabilities, the floating debts, and the nature of their fixed debts ; to report on the values of the assets, calling to his assistance proper appraisers ; to point out if depreciation has been allowed and a proper amount to meet wear and tear of fixtures and machinery, etc. ; to see that there is no forestalling of profits or income, and no deferring the charging of losses, without giving a reason therefor.

"On entering on his duties :

"(1). He should fully acquaint himself with the purposes of his employment.

"(2). He should ascertain the Books of Accounts and other books of the business, with their functions and their relationship, also any special modes of doing business.

"(3). He should also ascertain cash on hand, bank balances, the bills receivable and where they are, and the immediate liabilities.

"(4.) Also the interest receivable from interest bearing assets, and obtain a copy of the rents receivable.

"As to the method of conducting his audit that will depend on the purposes of his employment.

"As to the spirit of the audit, it should be liberal, not carping ; comprehensive, not petty ; and efficient and not slighting."

### KNOWLEDGE, COMMON SENSE AND TACT.

A Chartered Accountant of wide experience in business affairs, and who is well known to our readers by reason of articles which have appeared in these columns, writes us as follows :

"I assume that a man practising as a public accountant is well versed in the science of bookkeeping, and, from years of practical working at the books used in various lines of business, has a general idea of the practices of manufacturing, trading, and financial concerns. It follows that the duties of a public accountant and auditor consist in the exercising of his ability, common sense, and tact. His ability is to be shown in thoroughly grasping the methods of recording the business transactions of his clients, and, if necessary, to bring the same to a clearly defined and workable system—one that will show the true results of the business, in scrutinising the entries made in the several books by the office staff, so that the Revenue, Cost, and Capital Accounts are properly separated, and periodical statements correctly set forth the state of affairs. His tact will come into play in accomplishing the required changes without disorganising the business or the office staff, in discovering incorrect entries, in the methods he employs to verify the cash, and in the continuing of a straight course toward obtaining correct results without injuring the business or antagonising his clients' employees. Whatever work the auditor or public accountant sets out to do, he should do thoroughly, remembering that his reputation is both directly and indirectly bound up in the results of his work. With Court work, the statements prepared should be full in details, while the summary should clearly deal with the points under investigation. Clearness and simplicity in the compiling of the accounts is the object to be aimed at. Dealing with partnerships or firms in dissolution, the accountant would adhere strictly to the articles of partnership or incorporation in cases of differences, though the usual practice carried out by the parties before dissolution would give an indication of right satisfactory to both parties."

### DUTIES VARY WITH CIRCUMSTANCES.

The following very comprehensive reply reaches us from a prominent auditor in one of the Southern States, who is also an author of various works on accounting and mathematics :

" I doubt if you could have presented another question within the realms of accounting upon which a greater diversity of opinion exists, or upon which there is so much indefiniteness with American accountants as pertains to the subject of auditing. For more than a third of a century I have rendered service as an auditor, and in nearly every case the duties were varied and were determined largely by the circumstances of the case, modified by the instructions of the appointing authority—the judge of court, the directors of corporations, or the proprietor or partners of a business. The truth is, and pity 'tis, 'tis so, that in the States of our Union we have no special legislation on the subject of commercial auditing, and the accountants and business men of our country have not yet established a code of auditing rules and ethics that have the force of law by long custom and practice. Hence the great diversity of thought and action regarding the functions and powers of auditors.

" The laws of England create auditors and prescribe very clearly their rights, obligations and duties; and the strict accounting knowledge demanded of all auditors in England gives to the profession a uniformity and efficiency not always secured in this country.

" As we borrowed our common law, our language and our line of civilisation from England, so have we borrowed, very largely, our system of auditing. Of course the commercial auditor here, unless appointed and specially empowered by a court, has not the extended authority of the English auditor. But coming directly to your question, I would define, under the restrictions indicated above, the general duties of a commercial auditor in the United States to be approximately as follows :

" 1st. To qualify as a thorough and intelligent accountant. On this condition everything depends.

" 2nd. To call for all the books, financial statements, vouchers and other instruments connected with the business, the accounts of which he is to audit. To all of these he should give close inspection, and through the aid of the bookkeeper of the business, or the officers of the company, acquaint himself with the manner or system by which the books have been kept or the records of the business have been made. With this preparation, he can lay out his work and commence with the audit.

" 3rd. If the audit is to be a thorough one, he should proceed to examine each entry and verify all footings, extensions, postings and transfers, noting carefully whether any transposition or transplacement of figures has been made. Every item of every ledger account is to receive close inspection and verification.

" 4th. He should compare all items of cash receipts with the various sources from which they were received—Collectors' Books Department Cash Sales Books, Instalment Books, Rent Ledgers etc., etc., according to the character of the business. He should look constantly for omissions of cash receipt entries and for transposition of figures in the Cash Book.

" 5th. He should compare all items of cash disbursements with the vouchers or receipts, looking constantly for duplicate receipts for duplicate entries, for transposition of figures and for errors in transferring amounts.

" In the case of corporations, he should see that the disbursements of cash were authorised by a resolution of the board of directors, properly recorded in the Minute Book. He should examine all Bank, Pass, and Check Books, and see that the cash on hand and in bank agrees with the balance shown by the books.

" 6th. He should carefully consider bills receivable and personal accounts due, and see if the bills receivable are on hand and if there is any accrued interest thereon. In some cases the question of doubtful or worthless bills and accounts should be considered and proper adjusting entries made therefor, in case they have been omitted. Stocks, bonds, mortgages, and titles to real estate should also be examined and compared with the records. The collaterals held to protect loans should be seen by the auditor.

" 7th. He should see that all personal accounts and bills payable are shown in the books, and that no fictitious liabilities are presented. The accrued interest on the liabilities, if any, should also receive his attention.

" 8th. The valuation of all the property, the unearned rent, the unexpired insurance, taxes, advertising, anticipated dividends, etc. and the subjects of goodwill, copyright, trademark, franchise, etc. are questions to be considered by the auditor, in certain cases.

" 9th. The auditor of corporation accounts should see that the capital is no more or less than the charter specifies, and that there is no watered stock. He should direct his audit eyes and his ethical nature to treasury stock, preferred stock, guaranteed stock forfeited stock, operating capital, reserve funds, bonds, mortgages and the kinds of dividends declared,—instalment, cash, stock capital stock of fictitious dividends.

" Thus I could proceed and write a small book on the duties of auditors, about the size of Soule's Manual of Auditing. But I will forbear.

" *State Auditors.*—The duties of state auditors are numerous and are specified by law. They are bonded officers and generally faithful apostles of the political creed that honored them with office. They should be, but are often not, good accountants.

" *Special Corporation Auditors.*—Many large corporations like railroads, factories, mining and investment companies, often employ parties at a yearly salary to audit, at regular periods, the books and accounts of the different accounting officers of the company. It is also the custom of many business firms and companies to employ professional auditors to test the accuracy of their books and accounts by an audit, made monthly, quarterly, semi-annually, or annually. This is a prudent and wise measure and if it were univerally observed by business men it would prevent much of the defalcation and theft that is bringing ruin and dishonour to thousands.

" In conclusion, it is my experienced opinion that the duties of an auditor are onerous and responsible, requiring integrity and high professional ability. He should be a thoroughly qualified accountant ; not merely a self-assumed, superficial bookkeeper No person who is not proficient in the science and practice of accounts, familiar with business laws and strong in his ethics should ever be so unjust to his fellow men as to seek or accept the position of an auditor."

### AN ANALYTICAL STATEMENT.

An expert accountant, whose residence and field of work is in the extreme north-western State of the Union, discusses first the qualifications of an auditor, and second, his duties. The way in which he has analysed and arranged his reply is suggestive of the thorough system he applies to his work :

" First—The requisites. He should be of reputable character and absolutely honest; competent to advise, plan, devise direct, formulate, tabulate, analyse and summarise; possess a clear and accurate knowledge of mercantile law and that governing ublic and corporate offices, that he may be able to at once grasp any technical or hypothetical question that could or might arise; clear of perception and quick of discernment, that fraudulent designs be detected; honest, skilful and experienced.

" Second—Duties (in general.)

" 1. Searching for errors and correcting the same.

" 2. The supervising of inventories of stock.

" 3. Proper balancing of books.

" 4. Designing suitable systems of account books and forms for mercantile firms, any special business, state, county and city offices and their departments and for corporations; the opening and closing of the same.

" 5. Designing of labour-saving forms.

" 6. Examining and reporting upon the affairs of embarrassed and insolvent debtors.

" 7. Examining and reporting upon the financial condition, profits and losses of commercial, financial or manufacturing enterprises for prospective investors or purchasers.

" 8. The adjustment of partnership, joint or disputed accounts.

" 9. The adjustment of losses by fire.

" 10. The examination of the financial dealings and accounts between corporations or firms and their branches or agents.

" 11. The liquidation of the affairs of corporations, firms or individuals.

" 12. Auditing and certifying statements of corporations to their stockholders.

" 13. Examining and reporting upon the value of securities, comparing them with book entries.

" 14. The auditing of the accounts of state, county and city officials, of all corporations, firms and individuals.

" 15. Auditing and certifying receivers' and trustees' accounts for acceptance.

" 16. The preparation of accounts of executors, administrators, assignees, receivers or other officers of the Court, and assisting them in the performance of their duties.

" 17. Searching accounts by order of the Court or attorneys for the purpose of establishing evidence or for testing theories.

" 18. Assistance as adviser in causes of law involving accounts.

" 19. (Which covers all). Thorough, skilful, honest, impartial, (a) study; (b) examination; (c) analysis; (d) report."

### A REPRESENTATIVE OF OTHERS.

A Chartered Accountant, whose office is in Toronto, writes:

" In reply to the query, ' What are the Duties of an Auditor?' one's first impression is that a full reply would fill a good-sized book. But to put a general idea in a few words, I would say that, as an auditor is appointed to represent and to protect the financial interests of those who, for many reasons, cannot attend personally to examine into and prove the safety and profitableness of their investments, it is his duty to do everything that is necessary in order that he may certify with reasonable certainty to the accuracy and completeness of the statements prepared by himself or others, to show the condition of the business.

" He cannot do this unless he has the knowledge, skill, and ability necessary to detect all errors of omission or commission, either in principle, in fact, in authority, or in calculation, whether intentional or unintentional, nor can he do it honestly unless he has gone carefully over all the ground of the work for the period under audit.

" His duties are not necessarily confined to the books alone, but include all examinations which are necessary to satisfy him of the substantial truth of all matters set forth in the statements, and he should see that the statements exhibit not only the truth, but all the truth. Failing in this, he might find himself liable in damages to an investor who had made a loss through being misled by his certificate, and his incompetency would not be a good defence. No set plan can be set down for doing the work, for no two audits are likely to proceed alike. The auditor must be satisfied that all receipts and increase of property are accounted for, and that all payments and disposal of property have been on behalf of the business, and were duly authorised; that there has been no mingling of entries belonging to the loss and gain accounts with the accounts representing assets and liabilities, or vice versa; that the personal accounts are correct; that the assets reported are actually in possession of the business, and that due allowance has been made for changes in value by depreciation, loss, etc.; that the loss and gain have been properly closed off into the accounts representing capital, and, in the case of a company, that dividends have only been paid out of profits, etc., and he should be able to advise as to the best methods of bookkeeping for the purposes of the institution.

" To fill the requirements he should by all means be the equal or the superior in knowledge and skill of the officers whose work he is examining.

" I have tried to express my idea of the responsibility surrounding the certificate of an auditor.

" I consider that an audit made by one who is not properly fitted to undertake the task is a serious danger and wrong, as relying upon it creates an unfounded feeling of security.

" It is still very common for large interests to be entrusted to the scrutiny of untrained auditors, especially in public affairs where influence can be brought to bear, and it seems remarkable that such appointments are often made by business men who would not engage any but a good lawyer to watch their financial interests in even minor cases.

" There is, however, a rapidly-growing tendency among the larger financial and commercial companies to employ as auditors only those who, by making it a profession, having fitted themselves for the work, keep themselves also in constant practice."

### TO ASCERTAIN THAT EVERYTHING IS ALL RIGHT.

An accountant of wide experience and a prominent member of the Institute of Chartered Accountants of Ontario writes as follows:—

" The question, What are the duties of an auditor? will be answered differently by each of your correspondents. Perhaps the shortest answer will be—To ascertain and to satisfy himself and all concerned that everything is all right. Proper auditing is often prevented by appointments, directions, and limitations. Some auditors are contented with a mere checking of the accounts, if they have vouchers, and the Ledger is correctly posted. Some auditors are too complaisant, some fearful of non-reappointment, and some too trivial in fault-finding. I conceive that in all cases it is the duty of an auditor, first, to be sure that all expenditures and all payments are properly authorised (the sources and forms of authorisation will, of course, vary, some being personal and some legislative); second, to be sure that all are properly recorded; third, to be sure that all are clearly set forth in the published reports. An auditor should suggest and procure improvements and simplifications in methods of accounts. He should point out sources of danger of over-expense and of loss, so that failures may be avoided. In case of dissolution, of liquidation, or of reconstruction, he should, by his knowledge of previous errors, materially assist in the future prosperity. He should exercise great discretion in his manner of exposure of errors and faults, as he assumes grave responsibility in either alternative of silence or of publication."

### DUTIES CHANGE WITH EACH EMPLOYMENT.

A prominent accountant in Chicago says:

" I should think that the duties would change with each employment, and the auditor or accountant should first consider what is the result desired in his employment. His particular duties may perhaps be properly classified under the following general heads:

" 1. Investigating, to learn if positions of trust have been honestly administered.

" 2. To learn if accounts are properly kept so as to give the information required.

" 3. To show what has been the real earnings for a stated period of time.

" 4. To prepare a comprehensive statement of assets and liabilities.

" A public accountant should have both a thorough knowledge of accounts and some general business experience. If his experience has been entirely confined to accounts, he may fail to appreciate whether or not the accounts are so kept as to give all of the information desirable for the successful operation of the business and no more. In making up a statement of earnings he should note whether or not proper amounts have been charged off against depreciation. In making up a statement of assets it may not be sufficient to take them at their face value, and in addition, they should be shown at their fair value, and one competent to make such a statement will need to have some business knowledge, some idea as to the value of patents, plants, etc. In making up his report the accountant will consider the exact conditions, by whom he is employed and the reason for his employment, and his work will be more or less extensive, and his report more or less exhaustive, on certain points, according to the needs of the case. An experienced bookkeeper should be able to take any set of books and, taking the Ledger accounts at their face value, make up correct Balance Sheets and statements of loss and gain for any period desired, but to my mind, a public accountant and auditor should be able to do a good deal more than this, as I have indicated above."

# The Accountant

## THE ORGAN OF CHARTERED ACCOUNTANTS THROUGHOUT THE WORLD.

### (Awarded Silver Medal, Esposizione Italo-Americana, Genova 1892.)

Vol. XXII.—New Series.—No. 1114.                    Saturday, April 11, 1896.

## Leading Articles.

### The Present Position of Accountancy in view of Recent Legal Decisions.

A VERY important debate took place at a recent joint meeting of the Manchester Society of Chartered Accountants and the Manchester Students' Society, when the present position of accountancy in view of recent legal decisions was fully and most ably discussed.   A report of the proceedings duly appeared in our issue of the 21st ult.   The general question is of such paramount importance in the interests of the profession that it is most desirable that we should supplement the discussion which then took place with a few remarks upon the subject, not so much in order to note any impressions that we may have arrived at from our perusal of the report, but with a view to further emphasising the gravity of the questions at issue, with the object, if possible, of inciting further correspondence upon the subject in these columns.

We think that we may safely say that the impression of anyone who has carefully read the report of the meeting will be that the consensus of opinion was entirely and unconditionally in favour of the views which we have already expressed in these columns in respect of the two cases around which the discussion chiefly centred, viz., the *London and General Bank* case and the *Kingston Cotton Mills* case.   We think it particularly important to emphasise this point, having regard to the fact that the opinions which we have expressed upon these two cases have not been unconditionally accepted in London.

Our own opinion has always been that the continued prosperity of the profession depends entirely upon the ability of its members to convince the general public that the work which they are prepared to perform, and to certify to, is of such a nature as to be a real benefit to those in whose interests it is performed; and we have always maintained that no lasting good could result from any attempt to be-little the responsibilities of the profession. This is the view which has been invariably upheld by such leaders of the profession as Mr. FREDERICK WHINNEY, F.C.A., and others, to whom, undoubtedly—and to others like him—the profession owes much of the high position which it now occupies in the commercial world; and although we can quite appreciate the standpoint of some who consider that, now the Legislature and the Courts appear desirous of interpreting the liabilities of auditors from a much more exalted and rigid standpoint than had in previous years been thought desirable, it is expedient that the profession should seek to shelter itself whenever it can behind the bare legal limits of its responsibilities, yet we are convinced that, in the long run, this view of the matter is a suicidal one, which can only end in convincing the commercial world that a professional audit is of little or no practical value. Accountants possess—whether fortunately or unfortunately we leave it to the individual tastes of our readers to decide—no monopoly, and their continued employment rests entirely upon their being able to satisfy the public that their services are worth paying for; and, further, it may be laid down as a general rule that the public will be prepared to pay for these services in a precise proportion to their value to them. We hold, and always have held, that it is to the interest of the profession as a body that the services which it is able to render to the general public should not only be emphasised, but carried to the greatest possible extreme consistent with a reasonable amount of risk which attends every business enterprise. Without some form of risk it is practically impossible for any business man to earn a livelihood; and we think that the most capable members of the profession will be quite prepared to accept a *reasonable* amount of risk in connection with such certificates as they may give as auditors. We do not, of course, wish this to be interpreted into a suggestion that we are in favour of certificates being given by auditors in excess of that which they are prepared to certify to as being facts; but what we do wish to point out is that, in our view, neither of the two decisions which formed the discussion at the meeting in Manchester really go beyond the point which most auditors who hold a high idea as to the responsibility of the profession would be prepared to accept as the limit of their responsibility.

In general terms the *London and General Bank* decision amounted to nothing more than a statement that when the auditor had grave reasons for supposing that the value of the floating assets as stated in the Balance Sheet was excessive, and that consequently there were serious doubts that the profit shown in the accounts was the actual profit earned and available for distribution, it was incumbent upon such auditor to place before the shareholders his views upon the matter. Such views, we opine, need not under ordinary circumstances, where ordinary articles of association obtain, be necessarily stated in print so as to be available for the whole world. In the face of Lord Justice LINDLEY's *obiter dictum* that it is not sufficient for auditors to give the shareholders merely the *means* of information but to supply it, we should scarcely be prepared to contend that the auditor would have been safe had he made a special report to the directors, and in clear terms stated in his report to the shareholders that he had reported upon the matter more definitely to the directors themselves, and that he would by so doing have put himself right with the shareholders without incurring any risk in respect of subsequent misfeasance proceedings, while doing his best under the existing circumstances to avoid wantonly wrecking the company. We do not contend this, but nevertheless, we have doubts if this decision would have been come to had this been the case.

The position of the auditors of the London and General Bank, it will be remembered, was far otherwise, inasmuch as they consented to the suppression from their certificate of all reference to a separate report to the directors, upon the understanding that the chairman would verbally refer to such report at the meeting; while, as a matter of fact, although he did refer to the auditors having made a special report, he referred to it in such terms as to indicate that the report was confined to suggestions as to the *management* of the bank in the future, and not as to its financial position. Moreover, the position of the auditor as a defendant was further prejudiced by the fact that he was actually present at the meeting in question, and did not protest against the misrepresentations and suppressions contained in the chairman's speech.

The *Kingston Cotton Mills* case is, perhaps, a more difficult one to the lay mind, and particularly to those who may not unnaturally be assumed to be prejudiced in favour of the profession. It certainly does seem incomprehensible that, under any circumstances short of deliberate misrepresentations to the directors themselves, a case could possibly arise in which the auditors could be held liable and the directors not held liable; but we take it that in the articles which appeared in these columns shortly after the pronouncement of this decision, we have accurately reproduced the thoughts which must have been passing through the mind of the Judge at the time. No doubt he differed from us in his view that the certification of the value of the stock-in-trade is a matter upon which the directors were entitled to rely on the statement of the auditor; whereas we hold that the valuation of the stock-in-trade is not a matter of account but a matter peculiar to the precise style of business undertaken, upon which, we think, the directors might reasonably be considered as experts, while, in our opinion, it may, with an equal show of reason, be objected that the auditors were *not* experts. Still, with this singular irreconcilable difference of opinion, we take it that there is no very serious difficulty in following the line of reasoning adopted by Mr. Justice VAUGHAN WILLIAMS in respect of this case. He would appear to have been guided mainly by the expert evidence to the effect that by an examination of the books *alone* an auditor might have arrived at the conclusion that there were grave reasons for supposing that the stock had been over-estimated. We ourselves have shown that—even from the limited data at our disposal—there seemed to be very much in favour of this suggestion, and in so far as his Lordship's decision is based upon these circumstances, it merely reiterates the view which we have frequently expressed in these columns, that it is the duty of the auditor to, so far as possible, verify every item in the Balance Sheet, to take nothing for granted, but to form a mature and qualified opinion, as an expert in accounts, that the actual position as disclosed is really borne out by the facts of the case, so far as they are capable of verification by a professional accountant. The decision arrived at by the majority of the speakers at this meeting of the Manchester Society of Chartered Accountants and the Manchester Students' Society entirely supports this opinion.

# The Accountant

## THE ORGAN OF CHARTERED ACCOUNTANTS THROUGHOUT THE WORLD.

**(Awarded Silver Medal, Esposizione Italo-Americana, Genova 1892.)**

Vol. XXII.—New Series.—No. 1121.                    Saturday, May 30, 1896.

### Leading Articles.

#### Checking of Stock.

THE query raised by " O. P. Q." in our issue of the 9th inst. is of no little interest to accountants as being intimately connected with the points raised in the *Kingston Cotton Mill* case. It will be remembered that the President of the Institute (Mr. C. Fitch Kemp), in his recent presidential address, expressly cautioned members of the Institute to be very guarded indeed in placing their signature to a Balance Sheet under any circumstances, " unless they were fairly and " justly satisfied at the hands of those from whom " they could seek information that that informa- " tion properly conveyed the true position of the " concern." He further pointed out that, in his own view, there was certainly a limited duty imposed upon an accountant who had to deal with the figures which were before him, that he should be reasonably and fairly satisfied that the stock properly represented the amount at which it was taken in the Balance Sheet. We have already, upon various other occasions, expressed ourselves to very much the same effect. We fully agree that auditors cannot possibly be expected to be omniscient, and we further admit that, in the great majority of cases, it is unreasonable to expect them to form any such opinion as to the value of stocks as would justify them in putting forward their own views upon so technical a matter in contradiction of the opinions which had already been expressed by reliable experts. Notwithstanding all this, when an auditor accepts the statement of an expert as to the value of certain assets (and we think it immaterial whether or not such expert be or be not an officer of the company, or otherwise interested, so long as the shareholders are aware of the facts), we think it reasonable to argue that he should support such statement by *his own views* or make some such qualification as that appearing in our Weekly Note of last issue, page 425. It has, however, now been held by the Court of Appeal that the auditor who does not attempt to verify a manager's valuation of stock is not guilty of legal negligence. We must, of course, accept this ruling, but it does not estop us from enquiring whether a more thorough audit is not sometimes possible. The problem which has to be considered therefore is the extent to which it is practicable that an auditor shall carry his independent scrutiny of the valuations which are submitted to him of assets which, in the nature of things, it must be admitted he himself is not really competent to value; and so far as stock-in-trade is concerned, we pointed out in our issue of 25th January last how an auditor, by comparing the percentages of profits earned during different periods, may, up to a point, check the accuracy of the figures of stock-in-trade that have been submitted to him. The matter is dealt with in some detail in DICKSEE'S *Auditing*, pages 50 to 54 and 174, and in view of what we have already said upon the subject it is perhaps unnecessary that we should repeat here the general principles upon which the auditor's scrutiny should be founded. Suffice it to say that in every class of trade there is a percentage of gross profit which (within limits) will be found to be adhered to under all but abnormal circumstances, and *à fortiori* the same remark applies when one particular undertaking rather than one class of undertakings is considered. If therefore the auditor finds, upon a comparison of the

percentages of profit earned during different periods, that there is a material variation in the rate of such percentage, we think it may safely be taken that, whatever the actual law may be, it is expedient that he should look upon the occurrence as abnormal, and set himself to enquire as to what circumstances may have occurred during the period in question which could possibly account for such a variation in the percentage as has been observed. It may, of course, be that there exists a very excellent reason for the difference in question, and where the auditor after enquiry has satisfied himself that the reasons which have been advanced to him, and which he is convinced have actually existed, are sufficient to account for the variation, it must, we think, be admitted that he has done all that an auditor can do towards verifying the valuation of stock-in-trade which has been placed before him.

For the purposes of this comparison it is very much simpler—whether or not the method can be defended upon academical grounds—to arrive at the figure of gross profit by taking on the one side the opening stock, the purchases, and (in the case of manufacturers) the productive wages, and on the other side the sales and the closing stock, without any other elements of cost. It is, of course, easy to argue that the gross profit so arrived at in the vast majority of cases is no true gross profit at all; but that, from the present point of view, is entirely immaterial, all that is necessary being to ascertain whether the percentage is more or less *constant*. The figures we have referred to are much less likely to be influenced by outside circumstances, or by a marked increase or decrease in the turnover, than if elements of cost be introduced which, perhaps, ought properly to be taken into account before arriving at a true gross profit, but which in many cases would represent fixed charges that did not vary with the turnover, and consequently would be disturbing influences when periods of varying turnovers were compared with one another.

Like everything else connected with the audit of accounts, the test which we have been describing requires to be carefully and intelligently applied, with due regard to the circumstances of each particular trade and to all disturbing influences which might affect the profits earned during any particular period; but, if used with discretion, it will be found of the greatest possible value, and will, at all events, prevent any serious falsification of stock from being passed unsuspected.

In those industries, however, where the amount of sales is very large in proportion to the amount of stock the test becomes less sensitive, and proportionately less certain, but even this defect may be obviated if the directors can be induced to take stock at short intervals so that the amount of stock may bear a larger ratio to the amount of the turnover during the period. If there is really cause for suspicion, the auditor cannot do better than strongly recommend that the stock be taken again at the end of, say, one or two months after the previous stocktaking, for in so short a period as this any discrepancy of serious moment would be at once detected in almost every class of undertaking. Of course, on the other hand, the auditor has no power whatever to *require* the directors to take stock at an unusual period; but if he explains to the board his reasons for suggesting that such stock should be taken, we cannot but think that the onus would then lie upon them rather than upon him for any consequences that might ensue.

# The Accountant

THE ORGAN OF CHARTERED ACCOUNTANTS THROUGHOUT THE WORLD.

**(Awarded Silver Medal, Esposizione Italo-Americana, Genova 1892.)**

VOL. XXII.—NEW SERIES.—No. 1122.                    SATURDAY, JUNE 6, 1896.

## Leading Articles.

### The Liability of Auditors.

### The Kingston Cotton Mill Case.

IT will be remembered that in our issue of the 23rd ult. we placed before our readers a full report of the judgment of the Court of Appeal in this case, and commented at some length upon the decision and its possible effects, while in our last issue we pointed out that, in spite of this decision, it was desirable that auditors should do all that lay in their power to render their audit the most effective possible under the circumstances of each individual case. We have now to consider the manner in which this judgment has been received by those of our contemporaries who represent either the financial interest or the general public, for although these views are perhaps of little importance as throwing any real light upon the exact extent and limitations of the decision in question, yet they are of the greatest possible value to accountants, as showing the opinion of outsiders as to the general scope and value of an audit.

In view of the extreme importance of the judgment in question, it is not a little surprising that so few of our contemporaries should have thought it worth while to express any opinion at all upon the matter. One would have at least expected a *Times* leader upon the subject; the *Standard* also is silent; and it is perhaps even more astonishing that the *Westminster Gazette* and the *Pall Mall Gazette* (both of whom a year or two ago entered upon a crusade against auditors, which perhaps was more remarkable for its zeal than the discretion with which it was conducted) are also absolutely mute in respect of the judgment in this case. This shows beyond dispute —if indeed it was necessary to show so obvious a fact—that the majority of our lay contemporaries take no real interest in the subject on account of its intrinsic importance, but merely take it up when they think that by so doing they can increase their circulation, and as quickly drop it again when that end has been achieved. At the time when our two evening contemporaries devoted so much space to the discussion of the exact value of an audit, a large number of shareholders were smarting under the effects of recent losses, and the subject accordingly offered a fair market for any newspaper that was prepared to throw stones at any one who, by the greatest stretch of imagination, could be regarded as responsible for this state of affairs. Accordingly, the question of the liability of auditors was, for the time being, one of some little public importance, and therefore one which might profitably be discussed by those whose sole object was to interest their readers for the moment. Now, however, the main question has receded in importance, so these newspapers are no longer interested in the result. It seems especially desirable to point this out, because, in so far as it can be shown that our contemporaries are merely interested in pleasing their readers, it naturally takes away from the effectiveness of their criticism.

Turning now to the consideration of those articles discussing the *Kingston Cotton Mill* case which have appeared in the columns of our contemporaries, we find that unquestionably the most notable is the leading article which appeared in *The Financial Times* on the 21st ultimo. This article we print in full in another column of the present issue, and it is hardly necessary to criticise it in detail, beyond pointing out that in all essential respects it closely follows the line of argument which has consistently been upheld by ourselves. Our contemporary points out that the decision of the Court of Appeal is a direct endorsement of the view that the certificate of an auditor to the published accounts of a company does not necessarily mean that those accounts are absolutely true. This view has now been upheld by the Court of Appeal, which has decided that it does not necessarily follow, because it can be proved that the accounts certified by an auditor are not true, that the auditor has been guilty of negligence; and our contemporary proceeds to point out that "it is vitally important that the public " should understand this, and should attach " to auditors' certificates exactly what they " purport to certify, and no more." To this it may be added that it is entirely open to the shareholders of every company to prescribe exactly what they wish the auditor to certify. It is now settled law that it is no part of an auditor's ordinary duty to take stock; but if, on the other hand, the shareholders of any particular company resolve that the auditor shall certify the amount of their stock-in-trade, then it is a very easy matter for them to instruct him to do so; and, probably, there are few accountants in the United Kingdom who would not be prepared to certify as to stock, provided they were properly remunerated for so doing. At the same time, it may be pointed out that this would involve the employment of a properly qualified valuer by the auditor, and under these circumstances it is a question which each company will have to consider for itself, whether it would not be simpler (perhaps even cheaper) for the company itself to employ an independent expert to make the valuation, rather than to instruct the auditor to have such a valuation made upon his behalf. The question, however, is one entirely of contract between the company and the auditor, and for all practical purposes it makes little difference which course be adopted; but we agree with our contemporary that it is in the highest degree desirable that the shareholders of companies should fully understand that all that an auditor is actually required to do by law is to examine the accounts which are placed before him, and to verify them so far as the means at his disposal admit; with the further reservation that he is not bound to suspect everybody with whom he comes in contact of being a potential felon, unless something should occur which would arouse the suspicion of any ordinary man of business.

The views expressed by *The Financial Times* are very closely followed in the "money article" of *The Court Circular* of the 23rd ult., but a very different view is maintained by *The City Press* in an article which appeared in its issue of the same date. *The City Press* expresses the opinion that "a "great many people hold that Mr. Justice "WILLIAMS was right, and that the Court of "Appeal is wrong," and it bases this conclusion upon the argument that the auditors were "guilty "of a dereliction of duty in not discovering what "would have been obvious at a comparison of the "books at their command, that the stocks had "been grossly and fraudulently exaggerated." In arriving at this conclusion, our contemporary is probably under the mistaken impression that the Kingston Cotton Mills Co., Lim., actually kept proper stock books showing what had been purchased and what had been manufactured and sold. This, we believe, was not the case. As we pointed out at the commencement of the present year, it was only after an investigation extending over about two years that the Official Receiver's examiner was able to produce figures showing that the amount of cotton sold, together with the amount of cotton alleged to have been in stock at the close of the year, exceeded the amount which could possibly have been manufactured out of the yarn actually purchased together with stock at the commencement of the year. For what it is worth, such evidence no doubt goes to prove the admitted fact that the stock was overstated, but it does not in the least follow that the auditors were "guilty of a dereliction of duty" in not following up the matter to the same extent as the Official Receiver's examiner did when he was endeavouring to obtain evidence for a charge of fraud or misfeasance against the officers of the company. This, indeed, is the precise point which the Court of Appeal overruled when it stated that "an auditor is not "bound to be suspicious, as distinguished from "reasonably careful," and although, as we have stated upon more than one occasion, we believe that in this particular case the auditors might have found out the fraud of the managing director, yet it must always be remembered that

legislation is for the rule and not for the exception, and that to a very great extent the same principle must apply when legislation is interpreted by the Courts of law. The auditors in this particular case never professed to have gone behind the managing director's certificate, and the judgment of the Court of Appeal is in effect that, unless it can be shown that they did not choose to go behind the valuation of the managing director because they knew that if they had gone behind this valuation they would have found a discrepancy, they had not been guilty of misfeasance in the discharge of their duties. We have already shown that this is perhaps hardly the highest view which can be taken of the functions of an auditor, nor, we are convinced, is it the line upon which many accountants act in the discharge of their duties as auditors. Nevertheless, there is a vast distinction between failing to come up to the highest possible ideal and being guilty of such negligence as can only be justly punished by a fine of many thousands of pounds, and we are convinced that the Court of Appeal is well advised in drawing a hard line between these two points of view. It is absurd to suppose that such a judgment as that recently delivered amounts to more than a statement that, under all the circumstances, it would not be expedient to press the case too hardly against the auditors, and we are convinced that this sign of clemency upon the part of the Court of Appeal will neither take away from nor add to the actual responsibilities of those auditors who value their reputation and the esteem of their clients.

The view expressed by *The Liverpool Echo* in its issue of the 20th ult. (also printed in another column) is therefore quite uncalled for. Those shareholders who do not like to trust the directors they have appointed to look after their own interests have the matter in their own hands, and all that the Court of Appeal has laid down is that shareholders must not expect auditors to be more suspicious than they themselves think fit to be. Surely this is only common sense, and it is no short of an absolute misstatement of facts to suggest that it reduces the auditor to the level of a "mere calculating machine." Moreover, if this decision has the effect of making shareholders little more careful whom they elect as directors and as auditors, no one can pretend that the ultimate result will be other than beneficial to the community at large and to the profession in particular.

What is actually unfortunate about the whole matter is that a certain section of the public is so obstinate in its view as to the exact meaning of an auditor's certificate. Thus, a correspondent, writing to *The Eastern Morning News* on the 22nd ult., expressed the view that, " in the matter of stocktaking " the auditor should employ someone who " has a complete knowledge of each particular " business to superintend and book same." We have already pointed out that no accountant who was specially instructed to attend at the stocktaking and to certify stock regardless of expense would wish to obviate the fullest responsibility in connection with the matter ; but where an auditor has expressly pointed out to shareholders that he has not accepted any such responsibility in connection with the stock, it is absurd for the shareholders to suppose that they have been unfairly treated in the matter. Clearly, it is to the interest of accountants to magnify the scope of their duties as far as possible, in order that they may be entitled to increased remuneration for the discharge thereof ; but that is quite a different thing from saddling them with absolute responsibility for the correctness of every item when there has been no expressed or implied contract upon their part to accept such a liability.

It is greatly to be regretted that, at a time like the present, when the lay press might do so much to inform the general public as to the precise position of the law, it remains silent ; and the fact of its remaining silent upon such an occasion as this, in our view, throws upon it the whole blame of the misconception which undoubtedly exists. This misconception, as *The Financial Times* points out, can under the circumstances be only effectively removed by a definite enactment upon the subject. This enactment should be framed with three distinctive objects in view : (1) the protection of investors from vague and misleading statements ; (2) the protection of the auditor from misunderstanding as to his functions upon the part of the public, and from consequent obloquy ; (3) a declaration as to whether the auditor is the servant of the directors, the shareholders, of both, or of neither. These are points which it is desirable in the public interest as well as that of the profession should be settled without any further delay, for then at least auditors will be in a position to know precisely what is expected of them by the Legislature, while on the other hand the general public will be able to ascertain with equal facility what they can expect from the audit of a company's accounts.

## The Liabilities of Auditors.

(From the *Financial Times*.)

SOME four years ago in an address to the Chartered Accountants Students' Society, Mr. Frederick Whinney dealt with a number of vexed questions as to the legal responsibilities of auditors, and in the course of that address referred specifically to the danger and hardship which would result if it were decided that auditors were to be held responsible for wrong valuations by managers of departments. Mr. Whinney, an eminent accountant, laid stress on " the necessity of disabusing not simply the public mind, but " the official mind, of the idea that auditing means that the " accounts are absolutely true." We are still without an effective definition of an auditor, and his duties and responsibilities; but we have made an important step towards such a definition by the decision on Tuesday in the Court of Appeal in the case of the Kingston Cotton Mill Company. We are not at present concerned with the merits of the case itself, we have to treat it academically as regards our subject—the legal responsibilities of auditors. Certain auditors had been held liable to make good to the assets of the Company moneys improperly applied in dividends on the faith of certain Balance Sheets certified by the said auditors. Against this decision the auditors appealed, and have won their case, which shows that the law is not always " a hass." The whole question turned upon the issue as to whether or not auditors are responsible for valuations of stock-in-trade where such valuations are supplied under circumstances which do not give rise to suspicion. In this particular case the valuations were fraudulent, and it was sought to throw on the auditors the responsibility for not detecting these frauds. But the Court of Appeal very summarily brushed away that contention. It was pointed out in the case of the London and General Bank that an auditor's duty is to examine the books, ascertain that they are right, and to prepare a Balance Sheet showing the true financial position of the company at the time to which the Balance Sheet refers. But it was also pointed out that an auditor is not an insurer, and that in the discharge of his duty he is only bound to exercise a reasonable amount of care and skill. It was further pointed out that what in any particular case s a reasonable amount of care and skill depends on the circumstances of that case ; that if there is nothing which ought to excite suspicion, less care may properly be considered reasonable than could be so considered if suspicion was or ought to have been aroused. That is but another way of stating what Mr. Whinney said four years ago, that auditing does not mean that the accounts are absolutely true.

It is obviously out of the question that an auditor shall combine in his own person the qualifications of a valuer of all kinds and conditions of goods and goodwills. What he has to deal with are the figures submitted to him, and to check the accuracy of these figures. If, in the course of doing so, there arises anything to excite suspicion, then it is the manifest duty of the auditor to satisfy himself as to whether there is any ground for the suspicion before giving his certificate. But, says Lord Justice Lindley, " I protest against the notion that an auditor is bound to be suspicious as distinguished from reasonably careful." And therein every sensible person will agree with the learned Judge. In the case to which Lord Justice Lindley's dictum referred, the auditors had actually guarded themselves by stating that the entries questioned were " as per manager's certificate." That certificate they appear to have checked as far as possible from other books, but of course they did not undertake. to go through the business of stock-taking, which is not the duty of auditors. They did not profess to guarantee the correctness of that item ; and Lord Justice Lindley says : " I confess I cannot see that their omission " to check his returns was a breach of their duty to the company. " It is no part of an auditor's duty to take stock. No one contends " that it is. He must rely on other people for details of the stock- " in-trade in hand. In the case of a cotton-mill he must rely on " some skilled person for the materials necessary to enable him " to enter the stock-in-trade at its proper value in the balance- " sheet." That is surely plain enough and emphatic enough.

But there is in this matter another question to be considered—a question of vital importance to the investor. Mr. Whinney told us years ago, and the fact has been fully recognised amongst experts, that the public and official minds must be disabused of the idea that auditing means that the accounts are absolutely true. An auditor, to quote Lord Justice Lopes, is a watch-dog, but not a bloodhound. It is vitally important to the public that they should understand this, and should attach to auditors' certificates exactly what they purport to certify, and no more. In prospectuses great prominence is given to such certificates, and in established companies the auditors' certificate is seldom read as carefully as it ought to be. Reform is urgently called for, not now so much as to the responsibilities of auditors, which have been pretty clearly defined in the case under notice, as to the form in which certificates should be given. A definite enactment to regulate that would be a great boon, and would obviate many of the abuses to which the present inchoate state of our company law gives rise. The statutory form need not be a very long one ; but, without being verbose, it might be made comprehensive. In framing such a model certificate there would be three distinct objects to be aimed at :—(1) The protection of the investor from vague or misleading statements ; (2) the protection of the auditor from misunderstanding, on the part of the public, as to his functions ; (3) a declaration as to whether the auditor is a servant of the directors, of the shareholders, or of both ; or is responsible to neither, but holds an absolutely unfettered position.

(From the *Liverpool Echo*.)

The judgment of the Appeal Court in the case of the Kingston Cotton Mills will be received with feelings of relief by that not inconsiderable profession, the Chartered Accountants. In these days that profession enjoys almost a monopoly of the auditing of public and private business accounts, and the judgment of Mr. Justice Vaughan Williams undoubtedly imposes upon them very considerable responsibilities. The Appeal Court has now decided in effect that the auditor is not, as Mr. Justice Vaughan Williams held, a person whose duty it is to see that a business is being honestly carried on, but that he is a mere calculating machine, whose duty begins and ends when he has declared that the two and two found separately in the Day Book have been correctly added up and found to make four in the Ledger. It is clear that if the auditor is justified in taking for granted the stock-list presented to him by the manager of a public company, the value of his report as evidence of the financial condition of the company depends entirely upon the honesty and accuracy with which the stock-list has been made out. In cases of company frauds, the management are necessarily the delinquent parties, and therefore to place them in a position to hoodwink the auditor by presenting a "faked" stock-list is very like leaving the cream in the guardianship of the cat. The door is opened wide to this particular form of fraud by the decision at which the Court of Appeal has arrived, and it is to be regretted that they appear to have given so little weight to the considerations which led that extremely astute expert in company law, Judge Vaughan Williams, to decide in the manner appealed against. It is, of course, gratifying to auditors to find that they are not personally liable for failure to show the true condition of the affairs of companies whose accounts they audit, but there is no concealing the fact that this decision robs shareholders of what is practically the only real security they have against fraud on the part of those to whom they entrust their money. The case is one on which it is eminently desirable to have the judgment of the ultimate court, and it is to be hoped that, in the public interest, it will be carried before that august tribunal.

# An Auditor's Duties & Responsibilities.

Lecture by Mr. H. L. PRICE, A.S.A.A., Manchester.

[N.B.—This lecture was given prior to the decision of the Court of Appeal in the *Kingston Cotton Mills* case, and therefore the remarks relating to that case are out of date.]

UNTIL little more than a generation or two ago, the profession of accountancy as we know it to-day could scarcely be said to have had any separate existence. Handmaiden of the law, it was as a specific science ill-defined and tentative, and it spoke with something of "bated breath "and whispering humbleness." To-day it stands robustly and firmly upon its feet, demanding and obtaining recognition as a distinct entity among the learned professions.

Coincident with the adoption of free trade in England came an enormous extension of our commercial boundaries, and the earliest growth of the joint stock company laws; and without stopping to discuss the question whether the one stands to the other in the relation of cause to effect, we may at least relate the main, if not the initial, impulse given to our profession to the period of this new departure in politico-economics. Since then its growth, like Sam Weller's knowledge of London, has been extensive and peculiar, and until within the last twenty years it would have been easier to say what did not, rather than what did, fairly come within the scope of its operations. But as with all new institutions, its shape has been gradually moulded by circumstance, its limits approximately set; and although there is still within its horizon ample room for expansion, the duties and responsibilities of the professional accountant are daily becoming more fixed and definite factors.

In no branch of its work, perhaps, is this more true than in the audit of all classes of accounts; and so amply is this recognised by accountants themselves, and so forcibly have recent legal decisions emphasised its importance, that the discussion of it has of late been thrust into the forefront of the practical politics of the profession.

I fear I have little new light to throw upon a subject which has already fully engaged the attention of the "grave "and reverend seigneurs" of the profession. But, as truth need lose none of its force in the re-telling, I make no apology for its repetition. It is not by one blow, but many, that sound work is wrought; it is only by brick upon brick that the fabric of concrete knowledge of any science can be builded up, and you may, therefore, regard this as the contribution of my own particular brick.

The duties and responsibilities of an auditor are inseparable; each connotes the other. Duty without responsibility, or responsibility minus duty, are unimaginable items; and hence, in what I have to say, I treat them rather as parts of a whole than distinct or separable quantities. What, then, are the duties of an auditor, and what the responsibilities, moral and legal, which he incurs in their performance?

A humorous member of our profession—it almost sounds like a paradox to speak of humour in this connection—in a "funny" book recently published thus pokes fun. One of his characters had a friend, a bilious, discontented-looking man—an accountant—who was always saying life was not worth living. Asked to explain what auditing was like, he said, "It's all checking. It is most interesting. Imagine "being shut up in a stuffy office, say at a cotton mill, a "tannery, or a tallow manufacturer's from 10 a.m. to 5 p.m. "The atmosphere in such places is always odoriferous and "invigorating. You begin your audit: that is, you begin "checking each item from one book to another. One fellow "takes one book and another fellow takes another book. "The first fellow shouts out the reference folio in the other "fellow's book, and the amount of the item to be checked. "The other fellow turns to the said folio, and ticks off the "item, and says 'Right.' That's auditing."

Well, although such a process bears somewhat the same relation to auditing that bumble-puppy does to whist, it does not, I fear, unfairly represent the notion some people—dare I say some accountants?—hold of what constitutes the duties of an auditor. As if, forsooth, any bookkeeper in possession of a bottle of coloured ink, and the ability to make nice ticks, is fully equipped for the work. In point of fact, perhaps no other part of an accountant's duties calls for a greater combination of high business qualities—eyes and ears wide open, head clear, manner tactful and courteous, yet with the ability when needful to combine with the "*suaviter in modo*" the "*fortiter in re*." And to these our ideal auditor must add a well-balanced judgment and a sound integrity, accompanied by such a knowledge, both general and particular, of all classes of commercial accounts as to qualify him to become to his client, in matters financial, at once "guide, philosopher and friend."

I can imagine some of you thinking that such a paragon of all the intellectual virtues ought to be at least a Lord High Chancellor or a town councillor or something equally brilliant and distinguished instead of a struggling accountant, and yet I am glad to think that such men are by no means rare in the profession. I grant you the standard is high, but by no means an unattainable, one; but even if so, a high ideal is always provocative of emulation, and in the struggle to attain it, if we do not fully succeed, at least we catch something of its spirit. In this connection I look to the growth of Societies like our own, which, by granting admission to students through the door of stringent examination, ensures that the future of the profession shall be in the hands of men possessing at the outset sound scholastic attainments, and, in the result, a careful training as experts in accounts.

It lies in the nature of the case that the attitude of an auditor varies considerably with the circumstances under which his services are retained. He may, for instance, be called in to conduct:—

1. A complete or partial audit for a private trader.
2. An audit of partnership accounts.
3. A special audit for a sleeping partner; or
4. The audit of a public company, trust or corporation; and in no two of these capacities will his duties or responsi-

bilities run on parallel lines. While I am aware that any one of these sections contains within itself ample material for a lecture, it is unnecessary to do more than note very briefly and in outline the duties involved in what is known as a " private" audit, to distinguish these from the more public appointments under the Companies or Building Societies Acts, and then to pass on to the recent legal decisions affecting auditors.

### Private Audit.

In the audit of the accounts of a private trader, it is necessary that at the outset the auditor should obtain full and definite instructions as to the extent and scope of the audit, and while careful to give his client no needless cause of offence, to remember that, if he is to be asked to certify accounts, he may incur in that act a grave *moral* responsibility to the general public, even though no *legal* liability may attach. To illustrate my meaning. I have in mind as I speak an instance which came recently under my own observation, in which a Chartered Accountant had been called in by a trader to make up his books for the year, and to prepare a certified Balance Sheet. It transpired in the event that the stock figure—which was the main asset—was accepted by the auditor from his client without much question, although he did inspect the Stock Book, which confirmed the total given him. He consequently certified the Balance Sheet with the ancient formula, "Audited and found " correct," and therein put into the hands of the client an instrument for fraud. Instead of possessing the surplus disclosed by the accounts, the trader was hopelessly insolvent, and he suspended payment three months afterwards with a large deficiency. But in the interim, armed with a favourable Balance Sheet bearing the imprimatur of a highly reputable firm of accountants, he had succeeded not only in gaining time from pressing creditors, but in re-opening several credit accounts which had been long closed to him. It was but poor consolation to the creditors for the certifying accountant to urge, as urge he did, that, although the stock had been admittedly exaggerated to the extent of £15,000, " he, like they, had been misled," " that the Balance Sheet " had been prepared for the client's own use," and " that he " (the auditor) had no means of verifying the stock without " the client's sanction." One cannot resist the opinion that a precautionary foot-note to that effect, or a refusal to certify at all in such unqualified terms, would have obviated the whole difficulty, and saved an honourable professional man from the indignity of having to make feeble excuses for his methods. For if the account were prepared for the client's own eye, no injury could have resulted in the auditor stating in his certificate what the trader already knew, viz., that the auditor had accepted the stock figure without verification ; while if the Balance Sheet were intended for other uses, as in this case, then the *duty* rested upon the auditor of ensuring, as far as may be, that a false impression should not be created under the ægis of his name.

### Partnership Audit.

What I have said as to the audit of a private trader's accounts applies with equal force to partnership accounts,

but to this duty something is superadded ; because, assuming our auditor's appointment by the general concurrence of the partners, each of them becomes his client, and it is hence as much his duty to safeguard each against the other as the firm against third parties. It happens frequently that the work of each partner is departmental, without anything more than a general knowledge of the departments outside his own. The auditor, as a consequence, occupies the position of a scrutineer common to all, upon the impartiality and competence of whose work each partner relies. It is therefore necessary that, before commencing his work, he shall fully acquaint himself with the terms of the partnership deed, and take care that they are fully carried out or only varied by unanimous consent.

### Sleeping Partner.

But where, as often happens, he is the representative of only one partner—as in the case of a sleeping partner—his attitude is again somewhat different, and he is in the position of being able not only to insist, if he thinks it necessary, upon the fullest information, but to make recommendations as to the form of accounts to be kept, etc., which may be almost in the nature of instructions.

### Company's Accounts.

It is, however, in the audit of the accounts of public companies and of corporate bodies that the auditor finds his task not only most difficult and delicate, but where his responsibility already comes within the purview of the law. From legal decisions, from the obiter dicta of judges, from the pronunciamentos of accountants whose views are, from their standing and experience, entitled to respectful consideration ; and in other directions we have a mass of material, not possible of reproduction here, but from which we may—though it be imperfectly—venture to generalise.

It is, I think you will agree, almost impossible to overrate the importance of the auditor's duties in connection with company work. If it be permissible to talk of degrees of " thoroughness " in this relation, herein lies the necessity for the application of the superlative of that quality. But, given that, care must be taken that the public do not exalt the auditor's work into a fetish. There has, for some years past, been steadily growing up, on the part of the general public, a confiding trust in an auditor's signature and certificate which tends to become a source of embarrassment and unfairness to the profession, as well as a danger to the community itself. While such implicit faith in the sign manual of an accountant may be a very gracious tribute to the competence of the profession in the mass, the acceptance of everything appearing above an accountant's signature, as the sheerest gospel dictated by an inherent inspiration, is unreasonable, not to say absurd. For, though the public have a right to expect that the watchword of the competent professional accountant shall be " thorough," they have no right to look to him for miraculous qualities ; if they do so, they will inevitably be doomed to disappointment. The *absolute* prevention of error and fraud by audit it is as unwise to expect as it is impossible to assure. " An ac- " countant's certificate," said Mr. Whinney not long ago, " does not or ought not to profess to be more than the

.. experienced and mature opinion of an expert founded on .. facts in going through the books"; while again with epigrammatic directness he describes it as "a statement .. that figures are facts." To say that scores of accounts have been certified as accurate in which errors have subsequently been discovered is only to say that an accountant is human, and, therefore, liable to err. But what is claimed for an effective audit is, that it will and does minimise the chance of fraud; and to that extent it must be beneficial. If it were possible to collate the instances of fraud committed in case of audit or no audit, it would not be a difficult operation, I imagine, to forecast the result. For, as a general rule, in this as in other direction, it is

> Oft the sight of means to do ill deeds
> Makes ill deeds done.

Many a servant dishonest in principle remains honest from motives of policy, for the very reason that the auditor is known to be relentlessly following in his wake, with an ability at least as good as, and probably better than, his own to tread the maze of intricate account keeping.

Opposed to this, there is always the danger, of course, of auditing becoming too academical, and we may, in some measure, fairly lay to heart the opinion expressed by the *Birmingham Daily Post*, in its strictures upon the disclosures connected with the Liberator frauds, that "A little less " knowledge of the science of bookkeeping and balancing, " and a little more worldly common-sense in verifying receipts " and payments and valuations, would add many hundreds " per cent. to the value of an audit." Well, just as every tub must stand on its own bottom, so every audit must be dealt with on its own special lines; and there is no golden rule or set of rules to be laid down as limits for an auditor's work. Indeed, it is scarcely practicable, even if it were necessary, before a society such as this to do more than suggest some of the many points to which his attention should be directed. Generally, of course, he must be familiar with the various Acts of Parliament affecting joint stock companies, and should make himself fully acquainted with the articles of association of the particular company under review, that he may guard against any acts *ultra vires* on the part of the directors. Thus armed, he should approach the accounts with a determination to go back generally in his examination to the ultimate source of all figures coming within his purview. I say "generally," because there are occasions when such an examination of details is either unnecessary or impracticable. Thus, as between a railway company and its numerous stations, or between a bank and its branches, where the auditor is satisfied that there is such an examination by the head office of the detailed returns under conditions which, for practical purposes, eliminate almost the possibility of fraud, it would savour of "gilding " refined gold " to make the audit comprehend an examination of every particular item. But he should, at the same time, be ready to apply such expert's tests of the accuracy of even this *internal* work as his knowledge may dictate, remembering always that an audit has for its aim not only the detection of fraud but the remedy of technical errors and errors in principle.

Having satisfied himself of the correctness of details, the proof of their summary in Profit and Loss, and Revenue Accounts, and Balance Sheets, remains as the most important section of his work; for in this direction every word, letter, or figure, should be scrutinised with scrupulous care, if his work is to be worth anything, and if the auditor, personally, would avoid legal responsibility to his clientèle. First let us deal with the question of "Profits," and what is expected from an auditor in respect of them. Upon this head the recent decision by Mr. Justice Vaughan Williams, in the matter of the *London and General Bank, Lim.*, is a valuable and serious object lesson. In that matter the Official Receiver issued a misfeasance summons against the directors and auditors, under sec. 10 of the Companies (Winding-up) Act 1890, for recovery of dividends paid out of capital. Such a summons is only returnable against an *officer* of the company, and in addition to a defence upon the merits, the auditor raised the plea that he was not an officer of the company, but sub.-sec. 2, sec. 7, of the Companies Act 1879 provides that a director or *officer of the company* shall not be capable of being elected auditor of such company; yet Mr. Justice Williams held that upon his election the auditor did, under the articles, become an officer of the company, and therefore liable for misfeasance,—and after carefully following the terms of the judgment it would be difficult to resist the conclusion. Now, as to the misfeasance itself. Shortly stated, the facts were these: the bank in question was promoted, primarily to finance the companies now unenviably notorious as the "Balfour" group. Like most banks, their profits were derivable from interest and commission in respect of loans to customers, and the articles provided for payment of dividends out of profits only. These charges were made in the usual manner by debit to the customers' accounts current. The customers were in the main the companies or firms now known to have been the creatures or puppets of their promoters, and it was plain from the evidence that at the time such debits were made to their accounts, *i.e.*, at or about the period of audit, the accounts were in credit, and therefore *primâ facie* able to liquidate these charges, and upon this fact the auditor mainly relied in his defence. Treating the items in question as profits actually made, the bank from time to time declared dividends; but the contention of the Official Receiver as plaintiff was that everyone of the accounts in question, though largely in debit during the year, were put into credit at the end of the year by the old-fashioned process of everybody drawing bills on everybody else, and passing these bills to credit of each other's accounts as sound instruments The auditor was content in the main to leave the matter at that point, but Mr. Justice Vaughan Williams made it abundantly clear in his judgment that in his view the duty of the auditor was to go behind these credits and satisfy himself that they represented solid value. Without this, he contended, the auditor could not reasonably satisfy himself that profits had been made, and if the profits were a minus quantity, then the dividends must have come out of capital and were illegal payments, for which he held the auditor liable. It was in the course of this judgment that Mr. Justice

aughan Williams propounded the apparently questionable
theory (I say apparently, for other parts of the judgment
may be taken to modify that view) that profits must be
realised as well as earned before dividends may be paid out
of them. I admit that there is a technical accuracy in the
view that it is impossible to pay away what is not in
possession; but surely commercial usage must be taken
into account, and it is matter of common knowledge that it
would be as impracticable as it is unnecessary if the profits
have been bonâ fide earned, and funds exist which admit
of dividends being paid, to insist that before such payment
every customer shall have contributed to the coffers of the
company the mite representing his particular portion of the
profits earned.

But the judgment, so far as the auditor is concerned, did
more. The Judge showed, from the auditor's reports and
correspondence, that there was an uneasiness, and a growing
uneasiness, in the auditor's mind upon the subject of these
loans; that the auditor made reports and statements to the
directors which he lacked the courage or determination to
make to the shareholders, or as to which he permitted his
sound judgment to be turned from its original purpose by
persuasion of the board. Thus he specially reported the
board, calling their attention to the weakness of securities
representing nearly half a million, and adding, " We cannot
conclude without expressing the opinion unhesitatingly
that no dividend should be paid this year," and he informed
the directors that in his report to the shareholders he
proposed to say, inter alia, " The value of the assets as shown
on the Balance Sheet is dependent upon realisation,
and on this point we have reported specially to the
board." But this reference to the report to the board
with its criticism of securities, and objection to a dividend,
was, in the view of some of the directors, highly undesirable.
That special report may be called for by some enterprising
shareholder of a nasty inquiring turn of mind, and the
inevitable collapse be inconveniently anticipated. And
hence the auditor was plied with all kinds of reasons why
he should withdraw the sting from the tail of his report to
the shareholders, and letting " I dare not" wait upon
" I would," he at last consented to delete the objectionable
paragraph, with the result that another dividend was paid
out of capital, and the auditor added the corner stone to the
burden of his responsibility. I have dwelt thus at length
upon this judgment because it not only confirms the decision
in the Oxford Building Society, but is, together with the
more recent decision in Re The Kingston Mills Co.,
the most weighty of the recent decisions yet pronounced.
The case of the Kingston Mills Co. upon appeal, confirms
the decision in Re The London & General Bank, in
holding that auditors are officers of the company,
and though, perhaps, we may regard these two decisions as
embodying a correct interpretation of the law as it at present
stands, it is a matter for regret that upon neither of the issues
has the opinion of the ultimate Court of Appeal in the
House of Lords been sought.* In the course of The London

*Since this lecture was delivered, the decision in Re The Kingston
Mills Co. had been reversed on appeal.—H.L.P.

& General Bank judgment, the Judge lays down certain
definite opinions upon the duties which the law will, for the
future, be disposed to exact from auditors, and I commend
to you the reading of the full text of the report. Two points
stand out from the decision, viz., (1) That the profits must
be seen to have been well earned; and (2) That any assets
representing such profits must be ascertained to be sound
assets. From these as a corollary, I think we may fairly
say that among other duties the auditor must:—

1. Look to the due depreciation of assets and the liquidation, by sinking fund or otherwise, of what we may call
fictitious assets, such as goodwill, preliminary expenses,
and the like, which tend to perpetuate themselves without
anything tangible to represent them.

2. Shew upon the Balance Sheet specifically any items
due by directors or officials, or by any concern in which
they may be actively concerned.

3. Inspect carefully all securities representing assets.

It would be possible to enlarge to an almost indefinite
extent upon these and a score of other points which will
readily occur to you as practical men, but it would only be
to offend your good sense and occupy otherwise valuable time
in so doing. As was pointed out in this case, however, it
must not be forgotten that it is not the duty of an auditor to
manage the company nor even to express opinions upon its
management or operations, and hence nice discrimination is
necessary in his various acts. Nor is he, again, a valuer of
assets and securities. I have before endeavoured to show
that he cannot altogether afford to disregard entirely this
question of valuation. It happens not infrequently that
stock is taken and other assets are valued by directors or
managers about a concern who may have an interest, for
many readily imaginable reasons, in exaggerating values.
Our auditor's duty is, however, to be satisfied fully that the
basis of such valuations is a sound one, and, where possible,
to recommend a periodical revaluation by independent and
responsible men. The manager of a company of which I
have knowledge was recently sent to prison for frauds
committed in the manipulation of stock over a series of
years. Each half-year the directors presented to the auditor
a detailed stock account, taken by the manager and certified
as checked by them. The nature of the check adopted was
never inquired into by the auditor, and it was only when all
the mischief was done that he learned that the directors had,
for several years, been in the habit of counting as valuable
stock shelves upon shelves of empty boxes. In that case the
auditor, in my view, exhibited a lack of common-sense called
for by the Birmingham Post. For it should never be
forgotten that " the strength of a chain is only the strength
" of its weakest link," and hence the weak spot should not
only be made the subject of careful scrutiny, but every effort
made, by recommendation and—where, as is possible in
some rare cases—by insistence, towards the strengthening of
the feeble barrier against fraud. It may be convenient, in
sequence to this instance, to express my personal view, that
to the extent of his certificate the liability of an auditor should
be throughout legal as well as moral; and the more an auditor
acts as though this general principle were fact the sooner, I

am convinced, will the public recognise more fully than they do at present the importance and value of his work. It would be as impracticable as it is undesirable that there should be any statutory definition or limitation of an auditor's duties. But in the matter of the *Leeds Estate Co. v. Shepherd*, Mr. Justice Stirling stated broadly that he regarded " the duty of the auditor not to confine himself " merely to the task of verifying the *arithmetical* accuracy " of the Balance Sheet, but to inquire into its *substantial* " accuracy, and to ascertain that it . . . was properly " drawn up, so as to contain a true and correct representation " of the state of the company's affairs." And having done that and appended his certificate, in my view, the auditor puts upon the accounts a hall mark, by which he should be prepared to stand or fall. But if, without such complete examination, he permits himself loosely to append his unqualified certificate, he should not, as it appears to me, be permitted in the time of tribulation to repudiate the liability attaching to his deliberate or careless act.

We all know, of course, the difficulty which arises by reason of the appointment of the auditor being *nominally* that of the shareholders, but *actually* that of the board of directors, whose transactions it is his duty to check, and whose views it is at times his unpleasant but needful duty to traverse. If it were possible (even if it need be by legal enactment) to provide that these appointments should be made actually by the shareholders, of whose interests the auditor is the guardian and watch-dog, a partial remedy would be applied to the risk of an auditor tending to view the acts of directors, it may be quite unconsciously, in too favourable a light. Indeed, it is open to question whether directors should not be debarred, *qua* shareholders, from taking any part in the appointment of a scrutineer of their own dealings with the shareholders' estate. At present, however, to refuse concurrence in the directors' views, to qualify the audit certificate in too pronounced a manner, or to go the length of declining to certify at all, is usually to ensure the auditor being regarded as a recalcitrant, whose removal must be secured upon the earliest opportunity. And, unfortunately, as was pointed out in a recent lecture by Mr. Theodore Gregory, of Manchester, " so long as a " dividend is paid the shareholders usually support the " directors, and not the auditor, when an acute difference of " opinion arises. Possibly," he adds, " the time may come " when the Council of the Institute will take action to sup- " port accountants who are not re-elected in consequence of " the tone of their report, and after due inquiry into the " circumstances, and being satisfied that the auditor has " done his duty and *done it with discretion*, may take such " steps as will effectually prevent any other Chartered Ac- " countant accepting the vacant appointment." And if such a time does come, I venture to think our own Council will not be one whit behind the Institute in taking similar action. " Provided he has done his duty *with* " *discretion*." (The italics in each case are my own.) For there are undoubtedly indiscreet accountants who may, and would, unless restrained, do enormous harm. Take the case of any large undertaking—like a bank, for example—

the very breath of whose nostrils is an untarnished public reputation. One sees at a glance that an unfortunate expression in a report, published to the world, trumpeted in the financial press (some of whose organs are only too glad to catch an indefinite phrase in such a document and distort it for the benefit of the " bears" of the stock market), may, unless the utmost care is exercised, work in a moment incalculable mischief. And yet the auditor, upon whom rests not only this enormous responsibility on the one hand, but in the days of a company's misfortune, the risk of attack by an angry and splenetic body of shareholders, is, as a rule, thought to be sufficiently remunerated by a fee of a few guineas per annum. I fear, indeed, that this very fact lies more frequently at the root of the mischief resulting from inefficient auditing than we are at times disposed to imagine. I heard a Yankee say recently, when a buyer was seeking to cut down his profits, " My friend ! You " appear to forget that I am not in this business for my " health," and this applies equally to accountants. They are accountants mainly, often primarily, to gather shekels; and it is perhaps but natural that they should consider the relation between the fees received and the services rendered. Hence it has happened, and will happen again, that work which has been undertaken—perhaps through competition —at unremunerative rates has been " scamped" to make it pay. The pity, of course, is that it is practically impossible to fix a scale of fees upon a dead level, below or above which work should not be undertaken. In the mental, as in the labour market (only in greater degree), experience, ability, age and general reputation, will always command a higher price than their opposites. But it should be possible to fix *minimum* rates of remuneration, which will prevent a levelling down of fees to an equivalent of what is known in the labour world as " sweating prices." This may come in due time with the closing of the profession, but our time is not yet. Meanwhile, no honourable member of so honourable a calling, having once undertaken work at whatever price— if he has any feeling of *esprit de corps*—ought to permit himself to render to his clients any but the most thorough service of which he is capable. In this every man of sound integrity will be honest upon principle; but, taking the lower ground of policy, it does not and cannot pay in the long run, permanently to besmirch the fair fame of a whole profession for a temporal and personal gain. I would rather, however, take the higher ground and say with Ruskin in his *Crown of Wild Olive*, " With all brave and rightly-trained " men, their *work* is *first*, their *fee*, *second*—very important always, but still *second*."

# The Accountant

## THE ORGAN OF CHARTERED ACCOUNTANTS THROUGHOUT THE WORLD.

### (Awarded Silver Medal, Esposizione Italo-Americana, Genova 1892.)

Vol. XXII.—New Series.—No. 1134.        Saturday, August 29, 1896.

## Leading Articles.

### The Liabilities of Auditors.

IT is always a difficult matter for those who have not been actually present at the hearing to express any definite opinion upon the merits of a case from a perusal of the report, no matter how full the latter may be, and the case of *Ross & Co. v. Wright, Fitzsimons & Mayes* is no exception to the rule. We printed a full account of this case in our Law Reports of the 8th August, and although (being a decision of the Irish Court) it is not a precedent in this country, it is yet of sufficient interest to merit the close attention of our readers—especially as the various circumstances are by no means so unusual that a precisely similar case might not occur in this country—for although it is probable that in London, or in many of the larger provincial towns, no accountant would ever be asked to perform a partial audit which did not even allow him to inspect the Ledgers, there are many parts of the country where private traders are still sufficiently old-fashioned to be extremely careful to avoid taking even their auditors into their confidence.

The question before Lord Justice FITZGIBBON in the case which we are now considering was, first, as to whether the auditors had discharged the duties which they undertook to do, and, secondly, as to whether the losses complained of by the plaintiffs were a consequence of their failing to discharge those duties. If the truth be told, it seems to us that, although successful, the plaintiffs came rather badly out of the case. They had apparently been robbed upon a previous occasion by their cashier, and, with a view to preventing a recurrence of so unpleasant an incident, they arranged with a firm of accountants to make an audit of the Cash Book, although they were not prepared to incur the expense of the auditor's inspection of their Ledgers, still less the checking of their annual Trading Accounts and Balance Sheets. It is alleged by the defendants that they pointed out that it was undesirable that the cashier should post the Ledger without their being allowed to check the postings, but this is disputed by the plaintiffs; however that may be, it occurs to us that, inasmuch as by their own admission one member of the plaintiff's firm is held forth as a competent accountant, they must have been taken to know (whether the defendants explained it to them or not) that no effective audit could be performed in the manner which they prescribed, and that the audit which they contracted for was really nothing less than a farce, intended probably as a deterrent against fraud, rather than as a means of discovering it. Apparently, however, it failed to do either, for in due course the cashier swindled his employers out of nearly £700, for which offence we are informed that he is now suffering a long term of imprisonment. Had the plaintiff firm ever intelligently performed the audit which they represented to the accountants was performed half-yearly by one of their members, it seems to be beyond question that the frauds must have been discovered—at all events, when the half-yearly audit took place—and the fact that they were not so discovered is another proof of the futility of amateur audits, even when the auditor is directly interested in the effectiveness of his work. The incapacity of the plaintiffs, however, could not, of course, be regarded as any proper defence on the part of the defendants, and the question which the jury had to decide was as to whether or not they would have been able to discover the frauds had they properly discharged the specific duties which they undertook to do.

It seems that there were a considerable number of erasures in the Cash Book, a circumstance which is always reprehensible, and which should, of course, be invariably put a stop to, but which, when dealing with third and fourth-rate bookkeepers, is frequently practically unavoidable. Nevertheless, in the case in question, some of these erasures concealed a fraud; and that being so, it is difficult to see why it should not have been discovered by the auditors, even although we are prepared to admit that they were quite powerless to prevent the existence of erasures altogether. This appears to have been the view taken by his Lordship and by the jury. It is certainly the view suggested in his Lordship's summing-up, while the finding of the jury was that the defendants "did "not carry out the monthly audit with reasonable "care, skill, and diligence."

The next question which arose was, of course, the measure of damages to be incurred by the defendants under the circumstances, and in connection with this point, the summing-up of Lord Justice FITZGIBBON will be studied with interest, although we think it probable that most of our readers will hardly be inclined to admit the soundness of his Lordship's analogy. If a man were employed to make a gun and made one that would not shoot, we are told that the amount of the damage would be what was lost by getting a thing which was not worth what it purported to be; so that, if the auditing, in this case, was not worth £25 a year, the plaintiffs ought to get back the difference in value. It occurs to us that, in such a case as this, if the gun were altogether worthless, the purchaser would be entitled to return it and claim his money back; but the analogy does not seem to be particularly appropriate, inasmuch as it would be practically impossible for a firm to return his work to an auditor. Again, we are told that if the gunmaker made a gun which burst and blew off the purchaser's fingers, he would be responsible for the damage done. This, again, would only be so, provided there was no contributory negligence in the manner in which the plaintiff used the gun; and, in so far as the analogy is applicable, it would appear to suggest that, in this case, the defendants would be liable for the full amount of loss suffered by the plaintiffs. Yet his Lordship expressly directed the jury that the plaintiffs were not entitled to the same damages that they could have claimed, had they paid for a complete audit; which, if it meant anything at all, must, of course, have meant that they were not entitled to be recouped for the whole amount lost. Indeed, the more one examines his Lordship's summing-up, the more one is compelled to admit that there is nothing contained therein which was really of assistance to the jury in the matter; and the probability is that the £50 damages which the jury awarded was a sum roughly agreed upon, as representing something more than nominal, but considerably less than plenary, damages.

As the law stands at present, such actions as these are purely actions for non-performance of a contract, and as such one would have expected that the damages—if any—would invariably have been proportionate to the loss actually suffered. On the other hand, in almost all cases where such actions would arise, it would probably occur to any intelligent jury that damages so assessed would be unreasonably high, inasmuch as they would have the effect of constituting the auditor an " insurer," which it has been expressly laid down he is not. The probability is, therefore, that in all such cases the jury, in assessing damages, would have some regard to the amount which had been paid for the work contracted to be performed; and, without in any way assenting to the proposition that a poor remuneration may justifiably be repaid by indifferent work, we think that some such lines as these would be the fairest to go upon. In cases where a client has paid a liberal fee and given his auditors a free hand, he is, we think, clearly entitled to more damages than when he has starved the fee, and by his conduct throughout shown that he does not repose confidence in his auditors. When no confidence has been placed in the auditors, it seems to us that it is hardly open to a client, when it suits his purpose, to turn round upon them and say that his confidence has been abused; but it would not be expedient to carry even this view too far, because it would in effect amount to laying down as a principle that an auditor was justified in doing his work badly when he was badly paid.

If it could be done, which we doubt, it seems desirable that some definite principle should be settled upon which such cases could be dealt with in the future; but, on the other hand, we very much doubt whether any principle could be laid down which would not have the effect either of imposing too onerous a responsibility upon auditors, or of encouraging them to scamp their work; and that being so, it is probably best upon the whole that the existing system of leaving each case to the intelligence of a jury should be continued.

# The Accountant

## THE ORGAN OF CHARTERED ACCOUNTANTS THROUGHOUT THE WORLD.

### (Awarded Silver Medal, Esposizione Italo-Americana, Genova 1892.)

VOL. XXII.—NEW SERIES.—NO. 1138.        SATURDAY, SEPTEMBER 26, 1896.

## Leading Articles.

### The Value of an Audit.

A RECENT issue of *The Journal of Finance* contains an article dealing generally with the question of the value of audits by professional accountants, the subject having apparently been suggested by the action of the General Steam Navigation Company in making its retrograde move of adopting amateur in place of professional auditors. It will be remembered that we called attention to this in a note appearing in our issue of the 12th inst.

Our contemporary intimates that from the point of view of a limited company the value of an audit is dependent partly upon its cost and partly on the utility to the shareholders of the services rendered by the auditor, but appears to be unable to distinguish between the services which would, under all circumstances, be rendered by a responsible firm of accountants, and those services which have been defined as the strict duties of an auditor by recent legal decisions. From one aspect it is perhaps only businesslike to assume that the value of a professional audit would in all cases be reduced to the lowest level consistent with the strict letter of the legal responsibility of the auditor, but a very little consideration must, we think, show that in dealing with professional services this view is entirely erroneous. Indeed, were it not so we should be driven to the conclusion that the services of barristers—no matter how eminent—were in all cases valueless, seeing that counsel are not subject to any legal responsibility concerning their opinions. In dealing with the services of professional men it is indeed impossible to disregard the personal element ; and, as a matter of fact, no one ever really does disregard it. Professional auditors are invariably appointed not merely because they are accountants, but largely—and indeed principally— on account of the confidence which is reposed by those making the appointment in the particular accountant or firm of accountants selected, and it may, we think, safely be stated that this measure of confidence would be of the smallest if it were really thought that the particular firm employed would devote their energies to doing the least possible amount of work for their fee consistent with making themselves safe against the possibility of an action for negligence.

It seems to us that by many of our contemporaries an exaggerated importance has been attached to the fact, as per recent decisions, that there is *some* limit to the liabilities of an auditor. We should have thought that this interpretation of the law must have been obvious from the outset, and for our own part we do not think that as at present interpreted the law errs on the side of leniency towards auditors. It appears, however, that our contemporary attaches very great importance to the dicta of Lords Justices LINDLEY and LOPES, to the effect that an auditor is only bound to exercise reasonable care, and that it is no part of his duty to be animated by suspicion in pursuing his investigations. Our contemporary goes on to say that—

Were not the possibility of error or of fraud on the part of the directors, officers, or servants of the company to be entertained by the shareholders, why should they be compelled under the various Companies Acts to have the books and accounts of the company audited periodically ? And this being so it would be both absurd and unreasonable for an auditor to approach

his work in a spirit of foregone conclusion that everything is right, and that his duty merely consists in the distribution of red, blue, green, and yellow "ticks" over a certain number of Day Book and Ledger folios. If an auditor does not perform his work in the spirit of a detective, his work is of very little value, and, however much policy and convention dictate to him the necessity of concealing his true attitude and purpose from the officials of the company whose accounts engage his attention, it is as a detective of possible fraud more than as searcher for probable error, that the auditor must, and almost invariably does, approach his task.

The line of argument pursued by our contemporary is so illogical as to suggest that it has been advanced for the purpose of justifying a conclusion already arrived at, rather than of formulating a fair conclusion upon the whole matter. Surely it must be obvious that there is a vast distinction between an auditor not being " animated by suspicion" in pursuing his investigation, and his approaching his work in a spirit of " foregone conclusion that everything is right." We can quite understand that the distinction may not be very obvious to those who have no clear idea as to what the duties of an auditor are, or how he sets about discharging them, but we should certainly hesitate to place our contemporary under this category. If an auditor were to approach his work " in a spirit of foregone con- " clusion that everything was right," there would, of course, always be a serious danger—if not a certainty—that he would fail to detect anything wrong, which had been concealed with even ordinary caution ; and in this sense it may, perhaps, truly be said that if an auditor does not perform his work " in the spirit of a detective," his work is of very little value. There is, however, a wide difference between adopting the spirit of a detective and being " animated by " suspicion." In the former case, the frame of mind may be best described as one fully realising the possibility that there *may be* something wrong ; but this is very far removed from being actually suspicious as to what has occurred. An auditor is, of course, always conscious that anyone connected with the accounts which he is auditing may be guilty of fraud ; but that is quite a different thing from suspecting the whole of the staff of having already committed it. As regards the mere mechanical checking of entries, the point hardly arises one way or the other ; but the distinction is at once apparent when we come to consider the procedure in case an auditor thinks it desirable to call for some explanation with regard to entries which have been made. If he has a foregone conclusion that everything is right, the probability is that he would never make any enquiries. If, on the other hand, he is animated by suspicion as to the *bonâ fides* of the officers of the company, it seems a little objectless for him to ask *them* for any explanation as to their conduct. In point of fact, he could not rest contented with any reasons that they might give, unless he were able to verify them from outside sources, in which case it would have been altogether unprofitable to ask for explanations, while at the same time such a course would have had the disadvantage of putting a suspected person upon his guard. If the middle course be adopted, however, the auditor will naturally make such enquiries as appear to him to be necessary, and, being fully alive to the fact that he may be deceived, he will satisfy himself, not merely that the explanation which has been given to him *primâ facie* appears to meet the case, but he will further take steps to ascertain that it is correct. If possible from an independent source, but if not, in precisely the same manner as a Court of Justice satisfies itself with regard to the truth of evidence placed before it; namely, by cross-examination and the exercise of a little discretion.

Before leaving this point, however, we should like to state that we do not altogether accept the suggestion contained in the first sentence of the paragraph which we have quoted above. Apart from the possibility of error and of fraud, it would doubtless be unnecessary for auditors to be employed, but this is quite a different thing from suggesting that, because they are employed, they ought to be able to prevent the possibility of either contingency. So far as such errors and frauds may relate to the accounts, it is, no doubt, reasonable to expect that they could be discovered by an exhaustive examination of the books, but in point of fact—as has been shown of late—both error and fraud may sometimes arise which could not be detected by an examination of the accounts, and we are glad to notice that our contemporary practically admits this proposition, for a little further on in the same article it is stated that " the duties of auditors are practically im- " possible of definition, since they vary with every

" company by whom they are employed." This is a matter which has been dwelt upon in these columns. It will be remembered that a year or so ago some of our evening contemporaries devoted pages to the discussion of the question, and in various ways they displayed a most startling ignorance of the real requirements of the situation. These contemporaries must have applied at least a portion of the intervening period in acquiring a little more knowledge of the subject; otherwise it is inconceivable that they should have kept silence upon such important cases bearing upon the subject as the decisions in the cases of the *London and General Bank* and the *Kingston Cotton Mill Company*.

It seems to be now generally admitted that it is impracticable to frame an enactment exactly defining the duties of auditors to various classes of undertakings under all different circumstances; and, indeed, the impression appears now to prevail that the public is well protected against carelessness as well as fraud upon the part of auditors, and that there is therefore no need for legislation in the interest of the general public. Whether or not there is need for any reform of the existing law in the interests of accountants is, of course, altogether another matter, but up to the present at least there does not appear to be any demand on the part of accountants for legislative interference.

The only suggestion upon the whole matter which really appears to be worthy of careful consideration is that which was made by Mr. Justice VAUGHAN WILLIAMS at the Council dinner in May, viz., that the Council of the Institute should endeavour to formulate some rules for the guidance of its members. His Lordship expressed the view that the fact of such rules being in force would go far to protect auditors, inasmuch as it would then be capable of easy demonstration that the auditor had done all that under the circumstances the most experienced accountants would have deemed necessary. There are, doubtless, many difficulties in the way of drawing up a set of rules upon such a basis as this which would not do more harm than good by reason of their being wrongly or indiscreetly applied. But, even if this scheme should have to be abandoned as impracticable, it does occur to us that much might be done by the appointment of a committee, who would be prepared to deal with any points arising in the course of an audit that might be submitted to them by the auditor, and to express an opinion upon the right course to adopt under such circumstances. It is, of course, possible that, even where this was done, the auditor might have failed to properly disclose the facts, and this he would, of course, have to take the risk of. But where the circumstances were correctly stated, and where he had followed the advice of the committee, his position in the event of his being shot at would be greatly improved, inasmuch as he would be able to show, not only that the point had engaged his careful attention and that he had discharged his duties to the best of his ability, but he could produce, as evidence that he had done what was proper, the opinion which he had received, carrying with it the weight of a committee of authority, and we venture to think that only the most courageous of Judges would be inclined to fall foul of views so expressed.

## Chartered Accountants Students' Society of London.

### Notes on Auditing.

#### By Mr. John Paterson, F.C.A.

At a meeting of this Society, Mr. Francis W. Pixley, F.C.A., presiding, the following paper was read by Mr. Paterson :—

Of course, it is impossible in the course of an hour to say very much about Auditing, and I thought I would select two salient and prominent items in a Balance Sheet, and give you some notes on what I think is an auditor's duty in connection with these. We have recently had a case where an auditor escaped from liability in not checking the stock sheets : luckily for that auditor the Court of Appeal took a different view from Mr. Justice Vaughan Williams, and he was not found guilty of negligence. Still, I think it is sufficiently important to draw your attention to the fact that an auditor's duty does not end with the books, but he has a serious task in connection with the stock sheets.

In the first place, as regards the arithmetical accuracy of the stock sheets, I think the auditor ought to have these checked by his own clerks, but there are cases where this would be impossible to do considering the fee allowed. In cases where the auditor cannot check the extensions and the castings, I think he ought to get the various men in the company's employ to vouch the extensions and castings ; that is to say, the man who priced the stock ought to put his name to the sheet, and the man who did the extensions and additions should sign, and also the man who actually took the stock. By doing this you take all reasonable precautions against fraud. Let us assume that the manager was anxious to "cook" the stock sheets ; the other men would know something about it, and they would hesitate before they put their names to a cooked stock sheet. In addition to that, there is one thing which, I think, an auditor should do. He ought to look at the larger items in the stock sheet and see whether they are taken at cost. As regards a trader that is very easy to do, because the auditor can ask for the last invoice received for the goods, and compare it with the price in the stock sheets ; but in the case of a manufacturer the thing is much more difficult, because the question of what these goods cost is an intricate one. I will deal with that presently, and show you how, in different trades, that question of "cost" can be dealt with.

We will take the case of a manufacturer who uses raw materials, which may be cotton, lead, iron, or various other commodities. Take the case of cotton and metals, for example, the price of which fluctuates daily ; the question is whether, in the stock sheets, these raw materials should be put down at their original cost price, or at the market price of the day of the stocktaking. Take cotton or copper, the question is, what price should they be taken at ? A safe rule is to take them at cost price ; but that is sometimes subject to exceptions. One cannot always say the cost price is the right price ; it depends upon the quantity. For example, if there is a fall in price at the date of stocktaking, and there is a large quantity of the article, and the fall in price looks to be permanent, one ought to take the goods at the cost price of the day of stocktaking. Another question is whether, to the raw material cost, you have to add the cost of delivering to the works. With some items, the cost of carriage is much greater than the goods themselves. Take the case of coals delivered in London. If we were to take them in the stock sheets at 6s. per ton, the cost at the pit's mouth, this would be too low ; one has to add on the cost of carriage. This is clearly a case where carriage must be added ; but there are other cases which are not so clear. Take the case of a linen draper in London who buys goods in Manchester. Is the cost of these goods bought in Manchester, the cost price in Manchester, plus the carriage or not ? I think, in that case, the carriage ought not to be added to the cost price. This should be charged to Profit and Loss ; we ought not to treat that as an asset.

There is another thing you have to consider with reference to stock sheets. Are there any items in them which are old, or stale, or carried forward in the stock sheets for two or three years ? That happens in all businesses ; I can give you many instances, but we will take the case of a linen draper, or jeweller, or any other trade where the constant fluctuations of fashion depreciate the value of stock-in-trade. It is clear that, if the stocktaker in a business of that kind were to carry forward all the stock at the price paid for the goods, it would not be a fair price. The certificate of the stocktaker should run that the stock has been priced at cost or under. You must be particular to find out that the stale or depreciated items, which should be dealt with as under cost price, are properly dealt with. I do not say that the auditor is expected to go over every item in the stock sheets, but he can select salient items and test them by comparison with previous stock sheets and the invoices. By doing this he will be able to discover a great deal which it is necessary for him to discover.

Another thing which should be gone into is, any increase or decrease in stock as compared with the beginning of the year. If there is an increase in stock he must inquire what has been the necessity for it, and see the invoices to ascertain when the goods were purchased and why; or if the concern is a manufacturing concern, the question he must ask the maker is, Are you not making more stock than is necessary? Then, of course, that raises the question, If your stock is so increased, why cannot you sell it? Is it worth the price that you put upon it? Ought you not to take something off the cost price you have put on it in the stock sheets?

Another thing to note (it is almost unnecessary to mention) is that stock must not be taken at selling prices; but there have been cases made public where stock has been so taken. That happened with some American breweries which were sold to English companies. It is true this method of stock-taking did not affect the certificates of the accountants who gave the certificates of profits at the time, because the stock was practically the same in quantity at the beginning of the year as at the end, and so it did not affect the result. But when the same accountants certified subsequently to the Balance Sheet the stock of beer had to be written down to cost price.

There are, however, some exceptions to the rule, and you will see that there are cases where stock has to be taken at very nearly selling prices. We will take the case of seed crushers, where oil and oil cake are the product of the manufacture. One cannot tell what the oil costs to produce and what the oil cake. They are products of the same process, and the cost of manufacture applies to both. In that case, I think one would allow the stock to be taken at the selling price of the day, after deducting a percentage to represent the cost of selling and delivering that stock, and the interest which has to be deducted, to reduce the stock to cash value at the date of the Balance Sheet. I think, also, a maker of pig-iron and a lead or copper smelter, might be allowed to value his stock in this way, especially as there is a free and ready market for the sale of these commodities for cash. Where, however, there is no free market for cash, I think the cost price of the article produced is the proper price for the stock sheet. This cost price is not, however, always easy to ascertain, especially with firms who do not keep proper Cost Price Books. In that case, where the cost is only arrived at by a rough estimate, and not from an accurate cost sheet prepared from the actual expenditure on production, the auditor has to find out the selling price of the article produced, and the average gross profit on it, as shown from the Manufacturing or Trading Account, and deduct that percentage of gross profit from the selling price of the article. In the case of breweries, most brewers take care to keep a correct account of what each brew costs them, so that the cost of a barrel of beer is easily ascertained. There is usually no difficulty in ascertaining the cost price of a brewer's stock.

I give the case of agricultural implement makers as an illustration of the difficulty of ascertaining what is the cost of each article manufactured, because, unless a very correct dissection is made of the goods consumed and the wages paid in each department, the cost price cannot be accurately stated. Here it might be necessary to fall back on the gross profit test, and deduct the necessary percentage from the selling price, and in this way check the agricultural implement maker's rough statement of costs. A similar remark applies also to taking the stock of electric constructors. These stocks would be very difficult for anybody, even an expert, to value. The manufacturers ought to keep a Cost

Price Book showing what the stock cost; and then you must compare it with the gross profit and the selling price, as before explained.

There is another thing to keep in view in manufacturing concerns; they generally have reserve pieces of machinery. It is the custom with some concerns to charge the cost of these direct to the Trading Account, and, with others, it is the custom to charge the cost to capital expenditure, and write off so much for depreciation. While these reserve pieces of machinery have been charged to capital expenditure, they may have been taken credit for in the stock sheets as stock in hand.

A perusal of the stock sheets would soon discover this error. There are occasions where goods are omitted altogether from stock, and it might be that a comparison of the previous stocktaking with the present one would discover the omissions from the stocktaking.

There are many cases where the stock sheets are too voluminous for an auditor to effectively deal with. Take the case of Armstrong, Mitchell & Co.'s works, or even the Army and Navy Stores, or any large concern like that. Even in such cases some tests can be easily applied. It would be desirable, I think, to compare the totals of the various departmental stocks one year with the other, and see whether there are increases or decreases, and call for explanations of these. With reference to stock afloat, that is to say, on board ship, you can satisfy yourself by inspecting the invoices and bills of lading, and the date of arrival of the ship, to prevent this stock being twice taken. Where stock books are kept, as they are in many businesses, both wholesale and retail, one ought to see whether the stock sheets tally with the list of stock taken from the stock books. In dealing with stocks of wines and spirits, you come across a curious custom. In the case of spirits, it is the custom to add interest at the rate of 5 per cent. per annum, and sometimes at 6 per cent. to cover loss by evaporation. I think this is justifiable, because spirits improve by keeping, but it is doubtful with wines. Certainly it is not allowable with some wines. In the case of champagnes, it is the custom of manufacturers to add 5 per cent. per annum to the cost, as the wine takes three years to make ready for sale, but when it is ready for sale no further interest is added. A dealer cannot add any interest to his cost of champagne, except, perhaps, in the case of fine vintages, which only happen about once in every ten years. The same remark applies to clarets and ports. In the case of spirits, which are very often blended for sale, there is not much difficulty in arriving at the cost of blended spirits, because a blend book is kept, and you can see what has been the cost of the mixture. In some companies the stock-in-trade is taken annually by an outside valuer. In such cases you are relieved from difficulty in dealing with stocks, but even in such cases you should compare the stock sheets with those of the previous year, and make inquiries as to the increases or decreases. In connection with this question of stocks, I heard of a case where a wine merchant wanted a partner, but the last year's Profit and Loss Account showed, although the sales were about the same as previously, a larger rate of gross profit than had been made in the previous years.

On comparing the stock sheets it was discovered that the wine merchant had, at the last stocktaking, added interest at the rate of 5 per cent. per annum from the date of purchase, to the cost price of some wine which had been in bond for some years, and which was difficult to sell. On this being discovered the partnership negotiations were not proceeded with, as the profit as shown by the last year's Profit and Loss Account, was not a fair profit, having been fictitiously augmented by the added interest to the value of the stock.

Another thing you have to keep in mind when dealing with stocks, not in the owner's premises but in public warehouses or in bond, is that there are warehouse charges running on the stock. If you find in the stock sheet that the stock is in a public warehouse, you must ascertain when it was deposited there; and as it is not the custom to pay dock charges until the goods are cleared, it is frequently the case no account is taken of these charges in the owner's books till the stock is taken from the warehouse.

There have been occasional cases where the manager has "cooked" the stock sheets to cover defalcations. The most out-of-the-way case I have heard of was that of a wholesale perfumer, who had a manager who used to steal the essences which give the scent, and then, to make good his deficiencies, he put in a larger proportion of spirit than was usual. As most of this scent went abroad, it was not discovered for some time that he was shipping perfumery which had very little scent in it.

One has also to keep in mind that it is the custom, in some businesses, to make sales of goods for future delivery. These have to be taken into account, because occasionally they turn out to be bad sales or bad purchases. In dealing with this question of buying goods for future delivery, I heard of a case where the manager of a company used to buy a metal for use in the factory, and, when the contract for future delivery showed a profit, he never disclosed it to his company, but resold the metal, and it was only when the metal showed a loss that he disclosed the contract, and then the company had to take delivery of it.

I have now dealt with all the points on stocktaking and stock sheets that I can conveniently deal with in the short time allotted to me, and you will see that there are a great many things which an auditor can discover, by just using a little ordinary care and diligence in dealing with the stock sheets. It is not necessary that an auditor should be an expert in the particular business he is auditing, in order to discover what I have been telling you. Stock-in-trade is a very important item, for sometimes profits can be made to appear as if they had been earned when they have not been earned at all, and *vice versâ*, losses can be shown which have not really been made.

There are some businesses which have items in their Balance Sheets very difficult to deal with. I refer to the businesses of shipbuilders or contractors who take contracts. Of course, their stock-in-trade is small, but the question is with their Profit and Loss Account. If a contract extends over two or three years, all that you can do is to see that all the labour and materials spent on the job are charged to it; but you cannot do anything with that account, until the contract is finished, because it is only then that you know whether there has been a profit or a loss. One does not know which it will be; all one knows is that a certain amount has been expended on these contracts, but how much is required to finish them no one can tell, unless the contract is very near completion. What profit a contractor is making, I do not think anyone can say, if he has many contracts on hand. This must be a difficulty with shipbuilding companies to make up their Profit and Loss Account to the satisfaction of an auditor, and that brings me to this question, that an auditor in signing a Balance Sheet ought to say to himself, "Now, is this a Balance Sheet fairly, correctly, and properly "drawn up, and does it exhibit a true state of the company's "affairs, and if I were advising a client to join this concern, "could I honestly tell him that it is a true and fair Balance "Sheet?" If one puts a question like that to himself, one might hesitate before signing some Balance Sheets. There is always this recourse if an auditor has any doubt about it, he can put some qualifying words in the certificate to show doubt. If an auditor does that, I do not think he can be blamed in the case of a shipbuilding or contracting company passing profits which may not be ultimately earned.

I will now say something about another important item in a Balance Sheet, viz., book debts. I think in dealing with that item I would like to call your attention to this fact, that in some audits it is impossible to do all the work; that is to say, you have to select what is really the essential work, and what you can omit to do. If you report to your principals that you have done so and so, you would, under those circumstances, be exonerated, at any rate, so far as an action would lie against you for not discovering frauds. As regards the main essentials of a Balance Sheet, you would have to make sure that all the assets and liabilities were correct, and whether the company had done the trading represented. I think you would get out of any liability if you applied these tests.

In the French and German system of bookkeeping, they have a very good law which is practically to the effect that all the entries in connection with the bookkeeping must pass through the Journal. In many cases we don't do that, because we have Day Books, Purchases Books, &c., and we post direct from these and from Cash, Bill, and other books. You could also comply with the French system. You could put the totals of the Cash Book monthly into the Journal, and also the totals of the other subsidiary books from which postings are made. The French law also requires that when you take out your Trial Balance at the end of the year, you have to take it out in four columns, and you have to take out all the accounts which have been operated upon during the year. Our custom is only to take out the open balances; therefore, all closed accounts for the year do not appear in our Trial Balances. The object of the French system is to make the totals which you take out from Ledgers tally with the totals of your Journal. When you begin the year, you bring into your Journal the open balances which are closed in the Ledger at the end of the year and reopened at the beginning of the next year by an entry called "*Balance d'entrée.*" By that means all the debits and credits which have been in the Ledgers are brought into the Journal, as the opening entry of the year, and when you take out the Trial Balance at the end of the year, you take out all the accounts, including those which have no balances, but which have been operated on during the year.

The Trial Balance has, therefore, four columns. In the first is the total debits in the year; in the second, the total credits; in the third, the final debit balance, if any; and in the fourth, the final credit balance, if any.

In an English Trial Balance only the third and fourth columns are used; but with the four-columned French Trial Balance you can see at a glance, not only the existing balances at the end of the year, debit or credit, but also the total debits and credits on every account operated on during the year, whether closed or not. That is a useful form of Trial Balance, and the total debits in the first and second columns must agree with totals of the debit and credit columns in the Journal added up for the whole year.

You can see from this Trial Balance at a glance who are the largest customers of the firm and with whom the largest transactions take place.

In going through the Ledgers in connection with the book debts, it is very important to look at the debit side and see whether there are any debits for bills or cash. If you see such a debit in a Sales Ledger, you may be sure that there is something wrong with that account, and it will be necessary for you to make inquiries. Another thing you should do, with reference to an open debit balance, is to see whether it "letters" off, and what items or invoices make up that total. Sometimes you will find that a man has paid a later invoice, and the older one is left standing. You must also know what the terms of credit are, and whether the debtor has paid up or not in accordance with the credit allowed; if he has not, you must have explanations about it.

Another thing you must keep in view is, that when you come across a large debit balance you ought to investigate it carefully, and not only must you allow for the open balance, but you have to take into account the bills discounted which bear that man's name in order to see the total risk with any one customer. If you find the firm is running a large risk with one customer, you ought to satisfy yourself that it is a good account.  If there is an account, say, on which there is a risk of loss by bad debt of £5,000, you ought to make inquiry to know something about that man before you pass it as a good debt.  Some lawyers are of opinion that the accountant's way of making up a Profit and Loss Account is wrong ;  their idea is to get fees, and as they are generally paid that is their profit and loss.  If they do not get a fee they do not treat it as profit ; they say, "You take " credit in your Profit and Loss Account for amounts owing " by persons who have not paid."  That is a very proper comment, but the answer to it is, that in trading and commercial affairs, it is the custom to do so, and if due care is taken and the auditor sees that the ordinary risks are fair business ones, he is justified in taking those sales as proper sales to the credit of the Profit and Loss Account.  There are special businesses in which long credit is given—businesses which give credit extending over a period of two or three years—such, for example, as supplying implements and machines, payable by instalments.  I came across such a business in America, and I was simply amazed by the apparent risks which were run, but I found on investigation that the proportion of bad debts was comparatively a small percentage of the total business done.  It is clear that in making up a Balance Sheet of a business of this description you would have to make a very large discount from the face value of the debts to reduce them to the cash value ; whilst in an ordinary case of book debts you could say 2½ per cent. was the proper discount to reduce them to their cash value. You would in that case, perhaps, take off 15 per cent. or 20 per cent. to allow for various kinds of risks.  In all Balance Sheets where book debts appear it is not right to set down the gross value of the debts ; you ought to take off a discount varying according to the terms of credit, whether it is 5 per cent. or 2½ per cent.

With reference to the provision for bad and doubtful debts, I think it is a prudent practice that, in addition to making a reserve to cover all known bad or doubtful debts, a further reserve should be made for the good debts which may turn out " bad."  Assuming that your bad and doubtful debts came to £1,000, while you would reserve that £1,000 you would say, " I must make another reserve for debtors " who might go bad."  In that way your reserve would be greater than £1,000, but you then have your book debts always at fair value.   This is difficult to get some people to do at the start, but when once a start is made the Profit and Loss Account of subsequent years does not suffer ; it is only the first one which is affected.

With reference to bad debts, there are two ways of dealing with them—one is to let them stand in the Ledger until the last dividend is received and make a reserve for them ; and the other way is to write them clean off.  The latter is not quite such a good way, as they are apt to be overlooked, and if dividends are obtained they may be credited to the account in Bad Debts Ledger and the auditors might not look at it. If in the Balance Sheet you have such items as " Loans and "Mortgages," you must see that the interest debited has been paid.  There have been cases where the interest has not been debited, but collected and not accounted for.  If there are debtors for rents you must see that the rents are not in arrear.

I have already dealt with the question of a debtor owing a large amount.  The same remark applies to the Balance Sheet of a bank.  We had a case some short time ago, where one of our brothers was cast in damages because he had passed very large sums in the Balance Sheet by two or three companies.  That is an illustration of how one has to be careful in dealing with large amounts, and why every care should be taken and inquiry made before passing them.

Another question arises in dealing with debtors.  We will take the case of a foreign currency which fluctuates a great deal, for instance, the rupee or rouble.  Here the proper thing to do would be to take the rupee as of the exchange value at the date of your Balance Sheet.  I do not see any other method one can follow.

I think I have dealt with a few main points on the Balance Sheet.  I should like also to bring to your attention a thing which goes without saying, but which I do not think has ever been the subject of a lecture.  I think I can deal with it on the present occasion.  I refer to the point of professional secrecy.  It is very important, because there are a great many clients who are naturally afraid of trusting a knowledge of their monetary affairs to outsiders, and more especially are they careful of the accountant's clerks, who naturally get to know their affairs, and they are afraid their business may be talked about.  You will see what an injury is done to the profession if professional secrecy is violated. We have not such a severe law on this subject as the French have.  You well recollect about a year ago a doctor was defendant in an action for libel, for communicating something connected with his patient, which he had acquired in his professional capacity.  If that case had occurred in France, the action against that doctor would have been not only a civil action but a criminal one, because in the Penal Code Napoleon, which was promulgated in 1810, article 348, after enumerating the medical profession and kindred occupations, goes on " and all other persons depositaries, through " their occupation or profession, of secrets confided to them, " who (except in the case where the law compels them to " become informers) shall reveal these secrets will be " punished by imprisonment of from one to six months, and " by a fine of 100 to 500fr."

That is the law in France.  Unfortunately we have no such law here.  I do not know what remedy a client would have if we were to violate our professional secrecy ;  most likely we should not get employed again.  The other day a lady brought an action against a bank because it had violated the secrecy of the state of her banking account, with the result that the lady got £150 damages.  I do not think the lady suffered any damage, but the jury gave that amount.  It is very important that this question of professional secrecy should be highly impressed upon accountants and auditors, and that one should never talk of our clients' affairs to anybody, not even to our wives. (Laughter.)  This question also arises sometimes, where an auditor acts for two persons. There, I think, the secrecy is such that one ought not to communicate to the other client the knowledge which one acquires as the accountant to the other.

Another question sometimes discussed is, whether the auditor ought to take advantage of his knowledge of the company's affairs either to buy, sell, or traffic in the shares. It is clearly a wrong thing, because he has no right to use his knowledge acquired in his professional capacity to his own profit or advantage.  That is sometimes a good reason why the auditor should not be a shareholder in the company. I have been concerned with two lay auditors on two different occasions, and on one occasion we discovered that the company was in a hopeless financial condition, and it was not likely to last long.  Luckily I was not a shareholder, but my co-auditor was unfortunately, and what he did was, he immediately sold his shares, the result being that he was not re-elected on the next occasion.  I must also mention the case of another auditor, who was a stockbroker.  He held shares in a company which came to grief ; and although there was a large liability on his shares he held them all the time: and he said to me : "I often could have sold my " shares ; I knew the company was going wrong, but I have " stuck to my shares all through."

The right thing is never to take any advantage, nor to allow anyone else to take advantage, of your knowledge acquired in a professional capacity.  I do not think I have anything more to add to my remarks.  I am sorry I could not find time to write a paper and give you more connected remarks, but perhaps I have touched on sufficient points to interest you.

Mr. FRANCIS W. PIXLEY said they had had a most interesting and practical address.  The main part of it consisted of two very important points, viz., as to how an auditor should deal with stock-in-trade and with book debts in a

Balance Sheet.  It was practically possible in a trading concern of magnitude to make the profit or the loss anything
one liked by a very slight manipulation of the value of the
stock.   For example, by adding slightly to the value in the
detail of the stock, or by not writing off sufficient depreciation, in order to show too much profit, or by slightly reducing
the value of the items in the stock, or by writing off too
much depreciation if there was any desire to show a loss or
a profit less than that actually made.  The duty of an
auditor with regard to stock was very difficult to determine.
What would be possible to do in the way of checking where
the stock was small would probably be impracticable in
dealing with a large concern, and it was somewhat
dangerous to lay down any hard or fast line as to what
course should be adopted, considering the way the remarks
and writings of auditors were made use of in the present
day by Her Majesty's Judges.

With regard to the question as to whether auditors should
be shareholders, Mr. Pixley said that an auditor should not
be a shareholder—he should be an entirely disinterested
person ; in the same way that a Judge does not try a case in
which he is interested, so an auditor should not have any
bias or be in any way interested in the concern, other than
as auditor.

Votes of thanks having been accorded to Mr. Paterson for
his valuable address, and to Mr. Pixley for his presence in
the chair, the meeting terminated.

# The Accountant

### THE ORGAN OF CHARTERED ACCOUNTANTS THROUGHOUT THE WORLD

#### (Awarded Silver Medal, Esposizione Italo-Americana, Genova 1892.)

VOL. XXIII.—NEW SERIES.—No. 1172.    SATURDAY, MAY 22, 1897.

## Leading Articles.

### Directors v. Auditors.

A PROVINCIAL firm of accountants—who, however, desire their name kept in the background—have forwarded us some interesting information in connection with a dispute which recently arose between them and the managers of a "single-steamship" company, which, we think, can hardly fail to be instructive to our readers.

The firm in question had been appointed auditors to the company, and the first account that they were called upon to audit was a Voyage Account of the vessel, without any Balance Sheet appended. They examined the accounts in the usual manner and certified them as follows: "We "have examined the foregoing Voyage Account

" No. —, with the accounts and vouchers relating
" thereto, and find it in agreement therewith.
" No provision is made in the account for
" depreciation." We are informed that, before
adding this last clause to their certificate, the
auditors consulted their solicitors, who advised
them that, in view of recent decisions, and
apart altogether from the practice that many
single-steamship companies do not write off
depreciation or form a Reserve Fund, they considered it absolutely the duty of the auditors, in
the interests of the shareholders and probable
investors, as well as for their own protection, to
state in the certificate that no depreciation had
been written off.

There can be no doubt that, notwithstanding
the fact that single - ship companies do very
generally make no provision whatever in their
accounts for depreciation (either as such or in the
way of reserve), where depreciation has occurred
—which, for all practical purposes, may be taken
to be always the case—it would be most unwise
for auditors to neglect to call attention to the
circumstance upon the face of their certificate.
That being so, although, perhaps, to a practical
ship manager the clause may seem somewhat
redundant, yet, as a matter of fact, we are satisfied
that it is very necessary for the protection of the
auditor and for the information of the
shareholders. It may, further, even be added
that, in so far as it is necessary for the
protection of the auditor, it is at least equally
necessary for the protection of the managers.
This, however, does not appear to have been the
view taken of the matter by the managers of the
company in question, for we understand that they
immediately intimated to the auditors that at the
full board meeting their certificate was considered
and a resolution was come to, requesting the
auditors to reconsider the wording, and to omit
all reference to the absence of provision for depreciation. This the auditors declined to do, where-
upon the managers intimated that they would not
print the clause in the published accounts. The
auditors then pointed out that, if the managers

declined to publish the certificate as signed by
them, they would do so at their own risk; but,
notwithstanding this warning, the certificate was
eventually published without any reference to the
absence of provision for depreciation.

Naturally the auditors protested, and at once
sent in their resignation. In the correspondence
which followed the managers attempted to suggest
that the clause as it stood was inaccurate,
inasmuch as there was a Reserve Fund available
for the purposes of meeting depreciation; but
they seem to have lost sight of the fact that the
Reserve Fund was not *solely* available for this
purpose, and further that (even including undivided profits) it only amounts to £270, whereas
the cost of the vessel was something in excess of
£25,000, while it was only insured for about
£15,000—which we may take it would be the
maximum amount for which the underwriters
would insure it.

Some of the views expressed by the managers
as to their conception of the duties of auditors in
general appear to us to be not a little amusing.
Thus, in the correspondence which took place
between the parties, we find that they considered
the auditors were "going beyond their duty" in
dealing with depreciation, or offering any suggestions thereon. This, of course, was a matter
which the auditors did not feel called upon to
discuss at that particular juncture, and they
merely replied to the effect that after taking legal
advice upon the matter they had determined,
in the event of the directors still declining
to publish the full certificate, to take
proceedings to ensure its publication to the shareholders; in reply to which the managers stated
that they "took note" of the auditors' threat and
begged to give them notice that they would be
" held liable for anything which they might do or
" circulate to prejudice the standing of the direc-
" tors or interests of the company, or of the
" managers, directly or indirectly." The suggestion that an auditor should be held liable for publishing his certificate, when the directors and

managers of the company refused to do so, strikes us as particularly amusing; but, unfortunately for the interests of the profession, the matter seems never to have reached a stage when any authoritative decision might have been delivered thereon, for we learn that at the meeting of shareholders, which was called to receive the resignation of the auditors, they were again re-elected, and a strongly worded resolution was passed condemning the action of the managers and of the board.

It will thus be seen that, in this particular case, at all events, the shareholders were sufficiently enlightened to appreciate the importance of having auditors who not only had the courage of their own opinions, but also were prepared to take effective steps to see that those opinions were placed before the shareholders. We congratulate the shareholders of this particular company upon having the services of such auditors, and the auditors themselves upon being so fortunate with regard to the shareholders; as frequently the auditors receive no such support.

We remember a case in point, in which the shareholders of a large metropolitan water company were particularly annoyed with one of the auditors, because he wished to point out to them that certain expenses which he thought properly chargeable against the half-year had not been included. All the thanks that he got for so doing appear to have been in the shape of extreme indignation upon the part of the shareholders, and an expression of opinion that, had these expenses been included, their dividend would have been reduced 1 per cent.; and it was distinctly hinted that the matter would be remembered against the auditor when he next came up for election, which did not happen to be the case at that particular meeting.

Another case occurs to us, in which an auditor's certificate was suppressed, but unfortunately it was in the United States and not in this country, so that the result is of little practical importance to us as a guide. In this instance the firm of accountants (Messrs. BROAKER & CHAP-MAN, of New York) promptly took proceedings against those responsible for the suppression of a portion of their certificate, but the law in New York State is very different from the law in England, and the matter was allowed to hang fire for many weary months, after which the advocate employed by Messrs. BROAKER & CHAPMAN settled the case out of Court without their permission, so that it never really came on for hearing. What would have been the result had it been fought out it is difficult to say, but, probably, many other considerations than those which would be allowed to have weight in an English Court would have had to be regarded.

*An Auditor's Duties.*

The following note, which we reproduce from the columns of *The Warehouseman*, will be of interest to our readers, because it draws attention to the vagueness of the views entertained by many persons as to the respective functions of directors and auditors of companies—particularly the latter :—

That directors should "direct" and that auditors should "audit" is a truism, though it needs to be repeated because many directors consider that all their duties are discharged if they attend the board meetings simply in an ornamental capacity, and auditors have not infrequently been content with adding up the figures in a Balance Sheet and verifying the totals. All the same, there are obvious limits to the duties of auditors, who cannot or ought not to be expected to interfere with the functions of directors. They must themselves be responsible for the policy of the company. We make these remarks because a lengthened advertisement in the daily press calls attention to a Balance Sheet issued by a company, the name of which is not given, the auditor's certificate being as follows:—" Under reference to what is " stated in the prefixed report of the directors with regard to " the company's investments, the above Balance Sheet is, in " our opinion, a full and fair one." " Now, these words," the advertiser says, " cover an estimated loss or depreciation " in the value of the company's assets, as estimated by the " directors, of a sum of £170,000, and of such loss or deprecia- " tion there does not appear on the Balance Sheet itself any " indication whatever." And he asks whether the Balance Sheet can be truly declared a full and fair one. Well, we cannot, of course, answer the question, because we do not know anything about the company referred to, or even what its name is. We quote the advertisement simply for the purpose of reminding our readers, if they need reminding, that they must not expect too much of auditors. On the face of the statement made, we should say the auditors had done all that they need do. For some reason or other the directors have called attention to a possible, probable, or actual depreciation, temporary or otherwise, of the assets. The auditors are not apparently in a position to express a positive opinion, and they refer to the directors' statement as a qualification of their certificate, leaving the shareholders to settle the matter with the directors. We do not see what more could be asked.

## The Nature and Extent of an Auditor's Responsibility.

Mr. Wm. Robertson, C.A., F.F.A. (Edinburgh), next delivered a paper on "The Nature and Extent of an "Auditor's Responsibility." He said :—

"The Nature and Extent of an Auditor's Responsibility" is a subject of great importance to the professional accountant, and of considerable interest to the general public.

The view that may be taken will depend upon what is considered to be the duties of an auditor —the work required to be done to make an audit efficient. Much has been written on these subjects, and, although I do not suppose I shall have anything to say that is new, yet, as the views of those who have written on auditing and an auditor's duties and responsibilities vary considerably, and as it is only by discussing the matter that we can hope to arrive at some general rules applicable to most cases of auditing, I trust that this paper of mine by further airing the matter may be of some slight service.

So far as the audit of the accounts of private firms is concerned, I consider that it is a matter for arrangement between the auditor and the firm employing him as to the work to be done. In many of the audits of private firms' accounts the principal object is to act as a check upon cashiers and bookkeepers, and so prevent fraud. Again, in others, where we will say the sole partner, or one of the partners, attends personally to all cash transactions, and where, therefore, it might not be considered necessary to check Cash Book entries, vouchers, etc., so particularly, the services of a professional accountant are required as much to put the accounts in shape, and advise as to the books to be kept, as for anything else.

Of course, the auditor will advise the doing of what he considers necessary; but whatever arrangement is made between him and the firm should, I think, be embodied in a letter by the former to the latter, detailing clearly what work he proposes to do, and so by it defining his responsibility. If errors or defalcations are afterwards discovered which could not have been brought to light by the work he undertook to do, then clearly no responsibility can attach to him; and, on the other hand, he should, I think, be held responsible if the work he undertook (properly done) ought to have discovered the errors or defalcations.

It is, however, quite a different matter, the responsibility of the auditor of the accounts of public trading companies and corporations constituted by Act of Parliament or Royal Charter. The auditor is here, I think, the agent of the shareholders who elect him and to whom he has to report. He may have a duty to the general public, but his responsibility is only to the shareholders. As bearing on the subject I shall quote the following opinion of the Council of the Institute of Chartered Accountants in England and Wales :—

" The Council desire to point out that an auditor has no
" concern with the administrative management of a com-
" pany, except so far as to see that its operations have been
" within its statutory powers.  The duties of auditors must
" necessarily, to a greater or less extent, vary with every
" class of business, and with the constitution of the com-
" panies whose accounts are under review ; but an auditor
" will fail in his duty if he does not use reasonable care
" such as the circumstances of the case may allow or render
" necessary to satisfy himself as to the propriety of the
" figures contained in the books and Balance Sheet."

I think that this statement, which from its tenor
evidently applies more particularly to public companies, is
well worth keeping in mind, as, although it is necessarily
vague as to details, it states plainly enough the Council's
opinion of what an auditor should concern himself about
and what things are outside his province.

Several Acts of Parliament make the appointment of an
auditor compulsory, and define to some extent his duties.
Mr. Frederick Whinney, in a paper on Audits and Certificates, states very concisely and clearly the provisions
regarding auditors in those Acts where an attempt has been
made to define their duties.  The following is a list :—

> Companies Clauses Act 1845.
> City of London Sewers Act 1848.
> The Companies Act 1862.
> Mersey Docks Act 1867.
> The Railway Companies Act 1868.
> The Gas Companies Act 1869.
> The Metropolis Water Act 1871.
> The Banking Companies Act of 1879.

And the Acts relating to building societies and friendly
societies.

There are, besides, the Acts referring to insurance companies, savings banks, and county and parish councils.

Of these Acts of Parliament, amongst the principal are
those relating to—

> (a) Railway companies.
> (b) Banks.
> (c) Manufacturing and trading (or industrial) com-
> panies.

The clauses in them bearing upon auditing I shall briefly
discuss.

By the Railway Companies Act of 1867 the auditors are
required to certify that the accounts contain a true statement of the financial condition of the company, that the
dividends are *bonâ fide* due thereon, and that the Revenue
Account is correctly stated after charging all the expenses
which ought to be paid thereout. A usual form of certificate
is the following :—

The accounts of the company for the half-year ending
——— have, in the opinion of the auditors, been correctly
made out, and are in conformity with the Regulation of
Railways Act 1868.  The balance of net revenue amount
to £ ———.

The auditors certify that the accounts subscribed by
them contain a full and true statement of the financial
condition of the company as recorded in the company'
books, and that the dividends proposed to be declared ar
*bonâ fide* due thereon, after charging the revenue of the
half-year with all expenses which ought to be paid there
out.

Clearly, here, the auditor is responsible if any item of
expenditure properly chargeable to revenue is charge
against capital, in other words he is responsible if a dividend
is paid out of capital.

To a certain extent on account of the failure of the City
of Glasgow Bank in 1878 there was passed in 1879 an Act
limiting the liability of shareholders of banks, and, amongst
other things, providing for an annual audit by an auditor
independent of the company.  The clause relating to the
audit, besides allowing the auditor access to the books at all
reasonable times, gives him the power of examining the
directors or any other officer of the bank.  He has to report
to the shareholders :—

" That, in the auditor's opinion, the Balance Sheet is a
" full and fair Balance Sheet, properly drawn up, and
" exhibits a true and correct view of the bank's affairs a
" shown by the books."

A form of certificate adopted with more or less, commonly
slight, variations is the following :—

" We beg to report that we have examined the account
" of ——— for the year ended ———, and that we have
" satisfied ourselves of the correctness of the cash balance
" at head office and branches, verified the cash with London
" bankers, the securities for money at call and short notice
" the Government securities, and other investments
" Further, in accordance with the Companies Act 1879, we
" have examined the foregoing Balance Sheet and Profit and
" Loss Accounts with the books of the bank, and we hereby
" certify that, in our opinion, said accounts are properly
" drawn up so as to exhibit a true and correct view of the
" bank's affairs at ——— as shown by the books."

Here we see that the auditor defines his work, and, I think
as a natural consequence defines the extent of his responsibility.  If he has not done the work stated or not done it
efficiently, and loss to the shareholders has thereby accrued,
he should, I think, be held liable, along with the directors
and other servants of the bank who framed and approved the
accounts.

We come now to the Companies Acts 1862 to 1890, under
which the great majority of public companies are now
registered.  Table A in the first schedule of the Act of 1862
(Regulations for management of a company limited by
shares), by articles 83 to 94 thereof, provides for an annual
audit, and, amongst other things, states the duties of the
auditor.  Because of their importance, I shall give articles
92, 93, and 94 in full :—

Article 92.—Every auditor shall be supplied with a copy of the Balance Sheet, and it shall be his duty to examine the same with the accounts and vouchers relating thereto.

Article 93.—Every auditor shall have a list delivered to him of all books kept by the company, and shall at all reasonable times have access to the books and accounts of the company. He may at the expense of the company employ accountants or other persons to assist him in investigating such accounts, and he may, in relation to such accounts, examine the directors or other officer of the company.

Article 94.—The auditors shall make a report to the members upon the Balance Sheet and accounts, and in every such report they shall state whether in their opinion the Balance Sheet is a full and fair Balance Sheet, containing the particulars required by these regulations, and properly drawn up so as to exhibit a true and correct view of the state of the company's affairs, and in case they have called for explanations or information from the directors, whether such explanations or information have been given by the directors, and whether they have been satisfactory, and such report shall be read together with the report of the directors at the ordinary meeting.

Most companies registered under the Act of 1862 have articles of association in lieu of the regulations of Table A, but, speaking generally, the sections relating to audit vary very little from those of that Table. As a rule, therefore, in article 94 above quoted, you would have to substitute 'articles of association" for "these regulations."

Now, I think that these articles clearly indicate that the auditor's duty is to verify the Balance Sheet, and that he can be held responsible for nothing else.

In a former paper by me which appeared in the *Scottish Accountant* of July 1894, I stated that there were two things to be kept in view when making an audit—two questions which the auditor must answer :—1st, Does the Balance Sheet exhibit a true statement of the assets and liabilities of the company as at a certain date? 2nd, Has there been any misappropriation of funds, embezzlement, unauthorised expenditure, or otherwise, during the period over which the audit extends?

I consider that his principal duty is the first of these, and that only for errors in the Balance Sheet which ought to have been brought to light by his audit can he be held responsible.

The Balance Sheet may be quite correct and at the same time frauds have been committed, and I would here point out that to a very considerable extent the detection of fraud depends on the method of book-keeping and the way the accounts have been kept. I do not suppose an auditor could compel the books being kept by double entry; yet the Revenue Account, Profit and Loss Account or Trading Account (whatever name you give it), if tested carefully item by item should bring most cases of fraud to light. Of course, the auditor should endeavour to

discover cases of misappropriation and should advise the keeping of the accounts with a view to their ready detection; yet, at the same time, I do not think he can be held responsible even if frauds do occur. No doubt the circumstances of every case will vary, but the directors and other chief servants of the shareholders are, I think, in as good if not in a better position to detect fraud than the auditor. Naturally my remarks do not apply to an auditor aware of, and conniving at, irregularities. Let us assume, then, that an auditor's chief duty, for the proper performance of which he ought to be held responsible, is to verify the facts stated in the Balance Sheet. He can verify such assets as book debts by seeing that they agree with the Ledger balances, and that the Ledger itself has been correctly posted up from the Day Book, Cash Book, etc. Similarly with accounts due by the company. This, I take it, is the meaning of the phrase "as shown in the books," or "as recorded in the books of "the company," appearing in most certificates. Whether the book debts are worth what they stand at in the Ledger or the reverse, is a different matter, upon which I consider the auditor is not called to give an opinion. Similarly, if the "accounts owing by the company" are understated because of entries having been omitted to be passed through the books, he cannot be held responsible. With regard to such assets as stock-in-trade, plant and machinery, he must of necessity, I think, be guided by lists and valuations made by others. He can only see that extensions and additions are correct, and that the totals are those appearing in the Balance Sheet.

With regard to the legal aspect of the question of an auditor's responsibility, the law as it stands at present cannot be said to be in a very satisfactory state. There appears to have been no Court of Session case in Scotland; and, although there have been several cases tried in England, yet as none have been carried to the House of Lords, the law cannot be considered as settled.

In a paper in the *Juridical Review* for 1896, on "The "Legal Position of Auditors of Joint Stock Companies," discussing the cases *In re London and General Bank* and *In re The Kingston Cotton Mill Company*, the writer, Mr. R. Scott Brown, states :—" The law, therefore, in so far as it has "been laid down, may be summarised thus :—

"1.—An auditor is only responsible for reasonable care and "skill.

"2.—This reasonable care does not imply that he should "be suspicious of fraud or that he need make elaborate tests "to discover it where he has no prescience of its existence.

"3.—A failure to make certain calculations from the "books in his hands which would have exposed the fraud "was not a want of reasonable care, as such a comparison "would be naturally suggested only by suspicion."

Continuing, Mr. Brown says :—" I cannot help thinking "that the standard of care and skill, in so far as such a "standard has been laid down at all, is too low a one." "If "the decision is maintained, there is a great danger that an "auditor need only plead that he had no suspicions, and,

" therefore, did not do more than check the items in the
" Balance Sheet with the vouchers, and he must be held to
" have fulfilled his duty."

I quite agree with what he says further on regarding
auditors:—" They must be men of skill, and in the perform-
" ance of their duties they must apply that skill with
" reasonable care. We can only hope, in the interest of all
" concerned, whether auditors themselves, directors, or
" shareholders, that the standard of that care and skill will
" be more explicitly expounded than it is at present. Such
" an exposition is urgently required in order that all con-
" nected with companies may know precisely an auditor's
" legal position."

It is difficult to say what can be done to mend matters.
The certificate of an auditor is, I think, to a great extent the
opinion of that auditor founded upon his examination of the
books and the documents relating thereto, as also upon his
knowledge of the nature and trade usages of the business
whose accounts he is auditing, and can never be considered
as an absolute guarantee of the correctness of the accounts.

At the same time I think that it would be an improvement
if the auditor's certificate were fuller than, as a general rule,
it is at present; if it stated, for instance, the work that had
been done, as is the case with banks' accounts, and also
stated what figures, if any, had been accepted as correct,
and on what authority. Shareholders might thereby, if they
desired, get a better idea of the value of the audit.

In conclusion, I think the whole question one that might
very well be taken up with a view to its solution by the
respective councils of the various bodies of public accountants.

———

The CHAIRMAN, opening the discussion which followed
Mr. Robertson's address, characterised the paper as a most
admirable one. He was sure that those who heard him would
agree that Mr. Robertson had done full justice to the matter.
He trusted they would now have a discussion useful to the
members present.

Mr. R. LUMSDEN (Edinburgh)—the first to respond to the
Chairman's invitation—said the paper which they had just
listened to opened up a very wide field of discussion. But
Mr. Robertson might have gone a little farther than he did,
as many would like to know where the duties of auditors
began, and where they ended. (Laughter.) That appeared
to him a matter which might well occupy a good deal of
the discussion. It seemed to him that there were so many old
businesses being turned into joint stock companies that
auditors should know whether they were the officials of the
shareholders or of the directors. As a matter of fact, an
auditor might be the official of the shareholders, but unless
he could carry the directors with him, he would not be
retained. Unless he was prepared to go hand in hand with
the directors, very often he found himself deprived of office.
The fees allotted to auditors were also worthy of discussion.
The public, too often, did not understand what they had to

do. For instance, undertaking the auditing of a mercantile
trading company, the duty of the auditor was to see that
the Profit and Loss Account was derived from legitimate,
and not illegitimate, trading in connection with the
business. He had in his mind a company, regarding which,
some time ago, many people were surprised at the profits,
which advanced in one year 100 per cent. A number of
people outside were sceptical, and he made a little investigation, and found that the company had gone outside its
legitimate business, and thus accounted for the extraordinary
profit. That brought them back to the fact that the auditor
simply dealt with seen things, and that was a matter which
might be made very elastic. As regarded the railway
companies, under the old Railway Act of 1868 it was not
intended that outside parties should be auditors, as they
were bound to be shareholders. But an Act was passed in
1869, or thereabout, by which outsiders could be auditors.
Another point raised by Mr. Robertson was the question of
the dockets that should be appended to audits. He had
struck the proper line when he remarked that the auditor
ought to state what he had done, so that the shareholders
could know whether his work embraced any point they
would like to have information on. Mr. Robertson referred
particularly to Banking Accounts. In this connection, all
that the auditor could be held to speak to was the fact that
the books contained the figures in the Balance Sheet. But
as to the fact of there being good or bad debts, that was
entirely beyond his jurisdiction. The auditor could do no
more than certify that the figures in the books and in the
Balance Sheet corresponded, leaving the directors and others
to be responsible for any breach of duty.

Mr. YULE (Glasgow) thought they might take it that
audits could be divided into two classes—the audits of
private firms, and the audits of corporations and limited
companies, which formed another class. He quite agreed
with Mr. Robertson's observations in regard to the strong
advisability of having a distinct arrangement with the
private firm as to the audit which was to take place ; because
unless some such arrangement was made, a very great
responsibility rested upon the auditor. He quite agreed
that the arrangement should be put in writing, so as to be
distinct. They had an excellent example in what took
place in London the other day. An eminent firm of accountants—originally hailing from Glasgow—had for many years
audited the books of a firm of solicitors without a written
arrangement. The result was that about a year ago the
firm of solicitors found that one of their cashiers had been
defaulting, and about £1,700 or £1,800 was missing. The
firm of solicitors raised an action against the auditors, on
the ground that they had failed to be accurate and careful
in their duties. They said that they had been accurate and
careful in their duties, but it was found, when the case
came before the Court of the Queen's Bench, that one of the
partners in the firm of accountants, who had died, had
arranged to do a certain check, and the other partner,
mistaking that, only did a smaller portion. He frankly admitted in Court that if he had done his full share of the
work he would have detected the defalcations. Damages for

about £2,000 were given, as a result of this want of accurate arrangement. They should all, therefore, take into account what Mr. Robertson had put before them. It should be a principle that there should be a letter between parties, as the most advisable way in which to define the work that was to be done. (Applause.) The next point he might draw attention to was the auditing of public companies. He was of a very strong opinion—and he thought most of the others were as well—that there should be an amendment to the Companies Acts whereby it would be distinctly understood and made clear that the auditor was the servant of the shareholders, and ought to be appointed by the shareholders, and that he should have nothing to do with the directors, but be responsible to the shareholders alone, and, further, that he could not be dismissed by the directors. They would thus have a much more efficient audit than at the present moment. It would be perfectly plain that even the most conscientious auditor, whose appointment lay in the hands of the directors, might allow certain things to take place which otherwise would not take place. Then, in the auditing of a great many public companies, such as fire insurance and accident companies who had unexpired risks, it should be made clear for the benefit of the shareholders that a certain proportion in the Balance Sheet should be deducted for unexpired risks, otherwise the Balance Sheet did not represent the true state of the companies' affairs. For instance, take a company doing an extensive accident business; they might receive five or six thousand pounds premiums in the last quarter, and if they did not, make provision for the unexpired risk by holding over, the accounts undoubtedly would not show what they ought to do. No doubt a great many companies, counting their profits, allowed 33⅓ per cent. for unexpired risk, and carried that forward. If companies did not make an allowance, then their accounts did not represent the true state of affairs. In the interests of the shareholders and the auditors, there should be some arrangement made whereby the auditors could call the attention of the shareholders to the unexpired risk. If such an arrangement existed he was perfectly satisfied that it would save much money, as precautions would be taken to stop undue trading before a company found it necessary to stop for want of funds. These were matters to which all accountants might draw attention. (Applause.)

Mr. W. A. BINE (Perth) understood Mr. Robertson to say that the limit of responsibility should be defined by a letter from the auditor's client. He did not think the audit could be covered by that. If they took the responsibility of auditing the books, the books should be thoroughly examined and certified as correct, the auditor taking full responsibility. If they took less responsibility on themselves, let them take the work on as an investigation; but let them not call it an audit. If the fee was insufficient to pay them, it was their duty not to accept it. (Applause.) He noticed it frequently mentioned in *The Accountant* that the bulk of accountants in England and Wales were refusing to take audits without being properly remunerated for them. If a client distinctly says he will not give a certain amount,

then let the auditor decline to certify the books as an auditor. (Applause.) The last speaker mentioned something about unexpired risk in accident and insurance companies. He would like to say they had a Reserve Fund provided by accident companies to cover all unexpired risk. It was also stated, he thought, that the auditor was an official appointed by the directors. This was an incorrect idea, as, by the Companies Acts, they were appointed by the shareholders, although it might be that the directors had a great deal to say in the appointment of an auditor. He had great sympathy with the proposed amendment whereby directors could not dismiss the auditor unless for any wilful negligence.

Provost WATSON (Falkirk) said the last speaker had spoken very wisely on the responsibility of auditors. There was no doubt, further, that auditors in public companies were really appointed by the shareholders, although at the shareholders' general meeting there was invariably a sufficient holding among the directors to control the whole matter. As to the responsibility arising from defalcation which had been referred to by Mr. Robertson, the company with which he happened to be most intimately connected had a case similar to that already related, in which no blame whatever attached to the auditor. There was no blame attached to him, although there was a defalcation of £2,300 carried off by one of the directors. It was in this way. The company dealt in one instance with one firm to a very large extent, and in ordinary trade would have been owing continuously £2,500. It turned out that when the auditor went over the accounts and books the firm's debit stood in Ledger to that extent. No suspicion was aroused, and the auditor knew nothing whatever of it. Had the auditor sent out notices to all the debtors of the company—the way by which he could have discovered the defalcation—he might have raised suspicions that would have ruined the company. To take such a step as that would be extremely injudicious. If some means could be devised whereby all auditors would have something to keep them in check then it would be an immense advantage to the public.

Mr. LUMSDEN (Edinburgh) held that the only way to avoid such a state as that described was to insist that directors should not interfere with the accounts going out.

Mr. D. D. BUCHAN, S.S.C. (Edinburgh), asked to be allowed to mention one or two points from the legal point of view. (Applause.) He thought that what had fallen from the various speakers went to show that the question of the independence of the auditor—that was to say, his appointment by the shareholders—was really the crucial point. (Hear, hear.) It had been pointed out already that although many shareholders imagined they appointed the auditor—(laughter)—he was the nominee of the directors and under the control of the directors. (Hear, hear.) He did not think any reform would be possible unless there were further statutory powers given. He had a case recently where he was asked to advise an auditor. He was auditing the books of a company, partly manufacturing and partly buying in. It had business through a great many branches. It occurred to the auditor that the valuation of the stock was not sound. If it was sound, it showed an enormous profit. What was he to do? The managing director of the company considered himself *facile princeps*, and would not brook the idea of the valuation being doubted. The auditor required a good deal of courage to oppose the directors. However, by force of character, he succeeded in getting a valuation, with the result that the fabulous profits disappeared. It turned out that the company was perfectly sound, and winning reasonable profits, but nothing like the profits on Balance Sheet. In doing what he did, the auditor had to run the risk of being turned out. It came to be a question at one stage whether he was to go or the managing director was to go. (Laughter.) One could see quite well that, in a situation such as this, it was very difficult for the auditor to have the free hand wh'ch, in the interests of the shareholders, he ought to have. (Applause.) Perhaps this might be amended if the law appointed that no auditor, when once appointed, should be removed unless cause were shown. It was very probable that, before there was further legislation on this matter, there would be a Government Department to control joint stock companies, in regard to their Balance Sheets, in much the same way as friendly societies were controlled at present. Mr. Robertson rightly contended that the duty of an auditor did not extend to the business of the company. It was only necessary that he should see that the administration of the business was kept within the statutory powers. This was a duty which the auditor did not always keep in mind. He had known cases where the shareholders suffered far more from a failure to look at the legal question of statutory powers, than from defalcations of the officials of the company. He might refer to the issue of debentures, and of preference stock in many cases. An auditor, doing his duty by the shareholders, had to see that, so far as possible, according to the existing interpretation of the law, all the arrangements connected with the issue of stock were strictly legal. Something had been said about gentlemen not taking the responsibility of auditing because the fees were not adequate. In talking with a member of an English firm, which had a very large number of public companies' audits, a complaint was made, not with regard to the fees, but with regard to the time within which audits had to be completed. It seemed to be a regular practice in London to bring Balance Sheets to the auditor within a day or two of the time when notices must be issued for the annual meeting, and it was quite impossible for the auditor to make a proper audit. Under the circumstances he could only check what was given him. Even in Scotland auditors were very much pressed for time.

Mr. GEORGE WILSON (Aberdeen) remarked that in most cases the appointment of an auditor was a mere farce, so far as the shareholders had a voice in the matter. This, he thought, pointed, for one thing, to an alteration in the law as to proxies. Of course, this was a very difficult question, because the interests of the absent shareholders had to be safeguarded. On the other hand, the interests of the shareholders who took the trouble of being present at the meetings were not sufficiently safeguarded. There ought to be some limitation in the use of proxies by directors. Then the real voices of the shareholders who took the trouble to attend the meetings would be heard, and the result would be that many abuses in the keeping of accounts and the publication of false Balance Sheets would be ended. As proxies stood at present, they were mostly couched in general terms, but if there was a statutory enactment that they could only be used for a particular business before a particular meeting, that would do away with the abuse. Under the present system, the independence of the auditor was a mere farce. Of course, Mr. Robertson had properly defined what ought to be the relations between the auditor and the private employer. But, in regard to public companies, he was of opinion that the auditor's responsibilities did not end with the shareholders. He considered he had a responsibility towards the public. The auditor should consider himself a servant, not only of the shareholders, but of the public, and as an independent official. His audit should not merely be an audit, but also, as suggested, an investigation. (Applause.)

The CHAIRMAN, summing up the discussion, said that sometimes many difficult questions cropped up in the Balance Sheet. For instance, there might be a consignation made for a large amount of goods to some foreign country, or to one of the colonies. Of course, when sent out it was put down in the books at a certain sum. But perhaps it had not gone off, or it had not been sold, and it came up again in the second year. He himself had had differences of opinions with directors as to whether these consignations should be continued at the same value. One was rather inclined to think that, if a large amount of goods was sent to another country, and remained unsold, there was a risk of depreciation, and that when the auditor came to such an item for the second time it could not be of the same value. In such a case as that he had procured a minute from the directors, in which they themselves undertook to make the valuation, and to say that the auditor was to accept that sum as the amount they thought they would ultimately get. In a case he recalled, the goods when new were put down at £3,000 or £4,000, but the amount ultimately realised was only £700. However, as the auditor had got a minute from the directors he was safe. It would be well, if there was any doubt in the mind of the auditor, to get the directors as a buffer between him and the shareholders, in case the shareholders might afterwards reflect that the values were being continued at too high a figure. In regard to a Government Department having the control of audits, he was opposed to grandmotherly legislation. (Laughter.) It was very much against the accountants that the Government should step in and say, "I'll do the accountant business of the whole country." It did not give fair play to the individual accountant. They should resist the system of having a department in Edinburgh to swallow up the whole accountant business of the country.

Mr. BUCHAN repudiated any intention of conveying in the slightest a suggestion such as that now made. His reference to friendly societies, he said, would show that he did not profess to interfere with the official audits of individual companies. He suggested only that over and above this there might be a Government Department to take some cognisance of progress in regard to joint stock companies, just as they took cognisance of the progress of friendly societies and others. He did not propose to interfere with the individual audit of any joint stock company.

Mr. LUMSDEN (Edinburgh) said they would like if some parish auditors gave them their views. But no one responding,

The CHAIRMAN proposed a vote of thanks to Mr. Robertson for his paper. He thought Mr. Robertson balanced very fairly the responsibilities and duties of auditors. He dared say they all had often thought their emoluments not too high, and would be glad if they received any increase. In dealing with directors they must exercise prudence. While shareholders had the nominal appointment of the auditor, the real appointment lay with the directors. If they could get a minute, as he suggested, from directors, the latter taking responsibility, to some extent one of the difficulties they encountered would be solved. They must, however, as prudent men, take things as they found them at present, and he had no doubt that most of them did so.

Mr. JAMES DRUMMOND (Glasgow), seconding, said the paper to which they had listened had been both interesting and instructive. There were a good many things which could be said on the different points did time permit. In the matter of auditors' duties he thought there were certain responsibilities devolving on the directors, as well as the auditors. There should be a kind of dual responsibility on the part of directors and auditor in the matter, for example, of the assets of the company. Regarding such things as machinery and plant, it was impossible for the auditor alone to know whether they were properly stated. In fixing the auditor's responsibility, the amount of remuneration offered him should be kept in view. Too much was expected of the auditor for the very small fee offered. In regard to the general duty of an auditor, he did not think it was that of a detective or a policeman. Where an auditor exercised due and reasonable care in the performance of his duty, that was the most that could be expected from him. How could an auditor certify, for instance, as to the correctness of a Bank Account where there were thousands of accounts and many securities which he had no means of verifying for himself? There were the matters of waste assets, depreciation, and reserve funds. All these devolved from the general duty of the auditor.

The vote of thanks was heartily awarded.

Mr. ROBERTSON briefly thanked the members for the reception they had given his remarks.

Thereafter the first day's proceedings were brought to a close, and the company were photographed, grouped in front of the municipal buildings. The remaining part of the day was spent in visiting various places of interest in the vicinity of the town.

# The Duties of Auditors.

(From *The Economist.*)

Complaints are frequently made that auditors are too much under the control of directors, and thus fail to afford shareholders a sufficient amount of protection: but the weaker members of the auditing profession are not likely to be encouraged in an independent policy by the experience of Messrs. Carnaby Harrower, Barham & Co., at the recent meeting of the Britannia Motor Carriage Company. In that case the auditors found themselves in a position to give only a qualified certificate, pointing out in a report to the board that while the Balance Sheet was a correct abstract of the accounts as they appeared in the books of the company, its accuracy as disclosing the true position of the company was, in their opinion, subject to the clearing up of various matters as to the sale of patents and the absence of several vouchers and documents. At the meeting to which the accounts were presented, the chairman seems to have talked a good deal of nonsense about the erroneous view of their functions and duties taken by the auditors, and about accountants not being required to act as detectives; but he admitted that several of the receipts were missing, owing to their having been wilfully abstracted from the office, "possibly for the purpose of injuring "the company." There was a considerable excess of expenditure over income, and it is quite clear that the auditors could not properly have given a less qualified certificate under the circumstances, even to please the directors; and one would have thought that the frank explanations given by Messrs. Carnaby Harrower & Co. would have been welcomed by the shareholders in a company which has, so far, proved no exception to the unsatisfactory record of the motor companies. So far from displaying any gratitude, however, they refused to adjourn the meeting until the accounts could be fully investigated, and when the motion for the re-appointment of the auditors was brought forward, Messrs. Carnaby Harrower & Co. were "shunted" in favour of a fresh firm of accountants.

(From *Money.*)

We have commented often enough in *Money* on the laxity with which auditors of public companies too frequently do their work, and the need for reform in the law as affecting the responsibilities of the public company accountant. The reasons for the lax and perfunctory manner in which auditors walk through their part are not far to seek. In the case of an industrial concern in nine cases out of ten the auditor has been asked prior to the formation of the company to inspect the books of the business, and to give a certificate of profits for use in the prospectus. In this manner the future auditor of the company serves an apprenticeship as the servant of the promoter, and the man who is, in the legal fiction of the Companies Acts, supposed to stand between the directors and the shareholders to see fair play, is in the very nature of things on intimate terms with the directors, while in most cases absolutely unknown to his real masters—the shareholders of the company. Thus it happens that, unless there is something par-

ticularly flagrant, an auditor rarely goes out of his way to fall foul of the directors, and if he belongs to the time-serving party, as a great many auditors do, his chief endeavour is to smooth things over and pave the way for his re-election. For, although the appointment of the auditor is supposed to be the function of the shareholders, it is not a difficult matter for directors to get rid of a too inquiring auditor, or, if they cannot achieve that, to reduce his remuneration down to an amount which cannot possibly be a fair set-off for services rendered.

Additional force is lent to these contentions by what has recently taken place in connection with the Britannia Motor Company, Lim., where Messrs. Carnaby Harrower, Barham & Co., the auditors, have been indulging in some very plain speaking. The company was formed in March 1896, but no business appears to have been done until the spring of the present year. From the beginning the auditor states that the books have been in a very disorganised and muddled condition, and that, prior to commencing their audit, they had to write up the books for a period of quite six months. At the very outset of their duties they were met with the fact that a number of vouchers and other documents were not forthcoming—and, indeed, as long since as February 1897, when Messrs. Carnaby Harrower, Barham & Co. also appear to have been engaged in writing up the books, they state they called the attention of the directors to the fact that vouchers were missing. At the meeting held this week, when the accounts were submitted to the shareholders, matters were fought out, and the auditors only did their obvious duty in calling the attention of the shareholders to many curious circumstances which had come under their notice. The first thing to which they directed attention was the manner in which the sale of the patent and the obtaining of a licence to work had been carried through, dates having been omitted from the minutes; and it was also pointed out that in the letters on which the arrangement rested reference was only made to Great Britain and the Colonies, distressful Ireland being left out altogether—which, if not another injustice to Ireland, would be a singular injustice to the company. Then, later on, when an attempt was made to put matters right in a formal agreement, they would have none of it, and the matter had to rest on mere letters. This was a matter which the auditors considered ought to be made known to the shareholders —presumably as affecting the value of the company's assets. Another important matter was with regard to the payment of a commission for introducing the purchaser of the patent. The auditors contend that, inasmuch as the purchaser was known to the Britannia board, there was no need whatever for the payment of a commission of over £2,000. The auditor also pointed out that although a Mr. Davis was supposed to receive the commission a cash payment of £600 in that connection was made by bearer cheque, and it was therefore impossible to trace to whom the commission had been paid. Complaint was also made that no account was kept of petty cash, amounts being estimated, and written up in the Cash Book after a period of eighteen months had elapsed. Documents and vouchers vital to the audit were said to be missing altogether, and there were no particulars in the books as to the cost of materials and wages on which the item of stock could be valued. The auditors were compelled with regard to an important item of that sort to accept the mere estimate of the officials of the company, and this with a new business where the valuation of stocks is a particularly difficult matter. There were other things to which the auditors drew the attention of the shareholders; loans to an official of the company, who is said to be indebted to the company for calls to an amount of £500, while in the case of other shares allotted it is alleged that no application money has even been paid. Share certificates were also alleged to be missing. Altogether, the Britannia Motor Company, judged by the light thrown on its affairs by the auditors, appears to afford an object lesson in company mismanagement.

Now, one would naturally imagine that the shareholders would have been grateful to auditors who had called their attention to such grave irregularities. The auditors themselves contend that they have merely done their duty, and although the chairman of the company asserts that Messrs. Carnaby Harrower & Co. have been hypercritical, we prefer to accept the auditors' own definition of the revelations as a mere discharge of duty. That auditors should take this very definite view of their duties to shareholders is in itself rare enough to demand attention, but the sequel to their action certainly calls for general notice. Here are auditors who with a calm disregard of time and trouble ferret out a number of details with which it is desirable that the shareholders should be acquainted, and then the latter, instead of rallying to support their own interests, actually allow another firm to be appointed auditors, and send accountants who have done them good service to the right about. It is true that an amendment was moved that the accounts be not adopted, which was only defeated by a small majority, and it is equally true that the resolution appointing other auditors was seconded by an official of the company and also carried by only a narrow majority. This, however, does not affect the point on which we wish to insist— that it is useless to expect gratitude from shareholders. Facts like those brought forward by the auditors to the Britannia Motor Company appear to fall on deaf ears. If auditors, after this revelation of the temper of shareholders, are inclined to take a less serious view of their responsibilities, they are not to be blamed.

## What is an Auditor?

### His Duties to Shareholders.

#### THE TALK ABOUT REFORMS.

(From the *Bullionist*.)

THE position of the auditors in a joint stock company, and a definition of their duties and obligations, would appear to be a very simple question, and yet there is nothing more unsatisfactory or more undefined in the world of finance to-day than the exact status of the auditor. Ever since the passing of the Joint Stock Companies Act 1867, this has been a vexed subject. Constant undetected frauds, successfully carried on in many cases for years in spite of periodical professional audits, have not tended to inspire the absolute confidence in accountants which their status as a profession should demand. And recent disclosures have added fuel to an already fierce fire until there is a large section of the investing public who place no reliance whatever upon the auditor's certificate at the foot of a Balance Sheet, and look upon the fees paid to that official as so much money wasted.

I have made some careful investigations into this matter, and in a series of articles propose to thresh the subject out thoroughly from the shareholders' point of view, at the same time doing ample justice to the accountancy profession, whose general doings as regards the working of joint stock companies it will be necessary for us to examine closely, and criticise impartially but fearlessly.

What is an auditor?

Some people regard him as a nominee of the promoter, bound body and soul to look after the interests of that individual regardless of everyone else. We have had lots of auditors of this class, and know a few now. Others say he is the nominee and servant of the directors, and his certificate must be drawn to meet their views; while others maintain that he is a general watch dog, but so muzzled by a "long" board that his bark is never heard, and he never gets a chance to even snarl at a managing director or a general manager. He is regarded by another section of the public as a financial detective in plain clothes, employed to spy and report to the board; or a financial policeman, with a regular "beat," whose uniform is a moral force and preventative of fraud.

I venture to assert that a properly-qualified auditor answers to none of these descriptions, although he should possess, perhaps, many of the attributes referred to. The auditor should be the servant of the shareholders, responsible directly to them and to no one else.

There need be no clash between an honest directorate and an independent and impartial auditor. The functions of the latter should be to investigate the books, accounts and records of the company, and satisfy himself that the Balance Sheet the directors propose to lay before their shareholders is a full, fair and straightforward statement of the affairs of the company to date, without equivocation or reservation, and the certificate should be in a plain, simple form, pinning the auditor to the personal responsibility of the words over his signature, and not, as is now frequently the case, a certificate insulting to the common sense of the merest tyro in finance, meaning—and intentionally meaning

—nothing. I know that many of the larger firms of Chartered Accountants will say these strictures cannot apply to them—they are above any influence; to which may be replied that there are "more ways of killing a dog than hanging him," and there are more refined and artistic methods of assisting an auditor to obscure his vision than brutally requesting him to describe a spade as an implement of agriculture.

There have been many theories advocated during the past few months in the columns of the daily Press for the improvement of what is generally admitted to be a very serious state of affairs. Shareholders, directors, accountants and Board of Trade officials have all had their say, the latter particularly being conspicuous by their theoretical verbosity and absolute impracticability. The disease should be traced to its source, and a drastic remedy applied: one which settles once and for all the position of auditors, their responsibilities and remuneration, and renders impossible some of the most glaring defects of the present Companies Acts. These proposals, or part of them, will form the subject of my next contribution upon this subject.

AJAX.

# The Accountant

## THE ORGAN OF CHARTERED ACCOUNTANTS THROUGHOUT THE WORLD.

### (Awarded Silver Medal, Esposizione Italo-Americana, Genova 1892.)

Vol. XXV.—New Series.—No. 1284.             Saturday, July 15, 1899.

## Leading Articles.

### What is an Auditor?

IN our last issue we reproduced from the columns of the *Bullionist* the first of a series of contributed articles which our contemporary had announced upon the above subject, and the second of the series will be found in another column of this week's issue.

The first instalment dealt with the subject in general terms; and, so far as one was then in a position to judge, there appeared to be a likelihood that the series—if somewhat original—would be by no means unprofitable, while it was clear that they would at least possess the advantage, so far as our readers are concerned, of being written neither from the point of view of the profession, the Board of Trade, nor of disappointed shareholders. Whether the second instalment, which we reproduce this week, may be fairly regarded as carrying out the promise suggested by the first is, perhaps, an open question; and, indeed, we think it not impossible that some of our readers may wonder whether we could not utilise our space better than by reproducing it. From one point of view we have no doubt that we could; but it is well to bear in mind that for us to discontinue the series at the precise moment when the writer's views happened to be somewhat unpalatable, would undeniably be open to misconstruction, and as the article bristles with inaccuracies and misstatements which, if directed against a private individual, would undoubtedly require substantiating before a Court of Law, the better plan we thought would be to spend a little space in refuting the misstatements and erroneous conclusions.

The second article, it will be noted, is in itself contradictory, inasmuch as it states that there is no case on record of any member of the Institute being "disciplined" by the Council; while, further on, it expresses the view that were an Associate "struggling "to make a business, and taking a nominal "fee to obtain a connection," to do anything to which exception might be taken, "the "thunder of the Society might possibly be "broken over his head, and he would have "been made an example of." If the first statement were really one of fact, we are not aware of any justification for the second, which, in that event, would appear to attribute to the Council (without any suggestion as to why) a desire to inaugurate an entirely new policy so soon as what they thought to be a suitable opportunity arose. As a matter of fact, however, it is unnecessary for us to consider the latter contingency, because the first statement is wholly inaccurate.

It is unnecessary for us to quote chapter and verse for what we are about to say, because it is perfectly capable of independent verification. Without involving the necessity of raking up matters which, being now finished, might just as well be forgotten, the fact remains that the number of persons who have ceased to be members of the Institute —apart from those who have been struck off for non-payment of their fees—is sufficient to show that the disciplinary powers of the Council have been frequently exercised in the past on great and small, irrespective of their influence on the Council, and that without necessarily waiting for a public scandal to draw attention to the matter and create pressure from outside.

If we thought it worth while we might raise the question as to whether, in point of fact, it *was* easier to enforce a claim for negligence against a solicitor than an accountant; but as this is entirely a side-issue, and has, we think, been already sufficiently fully dealt with in these columns in the past, we prefer to leave it, and only to refer to this portion of the article appearing in our contemporary for the purpose of pointing out that, in point of fact, the Incorporated Law Society never takes action against its members while there is an action pending against them in the Courts of Justice. This is, of course, a very proper attitude to assume —and, indeed, the only attitude that could be assumed in fairness to the solicitor; and here the analogy between solicitors and accountants is sufficiently close to make a comparison profitable, and to point out that while an action is pending against an accountant for negligence, it would be entirely inconsistent with all English ideas of justice, for the governing body of an association of which that accountant was a member, to prejudge his case by pronouncing sentence upon him while the case is still pending. That being so, it appears to us to be unnecessary to comment further upon the "recent well-known" case referred to by our contemporary; nor is it necessary to ask who defended the accountant on the score of the smallness of his fee.

Before dismissing the subject, however, we may perhaps be allowed to state that it would have been impossible for so many misstatements to have appeared—presumably in all seriousness—in a public print, if the Council were to adopt the practice which we have so frequently suggested that they should, of publishing in a more prominent manner the names of members who are expelled, and, if possible, the reason why.

Another misstatement which, it seems to us, can only have arisen by a complete ignorance of the facts upon the part of the writer, is the one that the Society of Accountants and Auditors "has sprung into existence" in consequence of the initials "F.C.A." and "A.C.A." not being "accounted as valuable as they used "to be." The statement has been made not merely by ourselves and others, who might perhaps be regarded as interested parties, but also by such wholly independent persons as many of the leading occupants of the Bench, and others, that the position of the Institute has grown from year to year ever since its incorporation; and not merely those who are entirely familiar with commercial matters, but also even the outside public, are now becoming familiar with the status and position of Chartered Accountants. That being so, the formation of the Society of Accountants and Auditors must clearly be attributed to another cause. We have our own views as to what that cause was, and these also are not unknown to our readers; but, inasmuch as they have nothing whatever to do with the subject at issue, it is best not to complicate the discussion by a reference to them in the present article.

The next statement that the Institute of Chartered Accountants has done "absolutely "nothing to meet the unmistakeable demands "of the investing public" (presumably this has reference to Company matters) is equally unhappy and untrue, and we have only to point to the utterances of witnesses examined by the Select Committee of the House of Lords on the proposed Company Law Reform, and to the mass of papers and the number of addresses that have been read and given elsewhere to completely refute this charge.

Our contemporary's comments upon the utter futility of anticipating any good results from an official audit are to the point, and, for that reason, afford a somewhat startling contrast to the lack of information which appears to characterise—and to have given rise to—the first portion of the article under review.

The contents of the concluding paragraph, relating to the evils that occasionally result from directors of companies going to allotment upon insufficient capital, are also truisms. For our own part we are somewhat at a loss to see what they have to do with the subject under discussion; but, as we are assured that we shall be in a position to see the connection when the next article appears, we must perforce restrain our curiosity until then. The "to be continued

" in our next " style of literature strikes us, however, as being somewhat unsuitable, save when the matter under consideration is *admittedly* fiction.

## What is an Auditor?

### II.

(From *The Bullionist.*)

THE profession of accountancy is represented by the Institute of Chartered Accountants, an institution in many respects similar to the Incorporated Law Society. The " Institute " is eminently respectable, and, like many other societies, principally devotes its attention to the collection of heavy dues from its members. It has always been noted for its " cliques," and during the early years of its existence was a mutual admiration society of limited numbers. So far as the public are concerned it has never been of much use, as, I believe, there is no case on record of any member of the Institute being " disciplined " by the Council.

If a solicitor, for an utterly inadequate fee, agrees to examine an abstract of title, does so negligently, and in consequence of his act causes his client to lose a large sum of money, pleading insufficient remuneration as an excuse, that solicitor, apart from any personal liability, will probably have the Incorporated Law

311

Society to deal with for unprofessional conduct. Not so with the Chartered Accountant. A recent well-known case within the public recollection of an auditor who had been "hoodwinked" for years by a managing director was attempted to be excused on the ground that the fee paid to the auditor was only £26 5s. per annum! Is this any excuse? and what does the Council of an Institute with a very high-toned Charter and most exemplary bye-laws think of one of its members, enjoying a large practice and altogether a "leading light," who, for a most important audit, accepts a ridiculous fee, and avoids responsibility when a gigantic fraud is discovered by a speciously-worded certificate? Did the Council "discipline" this member or take any steps to place themselves right with the public? So far as I am aware, the answer must be "No." There are too many "pots" and "kettles" in the Council, and the "disciplined" one, if he be a big man, might make things warm for his tormentors. If the incident had involved a "small" man, say an Associate struggling to make a business and taking a nominal fee to obtain a connection, then all the thunder of the Society might possibly have broken over his head, and he would have been made an example of. Is it any wonder that F.C.A. and A.C.A. are not accounted as valuable as they used to be, and that another society of incor- porated accountants (about which I must confess I know very little) has sprung into existence?

I know these opinions are not only very generally held "out- "side," but that many Chartered Accountants are dissatisfied with their present situation, and would gladly hail any suggestion of reform. And any reform should emanate from the Institute of Chartered Accountants. It should come from within and not from without; but although presumably in possession of the best means of information, with ample resources and perfectly-equipped machinery at command, they have done and are doing absolutely nothing to meet the unmistakable demands of the investing public, and so benefit themselves and justify their existence as a corporate body.

Without doubt there are auditors who in too many cases are badly paid; indeed, not properly remunerated at all. The remedy, I maintain, does not lie entirely with themselves, when the fierce competition for business is remembered. It rests more with shareholders seeing their trusted auditors are sufficiently paid; but this question, and others that grow out of it, I must reserve for future discussion. The suggestion of a Government audit has been frequently mooted, and there is no doubt a pro- posal of this nature would find no small measure of public support. But experience teaches that "officialism" with regard to mercantile matters is most unsatisfactory.

There is no reason why the Government should "wet-nurse" creditors and shareholders more than any other class of the com- munity, and its present efforts in that direction by the medium of the Board of Trade are generally admitted to be a lamentable failure. As a "Government audit" would probably mean, there- fore, the employment of a further legion of juvenile Board of Trade officials, it is not likely to be seriously contemplated. I think, with very slight legislation, present organisations may be utilised and a satisfactory elucidation arrived at as regards the most pressing abuses under the Companies Acts.

One of the greatest scandals urgently calling for immediate attention is the common one of directors proceeding to allotment upon utterly insufficient capital. It is doubtful whether in any respect the Companies Acts have been so successfully used as a means of fraud as in this direction. Cases innumerable might be cited, for the ingenuity of the greatest rogues in the City has been exercised upon this point for years past. I suggest directors be prevented from going to allotment unless not less than three-fourths of the capital issued for subscription is *bona fide* applied for, and then only on condition that the purchase price of any property to be acquired by the company is *pro rata* diminished. If the directors are of opinion, in cases where less than three-fourths of the capital is applied for, that, by arrangements with vendors or otherwise, they may properly commence business, they should be obliged to convene a meeting of the subscribers, setting out full details in their notice of meeting, and let the subscribers decide.

But in connection with this rather summary proposal I have a new duty to suggest for the auditors, the details of which I will give in my next letter.

AJAX.

## What is an Auditor?

### III.

#### (From *The Bullionist.*)

IN previous letters I have dealt with the question of a Government audit and the necessity of preventing directors proceeding to allotment upon insufficient capital. I have indicated why audit by the distinguished nonentities of the Board of Trade is undesirable, and yet an official audit by some person or persons directly responsible to a Government department is sure to be highly acceptable to the general investing public. The two societies representing the profession of public accountants could, by combination, materially improve both the status and business of their members, and, at the same time, do good public service by adopting the suggestions I make.

At present the auditors are generally appointed by the promoters, occasionally by the directors, and rarely by the shareholders; but their functions, as a rule, do not commence until the first Balance Sheet is presented to the members of the company a year after incorporation.

Under existing Acts of Parliament the statutory meeting held four months after the incorporation of the company is more or less a legal farce. There are no statements of account before the meeting, and the directors usually either favour the shareholders with some fluent platitudes about the prospects of the company—hiding any personal responsibility for their statements behind generalities—or, as is more frequent, plead they have only just assumed the reins of government, and it is inexpedient, in the interests of the members of the company, to go into any details about the business. The co-partners in the undertaking, in six cases out of ten, receive *bona fide* information, and are treated fairly by their official representatives on the directorate; but in the other four instances it is a case of "confidence game" from the beginning, and the operation of the law, as it stands at present is all in favour of the dishonest promoter and director.

The statutory meeting, as defined by the Act, is a very weak-kneed affair; time and experience have made it practically lifeless. The reverse should be the case. In starting any business the primary matter of importance is the capital, and the shareholders at the statutory meeting should be in possession of a statement showing the exact position of the Capital Accounts, and that statement should be prepared and submitted, not by the board, but by an auditor or auditors appointed for that specific purpose in manner hereafter indicated. The present powers and duties of directors would not be changed, except as hereafter mentioned. Shareholders would simply have an independent assurance that the capital they subscribed to was fully issued, or, if a lesser amount, they were consulted before allotment.

It is a Utopian idea, but some day we may have attached to the Chancery Division of the High Court of Justice a Commercial Court for all cases in which companies incorporated under the Companies Acts are either plaintiffs or defendants, presided over by a Judge, say, of Mr. Justice Bigham's experience—a good all-round lawyer and a shrewd, common-sense man of business—assisted by a staff of chief clerks not necessarily all selected from the legal profession, but well-seasoned City men, accustomed to the work they would have to perform. The Judge of such Court might be assisted in certain cases by commercial assessors appointed by Chambers of Commerce, under conditions somewhat similar to Trinity Masters and the Court of Admiralty. If such a Court existed I would propose that all accountants who desired to be appointed public auditors should be required to register their names in such Court, and that they should be members of either one or the other Chartered or Incorporated Societies.

But at present there is no such Court, so I suggest the accountants file their names with the Registrar of Joint Stock Companies at Somerset House. Upon the registration of a new company it should be the duty of that official, having such names upon an alphabetical list, to appoint, in strict priority, the accountant whose name came next upon such list as public auditor until the statutory meeting, solely for the purpose of certifying to the Registrar of Joint Stock Companies and the shareholders the position of the Capital Account. Such auditor should be eligible for election as auditor for the year next ensuing, but debarred from canvassing or touting for the position, under penalty of forfeiting his fees and losing his position as a candidate for the appointment of a public auditor. Fees payable to such auditors would be paid to the Registrar at the time of registration, and should be upon a liberal basis or a graduated scale. The auditor would be entitled to draw his fees from the Registrar upon filing his certified accounts, with full details of the Capital Accounts of the company, within seven days of the statutory meeting. The Registrar would be entitled to deduct a small percentage from such fees for the extra expenses thrown upon his department.

The public auditor would be entitled to access to all the papers and records of the company at any time, and it would be his duty to see the books relating to the share capital were well and properly kept, as prescribed by the Act of Parliament, and to promptly after issue of the prospectus ascertain the amount of subscriptions, and in event of the capital being fully subscribed, so certify to the directors. Until they were in possession of the written certificate of the auditor the directors should have no power to proceed to allotment. In cases where the subscriptions amounted to three-fourths of the sum offered, the auditors would be bound to give a certificate so stating, and authorising the directors to proceed to allotment only upon condition that the purchase price to be paid for properties to be acquired by the company be *pro rata* reduced, but that the sum reserved as working capital in the prospectus be not diminished, the difference being provided by the vendors or promoters. Failing these conditions, the auditor would refuse his certificate, and the directors would be obliged to convene a meeting of the subscribers, as referred to in my last letter.

I have in bare outline indicated how by simple means the crying scandals that now exist of companies being registered with a capital of a million and going to allotment upon a subscription of £20,000, or even less, may be summarily stopped, and how, once and for all, the investor may know by independent means whether or not the capital for which he has partly subscribed is really fully subscribed or not; and, further, how he can be sure of finding at the statutory meeting a clear account with full details of the capital of the co-partnership of which he is a member, so that he starts fair, with information "up to date." Whether further details should be forthcoming at the statutory meeting is another question that may be discussed hereafter.

AJAX.

# The Accountant

## THE ORGAN OF CHARTERED ACCOUNTANTS THROUGHOUT THE WORLD.

### (Awarded Silver Medal, Esposizione Italo-Americana, Genova 1892.)

VOL. XXV.—NEW SERIES.—NO. 1287.　　　　　　　　SATURDAY, AUGUST 5, 1899.

### What is an Auditor?

### II.

THE third contribution of the correspondent signing himself "AJAX," to our contemporary *The Bullionist*, was reproduced in our issue of the 22nd ult., and will doubtless, in the opinion of our readers, be thought chiefly remarkable for its extreme inconsistency, as compared with his second effusion. It will be remembered that, in his second article, "AJAX" dealt with the constitution of the Institute of Chartered Accountants and of the Society of Accountants and Auditors, and the policy of their respective governing bodies; and, if his statements are to be summed up in a few words, we think it may fairly be stated that he thought that little—if anything—was too bad to be said with regard to either of them. As we pointed out in our previous article, his views upon this point were (to put it mildly) not justified by the misstatements of facts which he put forward, and it is, of course, conceivable that we may have succeeded in convincing him as to the entirely erroneous character of his previous conclusions. If so, it would, perhaps, be unfair for us to charge the writer in question with inconsistency; but under any other circumstances—and in view of the fact that the article which we reproduced in our issue of the 22nd ult. was doubtless penned before our own comments upon the previous articles were published, it is difficult to conceive that our ideas have in any way influenced the views of our contemporary's contributor—we may well inquire upon what basis of reasoning he justifies the suggestion that every company which may in future be registered should be compelled to requisition the services of either a Chartered or an Incorporated Accountant.

On the other hand, it is well to remember that in all essentials the suggestion of "AJAX," that certain returns in respect of the shares allotted by a new company, &c., should be submitted to the statutory meeting of shareholders, certified by a public accountant, is by no means a novelty, having been already incorporated in the draft Companies Bill, as amended by the Select Committee of the House of Lords, and the only point upon which his recommendation differs is that, whereas the Select Commitee provide that the return in question shall be certified by the company's auditor, "AJAX" advocates that it should be certified by a practising accountant, taken in strict rotation from a list of all practising accountants who are members of either the Institute of Chartered Accountants or the Society of Accountants and Auditors.

As we have already stated in these columns, we see no objection to the proposition put forward by the Select Committee. It only therefore remains for us to say whether, in our opinion, the modified proposal of "AJAX" is an improvement upon this suggestion. Without running any serious risk of being misunderstood, we think that we may safely say that, so far from being an improvement, we think that the alteration suggested by *The Bullionist's* correspondent is a most objectionable one, and this for the simple reason that it implies a state of affairs which is obviously non-existent, viz., that every Chartered Accountant and every Incorporated Accountant is *equally* competent to certify to a return of this description, no matter what the magnitude of the undertaking may be; and that, in point of fact, the certificate of every such practising accountant would be received by the investing public with equal attention. We think that we have only to express the matter in these terms to demonstrate its utter absurdity. But, lest it should be thought that, in making this statement, we are endeavouring in a covered way to attack the position of Incorporated, and to advance the status of Chartered Accountants, as such, we may add that, even among the membership of the latter, there are necessarily practitioners whose standing is not sufficiently high to justify their compulsory employment by companies of considerable magnitude.

There can, we think, be no question that the proposition of the Select Committee, providing for the return in question to be certified by the company's auditor, is a far more reasonable one; and although, of course, in practice the appointment of the first auditor of any public company is to a large extent—although by no means entirely—controlled by the promoter, it may in this connection be very properly borne in mind that—whether or not the capital of the undertaking is underwritten—in practice it is essential that the promoter should select his auditor with some regard to the professional standing of the latter and the magnitude of the undertaking concerned.　Consequently, the probabilities are greatly in favour of the auditor, selected by a promoter in connection with an important undertaking, being of better standing than the accountant who happened to be next in the order of rotation.　These chances are greatly emphasised by the fact that, if the fees had to be upon a fixed scale, having regard to the average record of companies, the probability is that the best firms of Chartered Accountants would decline to lay themselves out for business of this description, and that consequently the average standing of the practitioner available would be lower than the average standing of the profession as a whole.

As a scheme for distributing the available amount of work among all practising accountants the proposition of " AJAX " is undoubtedly ingenious, but, like all quasi-socialistic suggestions of this nature, it would have the twofold defect of diverting first-class business from first-class hands, and of substituting an average of mediocrity for an ability proportionate to the amount of responsibility involved.

## Ⅶbat is an Auditor?

### IV.

(From *The Bullionist*.)

MY search after a clear and simple answer to this apparently easy question is not meeting with much success in the quarter where, if anywhere, I am entitled to expect a prompt definition. Accountants, as a professional body, should certainly be able to answer so elementary a question as " What is an auditor?" and yet select six members of the Institute of Chartered Accountants, take them aside one by one, and put the query to them, and you will receive six most contradictory replies.

The organ of the profession, *The Accountant*, which has honoured me with five columns of leading article abuse, but which, I notice, reprints these letters with great regularity, in referring to a paper of an accountant who appears to have been floundering about in a slough of despond over this question, observes : " While in general terms agreeing with Mr. —— that " the public are apt to look upon the auditor of a company as " responsible, not merely for its *bona fides*, but also for the accu- " racy of all the statements contained in the prospectus (even if it " does not include a certificate as to profits at all), we differ from " him as to the reasonableness of this view and as to the desir- " ability of affording it any encouragement."

There is a widespread idea that certain prominent firms of accountants demand, and obtain, large fees for "going on a " prospectus " ; and so long as they can keep up the fiction that their names " draw " so much the better for them ; but I believe the investor of to-day pays very little heed to these prospectus ornaments. The long list of colossal failures of the last few years, graced with the names of some of the highest firms as " auditors," has changed public opinion. Not that I ignore the importance of the position of auditors, and the necessity for men of known probity and skill acting as such ; on the contrary, the measures I have already and am now suggesting, whilst primarily for the public benefit, are so obviously to the advantage of the accountancy profession that I fully expect at no distant date to find their journal supporting heartily the reforms I am advocating.

In my last letter I defined briefly—but, I trust, clearly—the position of the proposed public auditor. The duties of this official would, of course, in no case interfere with the accountant's report upon any examination of figures referred to in a prospectus. The law, as it stands at present, amply protects shareholders in this respect, if they only take proper care and read the certificates and avoid any company where specious and verbose certificates in meaningless terms are appended to a mass of estimated figures. As I observed in my second letter, "wet-nurse" legislation tending to restrict honest joint stock enterprise would be as unsatisfactory as the present "open "door" as regards some of the clauses of the Companies Acts now under discussion. Recent events point to the desirability not only of the official audit of share capital I have proposed, but also of a directors' report at the statutory meeting.

That miserable farce, the statutory meeting, as it exists at present should be abolished, and the shareholders should have, in addition to the public auditor's report, a statement from the directors dealing with the prospectus clause by clause, detailing what the board had done, were doing, or proposed to do with regard thereto. Four months is sufficient time in most cases for a directorate to do something more than meet their shareholders with the stereotyped, "This is a meeting convened to "comply with the Companies Acts, and we have no report or "accounts to submit," etc., etc. The appointment by the shareholders at the statutory meeting of the auditor or auditors for the ensuing year brings us back to the subject-matter of these letters, a subject so interwoven with scandals under the Companies Acts that occasional wanderings from the main point are not only excusable, but necessary.

I remember, some years ago—rather more than I care to think of now—being present at a very excited first ordinary meeting at the Cannon Street Hotel, where the question of the re-election of auditors caused a heated discussion that nearly ended in a free fight. The accounts were unsatisfactory, the Balance Sheet was meagre, the auditors' certificate was short, and in the following terms:—"Examined and found correct." The capital of the company was £100,000, and the auditors' fee was £42. I held and represented a large holding in the company, and in the course of my inquiries gleaned that the auditors had compared the Balance Sheet with the Private Ledger, and, finding the figures agreed, issued the above certificate; the so-called "accounts" had not been audited at all. The auditors, after being pressed, admitted it would cost at least £150 to properly audit the accounts. After a great deal of trouble and numerous adjournments, I obtained amended accounts, the resignation of a managing director, and the appointment of competent auditors, for whom I obtained £200 per annum, conditional upon a continuous audit taking place, with detailed reports to the directors at short periodical intervals. I have no hesitation in stating that that company, which was destined otherwise for an early wreck, was saved by those prompt measures.

I remember at that meeting defining a good auditor as a living insurance policy for shareholders, and a large subsequent experience has confirmed that opinion. Of one thing I am certain, an audit in the generally accepted understanding of the term is for the most part useless. The auditor, to be of practical good, must have constant access to the books and papers of the company, and the audit must be continuous. The moral effect of the visit of the auditor upon the clerical staff of a company at unexpected times cannot be overestimated, and the presence of the auditor with his private report at a board meeting once a month, or as required, should be of immense value to a directorate. I am fully aware that in many companies these plans prevail, but they are quite exceptional.

The question of remuneration is a difficult one, because the work involved is so various, both in amount and degree of responsibility, that no hard and fast rule can be laid down. The present rate of audit fees is, for the most part, ridiculously inadequate, and shareholders fully deserve in many cases the incomplete and unsatisfactory services they receive.

To give directors fees aggregating from £500 to £1,000 per annum, and pay the auditor £31 10s. or less, is paying a premium upon incompetency. In few cases should the auditor's fees be less than those of one of the directors, and in many instances this sum will be insufficient.

This question is one for shareholders to make their own, and it should raise no unpleasantness with the directorate, as a company in perfect working order possessing auditors appointed by, and responsible to, the shareholders are in reality giving their responsible managers the most valuable assistance in their power when they give them the services of a skilled, impartial, independent auditor.

AJAX.

# Duties and Responsibilities of Auditors.

IN our issue of the 16th inst. we printed an extract from the *Journal of Gas Lighting* on this question, and commented on the same. The editor of that paper now draws our attention to the fact that this excerpt is only one of a series of articles that have appeared during the last few months in that journal ; and, as he has furnished us with the copies of his paper containing these articles we append them, and shall comment on the same in another column :—

## Auditors.

THE doubts felt, and from time to time expressed, by the commercial world as to the value of the theoretical safeguard which shareholders possess in the certificate of their auditors, against the possible dishonesty of their managers and staff, have been greatly strengthened, and the confidence placed in that certificate by that most credulous and innocent minded person—the average shareholder—has been rudely shaken by the disclosures recently made public as to the state of the affairs of the Millwall Dock Company. Following, as they have, upon a series of statements made by auditors in the witness-box during enquiries into insolvent and fraudulent companies, as to the view commonly held by them in regard to the duties of their position and the meaning of their certificates, and revealing the possibility, under the present usual system of company auditing, of irregularities of startling magnitude going undetected for an extended period of years, these disclosures have naturally been the subject of anxious consideration by shareholders and of more or less uninstructed comment in the daily press. Misgivings have, moreover, or should have, been felt by the highly respectable and eminently worthy gentlemen who draw the auditing fees of the great joint stock trading companies of London, as to whether they could swear, on the authority of their examination, that no such irregularities have been committed or are possible in the companies whose accounts they light-heartedly certify as correct. Our view of what constitutes the duty of an auditor—the purpose for which he is paid by his fellow shareholders—is that he is appointed to determine to the best of his ability, and to report faithfully to the shareholders to whom he is responsible, whether or not the accounts of their business are kept honestly and accurately, and whether the Balance Sheet does truly represent the profits and the position of their enterprise. To take any lower view is impossible unless one is prepared to admit that shareholders appoint auditors merely with the object of finding them gentle and lucrative employment, rather than for the protection of the interests of the body of shareholders at large.

With the foregoing standard in mind we propose to examine the scope, method, and value of the system of auditing usually adopted and deemed sufficient by the auditors of joint stock companies, with special reference to gas undertakings of considerable size, and to consider whether any improvement in the system could be made, or any different plan adopted, whereby the certificate of the auditors might be rendered of greater value. We would, however, preface the examination with the remark that, in whatever criticism we make, we do not in the remotest degree impugn the honour or good intention of any auditors of any gas companies. They are, fortunately, above suspicion. It is the system which, in all good faith, has been adopted against which our criticisms will be directed.

The usual method of auditing the books and accounts of considerable gas undertakings and, *mutatis mutandis*, of all similar commercial concerns, seldom, we believe, varies materially in principle, from the following procedure. The audit generally commences with an examination of the Cash Book. This examination consists in comparing the entries therein with subsidiary books for the incomings, with receipts for all outgoings except dividends and wages, and with bank Pass Books for the balance. As to the accuracy of the returns of cash received (either for ready money or on credit transactions) and as to the genuine nature and correctness of the payments set out as made, the certificate of the staff of the company is usually accepted.

This, with regard to the incomings, means that no method is, under such a system, adopted of testing whether the quantities of coke and other residuals, which have been sold for cash, have been accounted for at the market prices of the day. If, therefore, the works staff agreed among themselves to sell coke at 1s. per cwt., and account for it at 10d., the shareholders would, so far as being protected by their auditors is concerned, be robbed with impunity. Again, it means that, if the cash received from the consumers of gas, or the credit purchasers of residuals, were not properly accounted for, and the amount owing by them were improperly set out in the books and overstated in the Balance Sheet—whether for the purpose of misappropriation of cash or of a false return of revenue—the auditors would, through not systematically testing the accuracy of the books in question, entirely fail to discover such irregularity. We may here ask a very pertinent question : Of the several cases of defalcations by servants of gas companies which have been reported in the newspapers, how many were discovered by the auditors ?

Such an overstatement of accounts owing by consumers as we have instanced as possible, would be a fraud of the same nature as the falsifications alleged to have been discovered in the accounts of the Millwall Dock Company. The following extract from the sworn information of Mr. W. Peate, one of the auditors of the company, will at once make this clear, and at the same time corroborate our estimate of the commonly adopted method of audit. (The italics are our own.)

I have made a preliminary examination of the books of the company, and have discovered that the Balance Sheets issued and circulated among the shareholders between June 30 1891 and June 30 1898, have been falsified in the most material particulars, in that there has constantly appeared on the asset side of them an item described as "import and export "rates due to the company" carried out at amounts varying between £147,000 and £232,000, which, as to a large part of such amounts at the date so entered, had no existence in fact. The preparation for audit of the said Balance Sheets was controlled absolutely by the said G. R. Birt; and *I, as one of the auditors of the said company, was dependent for the accuracy of the above items upon the certificate of G. R. Birt and the Indoor Superintendent, chief clerk, and Ledger clerk at the docks of the company.* If the figures shown as the real amount of the asset had been truly certified to me, the profits appearing in the said account as available for dividend would have been substantially less, and the profit taken by G. R. Birt during the time of his managing directorship under his commission of 2 per cent. would have been proportionately less. By means of the publication of the Balance Sheets above specifically referred to, the directors and shareholders of the said company have been deceived as to the true financial position of the company; and during the period over which they range, the profits of the company have been fraudulently over-estimated by some thousands of pounds in each year.

In respect of the outgoings, similar possibilities of fraud are not guarded against by such an audit as we are considering. No care is taken, as a rule, we fear, to test whether the receipts presented for audit represent genuine authorised payments—that is to say, whether the sums reported to have been paid have been actually debited to the accounts of the vendors, and are to meet corresponding credits for coal or other goods purchased; or, if so properly accounted for, whether these goods have been (or should have been) received and have been paid for at the fair market rates. How many auditors ever examine the accounts for coals purchased with the contracts entered into by the directors? Few, if any, we believe. So, if the staff of a gas company conspired to pay a coal merchant, for valuable consideration, a higher price for his coal than that at which the directors agreed to purchase, the shareholders would be without protection by their auditors. The same question, the same answer, and the same possibility, apply to all the purchases of plant and of materials used for construction, repairs, or purification.

Again, it is to be feared that few auditors take any steps to ascertain whether the figure which appears in the Cash Book as being the amount of dividends paid, actually does represent the aggregate of the dividends paid to the shareholders, or whether the amounts of the holdings of the proprietors as registered in the books total up to the actual capital of the company. The necessity for testing these figures arises from the fact that there is usually, in a big company, a sufficient balance of dividends awaiting the claim of ignorant or unknown proprietors to pay a considerable dividend to a fraudulent staff on non-existent capital.

What auditor of a company with over 2,000 shareholders has ever taken any step to test the accuracy of the dividends paid?

As to the wages bill (which usually represents an amount equal to, or greater than, the profit to the shareholders), the examination of it rarely amounts to more than a little practice in addition, in casting up the total weekly amounts reported to have been paid by the works officials. In how many instances do auditors test the rates of pay at which the men are reported to have been paid with the rate sanctioned by the board of directors? If, therefore, the works staff shows payments to stokers at 1d. a day more than the men have actually received or the directors approved, the auditors (and so the shareholders) are none the wiser.

After having in such fashion " satisfied " themselves as to the correctness of the Cash Book, the auditors (we are speaking throughout of what we believe to be the usual type of auditors) then proceed to the second stage of the process, which, when completed, justifies them, in their opinion, in certifying the accounts to be correct. This second stage consists in comparing most carefully and particularly, a few final books of the concern with each other and with the semi-final books, the accuracy of which the auditors apparently never dream of testing. For the correctness of these semi-final books, and of other subsidiary returns or accounts leading up thereto, the signatures of the very men whose honesty it is the auditors' duty to prove, are considered by them trustworthy and sufficient guarantee.

This audit—save the mark!—then terminates in the examination of the Balance Sheet with the final books, which have, as we have said, been carefully compared with semi-final books, whose contents might, as a rule, so far as the auditors, by their own examination, are aware, be falsified from start to finish. The accounts are then signed and presented to the shareholders, whose grateful thanks are returned to their able auditors, who are unanimously re-elected by an admiring general meeting.

To further demonstrate the value of such a system, let us for a moment consider one or two of the items in the statement of assets and liabilities.

*Coals, Residuals, and Stores in hand.* How do the auditors know, of their own personal knowledge, how many tons of coal, coke, or sulphate are in stock, or how do they ever practically test the statements of these and other stocks laid before them? (It is only necessary to turn to the proceedings at the recent general meeting of the Sheffield United Gaslight Company to see that this question is not merely academical.) We do not think that many works officials would know an auditor if they saw one. Further, are the valuation prices ever compared with market rates?

*Accounts due from Consumers and other Debtors and to Creditors.* Are these enormous figures ever efficiently tested? For instance, do the auditors ever in any practical way satisfy themselves that the quantity of gas reported to have been sold has been properly charged, at the proper prices, to the consumers, and that the amount shown as unpaid is actually owing by them? We are afraid that the answers to all these questions must, in most cases, be equally unsatisfactory.

The extreme importance of a proper audit of these items in the Balance Sheet will be realised by a glance at the following figures, taken from the accounts of the three Metropolitan Gas Companies for the half year ended December 31 1897:—

| Company | Stores in Hand | Accounts due to the Company | Accounts due by the Company | 1 per Cent. on Ordinary Stock for Half Year |
|---|---|---|---|---|
| | £ | £ | £ | £ |
| Gaslight and Coke .. | 540,591 | 1,003,182 | 367,402 | 29,611 |
| South Metropolitan.. | 184,089 | 329,653 | 144,036 | 11,062* |
| Commercial .. .. | 45,852 | 97,978 | 30,651 | 3,753 |
| Total .. .. | £770,532 | £1,430,813 | £542,089 | £44,426 |

* On stock prior to conversion.

These figures show that a falsification of either 5·8 per cent. on the stores in hand, 3·1 per cent. on the accounts due, 8·2 per cent. on the accounts owing, or of 1·6 per cent. on the aggregate of these several items, would have been sufficient to have enabled these companies to have paid the rate of dividends sanctioned by the sliding scale on their ordinary stocks for that half year, even if they had failed to earn them by 1 per cent. on those stocks.

We think we have now sufficiently demonstrated the absurdly futile character of the system of company auditing generally in vogue; and we need scarcely point out how valueless and, therefore, how mischievous are the certificates which are signed on the strength of such examinations.

We have confined our attention to, and drawn our instances from, the accounts of gas undertakings in the metropolis, not because we think they are any less efficiently audited than the generality of large trading companies, but rather because criticism is usually more useful if it be particular rather than general in its aim, and because the readers of the *Journal* are especially interested in, and acquainted with, the working of these companies. We, however, do not hesitate to assert that the same vital weakness to which we have throughout called attention renders more or less valueless the certificate attached to the Balance Sheets of nine out of ten public companies. This weakness, we must, at the risk of incurring the accusation of repeating ourselves, again point out, lies in the *unqualified* reliance placed, at some stage or other in the process of auditing, upon the certificate of the very servants against whose possible dishonesty the whole purpose of auditing is directed. And the larger the company the more closely does the stage in the accounts at which the certificate is accepted approach the final, and the more meaningless the audit.

It may then fairly be asked whether it is possible to devise any system of auditing the accounts of companies of such magnitude as those we have instanced, which shall be really effectual for its purpose, and which is practically within the limits of time and money usually expended thereon. Having given, we trust, every occasion for such a question to be asked, we hope to show that such an audit is both possible and practicable, not perhaps within the bounds of time and money which are now, but certainly within those which should be, devoted to the work in question. For first of all, it is necessary to put to the body of shareholders generally the question whether they are prepared to pay a fair and proper amount for an auditors' certificate which will really mean that they can rely upon the accuracy and straightforwardness of the accounts laid before them. If they are not, then they had much better keep in their pockets the

money that they at present pay for a certificate which, in most cases, is evidence merely that the auditors have spent a certain number of days at the offices of the companies, and have performed a few harmless evolutions amongst the books and accounts. But assuming, as we have little doubt, that shareholders would be willing, if necessary, to pay a higher price in order to obtain the safeguard of an audit worthy of the name, we will endeavour to point out how a satisfactory and efficient audit might be adopted in practice.

First we have to consider what qualifications auditors should possess, in addition to those of a certain holding in their company and time to devote to the duties of the office. The fundamental requirement of an auditor, over and above the foregoing, and in addition to the unimpeachable uprightness which is a *sine quâ non*, is, we hold, a thorough and detailed knowledge of the whole system on which the accounts he has to audit are kept. And by this we mean, not merely a knowledge of how the figures in the final books are derived from subsidiary books and welded together, but also of the source and meaning of every entry in every book which forms a material link in the chain leading up to the final entries in the Balance Sheet. Only by the possession of such knowledge will he be able to really test the accuracy and the straightforwardness with which each and every part of the whole has been constructed and put together.

We are afraid that very few companies' auditors—even after many years examination of the accounts in the accustomed fashion, much less at the time of their appointment—possess this most essential qualification; and it is this primary deficiency in their equipment that gives to even such examination as they do undertake a superficial and unsatisfactory character. We are led to the conclusion that only such men as have had years of experience of the system on which the books are kept of the particular (or analagous) classes of company which they are called upon to audit, are really qualified for the work. The only possible alternative is the appointment of Chartered Accountants, who, by their training, are better qualified than other men to grasp the details of a business with which they have had no previous acquaintance. But, unless the present system be materially amended, we decline to put any practical value upon the signature of any auditor, whether amateur or professional.

Hypothecating auditors of the necessary qualifications, we have to define the guiding principle upon which an audit should be conducted. It will be observed that we have, throughout, used the expression "take steps to *test* the accuracy of" this or that figure. That is the basis upon which we should found our whole system of auditing. Instead of a stereotyped method of merely examining regularly the few final books, and seeing that the subsidiary books are duly examined and certified by members of the staff, we would, in addition to such routine, adopt a plan of occasionally (at irregular, though at as short as possible, intervals) sampling the accuracy of every book or return which in any way formed part of the system of accounts. Under such a system no member of the staff of a company, from the lowest to the highest, would ever know whether or when any or every entry he made might be examined by the auditors. This is only applying, on an extended scale in a large matter, the system already in vogue on a small. Omnibus conductors never know when their vehicles will be boarded by road inspectors. They have, therefore, to be always certain that their tickets and waybills will bear auditing. So it should be with every Day Bookkeeper, every Ledger keeper, every storekeeper, collector, or other such servant in the employment of a company.

For example. Under this system the auditors of a gas company would, occasionally—at some time only previously known to themselves—visit the works of the company, and check approximately (or have checked under their supervision) the stocks of coals, residuals, or principal stores; compare these stocks with the figures returned to them by the works manager; and check, from outside sources, or from contracts approved by the directors, the book prices put upon them. At the same time they could observe and compare with the book figures the prices being charged to the public for residuals sold for cash. Again, at another time they would call for one of the consumers' Ledgers, examine, on one page here and another there, the charges for gas consumed with the meter-index returns, see that the cash for such accounts as had been paid had been properly accounted for, that only a normal percentage of the accounts showed at the commencement of a quarter more than the amount for the previous quarter as unpaid, test the castings of the Ledger, and see that the totals were properly carried into the Summary Books. The Summary Books would from time to time be tested for additions, and in due course checked into the final books. The same principle, applied throughout the system, so that the staff would be always wondering what their auditors might ask for next, would make auditors the terror instead of the laughing stock of dishonest servants, and would check, by the wholesome fear of discovery, any desire to falsify or manipulate the accounts.

It would be easy, had we space, to show, but we think it will readily be seen, that this plan would, if adopted and properly carried out, render certain the discovery, or, in most cases, the prevention, of such irregularities as we have indicated as possible under the present system. We believe that some such plan of check will be found to be in force in most well-managed companies, whereby each section of the staff is more or less checked by another. But, however it may satisfy the directors and head managers as to the correctness of the accounts, of the existence of such a plan auditors can have no satisfactory proof. Nor would such proof relieve them of one ounce of their own responsibility, because it would still leave untouched that possibility of collusion and conspiracy among the servants, of which we have recently had so striking an example. It would also leave undiminished the fundamental weakness of the present system which we have repeatedly emphasised—that of auditors, while attempting to fulfil their duty, putting faith in the honesty of any section or member of the staff.

We may further illustrate our view of what is, and also of what should be, the system of auditing by a reference to the procedure adopted by Parliament for the checking of the honesty of the metropolitan gas companies in respect of the illuminating power of the gas supplied. The candle-power of the gas sent out by the companies is frequently and regularly examined personally by public officials, whose duty it is to see that the statutory obligations of the companies in this respect are fulfilled. On the strength of their personal testing of samples of the distributed gas, and on that alone, the testers base their reports as to whether the bulk of the gas supplied is of standard illuminating power; and we contend that the personal sampling of the accuracy of all the materials from which a Balance Sheet has been constructed is the only method which can justify an auditor in certifying it as correct.

A certificate based upon such a system of auditing as we first outlined is of precisely as much value as would be that of the official gas-testers if, instead of themselves actually making the photametrical tests, they confined their attention to merely checking the final calculations based thereon, and accepted the certificates of officials of the companies for the accuracy of the candle-power readings, the rates of consumption of sperm, temperatures, and barometrical pressures. What would such a certificate be worth, and what would be said of the gas referees if they adopted such a method of procedure? What would then be said of the referees may fairly be said now of auditors who are satisfied with the system on which the accounts of many companies are examined. But we have indicated a system of "book testing" which, if applied in an intelligent manner by men of the necessary knowledge and experience, would, we believe, be of equal practical value to that adopted for the testing of gas.

As to the practicabilty of adopting such a comprehensive scheme in the case of large companies, we have no doubt. It would, of course, entail a considerable deal more time being given to their duties by the auditors than is given now; and this would necessarily entail some increase, although, we submit, not a proportionate increase, in their remuneration. The three metropolitan gas companies at present pay their auditors about £800 a year. For say £1,200 a year more, making a total charge for auditing of one-seventieth of a penny per 1,000 cubic feet of gas sold, we think that the shareholders of these companies might ask and expect that their accounts should be audited in some such adequate manner as we have outlined.*

If this attempt to demonstrate the futility of the present, and to suggest the possibility of an improved, system of company auditing leads to nothing further than a corrected estimate by the average shareholder of the value of auditors' certificates, we shall have achieved some measure of success; but we hope that it may be the means of sooner or later inducing him to insist upon getting something rather than nothing for his money.

---

* As to the auditor of the metropolitan gas companies appointed by the Board of Trade, we have said nothing. His duty is to satisfy Parliament, and not the shareholders; and if Parliament be satisfied, that is all that is required of him.

## The Duties and Responsibilities of Auditors.

———

PRESSURE of other matters has prevented us from replying earlier to an interesting article upon the above subject which appeared in our contemporary, the *Journal of Gas Lighting*, on the 10th ult.

The article deals, to a large extent, with the opinions which we put forward in our issue of the 30th September last. Our contemporary is, we understand, quite prepared to believe that an efficient system of audit is adopted by first-class firms of accountants, but it raises the question " How are the public to know which " are the first-class firms ? " The only reply to this is that, as in the case of other professions, so it is in the accountancy profession, the members obtain their reputation by their work ; and that reputation is not invariably to be measured by the magnitude of their operations. It may be pointed out that auditing is not an " exact science " in the sense that it is an occupation which anyone following a definite series of rules can necessarily efficiently perform ; and, that being so, it is not a matter upon which it is possible to say off-hand that this man performs his work " well," and that one " badly." On the other hand, the duties of an auditor are such that it does not by any means necessarily follow that even failure in an individual case must be fairly regarded as being the result of " criminal neglect." Such failure, where it occurs, may be the result of want of judgment, want of care, or want of skill. Either of the last two is sufficient to stamp a man as an undesirable auditor ; but an error of judgment, however important its consequences may be, does not necessarily make the same conclusion a reasonable one. Professional men of all kinds occasionally make an error of judgment, and, as a matter of fact, their reputation will (rightly or wrongly) inevitably suffer in consequence ; but we know of no profession, other than accountancy, in which it has ever been seriously suggested that a man should be debarred from attempting to earn his living in that particular capacity for ever afterwards merely because he has once happened to commit this mistake.

From the point of view of the public, it may be stated that—inasmuch as they are the employers of auditors—it is primarily *their* business to satisfy themselves as to the auditor's qualifications for the position which he is asked to fill. It may well be asked whether such an idea has ever yet occurred to a single shareholder when voting for the appointment of an auditor. The Institute, on the other hand, is not without responsibilities in the matter ; but its responsibilities are naturally limited by its powers. The Institute has power to refuse admission to accountants until they have satisfied the governing body as to their knowledge; this power, however, did not come into force until after all the original members had been admitted. After admission, the Institute has no power to make inquisitorial enquiries as to the manner in which its members transact their business, although it may take cognizance of complaints against the conduct of any member, from whatever source they are forwarded. The statement was recently made in another contemporary that this right to enquire into the actions of members whose conduct had been impugned was never exercised; and, in reply, we quoted figures, showing that every year some few members were removed for such causes.

Our contemporary then dealt with a supposed conflict of views enunciated by us on the subject of the valuation of stock, but this is quite capable of easy explanation. There are certain tests which an auditor can perform to enable him to satisfy *himself* as to the reasonableness of the valuation placed upon stock-in-trade, and these tests should (so far as they are available) invariably be employed. Certainly one of them would, in the case of a gas company, be to compare the price at which coal in stock was valued with the contract price which had actually been paid for it. Nevertheless, such a test, although useful, is by no means final; and, for that reason, an auditor, while seeking to satisfy himself as far as possible, should, in our opinion, always carefully abstain from attempting to give a definite valuation of assets. To take this particular example alone, it by no means follows that, because coal has been purchased at a certain price per ton, the amount of coal in stock at a particular date is really worth that amount. It

would, however, be impossible for a Chartered Accountant, or any other ordinary auditor, to state with any authority what the value of coal in stock might be, other than by testing it with the cost or market price. It would require an expert to say whether or not it was really worth this figure.

**The Duties and Responsibilities of Auditors.**

———

IN a recent issue our contemporary, *The Journal of Gas Lighting, Water Supply, etc.*, resumes what it very appropriately describes as its " friendly discussion " with ourselves upon this interesting subject.　Our last contribution thereto appeared in these columns so long ago as the 18th ult., and we fear, therefore, that our comments can no longer be very fresh in the minds of our readers.　Doubtless, however, they will be easily recalled by a perusal of our contemporary's article, which we reproduce in another column.　For the sake of convenience, rather than upon the score of logical sequence, we propose to deal with the various points raised by our contemporary in the order in which they appear in the article.

Our contemporary appears to cordially agree with our statement that the mere volume of business transacted by any particular firm of accountants, is not, of itself, any guarantee that the work which it undertakes will be performed with as much satisfaction to all concerned as might possibly have been the case had a firm in a smaller way of business been instructed ; but, in order to remove a very probable misconception, we should like to state at once that, in our opinion, no such reflection as that suggested by our contemporary can with justice be made against some of our largest practitioners.　The suggestion may, of course, be entirely un-conscious, but our contemporary would appear to imply that no good auditing work is to be expected from a firm where the bulk of it is left in the hands of clerks ; while the suggestion is emphasised by describing these clerks as " irresponsible," and " many of them as none " too well paid."　We should be straying too far from the direct matter at issue to deal fully with the points here suggested, but we think that we are in a position to state authoritatively that, although necessarily a very large amount of the work transacted by the largest firms is perforce left to the supervision of senior clerks, those clerks cannot accurately be described as either irresponsible—being in many cases A.C.A.'s themselves—or as being insufficiently remunerated to secure good work. It may further be added that, if there is one respect in which accountancy differs from other professions, it is that in which it calls for—and offers rewards for—the faculty of business organisation, by which a principal, without losing in any way his grip upon (or his responsibility for) all matters passing through his office, is able to arrange for each portion of the various detail work to be effectively performed without undue expense, while still retaining in his own hands the actual control of, as well as the legal responsibility for, the result.

Our contemporary speaks absolutely to the point when it states that auditing differs radically from the other professions, in that the value of the work done is intangible ; and, for this reason, we suppose that accountants must be content to remain unappreciated where their work is good, and to be unjustly condemned where the results turn out to be unfortunate. But, although our contemporary apparently assents in theory to our suggestion that, however difficult the task may be, it is the duty of shareholders to select a competent auditor, it seems to us that those of its readers who followed our contemporary's advice would merely become past-masters in the art of " how not to do it." By what process of reasoning our contemporary arrives at the conclusion that the best auditors for gas, water, or electric lighting companies would be the accountant book-keepers of rival companies, we are at a loss to perceive ; and—leaving on one side the disadvantageous results which would by no means improbably result from such rivalry—it is, we think, pertinent to enquire what possible advantage could reasonably be expected from the change. We will not go so far as to say that a very competent and conscientious auditor might not be chosen from this restricted field, if a selection were carefully made. But we do most definitely state that the chances of such a selection proving advantageous, as contrasted with the appointment of a professional accountant, are few and far between, more particularly until shareholders begin to look upon the appointment of an auditor (and the discharge by him of his duties after being appointed) as matters of serious import, rather than mere matters of form.

One would imagine, from the general tone of our contemporary's articles, that the auditing of the companies for which it specially caters, is, at the present time, in a very defective condition. We are prepared to admit that this is a point upon which our contemporary ought to possess better information than ourselves, but, at the risk of appearing ill-informed, we must admit that we are aware of no such condition of affairs ; while the one instance of importance which we recollect, as having occurred of recent years, directly tends to prove our own contentions with regard to the subject. Lest this case should have escaped the attention of our contemporary and its readers, we think it worth while to shortly recount the facts, although we dealt with them very fully at the time.

It will, no doubt, be remembered that, in the severe frost of the winter of 1894-5, most water companies (and especially the Metropolitan water companies) were put to considerable expense in connection with the repair of broken mains. In the case of one of these Metropolitan companies, the auditor drew attention to the fact that only half of the expenditure so incurred had been debited against the revenue for the current period ; and he deemed it his duty to acquaint the shareholders with the fact so that they might judge whether or not it was desirable to carry forward the other half of this purely revenue expenditure as an asset, or whether they would require the whole of the expenses to be debited to revenue before arriving at a profit available for dividend. We feel sure that our contemporary, with its high view of the importance of an efficient and independent audit, will agree with us that, in taking this view, the auditor did nothing more than his bare duty. As a matter of fact, however, by so doing he not merely offended the directors, but also the shareholders—the especial grievance of the latter apparently was that, if the auditor's recommendations had been taken into account, their dividend would have been reduced 1 per cent. Moreover, the opinion was very generally expressed at the shareholders' meeting, that these circumstances should be taken into consideration at the next meeting, when the auditor came up for re-election ! What happened at the next meeting we do not remember. By that time, very possibly, the shareholders had cooled down, and the auditor's re-election was unopposed ; but no one who read a verbatim report of the first meeting could have failed to form the impression that, had the auditor's election been then due, another auditor would inevitably have been appointed. Cases of this description are in our mind when we deliberately make the statement that it is from shareholders, rather than from auditors, that any improvement is to be expected in the direction of the increased independence of the audit of directors' accounts.

Passing on to another question, which our contemporary admits that it had not previously alluded to, we may point out that, before enquiring in how many cases the auditors of gas companies satisfy themselves as to whether the value of the works, land, and plant, of the undertakings is maintained at the figure representing the asset in the Balance Sheet, it is —to say the least of it—only fair to enquire what power auditors have to make any such enquiry whatever. The statutory form of accounts for gas companies, which is prescribed by the Gas Clauses Act 1871, takes no cognisance whatever of the depreciation of fixed assets, merely requiring that all repairs and renewals shall be charged against revenue. That being so, the question to which our contemporary alludes— vitally important as it may be—is not one within the purview of the auditor. Were it the auditor's duty to make any such enquiry, it would be reasonable to ask what facilities are afforded him (a man of no practical experience in the valuation of such assets) to verify the data placed before him. But, as matters stand, such a question is entirely unnecessary, and merely indicates that there is much confusion in the mind of the average layman as to what it is that an auditor is really responsible for. In the case of electric lighting companies, on the other hand, there *is* provision for a reserve being made for depreciation; and the auditor's duty to see that some such reserve is made is therefore clear. Here again, however, he cannot pose as a specialist in the value of land, plant, and machinery ; and, if he has the assurance of the directors and other responsible officials of the company that the reserve which has been made is, in their opinion, adequate, he would be a bold man to—in any normal case—put in his "inexpert" opinion against their opinion, which is at least supposed to be that of persons experienced in that particular class of business.

It still remains for us to deal with the two points mentioned at the conclusion of our contemporary's article, in connection with which it makes quotations from our issue of the 18th ult. With regard to the first of these quotations, we may point out that our contemporary's disclaimer against having adversely criticised an auditor for committing *one* error of judgment, falls to the ground, inasmuch as the second company concerned has expressly gone out of its way to absolve the auditor in question from any breach or neglect of duty. It seems to us that their deliberate conclusion upon a matter which so much more intimately concerns them than anyone else must in all fairness be accepted as final, and upon further reflection we feel convinced that our contemporary will agree with us upon this point.

With regard to our second quotation (in which we stated that although an auditor, not being an expert, could not be expected to be responsible for the valuation of stocks, there were certain tests which it was possible for him to perform to enable him to satisfy *himself* as to the reasonableness of the valuation adopted by the directors), our contemporary states, in effect, that it would be well satisfied if such a course were pursued, but that its complaint is that in very many cases this is not done. It is difficult to generalise in matters of this description, and we must say that we do not quite understand how it could be possible for our contemporary to be in possession of any definite information

thereon, seeing that it is one of the essential features of an audit that the staff of the company should—as far as possible—be kept in the dark as to its extent and scope. Any audits omitting these precautions, however, are not as complete as they might be; and we would suggest that, in the case of any individual company where it is known that no such precautions are taken by the auditor, it would be desirable that the shareholders should be acquainted with the facts, so that they might be in a position to consider whether or not it were desirable to continue the appointment. At the same time, we may add that we have a sufficient want of confidence in the manner in which shareholders discharge their duties in this respect to assert that, in all probability, it would make no difference whatever in their selection.

To avoid any possibility of further misunderstanding, we may state that, as a whole, the accountancy profession is both able and willing to afford to shareholders all the protection that they can reasonably require. If, up to the present, the ultimate result in any individual case has been unsatisfactory, the blame—if we be compelled to generalise—is far more due to the apathy and ignorance of shareholders than to the neglect or incompetence of accountants; and, that being so, if any material improvement is to be effected, it must for the most part be looked for among the former, rather than the latter.

## Shareholders and Auditors.

THE following is the extract from the *Journal of Gas Lighting* referred to in our leader.

IN their issue of the 18th ult., *The Accountant* continue their friendly discussion of the position taken up by the *Journal* in regard to the duties and responsibilities of auditors. In a previous article, we expressed our willingness to believe, on the authority of our contemporary, that an efficient system of audit is adopted by " first-class firms of accountants "; but we asked how the public were to know which were the " first-class firms " seeing that, as we contended, the fact that a candidate for an auditorship is a Chartered Accountant is not a sufficient guarantee of his fitness for the appointment. Our contemporary admits this contention, and tells us that the professional reputation of an accountant is the only guide to his fitness—adding, what we can readily believe, that the magnitude of the business done by a firm of accountants is not necessarily indicative of high reputation. It is, we should say, not infrequently the reverse; more work being undertaken than can be done properly and carefully, and the bulk of it being left in the hands of irresponsible clerks, many of them none too well paid. Our contemporary urges that, as in every other profession members obtain their reputation by their work, so in the profession of auditing reputation serves to distinguish the good from the indifferent. But we do not think that the parallel is by any means exact ; for auditing differs radically from the other professions, in that the value of the work done is not readily estimated. An auditor's work, unlike an architect's, is not necessarily productive of tangible results. If the books of a company be correctly and honestly kept, how is it possible for the outside public to tell whether the auditor of that company does his work in such a way that he would discover fraud, were it ever attempted ? Further, if fraud were perpetrated in the accounts of a company for twenty years without the auditor detecting it, might not that auditor enjoy an excellent reputation throughout the time ? It is, therefore, all the more necessary that negligent auditors should, when discovered, be severely criticised, and, we contend, much more sternly dealt with by the Institute than they are at present. Unless the Institute are prepared to take the necessary steps to make membership thereof a better guarantee of efficiency than it is at present, the value placed upon a Chartered Accountant's certificate by the business community will remain a low one. One step that we think might well be taken would be to prescribe in general terms the form of certificate that an auditor should attach to a Balance Sheet, to require every member of the Institute to forward thereto a copy of every published Balance Sheet bearing his signature, and to refuse to retain as member any auditor using an unsatisfactory form of certificate.

It remains, then, at present, for shareholders to judge of the fitness of a candidate for the post of auditor by his reputation, not merely as an auditor—that may be, and probably is in most cases, a matter of luck—but as a business man ; and they will therefore be best advised to select a man of good standing in the industry in which the company is engaged, preferably the accountant of another company. In connection with this question of appointing auditors, our contemporary very pertinently inquires whether the idea that—inasmuch as they are the employers of auditors—it is primarily the business of shareholders to satisfy themselves as to their auditors' qualifications, has ever occurred to a single shareholder when voting for the appointment of an auditor. It is unfortunately the case that little, if any, attention is ever paid to the election of the auditors of a company. This is, perhaps, partly due to the scepticism of the business world as to whether auditors are of much use ; but it is also largely owing to the apathy of shareholders to everything but the dividend. We shall not cease to urge upon them the importance of selecting able men for the post, and, further, of keeping them after their election alive to their responsibilities. We have quite recently pointed out the advisability of shareholders from time to time interrogating the auditors at the general meetings of companies, as to the extent and result of their inquiries into the reliability of the accounts they have signed. The difficulty is to find a shareholder sufficiently shrewd and public-spirited to raise his voice on this, or on any other, important question at the dreary function known as a general meeting of shareholders. This difficulty is greatest, of course, where the company in question is paying substantial dividends ; but it is not a whit the less necessary that the auditors of such a company should be roused to a sense of their responsibilities, because the vital question which a shareholder should be anxious to have answered, and which the auditor should be (but seldom is) able to satisfy, is whether the distribution of those substantial dividends is justified by the present and future position of the company.

There is one question, to which we have not previously alluded in connection with the duties of an auditor, but to which general reference was made in the *Journal* last week, and as to which shareholders should be especially inquisitive ---namely, the provision made in the accounts for depreciation of works and plant. In how many cases do the auditors of gas or electric lighting companies satisfy themselves as to whether the value of the works, land, and plant of the undertakings is maintained at the figure representing the asset in the Balance Sheet—that is to say, in most cases, at the actual original cost—or, where the system of replacing or renovating deteriorated works out of revenue is not adopted, whether an adequate amount has been written off for depreciation ? If, in the one case, the book value be higher than the true value, or in the other, a sufficient sum has not been written off for depreciation, then – in fact, if not in law —dividends are being paid out of capital. We say " if not " in law," because we have in mind, in this connection, the judgment delivered by the Master of the Rolls in the *National Bank of Wales* case, in which a distinction—somewhat too fine and subtle for the lay mind—was drawn between dividends paid out of profits augmented by charging bad debts to capital instead of to revenue, and dividends actually paid out of the cash subscribed by shareholders. This distinction, however, is only of practical value to lawyers. If a shareholder's capital is melting away without his knowledge, and each dividend he receives is made up partly of legitimate and partly of imaginary profits, he will care little, when the final crash comes, what name be given to the transaction by which he has been deceived. What he will want to know will be why the auditors whom he appointed to safeguard his interests did not enlighten him as to the true state of affairs. If shareholders would only occasionally remind their auditors of what they are appointed to do, there would probably be fewer occasions for futile abuse of them for having allowed the milk to be spilled.

That shareholders in electric light undertakings are in greater danger of finding they have been living in the particular fools' paradise in which shareholders in a concern with an insufficiently-depreciated Capital Account spend a more or less brief existence, than are the shareholders in the great majority of gas undertakings, we do not doubt ; but, for all that, the necessity for making assurance doubly sure cannot be too strongly urged. In this connection, the fifth and last of the recommendations of the Select Committee on Metropolitan Gas Companies Charges may be re-called : " That an effort should be made by any company having " obsolete or unproductive capital to redeem such capital " by sinking fund or otherwise." Is it not the duty of an auditor of a company, part of whose capital is " obsolete or " unproductive," to see that, of the amount shown as an asset in the Balance Sheet (the net capital expended), the proportion which, as a matter of fact, is non-existent or non-productive is specifically stated in the accounts ? In our opinion, if the cost of such valueless plant were not, as we think it should be, transferred from the Capital Account to a separate " dead Capital Account "—to which all sums charged against revenue by way of reduction of the dead capital would be carried—then the auditors should qualify their certificate by stating that of the capital raised and expended so much was no longer represented by realisable assets. This would specifically draw the attention of shareholders to the need for redeeming such capital " by sinking " fund or otherwise," and, in case some provision for such redemption had been made, would enable them to judge whether such provision were adequate.

The question of whether a company, a certain portion of whose capital has been lost, are justified in paying full, or any, dividends until that lost capital shall have been replaced out of revenue, or written off by reduction of capital, is one on which the law rightly refuses to generalise. It leaves the responsibility for deciding each case upon its merits to those responsible for the direction of the undertaking, who are, or should be, best qualified to judge of the way in which such a loss shall be met. The law will only undertake to punish any directors who have wilfully neglected to adequately provide for redeeming, and who fraudulently conceal from the shareholders, any loss of capital. It is the duty of the auditors, who are appointed to protect the shareholders against such fraudulent misrepresentation of the position of their business, to satisfy themselves that the true state of the Capital Account is revealed by the Balance Sheets, and to report to their constituents if they be not so satisfied. How many auditors of gas companies ever trouble themselves to properly perform this duty, or would be capable of so doing if they tried ?

Dealing with the question of what constitutes criminal neglect on the part of an auditor, *The Accountant* says :—

> Professional men of all kinds occasionally make an error of judgment ; and, as a matter of fact, their reputation will (rightly or wrongly) inevitably suffer in consequence. But we know of no profession, other than accountancy, in which it has ever been seriously suggested that a man should be debarred from attempting to earn his living in that particular capacity for ever afterwards merely because he has once happened to commit this mistake.

If, as would appear, this is intended to refer to any criticism made on any auditor in the *Journal*, we have to say that we have never adversely criticised an auditor for committing merely " one " error of judgment. We certainly have attacked, and have attempted to demonstrate the futility of the system of auditing commonly adopted by shareholders' auditors ; and if an entire failure to comprehend the duties and to realise the responsibilities of an auditor be agreed to constitute one error of judgment, we should maintain that such an error should disqualify a professional accountant from practising. But when we have referred to a specific case, it has been one in which, as we need scarcely remind our contemporary, the auditor had previously had warning of the necessity for adopting a more thorough system, in order to render an audit effective.

With reference to the checking of the valuation of coal stocks, the writer in *The Accountant* says :—

> Our contemporary (the *Journal*) then dealt with a supposed conflict of views enunciated by us on the subject of the valuation of stock ; but this is quite capable of easy explanation There are certain tests which an auditor can perform to enable him to satisfy *himself* as to the reasonableness of the valuation placed upon stock-in-trade ; and these tests should (so far as they are available) invariably be employed. Certainly one of them would, in the case of a gas company, be to compare the price at which coal in stock was valued with the contract price which had actually been paid for it. Nevertheless, such a test, although useful, is by no means final and, for that reason, an auditor, while seeking to satisfy himself as far as possible, should, in our opinion, always carefully abstain from attempting to give a definite valuation of assets To take this particular example alone, it by no means follows that, because coal has been purchased at a certain price per ton, the amount of coal in stock at a particular date is really worth that amount. It would, however, be impossible for a Chartered Accountant, or any other ordinary auditor, to state with any authority what the value of coal in stock might be other than by testing it with the cost or market price. It would require an expert to say whether or not it was really worth this figure.

We can assure our contemporary that we should be very well satisfied if the auditors of gas companies would occasionally ascertain that the quantity of coal shown in the accounts as in hand was actually in stock on the given date and was valued at its cost price. Our complaint is that in many cases, if not in most, they do neither.

## Points of Interest to Accountants.

### III.

*Audit of Companies.*

"THE duties and responsibilities of an auditor as regards valuation of stock-in-trade."

The leading decision upon this point is *The Kingston Cotton Mills* case, in which, as our readers will doubtless recollect, it was held that auditors were justified in placing reliance upon the deliberate statements of tried servants of the company, provided they had no reason to doubt their accuracy; but that they were obliged to independently enquire into the accuracy of such statements, and in the course of such enquiry to bring to bear a reasonable amount of care and skill. It might perhaps appear that this decision left one in very much the same place as that in which we started. But this is by no means the case, because in the first place it admits the principle of allowing an auditor, in the absence of suspicious circumstances, to adopt the valuations supplied to him by persons who are reasonably competent to make such valuations, and who, although not "independent," are reasonably supposed to be willing to do so upon *bonâ fide* lines. The question as to whether an auditor is himself required to take and assess the value of stock-in-trade is thus definitely set at rest. In connection with the amount of care and skill which an auditor should bring to bear upon the valuation of stock-in-trade submitted to him, one cannot do better than follow the lines indicated by Mr. FREDERICK WHINNEY, F.C.A., some time ago, when he pointed out that what auditors had to do with regard to statements put before them by the servants of a company was to "sift the evidence," presumably in exactly the same manner as a jury would be expected to do were such a valuation placed before them. The clerical accuracy of the work involved, it is, of course, readily within the capacity of the auditor to check, and he would no doubt be held responsible for any inaccuracies therein. As to the general principles involved, all that he can do is to see that they appear to be upon the right lines; that they are consistent with the principles employed upon previous occasions; and that the results shown by the accounts, as framed upon these principles, are consistent and reasonably probable in view of all the circumstances. At the time we devoted a series of articles to the discussion of the facts in connection with *The Kingston Cotton Mills* case from this point of view, and those of our readers who wish to pursue the subject further might with advantage refer to those articles.

### Preparation of Balance Sheets.

"What is an auditor's duty as regards the "intentional undervaluation of assets in a "Balance Sheet?"

Upon this point a somewhat voluminous discussion occurred quite recently in these columns, arising out of a lecture delivered at Manchester last year by Mr. EDWIN MOSS, F.C.A., to which attention might advan-. tageously be directed. From what then transpired it will be clear to our readers that the subject is one upon which authorities are by no means unanimous. The view which we ourselves hold, however, is that so long as the undervaluation is made in good faith and is not excessive, it is not for the auditor to interfere. Directors are clearly entitled to write down the value of assets to any reasonable extent in order to fully protect themselves against the charge of having overvalued them ; but it is equally clear that they are not entitled to juggle with the figures, with a view to equalising the profits of successive years when in point of fact true accounts would show that those profits were liable to serious fluctuations.

### Audit of Firms and Companies.

" How far should an auditor check details in " an audit ? "

Upon this point the view which we think most of our readers will be inclined to uphold is that it is the duty of the auditor to do whatever work may be necessary in order to satisfy himself that the figures which he certifies represent a correct summary of the transactions which have taken place during the period under review, so far as it is humanly possible to represent such transactions in figures at the time when the accounts are being prepared and audited. From this it will be seen that if an auditor omits to check any details in connection with the compilation of this summary, he does so at his own peril ; and, in spite of what may be said to the contrary, we feel ourselves that, in the interests of the public, no other view could possibly be safely held by the Courts in connection with the matter. It may of course be, and frequently is, the case that the enormous number of entries in connection with the accounts renders it absolutely impossible for each separate figure to be gone over by the auditor. But, as a matter of fact, it is, under any proper system of accounts a perfectly simple matter to make absolutely certain of the correctness of the summarised figures without going into every detail. It is in judging what must be checked in detail and what may be checked by total that a professional accountant is able to show his skill in accounts, and his superiority as an auditor over any laymen who may have been appointed to the same position. It would, we feel confident, be as disastrous to the interests of the profession as to those of the public to lay down any hard and fast rule absolving the auditor from the final and personal responsibility as to the selection of the detailed work which it is necessary for him to perform. Speaking generally, it may be stated that where there is a good system of internal check the detailed work may be left to look after itself. But in small undertakings, where the bulk of the transactions are recorded by one man (particularly where that same person has the control of the cash), it is essential that the verification of the accounts should be pursued in much greater detail. In any event, however, the transactions should be not merely checked in total, but a portion of the work should be taken at random and fully checked from beginning to end. By this means each member of the staff is kept in a state of constant uncertainty as to whether or not his particular section of the work will be checked by the auditors or not ; and the effect of this, if intelligently carried

out, is to secure all the advantages of a detailed check without anything like the same
expenditure of time as that would involve.

(*To be continued.*)

**Points of Interest to Accountants.**

### V.

*How can an Auditor best check outstanding*
*Book Debts ?*

THIS is a matter to which we have of late
devoted considerable attention, and we
need not recapitulate.   In the case of comparatively small undertakings a really effective
system of internal check is difficult, while
a complete check upon the part of the
auditor is comparatively simple, and therefore,
in such cases, a complete detailed audit is
unquestionably desirable. With really large
undertakings, however, such a complete audit
becomes practically impossible ; partly because
the time available is not sufficient, and partly
because great difficulty would usually be
experienced in arranging for an adequate fee.
We are not prepared to admit that this second
difficulty absolves the auditor from either his
legal or his moral responsibilities ; but, inasmuch as accountants should—above all things
—be practical, it may at least be stated that
such a position of affairs affords a powerful
inducement for them to consider whether it is
possible for them to meet the requirements of
the situation, and at the same time conduct
their business upon profitable lines.   We think
most of our readers will agree that this *is*
possible, if an effective system of internal check
be employed and the assistants selected for the
audit are sufficiently competent.   Such a
system of internal check should provide (1) for
the detailed checking of the Sold Ledgers by a
clerk in the client's employ, other than the
clerk responsible for the keeping of that particular Ledger; (2) for the frequent changing
of clerks from one Ledger to another ; (3) for

the cash not being handled by any of the Ledger clerks; (4) for the statements of account being ordinarily posted to the debtors by the various Ledger clerks themselves, but, from time to time and at unstated intervals, being checked over and posted by some more responsible official. With such a system of internal check, combined with an adequate system of Adjustment Accounts and self - balancing Ledgers, the auditor may rest satisfied if each Ledger balances separately within a certain small minimum allowed difference in books, and if one or two Ledgers (taken at random) are fully checked. The question of outstanding discounts and allowances for bad and doubtful debts will, of course, still have to be provided for ; but for this purpose the same principles will be found in practice to adequately apply. It has quite recently been held by the Irish Court of Appeal (and its decision would doubtless be endorsed by the English Court), that, if there is one point upon which an auditor is in the hands of the officers of a company, it is in connection with the provision for bad and doubtful debts. And, if the system of internal check requires each Ledger clerk to report (say, monthly) to his senior all accounts in arrear, and if these schedules are available for the auditor at the time of audit, there ought, we imagine, to be no difficulty in his settling with the managing director, or other responsible official, upon the reserve that should be made to meet all anticipated loss in connection with outstanding accounts.

*How far should an Auditor rely upon the statements of Officials as to outstanding Accounts?*

To a very large extent this point has already been dealt with by us, and it only remains for us to add that here—as in all other respects in connection with matters of fact outside the ordinary record of the transactions of a company—an auditor is entitled to rely upon the deliberate statements of trusted officials of the company, provided there are no reasonable grounds for suspecting their inaccuracy, arising either from an inspection of the books themselves, or from facts which may otherwise come to his knowledge. The general principles which should be applied we have already enumerated. It is, however, perhaps desirable to add that, although an auditor cannot be reasonably expected to be personally acquainted with the solvency, or otherwise, of any or all of the debtors of a company, yet, in the event of his happening to have any special knowledge upon the subject, it is quite clear that this knowledge must not be ignored. This, however, is only a particular way of stating the general principle that the auditor must act in good faith, and not merely give effect to certain definite sources of information available, but also utilise any casual information that may come into his possession ; and that he must honestly believe in the accuracy of the accounts which he certifies.

*(To be continued.)*

# The Accountant

### THE ORGAN OF CHARTERED ACCOUNTANTS THROUGHOUT THE WORLD.

#### (Awarded Silver Medal, Esposizione Italo-Americana, Genova 1892.)

Vol. XXVI.—New Series.—No. 1322.      Saturday, April 7, 1900.

## Leading Articles.

### Points of Interest to Accountants.

### VI.

CONTINUING this series of articles on the various matters raised at the meetings of the Chartered Accountants Students' Society of Edinburgh, we come to the report, which appeared in our issue of the 13th January last. The first point that calls for attention is the following :—

*Should Arrears of Cumulative Preference Dividend be entered in a Balance Sheet ?*

Inasmuch as this preference dividend does not become payable until sufficient profits have been earned to pay it, it is clear that the arrears cannot be treated as a liability, and in that sense they form no part of the accounts from which the Balance Sheet is compiled; but, at the same time, arrears of cumulative preference dividend are clearly a contingent liability, and should be stated as such upon the Balance Sheet by way of a note. Speaking generally, all contingent liabilities should be recorded in the Balance Sheet; but, even if some are occasionally omitted, upon the ground that there are always contingent liabilities of every undertaking which cannot be assessed, so special an item as arrears of preference dividend should, we think, invariably be specified.

### Trust Accounts.

Another interesting question deals with various points in connection with Trust Accounts, enquiring whether certain items should be charged against capital or income, or whether they are apportionable. The preparation of the trustee's account (where chargeable) is, we think, clearly apportionable in accordance with the subject-matter of the account itself. That is to say, if it dealt exclusively with capital items, the cost would be charged to capital; if it dealt exclusively with revenue items, the cost would be charged to income; and if (as would usually be the case) it dealt with both, then the charge should be apportioned. The same remarks apply to the fee paid for the audit of the trustee's accounts. In practice it is very usual to charge the first year's costs to capital, and those of subsequent years to income.

Another somewhat similar question deals with the case where a special fund has been set aside under a trust for a particular purpose, and enquires whether the cost of administering this special fund should come out of the income and capital of that fund, or out of the general estate. This is a question which could not possibly be answered without a careful perusal of the exact words of the trust deed. Any properly drawn trust deed would naturally provide for the matter, but, if the cost were not expressly provided for, it would be necessary to carefully peruse the exact wording, with a view to gathering the intention. Where the intention is that the whole of the income arising from certain investments should be applied for particular purposes, it may very well be held that the cost of administering the fund should come out of the general estate. Where, on the other hand, the intention is that a certain sum should be set aside for particular purposes, then it might be held that the amount to be charged against the general estate is limited to the fund so set aside, and that any cost of administering this particular fund should be paid for out of the fund itself.

### Can outlay for Advertising under any circumstances be entered as an Asset in the Balance Sheet?

The most obvious answer to a question of this kind is that unhesitatingly it "can" be so entered, and it would be quite possible to enter other even more unlikely items as assets. We take it that what is really intended is to enquire whether such outlay *may* properly be entered as an asset, and this is, of course, a question requiring more consideration. The justification for temporarily capitalising any portion of expenditure upon advertising cannot rest upon the allegation that the portion sought to be capitalised is a valuable asset. It must rather rest upon the ground that it is unfair to the revenue of that particular period that it should be charged with the whole cost incurred up to date. Where this proposition can be sustained, it is clearly permissible to spread the expenditure over a reasonable term of years; and it is, in our view, only under such circumstances, and upon such grounds, that it is permissible to hold in suspense any portion of the expenditure upon advertising that may have been incurred. Until the suspended balance is written off, it must, of course, in the nature of things, appear upon the assets' side of the Balance Sheet; but, at the same time, it cannot by any stretch of imagination, be said to *be* an asset, and the item should, therefore, be clearly explained on the face of the accounts.

### Should an Auditor check Cash in hand?

This question (if we may be allowed to say so without disrespect) strikes us as being childish in the extreme. Opinions of accountants may differ upon various matters in connection with auditing, both in theory and in practice; but if there is one point upon which we had imagined that all practitioners were agreed it is the vital importance of cash in hand being actually counted by an auditor, not merely once a year, when the annual Balance Sheet is being certified, but also at frequent intervals wherever a continuous audit takes place. The rule laid down in many accountants' offices is that, in the case of a continuous audit, the cash in hand is to be counted at every visit.

### Verifying the existence of Investments.

The last point with which we have now to deal asks whether an auditor is entitled to pass as a proper voucher a certificate written by a banker, or law agent, that certain securities are in his custody, or whether he should in all cases ask for the production of the securities. This, it seems to us, is largely a matter of degree. A banker's certificate (if accompanied, as it should be, by the qualification that the documents in question are held for safe custody only) would usually be regarded as sufficient; but, if the value of the securities in question is considerable, certainly no harm would be done by requiring them to be produced. Of course, in the case of a bank audit, the bankers' own certificate would be considered of no value. With regard to the question of the certificate of a law agent, here again much must be left to the discretion of the individual auditor. For comparatively small items his certificate might well be accepted, provided that, under all the circumstances of the case, it was reasonable that the documents in question should be with the solicitor; but it could never be thought unreasonable, if the auditor wished an actual inspection in each case. If anything went wrong, and he had not actually inspected the securities, the onus would rest with him to show that, under the circumstances, the precautions that he did take were reasonable. We may mention, however, that, where the securities in question are in the hands of third parties as cover for advances made, it would, under almost all circumstances, be reasonable to accept a certificate of the third party in question (or of their solicitors) that the securities were in their possession. The reason for this difference in practice is, however, not far to seek, inasmuch as any defalcation or misstatement would in such a case be made by outside parties, who are in no way interested in the audit, and who are therefore more entitled to be relied upon. Where, however, securities of considerable value had been deposited for a comparatively small loan, it would undoubtedly be wise to make an appointment to inspect them, in order to see that they remained intact.

*(To be continued.)*

## Directors v. Auditors.

### The Golden Grain Bread Company, Lim.

IN our issue of the 27th May last we drew attention at some length to the position of affairs then obtaining between the directors and shareholders of the Golden Grain Bread Company, Lim., and the company's auditors, Messrs. PRATT, NORTON & Co., Chartered Accountants. It will be remembered that, at the ordinary meeting of the company, held on the 15th May last, accounts were submitted showing a balance available for dividend of £2,913 10s. 5d., out of which the directors recommended that all preference dividends due up to date (amounting to 10½ per cent.) should be paid. The auditors, however, expressed the view that this balance was not available for dividend, on the ground that the assets were overstated in the Balance Sheet, and that losses actually incurred had not been made good out of revenue. The directors produced in support of their contention a valuation made some four years previously, in which the assets of the company (exclusive of goodwill) were assessed at £50,000. Mr. B. T. NORTON, F.C.A., pointed out, however, that the assets were valued in the Balance Sheet at £68,500, of which £18,000 represented an accumulation of expenditure on about 50 depôts opened at various times, 42 of which had since been closed without any provision being made in the accounts for the consequent loss in connection with the expenditure of fitting these depôts up. Buildings, plant, etc., represented £31,500, the valuation of which the auditors did not contest; while the remaining £19,000 was made up of Goodwill £15,000, and £4,000 for Establishment Account and repairs and renewals. These items Mr. NORTON described as "being "altogether fictitious when considered as an "asset."

The view adopted by the shareholders at this meeting was, as we pointed out at the time, somewhat unintelligible, inasmuch as they re-elected both the retiring directors and the auditors, but did not vote the payment of any dividend on the preference shares. But it is at least clear that they were then sufficiently impressed with the auditors' contention to accept their view of the situation that no dividend could properly be declared.

Considerable interest therefore attaches to the proceedings at the ordinary meeting, held this year on the 3rd inst. At this meeting the Chairman stated that, after writing off £4,000 from the leases, and £4,775, the amount of "accumulated discrepancies in the accounts of "former years," there remained an available sum of £2,665, out of which the directors recommended the payment of a dividend of 7 per cent. on the cumulative preference shares for the year ended 30th June 1898, carrying forward £515. It is not easy to trace the connection between these various figures and those presented a year ago, but we imagine that the so-called "asset" of £4,000 for Establishment Account and repairs and renewals has now been eliminated, and that the sum of £4,000 has been written off the item £18,000, which represents the expenditure upon 50 depôts, 42 of which have been closed. But, however that may be, the fact that after a lapse of twelve months it is only recommended that one year's preference dividend should be paid, whereas a year ago the directors wished to pay a preference dividend for the past eighteen months, is abundant justification of the attitude then taken up by the auditors, that these arrears of preference dividend ought not then to be paid, and the shareholders may reasonably congratulate themselves upon having had the good sense to fall in with this view.

With regard to the valuation of assets, the Chairman went on to state that they had had a further valuation made by Messrs. TOPLIS & HARDING, which fully bore out that previously made by Messrs. HOBSON, RICHARDS & Co., in that the company's loose plant, machinery, stables, horses, vans, &c. (exclusive of goodwill), were stated to be worth £51,952 as a going concern. The amount at which they appear on the Balance Sheet presented at the recent meeting is not clear from the report before us, but it is evident that there is a considerable discrepancy between the valuation of the tangible assets, and the total of the assets appearing in the accounts, which is presumably represented by the value placed upon the goodwill by the directors; while, bearing in mind the fact that the company's profits do not represent even 4 per cent. upon its total paid-up capital, it is clear that a strictly moderate estimate ought to be placed upon the present value of the item "Goodwill."

What view the company's auditors would have taken with regard to the matter in face of the recent re-valuation, it is, however, impossible to say, for the simple reason that the directors appear to have so little taken the auditors into their confidence that Mr. NORTON stated at the meeting that he heard from the Chairman's address for the first time that a re-valuation had been made at all. As to what it contained, and upon what it was based, he expressed himself as being entirely ignorant; but he pointed out that the original valuation of Messrs. HOBSON, RICHARDS & Co. (upon which his firm's observations were founded) had, in his opinion, been based upon data that were wrong.

One would imagine that where an apparently irreconcilable difference of opinion existed between a board of directors and a firm of auditors, both parties would gladly welcome the appointment of an independent committee of investigation to make full enquiry into all the circumstances, with the aid of such outside professional assistance as they might find necessary. A proposition to this effect was put forward at the meeting, but—this year as last—it was defeated; and, according to the report of the meeting appearing in *The Times*, it was defeated only by the directors making use of the proxies which had been sent in in their favour. The adoption of the report and accounts was then carried, and the payment of the proposed dividend sanctioned.

On the question of the re-appointment of auditors, the Chairman declared that Messrs. PRATT, NORTON & Co., were not re-elected on 'a show of hands, and, in answer to a shareholder, stated that if a poll were demanded the directors would use their proxies against the re-election of the former auditors. The meeting was accordingly adjourned for a week for the purpose of appointing these officers, and at the adjourned meeting Mr. J. F. LOVERING, F.C.A. (of the firm of JOHN F. LOVERING & Co.), and a Mr. GLENN were elected, the

Chairman explaining that the directors "re-"quired," in addition to the appointment of a Chartered Accountant, "the election of an "experienced commercial man well versed in "accounts."

It will be seen that, stated shortly, the position of affairs is that for some little time past there has been the widest difference of opinion between the directors and the auditors as to what items may properly be regarded as assets in the company's accounts, what values may be attached to these items, and what balance remained upon the Revenue Account as profit available for distribution. The directors have apparently vetoed any independent enquiry into the matter by a committee of representative shareholders, and have now, according to the report of the meeting, taken an active part in the dismissal of the auditors. It, of course, remains to be seen whether, under the circumstances, the auditors recently appointed will consent to act; but, even in the event of their doing so, it is, we think, impossible to justify the refusal of the directors that the dispute shall be referred to an independent committee—the more so as, in the event of its ever transpiring in the future that the stand taken by Messrs. PRATT, NORTON & Co. was justified, the directors will undoubtedly have incurred a very serious responsibility indeed in the payment of the dividend declared on the 3rd inst.

From the information before us, it seems quite clear that the directors have defended their omission to write off against revenue the items in dispute, by alleging that the actually existing assets of the company (including goodwill) are equal to, or in excess of, the book value of the assets appearing in the Balance Sheet. If it were merely a case of setting off the appreciation of some fixed assets against the depreciation of other fixed assets, such a policy could, of course, be easily defended, at all events to the extent of admitting that, in the present unsettled state of the law, there appears to be no compulsion upon the part of the company to provide for the depreciation of such fixed assets as have depreciated out of revenue. But that is not what we understand to be the position here. It seems clear that among other items that have been written up must be included the Goodwill Account; and, although in a sense goodwill is a "fixed" asset, it is perfectly clear that no appreciation of its value (even if clearly existent) could be properly taken into account so as to increase the total value of the assets appearing upon the face of the Balance Sheet.

The whole position of affairs is, it seems to us, one that demanded the utmost circumspection upon the part of the directors, more particularly in view of the fact that the payment of a preference dividend is—under all the circumstances—clearly an advantage given to the holders of preference shares at the expense of the holders of ordinary shares, in that by such payment the working capital of the company is depleted. If the balance of Revenue Account is legally available for the payment of such a dividend, nothing can of course be said against it; but so important a question ought not to be merely decided by the votes of shareholders, all of whom are naturally personally interested one way or the other. It is a question partly of law, and partly of account. The officers of the company responsible for its accounts had given it as their opinion that the proposed dividend ought not to be paid, while no mention is made of the company's solicitors having held a contrary view. In such a position it seems to us that the most prudent course for the directors to have adopted (and it is, perhaps, not too late to adopt it even now) would be to apply to the Court, by way of an application in the name of some holder of ordinary shares, for an injunction to restrain the company from paying the preference dividend. The matter could then be fully and fairly argued; and, whichever way the decision went, both the directors and the auditors would be absolved from all further responsibility.

## Auditors and Depreciation.

IT is, we think, desirable to draw attention to some of the remarks made by Mr. ARCHIBALD COATS (the Chairman of J. & P. COATS, Lim.) on the occasion of the recent annual meeting of that company.

In explaining some of the various items in the Balance Sheet, Mr. COATS stated that on the credit side "there was an item of about "£10,000 for renewals which had been de-"ducted from the depreciation." The auditors, he stated, would have preferred that only a portion of this £10,000 should have been so deducted, leaving about £3,000 to be taken from revenue; but the directors had not adopted this view because they considered that the rates of depreciation employed were quite ample to cover the total. Such questions as this, the Chairman stated, arose from time to time. They might discontinue using buildings or machinery, or make other changes which reduced the realisable value of certain assets, but if the value and earning capacity of others was correspondingly increased thereby, they did not propose to adjust the accounts in such a manner as to lead to the erroneous supposition that the aggregate value of their assets had undergone any change. Mr. COATS added that the matter was too complicated to enable him to go into details—and certainly his reported explanation is not particularly lucid;

but we gather that, in the opinion of the auditors, something like £3,000 should have been charged against revenue in respect of depreciation, which the directors have preferred to provide for out of reserve fund.

Mr. COATS added that he wished the shareholders to understand that the directors considered themselves the best judges of the extent to which mills and machinery depreciated; and that, whilst it was their duty to make ample provision for wear and tear, they were of opinion that no useful purpose was served by writing off more. No exception, can, of course, be taken to directors appreciating their responsibilities to the full. And inasmuch as every properly constituted board should of course (at all events theoretically) include practical men versed in every department of the business carried on, it is quite clear that a board of directors—as a board — may be reasonably expected to be able to express an authoritative opinion upon such a question as the amount of provision necessary for depreciation. It is probable that the shareholders of Messrs. J. & P. COATS, Lim., are exceptionally fortunate in the *personnel* of their board of directors; but such an attitude is one which, we think, is deserving. of general encouragement, and one which might with advantage be adopted by the directors of other companies.

But—and this is a very large "but"—we are by no means sure that Mr. COATS does not go too far when he adds that should any question of account arise which requires consideration it will be discussed with the auditors, but the directors reserve to themselves the right of deciding such question, and they accept full responsibility in connection therewith. It is, of course, quite clear that the accounts submitted to shareholders at general meetings are the accounts of the directors, and that it is their duty, as well as their right, to make these accounts correct to the best of *their* knowledge and belief. It may also be added that, whether they choose to accept the position or not, the full responsibility for the accuracy of the accounts must always rest with the directors. But, on the other hand, it should be remembered that the auditor has also his duties and his responsibilities in the matter. For our own part, as we have already stated, we consider that for all practical purposes the Companies Act, 1900, adds nothing to the previous responsibilities of company auditors. However that may be, auditors will, after the first January next (even if they are not required to do so now) have to definitely certify whether the Balance Sheet is properly drawn up so as to exhibit a true and correct view of the state of the company's affairs, as shown by its books. It is, therefore, quite a mistake to suppose that where the directors have discussed a question of accounting with the auditor, and — having disagreed with his opinions—have adopted their own views, the matter is then and there at an end. It is, as we have already stated, the directors, and not the auditor, who have to prepare the accounts, and they are responsible for the accuracy of the accounts which they submit, while in exceptional instances it may quite well be the case that upon some points the opinion of the board of directors is more entitled to consideration than that of the auditor. Nevertheless, certain duties and responsibilities are cast upon the auditor which must not be ignored, and which are not necessarily disposed of by his deferring his own opinion to that of the directors. We take it that in cases where there is a difference of opinion between the directors and the auditor, and neither is able to convince the other, it is the duty of the directors to frame the accounts in what they consider to be the proper manner, and for the auditor to report explicitly in what respects he considers that the accounts ought to have been differently treated.

In the case of a company like J. & P. COATS, Lim., the auditor very possibly may feel that he may quite safely leave the question of depreciation in the hands of the directors, but such an attitude would be by no means equally safe in connection with all other companies. The suggestion that after the directors have discussed the matter with the auditor they are free to adopt what course they choose, and no further enquiry is called for upon the part of the shareholders, is, we think, one which, if extended to other undertakings, might prove extremely dangerous.

## The Duties of Auditors under the Companies Act, 1900.

ALTHOUGH the new Companies Act has been very fully discussed for the past six years, and has been enacted for nearly the past six months, there would still appear to be some doubt as to what its precise effect will be upon the accountancy profession, particularly in respect of the duties of auditors thereunder. A correspondent, writing in our issue of the 8th inst., suggested that a series of articles dealing with the subject would probably be found of general interest, and we therefore propose to deal with the matter in this and the next issue, so that our comments may be available before the 1st January next, when the Act comes into full operation.

We are a little surprised to notice that at a recent company meeting a member of a well-known firm of Chartered Accountants frankly stated that he did not know what the effect of the new Act would be, and that he himself had hardly read it.

A careful perusal of the text of the Act is, indeed, most important for all practitioners, seeing that the Act comes into force in its entirety on the 1st January next; and this applies not merely to all companies registered after that date, but also to all companies then in existence. Inasmuch, therefore, as company auditing forms a very appreciable proportion of the connection of most practitioners, it is extremely desirable, to say the least of it, that they should be fully acquainted with the manner in which (if at all) this portion of their work is affected by the new legislation.

With regard to companies already in existence, where auditors have already been appointed these auditors continue office under the new Act until the next ordinary general meeting; but in future every company will be obliged to have auditors whether or not any have been appointed up to the present. And even those companies which have had auditors who, under their special articles of association, have been appointed by the directors, will now, at their next ordinary general meeting, have to place the appointment of auditors and their remuneration in the hands of the shareholders. Casual vacancies in the post of auditor may, however, now be filled up by the directors—and this even in the case of those companies which, by their articles of association, may require that an extraordinary general meeting be called for the purpose of making such appointment to fill any casual vacancy in the office of auditor. Where no appointment is otherwise made, the Act gives power to the Board of Trade to appoint an auditor and to fix his remuneration on the application of any shareholder.

So far as the appointment of an auditor is concerned the new regulations are in some respects ahead of the previous custom, and in some respects considerably behind it. The compulsory audit is undoubtedly a step in the right direction; but, as no provision whatever is made for qualified persons being appointed auditors, or for their receiving anything like an adequate remuneration, the improvement is more apparent than real—the more so as directors have now, in all cases, power to fill up any vacancy caused by the resignation of an auditor. The fact that the appointment is still an annual one, makes the continuance of the auditor in office for all practical purposes very largely dependent upon his continuing to please the directors—*i.e.*, the very persons whom he is expected to supervise.

*Primâ facie*, some improvement is effected by Section 21, which provides that no director or officer shall be elegible to be appointed an auditor; but the provision is distinctly unsatisfactory in that while apparently attempting to cope with an admitted abuse it fails to do so effectively. The probability is that a director or other officer is never auditor of the company unless it is a purely family concern, where no one is harmed by the dual appointment. But in public companies, cases are not unknown in which the partner of the auditor is a director or other officer; and this is a position of affairs which, apparently, will still be allowed to continue under the new Act, although it must very effectually interfere with the impartiality and independence of the audit.

As to the actual duties of auditors when appointed, these are provided for by Section 23, which reads as follows :—

> Every auditor of a company shall have a right of access at all times to the books and accounts and vouchers of the company, and shall be entitled to require from the directors and officers of the company such information and explanation as may be necessary for the performance of the duties of the auditors; and the auditors shall sign a certificate at the foot of the Balance Sheet stating whether or not all their requirements as auditors have been complied with, and shall make a report to the shareholders on the accounts examined by them, and on every Balance Sheet laid before the company in general meeting during their tenure of office; and in every such report shall state whether, in their opinion, the Balance Sheet referred to in the report is properly drawn up, so as to exhibit a true and correct view of the state of the company's affairs as shown by the books of the company; and such report shall be read before the company in general meeting.

These provisions are very similar in effect to those contained in the Companies Act, 1879, which relates to banking companies incorporated thereunder, and they are also very similar to what may be called the normal type of articles of association. That being so, it bears out our previous opinion that nothing has now been added to the duties of company auditors which had not been already anticipated by the best firms in the course of their usual practice. But the question has been raised—and it is one upon which there would appear to be some uncertainty—as to whether it is necessary for an auditor to *at all times* report to the shareholders, in addition to signing a certificate at the foot of the Balance Sheet. In this connection, an enquiry into the usual practice hitherto obtaining may not be found unprofitable. Directors and shareholders naturally prefer a short and unqualified

auditor's certificate to the accounts. As this preference is very generally shared by auditors, the custom has arisen for auditors not merely to examine the accounts in the form in which they are put before them, and to comment upon them in that form alone, but rather for them —where alterations appear to be necessary—to discuss the matter with the directors, and in general to get their recommendations adopted, so that in the end the accounts as rendered may be unconditionally certified as full and true. We imagine that, strictly speaking, it is no part of an auditor's duty to go out of his way to teach the directors the manner in which they should present their accounts for audit. He would be within the legal limits of his duties if he merely took the accounts submitted to him and investigated and reported upon them in their then existing form. But the effect of a qualified certificate—or of a report to the shareholders in the absence of any certificate at all—would be so serious that no auditor would care to see such a course adopted unless the facts showed it to be absolutely necessary. It is probable that not one company Balance Sheet in a hundred reaches the shareholders in exactly the same form as that in which it was put before the auditor; and those who are for ever asking " What is the value of an audit ? " would probably find the best answer to their question in a consideration as to what this statement implies. The most valuable audit is that which can achieve its end without the whole of the working being apparent to the outside world.

Having now briefly indicated the ordinary practice, we may point out that Section 23 appears to have been framed in ignorance of this custom. If an absolutely unqualified certificate is really all that an auditor has to report to the shareholders, then it is obvious that he will have nothing to add to the certificate as to the accuracy of the Balance Sheet, which the Act requires him to affix to the foot thereof, and no harm can possibly be done by omitting to give one. At the same time, now that the Legislature expressly requires that a report shall be addressed to the shareholders, considerable responsibility will necessarily rest with the auditor who omits to make such a report, especially if there is anything like a conflict of opinion as to whether or not anything ought to have been brought before the shareholders beyond the mere fact that the accounts, as rendered, are correct. For our own part, we think that it will not be necessary for an auditor to recount to the shareholders the various steps leading to his certification of the accounts. But if any outstanding points still remain in which there is a *bonâ fide* difference of opinion between the directors and the auditor, these will naturally very properly form the subject of a report to the shareholders. Inasmuch as the Act does not provide that this report shall be printed, but that it is merely to be read to the shareholders at the general meeting, the auditor will be freer to state to the shareholders exactly what is in his mind than would be the case were his report to be at once made public to the outside world. At the same time, it should be borne in mind that there is nothing particularly original about auditors specially reporting to shareholders. It is, we imagine, the usual custom to do so where it appears apparent that there is anything definite to be reported, and recent decisions have shown that the custom is by no means unknown to the Courts. We take it that such a report will now become more general, because, under the new Act, the onus will lie on the auditor to show that the report was entirely unnecessary if not given; but, at the same time, in cases where there is really nothing to add to a formal certification of the accounts as rendered, it would, we take it, be quite unnecessary to issue any separate report with regard to the matter. The certificate appended to the foot of the Balance Sheet should, however, we think, clearly state whether or not any further report has been made.

*(To be continued.)*

# The Accountant

**THE** ORGAN OF CHARTERED ACCOUNTANTS THROUGHOUT THE **WORLD.**

(Awarded Silver Medal, Esposizione Italo-Americana, Genova 1892.)

VOL. XXVI.—NEW SERIES.—NO. 1359.　　　SATURDAY, DECEMBER 22, 1900.

## Leading Articles.

### The Duties of Auditors under the Companies Act, 1900.

#### II.

IN our article on the above subject, which
appeared last week, we dealt with the
appointment of auditors under the new Companies Act, and their duties under Section 23
thereof. A perusal of our Correspondence
columns will have shown that there is some
difference of opinion, even among leading practitioners, as to the precise effect which this
section will have, and, in particular, as to
whether it will always necessitate a special
report to the shareholders of the company on

the accounts, in addition to a certificate at the foot of the published Balance Sheet that the auditor's requirements have been complied with. It is probably unnecessary for us to again go over the ground which we covered last week, but we should like to point out in particular that the strict letter of the Act does not require the certificate at the foot of the Balance Sheet to state whether or not the Balance Sheet is, in the opinion of the auditors, a full and truthful one, properly exhibiting the state of the company's affairs. Attention may also be profitably directed to the point raised by Mr. D. F. BASDEN, F.C.A., in his letter appearing in our last issue —namely, that the report mentioned in Section 23 is to cover not merely the Balance Sheet laid before the company in general meeting, but also whatever accounts have been examined by the auditors. This presumably would include not merely the Trading and Profit and Loss Accounts (one or both of which might be appended to the published accounts), but also the actual accounts, or books of account, of the company.

Another important point, which we do not remember to have seen commented upon as yet, is the provision that *every* Balance Sheet submitted to shareholders in general meeting must in future be reported upon by the auditors of the company for the time being. This will clearly apply not merely to annual meetings and annual accounts, but also to special or extraordinary general meetings, and anything in the nature of a Balance Sheet which may then be laid before the shareholders. This provision is extremely valuable, in view of the growing practice on the part of certain classes of companies of going into voluntary liquidation, or of passing resolutions for reconstruc-tion, without submitting audited accounts to their shareholders.

Another provision of the new Act which may prove of far-reaching importance is Section 21 (3), which provides that a director or officer of the company shall " not be capable of being " appointed " auditor of the company. *Per contra*, we take it that an auditor, having once been appointed, *ipso facto* vacates his post if he subsequently becomes a director or officer of the company. This point is, however, by no means clear, and it could be wished that the language of the Act had been more explicit. As we pointed out last week, the cases in which the same person is appointed the director or secretary of a company and also its auditor are extremely few, although provision might advantageously have been made for dealing with dual appointments held by partners of the same firm. But a question which will far more frequently arise in practice is as to whether it is now legally possible for the auditor of a company to be also its accountant—that is to say, whether or not Section 21 (3) prohibits auditors from doing any work in connection with the actual preparation of the accounts which they are afterwards called upon to verify. In the case of small companies which cannot afford the expense of a really qualified bookkeeper, there is much to be said in favour of the books being balanced and the final accounts prepared by the auditor or his staff ; but in the case of important concerns, where the motive of economy does not reasonably apply, these advantages are entirely over-balanced by the fact that the person who has actually kept the books and prepared the final accounts therefrom is not so well suited as a stranger to bring to bear upon those same accounts the critical inspection that an auditor ought always to have at his command. We think it extremely likely that the intention of the Legislature was to provide that the auditor should not come upon the scene until all the constructive work in connection with the accounts had been performed.

As to whether Section 21 (3) really achieves this object is, we think, doubtful, and depends very largely upon what is covered by the term " officer of the company," and also as to whether there is anything to compel an auditor to vacate his appointment if he subsequently becomes such an officer. There can, we think, be little doubt, in view of all the decisions that have been given, that a person who is regularly appointed to perform any specified piece of work of a recurring nature for a company *is* an " officer " of the company. That being so, a person who is employed to balance the company's books, or to prepare the final accounts from its books after they have been balanced, must be an officer of the company unless the appointment is of a casual description—*i.e.*, for one particular occasion only. If, therefore, the arrangement between the auditor and the company be that the remuneration which is paid to him is to cover the preparation of the final accounts in addition to the auditing of the books, it is clear that the auditor is acting in a dual capacity, more or less in contravention of Section 21 (3), according to how strictly the wording of that subsection may be interpreted. It seems to us that, in future, auditors will be wise to abstain from entering into any such arrangement. This is a point upon which a full discussion by practitioners would doubtless be found beneficial.

Another very important duty devolving upon auditors under the new Act arises under Section 12 (3), which requires the auditors, if they are appointed before the statutory meeting, to certify the report which the directors are required to forward to every member of the company at least seven days before the day on which such statutory meeting is held, in so far as the report relates to the shares allotted by the company, to the cash received in respect of such shares, and to the receipts and payments of the company on Capital Account. This, however, is absolutely straightforward work, dealing exclusively with facts readily capable of absolute verification, so that no difficulties are likely to arise in connection with the practical working of this subsection.

There is one point, however, which it seems to us has still not been dealt with by the Legislature—namely, as to what exactly constitutes the formal appointment of an auditor where such appointment is made prior to the statutory meeting. If made subsequently to the statutory meeting the appointment has to be with the shareholders, and a resolution of the shareholders in general meeting (or, failing that, an order by the Board of Trade) will actually constitute the appointment; but the auditors may be named in the prospectus of the company, or they may be appointed by the directors prior to the statutory meeting. If appointed by the directors, a resolution passed by the Board at one of their meetings will constitute the persons nominated the auditors of the company until the first annual general meeting; but where the auditors are named in the prospectus we are by no means clear as to whether that in itself constitutes their appointment. The prospectus is ordinarily settled by the promoter, and is frequently completed prior to the registration of the company. The mere adoption of an auditor's name in a prospectus under the old Act did not constitute the person so named the auditor of the company until he had been formally appointed by the directors. Section 9 (2) of the new Act, which requires the prospectus to be signed by every person named therein as a director, and to be filed on or before the date of its publication may—and very probably is intended to—act as a formal appointment of the auditor named therein by the directors. But, if so, the position might, we think, have been more clearly stated with advantage, as *primâ facie* there would be nothing to prevent the directors (so long as they acted in good faith) from changing their mind as to who should be the auditor of the company at any time before the statutory meeting, so long as they had not previously formally exercised their power on making an appointment. But, however this may be, there is at least this improvement upon the previous position of affairs, that the auditor named in the prospectus will, at all events, know where he stands before the date of the statutory meeting, instead of—as under the Act of 1862 —having to wait until the books are balanced for the first time if the directors are determined to keep him at arm's length in the meanwhile.

In conclusion, we may express the view that too narrow an interpretation of the provisions of this measure is to be deprecated. The intentions of the Legislature are, in general, sufficiently obvious, and accountants will be best advised to act up to them than to consider too closely the letter of the Act.

Since the above article has been in type, the Council of the Institute has published the opinion it has obtained from eminent counsel as to the interpretation of the audit clauses. This opinion appears in another column, and will form the subject of further comment next week.

# The Accountant

### THE ORGAN OF CHARTERED ACCOUNTANTS THROUGHOUT THE WORLD.

**(Awarded Silver Medal, Esposizione Italo-Americana, Genova 1892.)**

VOL. XXVI.—NEW SERIES.—NO. 1360.　　　　SATURDAY, DECEMBER 29, 1900.

## Leading Articles.

---

### The Duties of Auditors under the Companies Act, 1900.

---

### III.

IN our last issue we were able to give a copy of the joint opinion of Messrs. R. B. HALDANE, Q.C., M.P., C. SWINFEN EADY, Q.C., A. R. KIRBY, and F. B. PALMER, as to those clauses in the new Companies Act affecting the duties of auditors. This opinion did not reach us until after our last week's article was in type, but there are one or two points on which it appears desirable for us to add to what we have already stated.

Dealing with the paragraphs in the order in which they appear, we venture to think that, obscure as the new Act is in some of its sections, it is almost outried by Paragraph (1) in construction. It is difficult for ordinary laymen, unfamiliar with the technicalities of the subject, to interpret this paragraph. Having, however, some idea as to what would possibly have been passing through the minds of counsel at the time, we suggest that what they mean is that where either the Companies Act, 1879, or the articles of association or regulations of a company, have prescribed certain duties for the auditor, so far as these are not contradicted by the Act of 1900 they will continue to be in force, even although they may impose obligations beyond those imposed by the Act of 1900.

With regard to Paragraph (2), the view that Minute Books and Letter Books are "books of "the company" within the meaning of Section 23 is of interest, although, perhaps, the point was hardly seriously in doubt. There is, however, we think, this particular distinction, that whereas an auditor should in all cases carefully read through the whole of the Minute Book, he could never be seriously expected to adopt the same course in connection with the Letter Books.

In Paragraph (3) the opinion is expressed that the noun "requirements" employed in Section 23 has a much wider significance than the verb "require," used four lines previously. This may or may not be the case, but it would

no doubt be only prudent to attach the widest possible interpretation to both.

Paragraph (4) suggests that, even where there is no Balance Sheet in existence, it may be necessary for the auditors to issue a report. Such a case might, we suppose, arise; but it is extremely improbable, in the event of no Balance Sheet being prepared, that the auditors would be called upon to examine any accounts at all, and the Act only requires them to "report to the shareholders on the accounts "examined by them, and on every Balance "Sheet laid before the company in general "meeting."

In Paragraph (5) counsel confirm our previously expressed view that the certificate and the report referred to in Section 23 are intended by the Legislature to be separate entities; but we think it is carrying matters rather far to suggest that, even when both are placed at the foot of the Balance Sheet, they must be separate, and separately signed. We take it that, whatever the literal meaning of the words quoted from the section may be, there is no harm in employing a little common sense in their interpretation. If all that need be said can be conveniently said at the foot of the Balance Sheet, we think it rather straining a point to suggest that the Act would be infringed, if it be condensed into one statement over one signature instead of being separated into two statements, each of which is separately signed. We imagine, however, that the requirements with reference to the report arise from a knowledge that auditors do frequently find it desirable to report to shareholders, and that (as matters now stand) it does not appear that such reports invariably find their way to the shareholders. The essential provision of this portion of the section is, we take it, that such a report shall be given by the auditor where necessary, and that, where given, it shall be read at the general meeting.

With regard to Paragraph (6), suggesting *pro formâ* wording for the auditors' certificate and auditors' report, we can only express the view that, had it been considered that any stereotyped wording would be generally effective, a prescribed form would probably have been included in the Act itself.  In spite, therefore, of the authority of counsel, we think that no hard and fast form can be adhered to, save in cases where it is clearly adequate in view of the requirements.

The concluding paragraph, expressing the view that the words " as shown by the books " of the company " do not limit the auditor's duties to a comparison of the figures, is quite in accordance with the opinion previously expressed by other authorities.  As has been frequently pointed out, an investigation which has been limited to a comparison of the Balance Sheet with the books will be for every purpose valueless.  We take it, therefore, that, if these qualifying words 'have any meaning at all, it is merely that if the record contained in all the books consistently testifies to the correctness of the published accounts, the auditor should  not be held liable in cases of elaborate falsification which could not have been discovered by the exercise of reasonable diligence and skill.

Whatever its merits, however, the document has this important value -- that the auditor who acts upon it cannot be said to have acted without due care, even if it should subsequently transpire that the Courts took a different view as to the meaning of the Act.

356

## The Institute of Chartered Accountants in England and Wales.

THE Council of the Institute have had Counsel's opinion on the clauses of the new Companies Act affecting Auditors and Accountants, which is as follows :—

(1)　In our opinion the provisions contained in Sections 21, 22, and 23 of the Companies Act, 1900, are supplemental to and not in substitution for provisions as to audit contained in the Companies Act, 1879 (where applicable), and in Articles of Association or Regulations of a Company, and, accordingly, we are of opinion that the Act of 1900 does not relieve an Auditor from the necessity of complying with such provisions, even though the latter impose obligations beyond those imposed by the Act of 1900. In so far, however, as the Act of 1900 is inconsistent with the earlier provisions, the Act must, of course, prevail.

(2)　In our opinion the words " books of the Com- " pany " in Section 23, which gives to the Auditor a right of access at all times to the books and accounts and vouchers of the Company, mean all the books—not merely the books of account of the Company; the words, therefore, include the Minute Books and Letter Books.

(3)　In our opinion the word " requirements " in Section 23, which makes it necessary for the Auditor's Certificate to state whether or not his requirements as Auditor have been complied with, is used in its popular sense, and not as referring merely to what he is entitled to require under the preceding words of the section.

(4)　In our opinion where the auditor's requirements are not complied with the Auditor should specify in his Certificate in what respects they have not been complied with ; and if there is no Balance Sheet on which to place the Certificate then the Auditor should so specify in his Report. But if the specification of the instances of non-compliance be lengthy we see no objection to the Certificate stating that all the requirements have not been complied with without specification of details, provided that it refers to the report for the details.

(5)　In our opinion the Certificate and Report referred to in Section 23 must be separate and separately signed, even though both be placed on the Balance Sheet. There would, however, be no objection, if it be desired, to connect the Certificate with the Report by inserting in the Certificate a reference to the " subjoined " or " accompanying " Report ; and, as an alternative, where thought expedient, the Certificate might set out the Report verbatim, thus :—I certify, etc., and I report to the Shareholders that, etc. Signed A. B. If, however, this course be adopted it will, in our opinion, still be necessary that the Auditor should make and sign the Report separately, and send it in to the Directors to be placed before the Shareholders.

(6)　As regards the form of Certificate, it may run thus :—

#### AUDITOR'S CERTIFICATE.

In accordance with the provisions of the Companies Act, 1900, I certify that all my requirements as Auditor have been complied with.

And the Report might run thus :—

To the Shareholders of the　　　　Company, Lim.

#### AUDITOR'S REPORT.

I have audited the above Balance Sheet [or the Company's Balance Sheet dated the　　day of　　　　] and in my opinion such Balance Sheet is properly drawn up, so as to exhibit a true and correct view of the state of the Company's affairs as shown by the Books of the Company.

(7)　Section 23 of the Act of 1900 requires the Auditor to report whether the Balance Sheet is properly drawn up, so as to exhibit a true and correct view of the state of the Company's affairs, as shown by the Books of the Company. In our opinion, these words, " as shown by the Books of " the Company," do not limit the Auditor's duties to a comparison of the figures. No doubt he has to examine the Books, but as Lord Justice Lindley said, in *In re The London and General Bank* (1895, 2 Ch. 683) : " He does not discharge his duty by " doing this without enquiry, and without taking " any trouble to see that the Books themselves " show the Company's true position. He must " take reasonable care to ascertain that they do " so."

　　　　R. B. HALDANE.
　　　　C. SWINFEN EADY.
　　　　A. R. KIRBY.
　　　　FRANCIS B. PALMER.

*Lincoln's Inn, 12th December* 1900.